D0084881

PLANNING
ETHICALLY
RESPONSIBLE
RESEARCH

Applied Social Research Methods Series
Volume 31

APPLIED SOCIAL RESEARCH
METHODS SERIES

Series Editors:
LEONARD BICKMAN, Peabody College, Vanderbilt University, Nashville
DEBRA J. ROG, Vanderbilt University, Washington, DC

PLANNING ETHICALLY RESPONSIBLE RESEARCH

A Guide for Students and Internal Review Boards

Joan E. Sieber

Applied Social Research Methods Series
Volume 31

SAGE Publications
International Educational and Professional Publisher
Newbury Park   London   New Delhi

For information address:

SAGE Publications, Inc.
2455 Teller Road
Newbury Park, California 91320

SAGE Publications Ltd.
6 Bonhill Street
London EC2A 4PU
United Kingdom

SAGE Publications India Pvt. Ltd.
M-32 Market
Greater Kailash I
New Delhi 110 048 India

Printed in the United States of America

Library of Congress Cataloging-in-Publication Data

Sieber, Joan E.
    Planning ethically responsible research: a guide for students and
internal review boards/Joan E. Sieber.
        p. cm. — (Applied social research methods series : v. 31)
    Includes bibliographical references and index.
    ISBN 0-8039-3963-9 (cl.) — ISBN 0-8039-3964-7 (pb.)
    1. Research—Moral and ethical aspects—Handbooks, manuals, etc.
    I. Title. II. Series.
    Q180.55.M67S54 1992
    174'.93—dc20   92-15340
                                                                        CIP

92 93 94 95 10 9 8 7 6 5 4 3 2 1

Sage Production Editor: Judith L. Hunter

Contents

To the memory of my mentor,
John T. Lanzetta

Preface

This book was written to provide social scientists, their students, and members of research ethics committees with the theory and practical knowledge needed to plan ethically responsible social and behavioral research. It interprets current viewpoints on what ethical research is, especially those views presented in *The Belmont Report* (National Commission, 1978), a document set forth by the National Commission on the Protection of Human Subjects of Biomedical and Behavioral Research. It is also a practical handbook on how to translate ethical principles into valid research methods and procedures that satisfy both scientific and ethical standards. Parts of each chapter provide guidelines for satisfying federal regulations governing human research and for working with one's Institutional Review Board (IRB), or Human Subjects Committee, as such groups are variously called.

Federal regulations of human research require IRB review of research plans (protocols), but are sparse on the matter of how to meet IRB requirements. As IRB chair at California State University, Hayward (CSUH), I spent much time explaining to exasperated investigators how to revise their protocols. Because it is preferable for investigators to know what is required of them in the first place, I decided to write this book.

This book's unpublished predecessor, *The IRB Handbook,* was written, with partial support from CSUH, for CSUH investigators. A grant from the National Science Foundation (BBS-8911646) provided the resources for a needs assessment, consultation with social scientists and their students on the adequacy of an earlier draft of this book, and some released time for writing. To NSF, and to Rachelle Hollander and Vivian Weil, who have monitored this project, I express my gratitude. The needs assessment survey of social science IRBs indicated that chapters on research on children and on AIDS should be added. A grant from the Universitywide Task Force on AIDS, U. C. Berkeley (C89CSH01) provided funding for a conference that examined current solutions to problems of community-based social research related to AIDS.

I thank the many social scientists, IRB members, and students who have critiqued this book in its earlier stages. In particular, statistician Bruce Trumbo and psychologist Mary diSibio provided superb advice and editing throughout the manuscript preparation process. Others, each of whom provided reams of useful criticism of the penultimate manuscript, included Jeffrey Cohen, Ross Conner, Jane Croley, Mary deChesney, Jane Close Conoley, Joni Grey, Maureen Hester, Erica Heath, Carol Jablonski, Sue Hoppe, Paul Kakagawa, Gerald Koocher, Suzanne Kusserow, Paula Knudson, Gary B. Melton, Joan Porter, Pat Schwirian, Ada Sue Selwitz, Marlene Wagner, and Tammy Wall. Working with Sage series editor Debra Rog and senior editor C. Deborah Laughton has been a delight. To all who helped, I express my deep gratitude.

PART I

Research Ethics, Regulations, and the IRB

Research is a complicated activity in which it is easy for well-meaning investigators to overlook the interests of research participants—to the detriment of the participants, scientists, science, and society. To provide a broader ethical and legal perspective on research on human subjects, the federal government, with the help of scientists, philosophers, and lawyers, considered what ethical principles should govern human research. Federal regulations of human research were promulgated and Institutional Review Boards (IRBs) were mandated to review proposed research and ensure compliance with the regulations. IRBs are to be established at institutions where any federally funded research is conducted, except that an institution can, with federal approval and an interinstitutional agreement, use another institution's IRB.

Building on the ethical principles set forth, this book offers a logical ethical framework to guide investigators and those responsible for the ethical review of research. It shows how the methods and procedures of social science can be tailored to meet ethical and legal requirements.

Chapter 1 discusses why there is a broad-based concern for ethics in social and behavioral research, and why unethical social science is bad social science. It explains how and why IRBs were established and how the individual investigator relates to the IRB.

Chapter 2 introduces the "IRB protocol," that is, the written plan of action through which the investigator describes the research to the IRB, addresses its ethical considerations, and indicates what steps will be taken to comply with legal and ethical requirements. The elements of the IRB protocol are briefly presented, and the reader is directed to subsequent chapters of this book that deal with each element. Chapter 12 provides detailed instructions on development of an effective protocol.

Chapter 3 introduces the ethical principles of human research set forth by the National Commission for the Protection of Human Subjects of Biomedical and Behavioral Research (1978) in *The Belmont Report*. One need not be very astute to notice that these principles instruct one to "do it ethically," but they do not say how. The rest of this book is about how: Part II discusses methods of handling issues of consent, privacy, confidentiality, and deception. Part III shows how to assess risk and benefit, and optimize research outcomes. Part IV focuses on ways to respect the needs and interests of two particularly vulnerable research populations, children and the urban poor, with special attention to those at risk for HIV infection. Part V describes how to summarize pertinent ethical considerations in a research protocol.

1

Research Ethics and IRBs

1.1 ETHICS IN SOCIAL AND BEHAVIORAL RESEARCH

Ethics (from the Greek *ethos*, "character") is the systematic study of value concepts—"good," "bad," "right," "wrong"—and the general principles that justify applying these concepts.

Thus, the ethics of social research[1] is not about etiquette; nor is it about considering the poor hapless subject[2] at the expense of science or society. Rather, we study ethics to learn how to make social research "work" for all concerned. The ethical researcher creates a mutually respectful, win-win relationship with the research population; this is a relationship in which subjects are pleased to participate candidly, and the community at large regards the conclusions as constructive. Public policy implications of the research are presented in such a way that public sensibilities are unlikely to be offended and backlash is unlikely to occur.

In contrast, an ethically insensitive researcher may leave the research setting in pandemonium. The ensuing turmoil may harm the researcher, his or her institution, and even the cause he or she seeks to promote, as suggested by the following fictionalized case, adapted from an actual study.[3]

Case 1.1: Working at Cross-Purposes. A researcher sends bilingual research assistants to interview poor Chicano families in Texas about their attitudes toward their children's school. The purpose of her research is to gather information that will help local schools meet the needs of children from families that have recently moved there. Unbeknown to the researcher, many of those interviewed are illegal aliens, who suspect that the research is connected with the U. S. Immigration authorities. They fabricate many of their answers to hide their illegal status here, and they are especially careful to reveal nothing about their children's needs or problems with the school.

Others in that community carefully avoid the researcher, thus ruining the random sampling design.

A better scientist would have understood that community-based research cannot be planned or conducted unilaterally, and that culturally sensitive approaches are required. He or she would have enlisted community leaders in formulating the research procedures, trained appropriate members of the community to assist with conducting the interviews, and closely supervised the entire process, as exemplified in Case 1, Part III (page 77) and discussed in Chapter 11.

Research designs and procedures that result in failure to treat subjects with respect are likely to yield misleading, inconclusive, or biased results. Yet, enlightened self-interest does not come easily to social scientists because they have been trained, typically, to focus on their predetermined research agenda and to ignore the perceptions and expectations of their subjects and of society at large. This "get data" mentality often produces invalid data.

Selective perception plays an important role in the judgment of scientists who are involved in the intense and demanding enterprise of research. When a researcher is narrowly focused on completing a research project, it is easy to overlook some of the interests and perspectives of the research participants and of society at large. In settings where social scientists have unilateral power to conduct research, they may *appear* to get away with insensitivity to the perceptions and expectations of their subjects, but they do not. Insensitive researchers themselves become an integral part of the stimulus array; thus, it should come as no surprise that their subjects often respond with lies and subterfuge. Clearly, sound ethics and sound methodology go hand in hand.

Scientists, themselves, (e.g., Kelman, 1968; Vinacke, 1954) have critically examined some of the ethically questionable assumptions and practices of social research and recommended changes, but it was the federal government that finally brought these issues most forcibly to our attention. In 1974 the federal government mandated the establishment of Institutional Review Boards (IRBs) at all universities that accept funding from the Department of Health and Human Services (DHHS).[4] The role of the IRB is to examine all proposals for research involving human subjects to determine whether the rights and welfare of the subjects are adequately protected. Before starting research, the investigator submits a protocol to the IRB. The protocol describes the proposed research and the arrangements that have been made to ensure that the project adheres to sound ethical and scientific principles. The wise researcher uses the protocol as a guide for improving the research design and procedures. Chapter 2 briefly introduces the elements of a typical research protocol and directs attention to those parts of this book that will guide the researcher through each part of the protocol.

1.2 WHAT IS AN IRB?

An IRB, or Human Subjects Committee, is a committee mandated by the National Research Act, Public Law 93-348, to be established within each university or other organization that conducts biomedical or behavioral research involving human subjects and receives federal funding for research involving human subjects. The purpose of the IRB is to review all proposals for human research *before* the research is conducted to ascertain whether the research plan has adequately included the ethical dimensions of the project. The administration of IRBs by the DHHS is conducted by the Office for Protection from Research Risks (OPRR), except for drug-related research, which is administered by the Federal Drug Administration. OPRR is an office within the National Institutes of Health. That office answers any queries from local IRBs, provides information to assist IRBs in their functioning, receives and investigates complaints about research practices, investigates the functioning of local IRBs, as necessary, and recommends sanctions against institutions not in compliance with the law. Institutions not in compliance with the law may lose any federal funding of their programs, including funding of student programs (e.g., federal financial aid to students).

1.3 HOW FEDERAL REGULATIONS AND IRBs CAME ABOUT

Until the past two centuries, people in many cultures considered any kind of research on humans, or even on human cadavers, to be sinful, since they conceived of the spirit and soul as residing in the body.

These religious views about research involving humans largely disappeared with the rise of biomedical research in the 1700s. Research on human subjects gradually gained wide acceptance. However, by the middle of the twentieth century the ethical fallibility of well-meaning scientists was recognized. The world also came to recognize that atrocities could be committed in the name of science. After World War II, it was learned that Nazi scientists had used prisoners in brutal medical experiments, without the slightest regard for their lives, and had contributed nothing to science in the process. These crimes were investigated at the Nuremberg trials of Nazi war criminals. One consequence of these trials was the development of the Nuremburg Code of research involving humans, which emphasized that scientists must have the informed consent of any human participants in research. Katz (1972) presents a detailed discussion of the origins of political concern about use of human subjects in research.

In the United States, the next significant step in examining research ethics occurred during the 1970s, when the U. S. Congress created the National Commission for the Protection of Human Subjects in Biomedical and Behavioral Research. From 1974 to 1977, the National Commission conducted hearings on ethical problems in human research. On the basis of these hearings and long deliberations, the Commission formulated certain principles and recommendations concerning human research.

The most troubling cases that came to the attention of the National Commission concerned the involvement of human subjects in biomedical research, where concern for human life was sometimes overshadowed by concern for enrolling subjects, completing the research, or using the most rigorous design. To accomplish their scientific objectives, biomedical scientists have at times concealed from subjects circumstances relevant to the subjects' well-being. The following case illustrates how scientific zeal can interfere with ethical sensibilities:

Case 1.2: The Tuskegee Syphilis Study. A study was begun in 1932 to determine the course of syphilis from inception to death. Poor black men were recruited and offered thorough annual examinations and health care in return for serving as subjects in this study. Much information had already been gathered by 1943, when penicillin was identified as a cure for syphilis. However, the subjects were not told of the discovery of an effective treatment for syphilis and the study was allowed to continue until 1972, when an oversight committee finally recognized what was being done and halted the study (Heller, 1972). The details of this case are told in the book *Bad Blood* (Jones, 1982).

The problems that the National Commission observed in the social and behavioral sciences were not of this magnitude, but they were similar in character. In social science research prior to 1973, informed consent was rarely sought and subjects were rarely debriefed or desensitized (restored to an emotional condition at least as good as that with which they had entered the study) after research was performed. In some instances, electric shock was used as a punishing stimulus.

Deception was a standard and unquestioned social research technique, and the assumption seemed to be that subjects neither suspected deception nor could be harmed by it. In retrospect, we see that the harm, while subtle, was manifold. By the 1960s many of the people who participated in research (typically college subjects) actually *expected* deception and produced different results than unsuspecting subjects; see Diener and Crandall (1978, pp. 80-85) for discussion. Naturally, nondeceptive studies also become suspect in the minds of research participants; hence, even the data from studies not employing deception were tainted by the attitudes of subjects expecting to be deceived. Ironically, research validity was being jeopardized by the very procedures thought to promote validity.

Another prevalent problem in the social sciences was invasion of privacy.[5] Social scientists typically study persons who are relatively powerless to refuse (students, the elderly, minority populations), rather than persons who are in a position to limit scientists' access to them—precisely because it is inconvenient, difficult, and even impossible to study the powerful. Like deception, invasion of privacy is not only disrespectful of human subjects but also a cause of invalid data. Those who cannot refuse to participate have a secret weapon available for the protection of their privacy and autonomy—they can lie. Unfortunately, the real harm goes deeper than this apparent game of cat and mouse between investigator and subject. The reputation of social science itself becomes tainted. Consider the following commentary by journalist Nicholas von Hoffman (1970), which appeared in the *Washington Post*:

> We are so preoccupied with defending our privacy against insurance investigators, dope sleuths, counter-espionage men, divorce detectives and credit checkers that we overlook the social scientists behind the hunting blinds who're also peeping into what we thought were our most private and

secret lives. But there they are, studying us, taking notes, getting to know us, as indifferent as everybody else to the feeling that to be a complete human involves having an aspect of ourselves that's unknown.

Von Hoffman's remarks were about sociologist Laud Humphreys, whose research on "tearoom trade" raises the most difficult of all questions for social scientists: What if there seems to be no way to do an important study without wronging someone?

Case 1.3: Tearoom Trade. The public, as well as law-enforcement authorities, tend to hold simplistic stereotypes about men who commit impersonal sexual acts in public rest rooms. As a consequence, "tearoom sex," as fellatio in public rest rooms is called, used to account for the majority of "homosexual" arrests in the United States. Laud Humphreys, then a doctoral candidate in sociology at Washington University, sought to learn what kinds of men seek quick, impersonal sexual gratification and what motivates them to do so.

Humphreys gathered some of his data by stationing himself in "tearooms" and assuming the role of "watchqueen," the individual who keeps watch and coughs when a police car stops nearby or a stranger approaches. He played that role faithfully while observing hundreds of acts of fellatio. He gained the confidence of some of the men he observed, disclosed to them his role as a scientist, and persuaded them to tell him about the rest of their lives and about their motives for engaging in tearoom trade; but those who were willing to talk openly with him tended to be among the better educated members of the tearoom trade. To avoid socioeconomic class bias, Humphreys secretly followed some of the other men he observed and recorded the license numbers of their cars, which he then surreptitiously matched with Department of Motor Vehicle data to obtain names and addresses. Carefully disguised, Humphreys appeared at their homes a year later and claimed to be a health service interviewer. He interviewed them about their marital status, employment, and so on. Most of these interviews developed into quite personal discussions in which the men disclosed a great deal. Humphreys was aware that his data could be subpoenaed, an eventuality that probably would have led to the arrest of his subjects; he claims to have guarded the data with great care.

Humphreys' findings destroyed stereotypes: Fifty-four percent of his subjects were married and lived with their wives; superficial analysis would suggest that they were exemplary citizens who had satisfactory marriages. Most of these married men did not think of themselves either as bisexual or as homosexual. The marriages of these men were important to them, but were marked with tension. Most of these men or their wives were Catholic, and since the birth of their last child, conjugal relations had been rare, in most cases for reasons connected with family planning. Their alternative source of sexual gratification had to be quick, inexpensive, and impersonal. It could not entail involvement that would threaten their already unstable marriage, or jeopardize their most important asset, their standing as father of their children. They wanted some form of orgasm-producing action that was less lonely than masturbation and less involving than a love relationship. Only about 14% of Humphreys' subjects were members of the gay community and interested primarily in homosexual relations (Humphreys, 1970).

The gay community praised Humphreys' research for dispelling myths and stereotypes. Police departments in some cities responded to the knowledge he produced by ceasing to raid public rest rooms. Many social scientists have applauded Humphreys' research. The Society for the Study of Social Problems chose Humphreys' book for its prestigious annual C. Wright Mills Award. But for others, the study raised some very difficult questions: Is it ever justifiable to act contrary to the interests of subjects in order to obtain valuable knowledge? Does the importance of Humphreys' research justify spying on people and later visiting their homes and families and interviewing them under false pretexts?

Today, a study such as Humphreys' probably would be conducted differently. There are now legal mechanisms for protecting data from subpoena, as well as an emphasis on keeping data in anonymous form if feasible (see Chapter 6). While deception is not entirely ruled out, there is now a strong sentiment against the kinds of deception Humphreys employed (see Chapter 7). For respectful, straightforward approaches to subjects (see Chapter 4). For sensitive use of interview skills to learn about personal matters (see Chapter 11). Using an honest approach, sophisticated interview skills, and assurance of confidentiality, social scientists typically are able to obtain even the most personal information from respondents. Current approaches to research on persons with HIV infection (e.g., Melton, Levine, Koocher, Rosenthal, & Thompson, 1988; see Case 11.1) and on the sexual practices of persons at high risk for AIDS (McKusick, Wiley, & Coates, 1986) attest to the recent advances in social research methodology. Today researchers work with their IRB to develop ethically acceptable procedures.

1.4 HOW IRBs WORK

IRBs consist of five or more members, sometimes including the IRB administrator. The members are required by law to have:

[V]arying backgrounds to promote complete and adequate review of research activities commonly conducted by the institution. The IRB shall be sufficiently qualified through the experience and expertise of its members, and the diversity of the members' backgrounds including consideration of the racial and cultural backgrounds of members and sensitivity to such issues as community attitudes, to promote respect for its advice and counsel in safeguarding the rights and welfare of human subjects. (45 CFR 46.107, 1981)

The IRB meets periodically to review research protocols submitted by members of that institution and persons intending to do research at that institution. A research protocol of the kind that is submitted to an IRB is a description of the research and of the steps that will be taken to treat subjects respectfully and to reduce any risks involved. See Chapters 2 and 12 for a discussion of protocols. Ideally, the IRB administrator is available to researchers to answer questions and provide information about the IRB. The administrator receives protocols, sends them out for review, calls IRB meetings, and communicates the IRB's concerns or its approvals of protocols.

Human research, as it pertains to IRBs, refers to any study of persons that is a systematic investigation to develop generalizable knowledge. Administrative data gathering that has no scientific purpose is normally not reviewed by IRBs. Classroom demonstrations of research, done solely for pedagogical purposes, are not reviewed by IRBs. There is also a category of exempt research for which the federal government does not insist on IRB review; see Title 45 CFR Part 46.101 for exemptions. Most university IRBs, however, either do not exempt any scientific research from review, or else require that the investigator send a description of the research plan to the IRB to ascertain whether it is, indeed, exempt.

Investigators wishing to do human research should acquaint themselves with the requirements of their IRB at the time they begin planning their research. The IRB administrator can provide investigators with a statement of the requirements of that particular IRB, and of the federal government, concerning human research. While federal regulations outline the general procedures of IRBs, each IRB is responsible for developing its own specific policy statement.

A research protocol may be reviewed by either the full membership or an appropriate subgroup. A protocol must be submitted sufficiently far in advance of scheduled IRB meetings so that members can review it; the IRB administrator can provide information about the review schedule. Those who must begin their research by a particular time should submit their protocols well in advance.

When submitting research proposals under a deadline to a funding agency, it is usually possible to submit a preliminary protocol to the IRB and obtain a letter to the funding agency, stating that the research idea has been approved by the IRB and that a final protocol will be reviewed after the investigator has completed pilot testing and has worked out procedural details. The agency will not release funding until notified by the IRB that the final protocol has been approved.

In the review process, one or more of the reviewers may phone the investigator to clarify questions concerning the protocol. At that time, any problems reviewers have with the protocol can often be resolved. In any event, the investigator will receive a formal letter from the IRB (a) approving the protocol; (b) requesting changes or inquiring about problems; (c) approving the protocol, contingent on the investigator's making specified changes or solving certain problems to the satisfaction of the IRB; or (d) not approving the protocol. Protocols are rarely disapproved outright.

1.5 IS PILOT TESTING REVIEWED BY THE IRB?

Pilot testing refers to informal investigation with one or a few individuals to "fine tune" research procedures until they are satisfactory. For example, when a survey instrument is developed, it typically is tested on a few people and modified various times before it is satisfactory. These people typically are acquaintances of the investigator (e.g., students or colleagues) who have agreed to help with the study. Adequately performed pilot testing also provides an ideal opportunity to discover whether the interests and needs of subjects are adequately met.

Neither fine tuning a questionnaire nor testing equipment or a procedure with the help of a few acquaintances requires IRB review. However, most pilot studies—that is, exploratory studies to determine whether further research might be worthwhile—do require IRB review, as does the pilot testing of a risky procedure. A reviewer in doubt about whether review is required for a pilot activity should check with his or her IRB.

1.6 WHY IRBs HAVE BEEN CONTROVERSIAL

The knowledge required to design research that is both scientifically valid and respectful of human subjects is still not adequately taught in many methodology courses today. Some scientists do not know how to do research that is in compliance with federal regulations. Others find it difficult to describe their research in terms that IRBs readily understand.

Not surprisingly, some of these scientists find themselves in an adversarial relationship with their IRB and accuse the federal government of abridging the freedom of science.

IRBs are not perfect, either. An IRB that is unprepared to assist scientists in developing the most acceptable research procedures can only say what is unacceptable—hardly a popular enterprise! When that occurs, the scientist must become an effective ethical problem solver, and be able to communicate about that process with the IRB.

Finally, by establishing a decentralized review system, the federal government has not only given each IRB much autonomy in the interpretation of the regulations but also permits each to add requirements of its own. Thus different IRBs might decide the same case quite differently.

1.7 WHAT IF YOU THINK YOUR IRB MAY DISAPPROVE YOUR PROTOCOL?

Researchers who are aware that their intended research is ethically sensitive must educate themselves about the problems likely to be encountered. They should consult with several sources of information:

1. Scientists who have recently conducted related research.
2. Experts in the pertinent field. For example, if one wants to study the effects of caffeine on various kinds of learning, but realizes that some people have extreme physical reactions to caffeine, the appropriate person to consult may be the campus physician. Similarly, if one wishes to study abused children and is concerned about how they will respond to the intended questionnaire, an appropriate consultant would be a clinical psychologist who treats abused children.
3. Key members of one's own IRB.
4. *IRB, A Review of Human Subjects Research*, an excellent bimonthly journal that covers issues of concern to IRBs and scientists and is available in most university libraries or IRB offices.

In any event, the investigator who undertakes sensitive research must investigate possible risks and learn how to decrease or avoid them. The investigator then describes, in the protocol, the details of the consultation that has occurred, what has been learned about the nature of the possible risks, and what procedures have been selected to minimize those risks. Relevant literature should be discussed and cited.

The IRB may need to be educated. If so, the researcher should provide that needed education and not be adversarial. IRBs have heavy workloads and tire of arrogant colleagues. Besides, they have the last word.

NOTES

1. For the sake of brevity, the term *social research* will be used from here on in place of *social and behavioral research*.

2. Many have argued that the term *research participant* is more respectful than the term *subject*. For some purposes I would agree. For the purposes of this book, however, I would prefer to use a term that continually reminds the reader that the person being studied typically has less power than the researcher and must be accorded the protections that render this inequality morally acceptable.

3. The illustrative cases presented in this book include: (a) cases based on published work; (b) cases based on personal communication; and (c) actual cases known to the author, in which anonymity and deliberate alteration of details are appropriate.

4. The federal regulations governing the protection of human subjects are set forth in Title 45 Code of Federal Regulations (CFR) Part 46. A copy of the federal regulations of human research can be obtained through any university's research office or reference librarian, or from the Office for Protection From Research Risk, National Institutes of Health, Building 31, 9000 Rockville Pike, Bethesda, MD 20892; phone (301) 496-8101.

5. *Privacy* refers to the ability of persons to control intrusions into their personal life; *confidentiality* is an extension of the concept of privacy and refers to agreements governing what may be done with information about oneself. The implications of privacy and confidentiality for research planning are discussed extensively in Chapters 5 and 6.

2

The Research Protocol [1]

This chapter introduces the reader to the concept of the research protocol, and its relation to (a) planning ethically responsible research, (b) working with one's IRB, and (c) using the rest of this book to plan research and develop the protocol. It stresses the importance of using the protocol as a planning tool, not as a bureaucratic evil—a form to be tossed together at the last minute. The details that need to be considered in developing a protocol are discussed in subsequent chapters, and a full discussion of the protocol is presented in Chapter 12.

In research involving humans, as in any complex undertaking, the best way to develop an ethically responsible project is to consider systematically (in writing) the research rationale, methods, and procedures, and the steps that will be taken in response to ethical considerations. Just such a written plan—the protocol—is required by federal regulations of human research. The most effective way to develop an adequate protocol is to begin writing it when the research planning begins; thus, the investigator is reminded to think through the ethical considerations along with the methodological ones. The alternative is to treat ethical considerations as an afterthought and perhaps discover that the research plan is not workable.

2.1 WHAT IS A PROTOCOL?

The research protocol is an official account of the intended research methods and procedures, with special attention to how benefit is maximized and risk minimized, autonomy of subjects is respected, and fairness to subjects is ensured. Included is a brief discussion of the research problem and hypotheses, relevant literature, the research methods, and the investigator's background. This clarifies what is to be done, how, and why. Some other elements of the protocol (and chapters where these are discussed) include:

Subject selection, recruitment, and justification for the number and kind of subjects proposed: Chapters 3, 4, 5, and 12.

Benefits to subjects and others: Chapter 9.

Risks and how these will be minimized, including risks to privacy and confidentiality: Chapters 5, 6, 7, 8, 10, 11, and 12.

Informed consent: Chapters 4, 6, 9, 10, and 12 and Appendix A.

Obtaining permission of a parent or guardian, and subjects' assent, when subjects are minors: Chapter 10.

The protocol might consist of a one- or two-page statement and a consent form, if the project is simple and involves little risk. Or it might be considerably longer. The protocol is prepared by the researcher and submitted to the IRB. It reminds the researcher of many of the elements that are essential to scientifically and ethically sound research, and provides the information needed by an IRB to carry out its legal mandate. A protocol that has been tossed together at the last minute to request IRB approval is likely both to overlook important issues and result in delay of IRB approval.

The protocol enables the investigator and the IRB to ascertain at a glance whether certain matters are handled properly. For example, is the consent statement appropriate? The protocol discusses the purpose and procedures of the research, the characteristics of the research population, the risks and benefits, and the informed consent procedure. Thus, the IRB can observe whether the consent procedure describes the risks and safeguards, the benefits, and the general nature of the research—taking into account the perspective and background of the subjects. A consent statement that overlooks the perspective and background (e.g., culture, education, reading level) of subjects is disrespectful and may adversely affect response rate and cooperation.

The IRB may examine the feasibility of the sampling plan. The protocol states how many subjects will be recruited, from where, and how, and what inducements will be offered to subjects. Does the plan call for too few or too many subjects? Is the subject population suitable to the purpose of the research? Are there concrete plans to benefit those who participate in the research? Is exploitation avoided? In research conducted in an organization (e.g., a school, hospital, workplace, recreation center), the IRB will require the written permission of an authorized gatekeeper for the researcher to approach the subjects. It will require evidence that subjects are not coerced into participating by either the researcher or the gatekeeper. Other things to include depend on the nature of the research.

In a large interview project, one ought to indicate how hired interviewers are trained, and whether they are paid by the hour or "by the head," and why. These matters affect whether subjects are treated respectfully, the success of the sampling procedure, and the validity of the research.

Because the protocol directs the investigator's attention to problems intrinsic to the design and procedure of the research, it is seriously recommended that the investigator begin writing the protocol in the early stages of research planning.

2.2 CONTROL DOCUMENTATION

Institutions are legally responsible for research conducted within them—as are researchers and their supervisors. Therefore, IRB protocols must reflect what is *actually* done in the research. Once the IRB has approved a protocol for a particular project, the investigator is bound to follow that procedure, or to have the desired change of procedure approved by the IRB. *That is, the protocol becomes a control document, an official statement that specifies how the study is being conducted.*

This document becomes a vital part of an official "paper trail" showing that the research is acceptable to a legally constituted board of reviewers. Should anyone raise questions about the project, the approved protocol is powerful evidence that the project is of sufficient value to justify any risks or inconveniences involved.

Case 2.1: A (Fictionalized) Study of Moral Development. Dr. Knowall interviews school children about their understanding of right and wrong. A parent who gave permission for his child to participate in the research later regards the project as seeking to change his child's religious beliefs. He calls the newspaper, the ACLU, the mayor, the school board, and the governor to complain that Dr. Knowall's research violates the separation of church and state. The university is required to respond, and proffers the approved protocol, which would be powerful evidence in any legal proceeding that the project was socially and legally acceptable—

except for one thing: The researcher had slipped in a few questions about religion *after* receiving IRB approval. The researcher finds himself in serious trouble and without enthusiastic backing from his institution.

NOTE

1. The research or treatment protocol is a concept and practice from medicine in which the details of the presenting problem, the patient, and the intended treatment (research) are spelled out in great detail and reviewed by appropriate supervisors to ascertain that it meets the highest ethical, clinical, and research standards. It is developed at the outset, incorporated into the patient's chart, and followed throughout the treatment or research. Unfortunately, when social scientists began to develop protocols for their IRBs, most had no such tradition or training. Rather than use the protocol as a tool for planning and professional consultation, many social scientists regard the protocol as a piece of paperwork one does for the IRB.

3

General Ethical Principles of Research on Humans

The National Commission for the Protection of Human Subjects in Biomedical and Behavioral Research has identified ethical principles and scientific norms that should govern human research. A full discussion appears in *The Belmont Report* (National Commission, 1978). An understanding of these principles and norms will assist the researcher in the planning of research and in the development of the research protocol.

3.1 THREE ETHICAL PRINCIPLES: BENEFICENCE, RESPECT, AND JUSTICE

The following three ethical principles must guide human research:

A. *Beneficence*—maximizing good outcomes for science, humanity, and the individual research participants while avoiding or minimizing unnecessary risk, harm, or wrong.

B. *Respect*—protecting the autonomy of (autonomous) persons, with courtesy and respect for individuals as persons, including those who are not autonomous (e.g., infants, the mentally retarded, senile persons).

C. *Justice*—ensuring reasonable, nonexploitative, and carefully considered procedures and their fair administration; fair distribution of costs and benefits among persons and groups (i.e., those who bear the risks of research should be those who benefit from it).

3.2 SIX NORMS OF SCIENTIFIC RESEARCH

As discussed in *The Belmont Report*, these three basic ethical principles translate into the following six norms of scientific behavior (The letters in parentheses after each norm designate the specific principles upon which that norm is based.):

1. *Valid research design*: Only valid research yields correct results. Valid design takes account of relevant theory, methods, and prior findings; see Chapter 9 for details. (A, B)

2. *Competence of researcher*: The investigator must be capable of carrying out the procedures validly. (A, B)

3. *Identification of consequences*: An assessment of risks and benefits should be identified from relevant perspectives. Ethical research will adjust procedures to respect privacy, ensure confidentiality, maximize benefit, and minimize risk. (A, B, C)

4. *Selection of subjects*: The subjects must be appropriate to the purposes of the study, representative of the population that is to benefit from the research, and appropriate in number; see Chapter 9 for details. (A, B, C)

5. *Voluntary informed consent*: Voluntary informed consent of subjects should be obtained beforehand. *Voluntary* means freely, without threat or undue inducement. *Informed* means that the subject knows what a reasonable person in the same situation would want to know before giving consent. *Consent* means explicit agreement to participate. Informed consent requires clear communication that subjects comprehend, not complex technical explanations or legal jargon. See Chapter 4 for details. (A, B, C)

6. *Compensation for injury*: The researcher is responsible for what happens to subjects. Federal law requires that subjects be informed whether harm will be compensated, but does not require compensation. (A, B, C)

3.3 UNDERSTANDING THE RELATIONSHIP OF NORMS TO PRINCIPLES

These six norms of scientific behavior can be easily derived from the above three ethical principles. The full purpose of these norms cannot be grasped without an understanding of this relationship. To enable the reader to grasp these relationships, an explanation is provided here with respect to the last norm, compensation for injury.

As an exercise, the reader is urged to develop his or her own explanations of the relationships between the three ethical principles and the first five norms and to compare them with the explanations provided in 3.5. Note that these relationships may be explained in various ways.

The norm that the researcher is responsible for compensating participants for injury can best be understood through a simple example: Suppose the researcher intends to interview subjects, who were sexually abused as children, about their perception, as adults, of that experience. This is likely to be traumatic for some. Consequently, the consent statement should indicate (a) the purpose of the research, (b) the possibility that they might experience considerable upset from the interview, and (c) whether they are entitled to psychotherapy from a qualified therapist to work through the immediate sources of their upset.

How does such compensation for injury relate to each ethical principle? The principle of beneficence means maximizing good over harm. We shall assume that the study is well designed and hence may generate useful knowledge. We further assume that participating in the interview may provide an opportunity to recognize, reflect upon, and resolve remaining trauma pertaining to one's prior abuse. But what of the person who cannot resolve the frightening or unpleasant feelings that are generated? Anything that will help that person to reduce the upset engendered by the study would help maximize good over harm. However, psychotherapy for such an individual may take years and require the services of a specialist. Peace of mind might never be restored to some sexually abused individuals. What protection exists against such psychological harm to research subjects? Apart from avoiding trivial research on vulnerable subjects, and offering counseling to those who might need it where affordable to the project, voluntary informed consent provides the main means of protecting subjects.

Respect means both honoring the right of persons to choose whether to be in the study, and showing concern for their well-being. Adults who are competent to consent may choose to be in a study that is potentially upsetting, but the investigator must also respect their well-being. To cause upset and not take appropriate steps to restore the person's sense of well-being is disrespectful. It is unjust that some should be left to suffer as a result of their yielding valuable knowledge that may benefit others. Any steps that can be taken to observe when participants have been upset, and to offer them the resources required to achieve well-being, contribute to the achievement of justice.

3.4 APPLYING THESE PRINCIPLES AND NORMS
TO THE DESIGN OF RESEARCH

These norms and principles are powerful tools for identifying ethical issues in research. Practice in applying these principles to some hypothetical research plans will help prepare the reader for the application of these concepts to actual cases. Determine which norms apply to each problem. Evaluate what should be done about each research proposal.

1. A researcher plans to study the effects of competition on ability to solve math problems. Half of the subjects will be told that the researcher wants to see what approach they take in solving math problems. The other half will be told that the researcher wants to see which persons choose the *best* approach.

2. A researcher plans to compare the intellectual skills of retired people to those of college sophomores. To recruit the sophomores, she plans to arrange for volunteers to receive an A in their psychology course, and for nonvolunteers to have their grade lowered. To recruit retired people, she plans to go to a retirement community each evening, knock at people's doors, and ask them to work some puzzles, not explaining details of the study because most wouldn't understand. Because retired people are usually unwilling to participate, only three of them will be recruited.

3. A graduate student plans to compare cocaine use in college freshmen and seniors. Because she may want to reinterview some subjects later, she plans to write their names and phone numbers on their data sheets. She plans to promise confidentiality, so that subjects will trust her, and to keep the data in her dorm room in a locked file.

4. A researcher plans to study the effects of an educational (cable) TV curriculum on learning to read. He gives access to the cable TV programs to 100 homes with 5-year-olds, where the parents agree to allow their children to watch the TV curriculum daily. He obtains permission to test these 100 children in 2 months, along with 100 matched control children who will not have access to the cable TV.

5. To study self-esteem, a researcher plans to have 8-year-olds draw pictures of themselves and their friends and answer some questions. She plans to ask a teacher friend to let her test her students.

3.5 SOME ANSWERS TO THE EXERCISES IN 3.3

Norm 1. Invalid research cannot provide scientifically sound knowledge; in fact, it may provide misleading and thus socially harmful information. Such research does more harm than good and cannot be considered beneficent. It is disrespectful to use people for invalid research.

Norm 2. A researcher who is incompetent to carry out the research cannot produce good outcomes or involve subjects wisely. It is disrespectful to involve subjects in this way.

Norm 3. Beneficence requires discovery of ways to maximize benefits over risks. Research that is respectful of participants does not place them at unnecessary risk. It is unjust to subject persons to unnecessary risk to benefit others.

Norm 4. The validity, hence beneficence, of research depends on selection of the appropriate sample and number of subjects. It is disrespectful and wasteful of participants' time (a) to subject an inappropriate group or inappropriate-size sample to the inconvenience of being studied (for naught), and (b) to subject vulnerable people to procedures to which they are in no position to object. It is unfair to do research on a population that will not benefit from the knowledge gained, in order to benefit some other population. This is justified only when there is no other feasible way to do the research and the benefit to others promises to be great.

Norm 5. Voluntary informed consent is respectful of individuals' autonomy. It is also beneficent in that it gives persons the opportunity to decide for themselves whether participation would be a beneficial experience for them and whether it would involve any risks they are unwilling to take.

3.6 OTHER ETHICAL PRINCIPLES

The principles and norms set forth by the National Commission in *The Belmont Report* were intended to provide succinct guidelines to govern all of biomedical and behavioral research. Other groups (e.g., the American Psychological Association, the American Sociological Association, the American Anthropological Association) have set forth guidelines that are designed to guide research in their respective disciplines. While congruent with the principles and norms set forth by the National Commission, these guidelines explicitly address some additional issues that the National Commission did not mention. Given that each discipline tends to encounter somewhat different ethical problems in research, it is useful for investigators to be familiar with the guidelines intended for their own discipline. (The full text of the professional code of ethics of each association is available from the association office, in Washington, D. C.)

For example, the American Psychological Association (APA) recognizes that the researcher cannot always reveal the exact purpose of the research ahead of time and stresses the importance of debriefing and of removing any undesirable consequences for the individual participant. Information obtained from the research participant is considered confidential unless otherwise agreed upon in advance (APA, 1982).

The American Sociological Association (ASA) recognizes that its researchers often work to influence social policy. Accordingly, emphasis is placed on not misrepresenting one's abilities to conduct a particular research project, honest reporting, disclosure of all sources of financial support and special relations to the sponsor, and nonacceptance of grants that would violate the ASA code of ethics. Sociologists are to lend their expertise on a *pro bono* basis to organizations that cannot afford to fund them. In joint research projects, there should be explicit agreements on division of work, compensation, rights of authorship, access to data, and other rights and responsibilities.

The American Anthropological Association focuses on the context of fieldwork. Anthropologists work throughout the world in close personal association with people in developing countries. Consequently, their relationship with their sponsors, their own and host governments, their students, and the particular individuals and groups they study are unusually complex and fraught with potential for misunderstanding, conflict and possible harm to individuals, groups, and cultures. Anthropologists are exhorted not to pursue a particular piece of research if they cannot do so without damaging those they would study.

Various guidelines and casebooks that have been written for social science disciplines are described below.

RECOMMENDED READINGS

American Psychological Association. (1982). *Ethical principles in the conduct of research with human participants*. Washington, DC: Author. [This book examines the implications of each principle.]

24   PLANNING ETHICALLY RESPONSIBLE RESEARCH

Cassell, J., & Jacobs, S-E. (1987). *Handbook on ethical issues in anthropology.* Washington, DC: American Anthropological Association.

Fluehr-Lobbau, C. (Ed.). (1991). *Ethics and the profession of anthropology: Dialogue for a new era.* Philadelphia: University of Pennsylvania Press.

Keith-Spiegel, P., & Koocher, G. (1985). *Ethics in psychology: Professional standards and cases.* New York: Random House. [This comprehensive book examines a variety of ethical issues ranging from dual role relationships and psychological testing to research issues and mass media audiences.]

Sieber, J. (Ed.). (1982). *Vol. I: The ethics of social research: Surveys and experiments.* New York: Springer-Verlag.

Sieber, J. (Ed.). (1982). *Vol. II: The ethics of social research: Fieldwork, regulation and publication.* New York: Springer-Verlag.

PART II

Basic Ethical Issues in Social and Behavioral Research

The methods and ethics of research may be conceptually distinct topics, but in practice they are inseparable. Poor quality data are obtained when the investigator is insensitive to the needs and interests of subjects. This section answers the following questions:

What is the impact of informed consent on the ability to obtain high quality data? What are the psychological and legal elements of informed consent? How does one obtain consent and debrief subjects in the various settings where research may be performed?

How does an investigator become sensitive to what is private to subjects, and respect those privacies? What is the relationship of respect for privacy to validity of data?

What promises of confidentiality should and should not be made? How can an investigator assure the confidentiality that is promised? How do consent and confidentiality influence the kinds of information subjects are willing to provide to investigators?

When is the use of deception acceptable?

The more general but equally basic ethical question of how to minimize risk and maximize benefit is answered in Part III.

4

Voluntary Informed Consent and Debriefing

Voluntary informed consent is an ongoing, two-way communication process between subjects and the investigator, as well as a specific agreement about the conditions of the research participation. *Voluntary* means without threat or undue inducement. *Informed* means that the subject knows what a reasonable person in the same situation would want to know before giving consent. *Consent* means explicit agreement to participate. Informed consent requires clear communication, not complex technical explanations or legal jargon beyond the subject's ability to comprehend. Social scientists should draw upon their communication skills to ensure that the consent process fulfills these criteria and that communication lines remain open, even after the formal and legally mandated consent has occurred.

We will concentrate first on the communication process of obtaining informed consent, then on the legal requirements, and finally on debriefing. A few issues of consent and debriefing in community-based settings are introduced here, although extensive discussion of these issues is deferred until Chapter 11. Issues of consent for research on children are discussed in Chapter 10, and issues of debriefing in research involving deception are discussed in Chapter 7.

4.1 THE COMMUNICATION PROCESS OF VOLUNTARY INFORMED CONSENT

There are many aspects of the investigator's speech and behavior that communicate information to subjects. Body language, friendliness, a respectful attitude, and genuine empathy for the role of the subject are among the factors that may speak louder than words. To illustrate, imagine a potential subject who is waiting to participate in a study:

Scenario 1: The scientist arrives late, wearing a rumpled lab coat, and props himself in the doorway. He ascertains that the subject is indeed the person whose name is on his list. He reads the consent information without looking at the subject. The subject tries to discuss the information with the researcher, who seems not to hear. He reads off the possible risks. The nonverbal communication that has occurred is powerful. The subject feels resentful and suppresses an urge to storm out. What has been communicated most clearly is that the investigator does not care about the subject. The subject is sophisticated and recognizes that the researcher is immature, preoccupied, and lacking in social skills, yet he feels devalued. He silently succumbs to the pressures of this unequal status relationship to do "the right thing"; he signs the consent form amidst a rush of unpleasant emotions.

Scenario 2: The subject enters the anteroom and meets a researcher who is well groomed, stands straight and relaxed, and invites the subject to sit down with him. The researcher's eye contact, easy and relaxed approach, warm but professional manner, voice, breathing, and a host of other cues convey that he is comfortable communicating with the subject. He is friendly and direct as he describes the study. Through eye contact, he ascertains that the subject understands what he has said. He invites questions, and responds thoughtfully to any comments, questions or concerns. If the subject raises a scientific question about the study (no matter how naive), the scientist welcomes the subject's interest in the project and enters into a brief discussion, treating the subject as a respected peer. Finally, he indicates that there is a formal consent form to be signed and shows the subject that the consent form covers the issues that were discussed. He mentions that it is important that people not feel pressured to participate, but rather participate only if they really want to. The subject signs the form and receives a copy of the form to keep for himself.

Though the consent forms in the first and second case may have been identical, only the second case exemplified adequate, respectful informed consent. In that case, the researcher engendered a strong sense of rapport, trust, and mutual respect; he was responsive to the concerns of the subject and he facilitated adequate decision making. Let us analyze these and other elements of communication:

Rapport. Because informed consent procedures are administered to many subjects in some experiments, it is all too easy to turn the process into a singsong routine that is delivered without any sense of commitment to interpersonal communication. A friendly greeting, openness, positive body language, and a genuine willingness to hear what each subject has to say or ask about the study are crucial to establishing rapport. The amount of eye contact one should employ depends on various circumstances. Extensive eye contact can interfere with the subject's ability to think, and would be considered rude in some Asian cultures. Too little eye contact may signal avoidance, however. Lack of rapport communicates disrespect.

Congruence of verbal and body language. This is an important part of rapport. In the above two examples, the first researcher was highly incongruent: The words said one thing, the manner in which they were delivered said the opposite. The second researcher was highly congruent: All channels of his communication conveyed respect and openness. The congruent communicator of informed consent uses vocabulary that the subject can easily understand, speaks in gentle, direct tones at about the same rate of speech that the subject uses, breathes deeply and calmly, stands or sits straight and relaxed, and is accessible to eye contact. Even if the researcher was feeling stressed, he or she takes time to relax so as not to make distracting movements, show impatience, or laugh inappropriately. To communicate congruently, one's mind must be relatively clear of distracting thoughts.

Trust. If participants believe that the investigator may not understand or care about them, there will not be the sense of partnership needed to carry out the study satisfactorily. The issue of trust is particularly important when the investigator has considerably higher status than members of the target population, or is from a different ethnic group. It is often useful to ask representatives of the subject population to examine the research procedures and make sure they are respectful and acceptable to the target population, as the following example illustrates:

A Caucasian anthropologist wanted to interview families in San Francisco's Chinatown to determine what kinds of foods they eat, how their eating habits have changed since they immigrated here, and what incidence of cancer has been experienced in their family. She employed several Chinese-American women to learn whether her interview questions were appropriate and to translate them into Mandarin and Cantonese. First, the research assistants worked on the basis of their personal knowledge of the language and culture of Chinatown; they then tested their procedures on pilot subjects. There was considerable confusion among pilot subjects about the names of some Chinese vegetables; the researchers devised pictures of those vegetables so that subjects could confirm which ones they meant. The Chinese-American research assistants rewrote the questions and the consent statement until they were appropriate for the population that was to be interviewed, then conducted the interviews. Their appearance, language, and cultural background engendered a level of trust, mutual respect, and clear communication that the researcher herself could not have created.

Another way to have built trust and cooperation in that community would have been to identify legitimate leaders or gatekeepers, who are concerned about the health and welfare of community members, and to work with them to make the survey mutually useful. A gatekeeper is a person who lets researchers into the setting or keeps them out. Gatekeepers derive their power from their ability to negotiate conditions that are acceptable to those they serve. Only unscrupulous gatekeepers would grant a researcher privileges that would cause concern or harm to research participants or to the community. Gatekeepers may be scientists, such as a researcher who also directs a clinic. More frequently, they are nonscientists—principals or school-district superintendents, managers of companies, directors of agencies, ministers of local churches, or "street professionals," such as a recovered drug addict who now serves as a community outreach person to his own people.

Some anthropologists have offered to share data with their host community for its own policy-making purposes (e.g., Pelto, 1988; White, 1991). The community leaders or gatekeepers might request that certain items of interest to them be added to a survey and might subsequently need some assistance with specific analyses and interpretations of data. The net result could be a collaborative effort to achieve a shared goal, such as improve health and nutrition in that community. Ideally the collaboration and cooperation would be communicated explicitly to community members. For example, the community newspaper might print an article—including pictures of the interviewers who would soon appear at residents' doors. Interviewers might even carry copies of the newspaper article with them for purposes of identification.

There are many ways to enhance rapport, respect, and trust and increase the benefit to subjects of the research project, depending on the particular setting and circumstances. When planning research, especially in a field setting, it is useful to conduct focus groups from the target population (see Part III, and Stewart & Shamdasani, 1990), to consult with community gatekeepers (Chapter 11), or simply to consult with pilot subjects. The purpose of such consultation during planning is to learn how subjects are likely to react to the various possible research procedures and how to make the research most beneficial and acceptable to subjects. The rewards to the researcher for this effort include greater ease of recruiting, cooperative research participants, a research design that will work, and a community that evinces good will.

Relevance to the concerns of the research population. In developing consent statements, researchers usually try to address the concerns they think their subjects ought to have. However, it is important for the researcher to determine what the concerns of that subject population actually are. *Pilot subjects* from the research population should have the procedure explained to them and should be asked to try to imagine what concerns people would have about participating in the study. Often some of these concerns turn out to be very different from those the researcher would have imagined, and they are likely to affect the outcome of the research if they are not resolved, as the following case illustrates:

Case 4.1: Misinformed Consent. A Ph.D. student interviewed aged persons living in a publicly supported geriatric center on their perceptions of the center. At the time of the research, city budget cuts were occurring; rumors were rampant that eligibility criteria would change and many current residents would be evicted. Mrs. B., an amputee, was fearful that she would be moved if she were perceived as incompetent. Upon signing the informed consent form she began answering his questions:

"Can you recite the alphabet?"
"Backwards or forwards?" she asked to demonstrate her intellectual competence.
"How do you like the service here?"

"Oh, it's great!" she replied, although she constantly complained to her family about the poor service and bad food.

"How do you like the food here?"

"It's delicious," she replied.

Mrs. B.'s anxiety was rising and midway through the questioning she asked the student, "Did I pass the test?"

"What test?" he asked.

"The one for whether I can stay in the hospital."

"I'm not working for the hospital," he replied. With that, Mrs. B. spun her chair around and wheeled herself away. (Fisher & Rosendahl, 1990, pp. 47-48)

Comprehension. In addition to its relevance to the concerns of the research population, the consent must employ terms and concepts that they will understand. To check for understandability, pilot subjects should be asked to read the consent statement and explain it in their own words. It should be revised until it is correctly understood.

Adequacy of decision making. Even when rapport, comprehension, relevance, and trust are present, it is possible that a subject may fail to give adequate consideration to the decision to participate. Adequate decision making is important to both the subject and the researcher. The subject who regrets agreeing to participate in a study is likely to be late or fail to appear at all, to hurry through the procedures with less than full attention, or even to give dishonest answers.

When consent statements are presented as a plea for help, two factors may cause subjects to participate, even though they would rather not. The *volunteer effect* (Rosenthal & Rosnow, 1969) occurs when subjects feel that they ought to be helpful and agree to participate to do "the right thing." The other factor that predisposes people to be poor decision makers is being rushed into a decision. The following steps will help to avoid these two problems:

1. Present the consent statement well before subjects are to participate, so that they have ample time to consider their decision.

2. Especially if participation requires much time and effort, urge subjects to make the decision that best serves their own interests, as to do otherwise will serve no one's interests.

3. Provide a group context in which subjects discuss with the researcher the pros and cons of participating. This gives individuals exposure to much more information, both for and against participation, than individual decision makers would typically generate.

4. If the procedure is complicated and unusual, let subjects participate in a simulation, or show a videotape of another subject participating, to provide a concrete sense of what is involved.

5. If some or all of the intended subjects do not speak English, the consent statement should be translated by a bilingual person who fully understands the research and the research population. A second bilingual person should then translate the statement back to English to detect any possible misunderstandings in the original translation. Employ the first four procedures above, as appropriate, in the native language of the research population.

Competency and voluntariness in special populations. Although the competence to understand and make decisions about research participation is conceptually distinct from voluntariness, these qualities become blurred in the case of some "captive" research populations. Children, retarded adults, the poorly educated, and prisoners may fail to understand their right to refuse to participate in research when asked by someone of apparent authority. They may also fail to grasp the details relevant to their decision. Where competency is a legal issue, the matter is resolved by appointing an advocate for the research subject, in addition to obtaining the subject's assent. Children cannot legally consent to participate in research, but they can indicate whether they want to participate, and must be given veto power over adults who give permission for them to participate. This is called *assent*. (See Chapter 10 for a detailed discussion of assent and research on children.)

Competence to consent or assent and voluntariness are affected by the way the decision is presented (Melton & Stanley, 1991). For example, an individual's understanding of information presented in the consent procedure, and acceptance of his or her status as an autonomous decision maker, will be most powerfully influenced not by *what* he or she is told but by *how* he or she is engaged in the communication. See Stanley and Guido (1991) for a review of literature on competency and voluntariness.

Protection of privacy and confidentiality.[1] It is essential that researchers protect the privacy of research participants and the confidentiality of data to the extent possible, and communicate how this will be done (including limits on their ability to assure confidentiality) in the consent statement. This is discussed extensively in Chapter 5 (Privacy) and Chapter 6 (Confidentiality).

4.2 LEGAL ELEMENTS OF
VOLUNTARY INFORMED CONSENT

Federal law requires that the formal consent statement contain the following information:

1. An explanation of the purpose of the research, the expected duration of the subject's participation, and a description of the procedure. There is no need to describe the details of the design, especially if this will affect the subjects' responses in ways that jeopardize the validity of the research. If concealment is necessary, the subject should be told that not all of the details of the research can be revealed until later, at which time a full explanation will be given. It is necessary only to describe, in terms the subject understands, what the subject will experience. Jargon, legalistic terminology, and irrelevant explanations should be avoided.

2. A description of any foreseeable risk or discomfort. (See Chapter 8 for a full discussion of the meanings of *risk* and how it may be foreseen or assessed.)

3. A description of any benefits to subjects or others reasonably to be expected. (See Chapter 9.)

4. A description of alternatives to participation that might be advantageous to the subject. As examples, subject pool participants must be given viable alternatives to participation (e.g., Sieber & Saks, 1989); persons who have sought clinical treatment and are offered an experimental treatment must be offered the standard treatment as an alternative.

5. A description of how confidentiality or anonymity will be assured and the limits to such assurances if warranted—especially in sensitive research, such as AIDS research. (See 4.4 and Chapter 6 for details.)

6. For research involving more than minimal risk, a statement of whether compensation or treatment for harm or injury is available. This is more relevant to biomedical research in which physical harm is a distinct possibility. In social and behavioral research, the possible harms are more likely to be social and emotional. Thus, for example, if research may be upsetting, the investigator may be available for immediate counseling or may provide the services of an appropriate professional.

7. An explanation of whom to contact for answers to pertinent questions about the research and about subjects' rights, and whom to contact in the event of research-related harm.

8. Indication that participation is voluntary, that refusal to participate will involve no penalty or loss of benefits to which the subject would otherwise be entitled, and that the subject may discontinue participation at any time.

9. The subject should be given a copy of the consent statement.

Other elements that may be appropriate only to medical research are specified in 45 CFR 26.116 of the federal regulations. Common sense dictates that other elements be included in social research. For example, if the research is sponsored (and especially if it is sponsored by an organization that not everyone approves of), the investigator should disclose the identity of the sponsor.

4.3 EFFECTIVE CONSENT STATEMENTS

Although consent statements should explain the research to be undertaken and should fulfill legal requirements, they should also be simple and friendly in tone. Not surprisingly, some consent statements are written in scientific jargon, telling the subject more about the design than the subject cares to know, yet failing to mention things that a person would need to know in order to decide whether to participate. Others are written in harsh, legal-sounding language. An effective consent statement should translate a scientific proposal into simple, everyday language, omitting details that are unimportant to the subjects.

The following exercise provides an opportunity to translate a technical description of a research design into an adequate consent statement. Assume that you are a researcher who has been given permission to study taste perception at a hospital and has designed the following study. You now need to write a clear, friendly letter soliciting participation in the research. Here is the project, as described in scientific language. Translate this into a consent letter that uses plain English:

Eating disorders (e.g., cravings and aversions) have been observed among psychiatric patients receiving lithium treatment. Acuity for detecting and recognizing the four basic tastes (sweet, sour, salty, and bitter) and preference among these tastes will be measured among patients undergoing lithium therapy and a group of matched controls. It is hypothesized that lithium-medicated subjects have altered taste perception thresholds and taste preferences. The substances to be tasted will consist of pure water and small concentrations of the following substances diluted in water: sucrose (sweet), salt, citric acid (sour), and quinine sulfate (bitter). These substances are normally used as food additives at higher levels of concentration. Three small samples will be presented simultaneously, two identical and one different, with position varied so that odd and identical samples are tried equally often. Paired comparisons and an hedonic rating scale will be used to measure taste preference. Data acquired through taste testing will be analyzed in relation to age, sex, smoking history, duration of lithium administration, and current lithium concentration. Five sessions per subject, each 10 to 15 minutes long, are required. Three threshold tests for each of the four test substances will be conducted on separate days. On the fifth day, preference testing will be conducted.[2]

Make sure your letter contains all of the required elements of consent, is easy to understand, is friendly, and contains no unnecessary detail or jargon. Remember, you do not need to describe the study as though you were describing it to a scientist; rather, describe generally why the study is being done and what the subject will experience. Be sure to cover all of the elements of consent listed in 4.2. An appropriate letter probably should devote no more than two sentences to each of the following points of information:

1. Identification of the researcher.
2. Explanation of the purpose of the study.
3. Request for participation, mentioning right to withdraw at any time with impunity.
4. Explanation of research method.
5. Duration of research participation.
6. A description of how confidentiality will be maintained.
7. Mention of the subject's right of refusal without penalty.
8. Mention of right to withdraw own data at end of session.
9. Explanation of any risks.
10. Description of any feedback and benefits to subjects.
11. Information on how to contact the person designated to answer questions about subjects' rights or injuries.
12. Indication that subjects may keep a copy of the consent.

After drafting a consent letter, compare your own with the one that follows. Note the simplicity, friendliness, and lack of jargon:

(Letterhead of the Researcher's Institution)
Dear Patient,

I am a psychologist who specializes in the study of taste perception. I am currently working with the staff of your department to see if we can learn ways to enhance your enjoyment of the food served to you here. We need your help in a new study on how sensitive people are to different tastes and which tastes they prefer. The results of this study may help doctors and dietitians, here and at other hospitals, plan diets to improve health, and may add to the understanding of taste perception.

In this study, we will find out how readily persons detect and identify sweet, sour, salty, and bitter tastes, and which tastes are preferred. This information will be analyzed in relation to some information that I am given by the staff physician from participants' medical records about their age, sex, smoking history, duration of lithium administration, and current lithium concentration. Persons participating in this study can expect to spend about 20 minutes on each of five different days. Participants will be asked to taste plain water and samples of water mixed with small amounts of some safe substances that normally are used to season food; they will be asked to answer some questions about how the samples taste and which ones they prefer. There is no foreseeable risk or discomfort. Participants may withdraw their data at the end of their participation if they decide that they didn't want to participate after all.

Participants' identity and personal information will be kept confidential (locked in a file cabinet to which I alone have access) and will be destroyed as soon as the study is completed. The results will be published in a scientific journal. After the study, all participants will be invited to a presentation on how taste perception works. Then each participant will be given the results of his taste test, and an opportunity to sample foods having both typical and increased amounts of the preferred tastes. We hope you will find this information useful to you in seasoning your food in the cafeteria.

Your participation in this study is strictly voluntary. You may withdraw your participation at any time. Your decision as to whether to participate will have no effect on any benefits you now receive or may need to receive in the future from any agency. For answers to questions pertaining to the research, research participants' rights, or in the event of a research-related injury, you may contact me directly, at 555-1212; Dr. John Smith, Director of Research, at 555-1313; or Dr. Mary Doe, Hospital Director, at 555-1414.
Sincerely yours,
Mary Jones, Research Psychologist

Please indicate your consent by signing a copy of this letter and returning it to me. The other copy is for you to keep.

I have read this letter and consent to participate.
Signature:
Date:

Note that this letter not only fulfills the legal requirements for a consent statement but is also clear, friendly, and respectful of the recipient. Irrespective of whether the researcher is a Nobel Prize-winning scientist or a senior in college, the consent letter should treat the potential subject as an equal. Fanfare about the importance of the project is inappropriate. The letter should make an accurate, but brief, statement about the likely scientific value of the research. Information about the scientific legitimacy of the project is conveyed through the name of the research institution on the letterhead and mention of the researcher's official capacity below the signature (e.g., student, Professor of Sociology, Director).

4.4 CONSENT: SIGNED, ORAL, OR BEHAVIORAL?

Signed (or documented) consent proves that consent was obtained. In the case of some risky research, it may even be desirable to also have a witness sign. Most IRBs require signed consent, except in the following situations (as specified in the federal regulations):

1. When signed consent is intrusive or inconvenient and subjects can behaviorally refuse (e.g., by hanging up on a phone interviewer or by throwing out the survey that was received in the mail). In some cases, a letter or statement providing the information required for informed consent may be sufficient. For example, when phone surveys are conducted using random digit dialing, the researcher does not know the name or address of the subject, thus assuring anonymity; the subject, upon learning about the survey from a brief verbal description, can very easily say no, or simply hang up. The process of getting signed consent may be unduly cumbersome for both parties. Similarly, although a survey mailed to respondents should include a cover letter that contains all of the information required for informed consent, it is generally deemed unnecessary for the subject to actually sign and return a consent form. Returning the survey is the subject's way of consenting. Throwing it away is the subject's way of refusing.

2. When signed consent would jeopardize the well-being of subjects. For example, if the research is on criminal behavior, being recruited and agreeing to participate is evidence of one's illegal activity. When the research focuses on illegal or highly stigmatized aspects of the persons being studied, it is not in the subjects' best interest for the researcher to provide a paper trail that reveals the identity of the subjects. Such information could be subpoenaed by a local law enforcement authority (e.g., in connection with a labor dispute, or prosecution of suspected child abusers or drug dealers), or stolen (e.g., by blackmailers), placing subjects at serious risk. Examples of research in which subject lists might be subpoenaed include studies of drug users or drug dealers, prostitutes, child abusers, pornography producers, white-collar criminals, illegal aliens, and so on. Sometimes, certain information about persons, were it to become known, could also lead to personal, social, or economic discrimination, blackmail, or simply to embarrassment and worry. Having AIDS, being gay, having had an abortion, having been exposed to high levels of radiation—all such characterizations are potentially stigmatizing to individuals. Consequently, in research on populations vulnerable to stigmatizing effects, a signed consent form may well pose more danger than protection to the subjects who participate. (Also, see Chapter 6 [6.6] on legal protections of confidentiality.)

However, just because *signed* consent is not required does not mean that consent is not necessary. Consent is necessary and a copy of the consent statement may be given to the subject; only the signed agreement to participate is waived.

4.5 CONSENT AS AN ONGOING PROCESS

The researcher should regard the relationship with subjects as an open communication process and willingly answer questions from subjects and gatekeepers at any time. Especially in field research, where the researcher returns to the site on many occasions, it is easy for his or her welcome to wear thin. In organizational settings, the researcher should provide employees, administrators, and all other interested parties with a written statement (in layperson's language) about the topic of the research and should also furnish occasional updates, reporting on the current phase of work. The research team might also invite members of the organization to drop in at break time for a snack and discussion, questions, or complaints. The advantages of such openness and cordiality are enormous. Even the most sensitive research team gets in the way sometimes and causes unexpected inconvenience to ongoing operations. If people become irritated, but have no avenue for complaining, tensions may grow until they reach a breaking point, and the research is halted. In contrast, openness to any observations and complaints means that problems can be solved before they become serious.

Good communication and good sense require that openness and honesty also characterize the ongoing relationship with subjects, gatekeepers, and others in the research setting. In field settings (e.g., workplaces, schools, hospitals), such communication may occur not only with subjects but also with other key individuals within the setting, such as union representatives, managers, parents, and others who are part of that setting but not subjects. The researcher should be open to discussion of problems that the research raises for the various interests represented within a particular setting. Any communication with the press about the research should be cleared through the gatekeepers of the organization. Sensitivity and willingness to accommodate these interests, however inconvenient for the researcher, pay off in the long run. Insensitivity to such concerns has often resulted in a researcher being asked to leave the field before the project is completed.

4.6 DEBRIEFING AND DISCUSSION OF FINDINGS

"That's all. Thanks. 'Bye." Having gotten the data, the researcher's relationship with subjects has ended. Right? Wrong.

Of paramount importance is *debriefing*, or providing an opportunity for interaction with subjects and relevant others immediately following the research participation. Depending on the nature of the research and the amount of time required to complete the study and analysis, it may also be appropriate to provide an immediate opportunity for *discussion of the findings* of that particular study with subjects and relevant others. Debriefing when deception has occurred is discussed in Chapter 7.

Debriefing. Researchers often state that one benefit of their research is its educational or therapeutic value for participants. The other benefit, of course, is the knowledge gained from subjects. The debriefing process provides an appropriate time to consolidate the educational and therapeutic value to subjects through appropriate conversation and hand-outs. It is also a good time for the researcher to gain some more knowledge: What were subjects' perceptions of the research? Why did they respond as they did—especially those whose responses were unusual? How do subjects' views of the usefulness of the findings comport with those of the researcher? Typically, the interpretation and application of findings are strengthened by thoughtful discussion with participants. Many a perceptive researcher has learned more from the debriefing process than the data alone could ever reveal.

Debriefing should be a two-way street: Subjects deserve an opportunity to ask questions and express reactions, as well as a few minutes in which to interact with a truly appreciative investigator. The researcher should be listening.

All too often researchers duck their responsibility to debrief by glibly promising to make the results of the study available to subjects. It is rarely a good idea to promise to give subjects the results of the research. The time and logistics involved in doing so can be prohibitive, hence this promise is often broken. Besides, the findings of a single study typically are of limited interest to the participants. Of greater interest and usefulness is the knowledge that the researcher gained from the literature search that (should have) preceded the study, and that can easily be provided during the debriefing. The educational discussion offered after participation should emphasize what is already known, with only secondary attention given to what might be learned from the current study. To do otherwise is to make unwarranted assumptions about the importance of one's research.

The debriefing period should be planned and scheduled as an integral part of the research process. The timing and nature of the debriefing should be appropriate to the circumstances. If the research deals with private or sensitive matters, the debriefing should take place privately with each subject. The complicated study of problem solving in children, described in 4.7, involved four debriefings: (a) several minutes taken with each child after a session, (b) a presentation to the teaching staff at a faculty meeting, (c) a presentation to parents at a PTA meeting, and (d) a brief written presentation mailed to parents. By contrast, in the typical case of research on college students, the debriefing might include a brief, nontechnical presentation on (a) the purpose of the study, (b) the relation of the purpose to the condition(s) in which subjects participated, (c) what is known about the problem and what hypotheses were being tested, (d) the dependent and independent variables, and (e) why the study is of theoretical or practical importance. At this time, subjects also might be given a one- or two-page description of the topic and the research, expanding upon what they had already been told.

The debriefing period is also an appropriate time for such administrative tasks as addressing an envelope for sending a summary of the results when they are ready, paying subjects, and so on.

Discussion of findings. Researchers often appeal for access to a research population on grounds that their research will yield answers that will benefit that population. But after receiving permission to do the research, some researchers forget the implied promise to discuss their findings with those who made the study possible. Publishing the results is not equivalent to first-hand discussion with the research population.

In applied field research in which access is gained through community representatives, arrangements should be made for discussing the findings with appropriate members of the community. Typically, the same gatekeepers who consented to the research decide when, and with whom, the discussion of results should be held. As described in 4.7, preliminary planning of the community presentation occurs as part of the consent process, and final plans are worked out when the presentation of findings is made to the primary gatekeepers. If the results might stigmatize the members of the research population, agreements should be made ahead of time about how such results will be handled; censorship and stigma are to be avoided.

4.7 CONSENT AND DEBRIEFING IN COMMUNITY-BASED RESEARCH

Schools, workplaces, hospitals, prisons, social service agencies, churches, and residential neighborhoods are but a few of the community-based settings where applied research is conducted, and where the researcher must obtain the consent of gatekeepers before seeking the consent of individual subjects. To gain entrée and obtain valid data, the researcher must learn about the culture of the organization in which the research occurs, as well as that of the individuals within it. Thus, the problems discussed in 4.1—the communication elements of consent—

become cross-cultural problems: the scientific and personal culture of the researcher versus the organizational and individual cultures of the gatekeepers and subjects. In some community-based research, such as research on drug addicts at risk for HIV (topics discussed in Chapter 11), the difficulties of comprehending and responding sensitively to these cultures can be overwhelming, even to the experienced community-based researcher. Another problem is that of the unscrupulous or insensitive gatekeeper, who may coerce participation or expect to have access to personal information that the researcher obtains.

The example of consent and debriefing in community-based research presented here is an easy one compared to those discussed in Chapter 11. It is based on my own research on test anxiety and problem solving, conducted in a suburban elementary school on children whose upwardly mobile parents pressured them unduly for good grades. (See Chapter 10 for further discussion of issues of consent for research on children.) Although relatively simple in many respects, the issues of consent and debriefing in this study are similar to most of the questions that must be answered in more difficult settings:

1. *Who is the key gatekeeper? How can needs of the gatekeeper and community be met through the research?* The principal, a mature and understanding woman, had been searching for ways to demonstrate to parents the importance of easing up on their children. She regarded my research as a way to achieve some parent education, provided that I communicated my scientific findings sensitively to parents.

2. *Who are the other gatekeepers? How are they reached?* The school board and superintendent had to approve the research. The teachers had to be satisfied that it would not interfere unduly with their activities. Finally, parents had to consent for their children to participate, and the children, themselves, had to assent. The principal arranged for me to meet with the school board and to attend a teachers' meeting. I drafted a consent letter to parents, and revised it in response to the principal's suggestions.

3. *What flexibility is needed to fit the research plans with the needs of the community?* There was no extra room in the school to accommodate my research; a trailer had to be rented. The schedule, according to which I took students from their classrooms, was worked out in collaboration with their teachers and was subsequently revised as new school events were scheduled. The teachers were concerned that students might think they had not done well on the problem-solving tasks given to them in the

research, so they helped devise the debriefing explanation procedure given to each child after participation.

4. *How should communication and dissemination be handled?* I promised the principal that I would discuss my findings with teachers and parents. The principal subsequently responded to polite inquiries from parents by inviting them to the discussion of the findings at a PTA meeting "sometime in the spring." I reviewed my results and conclusions with the principal, whose astute observations resulted in some constructive changes in my conclusions. I showed her a discussion of my research problem written in layman's language, including a summary of the literature and of my findings, along with some tactful suggestions for helping children overcome test anxiety. After incorporating her suggestions, this paper was sent to parents and teachers, together with a cover letter expressing our gratitude for their cooperation. We also scheduled a presentation of the findings to teachers, and then one to parents at a PTA meeting. I received some nice notes and phone calls from parents and teachers, offering additional comments and thanking me. By the time I wrote the published version of the research, I had gained a perspective that I could not possibly have attained without my conversations with teachers and parents. I also knew that I would be welcome in that school district if I ever wanted to do research there again.

NOTES

1. Throughout this book, *privacy* refers to the interest that persons have in controlling others' access to themselves. *Confidentiality* refers to the agreement between researcher and subject about access by others to the data. *Anonymity* refers to data that include no unique identifiers such as name or Social Security number.

2. I am indebted to Winifred Westberg for this description.

RECOMMENDED READING

Katz, J. (1984). *Silent world of doctor and patient*. New York: Free Press. [Provides excellent illustrations of the process of communication in informed consent.]

5

Privacy

*"I know it when I feel it." A gut sense of personal violation may be
the tie that binds such disparate events as being subjected to a body
search, being the subject of gossip, having one's mail read, being
asked one's income, or having one's house entered without
permission. It should come as no surprise that such an intensely
personal construct is difficult to define.*

Melton, 1991, p. 66

We certainly know when our own privacy has been invaded, but do we
know when a subject's privacy is likely to be invaded? An interview
that asks respondents about matters of love and friendship will produce
very different "gut reactions" in someone who has a happy family life
versus someone who has just been dumped and is barely controlling
feelings of hysteria and despair. How can investigators protect subjects
from the pain of invaded privacy? How can investigators guard the
integrity of their research against the lies and subterfuges that subjects
will employ to hide some private truth or guard against an intrusion?

The purpose of this chapter is to provide a framework for understanding
how to respect the privacy of research subjects.

5.1 HOW DO PRIVACY, CONFIDENTIALITY, AND ANONYMITY DIFFER?

Privacy refers to *persons* and to their interest in controlling the access
of others to themselves. Confidentiality is an extension of the concept
of privacy; it refers to *data* (some record about the person, such as notes
or a videotape of the person) and to how data are to be handled in
keeping with subjects' interest in controlling the access of others to
information about themselves. Ideally, confidentiality is handled in an
informed consent agreement between researcher and subject; the agree-

ment states what may be done with private information that the subject conveys to the researcher. The terms of the confidentiality agreement need to be tailored to the particular situation. Anonymity means that the names and other unique identifiers (e.g., Social Security number, address) of subjects are never attached to the data or even known to the researcher.

5.2 WHY IS PRIVACY AN ISSUE IN RESEARCH?

Privacy, that is, subjects' degree of control of the access that others have to them and to information about them, affects their willingness to participate in research and to give honest responses. An understanding of the privacy concerns of potential subjects enables the researcher to communicate an awareness of and respect for those concerns, and to protect subjects from invasion of their privacy. Because privacy issues are often subtle and not understood by the researcher, appropriate awareness and safeguards may be omitted, with unfortunate results. Here are some examples:

A researcher interviews poor Chicano families in Los Angeles about their attitudes concerning AIDS. Unknown to the researcher, these people consider it immoral, and sacrilegious, to even talk about homosexuality or AIDS. Most pretend not to understand his questions.

A researcher gets access to medical records, discovers which persons have asthma, and contacts them directly to ask them to participate in research on coping strategies of asthmatics. "How did you get my name?" "What were you doing with my medical records?" were the thoughts, if not the actual questions, of most of those called. Most refused to participate. The researcher should have asked physicians to send their asthmatic patients a letter (drafted and paid for by the researcher), asking if they would be interested in participating, and if so, the physician would release their names to the researcher.

A researcher interviews families about their child-rearing practices. She establishes such excellent rapport that some pour out details of physical and sexual abuse of children by other members of their families, all of which the researcher is required by law to report, even though she has promised confidentiality.

A researcher interviews children about their moral beliefs. Believing that the children would want privacy, he interviews 5-year-olds alone. However, they are sufficiently afraid to be alone that they do not respond as well as they would have if their mothers had been present. Recognizing his error, the researcher then makes sure that subjects from the next group, 8-year-olds, are accompanied by their mothers. However, the 8-year-olds have entered that stage of development in which some privacy from parents is important. Consequently, they do not answer all of his questions honestly.

A researcher decides to use telephone interviews to learn about the health history of lower-class older people, as the phone typically offers greater privacy than the face-to-face interview. She fails to recognize, however, that poor elderly people rarely live alone or have privacy from their families when they use the phone, and many keep health secrets from their family.

A researcher interviews minority children about their nutritional habits. Because another scientist has made known to the press the opinion that this community does not responsibly feed its children, a small group of activists in the community breaks into the researcher's files and steals his data.

In each case, the researcher has been insensitive to privacy issues idiosyncratic to the research population and has not addressed the problems these issues pose for his or her research. Had he or she consulted with community gatekeepers or others familiar with the research population, these problems might have been identified and solved. Most of the research topics that interest social scientists concern somewhat private or personal matters. Yet most topics, however private, can be effectively and responsibly researched if the researcher employs appropriate sensitivity and safeguards.

5.3 IS THERE A RIGHT TO PRIVACY?

An individual's right to privacy from research inquiry is protected by the right to refuse to participate in research. An investigator is free to do research on consenting subjects or on publicly available information, including unobtrusive observation of people in public places. May a researcher videotape or photograph behavior in public without obtaining informed consent? There is no law against this, but common courtesy and sensitivity to local norms should be heeded. Intimate acts, such as goodbyes at airports, should be regarded as private, even though performed in public.

Constitutional and federal laws have little to say directly about privacy and social research. The only definitive federal privacy laws governing social research are the following: The Buckley Amendment prohibits access to children's school records without parental consent. The Hatch Act prohibits asking children questions about religion, sex, or family life without parental permission. And the National Research Act requires parental permission for research on children.

Tort law provides a mechanism under which persons might take action against an investigator alleged to have invaded privacy. In such an action, the law defines privacy in relation to other interests. It expects behavioral scientists to be sensitive to persons' claims to privacy, but recognizes that claims to privacy must sometimes yield to competing claims. Any subject may file a suit against a researcher for "invasion of privacy," but courts of law are sensitive to the value of research as well as the value of privacy.

An important protection against such a suit is an adequate informed consent statement signed by each participant, as well as parental permission for research participation by children. However, persons other than the research participant may consider their privacy invaded by the research. For example, family members who are not participants in the research may feel that the investigation also probed their affairs. If the research is socially important and validly designed, if the researcher has taken reasonable precautions to respect the privacy needs of typical subjects and others associated with the research, and if the project has been approved by an IRB, such a suit is likely to be dismissed. But what exactly is this privacy about which researchers need to be so careful?

5.4 A BEHAVIORAL DEFINITION OF PRIVACY

As a behavioral phenomenon, privacy refers to certain needs to establish personal boundaries; these needs seem to be basic and universal, but they are manifested differently, depending on learning and cultural and developmental factors. Privacy does not simply mean being left alone. Some people have too little opportunity to share life with others, or to bask in public attention. When treated respectfully, many are pleased that an investigator is interested in hearing about their personal lives. Because of this desire on the part of lonely people for understanding and attention, competent survey investigators often have more difficulty exiting people's homes than entering.

A different kind of unwanted privacy was found by Klockars (1974), a criminologist, when he undertook a case study of a well-known "fence." The fence was an elderly pawnshop owner, who had stolen or fenced vast amounts of goods in the course of his life. Klockars told the fence that he would like to document the details of his career, as the world has little biographical information about the lives of famous thieves. The fence wanted to go down in history and offered to tell all, provided that Klockars used the fence's real name and address in his writing and published the entire account in a book (Klockars, 1974). This was done, and the aging fence proudly decorated his pawnshop with clippings from the book.

Privacy is invaded when people are given unwanted information: A subject's privacy may be breached by showing him pornography, or requiring him to listen to more about some other person's sex life than he would care to hear. Privacy is also invaded when people are deprived of their normal flow of information, as when unconsenting subjects (who did not realize they were participating in a study) were deprived of information that they would ordinarily use to make important decisions.

Thus, many claims to privacy are also claims to autonomy. For example, subjects' privacy and autonomy are violated when their self-report data on marijuana use become the basis for their arrest, when IQ data are disclosed to school teachers who would use it to track students, or when organizational research data disclosed to managers become the basis for firing or transferring employees. The most dramatic cases in which invasion of privacy results in lowered autonomy are those in which something is done to one's thought processes—the most private part of oneself—through behavior control techniques: for example, psychopharmacology, brainwashing, and subliminal advertising.

5.5 PRIVACY AND INFORMED CONSENT

A research experience regarded by some as a delightful opportunity for self-disclosure could constitute an unbearable invasion of privacy for others. Informed consent is an important way to respect these individual differences. The investigator specifies the kinds of things that will occur in the study, the kinds of information that will be sought and given, and the procedures that will be used to assure anonymity or confidentiality. The subject then decides whether to participate under these conditions. One who considers a given research procedure an invasion of privacy can simply decline to participate.

However, informed consent is not the entire solution. One who is insensitive to the privacy needs of the research population may be unprepared to offer the subjects the forms of respect and protection they want.

5.6 GAINING SENSITIVITY TO PRIVACY INTERESTS OF SUBJECTS

Although there is no way to be sure of the privacy interests of all members of a given research population, the researcher can learn how typical members would feel. If the typical member considers the research activity an invasion of privacy, the data will be badly flawed. Evasion, lying, and dropping out of the study are sure to occur, and those who answer honestly will worry about the consequences.

The best ways to learn about the privacy interests of your research population are as follows: (1) Ask someone who works with that population regularly. For example, ask teachers and parents about the privacy interests of their children, ask a child psychotherapist about the privacy interests of abused children, ask a social worker about the privacy interests of low socioeconomic-status parents; (2) ask an investigator who has had much experience working with that same population; and (3) ask members of the population what they think other people in their group might consider private in relation to the intended study.

5.7 "BROKERED" DATA

Researchers may lack access to a given population for a variety of privacy-related reasons. For example, a researcher may wish to survey people who go to an HIV testing clinic, but the clinic may not want him or her on the premises since his or her presence would reduce clients' sense of privacy and frighten some away. However, the physicians who administer the tests may be willing to hand an anonymous questionnaire to the clients and ask them if they would be willing to respond and mail the questionnaire back at their convenience. The investigator may have to offer some incentive, such as a financial contribution to the clinic, to achieve the necessary cooperation from its staff.

The term *broker* refers to any person who works in some trusted capacity with a population to which the researcher does not have access, and who obtains data from that population for a researcher. For example, the broker may be a psychotherapist or a physician who asks patients if they would provide data for important research being conducted elsewhere. A broker may serve other functions in addition to gathering data for the researcher:

"Broker sanitized" responses. There may be concern that some aspect of the response will enable the investigator to deduce the identity of the respondent. For example, if a survey is sent to organization leaders in various parts of the country, the postmark on the envelope might enable someone to deduce the identity of some respondents. To prevent this, a mutually agreed upon third party may receive all of the responses, remove and destroy the envelopes, then send the responses to the investigator.

Brokers and aliases. Sometimes lists of potential respondents are unavailable directly to the researcher. For example, the researcher wishing to study the attitudes of psychiatric patients at various stages of their therapy may not be privy to their names. Rather, the treating psychiatrists may agree to serve as brokers. The psychiatrists then obtain the informed consent of their patients and periodically gather data from those who consent. Each patient is given an alias. Each time data are gathered, the psychiatrist refers to a list for the alias, substitutes it for the patient's real name, and transmits the completed questionnaire back to the researcher.

Additional roles for the broker. The broker may (a) examine responses for information that might permit deductive disclosure of the identity of the respondent, and remove that information; (b) add information (e.g., a professional evaluation of the respondent); or (c) check responses for accuracy or completeness.

RECOMMENDED READINGS

Laufer, R. S., & Wolfe, M. (1977). Privacy as a concept and a social issue: A multidimensional developmental theory. *Journal of Social Issues, 33*, 44-87. [This elegant theory provides ways of understanding what privacy means to persons in age groups, cultures, and circumstances different from one's own.]

Melton, G. B. (1990). Brief research report: Certificate of confidentiality under the Public Health Service Act: Strong protection but not enough. *Violence and Victims, 5*(1), 67-70. [This paper outlines advantages and problems in the use of the certificate of confidentiality.]

6

Strategies for Assuring Confidentiality

The terms *privacy* and *confidentiality* are often used as though they were interchangeable. They are not. Close attention to the definition of confidentiality is important.

6.1 WHAT IS CONFIDENTIALITY?

Confidentiality refers to agreements with persons about what may be done with their data. The confidentiality agreement between a researcher and subject is part of the informed consent agreement. For example, the following is a confidentiality agreement that might be included in the consent letter of a scientist (or thesis student) seeking to interview families in counseling:

To protect your privacy, the following measures will ensure that others do not learn your identity or what you tell me.

1. No names will be used in transcribing from the audio tape, or in writing up the case study. Each person will be assigned a letter name as follows: M for mother, F for father, MS1 for male first sibling, and so on.

2. All identifying characteristics, such as occupation, city, and ethnic background, will be changed.

3. The audio tapes will be reviewed only in my home (and in the office of my thesis adviser).

4. The tapes and notes will be destroyed after my report of this research has been accepted for publication (or in the case of an unpublished thesis—after my thesis has been accepted by the university).

5. What is discussed during our session will be kept confidential with two exceptions: I am compelled by law to inform an appropriate other person if I hear and believe that you are in danger of hurting yourself or someone else, or if there is reasonable suspicion that a child, elder, or dependent adult has been abused.[1]

Noteworthy characteristics of this agreement are: (a) that it recognizes the privacy of some of the information likely to be conveyed; (b) that it states what steps will be taken to ensure that others are not privy to the identity of subjects or to identifiable details about individuals; and (c) that it states legal limitations to the assurance of confidentiality.

6.2 WHY IS CONFIDENTIALITY AN ISSUE IN RESEARCH?

Subjects may be willing to share highly personal information with a researcher if there is a believable confidentiality statement, or if the data are anonymous. Unfortunately, many researchers make glib promises of confidentiality without understanding the ways in which confidentiality may be breached. Subjects, acting on a belief in the researcher's ability to keep the promise, may then be harmed by unintended disclosures. The following examples of broken promises are fictionalized accounts of leaks that have actually occurred in research:

Case 6.1: Blackmail. A researcher studied attitudes concerning morality and asked questions, such as whether subjects had cheated on their income tax, used illegal drugs, had extramarital affairs, or filched supplies from their employers. He also gathered data on the attitudes these persons had expressed at an adult fellowship meeting at their church. He entered each data set into a mainframe computer file, identifying subjects by number. In a separate computer file of that mainframe computer, he kept the linkage of names and numbers. A computer hacker accessed his files. Several subjects were blackmailed. [When storing data on computers to which others have access, identifiers must be stored elsewhere, such as in a safe deposit box.]

Case 6.2: Personnel Action. In a study involving about 200 middle management employees at a large firm, a researcher collected information on drug abuse and financial difficulties, along with employment histories and demographic information such as race, age, and sex. Although no names were used in the final report, it was possible to deduce from the table of summary statistics that a particular employee was a cocaine addict who was about to lose his home because of financial problems. This deduction was possible because he was the only Asian male who had worked continuously in the same division of the company for more than 5 years. He was laid off during the next reduction in work force. [Provide only those summary tables that serve a purpose, and make categories broad enough to prevent singling out of individuals.]

Case 6.3: Subpoena. A researcher interviewed women who had taken medication that was later found to cause birth defects. One of the interview questions was whether respondents remembered reading the warnings of possible side effects in the literature accompanying the drug. In connection with a multimillion-dollar lawsuit against the drug company, the data were subpoenaed to prove that some of the plaintiffs had been aware of the risk they were taking, contrary to what had been stated in the class action suit against the drug company. [This problem would not be solved by destroying unique identifiers. One must be sensitive to when data might be of interest in a law suit. That survey question should never have been asked.]

Case 6.4: Incest. For her master's thesis, a social work student did a case study of a family that had been part of her client load. Fifteen years later, the youngest son in that family entered college and, in connection with a sociology assignment, read the thesis, recognized that it was about his family, and learned that he was actually the son of his eldest sister and their father. [When reporting case studies, the names of persons, places, special events, occupations, ethnic background, and so on should be changed. Any special characteristic of subjects should be changed slightly so that individuals cannot be identified.]

Case 6.5: Computer Problems. A part-time MBA student received permission from the president of the company where she worked to study employee morale while office automation was being introduced. Employees were candid with the researcher because she promised confidentiality and was their trusted co-worker. Some employees complained bitterly to her about the automation system, indicating their conviction that it would fail. She kept the data locked in her office at work, an office to which top executives had skeleton keys. The persons who had complained most bitterly were laid off during the next reduction in staff. [The data should have been kept at home, and codes should have been used, with the code key kept separately.]

In each case, the researcher was responsible for the harm to participants and might have been sued by them. The investigators should have assessed these risks and taken effective precautions. In assessing risk to confidentiality, it is important to remember that attitudes change; the political pendulum swings between conservative and liberal extremes. Consider the following:

Case 6.6: Seizure of Records. (This hypothetical case is based on a police seizure of biomedical research records thought to contain information that would assist in the identification of a bank robber.) A researcher began gathering longitudinal data on the life-style of persons known to be HIV-positive. The data were kept in locked files in a locked office. Three years later, during a conservative political era, a sheriff seeking information on suspected drug dealers issued a search warrant, conducted a "midnight raid," handcuffed the investigator to his desk, and removed his AIDS research files. [Because this is longitudinal research, unique identifiers are needed. When the political climate changed, the researcher should have removed all real names from records in this country and sent the original files to a colleague in another country.]

Adequate safeguards of confidentiality must be employed and described in specific terms in the consent statement. Many people, especially members of minority populations (Turner, 1982), doubt such promises unless the details are spelled out clearly.

6.3 CONFIDENTIALITY OR ANONYMITY?

Anonymity means that the researcher acquires no unique identifiers, such as the subject's name, Social Security number, or driver's license number. When designing the research, one should decide whether the data can be gathered anonymously. Five major reasons for gathering unique identifiers are as follows:

1. So that subjects can be recontacted if their data indicate that they need help or information.

2. So that data sets from the same individual can be linked to one another. (This problem might be solved with code names.)

3. So that results can be mailed to the subject. (This problem can be solved by having each subject address an envelope to himself or herself. Envelopes are stored apart from the data. After results are mailed out, no record of the names of subjects remains.)

4. So that signatures may be obtained on the consent form. (Signed consent may be waived when signatures pose a risk to subjects, as when subjects have been selected because they have engaged in some illegal or socially stigmatizing activity.)

5. So that a low base-rate sample can be identified when a large sample is screened on some measures.

Note that for the first two reasons, the issue is whether to have names associated with subjects' data; for the second two reasons, the issue is whether to have names on file at all. In the fifth case, identifiers may be expunged from the succeeding study as soon as those data are gathered. If the data can be gathered anonymously, subjects will be more forthcoming, and the researcher will be relieved of some responsibilities connected with assuring confidentiality. If the research cannot be done anonymously, the researcher must consider procedural, statistical, and legal methods for assuring confidentiality. Readers who want to investigate methods beyond those presented here are referred to *Assuring the Confidentiality of Social Research Data* (Boruch & Cecil, 1979).

6.4 PROCEDURAL APPROACHES
TO ASSURING CONFIDENTIALITY

Certain procedural approaches eliminate or minimize the link between the identifiers and the data. Various procedures are appropriate, depending on whether the research is cross-sectional, longitudinal, or experimental.

6.4.1 Cross-Sectional Research

In cross-sectional research, there is no attempt to link individual data gathered at one time to data gathered at another. Three simple methods of preventing disclosure of unique identifiers in cross-sectional research are as follows:

Anonymity. The researcher has no record of the identity of the respondents. For example, have respondents mail back their questionnaires or hand them back in a group, without names or other unique identifiers.

Temporarily identified responses. It is sometimes important to ensure that only the appropriate persons have responded and that their responses are complete. After checking names against a list or making sure responses are complete, the names are destroyed, as is done at polling places.

Separately identified responses. In mail surveys, it is sometimes necessary to know who has responded and who has not. To accomplish this with an anonymous survey, respondents may be asked to mail back the completed survey anonymously, and to mail separately a postcard with his or her name on it. This method enables the researcher to check off those who have responded and to send another wave of questionnaires to those who have not.

Any of these three methods could be put to corrupt use if the researcher were so inclined. Because people are sensitive to corrupt practices, the honest researcher must demonstrate integrity. The researcher's good name and that of the research institution may reduce suspicion.

6.4.2 Longitudinal Data

In longitudinal studies, one must somehow link together the various responses of a given person. Boruch and Cecil (1979) suggest many approaches, including the following:

Aliases. Subjects use an easily remembered code, such as their mother's birth date, as an alias. The researcher makes sure there are not duplicate codes among respondents. Note that the adequacy of this method depends upon subjects' ability to remember an alias. Inner-city drug addicts are an example of a population that may not remember; in cases where remembering the wrong alias might seriously affect the research or the subject (e.g., the subject gets back the wrong HIV test result), this method of linking data would be clearly inappropriate.

6.4.3 Interfile Linkage

Sometimes a researcher wants to link research records on persons with some other independently stored records on those same persons (exact matching) or else on persons who are similar on some attributes (statistical matching). An example would be court-mandated research on the relationship between academic accomplishment and subsequent arrest records of juveniles who have been sentenced to one of three experimental rehabilitation programs. The court may be unwilling to grant the researcher access to the records involved, but may be willing to arrange for a court clerk to gather all of the relevant data on each subject, then remove identifiers, and give the anonymous files to the researcher. The obvious advantages of exact matching are the ability to obtain data that would be difficult or impossible to obtain otherwise and the ability to construct a longitudinal file.

Statistical matching enables the researcher to create matched comparison groups. An example of statistical matching would be if each boy having a certain test profile were matched with a girl having a similar test profile. Statistical matching may also permit imputation—estimation of the values of missing data—by revealing how similar persons would answer the item. Interfile linkage is a complex set of techniques, the details of which are beyond the purview of this chapter. The interested reader is referred to Campbell, Boruch, Schwartz, and Steinberg (1977) and to Cox and Boruch (1986).

6.5 STATISTICAL STRATEGIES FOR ASSURING CONFIDENTIALITY

It is folly to ask respondents directly if they have engaged in illegal behavior—for example, used cocaine, beaten their children, or cheated on taxes. Respondents are unlikely to answer honestly, and if they did, they would place themselves in legal jeopardy.

Methods of randomized response, or error inoculation, provide a strategy for asking questions in such a way that no one can know who has given incriminating responses. Because they decrease effective sample size and do not work with all populations, these methods should be used only when necessary and appropriate. This procedure is intended to assure subjects, but it arouses suspicion in some populations and diminishes truthfulness.

The simplest variant of this strategy is to give each subject a die to roll before answering a "yes" or "no" question. The respondent might be instructed to answer untruthfully if the die comes up, say, two. Otherwise, he is to answer truthfully. The respondent does not let the researcher see how the die comes up. He then gives his answer according to instructions. The researcher knows that one response in six is false. The following example shows how the data are analyzed:

Suppose the researcher interviews 100 people and asks each if he or she has cheated on income tax; 36 indicate that they have cheated. The following equation enables one to estimate the true proportion of persons who have cheated on their tax:

$$\text{Estimated true proportion} = (Py - Pfp)/(1 - Pfp - Pfn).$$
Where Py = observed proportion of "yes" responses
Pfp = probability of false positive responses (here 1/6)
Pfn = probability of false negative responses (here 1/6)
$$\text{Estimated true proportion} = (.36 - .167)/(1 - .167 - .167)$$
$$= .193/.666 = .29$$

An estimated 29% of this sample have cheated on their income tax.

There are many variations of this procedure, and a considerable literature on its efficacy. See Boruch and Cecil (1979, 1982) or Fox and Tracy (1986) for details.

6.6 CERTIFICATES OF CONFIDENTIALITY

Members of certain professions, such as priests, physicians, and lawyers, have testimonial privilege. That is, under certain circumstances they may not be required to reveal to a court of law the identity of their clients or sources of information. This privilege does *not* extend to researchers. As indicated earlier, prosecutors, grand juries, legislative bodies, civil litigants, and administrative agencies can use their subpoena powers to compel disclosure of confidential research information. What is to protect the researcher and subjects from this intrusion? Anonymous data, aliases, colleagues in foreign countries, and statistical strategies are not always satisfactory solutions. The most effective and yet underutilized protection against subpoena is the certificate of confidentiality.

In 1988 Congress enacted a law providing for an apparently absolute researcher-participant privilege when it is covered by a certificate of confidentiality issued by the Department of Health and Human Services. The provisions of this relatively new law authorize:

> [P]ersons engaged in biomedical, behavioral, clinical or other research (including research on the use and effect of alcohol and other psychoactive drugs) to protect the privacy of individuals who are the subject of such research by withholding from all persons not connected with the conduct of such research the names, or other identifying characteristics of such individuals. Persons so authorized to protect the privacy of such individuals may not be compelled in any Federal, State, or local civil, criminal administrative, legislative, or other proceedings to identify such individuals. (Public Health Service Act, 301(d), 42 USC 242a)

Certificates of confidentiality are granted on request for any *bona fide* research project of a sensitive nature, in which protection of confidentiality is judged necessary to achieve the research objectives. The research need not be funded or connected with any federal agency. Some government funders also issue certificates of confidentiality to their grantees upon request. Persons interested in learning more about certificates of confidentiality are referred to the Office for Protection from Research Risks, NIH; phone (301) 496-8101; or to the Office of Health Planning and Evaluation, Office of the Assistant Secretary of Health; phone (301) 472-7911.

6.7 CONFIDENTIALITY AND CONSENT

An adequate consent statement shows the subject that the researcher has conducted a thorough analysis of the risks to confidentiality and has acted with the well-being of the subject foremost in mind. The consent statement must specify any promises of confidentiality that the researcher *cannot* make. Typically, these have to do with reporting laws pertaining to child abuse, child molestation, and threats of harm to others. Reporting laws vary from state to state, so the researcher should be familiar with laws in the state where the research is to be conducted. Thus, the consent statement warns the subject not to reveal certain kinds of information to the researcher. A skilled researcher can establish rapport and convince subjects to reveal almost anything, including things the researcher may not want to be responsible for knowing.

There are many ways in which confidentiality might be discussed in a consent statement. A few examples are as follows:

Example 1. To protect your privacy, this research is conducted anonymously. No record of your participation will be kept. Do not sign this consent or put your name on the survey.

Example 2. This is an anonymous study of teacher attitudes and achievements. No names of people, schools, or districts will be gathered. The results will be reported in the form of statistical summaries of group results.

Example 3. The data will be anonymous. You are asked to write your name on the cover sheet because it is essential that I make sure your responses are complete. As soon as you hand in your questionnaire, I will check your responses for completeness and ask you to complete any incomplete items. I will then tear off and destroy the cover sheet. There will be no way anyone else can associate your name with your data.

Example 4. This survey is anonymous. Please complete it and return it unsigned in the enclosed, postage-paid envelope. At the same time, please return the postcard bearing your name. That way we will know you responded, but we will not know which survey is yours.

Example 5. This anonymous study of persons who have decided to be tested for HIV infection is being conducted by Dr. Jan Smith, at Newton University. Because we do not want to intrude on your privacy in any way, Dr. Barry Wray, at the AIDS Testing Center, has agreed to ask you if you would be willing to respond to this survey. Please look it over. If you think you would be willing to respond, take it home, answer the questions, and mail it back to me in the attached, stamped, self-addressed envelope. If you are interested in knowing the results of the study, please write to me at the above address, or stop by the AIDS Testing Center and ask for a copy of the results, which will be available after May 1.

Example 6. Because this is a study in which we hope to track your progress in coping with an incurable disease and your responses to psychotherapy designed to help you in that effort, we will need to interview you every 2 months and match your new interview data with your prior data. To keep your file strictly anonymous, we need to give you an alias. Think of one or more code names you might like to use. Make sure it is a name you will remember, such as the name of a close high school friend, a pet, or a favorite movie star. You will need to check with the researcher to make sure that no other participant has chosen the same name. The name you choose will be the only name that is ever associated with your file. We will be unable to contact you, so we hope you will be sure to keep in touch with us. If you decide to drop out of the study, we would be grateful if you would let us know.

Example 7. In this study, I will examine the relationship between your child's SAT scores and his attitude toward specific areas of study. I respect the privacy of your child. If you give me permission to do so, I will ask your child to fill out an attitude survey. I will then give that survey to the school secretary, who will write your child's SAT subscores on it and erase your child's name from it. That way, I will have attitude and SAT data for each child, but will not know the names of any child. The data will then be statistically analyzed and reported as group data.

These are merely examples. Careful consideration needs to be given to the content and wording of each consent statement.

6.8 DATA SHARING

If research is published, the investigator is accountable for the results and is normally required to keep the data for 5 to 10 years. The editor may ask to see the raw data to check its veracity. Some funders require that the documented data be archived in user-friendly form and made available to other scientists. Data sharing, if done with due respect for confidentiality, is regarded positively by most subjects, who would prefer to think of their data as a contribution to science and available to other legitimate scientists to examine, critique, and build upon.

When data are shared via a public archive, all identifiers must be removed, and the researcher must ensure that there is no way to deduce identity. For example, if data about teachers reveal the name of the district, along with teacher age, sex, and years of teaching, it may be easy for someone with access to school personnel records to deduce identities.

Techniques for rendering data immune to deductive disclosure. A variety of techniques have been developed to transform raw data into a form that prevents deductive disclosure. Variables or cases with easily identifiable characteristics are removed. Random error can be implanted into the data, introducing enough noise to foil attempts at deductive disclosure, but not enough to obscure conclusions. Micro-aggregation creates synthetic individuals; instead of releasing the individual data on 2,000 participants in a study of small business owners, one might group the data into 500 sets of four subjects each, and release average data on every variable for each set, along with the within-variance data. Outside users could do secondary analyses on these 500 synthetic small business owners. For details, see Gates (1988), Kim (1986), Duncan and Lambert (1987), and Boruch and Cecil (1979).

NOTE

1. This was adapted from a statement developed by David H. Ruja, and is discussed in E. Gil. *The California Child Abuse Reporting Law: Issues and Answers for Professionals* [Publication 132(10/86)]. This booklet is printed and distributed by the State of California Department of Social Services, Office of Child Abuse Prevention, 744 P Street, M.S.9-100, Sacramento, CA 95814.

RECOMMENDED READINGS

Boruch R. F., & Cecil, J. S. (1979). *Assuring the confidentiality of social research data.* Philadelphia: University of Pennsylvania Press.

Campbell, D. T., Boruch, R. F., Schwartz, R. D., & Steinberg, J. (1977). Confidentiality-preserving modes of access to files and to interfile exchange for useful statistical analysis. *Evaluation Quarterly, 1*(2), 269-300.

7

Deception Research

In deception research, the researcher studies reactions of subjects who are purposely led to have false beliefs or assumptions. Although deception is essential for the study of some kinds of behavior, there are serious objections to its use. Deception research may deny subjects their right of self-determination, causing a generalized suspicion of research and disrespect for science. It may invade privacy; it may use powerful methods to induce people to do things they regret doing; and it may create a great deal of upset on the part of subjects and society. The routine use of deception can result in poorly crafted and trivial experiments that are unjustifiable. This chapter examines the factors that may make deception research wrongful and harmful. It indicates ways to achieve valid research objectives without wronging or harming subjects and discusses the appropriate uses of dehoaxing and desensitizing.

7.1 WHY IS DECEPTION USED IN RESEARCH?

There are four defensible justifications for deception research. Deception may be the only viable way to accomplish the following research objectives:

1. To achieve stimulus control or random assignment of subjects.
2. To study responses to low-frequency events.
3. To obtain valid data without serious risk to subjects. For example, in research on conflict, one may employ an accomplice or confederates who will not escalate the conflict beyond the level needed for the purposes of the research.
4. To obtain information that would otherwise be unobtainable because of subjects' defensiveness, embarrassment, shame, or fear of reprisal.

An indefensible rationale for deception is to trick people into research participation that they would find unacceptable if they correctly understood it. *If it is to be acceptable at all, deception research should not involve people in ways that members of the subject population would find unacceptable.*

A flawed rationale is to promote spontaneous behavior in a laboratory setting. There is abundant evidence that participants in laboratory research, especially college students, typically assume that deception will occur and engage in deceptive hypothesis testing of their own (Geller, 1982; Orne, 1969). Contrary to what many researchers claim, subjects are respectful of consent procedures in which they are asked to permit the researcher to withhold some information until after they have participated, with a sincere promise of full debriefing afterward.

Case 7.1: Deceiving to Study Conformity. Solomon Asch (1956) studied conformity by telling subjects that they were participating in a perception experiment, in which each member of their group would select the line believed to be the same length as the standard line. Unknown to the subject, the other seven members of the group were confederates. On the first two trials, most of the seven confederates made the correct match. From the third trial on, the confederates all agreed on the wrong answer. Asch reported that the (real) subjects looked bewildered and anxious. Thirty-three percent of them gave the same wrong answer as the confederates, while the rest gave the correct answer despite obvious feelings of discomfort and confusion. The 33% error rate in the false majority condition was in sharp contrast to the 7% error rate in the condition without the confederates. Most subjects doubted their own judgment, and one-third of them caved in to the majority opinion. Following each subject's participation, a sensitive debriefing was conducted in which the procedure was fully explained and subjects were assured that their responses to conformity pressures were normal.

Asch's conformity study required deception for all four of the defensible reasons mentioned above. The first three rationales for Asch's deception—control and random assignment, study of a low-frequency event, and avoidance of real, and possibly dangerous, interpersonal conflict—obviously apply, but the reader might wonder whether the fourth rationale is pertinent: Are people that defensive about their conformity? Would self-report data have been as accurate? Apparently not. Wolosin, Sherman, and Mynatt (1972) found that individuals perceive most other people as conforming sheep, but report that they themselves are independent of group influence.

Did Asch's subjects see through the deception? Since the research was performed nearly a half-century ago, before deception became a method of choice among social psychologists, the subjects may actually have been naive and spontaneous.

7.2 ALTERNATIVES TO DECEPTION

The ethical and methodological problems of deception research have received much attention in recent decades (e.g., Geller, 1982; Kelman, 1967, 1972; Seeman, 1969). The emphasis in social research has shifted increasingly to field settings where deception is not tolerated (see, for example, Chapter 11, on community-based research). Also, the rise of IRBs has caused researchers to think twice about their methods, rather than regard deception as the unquestioned method of choice. Out of this confluence of events, three main alternatives have emerged.

1. Simulations—mock situations in which subjects are asked to act as if the situation were real—are effective ways of exploring social behavior. Three basic types of simulations have been developed: game simulations, field simulations, and role-playing simulations; each has taken an important place in research.

In game simulations, subjects take roles under a particular set of rules and maintain them until a desired outcome is reached. For example, mock trials have been convened, using real jury candidates, real judges, and real cases (Boruch, 1976). Such simulations are highly realistic.

Field simulations lack firm rules, use highly realistic staged settings, and encourage subjects to believe they are participating in a natural event. For example, the Stanford prison study (Zimbardo, Haney, Banks, & Jaffe, 1973) involved students who volunteered but did not know whether they would play prisoners or guards. The students were unexpectedly picked up in real Palo Alto police cars and booked at the police station before being reminded that this was the study for which they had volunteered. Field simulations, which may last for days, are so highly involving as to produce extreme behavioral and emotional responses; although avoiding deception, therefore, such simulations may well raise other kinds of ethical concerns.

Role playing is the type of simulation that is best suited for the kind of experimentation in which deception has typically been used. The role player knows of any illusions that are created in the setting and is asked to act spontaneously, as if the situation were real. Like a method actor, the role player attempts to do what one would actually do in a particular (contrived) situation. When realistic props are used, as in a deception experiment, the behavior of role-playing subjects is often indistinguishable from that of their counterparts in deception experiments (Geller, 1978).

2. Ethnographic or participant observation methods, coupled with self-report, are used increasingly to study real behavior. As described in Chapter 11, most community-based research involves the researcher deeply enough in field settings that it is feasible to validate self-report against observations of naturally occurring behavior. In such settings, the key to accuracy is not the technical cleverness of deception, but rapport, trust, and good ethnographic and interviewing skills.

3. Consent to concealment may be obtained. There is now ample evidence that most subjects will gladly participate in research with the understanding that some details must be withheld until after they have participated, and that a full debriefing will follow. We turn now to a fuller discussion of concealment versus deception strategies.

7.3 CONSENT TO CONCEAL VERSUS DECEPTION

Five kinds of deception or concealment may be used to achieve the objectives discussed in 7.1. Three approaches involve consent and concealment. Note that only two of the approaches listed below actually deny subjects their right of self-determination and involve deception.

1. *Informed consent to participate in one of various conditions.* The various conditions to which subjects may be assigned are clearly described to subjects ahead of time. For example, most studies employing a placebo use this consent approach. Subjects know that they cannot be told the particular condition to which they will be assigned, as this knowledge would affect their response. Complete debriefing is given afterward. Subjects who do not wish to participate under these conditions may decline to participate.

2. *Consent to deception.* Subjects are told that there may be misleading aspects of the study that will not be explained to them until after they have participated. A full debriefing is given as promised.

3. *Consent to waive the right to be informed.* Subjects waive the right to be informed and are not explicitly forewarned of the possibility of deception. They receive a full debriefing afterward.

4. *Consent and false informing*. Subjects consent to participate and are falsely informed about the nature of the research.

5. *No informing and no consent.* Subjects do not know that research is occurring. Subjects assume that they are just engaging in "real life." The setting may be contrived, or it may be a natural setting in all respects but one—it may contain a spy.

Most research requiring deception can be done about as well with one of the first three forms of deception as with the latter two. In the two cases that follow, consider how a researcher's decision to apply the first, rather than the fifth, form of deception might influence the consequences of a study of the behavioral effects of LSD:

> *(Hypothetical case).* Subjects are asked to participate in a study of the effects of LSD on specified behaviors. They are told they will receive either a salt tablet (a placebo) or an LSD tablet, but that they cannot be told ahead of time which they will receive. Subjects experience affective states and may incorrectly attribute the cause—hence the need for a placebo group. Before being released, subjects are monitored for a period of one week in a hospital setting, to ensure that the treatment effects, if any, are gone. All subjects are debriefed on the fifth day.

> *Case 7.2: CIA Research on LSD.* A true example of deception with no consent or debriefing is the following study, which was supported by the CIA: The investigators set up an elaborate laboratory in a brothel. As clients arrived, they were given drinks containing LSD. The men's behavior was then filmed from behind a two-way mirror. The subjects were never debriefed. One subject committed suicide while under the influence of LSD. The cause of his suicide and details of the research remained secret until many years later when the victim's family found clues that led to the truth (Goldman, Clark, & Marro, 1975).

These examples are informative. The first four forms of deception readily permit the research to be conducted in a setting where accurate measurements, proper controls, and all necessary safeguards are readily at hand. However, the form of deception in which subjects do not realize that they are participating in research is more likely to occur in field settings where assurances of privacy and confidentiality, adequate standby medical aid, and other features of scientifically and ethically sound research simply cannot be provided.

The fact that there is no informing and no consent in a field setting, however, does not necessarily mean that the research would be judged harmful or wrongful. Rather, it is how society evaluates the behavior studied that largely determines the attribution of harm or wrong, as the following example might suggest:

> *Case 7.3: Cookies and Kindness.* Isen and Levin (1972) investigated the effects of a person's positive affective state on subsequent willingness to help others. Feeling good was induced in half the subjects by handing out free cookies to them while they were studying in the library. The other half did not receive cookies. Half the subjects in each group were then approached by another person and asked if they would volunteer to serve as confederates in a psychology experiment designed to study creativity in students at examination time, as compared to other times of the year. There were also told that the experimental procedure was something students would find helpful. The other half of the subjects were asked if they would volunteer to serve as confederates in a study requiring that they drop books, make noises, and so on while the experimenter unobtrusively recorded students' reactions to distraction at examination time, as compared to other times of the year. They were also told that the distraction would be generally regarded by students as an unpleasant annoyance. The results of this study indicate that students who received cookies were far more willing to engage in helpful behavior and less willing to engage in distracting behavior than those who did not receive cookies. A debriefing and discussion period followed each subject's reply. Subjects indicated that they had regarded the handing out of cookies as a kind gesture, unrelated to the subsequent request.

The deception employed in Case 7.3 mildly induced good public behavior. But what of field research that powerfully induces bad behavior? Who wants to be spied upon, especially when engaging in private behavior, and even more so when engaging in bad behavior? Going a step further, who wants to be tricked (induced) into performing private deeds or bad deeds for the express purpose of affording someone else the opportunity to spy and record those deeds? Such treatment, obviously, should not be foisted upon those who would object. But for the sake of social science, some hearty souls might willingly sacrifice a bit of their dignity and privacy, and consent to research procedures involving concealment and powerful induction of private behavior, especially if the research were of considerable social importance and were competently performed. At this point, *confidentiality* becomes a critical means of preventing harm. Whenever possible, data should be gathered anonymously. If unique identifiers must be gathered, however, all possible precautions must be taken to ensure confidentiality (see Chapter 6).

7.4 MINIMIZING WRONG AND HARM

In writing this chapter for a broad audience—including some who conduct deception research for a living and others who are dead set against it—I can only hope that I have brought all readers to recognize two things: (a) Some important forms of behavior vanish under obvious scrutiny; concealment or deception is sometimes necessary in research, and (b) the more objectionable forms of deception are unnecessary. If I have succeeded thus far, we can now list some questions one should ask before setting out to study one of these more elusive forms of behavior that call for deception or concealment.

1. Is participant observation, an interview, or a simulation method likely to produce valid and informative results?

2. Would one of the "consent to concealment" procedures work?

3. Is privacy invaded? If so, have subjects consented to something like this, and have members of the subject population who understand the procedure decided that they would be willing to participate in such a study? Is confidentiality or anonymity absolutely assured?

4. If studying bad behavior, have subjects consented to something like this, and have members of the subject population who understand the procedure decided that they would be willing to participate in such a study? Is confidentiality or anonymity assured?

5. If studying private or bad behavior, is it induced? How strongly?

6. Is debriefing impossible? Debriefing deception research includes dehoaxing (revealing the deception) and desensitizing (removing any undesirable emotional consequences of the research).

7. Is the study of such overriding importance and so well designed that deception is justified?

7.5 DEHOAXING

An obvious advantage of the first three concealment methods described in 7.4 is that they are easily dehoaxed. When the latter two methods are used (consent and false informing, or no consent and no informing), dehoaxing is not always easily accomplished. Having been deceived once, why should subjects believe the next thing they are told?

Whatever the device used to deceive, it should be demonstrated to be fraudulent. When technical deception (misrepresentation of objects or procedures) is employed, a convincing demonstration of the deception is usually easy to arrange. For example, when a subject is given false feedback, supposedly based on a test performance, the dehoaxing might include returning to subjects their own tests, still in sealed envelopes, just as the subjects turned them in (Holmes, 1976). When role deception is used, the dehoaxing should include an introduction of subjects to the real person, along with the presentation of whatever information is needed to establish the person's real identity. Implicit deception (in which subjects naturally generate wrong assumptions that the investigator is careful not to correct) is the most difficult to dehoax, since essentially subjects have misinformed themselves. Here, it is tactful and beneficial to assure subjects that anyone would misinterpret the situation and that the research was designed so that misinterpretation would occur.

After dehoaxing, the rest of the debriefing procedure, as described in Chapter 4 (4.6), should be carried out, including a discussion of the nature of the observation, the data collection, the design, and a fairly detailed explanation of the purpose of the research.

Generalized mistrust is psychologically harmful, and the social scientist is obligated to prevent its occurrence or to remove any generalized mistrust engendered by the research. Hence, the practice of double deception is particularly harmful:

> This practice involves a second deception presented as a part of what the participant thinks is the official post-investigation clarification procedure. Then some further measurement is made, usually using covert means to assess the impact of the conditions upon the true dependent variable. In such cases there is a particular danger that the participant, when finally provided with a full and accurate clarification, will remain unconvinced and possibly resentful. Here, confidence in the trustworthiness of psychologists has realistically been shaken. (American Psychological Association, 1973, p. 80)

However, dehoaxing does not necessarily return subjects to their prior emotional state, and may even cause emotional difficulties.

7.6 DESENSITIZING

The investigator should detect any undesirable emotional consequence of the research for participants and restore them to a frame of mind that is at least as positive and constructive as it was when they entered the study. Deception research may induce subjects to reveal information they would prefer to have kept secret, or it may inflict on them new insights about their own personal weaknesses. Embarrassment, self-doubt, guilt, fear of damage to one's reputation, and other negative emotional consequences may ensue. Desensitizing should alter subjects' feelings concerning the way they behaved or were treated in the study, so that they are restored to a state of emotional well-being. The investigator should have adequate facilities to handle any emotional reactions to stress that may arise from participation in the study or the debriefing. In addition to providing effective and caring desensitization immediately after the research session, the researcher should make other sources of counseling or psychotherapy available to the subjects.

As discussed at length by Holmes (1976), it is not clear that desensitizing efforts always succeed in removing all of the self-doubt engendered by some deception. Hence, it is important that studies not involve treatments that are damaging to self-esteem in the first place. In any event, whatever desensitizing procedures are used, they should include processes or material designed to address the following concerns:

Confidence in science. Subjects should receive adequate explanation so that they will consider the research reasonable and will feel no loss of confidence in either the investigator or science.

Risk control. Subjects should be informed of any risks the researcher has anticipated, and of the steps taken to minimize them (e.g., use of confidentiality-assuring procedures). Any unwarranted concerns subjects may have about harm that could result from their participation should be detected, fully discussed, and allayed. The researcher should be receptive to subjects' concerns about unanticipated forms of harm and should be prepared to do everything possible to prevent such harms from materializing.

Questions. Subjects should be given an opportunity to ask questions about the study, and to have their questions answered satisfactorily.

Withdrawal of data. Subjects should be given an opportunity to withdraw their data from the study. This ethical requirement follows from the principle of respect for persons and is codified in the American Psychological Association's Principle 5, which states:

> Ethical research practice requires the investigator to respect the individual's freedom to decline to participate in research or to discontinue participation at any time. The obligation to protect this freedom requires special vigilance when the investigator is in a position of power over the participant. The decision to limit this freedom increases the investigator's responsibility to protect the participant's dignity and welfare.

The American Psychological Association's Ad Hoc Committee on Ethical Standards in Psychological Research notes that if the investigator has withheld or distorted information that would influence the participant's consent to participate, the right to withdraw data substitutes for the right to refuse to consent to participate (1973).

The right to withdraw one's data is particularly important when data on private behavior are gathered, and subjects experience discomfort about having revealed things that they would prefer not to have revealed. Just as respondents to an in-depth interview may regret having been skillfully drawn into a discussion in which they revealed more personal data than they would have wanted to reveal, so may participants in deception research discover, upon being debriefed, that they have revealed something about themselves that they would not have chosen to reveal if fully informed. In either case, subjects should have the option of withdrawing their data.

7.7 WHEN NOT TO DEHOAX

When studying behavior that is socially perceived as negative and when the behavior is typical of the subject, desensitizing is usually unnecessary, and dehoaxing may even be harmful.

Example 1: As any parent or child psychologist knows, young children steal—often innocently and without a sense that stealing is wrong. Suppose a researcher studies stealing in young children by making toys or coins available for stealing. After observing the children stealing, should the researcher then debrief them, by telling them that they were observed stealing, or by telling them that the study was about stealing? The researcher's business is not to punish, to shame, or to try to produce accelerated moral development, but only to study how children behave. The ethical guidelines of the American Psychological Association hold that children should not be debriefed when debriefing would upset them.

This example raises another problem: In obtaining parental permission to perform the research, should the researcher agree to inform parents of their child's response? Not necessarily. If such an agreement is made, however, the researcher must also give parents information about *typical* behavior for children of that age, and about *appropriate* parental responses to stealing by children of that age. With this background, most parents would handle feedback about their own children responsibly. However, the researcher must be sensitive to the needs of particular parents and children, and seek consultation about the handling of difficult cases.

Example 2: Some adults have attitudes or habits that the researcher (and most of society) would deem undesirable, but which the adults in question view positively and would not readily change. After participating in a deception study of parental authoritarianism, for example, should subjects be told that their authoritarian child-rearing practices have been studied? In all cases, debriefing should be done without demeaning subjects.

RECOMMENDED READINGS

Sieber, J. E. (1982, November). Deception in social research I: Kinds of deception and the wrongs they may involve. *IRB: A Review of Human Subjects Research*, 1-2, 12.
Sieber, J. E. (1983, January). Deception in social research II: Factors influencing the magnitude of potential for harm or wrong. *IRB: A Review of Human Subjects Research*, 1-3, 12.

PART III

Risk/Benefit Assessment and Planning

Prior chapters have discussed issues of research risk and benefit. This section examines how risk and benefit are assessed.

WHY ASSESS RISK AND BENEFIT?

To minimize or avoid risk and to maximize the benefit that may result from research, one must first identify the kinds of risk and the kinds of benefit that are possible within a study. A discussion in the protocol of the findings of this assessment and the methods and procedures to be employed to maximize benefit and minimize risk are crucial to the IRB's evaluation of the research plan.

Some vitally important social research, such as research on runaways, child prostitutes, or drug dealers, may necessarily involve risk. Such research is acceptable if it is well designed, if it is conducted by a competent investigator, and if risk/benefit assessment and planning have occurred. Minimal harm, valuable knowledge, a publication, and enlightened public policy would be among the expected outcomes. A similar amount of risk would not be acceptable in an undergraduate project.

MISCONCEPTIONS ABOUT RISK/BENEFIT ASSESSMENT

The term *risk/benefit assessment* invites misconceptions. These should be corrected now:

1. A ratio is not actually computed; most risks and benefits of research cannot be quantified.

2. Some risks and benefits cannot be identified accurately before the research is performed.

3. It is impossible to consider all possible risks and benefits. There are many forms of good that people want to enjoy and many harms they wish to avoid. Forms of good (e.g., freedom, self-respect, friendship, contentment, health, self-expression, understanding, pleasure) and the harm implied by loss of each are merely abstractions of the many specific emotional, physical, social, legal, and economic forms of good and harm that could arise in connection with research. In assessing social sensitivity, risk, and benefit, the researcher seeks to focus upon the most important of these, but cannot possibly anticipate everything.

4. Risk and benefit cannot be identified for each subject individually. One subject's risk may be another's benefit.

WHAT IS RISK/BENEFIT ASSESSMENT?

Risk/benefit assessment weighs the risks, or costs, of the research to subjects and to society, against its benefits. These risks and costs include ones incurred when socially sensitive research offends some sector of society, resulting in backlash against the subjects, the researcher, the participating institutions, and the cause the researcher had hoped to promote. IRBs assess risk to subjects only, as opposed to risk to groups in society or risk of offending persons who happened to hear about the research.[1]

A risk/benefit assessment is based on most of the same forms of inquiry that should inform other aspects of research design, including common sense, a review of the literature, knowledge of research methodology, ethnographic knowledge of the subject population, perceptions of pilot subjects and gatekeepers, experience from serving as a pilot subject oneself, and input from researchers who have worked in similar research settings.

Two keys to risk/benefit assessment and planning are (a) knowing where to look for potential risks (costs, harms) and benefits, and (b) engaging a wide spectrum of players in the risk/benefit assessment to obtain diverse perspectives and value orientations. No single source can say what potential risks and benefits inhere in a particular study. Risk, and the ethical issues raised by risk, cannot be defined by a few specifiable dimensions. The benefit and justifiability of research depend on the whole nature of the research process and on the values of the persons who judge the research. Thus, a researcher, those with whom he or she consults, and the IRB can only estimate whether a proposed project would turn out well. However, the potential for risk and benefit can be assessed in advance, and throughout the research process:

Case 1: In consultation with the IRB, with colleagues in his field, and with a local community-based drug treatment program, an investigator began the design of survey research on black teenage crack users.[2] After some initial planning, he invited prospective subjects to focus group meetings. For the design of the interview, he needed to know their beliefs about crack, where they got it and how they used it, their knowledge and practice of safe sex, and their sexual behavior in general. He was not sure how to recruit subjects, establish rapport, or phrase the interview questions, but he knew he could relate effectively to focus group members; he is a black man who easily engages youth in conversation.

The focus groups met regularly over lunch. Drug abusers often neglect nutrition, but when given food, may be ravenously hungry. The investigator learned their concerns about their lives and mentioned ways he would like to help them. He asked their advice on how to organize the interviews, what to ask, and what fears respondents would have about participating candidly. He asked what they, and the actual subjects, would like to have in return for their efforts. The investigator found that many focus group participants wanted to learn to be interviewers and some wanted drug treatment. These participants helped develop the interview questions, the recruitment strategy, and strategies for providing desired services to participants and interviewers. Those who were trained to become interviewers had access to crack houses where the investigator could not go. As community members, they could get candid responses to interview questions. As interviewing ensued, supervision revealed that an interviewer had regaled his sister with details of an interview in which a man they knew had named all the women in the neighborhood with whom (he said) he had slept. More discussions of confidentiality were held with the assistants, and the interviews were resumed. This research culminated in the publication of useful information about the relationship of crack use to high risk sexual behaviors. The results have been useful to drug treatment programs.

HOW DOES AN INVESTIGATOR
IDENTIFY RISKS AND PLAN BENEFITS?

Throughout Part III and other parts of this book, issues of social sensitivity are raised. The federal regulations governing IRBs are not concerned with social sensitivity, but only with harm to human subjects. However, the investigator who ignores the sensitivities of gatekeepers, community members, and society at large risks having the research prevented, interrupted, or maligned by powerful forces other than the IRB.

NOTES

1. CFR 46.111 states: The IRB should not consider the possible long-range effects of applying knowledge gained in the research as among those research risks that fall within the purview of its responsibility. However, no researcher would want to invite the destruction that can result from offending social sensitivities.

2. Under 46.408 of the Federal Regulations governing human research, one need not obtain permission for research on minors, provided parents or guardians are unreachable, or unlikely to act in the best interests of their children. (See Chapter 10.) Young crack users and dealers often live apart from any parents or guardians, who would likely be unreachable in any case. IRB consent was given to conduct the study without seeking parental approval. However, some laws in some states are more restrictive.

8

Recognizing Elements of Risk

All ethical codes governing human research require that investigators identify possible risks ahead of time and plan their research so that subjects' rights are protected. For example, the Code of Ethics of the American Psychological Association (Principle 9G) states that:

> The investigator protects the participant from physical and mental discomfort, harm, and danger that may arise from research procedures. If risks of such consequences exist, the investigator informs the participant of that fact. Research procedures likely to cause serious or lasting harm to a participant are not used unless the failure to use these procedures might expose the participant to risk of greater harm or unless the research has great potential benefit and fully informed and voluntary consent is obtained from each participant. The participant should be informed of procedures for contacting the investigator within a reasonable time period following participation should stress, potential harm, or related questions or concerns arise. (APA, 1982, p. 6.)

Few things concern an IRB more than an investigator who blithely states that no risk is involved in proposed research, when risk is evident to the IRB. Such a naive assurance suggests that the investigator is insensitive and likely to cause needless harm and upset.

One reason some researchers make no attempt at risk assessment is that the task seems impossible. It is indeed impossible to identify all relevant risk, but it is important to consider possible risks and be prepared for dialogue with the IRB. Because of the complexity of risk assessment, no two people will arrive at exactly the same conclusions. Unfortunately, investigators often become angry and defensive when the IRB raises the possibility of risks that the investigator has not considered. One purpose of this chapter is to provide a framework for identifying possible risks, thus creating a basis for dialogue, rather than defensiveness.

8.1 WHAT IS RESEARCH RISK?

Risk refers to the possibility that some harm, loss, or damage may occur. There are various kinds of risk in research, including the following:

- *mere inconvenience*, such as boredom, frustration, and taking up time that the subject might more profitably spend otherwise.
- *physical risk*, such as the possibility that one will get a black eye from participation in an exercise physiology experiment.
- *psychological risk*, such as the possibility of getting a black eye and becoming depressed about attending events wherein wrong inferences may be drawn about the cause of the black eye.
- *social risk*, being rejected for having that black eye.
- *economic risk*, being passed over for employment in favor of another candidate who interviewed without a black eye.
- *legal risk*, being arrested and interrogated about the possible connection between the black eye and a brutal assault that left a neighbor comatose.

These examples illustrate risks to subjects. As we shall see, however, these kinds of risks may apply to others as well, including the researcher and other persons associated with the research, the setting where the research is performed, and other settings and populations that are somehow affected by the research.

8.2 WHY RESEARCH RISK IS DIFFICULT TO ASSESS

Risk assessment is not intuitively easy. Most investigators are sensitive only to the risks they have already encountered and may fail to assess major risks in new research settings. Even a chapter such as this cannot point to all possible research risks. The goal of this chapter is to present a model that enables one to recognize circumstances likely to produce risk.

The model can be illustrated as shown in Figure 8.1, whose three dimensions consist of the following: (a) four aspects of scientific activity, (b) eight risk-related issues, and (c) seven general kinds of vulnerable entities. A quick mental calculation shows why each kind of risk is not illustrated here by a case study. The $4 \times 8 \times 7$ matrix yields

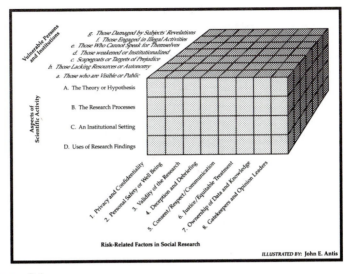

Figure 8.1.

224 cells, each containing the elements of a distinctly different case scenario.

The model should be read as follows, taking as an example a risk occurring at the intersection of *C, 1, d*. Because of an *aspect* of scientific activity (e.g., its setting—university administrative offices), a *risk* arises (involving, e.g., confidentiality—the interviewers are members of the university community), and this risk is serious because the *subjects* are weak members of the institutional setting (i.e., nonmanagerial employees who are being interviewed about their supervisors). Let us examine one more cell intersection:

Cell B, 6, b: A research process is unjust to nonautonomous persons who cannot complain effectively. Hypothetical example: In a program of applied research on math learning, children are randomly assigned to various 4-month cable-TV viewing conditions. Condition A is far superior to the standard curriculum, while Condition B has a damaging effect on math learning. After the 4-month program, all students go on with the standard curriculum. (Effects should be monitored, and all subjects should be provided with the superior or desired program after the data have been gathered. In treatment programs that could cause irreversible harm, subjects should be closely monitored and switched to the desirable program as soon as undesirable effects are observed [Conner, 1982].)

The reader is urged to refer to the matrix in Figure 8.1 while reading sections 8.3 through 8.5, which describe the matrix and illustrate ways in which risk may arise.

8.3 STAGES OR ASPECTS OF SCIENTIFIC ACTIVITY THAT MAY INVOLVE RISK

Four aspects of scientific activity may involve risk: (1) the theory or research idea, (2) the actual research process, (3) the setting of the research, and (4) the dissemination or uses of the research. The federal regulations are concerned only with 2 and 3, but any conscientious researcher will consider 1 and 4 as well.

8.3.1 The Theory or Research Idea

A new idea may change cultural values in fundamental ways, as occurred in response to the theories of Freud, Darwin, and Copernicus. Examples are plentiful. To avoid confusing the effects of ideas with the effects of research results, consider an idea of Freud's that was unsupported by research:

> Many of Freud's adult clients told him that they had been sexually abused by their parents. Freud announced this finding to his colleagues, who expressed shock and dismay that he would believe this of fine Christian parents. In response to his critics, Freud theorized that children's accounts of being sexually abused are products of fantasy.
>
> It is now recognized that approximately one child in three has experienced sexual abuse, either at the hands of adults or of older children, and that young children are incapable of describing sexual abuse based on fantasy alone. Moreover, until a decade ago, claims of sexual abuse in childhood were not taken seriously, largely because of Freud's ideas.

One might suppose that Freud's theory was so damaging because it was untested. This is not necessarily so; scientists often find what they seek, even when it is not there (Mitroff & Kilmann, 1979). But even if science were always self-correcting, research can still cause damaging misinformation. Consider a hypothetical case involving cells $A, C, D, 5, b, d$:

> A researcher is personally persuaded that boys are innately inferior to girls in social skills. In the course of obtaining informed consent, he describes his hypotheses to principals, teachers, and parents so persuasively that they become sensitized to evidence of poor social skills in boys. Consequently, some fail to challenge boys to develop social skills. Others decide that it is best to cultivate "the brutishness of the male." Will the research results correct these misconceptions? Probably not. Most researchers forget to give gatekeepers and subjects feedback after the data have been analyzed.

Four ways to reduce the risk of false confirmation or dissemination of damaging ideas are available to the researcher: (a) Recognize that the null hypothesis may very well be true; (b) design the research so that each theoretical orientation is tested fairly (Mitroff & Kilmann, 1979), or identify and develop competing hypotheses, consulting or collaborating with scientists who support alternative hypotheses; (c) remember the limitations of the models and measures employed, always announcing up front and reminding yourself and others that application and generalization to other populations must be done with caution; (d) upon completion of the research, share the documented data with other scientists who want to verify the findings or test alternative hypotheses with the data (Fienberg, Martin, & Straf, 1985).

8.3.2 The Research Process

The research process refers to steps involved in the actual conduct of empirical study. These steps typically include designing the research, recruiting the subjects, obtaining informed consent, administering the treatments (tests, interviews, and so on), gathering the data, and analyzing and interpreting the results. The following examples illustrate issues arising in the research process:

Recruitment. Inner-city men who have tested positive for sexually transmitted diseases are recruited for a study of safe sex practices. Community members figure out why people are being recruited, and the grapevine goes to work. Those recruited become stigmatized in their community; they do not return for interviews (Case, personal communication).

Induction. Subjects are invited to appear for on-campus job interviews. In fact, a deceptive study of self-presentation is being conducted. A student with financial problems has his suit dry cleaned, buys new shoes, and takes a day off from work to attend the interview, hoping to get a better-paying job so that he can complete school. Upon debriefing, he becomes so angry at the investigator that he vows to find and tell every prospective subject about the deception.

Consent and experimental treatment. Subjects in a study of correlates of drug abuse do not like the questions they are being asked. The questions seem different from what they agreed to. Because the research design was not adequately explained to them, they do not understand why some of their friends are asked different questions. They are suspicious about how their data might be used against them, and decide to quit the outpatient drug recovery program that sponsored the research.

Data gathering. Research assistants know the subjects and gossip about confidential information.

Debriefing. The researcher explains to parents who have just been studied in interaction with their young children that the research is designed to demonstrate how certain patterns of interaction produce unruly youngsters. As most children spend some time being unruly, many of the parents go away blaming themselves, their spouses, or other household members.

Data analysis. When cell size is too small to yield meaningful information, the researcher nevertheless fails to collapse cells and reports unreliable conclusions. Data summaries are published in which some cells contain so few cases that people familiar with the setting can deduce the identity of certain anonymous respondents, who have reported engaging in undesirable behavior.

Data sharing. The raw data are archived, without removal of unique identifiers, at the university library, where they are available to students and faculty. A blackmailer puts some of the juicier personal data to lucrative use.

These are only a few of the many kinds of risk that may arise because of the research process. Other kinds of risk arising within the research process are discussed elsewhere in this book.

8.3.3 The Institutional Setting of the Research

One readily thinks of research as a matter between researcher and subject. However, there usually is a "third party"—the setting or organization in which the research occurs. Aspects of the research that would otherwise be harmless may be risky because of the nature of the setting. The setting may be a community, a workplace, a hospital or clinic, a prison, a school, a church, a service organization, a professional organization, a recreational setting—any setting that has some kind of structure, culture, or interests of its own.

In most cases, settings have gatekeepers and impose rules on those who want to do research therein. When the research is done in one's own institution, the gatekeepers may be the subject pool coordinator, the IRB, the office of sponsored projects, and so on. In field research, gatekeepers are representatives of the setting the researcher wants to enter, for example, a school principal, a retirement home director, or a recovered drug addict who works as an advocate and community outreach person to street addicts whom the researcher hopes to interview.

Gatekeepers have the power to help researchers understand and establish rapport with the research population. They also have the power to negotiate conditions that are acceptable to those they serve. Thus, the researcher may expect to have to change some details of the research plans to suit the priorities of the setting and to contribute positively to that setting. Be aware, however, that gatekeepers and those they serve are not always interested in objectivity. They would not want the researcher to discover something that would be damaging to them or to their organization. They may even pressure the researcher to produce results that make them look good; hence, the researcher must be careful not to enter into unethical agreements with gatekeepers. In any case, gatekeepers will want the researcher to leave the setting, its staff, and its clientele in a positive state.

The following are two examples of risk and harm by an outside researcher who failed to understand or care sufficiently about the culture and interests of the setting:

> Organizational research is often conducted in a corporation by an academic social scientist who is more attuned to the norms of academia than to those of the corporation. Because both the investigator and the corporate officers have considerable autonomy, there is much potential for conflict and harm. The organization may make personnel decisions based on data that the investigator obtained from employees with a well-intended promise of confidentiality given by the investigator. Later, the investigator may release news about the research findings to a reporter. The news publication may harm the organization's standing with its customers, stockholders, personnel, competitors, or the government. The officers of the organization may halt a long-term research program in midstream and thus harm both science and the career of the scientist. (Based on an actual case described by Mirvis, 1982)

> Because medical and psychiatric clinics have their own concerns about maintaining their services uninterrupted and protecting confidentiality, they provide entrée to outside researchers only after a lengthy negotiation and approval process (Sieber & Sorensen, 1992). The following is a hypothetical case of the kind that clinic directors hope to avoid: Given entrée to a clinic that serves pregnant teenagers, researchers conduct a repeated measures study of the development of attitudes toward maternal and infant health care. In violation of their agreement with the clinic, the researchers add sensitive personal questions that the subjects find highly objectionable. Not knowing that the researchers are solely to blame, the subjects fear to complain, lest their medical care be curtailed. Some solve the problem by giving dishonest responses to those questions. Some drop out of the study. Some drop out of the clinic program. Finally a particularly assertive teenager tells the clinic director what she thinks of the research. The researchers are asked to leave.

In other cases, the researcher may be an insider who is more powerful than any gatekeepers or there may be no effective gatekeepers or subject-advocates. Thus, mental hospitals have, in the past, experimented with behavior modification approaches designed to make patients easier to handle; students may be required to participate in a subject pool with no real opportunity to decline; men and women serving in the military may be required to serve as subjects in sleep deprivation research; and courts of law may seek to study the effects of various sentencing, parole, and treatment conditions on juvenile delinquents who are randomly assigned to appropriate but different conditions.

Because individuals vary in their degree of personal autonomy, and institutions in their degree of control and coercive power, the kinds of harm that may result from research in institutional settings range from the killing of prisoners in Nazi concentration camps and the imprisonment of scientists as war criminals, to the inconveniencing of college sophomores and tarnishing of reputations of faculty members. As these examples suggest, the degree of harm that can occur because of the coercive power of the institution is affected by the nature of the research process itself, and can be further compounded if the research idea is intrinsically insulting or damaging to persons.

8.3.4 Uses of the Research Findings

If mere ideas can influence world events, "proven" ones can be even more influential. In our enthusiasm to use what we have learned from research, it is easy to forget that many findings are based on measures of dubious reliability, or account for so little of the variance in these measures that they should not be considered practically useful. Findings based on one population or setting may not generalize to other populations or settings. Findings that are useful for one purpose may be misused in other instances. The social sciences deal with ideas that readily appeal to our personal values or politics. Scientists themselves are often incapable of separating their personal values and perceptions from objective observation (Doris, 1982). A good example is found in the early twentieth century, when public policy was adopted on the basis of the various ideas that scientists promoted regarding the mentally retarded. As a result of that public policy, the mentally retarded were treated inhumanly; vestiges of that public policy linger today. The case is old, but the lessons to be learned remain current.

Around the beginning of the twentieth century, many social scientists considered mental retardation the most serious problem in the United States (Davies, 1930). They warned policymakers that unless the retarded were prevented from reproducing, mental retardation would assume greater and greater proportions with each new generation, leading to more crime, alcoholism, prostitution, poverty, and ultimately, the extinction of Western civilization.

Sarason and Doris (1969) have shown that this concern about mental retardation is attributable to two advances in psychology: the rediscovery and extension by psychologists of Mendel's theory of inheritance, and Binet's development of a measure of children's intelligence. Both Goddard at the Vineland Training School and Kuhlman at the Minnesota Institution for the Feebleminded showed how quickly and conveniently the IQ test could be used to classify the mentally retarded. Goddard's study of the Kallikak family in 1912, coupled with a reanalysis of his data by the great Harvard geneticist, E. M. East, was put forward as proof that feeblemindedness is hereditary and is transmitted in accordance with the Mendelian model of recessive traits—a conclusion that is now thoroughly discredited.

Goddard then administered IQ tests in English to non-English-speaking immigrants passing through Ellis Island. Based on their performance, Goddard claimed to have discovered that emigrating Jews, Italians, Russians, and Poles would contribute to the intellectual deterioration of the American populace. During the 1920s Congress enacted the most restrictive immigration laws this country has seen. Noted psychologists, geneticists, sociologists, and psychiatrists advocated institutionalization and involuntary sterilization to remove the mentally retarded from society and prevent their reproduction. From 1910 to 1923, institutionalization rates for retardates more than doubled, and between 1907 and 1926, 26 states passed sterilization laws (Doris, 1982).

The combined power of the ideas and the public policies that came into existence at the beginning of this century made it difficult for valid opposing ideas to gain visibility. Doris (1982, p. 205) comments that Goddard and others:

[H]ad created in the early decades of this century such a climate in the scientific and professional communities that Walter Fernald (1919), director of the Waverly Institution for the Feebleminded, withheld for two years research data demonstrating that former inmates of his institution—who for the most part had left without official blessing—had, in fact, adjusted quite well to the social and economic demands of the outside world. His defense was that the data were so contrary to the accepted theory for the management of the feebleminded that he hesitated to make them public. (Davies, 1930)

By the 1930s social attitudes were changing. The Great Depression caused people to realize that economic failure and unemployment were not necessarily because of bad genes. In addition to the new social zeitgeist, new data and better application of theory also caused social scientists to question earlier ideas. Attitudes toward the retarded began to change. Due to financial limitations, institutionalization had not occurred to the degree advocated, and squeamish local authorities had not enforced sterilization laws strictly. However, special education classes for the retarded continued to grow (Grant & Eiden, 1980). Although leading social scientists advocated segregated special education classes, their advocacy was not empirically based. There was no attempt to examine rigorously the relative merits of special education versus regular class placement (Sarason & Doris, 1979).

Within the past two decades, a new wave of scientists has supported the deinstitutionalization and mainstreaming of the mentally retarded. No research has ever conclusively supported claims either for institutionalization or for deinstitutionalization. However, a lack of conclusive research evidence is not always enough to keep scientists from speaking authoritatively when advocating ideas that are in keeping with their own values and that society is ready to hear.

New issues of equal or greater sensitivity continue to arise. A decade ago some research suggested a greater than chance association between the XYY chromosomes and criminal behavior. This finding led some politicians to propose that XYY-type children be identified and placed in a special treatment environment designed to prevent them from becoming criminals (Hook, 1973; Wiener & Sutherland, 1968). Today it is proposed by some that all members of our society be tested for AIDS antibodies. Note that universal screening for AIDS antibodies and XYY chromosomes, were they to occur, would involve a concatenation of problems: Imperfect research designs and inaccurate measurement methods would be used to identify persons who would then become objects of prejudice; powerful administering and enforcing institutions, social and economic sanctions, and the possibility of quarantine laws could be ruinous to those who test positive.

8.4 RISK-RELATED FACTORS IN SOCIAL RESEARCH

Eight key risk-related issues may arise in each of the above four stages of the scientific process and may affect any persons, institutions, or populations connected with the research. Through responsible planning, any of these issues might be transformed into a benefit. For example, a frail elderly woman might find it a frightening invasion of her privacy to be asked many personal questions by an unsympathetic interviewer from another ethnic group, yet she might be flattered and delighted by the attention of an attractive young researcher of her own culture, who also speaks her dialect (e.g., Loo, 1982).

8.4.1 Privacy and Confidentiality

A theory may invade privacy and diminish autonomy of persons by causing others to perceive them negatively. In the research process, a skilled investigator may extract more information than the subject intended to give. This invasion of privacy may be easier for investigators to accomplish if the research is done in an institution where the subject suspects that the information is available anyhow, and that lying might be punished. If the research is translated into public policy, prying into millions of people's lives (e.g., AIDS antibody testing and quarantine) could be legally mandated.

The ways in which issues of confidentiality may arise at each aspect of scientific activity are analogous to those of privacy. Fundamental to ethical research is an agreement between subject and researcher about how the data generated by the research will be controlled. See Chapter 6 for methods of assuring confidentiality.

8.4.2 Personal Safety and Well-Being

This is the least subtle of risk-related issues, and is included here for the sake of completeness. Might the theory reduce individual's safety, as in Freud's theory that children fantasize sexual abuse by parents? Does the research procedure contain elements that may cause direct physical or emotional harm (e.g., a torn muscle, extreme stress, damaged clothing)? Is the research setting unsafe (e.g., in a physically dangerous or frightening place)? Does the use of the findings cause physical harm?

8.4.3 Lack of Validity

Invalid research is bad science. It produces wrong information, the application of which may cause harm.

8.4.4 Deception and Debriefing

The very idea of deception in research damages the reputation of social science and may produce disingenuous responses from suspicious subjects, even in studies where deception is not employed. Some subjects may see through the deception all along, while others may be so deeply convinced by an induction (e.g., one that makes them feel inadequate) that no amount of debriefing removes the induction effects. In an institutional setting, the use of deception may destroy trust in the institution. The dissemination of socially sensitive studies involving deception may create considerable public backlash against social science and the funding of research. See Chapter 7 for solutions to these problems.

8.4.5 Informed Consent, Respectful Communication, and Consultation

What is communicated and not communicated by the researcher at each stage of the research process is critical. In the introduction to Part III, Case 1 provides an excellent example of effective communication (via focus groups) that quickly reached the entire research population through the community grapevine. Because the informed consent statement merely reinforced what people already knew, it was readily understood and believed. This communication process shaped the research idea, the research procedure, the relationship of the research to the community context, and the application of results within the community.

8.4.6 Justice and Equitable Treatment

Issues of procedural and distributive justice may arise at any stage of the research process. An idea that prejudices us against some sector of society is unfair, as is an experimental treatment in which resources known to be vital to subjects' well-being are withheld from subjects in one group and given to subjects in another. Such problems are compounded when they occur within an organization. If a vitally important treatment must be withheld from control group members during an experiment, it should be offered to them as soon thereafter as possible. Injustice may also occur in a variety of ways at the dissemination end of the process, as when the researcher takes no steps to encourage the dissemination of valuable knowledge to those who stand in greatest need. An excellent example of justice in dissemination is the fieldwork of Pelto (1988) on infant nutrition in various developing countries: Pelto routinely shares his data with appropriate governmental representatives so that the information can be used for the countries' own public policy purposes. He also provides training and consultation in data analysis, all as a way of repaying the host culture for its cooperation.

8.4.7 Ownership of Data and Knowledge

Ownership of data and knowledge refers to a complex of concerns about openness and democratic use of science that may arise at any point in the scientific process. Openness is vital to science. However, in some research for hire, the sponsor claims exclusive ownership of the data and the right to edit the results. The discerning reader may note a possible conflict between the principle of openness, or scientific freedom, and the need of applied researchers to accommodate the interests of gatekeepers in community settings where the findings may have political consequences. The researcher should gain all possible awareness of these concerns ahead of time in order to decide, in consultation with the gatekeepers, how they may be addressed without violating principles of openness or honesty. Often the problem is not what results are reported, but how they are framed.

Another possible conflict between openness and confidentiality arises when scientific data are shared. Most major funding agencies now require that researchers make their documented raw data available to other scientists, via either public archive or private arrangement. The legal rights of property ownership (e.g., to sell for profit, to withhold, to alter, to destroy) do not necessarily pertain to data that form the basis of publication, as these data are the basis of the researcher's claim to the validity of findings. Issues of data ownership and sharing are discussed in Sieber (1989) and touched upon in Chapter 6 (6.8).

8.4.8 Gatekeepers and Opinion Leaders

Most research is influenced in various ways by gatekeepers and opinion leaders. *Gatekeepers* function at each stage of the scientific process and include those who provide access to a research site, colleagues who will decide on one's promotion, IRBs, funders, and journal editors, to name but a few. *Opinion leaders* include those who create and support prevailing attitudes about scientific activity, who decide which theories are important and which research methods are "scientific," who are likely to object to socially sensitive research, or who would harass a scientist for his or her views or methods of research. Some specific opinion leaders include the press, advocates for one or another cause, politicians, senior scientists, religious leaders, editors, and science gadflies.

As an investigator, one must be sensitive to the views and influences of gatekeepers, yet one is also obligated to question and decide for oneself what is valid and ethical. For example, useless research efforts may result from employing methods that currently have high status in science, but are not appropriate or ethical for a given problem.

The scientist who ignores gatekeepers and opinion leaders runs three serious risks: (a) being unduly influenced by unrecognized forces in the research environment, (b) failing to create an explicit and constructive relationship with those who might have valuable input, and (c) being unprepared for possible criticism by gatekeepers and opinion leaders of a different persuasion.

8.5 PERSONS OR INSTITUTIONS THAT MAY BE VULNERABLE

Depending on circumstances, any person or institution may be vulnerable to research risk. Recognition of these vulnerabilities is vital to effective risk assessment. This chapter presents seven main kinds of vulnerability and approximately seven kinds of people within each. This amounts to about 50 categories of vulnerable people; obviously there are more.

Some are vulnerable because they are visible, famous, have deep pockets (i.e., are targets for lawsuits claiming damages), or may not have public sympathy. This category includes the investigator (who is visible), the research institution and other organizations (which have deep pockets), identified and well-known members of the population sampled in the research (whose reputation and opportunities may be altered by the generalizations about them that ensue from the research), well-known persons closely associated with the research participants about whom private information may be revealed, as well as certain kinds of research participants: the rich and the well-known.

Some are vulnerable because they lack resources or autonomy. This category includes the aged, minors, students, the poor, the uneducated, the mentally ill, the retarded, and the homeless.

Some are vulnerable because they are stigmatized. This category includes people with AIDS, with prison records, and with sexually transmitted diseases: minorities, homosexuals, women, rape victims, and the unemployed.

Some are vulnerable because they are in a weakened position, and perhaps in an institutional setting. This category includes alcoholics, prisoners, the hospitalized, military personnel, school children, employees, psychotherapy patients, and persons in crisis.

Some are vulnerable because they cannot speak for themselves. This category includes the dying, fetuses, and brain dead persons. It also includes persons who may be unable to assert their rights effectively: including illiterates, non-Western peoples, non-English-speaking people, primitive people, infants, and low-status people.

Some are vulnerable because their illegal activities may become known to law enforcement authorities through the research. This category includes drug abusers, juvenile delinquents, child molesters, wife beaters, illegal aliens, tax evaders, and political activists.

Some are vulnerable because they are associated with those who are studied, and may be damaged by information revealed about them. This category includes community members, family members, group therapy members, and co-workers of the research participants.

8.6 RESEARCHERS' PERCEPTION OF RISK

Having just reviewed the parts of the matrix in Figure 8.1, it is easy to understand that researchers who are narrowly focused on their research aims may readily lose perspective on risk factors. Researchers must balance complex roles, as scientists, individuals, and members of society, in which they are

> [S]ubject to the same societal processes as other members of society—the same economic pressures, the same social motivations and prejudices. A scientist may be a bigot; be personally exploitative of family, friends, and co-workers; be a supernationalist patriot; believe in war as a solution to international political conflict; or, be an anarchist, pacifist, militant radical, liberal dissenter, or outstanding altruist. These attitudes and behavior patterns may play some

role in the choosing of a research problem or theoretical position. The value systems and attitudes of the individual may be more significant in the choice of colleagues, students and assistants. They are likely to be most relevant to the uses to which the scientist is willing to put the results of the work done. (Tobach, Gianutsos, Topoff, & Gross, 1974, p. 16)

Researchers' conceptualization, execution, and dissemination of research are not independent of the institutions or social settings in which it occurs (Kevles, 1970). Even apart from researchers' own values, society dictates what kind of research is supported, where it takes place, and the uses to which its results are applied. In the midst of all these influences and distortions, the scientist must seek an objective view of risk factors. IRBs look for evidence that investigators are:

- aware of possible sources of risk and have employed appropriate approaches to reducing those risks,
- in consultation with those who can help them understand and reduce risk,
- aware of their own biases and of alternative points of view,
- aware of the assumptions underlying their theories and methods and the limitations of their findings, and
- aware of how the media and other opinion leaders may translate their statements into flashy and dangerous generalizations.

9

Maximizing Benefit

When researchers vaguely promise benefit to science and society, they approach being silly. These are the least probable of good outcomes. Researchers typically overlook the more likely and more immediate benefits, which are the precursors of social and scientific benefit. Some of the most immediate benefits are those to subjects and—in the case of some community-based research—to their communities. These are not only easy to bring about, but are also owed and may facilitate future research access to that population. The *intermediate benefits*—to the researcher, the research institution and the funder, if any—are ones that any talented investigator with an ongoing research program can produce in some measure. It is upon these immediate and intermediate goals or benefits that any ultimate scientific and social benefits are likely to be based.

> *Case 9.1: A (Semi-Fictitious) Tale of Two Researchers.* Psychologist A and Psychologist B each started an externally funded school-based experiment with instructional methods designed to improve the performance of students identified as learning disabled. Each sought to develop diagnostic and teaching procedures that could ultimately be used by school personnel.
>
> Psychologist A began by discussing her intervention and research plans with school administrators, teachers, parents, and students and asking them to describe problems with which they would like to have assistance. Where feasible, she made slight alterations in her program to accommodate their wishes. She integrated the research program with a graduate course so that her students received extensive training in the conduct of research in the school setting, under her rigorous supervision. Part of the graduate students' activities involved video documentation of the steps taken to establish this research in the school setting, with appropriate concern for issues of confidentiality. This material was incorporated into her department's research curriculum.

Psychologist A provided the school faculty with various published materials on learning disabilities. She gave bag-lunch workshops and presentations on her project for school personnel. Some teachers became interested in trying her approaches in their classrooms. She showed them how to implement the approaches she was using in her research. Respecting their special knowledge of their students and subject matter, she urged these teachers to adapt and modify her approaches, as they deemed appropriate, and asked that they let her know the outcome. Together, they pilot tested adaptations of the methods concurrently with the formal experiments. All aspects of the project were videotaped. The tapes were edited into usable materials for teaching university courses in research methods, and for teaching teachers to work with learning disabled (LD) children.

Each set of LD children who participated in the various one-month training programs received special recognition for willingness to participate, and each received both the experimental training and training in how to assist other students with similar problems. At the end of each one-month session, each child received a certificate, a workbook on how to use the techniques on future lessons, and a manual on teaching the techniques to other students. These children also received opportunities to work with younger students, using the methods they had learned.

Two newspaper articles about the program brought highly favorable publicity to the researcher, the school, and the researcher's university. This recognition further increased the already high morale of students, teachers, and the researcher.

Unfortunately, of the six procedures employed, only two showed significant long-term gains after 6 months on standardized tests of learning and problem solving. However, the teachers who had been involved with pilot testing of variations on the treatments were highly enthusiastic about the success of these variations. When renewal of funding was sought, the funder was dissatisfied with the formal findings, but highly impressed that the school district and the university, together, had offered to provide in-kind matching funds. The school administrators wrote a glowing testimony to the promise of both the new pilot procedures and the overall approach. The funder supported the project for a second year. The results of the second year, based on modified procedures, were much stronger. Given the structure that had been created, it was easy to document the entire procedure on videotape and disseminate it widely. The funder provided seed money to permit the researcher, her graduate students, and the teachers who had collaborated on pilot testing to start a national-level traveling workshop, which quickly became self-supporting. This additional support provided summer salary to Psychologist A, to teachers, and to graduate students for several years.

Researcher B made no attempt to benefit others, except by hoping that her experimental procedures would be successful. Her initial treatment effects were even weaker than those of Researcher A, because of the difficulties of operating in a setting where she interfered with ongoing activities. The first year of her project was also the last. There were no publishable results.

This tale of providing benefits to the many stakeholders in the research process is not strictly relevant to all research. Not every researcher does field research designed to benefit a community. In some settings, too much missionary zeal to include others in "helping" may expose some subjects to serious risk, such as breach of confidentiality. Also, not all research is funded or involves student assistants. For example, many researchers engage in simple, unfunded, unassisted one-time laboratory studies to test theory. Even in such uncomplicated research, however, any benefit to the institution (e.g., a Science Day research demonstration) may favorably influence the institution to provide resources for future research; and efforts to benefit subjects will be repaid with their cooperation and respect.

9.1 THE RISK/BENEFIT REQUIREMENT

The ethical principle of *beneficence* requires a favorable balance of benefits to risks. The Federal Regulations 45 CFR 46.111(a) contain the following statement: "Risks to subjects (must be) reasonable in relation to anticipated benefits, if any, to subjects, and the importance of the knowledge that may reasonably be expected to result." In balancing risk and benefit, it is important to take those steps that make real benefit a distinct possibility.

	Subjects	Community	Researcher	Institution	Funder	Science	Society
Relationships	Respect of Researcher	Ties to University	Future Access to Community Site	Improved Town-Gown Relationships	Ties With a Successful Project	Ideas Shared With Other Scientists	Access to Trained LD Teachers
Knowledge/ Education	Informative Debriefing	Understanding of Learning Disability (LD)	Understand Research on LD	Improved Graduate Research	Outstanding Final Report	National LD Symposium	Media LD Presentations
Material Resources	Workbook	Books	Grant Support	Videotapes	Instructional Materials	Refereed Publications	Popular LD Literature
Training Opportunity	Tutoring Skills	Teacher Training	Greater Research Expertise	Graduate Student Training	Model Project for Grant Applications	Workshop at National Meetings	LD Training for Teachers and Parents Nationally
Do Good/ Earn Esteem	Esteem of Tutored Peers	Parents' Enthusiasm for LD Program	Professional Respect	Esteem of Local Schools	Satisfaction of Funder Overseers	Recognition of Scientific Contributions	Greater Sucess and Respect for Teachers
Empowerment	Leadership Status as Tutor	Prestige From Effective LD Program	National Reputation	Good Reputation With Funder	Congressional Increases in Funder Funding	Increased Prestige of Educational Psychology	Increased Power to Help LD Children
Scientific/ Clinical Success	Improved Learning Ability	Effective LD Program	Leadership Opportunities in National LD Program	Headquarters for National LD Teacher Training	Proven Success of Funded Treatment Program	Improved LD Training via Workshops	Nationally Successful LD Programs

Figure 9.1. An Example of a Benefit Matrix Based on Case 9.1: The Learning Disability (LD) Experiment

As we have seen in Chapter 8, there are many risks to be considered. Most can be minimized or avoided, and some can be transformed into benefits. The potential benefits of research are also of many kinds, including benefits to subjects, to communities, to institutions of various kinds, and, ultimately, to science and society. Just as a risk is a possible harm that one takes steps to avoid, a benefit, at the time it is discussed in the protocol, is only a potential or hoped-for good outcome that one then seeks to bring about.

This chapter examines the kinds of possible benefits, and presents a matrix of benefits and of benefit recipients; see Figure 9.1, which illustrates the matrix and specifies some of the benefits that might be developed relative to Case 9.1. Thoughtful perusal of the matrix readily suggests (a) the kinds of benefit and beneficiaries to incorporate into one's research plans, and (b) the importance of planning for specific kinds of benefit when constructing one's research proposal, rather than leaving the occurrence of benefit to happenstance. These considerations are especially important in field research where intrusion into the daily life of subjects and their community calls for reciprocity, and in risky research where commensurate benefit is required by federal law.

9.2 FEASIBLE BENEFITS AND FALSE PROMISES

Research requires much effort, and part of the spirit that carries the investigator along is the hope or belief that the research will do some good. But one should go beyond vague hope and take the necessary steps to identify and bring about as many of the potential benefits as feasible. One begins by considering the kinds of benefits that are possible and asking which of these are feasible and which can be responsibly promised in the case of one's own intended research.

9.2.1 False Promises

Benefit to society is one of the two most frequently promised benefits of research. However, most research does not lead demonstrably to an improvement in the condition of humankind. Most theses and dissertations are not even published. And most important ideas in the social sciences do not receive the follow-up required to implement them effectively in society (Sarason, 1981). Thus, one must conclude that most promises of benefit to society are based on the vague hope that all research is bound to help—somehow. Most real-world benefits to society are predicated upon more specific benefits to subjects, to the researcher, to institutions, and to science.

Benefit to science is the other most frequently promised benefit of research. To constitute such a contribution, the proposed research must address a significant problem, be based on current literature and methods, employ a valid research design, and be of such quality as to be acceptable for publication in a refereed scientific journal. (Any research that entails significant risk to subjects must meet these standards to receive IRB approval.) In short, it is unrealistic and irresponsible to promise benefit to science unless the above conditions are met.

9.2.2 Feasible Benefits

Benefit to subjects is easier to bring about than benefit to science or society. Moreover, it is the duty of researchers to give subjects something in return for their efforts. The duty to benefit subjects is particularly important in field research, wherein (a) the research represents an intrusion into subjects' daily lives, and (b) participants were given to expect some benefit when they volunteered. Much of the value of a research benefit derives from the way it is given. Thus, care, cultural sensitivity, good rapport, and good communication are vital. Important, also, is the scientific integrity of what is provided.

Scientific knowledge is a most appropriate benefit to give in return for research participation. Unfortunately, researchers often promise to give subjects the results of their study, failing to either recognize or admit (a) that the results may not be available for a long time, (b) that the results may not turn out to be very interesting or useful to subjects or to anyone else, and (c) that researchers often forget to keep such promises. Research should be based on a literature review. Hence, researchers should be able to give subjects a balanced and interesting summary of relevant knowledge at the time of their participation. That summary might take the form of a handout that is carefully edited, clear, simple, and devoid of professional jargon. The researcher should also make a cheerful and friendly offer to discuss any of the material with subjects, if they so desire. Such discussions are gratifying to subjects, and sometimes provide researchers with valuable anecdotal information that is useful in planning the next study or understanding the results of the current study. (See 4.6 for relevant discussion of debriefing.)

Personally relevant benefits are sometimes more important than scientific knowledge to subjects. Depending on the nature of the research, various kinds of personal benefits may be possible, ranging from a successful intervention that helps the subject with a personal problem, to a list of reputable local services, or an annotated bibliography that the subject would likely find useful. In the case of needy subjects, especially in community settings, personally relevant benefits might also include money, food, or medical/mental health services. Information and referrals should be offered respectfully and without implying that the subject has problems or is ignorant.

Insight, training, learning, role modeling, empowerment, and future opportunities may be natural outcomes of participation in a treatment or intervention. Opportunities for follow-up experiences or applications should be discussed with subjects. Case 1, Part III, on focus groups with crack users, exemplifies valuable benefits of this kind.

Psychosocial benefits include the benefits of (a) altruism—giving of one's time to benefit others, (b) participation in an experiment that makes one feel worthwhile, and (c) receiving favorable attention and esteem from a skilled investigator. These are typical outcomes of receiving professional and respectful treatment.

Kinship benefits include the feeling of closeness to persons, or the reduction of alienation. Research participation often relates to significant persons in the subject's life, or to people in general, and provides an opportunity to reflect on these relationships. People who are selected for participation because they have something in common—such as a learning problem, musical talent, or being a twin—may enjoy feeling that they have an opportunity, through the research, to enhance the lives of others with whom they share some human bond.

Benefits to the community or organization that is the site of field research (e.g., the subjects' school, home, neighborhood, clinic, workplace) may derive from many sources, including an actual intervention and the resources it provides, staff development, improved morale, insight into problems that need to be solved, collection of data that can be useful for policy-making or political purposes, development of new opportunities and relationships with powerful outsiders, prestige, and new abilities to serve community members. Benefits may result from a Hawthorne effect in which respect and attention paid to members of the community improve their outlook and performance. Even if a community intervention fails to produce the desired experimental effects, the project may still benefit the community in various ways.

Community-based research inevitably gets in the way of ongoing activities. The wise researcher spends considerable time learning from community gatekeepers how to accommodate to community needs and how to provide benefits expressly sought by the community—not just benefits the researcher thinks would be good for the community. The planning, and delivery, of benefits is often a condition of access to the community. Such planning is also vital to the success of an intervention, since displeased community members can sink a project; to public perception of the project; and to continuing access to that research site.

Benefits to the research institution, the researcher, and the funder are also attainable with proper planning. Equipment; ongoing training of students and qualified researchers; productive relationships with collaborators elsewhere; development of appropriate methodology; production, peer review, and publication of respected intellectual products; and public recognition of the value of the research program are needed to sustain major research programs. These kinds of benefits are not explicitly required in an IRB protocol and are rarely addressed explicitly there; and they may even be irrelevant to student projects or to isolated studies. However, IRBs understand that the researcher must build some kind of research infrastructure to sustain a research program and ultimately yield significant scientific and social benefits. Obvious neglect of the underpinnings of a research program casts doubt on promises of significant scientific and social benefit.

9.3 A MATRIX OF RESEARCH BENEFITS AND BENEFICIARIES

Significant contribution to science and society is not a one-shot activity. Rather, such contribution is typically based on a series of competently designed research or intervention efforts, which themselves are possible only because the researcher has developed appropriate institutional or community infrastructures and has disseminated the findings in a timely and effective way. Benefit to society also depends on widespread implementation, which, in turn, depends on the goodwill, support, and collective wisdom of many specific individuals, including politicians, funders, other professionals, and community leaders. Thus, the successful contributor to science and society is a builder of many benefits and a provider of those benefits to various constituencies, even if the conduct of the research per se is a solo operation.

9.3.1 The Hierarchy of Benefits

Research benefits may be divided into seven (nonexclusive) categories, ranging from those that are relatively easy to provide, through those that are extremely difficult. As shown in Figure 9.1, these seven kinds of benefits, in turn, might accrue to any of seven kinds of recipients: subjects, communities, investigators, research institutions, funders, science, or society in general. As listed below, the seven categories of benefit are described as they might pertain to a community that is the site of field research:

Valuable relationships: The community establishes ties with helping institutions and funders.

Knowledge or education: The community develops a better understanding of its own problems.

Material resources: The community makes use of research materials, equipment, and funding.

Training, employment, opportunity for advancement: Community members receive training and continue to serve as professionals or paraprofessionals within the ongoing project.

Opportunity to do good and to receive the esteem of others: The community learns how to better serve its members.

Empowerment (personal, political, and so on): The community uses findings for policy purposes; gains favorable attention of the press, politicians, and the like.

Scientific/clinical outcomes: The community provides treatment to its members (assuming that the research or intervention is successful).

Note that even if the experiment or intervention yielded disappointing results, all but the last benefit might be available to the community, as well as to individual subjects.

9.3.2 The Hierarchy of Beneficiaries

Before examining the varied forms that each of these kinds of benefits might take, let us look closer at the seven kinds of beneficiaries:

The subjects (Column 1 of Figure 9.1) are the actual research participants, whose benefits may include such things as the respect of the researcher, an interesting debriefing, money, treatment, or future opportunities for advancement. Entries in Column 1 indicate ways to enrich the lives of the subjects, engender their goodwill toward the project, and enhance their respect for science.

The community or institution (Column 2) that provides the setting for field research may include the subjects' homes, neighborhood, clinic, workplace, or recreation center. A community includes its members, gatekeepers, leaders, staff, professionals, clientele, and peers or family of the subjects. Some examples of the kinds of benefits that the community may receive have already been mentioned, both in the above example of a hierarchy of benefits (9.3.1), and in Case 9.1. Sometimes community members also serve as research assistants and so would receive benefits associated with those of the next category of recipients as well. Column 2 indicates what can be done to leave the research site a better place, satisfy community gatekeepers, and pave the way for future research.

The researcher, as well as research assistants and others who are associated with the project (Column 3), may gain valuable relationships, knowledge, expertise, access to funding, scientific recognition, and so on, if the research is competently conducted, and especially if it produces the desired result or some other dramatic outcome. By creating these benefits for oneself and other members of the research team, the investigator gains the credibility needed to go forward with a research program and to exert a significant influence upon science and society.

The research institution (Column 4) may benefit along with the researcher. Institutional benefits are more likely to be described as good university-community relations, educational leadership, funding of overhead costs, equipment, and a good scientific reputation for scientists, funders, government, and the scientific establishment. Such benefits increase a university's willingness to provide the kinds of support (e.g., space, clerical assistance, small grants, equipment, matching funds) that enable the researcher to move the research program forward with a minimum of chaos.

The funder (Column 5) is vital to the success of a major research program and hopes to receive benefits such as the following, if only the researcher remembers to provide them: ties to a good project and its constituents, well-written intellectual products promptly and effectively disseminated, good publicity, evidence of useful outcomes, good ideas to share with other scientists, and good impressions made on politicians and others who have power to reward the funder. Such benefits make a funder proud to have funded the project, eager to advertise it, and favorably disposed to funding future research of that investigator.

Science refers to the disciplines involved, and to the scientists within them, their scientific societies, and their publications. Benefits to science parallel benefits to funders and depend on the importance, rigor, and productivity of the investigation. Development of useful insights and methods may serve science, even in the absence of findings that might benefit society. Column 6 represents the kinds of events that give scientific visibility to one's ideas and empirical findings. Initial papers and symposia give way to publications and invited addresses. Others evaluate, replicate, promote, and build upon the work, thus earning it a place in the realm of scientific ideas. *A single publication upon which no one builds is not a contribution to science.*

Society, including the target population from which subjects were sampled and to which the results are to be generalized, is the one group that benefits only when the hoped-for scientific outcome occurs and is generalizable to other settings. Column 7 represents the most abstract level of benefit possible; it also reflects the most advanced developmental stage of any given research project. By the time benefits of this magnitude have accrued, the researcher or others have already adapted and broadly implemented the idea in society. The idea has begun to take on a life of its own, be modified to a variety of uses, and be adapted, used, and even claimed by many others.

The conjunction of seven kinds of benefits and seven kinds of beneficiaries yields a 49-cell matrix that is useful in research planning. This matrix suggests that turning a research idea into a scientific and social contribution requires that benefits be developed at each stage of the process. It is useful to design a tentative matrix of benefits as the basic research idea and design are being formulated and to continue planning the benefits as the project proceeds. Many valuable benefits may be easily incorporated, provided that one is attuned to opportunities for doing so.

9.4 USING THE MATRIX TO PLAN PROTOCOLS AND PROPOSALS

The ethical investigator understands the necessity of identifying the intended benefits and beneficiaries and actively striving to make those benefits a reality. Some benefits are ones that can be produced directly and easily. Others are difficult to produce, and one's best efforts to produce them may be foiled by happenstance, politics, or contrary empirical findings. Systematic planning of relevant benefit is integral to designing the research, writing the research proposal, and writing the IRB protocol. It is this specific planning process to which we now turn.

The matrix contains seven benefits, ordered approximately according to the difficulty of producing each, and seven beneficiaries, ordered approximately according to the difficulty of serving each. It provides a heuristic tool for planning to provide feasible benefits. The upper left corner of the matrix readily suggests benefits one can most responsibly promise. As one approaches the lower right corner of the matrix, one's hoped-for benefits increasingly depend upon success at prior stages of the research, on the investigator's future hard work, and on events outside the investigator's own direct control. All 49 of these kinds of benefit are valuable, though some are inapplicable to certain kinds of research. Each represents a special kind of opportunity for success; but unless these opportunities are identified and planned for, they are unlikely to materialize. Each of these kinds of benefits may be important to mention in an application for funding. Many kinds of benefits, especially those to subjects and their communities, are important to mention in the IRB protocol.

The specific benefits that one designates within the matrix depend upon the nature and magnitude of one's project. Case 9.1 provides an interesting opportunity for the reader to try out skills of identifying benefits, as this case readily yields various entries for each of the 49 cells. Figure 9.1 illustrates 49 examples of benefits that might follow from Case 9.1. The reader can no doubt identify others, and will note that certain events may pertain to more than one beneficiary and provide more than one kind of benefit.

9.4.1 The Discussion of Benefits
in the IRB Protocol

The discussion of benefits in the IRB protocol should focus primarily on the benefits that are within the researcher's power and willingness to provide, especially those benefits pertaining to subjects and their community. The protocol should also allude, with appropriate modesty, to the possible scientific and social benefits that the researcher hopes will ensue from the project. This should be accompanied by a description of the methodology that demonstrates the rigor of the research and the specific anticipated products.

Perhaps the project is a major one that has developed the resources needed to undertake a ground-breaking effort that probably will influence science and social policy. Will an IRB permit the research to go forth if it necessarily involves risk? To show that the project has a distinct possibility of benefiting science and society, relevant parts of the entire matrix might be mentioned: the community goodwill and resources developed so far, the prior research and proven validity of the design and procedures, the competently trained assistants, the noteworthy prior publications, and the institutional commitment of needed resources. Thus, the IRB can see that the promise of social and scientific benefit is believable.

Or perhaps the project is a master's thesis, which is unlikely to be published. Such a project has only a slim likelihood of benefiting science and society. Therefore, the emphasis in the protocol discussion of benefit should be on what, realistically, will be done to benefit subjects, the community, and the researcher, with only modest mention of hoped-for benefits to science and society.

9.4.2 The Discussion of Benefits
in the Research Proposal

Protocols should mention relevant elements from the benefit matrix: What will be done to assure benefit to subjects and the host community, to assure their ethical treatment, and to enlist their cooperation? What competencies does the investigator bring? What resources will the institution provide? What additional resources are needed? If funding is sought, what intellectual products and other benefits will the funder, science, and society receive? Who will review and evaluate these products for scientific of social merit?

PART IV

Vulnerable Populations

It is beyond the scope of this book to discuss issues and safeguards pertinent to all of the vulnerable populations mentioned in Chapter 8 (8.5). However, two vulnerable groups in particular are the topics of much research, are especially vulnerable, and are discussed here: minors and disenfranchised urban populations.

In research on youngsters, issues of risk assessment, parental permission, assent, and confidentiality are far more complex than in research with adults. These problems are discussed in Chapter 10.

Disenfranchised persons who are at risk for HIV infection include the homeless, members of the urban drug culture, poor minorities, prostitutes, runaway children, gay males, and the mentally ill. These persons pose special problems because most researchers are typically not sensitive to the culture—the beliefs, worldview, time frame, language, social structure, needs, and fears—of these people. Consider the special needs and fears that an investigator must respect in research on runaway gay male children who are homeless minorities, mentally ill, and sell their bodies for drugs. No social scientist has enough natural empathy to know how to communicate effectively with such populations and how to translate ethical principles appropriately. Chapter 11 orients the reader to ethical and procedural issues in community-based research on these populations, including ways to increase one's empathy and cultural sensitivity to such research populations.

Various other vulnerable research populations require special consideration, such as the dying, sick newborns, medically indigent populations in public hospitals, institutionalized mentally infirm, prisoners, the physically handicapped, and those in advanced stages of HIV infection. Although these populations are typically the focus of medical research, social scientists are becoming increasingly involved. Some of the same guidelines for cultural sensitivity presented in Chapter 11 apply to these populations as well. However, it is beyond the scope of this slim volume to provide the additional chapters that would be required both to present case examples and adequately describe the problems of studying these other vulnerable populations. The interested reader is referred to the following excellent sources on these and related vulnerable populations: Bermant and Wheeler (1987); Gallagher (1990); Koocher and Keith-Spiegel (1990); Levine (1986); Macklin (1987); Pope and Basque (1991); and Rothman (1991).

10

Research on Children and Adolescents [1]

As a research population, children and adolescents are special in several respects: (a) They have a limited psychological, as well as legal, capacity to give informed consent; (b) they may be cognitively, socially, and emotionally immature; (c) there are external constraints on their self-determination and independent decision making; (d) they have unequal power in relation to authorities, such as parents, teachers, and researchers; (e) parents and institutions, as well as the youngsters themselves, have an interest in their research participation; and (f) national priorities for research on children and adolescents include research on drug users, runaways, pregnant teenagers, and other sensitive topics, compounding the ethical and legal problems surrounding research on minors.

Regulations governing research respond to these characteristics of youngsters by requiring that they have special protections and that parental rights be respected. The law also expects social scientists to respond to these characteristics by using knowledge of human development to reduce risk and vulnerability.

10.1 LEGAL CONSTRAINTS ON RESEARCH ON MINORS

In 1983 the Department of Health and Human Services adopted federal regulations governing behavioral research on persons under the age of consent, 18 years.[2] These regulations include the following requirements: (a) IRB approval; (b) the documented permission of a parent or guardian, and the assent of the child–in the case of risky research or at the IRB's discretion, consent of both parents is required–and (c) that the research involve no greater risks than those ordinarily encountered in the child's daily life, except when the IRB finds that the risk is justified by anticipated benefit to the subjects (as discussed in

111

45 CFR 46.405). However, some research is exempted from review at the discretion of the IRB, and some of these exemptions are especially relevant to school children. Hence, a partial list of the exemptions contained in 45 CFR 46.101(b) is provided here. The reader is referred to the full set of regulations for further details. Research of the following kinds is exempted:

1. Research conducted in established or commonly accepted educational settings, involving normal educational practices such as (i) research on regular and special education instructional strategies, or (ii) research on the effectiveness of, or the comparison among, instructional techniques, curricula, or classroom management methods.

2. Research involving the use of educational tests (cognitive, diagnostic, aptitude, achievement), if information taken from these sources is recorded in such a manner that subjects cannot be identified, directly or through identifiers linked to the subjects.

Waiver of parental permission. There are two circumstances under which parental or guardian permission may be waived, at the discretion of the IRB:

1. Parental permission may be waived for research involving only minimal risk (i.e., no greater than the risks of everyday life), provided the research will not adversely affect the rights or welfare of the subjects, and provided the research could not practically be carried out without the waiver. There are various circumstances in which it is impossible or impractical to contact the parents. For example, street children who are drug dealers may or may not have parents who are available or even living; and the subjects would probably make it impossible for the researcher to make, or act on, this determination in any case.

2. Parental permission may be waived if it will not operate to protect the child. For example, abusive or neglectful parents cannot be counted on to act in their child's best interests. Parents who are in an adversarial stance vis-à-vis their child present a different problem; typically they are feeling angry or punitive because of the youngster's misbehavior. Waiver of parental permission may be appropriate under these conditions, especially when the youngster is being treated for abuse or neglect, is identified legally as incorrigible or delinquent, or is in the custody of a hospital or other institution.

Although not recognized in the federal regulations, the National Commission for the Protection of Human Subjects of Biomedical and

Behavioral Research identified four other circumstances in which waiver or modification of the parental permission might be appropriate:

1. Research designed to identify factors related to the incidence or treatment of certain conditions in adolescents for which, in certain jurisdictions, they may legally receive treatment without parental permission.
2. Research in which the subjects are mature minors, and the procedures involved entail essentially no more than minimal risk of the kind that such individuals might reasonable assume on their own.
3. Research designed to understand and meet the needs of neglected or abused children, or children designated by their parents as "in need of supervision."
4. Research involving children whose parents are legally or functionally incompetent.

The National Commission's report goes on to say that

[T]here is no single mechanism that can be substituted for parental permission in every instance. In some cases the consent of mature minors should be sufficient. . . .

In other cases, court approval may be required. Another alternative might be to appoint a social worker, nurse, or physician to act as surrogate parent when the research is designed, for example, to study neglected or battered children. Such surrogate parents would be expected to participate not only in the process of soliciting the children's cooperation, but also in the conduct of the research, in order to provide reassurance for the subjects and to intervene or support their desires to withdraw if participation should become too stressful. (43 Federal Register 2084, 1978)

In interpreting these regulations and recommendations, the Task Force for Research on Children (see Stanley & Sieber, 1991) concluded that parental incompetence is unlikely to be an adequate reason, by itself, for waiving the requirement of parental permission. Children of legally incompetent parents have guardians whose permission should be sought. When parents' deficiencies are not sufficient to result in appointment of guardians, their deficiencies probably are not grounds for abrogating their right to decide whether their children may participate in research.

The determination of "mature minor" must be made on a case-by-case basis, rather than by category. For example, a state may not rule that all 17-year-olds are mature for purposes of exercising a particular right, such as the right to abortion. Although many states grant certain rights to mature minors, all state laws concerning the rights of mature minors are silent on the subject of participation in research. Thus, there is no clear legal definition of a mature minor with respect to research participation.

Waiver of child's assent. The IRB may waive the requirement of assent if it determines that the child is incapable of assenting, due to age, level of maturity, or psychological state, or if obtaining assent would render the research impossible. However, waiver of assent is permitted only if the research involves minimal risk, or if it holds out the prospect of direct benefit to the child that is not obtainable otherwise.

Research involving greater than minimal risk. Recognizing that there may be appropriate research interventions or treatments that involve greater than minimal risk, these are permitted if they present the prospect of direct benefit to the child, if the risk is justified by the anticipated benefit, and if there are no reasonable alternatives presenting less risk. If there is no prospect of direct benefit to the subject, the research may be conducted only if (a) the intervention or procedure presents experiences to subjects that are commensurate with those of their actual or expected medical, dental, psychological, social, or educational situations, or (b) it is likely to yield vitally important generalizable knowledge about the subjects' condition.

Research involving more than minor risk beyond minimal risk, without any direct benefit, may be conducted only if approved by a panel of experts appointed by the Secretary of Health and Human Services (45 CFR 46.406).

Beyond the explicit legal provisions governing research on children, researchers are required to adhere to the general provisions governing human subject research—including consideration of risk and benefit, privacy and confidentiality, and consent. Because children are different from adults in many ways, sensitivity to developmental issues is critical; this is the topic to which we turn next.

10.2 RISK FROM A DEVELOPMENTAL PERSPECTIVE

The question to ask about vulnerability to research risk is not: At what age does a youngster cease to be especially vulnerable? Rather, it is: *How do type of risk and maturity interact?* For example, the young child, in contrast to the adolescent, is not easily embarrassed and is unlikely to be stressed by concern about the researcher's intentions, given his or her lack of capacity for self-referent thinking. He or she is unlikely even to be aware of deception, given his or her lack of suspicion of authority figures, and probably cannot effectively be dehoaxed. In contrast, the adolescent would be highly sensitive to cues that might possibly indicate the researcher's intentions. He or she would be likely to react strongly to the knowledge that he or she had been deceived, yet would be somewhat protected by his or her skepticism. He or she would require careful debriefing (see 12.7, 12.8).

Thompson (1991), drawing on Maccoby (1983), has summarized the kinds of age by vulnerability interactions that should guide risk assessment in research on minors. The reader is referred to Thompson's excellent chapter for details; the following is a summary of that discussion:

1. Younger children are more likely to experience greater behavioral and socio-emotional disorganization accompanying stress; the older child is better able to cope and more reliant on self than on caregivers. The parent's presence may buffer the young child from stress in the research setting, but may even exacerbate the older child's stress.

2. Self-conscious emotional reactions, such as shame, guilt, and pride, emerge in the preschool years, and young children have an immature understanding of these feelings. For example, young children are likely to feel guilty in negative situations for which they are not responsible. It is not until the age of 7 or 8 that children begin to restrict these feelings to appropriate circumstances.

3. Young children's trust of authority renders them especially vulnerable to coercive manipulations and to deception. With age comes understanding of individual rights and skepticism about authority.

4. Because of their limited conceptual development, younger children may benefit relatively less from feedback, dehoaxing, and debriefing.

Because of their continuing trust in authorities, they may also be less vulnerable to heightened future sensitivity to deceit in research.

5. Older children are more vulnerable to implicit cues and pressures, but they also approach the research task with more skepticism than younger children.

6. Threats to self-concept become more stressful with age. Between about 7 and 9, when children develop an integrated self-image, the evaluations of others become increasingly important (Harter, 1983). Social comparison information begins to affect self-evaluation, and ability comes to be viewed as an enduring personal quality (Nicholls, 1978). Although young children may remain optimistic in the face of negative ability attributions, older children are likely to engage in worried self-reflection and to experience lowered self-esteem.

7. As they grow older, children become increasingly sensitive to cultural and socioeconomic biases that reflect negatively on their background, family, or prior experiences.

8. As children grow older, their concern about privacy and autonomy increases. This is a major topic, which is discussed in the next section.

10.3 PRIVACY AND AUTONOMY
FROM A DEVELOPMENTAL PERSPECTIVE

As we have seen in Chapter 5, privacy is a personal and idiosyncratic matter, having to do with control of the access of others to oneself. This problem is compounded in the case of children, as parents, teachers, and others also presume to have access to the child. This topic has been treated extensively by Melton (1983, 1991), and can be touched on only briefly here.

It is unclear when access to a child becomes invasive. From the time of his or her birth, caretakers have intimate physical and psychological access to the child. Gradually, the youngster takes control of his or her privacy, first through concern for privacy of possessions and space, later through concern for privacy of information. In fact, children sometimes seize control with "Keep Out" signs and locked drawers when they begin to experience the invasiveness of others. How sensitive are researchers to children's needs for privacy? Macklin (1991) offers the following test of our respect for children's privacy: Some parents install a speaker system between the baby's bedroom and the rest of the house, so they can hear the baby cry or call. This is clearly not an invasion of a 1-year-old's privacy, but what about a 5-year-old, or an 8-year-old? What are the implications for research?

A second complication arises because research on the child is often research on the family. Researchers who are accustomed to discussing (other people's) family life often fail to recognize the degree of privacy some people accord to family matters. Melton (1991) points out that even a simple task, such an essay to be written by 8-year-old on "how I spent my summer vacation," may be an implicit request for information about his or her associations and activities; it may also intrude into private family matters, as when the child spends the summer commuting between divorced parents.

Although children's privacy is easily and often invaded, privacy is clearly important even to primary school children. Indeed, children evaluate the quality of living situations by the degree of invasion of privacy and infringement of liberty present within them (e.g., Rivlin & Wolfe, 1985). Given the significance of privacy for the maintenance of self-esteem and the development of personal identity, it is extremely important to respect children's privacy by making research no more intrusive than necessary and by obtaining children's assent before entering a zone of privacy.

As we have seen in Chapter 5, privacy is intimately connected with autonomy. Children's ability to make reasoned decisions and avoid coercion with respect to research participation does not reach adult-like levels until mid-adolescence (Weithorn, 1983). However, their ability to know when someone is intolerably "in their space," or invading their privacy, exists by about the age of 6 or 7; it is appropriate, therefore, that the federal regulations of research give children veto power over their parents' permission for research participation.

Although the age of legal consent is 18, children's ability to make rational decisions is well developed before then and is not the main issue. Thus, rationality is not the main concern. At issue, rather, is the right of parents to have a say in what happens to their children. Herein lies a set of difficult issues for the researcher. As children grow older, the expression of privacy becomes an active choice; by adolescence it is a marker of independence, and the control of information becomes very important. But what of the parent? Often, the behavior being studied is rebellious and performed without the parent's knowledge. In some cases parental permission must be waived, as the youngster would never agree to having the parent informed of his or her behavior. In other cases, the behavior and the research are known to the parent, and the youngster reveals information to the researcher that the parent might wish to know about—for example, drug abuse, sexual behavior, or risk of HIV infection. Should such information be kept confidential from the parents? Do parents have a right to know? In many cases, release of such information would actually increase the risk to the youngsters. Macklin (1991) argues persuasively that a parent's desire to know does not constitute a right, and that the only ethical grounds for disclosing such information to parents is when it is only through such action that urgent help can be obtained for the youngster.

10.4 ASSENT, CONSENT, AND PARENTAL PERMISSION

Assent is defined as a child's affirmative agreement to participate in research; mere failure to object should not be construed as assent. The standard for assent is the ability to understand, to some degree, the purpose of the research and what will happen if one participates in it.

Consent requires that persons understand the consequences of their participation and be able to weigh these consequences. By tradition, the age of consent is 18, although by early adolescence most youngsters can make adult-like decisions. Some exceptions to the age of consent include full or partial emancipation, as through marriage or living apart and being self-supporting; being declared a mature minor; or being a member of the military.

Permission means the agreement of parent(s) or guardian to the participation of the child or ward in research. *Parent* means a child's biological or adoptive parent. *Guardian* means an individual who is authorized, under applicable state or local law, to consent on behalf of a child. Parental or guardian permission must fulfill the conditions of informed consent stated in Chapter 4, and documentation of the permission is required. (Exceptions are found in individual IRB policies; for example, for unobtrusive observation of school children, written permission of the school, but not the parents, may be acceptable.)

Obtaining adequate assent calls for sensitivity to maturational factors. Tymchuk (1991) suggests several ways to adapt the assent process for use with young children:

1. The level of difficulty of the information presented should be commensurate with the child's level of understanding, and his or her comprehension of the material should be assessed.
2. The format should be appropriate. A storybook or videotape format may be appropriate for young children or retarded children. Repeated presentations may be needed.
3. Training in the ability to use information to make decisions will probably yield better decision making by children.

A recommended procedure. What does one say to a child of about 5 to 12 years of age when seeking assent? Here is one possibility:

Hi, [child's name].

My name is [your name], and I am trying to learn about [describe project briefly in appropriate language].

I would like you to [describe what you would ask the child to do. Use a videotape or storybook format, if appropriate. Don't use words like "help" or "cooperate," which can imply a subtle form of coercion].

Do you want to do this? [If the child does not give clear affirmative agreement to participate, you may not continue with this child.]

Do you have any questions before we start? [Answer questions clearly.]

If you want to stop at any time, just tell me. [If the child says to stop, you must stop.]

10.5 HIGH-RISK BEHAVIOR

In consequence of the tendency of troubled youngsters to defy their parents or to run away, the law recognizes that parental consent may be waived by the IRB under certain circumstances (see 10.1). In most cases, the research is conducted within an institution, such as an HIV testing site, an abortion clinic, a youth detention center, a shelter for runaway children, or a drug treatment center. The problems of obtaining meaningful consent are manifold. These problems have been discussed extensively by Grisso (1991), who focuses on issues surrounding waiver of parental permission, and by Rotheram-Borus and Koopman (1991), who are concerned primarily with consent issues in the research and treatment of runaway, gay, and heterosexually active youth, whose relationships with their parents are often marked by secrecy, conflict, and long absences. The following is a summary of some of their main points:

1. The youngster is unlikely to believe that the research is independent of the institution or that he or she may decline to participate with impunity.
2. The youngster is unlikely to believe promises of confidentiality, especially when he or she is in trouble with his or her parents and other authorities.
3. Issues of privacy, which are normally salient for adolescents, are likely to be even more heightened for this population.
4. Maltreated youngsters are likely to experience the research as more stressful than normal children. If the researcher effectively establishes rapport, the youngster may reach out for help; the researcher must be prepared to respond helpfully.

Clearly, the researcher ignores the issues of privacy and autonomy for minors only at great peril. Both the youngster and the quality of the research will be harmed unless appropriate safeguards are employed. Adequate assent procedures, in particular, are essential. Grisso (1991) has suggested a pilot assent procedure to satisfy some of these concerns.

In the pilot assent, the researcher describes the actual research process to members of the research population in the social context where the study is to be performed. (For example, he or she obtains permission to talk to adolescent clients in an abortion clinic.) He or she then asks them a set of questions to find out if they understand what concerns such research would raise for them, and so on. In so doing, the researcher (a) refines the assent process to maximize understanding, (b) provides the IRB with documentation of adequate assent, (c) discovers possible ways to improve adolescents' assent capacities, and (d) develops the actual assent form to be employed.

In addition, Rotheram-Borus and Koopman (1991) suggest that researchers of high-risk behavior should observe the following:

1. Anticipate ethical dilemmas. Keep logs of critical incidents as an aid to formulating effective problem-solving strategies and policies.
2. Hold frequent staff meetings to discuss emerging or possible problems and to train members of the group in ethical decision making.
3. Secure assent whenever possible from the youngsters, and consent from community agency staff and parents. Parental consent should be avoided only when to seek it would jeopardize the health or well-being of the youngster.

4. Take special precautions to protect confidentiality. Whenever possible, collect data anonymously.
5. Involve the community in the design of interventions. Respect community values and perspectives; otherwise, the community can prevent successful implementation of an intervention.

Much research on high-risk behavior in youngsters is conducted in community-based settings, which themselves present special challenges; research in such settings is the topic of the next chapter.

10.6 SCHOOL SETTINGS

Schools provide a convenient entry point for researchers who want to study children. Some of the kinds of research possible through schools involve minimal risk, including noninteractive anonymous observation of public behavior, secondary analysis of data, observation of classroom behavior, testing of curriculum or teaching methods, and research based on educational testing. Often IRBs will permit such research with school permission and without parental permission. However, IRBs cannot approve research unless it complies with the Buckley Amendment.

The Family Educational Rights and Privacy Act of 1979 (the Buckley Amendment) states that: "An educational agency or institution shall obtain the written consent of the parent of a student or the eligible student [if 18 or older] before disclosing personally identifiable information from educational records of a student, other than directory information . . ." Thus, for any research that involves obtaining identifiable (as opposed to anonymous) information from student records, the investigator must obtain written permission from the parents for the specific information to be released (not blanket permission giving access to any information).

Research that involves direct intervention with school children, such as research on behavior, interviews and surveys, or introduction of special classroom activities, typically requires permission from the school district and parents, as well as the assent of each child. Research that involves risk to children, but also offers the possibility of special benefits (e.g., counseling research on abused children), might require, in addition, an IRB-appointed child advocate to monitor the consent process, and perhaps also to monitor the research. At the discretion of the IRB, the advocate might be an outside therapist specializing in the treatment of children, or a school counselor. Given the bias of researchers in favor of their own experimental treatments, the IRB might ask an independent expert to judge the likely benefit to subjects of risky research.

Example of letters requesting parental permission and child's assent appear in Appendix A.

School permission must come from the school district, not from a teacher, and must be presented to the IRB in writing, on district letterhead. Investigators should check with the district office to learn the appropriate procedure for obtaining school permission. However, schools do not have the authority to consent for children to participate in research, except as stated in the first paragraph of 10.6, above.

Avoiding coercion is especially important in school research, where peer and authority pressures are especially salient. To assure that each child's participation is truly voluntary, the researcher must implement the following objectives:

1. Minimize the coercion implicit in a request to participate from parents, teachers, or other adults.
2. Minimize peer pressure and fear of ridicule for not participating.
3. Keep any reward for participating small and not valuable.

NOTES

1. I am grateful to my fellow members of the Task Force on Research on Minors, Office for Protection from Research Risks, NIH, for contributing to my knowledge of this subject, especially to Barbara Stanley, Gary Melton, and Charles MacKay, with whom I worked most closely. This chapter draws heavily on the findings of the task force.

2. Research is also governed by state law. However, the requirements of state law are almost certain to be satisfied if parental permission is obtained. Only when a researcher wants to waive parental permission is state law likely to be more restrictive than federal regulations (Areen, 1991). Most state laws are silent on the topic of participation of minors in behavioral research, but vary in their authorization of minors to obtain various types of medical treatment without parental consent.

RECOMMENDED READINGS

Fisher, C. B., & Tryon, W. W. (Eds.). (1990). *Ethics in applied developmental psychology: Emerging issues in an emerging field.* Advances in Applied Developmental Psychology. Volume 4. Norwood, NJ: Ablex.

Keith-Spiegel, P. C., & Koocher, G. P. (1990). *Children, ethics and the law.* Lincoln: University of Nebraska Press. [This comprehensive discussion of professional issues and cases includes issues surrounding psychotherapy with children, children and the courts, and other issues that are beyond the purview of this book.]

Stanley, B., & Sieber, J. E. (Eds.). (1991). *Social research on children and adolescents: Ethical issues.* Newbury Park, CA: Sage. [This book focuses on socially sensitive research in applied settings.]

11

Community-Based Research on Vulnerable Urban Populations and AIDS

Some of the most serious social problems facing our society today arise in urban community settings among such disadvantaged populations as homeless street people, runaways, unassimilated ethnic minorities, prostitutes, intravenous drug and crack users, gay men, dual-diagnosis mentally ill, alcoholics, and the developmentally disabled. Compounding their experience of poverty, lack of education, poor mental and physical health, violence, and marginality in our culture, these populations are at high risk for HIV infection. Increasingly, researchers are seeking to help members of these groups prevent the spread of AIDS, but typically lack the cultural sensitivity required to adapt methodological and ethical principles to these settings.

The purpose of this chapter is to provide insight into ways of developing respectful and effective community-based research approaches with vulnerable urban populations. It uses, as a context, AIDS-related research, which involves ethical and methodological worst cases. This chapter focuses on disenfranchised urban populations and on the kinds of attitudes and life-styles that bring these populations into conflict with the law and complicate community-based AIDS research. Procedures are discussed for creating rapport, access, and trust within cultures that are ordinarily closed to research. This chapter emphasizes the need for cultural sensitivity, collaboration, respect, and the tailoring of research procedures to the population being studied. However, this chapter also contains lessons about community-based research that are applicable to middle-class populations.

Interventions need to be created that take into account the epidemic nature of AIDS, its 8- to 11-year latency from exposure to expression, the characteristics of the populations affected, and people's capacity to believe themselves safe. Sexually active people become vulnerable to HIV infection when their partners inject drugs or are exposed to infected individuals. Yet they are likely to ignore risk until it is too late—to believe that risky activities with one's healthy-looking partner could not be dangerous, that condoms are unacceptable, and that participation in AIDS intervention is an invasion of their privacy. Further complicating matters for researchers is the fact that the epidemic moves from one distinct population or culture to another. The specific approaches that work with one population may fail with the next.

When AIDS was first discovered, it was identified as a gay disease. Since gay males may be born into any ethnic or socioeconomic group, they include many who are educated, affluent, and hold powerful positions in society—physicians, lawyers, teachers, scientists, and other professionals. Gay men were hard hit, physically and psychologically, by the epidemic and were often brutally stigmatized by others who assumed themselves to be invulnerable to AIDS. But gay men quickly mobilized effective educational campaigns based upon scientific facts, and many members of the gay community modified their behavior so that the epidemic in this population has now reached a plateau. Gay men have also demanded a say in their treatment in medical trials:

> *Case 11.1: Community Consent.* The gay community in cities where AZT trials were scheduled did not like being guinea pigs in clinical trials that seemed to them like Russian roulette. Knowing that there were blind placebo controls, they worked as a nationwide network to develop an elaborate scheme for exchanging half doses so that each might receive possible life-saving treatment. Although this plan resulted in giving each subject an effective treatment, it foiled the toxicity-testing portion of the experimental design. In response to this research dilemma, Melton, Levine, Koocher, Rosenthal, and Thompson (1988) suggested that researchers hold forums with representatives of the subject population to plan and design the research. Medical researchers did not readily accept this idea. Consequently, key members of the gay community announced to the administration of a major medical school that they could expect no participants in AIDS research unless a regular forum were held for the gay community to negotiate the research agreements with the investigators. They expected to be in on the planning stages of the research. The prestigious investigators who met with them had never before participated in bilateral research planning with subjects. They were particularly offended when members of the gay community criticized the statistical design of their research and suggested a better design. Sessions were not very

friendly. However, the physicians involved received excellent and well-reasoned advice, and ultimately incorporated that advice into their research plans (Morin, 1990).

Such well-educated and powerful contingents were not to be found in the next populations to which the epidemic spread.

Because AIDS was mistakenly considered a gay disease, the next populations to which the epidemic spread—the inner-city poor, especially blacks, Latinos, and Asians who are intravenous drug users—had no idea that they were at risk; nor were these victims acknowledged or treated with compassion by members of their own group. In the course of this second epidemic, AIDS spread to women and, since blood is exchanged between mother and fetus, to their children. Now, as the AIDS epidemic sweeps through populations of disenfranchised and uneducated people in urban areas, it begins to enter another population that is even less willing to acknowledge its vulnerability and mortality—sexually active teenagers of all ethnic and socioeconomic groups.

11.1 COMMUNITY-BASED INTERVENTION RESEARCH

The community-based scientist works collaboratively within the existing social structure of the community, focusing on prevention (rather than cure), competence building, social support, empowerment, and mutual help. Empowerment means enabling persons and groups to solve their problems and meet their needs in their own cultural context; community researchers serve and build constituencies among community members (Gesten & Jason, 1987).

The methods of community research are often experimental and behavioral and may involve types of statistical design and analysis unfamiliar to social scientists. These include time-series analyses (Steiner & Mark, 1985), social-impact assessment and nonequivalent group designs (Meissen & Cipriani, 1984), and diverse qualitative methods (e.g., Susskind & Klein, 1985).

11.1.1 Settings for Community-Based AIDS Research

The researcher typically begins with a particular intervention research objective and target population in mind. For example, the researcher may want to teach safe sex practices to prostitutes, to develop a social support system for persons seeking to stay off drugs, or to provide a needle exchange program for drug-addicted homeless people. Community-based AIDS and drug-abuse research typically occurs on the street, in the living situation of the subject, in a drug-treatment or health-care setting, or under the auspices of some existing community organization.

Street-based research means working with people such as the homeless, drug users, and runaway children to create an intervention that promises to improve their lives. The cultures and informal gatekeepers of the streets are difficult for the typical researcher to get to know. Street people distrust outsiders, even researchers of the same ethnic background who speak the same language and are formerly of the same group (e.g., former prostitutes or drug addicts). An important survival skill of street people is to take on whatever persona is needed to get what they want. The middle-class researcher is often taken in by life stories that are simply untrue. Because of the difficulties of becoming an insider to street culture, researchers often turn to community organizations for access to communities.

Community organizations, such as churches or schools, may welcome the resources of a social scientist who is willing to work within their agenda. Such organizations may have considerable power to facilitate community interventions. Thus, if the researcher becomes a trusted and integral part of the organization and empowers people within their own culture, it may be possible to create an effective and lasting intervention. The costs to the researcher may include placing members of the community organization on the project payroll, doing community service work, and assisting the community organization in obtaining its own funding. A danger of working within community organizations is that they may want to modify results in order to look good in the eyes of funders, or to base interventions on beliefs or values that blame the victim (Ryan, 1971). Some community churches, for example, believe that AIDS represents the wrath of God, and will not work compassionately with AIDS victims or persons at risk for AIDS.

Clinic-based research offers a more scientifically oriented setting for research and interventions on hospitalized or outpatient subjects. Community-based physicians and drug-abuse treatment programs offer an excellent opportunity for the researcher to work with persons who have AIDS or are at risk for AIDS, and who have a trusting relationship with the staff of a clinic that provides their health care. Like indigenous community organizations, however, clinics have their own priorities and programs. Clinics will not permit research that might reduce the level of trust between patients and clinic staff, interfere with ongoing clinic activities, violate clinic rules, or create bad public relations.

11.1.2 Community Gatekeepers

All community settings have gatekeepers. These are persons who can help the researcher to learn the community culture and enter into effective working relationships with community members—or who can keep the researcher out. A gatekeeper is a leader with the power to decide whether an outsider has the potential to bring benefit to the community and should be admitted, though an unscrupulous gatekeeper may allow research that serves the gatekeeper's needs at a cost to the community. There are also informal gatekeepers, people who have the power to sink a project if they disagree with the formal gatekeeper's decision. Thus, the wise researcher tries to try to work out cooperative arrangements that suit all of the formal and informal gatekeepers, and seeks another community site if that effort proves unsuccessful.

Gatekeepers may be scientists, such as a researcher who also directs a clinic; they may be street professionals, such as a recovered drug addict who serves as an outreach person for his own people; or they may be nonscientist professionals, such as a school principal or a minister. The gatekeeper introduces the researcher to the community culture and negotiates the terms under which the researcher may fit in.

11.1.3 Community Cultures

The most serious error a neophyte community researcher can make is to assume that street people, unemployed drug addicts, homeless run-aways, and other disenfranchised members of society are necessarily unintelligent, or are out there alone. Such people live within a culture that has well-defined rules of conduct, communication, and attitudes toward outsiders. Members of the community look out for one another. They have a grapevine that rapidly spreads news about outsiders, as well as about one another; hence, clear communication and concern for the privacy of research participants are vital to the success of any program. Although many street people have unorthodox life-styles, they may be highly intelligent.

Communities of disenfranchised persons tend to distrust researchers and other professionals. Even runaway children who may be in imminent danger of being murdered tend to survive on bravado, believing that it is safer to sell their bodies for food or drugs than to trust a stranger who claims to be a helping professional. It takes a thoughtfully negotiated relationship with a gatekeeper to become trusted and accepted, as discussed in 11.4.

In clinic-based research researchers must learn to obey staff rules, get along with staff members individually, and contribute to the achievement of clinic goals. They must also understand the needs, attitudes, and behavior of the clients who might be, for example, street-wise, unruly, paranoid, manipulative, or frightened. Researchers must also respect and contribute to the clients' relationship of trust and rapport with clinic staff, which the clinic has worked hard to build, and must do nothing that would damage that trust, such as failing to respect clients' privacy or employing procedures that the clients might misunderstand or find objectionable.

To intervene and empower community members, one needs not only to get *access*, but also to *intervene effectively*. How can Latina women be enabled to persuade Latino men to use condoms? How can gay Asian men be enabled to form support groups that encourage safe sex? How can teenagers be effectively educated about birth control and safe sex? How can anyone be educated to understand that healthy-looking persons may carry the HIV virus? The simple rational educational approaches that readily occur to middle-class social scientists have often proved to be ineffective. A knowledge of the literature on intervention and cultural sensitivity (e.g., Bowser, 1990; Marin & Marin, 1991; Peterson & Marin, 1988), coupled with personal ethnographic efforts in the target community, are essential to successful intervention. The literature on AIDS and culturally sensitive intervention is growing so rapidly that perhaps the best advice to give here is to consult the most recent *Psychological Abstracts* and *Sociological Abstracts* and conduct computerized searches in the social/behavioral and medical science literatures.

11.2 WHAT IS CULTURAL SENSITIVITY?

In research on vulnerable populations, cultural sensitivity has almost nothing to do with the art and music of a culture, and almost everything to do with respect, shared decision making, and effective communication. Too often, researchers ignore the values, the life-style, and the cognitive and affective world of the subjects. They impose their own, perhaps in an attempt to reform people whose culture they would like to eradicate, or perhaps simply out of ignorance about the subjects' reality. This chapter provides various approaches to gaining cultural sensitivity. But first, what are the major sensitivities the researcher needs to gain?

Any communication or intervention must be couched in terms of the subjects' basic assumptions (not the researcher's) about such things as health, illness, AIDS, sexuality, personal adequacy and self-worth, sin and salvation, science, whose advice to take about medical or sexual matters, masculinity, femininity, and any other topic that the research touches upon. In addition, the researcher must have open lines of communication through which not only to learn community members' current views about the researcher's motives, the risks or benefits of participation, and so on, but also effectively address misconceptions. The needs and fears of the target population must be both understood and alleviated to the extend possible by the project. The social, religious, political, economic, and psychological barriers to communicating about AIDS, sexuality, illness, or other sensitive topics addressed by the research must be taken into account, and ways must be found to overcome these barriers. Knowing the subjects' time frame is vital; promises about "next year" mean nothing to people who live in the present. Knowing their family structure and dynamics are essential to knowing whose advice and authority are influential.

Concerns about control, autonomy, and exploitation will be raised by interventions that attempt to influence sexual or other life-style characteristics. It is essential to build trust, multilateral and shared decision making, and an equal-status relationship between intervener and target population. The project members who come in contact with the research participants must be acceptable to the community.

There is much potential for miscommunication when talking about sexuality, disease, and other personal topics where private or idiosyncratic vocabularies tend to abound; persons may be embarrassed to ask for clarification or to reveal their own beliefs. Ways must be found to discover and use the terminology of the target populations. Where English is not spoken fluently, the communication must be in the language of the target population.

11.3 WHY IS AIDS-RELATED RESEARCH
PROBLEMATIC?

Many problematic aspects of AIDS-related research have already been illustrated. Other problems include informed consent, especially with youngsters; the illegality of the activities of many of the populations at risk for AIDS; the stigma of AIDS; problems surrounding AIDS testing; sampling problems; and the difficulty of directly observing the behaviors conducive to AIDS.

Informed consent. The requirement of parental permission for research participation (discussed in Chapter 10) may be waived by the IRB when parents are unavailable or unlikely to act in their child's best interests, or when parental consent cannot feasibly be obtained and the research promises significant benefit at little risk (Rotheram-Borus & Koopman, 1991). Waiver of parental permission is often necessary since many of the populations at risk for AIDS are youngsters who are runaways, or whose sexual orientation, sexual activity, or drug use are not known to their parents. Some of these youngsters are simply engaging in a temporary (even if unprecedentedly risky) rebellious phase designed to separate themselves from their parents. For others, the problems are deeper, involving dysfunctional families, mental illness, or mental retardation. These matters, of course, complicate intervention as well as consent. However, the problems of intervention among adolescents are beyond the scope of this chapter; the reader is referred to Woodruff, Doherty, and Athey (1989).

Other consent issues involve problems of language and culture. Any consent statement must be administered in a style entirely understandable to subjects, taking into account their perception of the risks and the benefits they wish to receive for their participation. It must be in the subjects' primary language and communicated in a way that they understand and accept. The standard consent procedure may be replaced by a consent *forum* such as a focus group, community consent, or so-called hot dog ethnography, which are described below in section 11.4. In these situations, the standard consent form is largely a formality to satisfy federal law, as the consent agreement has already been discussed and decided by the community.

The illegal activities of some populations at risk for AIDS raise additional problems concerning consent, payment of subjects, police harassment, and the psychology of fugitive populations. When community research populations are engaged in illegal behavior (e.g., prostitution, drug use) or are members of stigmatized groups (e.g., gay men, people with AIDS), it may be unreasonable to obtain signed consent. A signed consent form on file may represent a potential threat to the well-being of the subject or, more likely, it may have been signed with a pseudonym. If signatures are obtained, a certificate of confidentiality should be obtained, and the signed consent forms should be kept in a secure place, such as the investigator's safe deposit box.

Since drug addicts may be willing to do anything for money, the issue of subtle coercion must be addressed. It is widely recognized that if some form of payment is not offered, drug addicts will not participate in research. Food is an important alternative form of payment to addicts and other street populations. Although most members of street populations neglect nutrition, they typically are ravenously hungry when presented with a good meal, and eating forms an important bonding ritual between them and the research team. However, this presents a second problem for researchers: Most funders do not allow food as a line item on a budget since it normally would not be used in this way. Hence some new terminology, such as "in-kind payment," usually must be used in budgeting for food.

Police harassment of subjects and researchers is a distinct possibility. For example, at an early point in a program of prostitute education, San Francisco police seized the condoms given to prostitutes, photocopied them to use as evidence of prostitution, then punched holes in them before returning them (Lockett, 1990). Researchers should gain city support for their projects whenever possible, for example, via the mayor's office or other powerful city agencies such as the city health department. In Lockett's case, above, a trip to the mayor's office stopped police seizure of condoms.

The psychology of fugitive populations involves endless paranoia and subterfuge. For this reason, only the most experienced researchers may be able to work with their target population without the aid of gatekeepers who understand that population's perceptions, fears, and strategies.

The stigma of AIDS and other sexually transmitted diseases means that many AIDS-related projects must state their purpose in euphemistic terms—for example, The Janesville Health Study, rather than The Janesville AIDS or Syphilis Study. Communities may reject members thought to have AIDS. People fear that AIDS testing could result in notification of their sexual partners or a government agency, quarantine, arrest, curtailment of insurance and employment, or other harm. People fear that they will be found to have a sexually transmitted disease and that other members of the community will learn about it. Consequently, the privacy of participants in AIDS-related research must be protected in every conceivable way, and every effort must be made to let subjects know that they will not be stigmatized by their participation. Even the location and architecture of the building where the program is housed should be planned to shield subjects' participation in the research program from the scrutiny of community members and others who might gossip.

AIDS testing itself is surrounded by problems. Many persons do not want to know their test results. When giving test results, it is essential, and required by federal law governing human research, that results be accompanied by adequate counseling. The topics of AIDS testing and counseling are beyond the scope of this chapter; the reader is referred to Fawzy, Namir, Wolcott, Mitsuyasu, and Gottlieb (1989); Meinhart (1989); Morin (1990); and Pope and Morin (1990).

Sampling problems in some populations at risk for AIDS are unresolvable. There are no adequate sampling frames for intravenous drug users, prostitutes, runaway youngsters, and so on. In some cases, the populations are transient, moving from one part of a city to another as the availability of drugs or services changes, so that even a geographically based sampling scheme would be inadequate. In other cases, these populations are hidden (Bowser, 1990). Such populations include intravenous drug users who are successful in the straight world and do not see themselves as drug addicts; closeted Latino and Asian homosexuals who hide their orientation from their community; and men who view themselves as heterosexuals, but engage in occasional sex with men. These hidden populations are difficult to reach. They are not clearly defined and may not define themselves as risk-takers. Their behavior (were it known to others) would be negatively viewed by the general public. Hence, they are underground in a private world.

The most rigorous sampling methods are not workable with some populations at risk for AIDS. Samples of subjects are often gathered through community recruitment; by posting an ad on a community bulletin board; or by being where the action is, for example, at a needle exchange site, at a place where condoms and food are handed out, or at a lunch and rap session. Even after obtaining volunteers, however, investigators often need to maintain careful observation to ascertain that they indeed meet the sampling criteria. A screening interview, for which all volunteers are paid, might be used to try to identify those who falsified some characteristic simply to be paid (e.g., gays who said they were straight, sexually active girls who claimed to be virgins).

Behaviors associated with AIDS, for example, injection drug use and sexual behavior, cannot acceptably be studied by unobtrusive methods and typically are not behaviors that persons discuss candidly. Clinic-based research may be essential for determining persons' actual status or behavior. For example, youngsters who go to a clinic for family planning, venereal disease, or drug-abuse may participate candidly in research, but in other contexts may be unwilling to reveal their sexual activity or drug abuse. The National Institute of Allergies and Infectious Diseases has published a useful paper suggesting ways to combine behavioral and epidemiological strategies for intervention research on these behaviors.

11.4 TECHNIQUES FOR CREATING CONSENT AND SHARED TRUST

Collaboration and shared trust are essential to community-based interventions. A consent *forum*, rather than a consent form, is required. Three basic kinds of forums are described here. In 11.5, these ideas are further developed in descriptions of relationships with various kinds of community gatekeepers.

11.4.1 Community Consultation and Consent

Effective community research requires consultation with the target population. The basic idea is that accepted representatives are chosen by their community to negotiate the conditions of the research in an open forum with the researcher. The objectives and concerns of the researcher, subjects, and target population are examined. Goals, methods, and procedures are revised until they are acceptable to both sides. Few traditionally trained researchers expect to take advice from subjects on matters of research design and procedure.

However, the rules are different in community-based research, and often the quality of research and subject cooperation are improved with community consultation. Community consultation is discussed extensively by Melton et al. (1988), and an example of subject-initiated community consent was described in Case 11.1 (the gay community's negotiations with a medical school). Consent forums with less educated populations are described in 11.4.2 and 11.4.3.

11.4.2 Focus Groups

Focus group techniques are useful for learning the views and concerns of one's target population. The use of focus groups to achieve the purposes of community consent have already been discussed in Case 1, Part III (Bowser's use of focus groups with teen crack users). Focus groups, especially centered around a meal, are an outstanding way for a researcher to learn about a population and its community, and to develop collaborative research or intervention plans. In the process, trust and rapport are developed. The plans that are formulated in focus group meetings are sure to be disseminated throughout the community via the grapevine, resulting in further feedback from the community. Focus group techniques are discussed more extensively in Morgan (1988) and Stewart and Shamdasani (1990).

11.4.3 "Hot Dog Ethnography"

A simple consent forum consists of giving a picnic for one's target population and inviting its collaboration in a project:

Case 11.2: Hot Dog Ethnography. A researcher/intervener wanted to establish a needle exchange program among street people and needed to know about her clientele and their concerns: Are they diverse populations or are they homogeneous? How will she identify individuals for repeated measures (i.e., whether they continue to exchange needles)? How can she best arrange to meet with them and avoid police arrest for exchanging needles? What are their needs and concerns? Which of these can she satisfy?

There was no established gatekeeper except some street people who were respected by their peers. (The researcher subsequently served as gatekeeper for others who became involved in the needle exchange program.) After some conversations with individuals in the area where she considered establishing the needle exchange, she issued a word-of-mouth invitation to dinner. She rented a hotel room in a flophouse and cooked hot dogs, sauerkraut, and soup; she also served cake, donuts, and soda pop in abundance. Her hot dog ethnography, as it has been called, was a great success. Most street people are quite hungry. About 40 people attended, which is surprising, given that they are a stigmatized population and police entrapment was a possibility. The researcher was known to them from her previous outreach efforts, which helped engender trust. The researcher learned that some of her clientele lived in flophouses and preferred to come to a designated place for the weekly needle exchange. Others lived on the streets and wanted a floating exchange place where the police would be less likely to wait for them. The willingness of the researcher to risk arrest was testimony to her caring for the population she sought to serve. A successful needle exchange program was established and has lasted for 4 years (Case, 1990).

11.5 WORKING WITH GATEKEEPERS

We turn now to specific examples of work with gatekeepers.

11.5.1 Street-Based Research

Locating a street-based gatekeeper who will welcome one's particular approach to intervention and research is partly a matter of being referred to the appropriate gatekeeper and partly a matter of negotiation. There might be a referral from a social agency, a community intervener, a researcher, or the street people themselves. The negotiation is a matter of learning whether the match between gatekeeper and researcher can be made into a compatible one. Each negotiation is different, but the following case is illustrative:

Case 11.3: Food and Condoms. A researcher wanted to learn what prostitutes understand about safe sex, whether it is possible to get them to use condoms, how many are seropositive, and whether drug-addicted prostitutes differ in their sexual behavior from career prostitutes. She established a working relationship with the director of a prostitute education and advocacy organization. The director, a black ex-prostitute, employs the following procedure to serve her clientele. She meets with groups of prostitutes and (a) serves them food, (b) asks them what she may do to help them, (c) finds out particular problems they may be experiencing, (d) works out ways to solve the problems, (e) assesses kinds of education they may need and enjoyable ways to provide that education (e.g., quizzes on safe sex, with nice prizes for those who get all the answers right), and (f) establishes regular places for prostitutes to meet, eat, voice concerns, and obtain needed resources. But what about the researcher? She made her research approach fit within this context of helping and educating, worked as a faithful team member with the gatekeeper, and achieved her objectives of survey research, HIV testing, and AIDS education (Lockett, 1990).

11.5.2 Clinic-Based Research

Clinics and their gatekeepers have many serious concerns the researcher must satisfy. Among these are concern for maintaining confidentiality of treatment files, managing their potentially unruly clients, keeping the researcher from interfering with the duties of the staff, making sure the clients are treated respectfully, and ensuring that nothing is done that casts doubt on the loyalty of the clinic to its clients. In addition, most clinics receive some federal funding and are prohibited by the government from permitting certain activities on their premises; for example, needle exchange research is prohibited at the time of this writing. Sorensen (1991) suggests a four-step approach to working with clinic-based gatekeepers:

1. Approach the clinic's research coordinator before proposing the study for funding, or IRB approval. Explain the research idea and its potential benefits to patients, the clinic, and science, as well as risks or inconveniences it may entail. Learn whether the idea is at all acceptable and the conditions under which the clinic is likely to participate.

2. Obtain a letter of contingent approval—a letter granting approval provided that certain conditions are met (e.g., time, space, clinic management and staff approval, funding, IRB approval).

3. Obtain consent from the administrative group that conveys actual clinic approval of research. At this stage, details will be worked out,

such as researcher access to patient charts, approval from a local research committee, number and kind of subjects to be made available to the researcher, and so on. If these negotiations are successful, obtain a letter of intent to cooperate, stating not only what each party will give and receive through the study but also any further issues to be negotiated. This letter should accompany any request for funding or IRB approval, and should be signed by both the clinic leader and the researcher.

4. Begin meeting with the staff to resolve such issues as who may participate, how much time the clinic will allot for each interview, and when and where interviews will occur. Unless the researcher is attentive to the needs of the staff, their passive resistance will destroy the study. The wise researcher attends all clinic staff meetings and works to make the research an integral service of the clinic's program, rather than an extra burden for staff and patients. Careful attention to Columns 1 and 2 of the benefit matrix (Figure 9.1) is amply repaid.

11.5.3 Other Agencies and Institutions

Although other agencies and institutions may have fewer rules than clinics, that may only be because they are unaccustomed to accommodating researchers. The lack of formal rules may result in misunderstanding and a premature end to the research program. It is better to try to go through steps such as those described for clinic-based research and to get the agreement in writing than to leave matters to chance. In nonscientific settings, it is especially important to reach a signed agreement on who has the right to decide on the formal content of presentations of the findings, and who has access to confidential data.

11.6 RESEARCH DESIGN

Some design considerations follow from the characteristics of the vulnerable populations described here (Sieber & Sorensen, 1992). Many of the theories and methods of traditional social science are unacceptable, including research that blames the victim (Ryan, 1971), deception strategies, procedures that may raise suspicions, studies requiring much reading or writing, research that provides no benefit for subjects, and some uses of standard psychological tests (Huang, Watters,

& Case, 1988). Extensive pilot testing is always advisable, and the researcher should build into the timetable provision for various redesigns of the study, including ones necessitated after the formal research has begun. Community-based research is full of surprises that threaten the validity of the research.

Long-term follow-up and random assignment may be difficult to employ. Drug users are difficult to locate for repeated measures unless one works out a strategy for doing so during the initial testing. For example, subjects may be asked for information on how to reach someone who will always know where they are. Subjects should be promised sufficient payment for the follow-up to motivate them to return when contacted.

Random assignment should not deprive anyone of desired benefits, and should be explained clearly. Otherwise, subjects will suspect deception and may engage in subterfuge to obtain the sought-after benefit.

11.7 WHAT TO DISCUSS IN THE PROTOCOL

In addition to the usual contents of a protocol, the IRB will need to know how access to the research population was obtained and what agreements were made with gatekeepers. They will want to be sure that the researcher has adequate knowledge of the target population; has done some pilot testing; and understands the actual risks to subjects, their fears of risk, and risks to the researcher.

The protocol should describe whatever kind of consent forum has been used, for example, focus groups, hot dog ethnography, meetings with gatekeepers. Written consent of gatekeepers should be presented, where appropriate. The actual consent form should reflect the agreements that were worked out in the consent forum.

Confidentiality is always a concern in community research, and every step that has been taken to ensure confidentiality should be described, including the location and configuration of the research site, the training of research assistants, agreements with gatekeepers, and the safekeeping of data. Where repeated measures are involved, special attention should be given to ways of maintaining anonymity or confidentiality while matching pre- and post-test data (see Chapter 6). Street people, especially those on drugs, are likely to forget which pseudonym they used on the pretest, or to lose the sheet of paper containing their code number.

Researchers using repeated measures sometimes use informal methods for matching pre- and post-test data, such as a private written description of individuals in conjunction with their names or code numbers. One does not want to mix up data, and in particular one does not want to mix up the results of HIV tests.

Special arrangements, such as waiver of signed consent by subjects, waiver of parental permission, or the obtaining of a certificate of confidentiality, may be necessary and should be explained and justified in full.

The IRB may be unfamiliar with the research population, the complexities of community-based research, and the gatekeepers who control the setting. Thus, for example, the researcher may need to educate the IRB about such things as the fact that research procedures may need to be changed in response to new problems, and that gatekeepers may later raise new issues not reflected in the original protocol. It is not unusual, in community-based research, for a researcher to need to submit a preliminary protocol, followed by modifications. The researcher who does a conscientious job of submitting the initial protocol will likely have the full cooperation and sympathy of the IRB when modifications need to be approved later.

RECOMMENDED READINGS

Edwards, J., Tindale, R. S., Heath, L., & Posavac, E. J. (Eds.). (1992). *Social psychological applications to social issues: Vol. 2. Methodological issues in applied social psychology*. New York: Plenum.

Herdt, G., & Lindenbaum, S. (Eds.). (1991). *Social analysis in the time of AIDS*. Newbury Park, CA: Sage.

Marin, G., & Marin, B. (1991). *Research with Hispanic populations*. Newbury Park, CA: Sage.

PART V

Developing an Effective Human Subjects Protocol

The protocol demonstrates to the IRB, and to anyone who might inquire, that the research is respectful of the needs and interests of the subjects, that risks have been reduced to a minimum, and that the benefits of the research more than justify any risk, inconvenience, or other cost it might create. The key to developing an effective protocol is to incorporate relevant ethical considerations into one's early planning of the project, and to begin writing the protocol along with the research proposal. Chapter 12 provides guidelines for developing a protocol, but cannot substitute for careful incorporation of the ideas from Chapters 3 through 11 into the research plan.

12

Developing a Research Protocol

The protocol format and reminders offered in this chapter combine the best of many of the forms used around the nation and will be useful even if the reader's own institution has a specific form. An IRB may raise any questions pertinent to the specific research project, even if those questions are not specifically addressed in their particular protocol format or instructions. This chapter, and its references to the rest of the book, enable the reader to answer such questions.

12.1 SUGGESTED ELEMENTS OF A PROTOCOL

One's individual protocol should reflect the requirements of one's department and IRB and should contain any additional information pertinent to the evaluation of the particular project. The following protocol elements meet federal requirements and include additional features that many institutions have found useful.

1. A *cover sheet* should include (a) the name and department of the principal investigator (PI), (b) his or her faculty rank or student status, (c) home and office phone number(s) and (d) address(es) of the investigator. This information enables the IRB reviewer to contact the investigator informally about questions that arise when reading the protocol, and perhaps to provide verbal approval before the formal approval is mailed. The cover sheet should also indicate (e) the project title; (f) the type of project, such as faculty research, externally funded project (with name of funder), student directed research (with name of faculty adviser, thesis, dissertation, course requirement—give course number and faculty name); and (g) the intended project starting and ending dates. It is useful to mention one's qualifications to conduct the specified research in a paragraph or two on the cover sheet, via an attached curriculum vitae, or with the description of the methodology. The cover sheet must contain (h) the signature of the principal investigator, and if the PI is a student, (i) the adviser. Some institutions also designate departmental or school representatives to review and sign off on protocols.

2. A *description of the research*, which includes the following: (a) the purpose of the research and the hypotheses to be tested; (b) the historical background of the research, referring to pertinent scientific literature (in brief, as in an abstract); (c) an orderly account of the research method, design, and mode of analysis, detailed enough that reviewers can assess scientific validity, including a fully detailed account of procedures that directly affect subjects; (d) a realistic statement of the value of the research, including both what the researcher expects to learn from the research and what value it will have for the participants and their community, the research institution, the funder, or science (Research is not of value to science unless it is of publishable quality. See Chapter 9.); (e) the location of the research—specifying the exact laboratory, community, institution, and so on where various components of the research are to be performed, the reason why that setting was chosen and how the researcher happens to have access to it; (Is the researcher employed there? Did he or she do volunteer work there? Is it his or her old neighborhood or an organization to which he or she belongs?; (f) duration of the project and how this window of time coincides with such other time constraints as the duration of funding, the periods of the school year when research can reasonably be carried out in a school, the period of time before an election when voting attitudes might be examined.

3. A *description of the prospective subject population* should include, where relevant, ethnic background, sex, age, and state of health. It should explain why that particular population is being used, the source(s) from which it will be obtained, and a statement of the selection criteria. If vulnerable populations are included, such as pregnant women, children, institutionalized mentally disabled, prisoners, or those whose ability to give voluntary informed consent is in question, the rationale for using such subjects should be stated. If the research is conducted in an institutional setting (e.g., a school, a club, a church, a home for the aged), written permission of the person in charge must accompany the protocol.

The expected number of subjects should be specified, and a statistical justification of the number of subjects should be provided either here or in the description of the research design. The researcher is urged to consult Kraemer and Thiemann (1987) and Lipsey (1990) for guidelines to deciding how many subjects to use.

4. The *discussion of possible risks* should include inconveniences or discomforts, especially to the subject, and where possible, an estimate

of the likelihood and magnitude of harm. Most IRB members are highly skilled risk assessors and take a dim view of researchers who ignore minor risks or inconveniences and blithely write "no risk." There are many forms of risk to subjects and others connected with the research, including the investigator, the community, and the institution. These are discussed in Chapters 5 (Privacy), 6 (Confidentiality), 7 (Deception), 8 (Categories of Risk), 10 (Research on Children), and 11 (Community-Based Research).

Discussion of risks should involve both objective risks and what subjects might perceive as risks (as in Case 1.1), and should indicate what will be done to allay each actual risk or unwarranted worry. As appropriate, the researcher might describe alternative methods that could have been used to minimize risk, stating why they were rejected. For example, IRBs are always quick to urge that data be collected anonymously to prevent breach of confidentiality; however, the researcher may have good reasons to collect unique identifiers.

5. *Discussion of inducements and benefits* to the subject and others should take into account the concepts regarding benefit, presented in Chapter 9, and field research, in Chapter 11.

6. *Freedom of subjects to withdraw with impunity* is a right that must, by law, be respected. If the subject is not free to withdraw from the research at any time, the protocol should both explain why and state when the subject is free to withdraw. Pertinent details of subjects' freedom to withdraw should appear in the consent statement.

7. *Source and amount of compensation*, if any, to be received by a subject or beneficiary in the event of injury is typically not addressed in social research protocols, where chances of injury are very small and liability for incidental injury is often covered by the university's workmen's compensation insurance.

8. *Analyses of risks and benefits* are to be summarized, and any risk must be shown to be substantially offset by benefits that the researcher has arranged to produce.

9. The *informed consent* procedure should be described, including how, where, and by whom informed consent will be negotiated, and how debriefing will be conducted (see Chapter 4). In Chapter 10, problems of obtaining children's assent and parental or guardian permission for research are discussed.

The actual consent form, if any, should be attached to the protocol. If consent is negotiated orally and not documented in writing, a statement should be attached regarding the information that is to be presented to prospective subjects orally. The content of the debriefing should also be described.

10. *Attachments*—such as any letters of permission, the consent form, interview or survey questions, materials to be presented to subjects, tests, or other items connected with the research—should be attached to the protocol, if they might be pertinent to the IRB's evaluation of the project.

12.2 SUPPLEMENTAL PROTOCOL CHECKLIST

The following is a list of typical problems that IRBs encounter, and tips on how to cure them:

"Rubber stamp" signatures. Those who sign off on the cover sheet of the protocol have a legal responsibility to have evaluated the protocol for legality, clarity, accuracy, and good writing. Students dissatisfied with their formal supervision should seek other help with the protocol and the design and analysis of the research, and consult research methods texts as needed.

Failure to mention investigator qualifications. This is especially serious in the case of inexperienced investigators. This statement should be clear, specific, and relevant. It might include prior research training and experience, membership in or special knowledge of the research population, or qualifications for counseling subjects as appropriate.

Too many generalities about the purpose of the research. IRBs are suspicious of protocols that devote much space to extolling the importance of the research, but fail to describe the methods and procedures adequately.

Vagueness about research location and permission. The protocol should be specific about where the research will be performed and how the investigator got permission to do the research. It should include letter(s) of permission from the relevant gatekeepers and discussion of what the researcher has agreed to do in return for that permission.

Vagueness about sampling procedure. Arrangements for access to subjects and for sampling should be complete before submitting the protocol. The protocol should be exact in the description of the sample frame, how it was obtained, and exactly what sampling procedure will be employed (e.g., a two-phase random sample using a table of random numbers, a random sample stratified on ethnic group with oversampling of Native Americans, a convenience sample); see, for example, Babbie

(1979) or Kidder (1981). If the sample frame consists of members of a private group, the IRB will want to know if the list of names is public information, and if not, how the researcher obtained that list and what permission was obtained to use it. Depending on the sensitivity of the research, some sampling strategies may pose objectionable threats to privacy; see Hartley (1982) for details.

Vagueness about the research design. The protocol should state exactly what general design or method is to be employed; for unusual procedures, it should describe any work previously done to test the procedure. Complex research designs might be accompanied with diagrams, if necessary, to show who gets what treatment and when, and when measurements are taken. For survey research, specify who and how many are to be surveyed, when and by what method they are to be surveyed, and what key cross-tabulations are planned. For case studies, state whether it is a behavioral single-subject design or a clinical case study; indicate how the raw data will be obtained and how the case study will be derived from those data, perhaps citing a methodology text that sets forth the rules. Protocols for action research should state why the action research is called for, the specific goals, the activities that are expected to achieve those goals, and how those goals are expected to come about. The goals of the action research should be ones jointly developed with the subjects, not goals foisted on subjects.

Omission of information about the political context of the research. Often, applied social research is done because there are conflicts, problems, or disagreements between parties at the research site. Perhaps the research is done to understand something about the problem, or to intervene. It is essential that the political context of the research be described accurately in the protocol.

"Fitting the format." Most protocol formats are designed for experimental or descriptive research, not for action or intervention research. In order to "fit the protocol," researchers sometimes make their project look like it is an experimental or descriptive study when it is actually action or intervention research. The protocol should state clearly what the purpose of the research is, even if the protocol format seems designed for describing something else.

Ignoring risk. Most social research involves some risk, if only that a survey may ask people to think about things that will make them uncomfortable, or that the data on some subjects, were it to fall into the hands of a malicious gossip, could cause trouble for the subjects. IRBs recognize that some risk is inevitable and acceptable; what they find unacceptable is the researcher who fails to recognize risk.

Insensitivity to issues of coercion in dual-role relationships. It is often easiest to arrange to do research in familiar settings; however, this is likely to involve a dual-role relationship. For example, one might study one's own clients, students, or employees or do participant observation research in a group of which one is a part. Or one may arrange to do research in a group where the gatekeeper takes unscrupulous advantage of the situation (perhaps coercing members of his or her organization to participate, or seeking access to confidential data in return for permitting the researcher access to the setting).

IRBs recognize that the only feasible way to do some important kinds of applied research is in a dual-role relationship. For example, a graduate student cannot easily arrange to try out a teaching intervention on someone else's class, or to try out a therapy intervention on someone else's patients. In such situations, however, special precautions must be taken:

- Every step must be taken to assure that subjects know that their participation is strictly voluntary—that they will lose no advantage and will fully retain the respect and goodwill of the researcher and gatekeeper if they refuse to participate.
- Subjects must have a neutral source to whom they can turn in case of problems. For example, if free counseling is offered to anyone who is upset by his or her research participation, the counseling must be available from an independent third party, not the researcher or the gatekeeper.
- Where feasible, participation should be anonymous, so that the researcher or gatekeeper does not know who participated or who did not.

A second kind of dual role is that in which the researcher is also an intervener. The researcher needs to be clear about what he or she and others consider to be his or her primary role. If the researcher is primarily an intervener—one who provides a service—then relevant other services may not be withheld from subjects.

Dual-role relationships introduce potential conflicts, which should be recognized at the outset and discussed not only with experienced members of one's IRB but also with experienced researchers who have had to work in dual-role situations.

Using data generated by others. When some or all of one's data have been generated by others, the IRB will want to know both the source of the data (e.g., a public archive, an individual scientist, a school or university student testing program) and who released the data and authorized their use in the proposed research. A letter of authorization may be required.

Research on physical and physiological qualities. Research on the effects of, say, caffeine or physical exertion may be safe for most, but not all, subjects. The IRB will want to know that the campus physician or some other medically qualified individual has reviewed and approved the research plan.

Research that stigmatizes persons. The researcher who is intent on helping persons who are in need of some intervention is likely to overlook the fact that research participation may stigmatize the subjects. So-called prevention research, community interventions, behavior modification programs, and research on people who already occupy a status to which stigma is attached may heighten the visibility of the these people's stigma. Every effort must be made to ensure the privacy of such individuals.

Appendix:
Sample Consent and Assent Forms
for Use With Older Children

The following sample letters were adapted from ones developed by the IRB at SUNY Albany:

PARENTAL PERMISSION FORM

[School Letterhead]

Date:_____

Student's Name: _____   Grade:_____

Dear Parent:

Our school is participating in a study conducted by Jane Jones, a graduate student at Western University. The project is titled: Verbal Processing in Elementary School Readers. The study compares children reading below grade level with those reading at or above grade level on various measures of learning and memory.

Your child has been selected based on the testing to which you previously agreed.

With your permission, your child will work with a person from the Study Center on six occasions, for approximately 20 to 30 minutes each time.

During each session, your child will be presented with a variety of tasks designed to measure attention, memory, language, learning, visual-spatial, and motor ability. The tasks are not difficult and in most instances the children find them quite enjoyable.

Each child will be seen on a one-to-one basis, and scheduling will be arranged with the teacher to make sure your child does not miss important classroom activities. Performance on all of the tasks will be kept confidential.

If you have any questions regarding the study, please contact Ms. Smith, Research Coordinator, at 555-1111.

Below is a form for you to sign. Please indicate whether you agree to have your child participate, and have your child return the form to school tomorrow.

Your cooperation in this research would be greatly appreciated.
Sincerely,

Principal

_____

I ____ give
____ do not give permission to have my child,_____
                                                    (child's name)
participate in the study involving verbal memory. I understand the nature
of the study and the amount of time involved.

STUDENT ASSENT

Student's Name:_____ School:_____

[The researcher sits down with each child separately, hands the child the
following written material, and reads it aloud as the child follows along.]

Do you remember the permission slip you took home for your parents
to sign a few days ago?

The people I work with and I are interested in how people learn about
words. We are asking you and other kids to help us find out about it.

If you agree, I will need you to help me six times: today, and five more
times over the next few weeks. We will work together for about 20 to 30
minutes each time. We will be doing something different each time, but
you shouldn't have any difficulty with any of the things we do. Sometimes
we'll ask you to find certain letters or numbers on a page or to remember
letters of words that you see or hear. Other times, I'll ask you to draw some
figures, follow directions from a map, tell some stories, and listen to some
sentences to tell me what they mean.

This is not a test like you usually have in school. All you have to do is
try as hard as you can to do the things I ask and you'll do fine. Your teachers
and parents and the other children will not know how well you do. It will
be just between you and me and the people I work with.

I would really appreciate it if you would help me to find out about these
things, but, if for some reason you feel like you really don't want to do this,
just tell me. You may quit at any time.

Do you have any questions? [The researcher should answer any questions the child asks, without discussing specific test items.]

If you agree to work on these reading tasks with me, I would like you
to sign this paper. It says: [Researcher reads assent statement.]

Date:_____

The information above has been read to me and any questions I had have been answered. I would like to take part in the activities that have just been described to me.

_____

Student's Signature

[Note: A signed Assent Form is not always appropriate and depends on the age of the child and the nature of the research. Consult your IRB about obtaining children's signatures.]

References

American Psychological Association. (1973). *Ethical principles in the conduct of research with human participants.* Washington, DC: Author.

American Psychological Association. (1982). *Ethical principles in the conduct of research with human participants.* Washington, DC: Author.

Areen, J. (1991). Legal constraints on research on children. In B. Stanley & J. E. Sieber (Eds.), *The ethics of research on children and adolescents.* Newbury Park, CA: Sage.

Asch, S. (1956). Studies of independence and conformity: A minority of one against a unanimous majority. *Psychological Monographs, 76*(9), Whole 416.

Babbie, E. R. (1979). *The practice of social research.* Belmont, CA: Wadsworth.

Bermant, G., & Wheeler, R. R. (1987). From within the system: Educational and research programs at the Federal Judicial Center. In G. B. Melton (Ed.), *Reforming the law* (pp. 102-145). New York: Guilford Press.

Boruch, R. F. (1976). *Methodological techniques for assuring personal integrity in social research.* Unpublished manuscript (NIE-C63).

Boruch, R. F., & Cecil, J. S. (1979). *Assuring the confidentiality of social research data.* Philadelphia: University of Pennsylvania Press.

Boruch, R. F., & Cecil, J. S. (1982). Statistical strategies for preserving privacy in direct inquiry. In J. E. Sieber (Ed.), *The ethics of social research: Surveys and experiments.* New York: Springer-Verlag.

Bowser, B. P. (1990). AIDS and "hidden" populations. *MIRA: Multicultural Inquiry and Research on AIDS, 4*(1), 1-2.

Campbell, D. T., Boruch, R. F., Schwartz, R. D., & Steinberg, J. (1977). Confidentiality-preserving modes of access to files and to interfile exchange for useful statistical analysis. *Evaluation Quarterly, 1*(2), 269-300.

Case, P. (1990). The prevention point needle exchange program. In J. E. Sieber, Y. Song-Kim, & P. Kelzer (Eds.), *Vulnerable populations and AIDS: Ethical and procedural requirements for social and behavioral research and intervention.* Hayward, CA: Pioneer Bookstore.

Conner, R. F. (1982). Random assignment of clients in social experimentation. In J. E. Sieber (Ed.), *The ethics of social research: Surveys and experiments* (pp. 55-77). New York: Springer-Verlag.

Cox, L. H., & Boruch, R. F. (1986). Emerging policy issues in record linkage and privacy. In *Proceedings of the international statistical institute* (pp. 9.2.1-9.2.16). Amsterdam:ISI.

Davies, S. P. (1930). *Social control of the mentally deficient.* New York: Thomas Y. Crowell.

Diener, E., & Crandall, R. (1978). *Ethics in social and behavioral research.* Chicago: University of Chicago Press.

Doris, J. (1982). Social science and advocacy: A case study. In J. Sieber (Ed.), Values and applied social science [Special Issue]. *American Behavioral Scientist, 26,* 199-233.

Duncan, G., & Lambert, D. (1987, April). The risk of disclosure for microdata. *Proceedings of the Third Annual Research Conference.* U. S. Bureau of the Census.

Fawzy, F. I., Namir, S., Wolcott, D. L., Mitsuyasu, R. T., & Gottlieb, M. S. (1989). The relationship between medical and psychological status in newly diagnosed gay men with AIDS. *Psychiatric Medicine, 7*, 23-33.

Fernald, W. E. (1919). A state program for the care of the mentally defective. *Mental Hygiene, 3*, 566-574.

Fienberg, S., Martin, M., & Straf, M. (1985). *Sharing research data.* Washington, DC: National Academy Press.

Fisher, C. B., & Rosendahl, S. A. (1990). Psychological risks and remedies of research participation. In C. G. Fisher & W. W. Tryon (Eds.), *Ethics in applied developmental psychology: Emerging issues in an emerging field. Advances in Applied Developmental Psychology. Volume 4* (pp. 43-59). Norwood, NJ: Ablex.

Fox, J. A., & Tracy, P. E. (1986). *Randomized response: A method for sensitive surveys.* Beverly Hills, CA: Sage.

Gallagher, H. G. (1990). *By trust betrayed: Patient-physician and the license to kill in the Third Reich.* New York: Holt, Rinehart & Winston.

Gates, G. W. (1988, August). *Census Bureau microdata: Providing useful research data while protecting the anonymity of respondents.* Paper presented at the annual meeting of the American Statistical Association, New Orleans.

Geller, D. (1978). Involvement in role-playing simulations: A demonstration with studies on obedience. *Journal of Personality and Social Psychology, 36*, 219-235.

Geller, D. (1982). Alternatives to deception: Why, what and how? In Sieber, J. E. (Ed.), *The ethics of social research: Surveys and experiments* (pp. 38-55). New York: Springer-Verlag.

Gesten, E. L., & Jason, L. A. (1987). Social and community interventions. *Annual Review of Psychology, 38*, 427-460.

Goldman, P., Clark, E., & Marro, A. (1975, July 21). No one told them: Suicide of F. R. Olson linked to CIA drug experiment. *Time,* pp. 15-19.

Grant, W. V., & Eiden, L. J. (1980). *Digest of Education Statistics, 26,* 199-233.

Greenawalt, K. (1974). Privacy and its legal protections. *Hastings Center Studies, 2,* 45-68.

Grisso, T. (1991). Minors' assent to behavioral research without parental permission. In B. Stanley & J. E. Sieber (Eds.), *The ethics of research on children and adolescents* (pp. 109-127). Newbury Park, CA: Sage.

Harter, S. (1983). Developmental perspectives on the self-system. In P. H. Mussen (Ed.) (E. M. Hetherington, Vol. Ed.), *Handbook of child psychology, Vol IV. Socialization, personality, and social development* (pp. 275-385). New York: John Wiley.

Hartley, S. F. (1982). Sampling strategies and the threat to privacy. In J. E. Sieber (Ed.), *The ethics of social research: Surveys and experiments* (pp. 167-189). New York: Springer-Verlag.

Heller, J. (1972, July 26). Syphilis victims in US study without therapy for 40 years. *The New York Times,* pp. 1, 8.

Holmes, D. (1976). Debriefing after psychological experiments: Effectiveness of post experimental desensitizing. *American Psychologist, 32,* 868-875.

Hook, E. G. (1973). Behavioral implications of the human XYY genotype. *Science, 179,* 139-150.

Huang, K.H.C., Watters, J., & Case, P. (1988). Psychological assessment and AIDS research with intravenous drug users: Challenges in measurement. *Journal of Psychoactive Drugs, 20,* 191-195.

Humphreys, L. (1970). *Tearoom trade: Impersonal sex in public places.* Chicago: Aldine.

Isen, A., & Levin, P. (1972). Effect of feeling good on helping: Cookies and kindness. *Journal of Personality and Social Psychology, 21,* 384-388.

Jones, J. (1982). *Bad blood.* New York: Free Press.

Katz, J. (1972). *Experimentation with human beings.* New York: Russell Sage.

Kelman, H. (1967). Human use of human subjects: The problem of deception in social psychological experiments. *Psychological Bulletin, 67,* 1-11.

Kelman, H. (1972). The rights of the subject in social research: An analysis in terms of relative power and legitimacy. *American Psychologist, 27,* 989-1016.

Kelman, H. C. (1968). *A time to speak: On human values and social research.* San Francisco: Jossey-Bass.

Kevles, D. J. (1970). Into hostile political camps: The reorganization of international science in World War I. *Isis, 62,* 47-60.

Kidder, L. H. (1981). *Research methods in social relations.* New York: Holt, Rinehart & Winston.

Kim, J. (1986). A method for limiting disclosure in microdata based on random noise and transformation. *1986 Proceedings of the Survey Methodology Research Section* (pp. 370-374). Washington, DC: American Statistical Association.

Klockars, C. B. (1974). *The professional fence.* New York: Free Press.

Koocher, G. P., & Keith-Speigel, P. C. (1990). *Children, ethics and the law: Professional issues and cases.* Lincoln: University of Nebraska Press.

Kraemer, H. C., & Thiemann, S. (1987). *How many subjects? Statistical power analysis in research.* Newbury Park, CA: Sage.

Laufer, R. S., & Wolfe, M. (1977). Privacy as a concept and a social issue: A multidimensional developmental theory. *Journal of Social Issues, 33,* 44-87.

Levine, R. J. (1986). *Ethics and regulation of clinical research.* Baltimore, MD: Urban & Schwarzenberg.

Lipsey, M. (1990). *Design sensitivity: Statistical power for experimental research.* Newbury Park, CA: Sage.

Lockett, G. (1990). AIDS prevention with Cal-PEP, COYOTE, and Project Aware. In J. E. Sieber, Y. Song-Kim, & P. Kelzer (Eds.), *Vulnerable populations and AIDS: Ethical and procedural requirements for social and behavioral research and intervetions.* Hayward, CA: Pioneer Bookstore.

Loo, C. M. (1982). Vulnerable populations: Case studies in crowding research. In J. E. Sieber (Ed.), *The ethics of social research: Surveys and experiments.* New York: Springer-Verlag.

Maccoby, E. E. (1983). Social-emotional development and response to stressors. In N. Garmezy & M. Rutter (Eds.), *Stress, coping and development in children* (pp. 217-234). New York: McGraw-Hill.

Macklin, R. (1987). *Mortal choices: Bioethics in today's world.* New York: Pantheon.

Macklin, R. (1991). Autonomy, beneficence and child development: An ethical analysis. In B. Stanley & J. E. Sieber (Eds.), *The ethics of research on children and adolescents.* Newbury Park, CA: Sage.

Marin, G., & Marin, B. V. (1991). *Research with Hispanic populations.* Newbury Park, CA: Sage.

McKusick, L., Wiley, J., & Coates, T. J. (1985). AIDS and the sexual behavior reported by gay men in San Francisco. *American Journal of Public Health, 75*, 493-496.

Meinhart, R. A. (1989, November). AIDS and issues of partner notification. *FOCUS: A Guide to AIDS Research and Counseling*, 1-2.

Meissen, G. J., & Cipriani, J. A. (1984). Community psychology and social impact assessment: An action model. *Journal of Community Psychology, 12*, 369-386.

Melton, G. B. (1983). Minors and privacy: Are legal and psychological concepts compatible? *Nebraska Law Review, 62*, 455-493.

Melton, G. B. (1990). Brief research report: Certificate of confidentiality under the Public Health Service Act: Strong protection but not enough. *Violence and Victims, 5*(1), 67-70.

Melton, G. B. (1991). Respecting boundaries: Minors, privacy and behavioral research. In B. Stanley & J. E. Sieber (Eds.), *The ethics of research on children and adolescents*. Newbury Park, CA: Sage.

Melton, G. B., Levine, R. J., Koocher, G. P., Rosenthal, R., & Thompson, W. C. (1988). Community consultation in socially sensitive research: Lessons from clinical trials on treatments for AIDS. *American Psychologist, 43*, 573-581.

Melton, G. B., & Stanley, B. H. (1991). Research involving special populations. In B. H. Stanley, J. E. Sieber, & G. B. Melton (Eds), *Psychology and research ethics*. Lincoln: University of Nebraska Press.

Mirvis, P. H. (1982). Know thyself and what thou art doing. *American Behavioral Scientist, 26*(2), 177-197.

Mitroff, I. I., & Kilmann, R. H. (1979). *Methodological approaches to social science*. San Francisco: Jossey-Bass.

Morgan, D. L. (1988). *Focus groups as qualitative research*. Newbury Park, CA: Sage.

Morin, S. (1990). Behavioral research on gay men in San Francisco. In J. E. Sieber, Y. Song-Kim, & P. Kelzer (Eds.), *Vulnerable populations and AIDS: Ethical and procedural requirements for social and behavioral research and intervention*. Hayward, CA: Pioneer Bookstore.

National Commission for Protection of Human Subjects of Biomedical and Behavioral Research. (1978). *The Belmont Report: Ethical principles and guidelines for the protection of human subjects of research* (DHEW Publication No. (OS) 78-0012). Washington, DC: Government Printing Office.

Nicholls, J. G. (1978). The development of the concepts of effort and ability, perception of academic attainment, and the understanding that difficult tasks require more ability. *Child Development, 49*, 800-814.

Orne, M. (1969). Demand characteristics and the concept of quasi-controls. In R. Rosenthal & R. Rosnow (Eds.), *Artifacts in behavioral research*. New York: Academic Press.

Pelto, P. J. (1988, February 18-20). In J. E. Sieber (Ed.), *Proceedings of a conference on sharing social research data*. National Science Foundation/American Association for the Advancement of Science, Washington, DC. Unpublished.

Peterson, J., & Marin, G. (1988). Issues in the prevention of AIDS among black and Hispanic men. *American Psychologist, 43*, 871-877.

Pope, K. S., & Basque, M.J.T. (1991). *Ethics of psychotherapy and counseling: A practical guide for psychologists*. San Francisco: Jossey Bass.

Pope, K. S., & Morin, S. F. (1990). AIDS and HIV infection update: New research, ethical responsibilities, evolving legal frameworks, and published resources. *The Independent Practitioner, 10*, 43-53.

Rivlin, L. G., & Wolfe, M. (1985). *Institutional settings in children's lives*. New York: John Wiley.

Rosenthal, R., & Rosnow, R. L. (1969). *Artifact and behavioral research*. New York: Academic Press.

Rotheram-Borus, M. J., & Koopman, C. (1991). Protecting children's rights in AIDS research. In B. Stanley & J. E. Sieber (Eds.), *The ethics of research on children and adolescents*. Newbury Park, CA: Sage.

Rothman, D. J. (1991). *Strangers at the bedside: A history of how law and bioethics transformed medical decision making*. New York: Basic Books.

Ryan, W. (1971). *Blaming the victim*. New York: Pantheon.

Sarason, S. B. (1981). *Psychology misdirected*. New York: Free Press.

Sarason, S. B., & Doris, J. (1969). *Psychological problems in mental deficiency*. New York: Harper & Row.

Sarason, S. B., & Doris, J. (1979). *Educational handicap, public policy, and social history*. New York: Free Press.

Seeman, J. (1969). Deception in psychological research. *American Psychologist, 24*, 1025-1028.

Sieber, J. E. (1989). Sharing scientific data. I: New problems for IRBs to solve. *IRB: A Review of Human Subjects Research, 11*(6), 4-7.

Sieber, J. E., & Saks, M. J. (1989). A census of subject pool characteristics and policies. *American Psychologist, 44*(7), 1051-1063.

Sieber, J. E., & Sorensen, J. L. (1992). Ethical issues in community-based research and intervention. In J. Edwards, R. S. Tindale, L. Heath, & E. J. Posavac (Eds.), *Social psychology applications to social issues. Vol. 2: Methodological issues in applied social psychology*. New York: Plenum.

Sorensen, J. L. (1991). Gatekeeping AIDS research in drug treatment programs. In J. E. Sieber, Y. Song-Kim, & P. Kelzer (Eds.), *Vulnerable populations and AIDS: Ethical and procedural requirements for social and behavioral research and intervention*. Hayward, CA: Pioneer Bookstore.

Stanley, B., & Sieber, J. E. (1991). Epilogue. In B. Stanley & J. E. Sieber (Eds.), *The ethics of research on children and adolescents*. Newbury Park, CA: Sage.

Stanley, B. H., & Guido, J. R. (1991). Informed consent: Psychological and empirical issues. In B. H. Stanley, J. E. Sieber, & G. B. Melton (Eds.), *Psychology and research ethics*. Lincoln: University of Nebraska Press.

Steiner, D. D., & Mark, M. M. (1985). The impact of a community action group: An illustration of the potential of time series analysis of for the study of community groups. *American Journal of Community Psychology, 13*, 13-30.

Stewart, D. W., & Shamdasani, P. N. (1990). *Focus groups: Theory and practice*. Newbury Park, CA: Sage.

Susskind, E. C., & Klein, D. C. (Eds.), (1985). *Community research: Methods, paradigms, and applications*. New York: Praeger.

Thompson, R. A. (1991). Vulnerability in research; A developmental perspective on research risk. In B. Stanley & J. E. Sieber (Eds.), *The ethics of research on children and adolescents*. Newbury Park, CA: Sage.

Tobach, E., Gianutsos, J., Topoff, H. R., & Gross, C. G. (1974). *The four horsemen: Racism, sexism, militarism and social Darwinism.* New York: Behavioral Publications.

Turner, A. G. (1982). What subjects of survey research believe about confidentiality. In J. E. Sieber (Ed.), *The ethics of social research: Surveys and experiments* (pp. 151-166). New York: Springer-Verlag.

Tymchuk, A. J. (1991). Assent processes. In B. Stanley & J. E. Sieber (Eds.), *Social research on children and adolescents: Ethical issues.* Newbury Park, CA: Sage.

Vinacke, W. (1954). Deceiving experimental subjects. *American Psychologist, 9,* 155.

von Hoffman, N. (1970, January 30). Sociological snoopers. *Washington Post,* pp. B1, B9.

Weithorn, L. (1983). Children's capacities to decide about participation in research. *IRB: A Review of Human Subjects Research, 5,* 1-5.

White, D. (1991). Sharing anthropological data with peers and third world host countries. In J. E. Sieber (Ed.), *Sharing social science data: Advantages and challenges.* Newbury Park, CA: Sage.

Wiener, S., & Sutherland, G. (1968). A normal XYY man. *Lancet,* 1359.

Wolosin, R., Sherman, S., & Mynatt, C. (1972). Perceived social influence in a conformity situation. *Journal of Personality and Social Psychology, 23,* 184-191.

Woodruff, J. O., Doherty, D., & Athey, J. G. (1989). *Troubled adolescents and HIV infection: Issues in prevention and treatment.* Washington, DC: CASSP Technical Assistance Center, Georgetown University Child Development Center.

Zimbardo, P., Haney, C., Banks, W., & Jaffe, D. (1973, April 8). The mind is a formidable jailer: A Pirandellian prison. *The New York Times Magazine,* pp. 38-60.

Author Index

Subject Index

Little Holocaust Survivors

Little Holocaust Survivors

And the English School that Saved Them

Barbara Wolfenden

Greenwood World Publishing

Oxford/Westport, Connecticut

2008

First published in 2008 by Greenwood World Publishing

1 2 3 4 5 6 7 8 9 10

Greenwood World Publishing
Wilkinson House
Jordan Hill
Oxford OX2 8EJ
An imprint of Greenwood Publishing Group, Inc
www.greenwood.com

Library of Congress Cataloging-in-Publication Data

Wolfenden, Barbara.
    Little Holocaust survivors : and the English school that saved them / Barbara Wolfenden.
        p. cm.
    Includes bibliographical references and index.
    ISBN 978-1-84645-053-2 (alk. paper)
    1. Jews – England – Surrey – Biography. 2. Holocaust survivors – England – Surrey – Biography. 3. Refugees, Jewish – England – Surrey – Biography. 4. Jews, German – England – Surrey – Biography. 5. Stoatley Rough School (Surrey, England) – Biography. I. Title.

    DS135.E6A186 2008
    940.53'1809224221 – dc22

                                                        2008020759

ISBN 978-1-84645-053-2

Designed by Fraser Muggeridge studio
Typeset by TexTech International
Printed and bound by South China Printing Company

To the memory of my sister, Linda Kirk Cohen (1942–2003)

Contents

Acknowledgements

I am indebted to a number of people for their generosity in giving me their time, providing me with information and reviewing the text of this book. First, I thank my husband, Martin Owens, not only for being my forbearing and sharp-sighted first reader, but for sharing me – my time and attention – for the four years that I worked on this project. (We can go bowling now, Honey.) I owe the authenticity of the story to the many Roughians, living or now gone, who documented their memories in alumni Newsletters and other collections with the heartfelt candour of witnesses. I thank the Hut Boys for inspiring me with their joyful stories: John Obermeyer, Peter Gaupp, Dieter Gaupp, John Goldmeier, Martin (of course) and especially Wolf Elston. He corrected my facts and opened up special little avenues with new details, often interrupting his full work schedule to provide clarification with unfailing courtesy and grace. Edith Hubacher Christoffel and Renate Dorpalen-Brocksieper not only helped me to understand the role of the Household Girls but provided me with reliable glimpses into the trials of the adults at the school. Hans Loeser and Herta Lewent [Loeser] understood the weight of history by capturing invaluable oral histories and collections. They were ever happy to answer my questions throughout the project.

I am grateful to those who made this book a tangible thing. My editor, Simon Mason, guided me with impeccable courtesy and genuine warmth from his office across the Atlantic Ocean. Peter Neivert created high-resolution copies of archived photographs which would never have made it into the book without his most generous support. Sue Donnelly, archivist at the London School of Economics, gave me access to all the documentation that I needed. The people of the Stoatley Rough School History Steering Committee deserve my gratitude for cataloguing in 1990 the names of pupils in a painstaking and tedious search through the hundreds of archived documents and files. Without those names and the dates in which children entered and left the school, I would not have been able to compile any kind of statistics on total yearly enrolments or to draw any of the several conclusions about the evolution of the school. These people I believe to be Ilse Bauer [Feldstein], Gina Schaefer [Mackenzie], Franceska Amerikaner [Rapkin], Hannah Giblanski [Wurzburger], Dr Margot Silverbach [Kogut], Susie Weissrock [Rice], Katharine Mayer [Whitaker] and Ann Funk [Steiner]. I apologise if I have failed to list any who helped in this valuable work. Finally, Seetha Srinivasan, head of the University Press of the State of Mississippi, since retired, and the other grandmother to my grandsons, Jackson and Joseph Srinivasan, shared generously her knowledge of publishing and gave me good advice and encouragement.

Preface

In the fall of 1998, on board a cruise ship en route to Alaska, I was
regaled night after night with stories of five friends who, sixty years
earlier, had come together for a brief time in England after Germany and
Austria had declared them unfit to be citizens of their own countries.
They were celebrating their seventieth birthdays. As the ship moved
among the glass-green icebergs, the men returned again and again to
the years 1938–1945. It was clear that they had received more than just
refuge at a very special place, Stoatley Rough School in Surrey, England.
Just ten years old when they arrived, they spent the next several years at
the school, growing up. Each of them had experienced persecution and
had lost family members to the Holocaust, yet each talked of a weekly
task roster, a morning run, and of how they learned to do a job right and
to take responsibility for the younger and less able ones in their midst.
The men expressed gratitude to the women (refugees themselves) who
ran the school. The men acknowledged how the communal living, daily
routines and strict boundaries, coupled with kindness, healthy exercise
and, above all, the sense of security, delivered to them a comforting
sanctuary. Overlaying the personal reminiscences came many anecdotes
and impressions of watching the Second World War unfold 40 miles
(64.37 kilometres) from London.

I am an educator and have taught public and private school children
from elementary through college level, and at one point in my life,
I helped to found a school. As the first Director of Studies for the Tampa
Preparatory School, Tampa, Florida, I understand the unique challenges
of starting a school. Listening to my husband's friends on that cruise
ship, I was struck by the odds against success of such a venture. The
Headmistress and her Board not only had to build a curriculum and
acquire teachers, books and materials, but they also needed to establish
a nurturing environment for parentless children in what, for them all,
was a foreign country. That the leaders were flexible enough to grow,
reset goals and conform to a constantly changing wartime environment
rife with rationing, lack of adequate heat, scarce funding and the
ever-present potential for emotional meltdown within each child,
was remarkable.

As we older folks sat in the large salon considering the merits of
French toast versus eggs Benedict, the ship's waiters hovering nearby,
the men recalled their daily fare of breakfast porridge which, as young

newcomers, they were assigned to stir with a wooden paddle while standing on a stool next to the wood-burning stove. They spoke of fun and mischief, of pranks, of discovering girls and watching the Royal Air Force (RAF) battle the Messerschmitts. I listened to the men express over and over again that their few years in England were of profound importance to them and it was then that I realised their story needed to be documented.

I have tried to knit together the skeins of the many anecdotes that I heard then and since, along with others I have read, to recreate that very special place. At the same time I have tried to capture some of the features of everyday life in mid-twentieth-century England and the Continent. The book tells the story by focusing on a few representative groups. The friends of my husband with whom we travelled call themselves Hut Boys (because they lived their best years in a Hut on the premises of the school) and it is their story that forms the core of the book. The Hut Boys were Martin Friedenfeld [Owens], Hans [Obo] Obermeyer, Wolf Edelstein [Elston], Peter and Dieter Gaupp, Tom Wongtschowski and Hans [Goldie] Goldmeier. Equally compelling were the stories of the child workers such as Renate Dorpalen [Dorpalen-Brocksieper], Edith Hubacher Christoffel and Herta Lewent Loeser, older pupils who helped keep the school running. Hans Loeser arrived a German teenager and ended up an officer in the US Army in time to take part in the Battle of the Bulge. Many other people helped me to tell the story of the school through recollections they recorded in a series of alumni Newsletters. I have also tried to represent fairly the remarkable personalities of the five German women who as educators and substitute parents maintained the healing environment that was Stoatley Rough School.

Finally, this is the story of a beautiful old manor house that still sits in its Surrey eyrie, high on what the English call a hanger or bluff. It is no longer a school and for several years in the late 90s, it lay dormant and neglected. Yet today it stands in its former glory, restored and inhabited. I see the house as a sturdy and steadfast reminder that England, although itself at the time was under siege, found a way to offer safe haven and so much that cannot be articulated, to stranded and desperate children.

Chapter 1
Sanctuary

Martin's heart was beating too fast. Why was he being sent away? He understood that his parents were trying to protect him from people in Austria who did not like Jews. But why would they not come to England with him? The sight of his mother's efforts to hold back her tears almost swamped his own resolve not to cry. From the corner of his eye he saw the big black engine chuffing and hissing, impatient to get going. He was excited by the acrid smell of hot tar and jets of steam coming from under the black undercarriage. Above him, his father droned on with more instructions for the journey. Then it was time to mount the steep stairs into the railway car. His mother had the saddest look on her face.

Martin found a seat by the window, and turned to wave but his dear *Mutti* had turned away. The train pulled out and the buildings of Vienna began to slip away, faster and faster. Martin soon got tired of looking out the window and pulled down his backpack from the overhead rack. 'Let me see what *Mutti* gave me', he thought. There was a bottle of 4711 Cologne. He sniffed it and put a drop on his cheek. He took a bite from an apple and put it back. He was not really hungry. There, under the lunch bag, was the stupid cardboard sign with his name on it. He was supposed to wear it around his neck when he got to England. Other children on the train were already wearing theirs. The older girl across from him asked if he wanted her to read to him from his book. He scoffed. Why did everybody think he was a baby? He returned his backpack to the over-head rack while outside his window telephone poles raced by in hypnotic regularity. There was a little girl sitting in his compartment and she began to cry. He thought, 'I am not going to cry', but within minutes, he was also in tears. The big girl pulled out *Der Letze Mohikaner* [The Last of the Mohicans] and read them both a chapter.

Martin got up to explore. At ten, he was wiry, with a frail body spread too thin over big bones. His hands and feet were growing ahead of the rest of him and his broad shoulders rescued him from looking like a waif. He had a wide mouth with full lips and pale blue eyes, and his nose, while not a beak, was the most pronounced part of his sharp little face. He was an observant, sensible boy, and every time his heart began to hurt again, he told himself that this was an adventure. It was going to be fun acting like a grown up.

He knew the trip was related to what had happened last March. His nanny, Millie, had taken him downtown on the trolley. Afterwards, he had told his parents about the exciting thing that had happened. First, they had gone to the *Kaertnerstrasse* and there were probably a hundred or maybe even a million people. They were yelling out the colours of the Austrian flag – '*Rot, Weiss, Rot bis in den Tod*' [Red, white, red until death]. Later he had asked about the death part, but his parents had just smiled in a sad way. And then the next day, Millie took him downtown again and this time they got to watch a long parade. Tanks, trucks, all kinds of guns on wheels, hundreds of soldiers and a whole pack of huge red flags swept by, rows and rows of them. He had yelled '*Heil Hitler*' too when the *Führer* came into view but then he had felt scared being in the midst of so many people all squeezed together. Their shouting grew louder as the *Führer* began to speak, and the crowd made a bigger noise than he had ever heard, a noise that rolled across the *Platz* in thundering waves. He had been glad his nanny kept a tight grip on his hand.

Martin slept. The shriek of the engine occasionally roused him as his train pushed across Germany, but the rhythmic clacking of the wheels always lulled him back to sleep. At one point, uniformed men boarded to check his papers. He slept again; then it was morning, and nice ladies were passing around rolls and hot chocolate and speaking a language he did not understand. Then he was in a line with other children walking up a gangway and onto a ship.

The air was brisk. He stood at the ship's rail watching all the fishing boats, freighters and warships as the pale cliffs in the distance grew larger. The water was pea green and sticky looking, like gelatin. Or snot. 'Snot'. He wished Rudi were there – he'd laugh like crazy. Martin jumped when his ship, a large ferry, loomed up over a smaller one and let out two long blasts. 'Out of my way!' His mother would have insisted he bundle up in six layers of clothes and two hats and three mufflers but his mother was not here to tell him what to do. Martin was not cold at all. He could stand here without his mittens as long as he wanted. His mother was far away now. A seagull swooped and screamed a harsh sound, like a cat. Martin's throat started to hurt and he wiped his eyes. He was going away to be safe; she'd said. They'd all meet again. The ship bellowed again, and the little ferry it had been tracking moved away. The people who had been playing shuffleboard quit their game and moved to the rail.

The ship docked, Martin was put on a train to London with his cardboard sign around his neck and before he knew it, he found himself in a small train leaving the bustle of Paddington Station and heading into the darkness, a warm little cocoon on rails. He wondered if his parents were eating dinner, if his little sister were getting into his toy soldiers. His mother had promised she would keep Liesel out of his room. He started to worry about his things. Then the conductor appeared, motioning to him to get ready to leave the train. Before he knew it, Martin was standing alone on the dark platform. What if nobody came for him? He frantically searched his memory for an English word, any word that Frau Pfniesl had made him repeat during the last weeks of preparations in Vienna. What was the word for bathroom? Nothing came.

From around a corner of the station house, a small woman bustled up. '*hallo, kleine Mann. Du must ja Martin Friedenfeld sein? Wilkommen. Mein Name ist Freulein Astfalck.*'

He unclenched his fists.

The next morning, in the kitchen, he saw large bowls of brown sugar and stewed fruit on a table. Some big boys stood near the outside door in rubber boots ogling the girls until the cook told them to leave. Just outside the half door that led down a corridor, he saw children carrying spoons and napkins; then a big girl started handing out pitchers of milk to the children. Everybody was working. Martin's job was to stand on a chair next to the stove and stir the porridge with a long-handled spoon. He peered into the gloppy stuff and thought of the hard roll, butter and mug of cocoa Cook always placed before him every morning back home. The big girl in charge of him said, '*Du must das Porridge rueren so das es nicht verbrent. Nein Nein, micht so schnell! Das musst du mit dem loeffel....*' He stopped listening. The edges of the pot got blurry and in spite of trying with all his might, he began to cry. The big girl lifted him off the stool and gave him a glass of milk. 'There, it's your first day after all; you'll be all right, we all had to leave our parents but you get used to it. Somebody go get Miss Astfalck.'

The Austrians

On Martin's first morning at Stoatley Rough, the school's Headmistress, Dr Hilde Lion, was sipping her morning tea in the dining room alongside her second in command, Dr Emmy Wolff. Dr Lion did not look like a headmistress with her roly-poly figure and short stature. The small had an impressive intellect but was something of the absent-minded professor who sometimes wore unmatched socks with her sensible lace-up shoes. Renate Dorpalen [Dorpalen-Brocksieper], one of the girls in charge of clean-up that morning, saw Dr Lion as 'a heavy-set short woman with sad eyes that rarely looked directly at people. Her greying hair was severely pulled back and managed to come undone during the day. Her dress was careless, clothing spotted with food or ashes from her ever-present cigarette. A nervous variety of vocal tics increased in intensity under pressure. She spoke in heavily accented English, and often left sentences unfinished.' Many former pupils have written about that vocal tic, little self-reassuring humming noises that the children gleefully mimicked behind her back ('*Hmm, hmm, my dearchen*'). Dr Lion poured herself more tea and took a bite of toast. (She and the staff did not always eat the same fare as the children.) She was worried. The arrival of the new little boy from Vienna, Martin Friedenfeld, reminded her that her boarding school was already strained to capacity. Where would they put Martin and the others who kept arriving? Stoatley Rough was now up to sixty-two pupils, double the enrolment of last year, and she feared it would double again in 1939. Dr Lion was also housing temporary evacuees; children moved out of London to safety because the country was gearing up for war with Germany. She had said at her most recent meeting of the Committee, 'They have got to be taken ...'. Dr Lion had a plan to house the Austrian children, ready to present to the Committee that very evening. Thursley Copse, a grand country house like Stoatley Rough just down Farnham Lane on the other side of the road, was available for rent. Dr Wolff was listening. Yes, she knew of the house, only half a mile or so from Stoatley Rough. It was just past what is now Woodland Trust land. Dr Wolff had walked many times across the Heath, sometimes called the Commons, an ancient pasturage once shared by neighbours. Everybody used the Heath to get to the small town of Hindhead or as a pleasant venue to take a walk. Children sometimes played football at its highest point, Gibbet Hill, a beautiful site that overlooked another protected swath of far-reaching land called the Devil's Punchbowl. Dr Wolff thought Hilde's idea a fine one and recalled that Thursley Copse stood next to a real copse of bushes through which ran a path to the tiny part of Haslemere known as Shottermill. After four years in England, the intellectually curious woman had learned that the English liked to bestow their estates names with historic weight. 'Stoatley', for example,

was borrowed from the nearby Great and Little Stoatley Farms, and
'stoatley' was composed of the Old English words 'stott' and 'leah'
meaning 'clearing' for horses or bullocks, and not, as she had guessed
originally, from the English word for the little weasel-like stoat that
populated the countryside. She nodded her agreement with Dr Lion's
plan. She needed to know what was going on. Dr Wolff placed her spoon
on her plate, folded her napkin and prepared to leave. She was as well
groomed as Dr Lion was untidy. Like Hilde Lion, Emmy Wolff wore her
red-brown hair in a bun at the nape of her neck. But unlike her friend, she
carried herself with dignity, her aquiline, patrician features composed. As
the two women left the dining room, Dr Wolff said she thought Dr Lion's
idea was marvellous. Dr Lion went on to say that she had already
contacted Thesi von Gierke, the niece of Anna Von Gierke, former
director of the *Jugenheim Charlottenburg* [Youth Home in the district
of Charlottenburg] in Berlin where Dr Lion and Dr Wolff had worked
and first met. Yes, Dr Wolff agreed, young Thesi would bring order
to the new residence.

Three months later, during the coldest winter recorded in England,
Martin and nineteen other Austrian children moved into Thursley
Copse. They would sleep there but take their dinner in the main house
at Stoatley Rough, an arrangement that lasted for the next two years.

Martin and the others had come to England because Germany had
marched into their country to claim it for itself. At the time, only six
months earlier, Martin's parents understood at once that Austrian Jews
were no longer safe. How had Austria been taken over by Germany?
If Martin, only ten years old at the time, had been old enough, he might
have learned in history class that almost a hundred years earlier, Austria,
while part of the powerful Austro–Hungarian Empire, had also belonged
to an alliance called the German Confederation. After being kicked
out of the Confederation by the great Prussian leader, Bismarck, many
Austrians yearned to return to the fold, seeing Germany as a kind
of superior big brother. The decade after the First World War had
brought misery and deprivation, inflation and unemployment, making
both Germany and Austria ripe for ultra-nationalism and political
infighting. In 1933, Hitler's party won control and began to re-arm and
strengthen the German economy. Austrian political parties jockeyed
for power throughout the 1920s, among them their own brand of Nazis.
In 1934, the Austrian Nazis assassinated Austria's Chancellor Dollfus,
paving the way for them to gain control. The country was beset by

violence. Nazi thugs set off stink bombs in the *Staatsoper* [Opera House]
while Martin sat with his grandmother watching a performance
of *Hänsel und Gretel*. By 1938, nine-year-old Martin was witness
to a democracy in its death throes. He would not forget the crowds,
the powerful roaring voices, the force of mob mentality, the thrill
of how one man could make whole crowds of people shriek and swoon.

Life in Vienna had been rather nice. Martin was born to upper-middle-
class, non-religious Jewish parents, who, as many Viennese of their
station, were fond of the opera, *Sachertorte* (a special type of chocolate
cake) and fancy dress balls. His mother had been baptised and educated
as a Christian, while his father, wishing Martin to have a Jewish identity,
took him to the temple on high holidays. 'My family lived in a sunny
apartment on the banks of the Danube in the second (Jewish) District
of Vienna. I remember that I had a beautifully decorated room with a
balcony overlooking the Danube. There was a large advertisement sign for
Persil (laundry soap) across the river.' When he was five, the Depression
was at its worst, and his father lost his job working in his grandfather's
wholesale fur business. His family went to live with his maternal
grandparents, where one aunt, two maids, a cook and the nanny also
lived. Martin was a quiet, tidy child, even handsome, winning first prize in
a beauty contest when he was three. He liked to play with his toy soldiers,
his large wooden castle and his trains. Martin spoke soft Austrian German
in cool, unemotional tones. (He was always quiet and unthreatening.
When he grew older at Stoatley Rough, the girls characterised him as
sweet, and he was the first of his friends to have a girlfriend.)

In 1934, six-year-old Martin started school at the *Pedagogium*,
a teacher training school on the *Hegelgasse* in the first District. In the
afternoons, his mother or grandfather took him to the *Stadtpark*, the
big municipal park in the centre of the city, where he fed the swans. He
revered his grandfather, his *Opi*, a handsome man with an erect bearing
and handlebar moustache who, like Martin's father, had served in First
World War, building a railroad line from Croatia to Turkey. *Opi* remained
a major in the Austrian Army Reserve Corps and a loyal monarchist
despite Austria's transition to democracy. Military officers in Europe at
that time held high social rank, a fact that delayed the departure of some
Jewish officers under Nazism until it was too late, never believing their
country would turn on them. 'My *Opi* taught me to ride a bike in the
Prater, Vienna's amusement park and city park, the one with the Ferris

wheel that features in Orson Welles' classic movie, "The Third Man". He used to take me there to shoot in the shooting galleries, where I got to be pretty proficient. I learned to hit the *Watschenman*, a dummy that you hit with all your might, wearing a very thick mitt, in order to obtain as high a score as possible. We used to visit the marionette theatre and also *Lilliput Stadt*, a village of tiny houses occupied by dwarves.' Martin's *Grosse Omi* [Big Grandma], his father's mother, lived nearby. He liked to watch her make apple strudel on her big kitchen table. Each season the family lit real candles on the Christmas tree. The summer before he started school, Martin stayed with the parents of one of the family's maids in the country and remembers watching deer at a salt lick and the force feeding of a goose that habitually terrorised him by snapping at his *lederhosen*. His maid read him one of his favourite books, *Der Struwwelpeter* [Peter with the Dishevelled Hair], thrilling him with the horrific punishments meted out to naughty children, each illustrated in bright reds, greens, blues and yellows. It had pictures of a tailor with huge scissors who cuts off a naughty girl's thumb as bright red drops of blood fall to the ground; a girl is burned to ashes for torturing cats while the cats wipe tears from their eyes with little handkerchiefs; other children are thrown into the water to drown, or are starved, bitten by a dog or shot. He was only slightly disappointed that he didn't get a St. Bernard instead. When Martin came home from the farm, he found he had a new little sister.

'I was nine when the ugly realities sank in as to the future of Jews in Austria. I was with my nanny one day and we joined a circle around some activity going on in the street. Brown-uniformed SA men with swastikas on their armbands had made elderly Jewish men and women kneel down and scrub the streets.' Going out with his nanny was not fun any more when she made him and Liesel sit on benches in the park he knew were prohibited to Jews.

Getting Martin out of Austria was not easy. Martin's mother stood in line for hours to get the countless forms from the German bureaucracy that had quickly taken root in Vienna. Since Jews were barred from almost all legitimate work, Martin's father joined forces with an 'Aryan' friend to help people send money illegally out of the country, involving forgeries of documents. It was very risky, but it brought in money. Six months after the German takeover, permission came through from both England and German governments. On 22 September 1938, the family stood on the *Bahnhof* platform to see Martin off.

Dr Lion remembers

With two houses full of refugees, Dr Lion had much to do. After four
years in England, however, she felt confident she could manage. She hung
up her coat in her room in the bungalow and prepared to return to her
office, musing about her own emigration from Berlin in 1934, just four
years earlier. A rising star in those days, she had lost everything to Nazi
hatred when they banned Jews from holding positions of responsibility
in governmental agencies. Forty years old and out of work, how had she
ended up in England running a school for refugee children?

Dr Lion's youth had been shaped by the war of her own generation,
the First World War. Born on 14 May 1893, into a wealthy, non-religious
Jewish merchant family of Hamburg, Hilde and her older sister grew
up in a genteel and stratified society. Dr Lion's early years, steeped in
Edwardian conventionality, were not happy after her parents divorced.
As she matured, she refused to consider any suitor for her hand and
then shocked her family by declaring she would never marry. In an
unpublished autobiography, she described the reaction to her radical
decision. 'My relatives and my parents' friends regarded my intention
of taking up a career as highly unsuitable, and there were rumours that
my father could not be well off if he permitted me to take up teaching....
My parents were aghast when I told them that I wanted to be a teacher,
be financially independent and avoid having to make a marriage of
convenience.'[1] Men were never to play any role in her personal life.
Hilde doted on her sister's two sons and the half-brother who was born
to her father's new wife in the ensuing years. But she was not to find
a love of her own so easily, and insecurity dogged her throughout her life.
She entered the Hamburg Social Pedagogical Institute in 1917, a year
before the First World War ended. There, she met feminists whose goals
were to advance a woman's right to economic equality with men. She
joined the movement to change such rules as society's stricture against
women taking jobs outside the home in any field other than teaching,
nursing or social work, the only acceptable roles deemed proper. Life was
slower then, less complicated, with the telephone, refrigeration and even
the lowly zipper still to be invented. There were strict gender roles, and
women were certainly not expected to behave and think like men. But the
war changed everything. Soon, social norms, and even radical changes in
fashion electrified a continent. Picasso's Cubism came onto the scene even
before the war; and by the time Hilde reached her twentieth birthday,

Stravinsky's *The Rite of Spring* had stunned concert audiences. Coco Chanel's loose line of clothing revolutionised women's fashion. In 1920, feminists earned women the right to vote (a year before the United States passed its own Nineteenth Amendment to the Constitution). While other girls her age might have thought it daring to smoke in public or cut their hair short, young Hilde Lion was becoming radicalised, recording the minutes at activist meetings, writing pamphlets, planning how best to advance women's rights. But her idealism soon flagged when she understood that women would not truly share political power overnight. She entered the University of Cologne, and in 1924, she earned a doctorate in social welfare, an extraordinary achievement at the time for a woman. In 1925, she began to teach at the *Jugendheim Charlottenburg*, part of a government-funded network of facilities and services.[2] In 1929, Dr Lion was appointed Director of another institution, the *Deutsche Akademie für Soziale und Paedagogische Frauenarbeit* [German Academy of Women's Social and Pedagogical Work], another government-funded institution established by the prominent German feminist Dr Alice Salomon. The academy offered university-level training of both practical and interdisciplinary value. Dr Lion found great satisfaction in helping the impoverished victims of the Depression, convinced that women could find dignity in volunteer work. She created a programme for volunteers called The Mother's Help Services for middle-class female social workers, to protect them from the 'narrow-mindedness, wretchedness and early bitterness' of unemployment.

Her belief in the intrinsic value of work in Germany became a corner-stone of the governing philosophy at Stoatley Rough, where everyone shared in the work, students and staff alike. Communal work provided the pupils a sense of purpose and predictability while at the same time imparting citizenship and fair play. One pupil wrote, 'the disciplines they imposed were so logical that I soon realised that resistance to them was pointless and unprofitable.'[3] By requiring the children to take part in running their own school and in having a stake in it through their participation, Dr Lion gave her displaced children a sense of purpose, the security of being needed. These values helped to save the Stoatley Rough children exactly as it had saved Depression women in Germany, from self-pity, despair and defeat.

Dr Lion sat down heavily at her desk and picked up her calendar, remembering the worried look on young Martin Friedenfeld's face as he had wandered from the breakfast room that morning. A little lost soul.

She, too, had suffered at the hands of the Nazis, back in 1933, when they took power in Germany. Almost immediate racial laws prohibited any Jew, or 'non-Aryan', from prominent positions in any of the hundreds of governmental agencies and organisations. Thousands of educators, artists, scientists, musicians and social workers were thrown out of work. Dr Lion and others of her prominence began to leave the country. In 1934 alone, some 60,000 people left Germany.

Dr Lion looked forward to the Committee meeting. It would be held in London that evening. She had enormous respect for the founders of the school, and was grateful they gave her leeway to put into practise their shared values for the school. She recalled how ardently they had all worked to establish Stoatley Rough School in the first place.

The idea had come from a group of British refugee workers attuned to the plight of the German–Jewish children arriving in their country in 1933. These advocates for refugees wanted to teach the English language and English customs to prepare the children to work overseas in British colonies. Strict laws dictated that immigrants could only work as house-keeper, maid, butler, valet or farm worker. Britain might be willing to accept foreigners but was not about to give up any of its good jobs to non-citizens. Members of the Quaker German Emergency Committee and the Jewish Refugee Committee, along with other concerned activists, formed a group to plan and raise money for a school. Quaker activist Miss Bertha Bracey, who shuttled between Berlin and London on behalf of German–Jewish children, met Dr Lion on one of her trips to Berlin and knew right away Dr Lion was just the person she had been looking for.[4] It was not long before she arranged for Dr Lion to receive a grant from the British Federation of University Women to come to England. Dr Lion was supposed to write about the 'intellectual and emotional readjustment of children to a new environment' but Miss Bracey had bigger plans. Dr Lion was legally forbidden to accept wages in England but her talents fit the plans of the Committee and they would take care of her. Dr Lion moved into the University Women's Club in Crosby Road, Chelsea, and plunged into helping Miss Bracey and her group. Eleonore Astfalck, the school's first Matron, wrote about Dr Lion's early activities in England. 'Hilde Lion ... had no money, nowhere to live, and [did not know] how to find a job or how to start her studies. In 1934 ... she was only interested in finding jobs for people.'[5]

Dr Lion recalled the luck the Committee had had (fuelled of course by their tireless efforts) in bringing the school into existence. Finances were the issue back then and, as far as she could tell, would always be her primary concern as headmistress. Back in 1934, neither the Quakers nor the Jewish Women's Committee could fund a new school, but the Inter-Aid Committee for Children contributed substantially, along with the Jewish Refugee Committee (£60 per annum), and the Mayor of Guildford Refugee Committee (£52 per annum). It was not enough so they turned to the very wealthy members of the peerage who agreed to form a temporary oversight council to monitor their investment.[6] A steering committee (all female) made up of the original group of founding activists would tend to the everyday business of the school.[7] Within a few months they raised around £531 (roughly $2,665), some of which was a loan to be repaid within the year. Wolf Edelstein [Elston] helps us understand the relative value of the sum raised for the school. 'In 1935, £5/week was a good middle class income. £531 would have been two–three years' pay for an industrial worker.' The committee worked out the fee to charge students for tuition, room and board: £100 per annum, with ongoing support to be sought, for those who needed it, from various refugee and charitable agencies. To put this fee into context: a Member of Parliament in 1934 was paid £600; a teacher at Stoatley Rough £50 per annum plus room and board.

Everything was set. The new school had a committee, a financial board, a headmistress and the financing. But where would the children live and study? At this critical juncture entered a small, self-assured, very wealthy and well-connected woman who was neither Quaker nor Jewish but rather a devout Anglican. Mrs Marjorie Vernon owned a country estate, Stoatley Rough, lying virtually empty out in Haslemere, Surrey, 40 miles (64.37 kilometres) south-west of London. She had inherited this lovely place from her father in the 1920s but now spent most of her weekends in another, more elegant residence in Hampshire. She wondered if Stoatley Rough might do. She checked with her husband, Roland Venables Vernon, Undersecretary in the British Colonial Office, whose family boasted baronetcies and titles of nobility dating from the twelfth century. He approved. After all, Marjorie devoted herself to charitable work and accompanied her husband in his travels; they hardly ever went to Stoatley Rough these days now that their only child had grown up and left home.[8] In one unforgettable act of generosity, Mrs Vernon handed over her estate lock, stock and barrel.

The beautiful Stoatley Rough was instantly deemed satisfactory by the grateful Committee. Mrs Vernon's terms were simple: the new school would retain the gardener and his wife, Mr and Mrs Phillips, who would continue to live in the carriage house ('The Lodge') for their lifetimes. (Mr Phillips and his wife, who never appeared in public without her hat, would live at Stoatley Rough for over forty years.[9]) Mr Phillips was to continue to maintain the grounds; the school would pay for all maintenance and upkeep of the property; and the gift of the house would be re-examined after three years.

Dr Lion settled in at her desk to begin her day's work. She wondered what Miss Fry, the lady originally in charge of things while Dr Lion acclimatised herself to England, was doing in her retirement. Probably travelling. Isabel Fry, a Quaker who had taught school for many years, had taken the helm on a temporary basis while Dr Lion recruited staff and pupils, and had long since dropped out of sight. Dr Lion wondered about her own future. Would she ever have the funds to travel? How long would she last at this new school? The irony was not lost on her. She who had dedicated herself to helping the impoverished and unemployed in Germany, might have been impoverished and unemployed as well had it not been for Miss Bracey, Miss Fry and the others.

She looked up. Mr Phillips stood awkwardly in the doorway to the tiny office. What did he want? He only delivered fresh flowers to Dr Lion's room during the summer months. Hat in hand, he asked if Dr Lion had special plans for the eastern edge of the second tennis court? He had some ideas for new shrubbery if she approved. After he left her office, Dr Lion remembered the day Mrs Vernon had to deliver the news to the crusty old gentleman that his sanctuary was about to be invaded. A Cockney with a green thumb and short temper, he was used to a quiet life at Stoatley Rough. Mrs Vernon knew he would be fearful of little feet trampling his prized flowers. Wolf [Edelstein] Elston recalled, 'At first I was afraid of that gruff old man, especially when he grumbled about "them bloomin' nippers, runnin' across me flower beds, Oi'll givem the shtick, Oi will!" ' But Mr Phillips was special. 'To me, he epitomised the sturdy English yeoman. In England, people don't talk much about themselves and only in his obituary in the *Haslemere Herald*, years later, did I learn that Mr Phillips had been a prominent local citizen, the respected member of boards and councils.'

Mr Phillips would have been proud to know how the pupils revered the school and its lovely grounds. The estate had been built by Mrs Vernon's father, Mr Arthur Leon, a stockbroker, philanthropist and wealthy civil servant, in 1898 along a ridge south of the small prosperous town of Haslemere. The 17 acres (6.88 hectares) offered a spectacular view of the forested South Downs, starting 750 feet (228.6 metres) above sea level along a promontory, then swooping 570 feet (173.74 metres) down at a steep angle to a small stream that trickled through lush farmland. Mr Leon hired the prominent London architect Falconer Macdonald to design his house, intending to mirror and perhaps exceed the grandeur of the other two Macdonald houses in the neighbourhood, Thursley Hall and Dunrozel. Like the Vernon house, the two were at once stately and sensible, neither too flashy nor humble, but quietly elegant, and were expensive dwellings that exuded stability and prosperity with their red-brick chimneys, slate roofs, gables and large bay windows. Mr Leon's property soon bloomed with gardens and shrubbery, two tennis courts and a winding path that led down the steep slope to the farmland.[10]

Improvements followed. Mr and Mrs Vernon added a gardener's cottage, stables and two small houses in the valley that they rented out to working class families. By the 1930s, however, the Vernons rarely used Stoatley Rough except to fill it with mementos of their extensive travels, allowing it to sit in splendid isolation, its view of the South Downs enjoyed only by the birds and small creatures that lived among the trees and shrubbery.[11] The view from the terrace encompassed Witley Forest and the high ridge dozens of miles away known as Blackdown where once Alfred Lord Tennyson made his home. On a clear day, one could even peer into Hampshire county.

Mrs Vernon's gift had an extraordinary influence on its students and refugee teachers because it imparted tranquillity and healing to traumatised and homesick children. Edith Hubacher [Christoffel-Hubacher] wrote, '[I recall] the magnificent garden, so lovingly and competently tended by Mr Phillips ...; the garden in which one could always find a lovely and quiet place to read or do one's prep. The Flowers! The age-old pine trees under whose branches one hid because they came down to the ground, forming the compact sides of a hut! The wide sweep of the path down to the tennis-court where we did our gymnastics! The Rhododendrons! The old wall below the house overgrown with wisteria, viburnum and wild roses, with the wide grassy path beneath! It's all gone, but the memories remain.' Ruth Ultman [Muessig] chose her new house in America based upon her memories of Stoatley Rough. 'One reason my little house here in Connecticut attracted me right away was that it faces a mountain, the Sleeping Giant, and it looks remarkably like the Surrey Downs.'[12]

Dr Lion picked up her day book. She noted that on the same day
in 1921, the German government had granted women the right to vote.
She smiled wistfully. So long ago, and in a place so far away, she had been
a part of that great moment in history.

Too many separations

Martin was starting to make friends with some of the children living
in the main house at Stoatley Rough. At least there were others just like
him who liked the same toys and games as he. In December, however,
he packed up the belongings he had stowed in the large dormitory on the
top floor of the country house and moved down the street into Thursley
Copse. Nineteen other children, mostly Austrians, filled the house within
weeks. He had barely gotten himself settled when the school closed for
the Christmas holidays and the thirty-five children who could not return
to Germany were placed into the homes of English friends and supporters
of the school. Martin said of his hosts that Christmas that, 'They spoke no
German and my English was somewhere between poor and non-existent.
I learned a lot of English from these kind people … for Christmas they
gave me a Dinky Toy dust lorry (garbage truck) which I treasured and
kept for many years.' Sometimes the children landed in the homes of
well-connected citizens, such as Gerhard [Gad] Wolff, who lived with
a successful playwright, Miss Olive Popplewell, not only a friend of
G. B. Shaw, but 'a kind-hearted Quaker lady, who also got us invitations
to tea parties and provided us with tickets to *Snow White*'. The thirteen-
year-old recalled that he had tried to convince Miss Popplewell and her
friends of Hitler's war build-up but his words 'were met with disbelief'.[13]

When Martin returned to the school in January 1939, there was
a surprise in store for him. He learned that he would not attend classes
with the other children his age at Stoatley Rough. Along with a few others,
he was going to attend a government-run boys' school, the Shottermill
County Council School. Classes in the main house at Stoatley Rough,
then averaging from between five to ten pupils who sat with their
teachers around big tables, were filled to capacity.

Martin would be separated from the boys he was just starting to make
friends with. And he would miss the Matron, Miss Astfalck, a very nice
lady who seemed to come around to check up on him in the kindest way
just when he felt most depressed. He had no choice. He would have to do

as he was told. Miss Astfalck tried to assuage his fears, noting that
he would still have many of his meals with the others in the big house.
The youngest of the German teachers and also the hardest working, Nore
Astfalck was a diminutive Mary Poppins – diligent, crisp, cheerful and
relentlessly efficient. Unlike Dr Lion, who was only seven years her senior
and something of a butterball, thirty-eight-year- old Nore was spare and
physically fit. Her features were finely sculpted, with clear blue eyes that
had a disarmingly direct gaze; an oval face with a long, aquiline nose and
short wavy hair swept back off her high forehead. Nothing happened in
the school that Miss Astfalck was not privy to, and the children knew it.
Nobody could duck responsibility. She'd know if you had not brushed
your teeth.

In one important way, Martin was lucky at Thursley Copse. At least
they had enough bathrooms. Stoatley Rough had only one sink for
girls, a toilet each for the girls, boys and teachers, and one boys' and one
girls' bathing room. When the school was new and enrolment small, the
facilities had been adequate, but by 1939, the residential population had
grown to over seventy. Wolf recalled, 'After the morning run came a rush
for the toilet and the sink – the singulars are deliberate. Stoatley Rough
had been a private home and there had been one indoor toilet for the
family ... and another in an unheated annex behind the kitchen, for the
servants (now used by boys). Mercifully, boys were allowed to use the girl's
facility at night.'

Martin began school that January, walking with another boy from
Austria, ten-year-old Richard Gruenzweig [Green]. From Farnham
Lane, they cut through the copse downhill to reach the school (which
incidentally had been built as a gift to the town by Marjorie Vernon's
father in the first decade of the twentieth century). Richard Gruenzweig
was bigger than Martin and something of a bully. Over time, the larger
boy started forcing Martin into fistfights along the way, but Martin never
complained to his elders. (Later Martin acquired a bike on which he flew
down Farnham Lane to school at high speed in the mornings and slowly
rode back up the hill on his return in the afternoons, carving out a zigzag
pattern in a slow, steady slog uphill.) At Shottermill, Martin studied
English, maths, history and science. He especially enjoyed the woodworking and gardening. 'It was a rough school. If you got out of line, you
were caned and the rules were strict. We all had Victory Gardens in which
we grew vegetables. We were not allowed to talk while gardening. One
day, the class clown told a joke and I burst out laughing. I was caught

and caned across my fingertips, whereas he escaped unpunished. It was a very painful experience.'[14] Martin yearned to take classes at Stoatley Rough where no corporal punishment was tolerated. The worst punishment anyone ever received was to be sent to Dr Lion for a talking to. But Martin kept his silence. As young as he was, he was grateful to be safe from whatever the Nazis planned to do to hurt the Jews back in Austria.

Dr Lion seems not to have been aware of any problems. When she wrote to the headmaster of the all-boys school, she merely commented, 'Richard is rather a wild young fellow, and we should recommend to have an eye on him especially. Martin is a little frail, and we would appreciate it if the school doctor could see him before he begins swimming. He tells me he has been swimming since his eighth year however.'[15] Dr Lion never overlooked any free services she could extract. In a note to the same principal the following year, Dr Lion asked if Shottermill's dentist would take care of Martin's toothache 'as we have very limited funds, it would mean a great help'.[16]

Martin was thus consigned to living a disjointed life, sleeping at Thursley Copse, dining at Stoatley Rough and taking classes at Shottermill. English children left the government school system of basic education at fourteen, and accordingly, Martin graduated from Shottermill and joined his peers at Stoatley Rough to live and study for another three years. He believes today that his formal education was not harmed by attending the government school, but he suspects that his lifelong fear of separation from loved ones may stem from leaving his parents, losing the girl who looked after him (Gertrud Gans), being segregated from the other children by attending Shottermill School and living in Thursley Copse, all within four months of his arrival in England.

In the summer of 1939, Martin's father and his partner were arrested for selling forged documents and were shipped off to a prison in Berlin to await trial. During this time, SS men regularly came to the apartment in Vienna to harass Martin's mother and to take her in for questioning, leaving Liesel behind screaming at the window. When the case came to trial, his father's partner accepted the lion's share of blame. The verdict was particularly perverse: Martin's father was sentenced to continued imprisonment while the Aryan who had committed the unforgivable crime of collaborating with a Jew was given the death sentence and was shot at once.[17] Months later, his mother miraculously managed to get the paperwork together to get her husband out of jail, out of Berlin and out of the country to safety in the United States.

The adult Martin does not remember many details from his past, particularly the trauma of his abrupt move from Vienna to England. Harvard-based researchers Gerald Holton and Gerhard Sonnert make the case that the Austrian Jews were more intensely affected than German Jews, since the *Anschluss* came so suddenly upon them. Theirs was not necessarily a worse experience, but one that was experienced with more intensity. In Germany, the persecution was inflicted a little bit at a time under official dicta, while in Austria, the official harassments and loss of status occurred to the Jewish population almost overnight. Today, Martin is relatively well-adjusted, displaying only the occasional eccentricity in such ways as packing for a trip several days before leaving, needing to arrive at events exactly on time or to be first in line. He is sanguine about his eccentricities and would agree that, in part, his introspective nature, fear of abandonment and need to be ready for any emergency seem to confirm that there was more than an element of trauma in his experience with the events during and after the *Anschluss*.[18]

In January 1939, while Martin was struggling to learn the tricky English verbs at Shottermill, other boys his age who would come to Stoatley Rough were still in Germany, reeling from *Kristallnacht* [the Night of the Brok Glass], which occurred on 5/6 November 1938, a month after Martin arrived at Stoatley Rough. On that night, Hitler's thugs set fire to Jewish businesses and synagogues across Germany and Austria as officials stood by. The pogrom was an unmistakable sign. Nazi hatred was out in the open. German–Jewish families began to search for ways to get themselves and their children to safety. Only a few children would be lucky enough to land in the welcoming lap of Stoatley Rough School.

One cold day in January, a boy from Berlin was assigned to Martin's table for the week, a boy his own age. Wolf Edelstein [Elston] was a big-boned, sometimes clumsy boy, with a handsome, somewhat melancholic face. The quiet and introspective Martin soon discovered his new friend was anything but moody. Wolf was an inveterate prankster who frequently indulged his impulse to utter witty, audacious or irreverent remarks, even to adults. Such bravado astonished Martin but apparently did no harm to his own standing with the powers that be. Wolf quickly became the darling of Dr Lion and Dr Wolff, the former a very distant cousin on his father's side. Dr Wolff even (unwisely) tried to get Wolf to address her in the familiar *Du*, the form of 'you' Germans use for children, servants and God, instead of the appropriate formal *Sie* as in '*Sprechen Sie*

Deutsch?' Wolf sensibly resisted being singled out. He was already
wildly happy with his new life in England after having suffered at the
hands of Nazi classroom martinets. He was all too aware of the ill-effects
of favouritism in school.

A perversion of education

Wolfgang Edelstein was happiest when he was dressed in old clothes.
At home, things had been different, when the highly intelligent and
independent boy regularly chafed at the fussier social conventions of his
upper-middle-class station. He especially hated his own birthday, when
his parents made him dress up in a little Lord Fauntleroy suit and bow
to the little girls in frilly dresses who came to his parties, adults atwitter
in the background. Stoatley Rough freed him of all that nonsense.
A notation in his personal file during his first term (1939) under the
headings 'Tidiness' and 'Personal Neatness' read: 'Improving but not
yet satisfactory'. Someone else had taken a black marker to cross out
the evaluation and had written 'BAD'.
   Wolf had grown up with his parents and his brother, Gerd, in
a comfortable apartment in Grunewald, a tony neighbourhood near
a forest of scotch fir and birch. The forest bordered the Havel River that
flowed gently into the lake that became notorious as the site of the 1942
Wannsee Conference where the Nazis formulated their plans for the Final
Solution of the Jewish Question. Wolf's mother conducted her practise
in Paediatrics in their apartment, having been one of the first women in
Germany to study medicine. (In the United States, at the age of forty-six,
this remarkable woman prepared for and passed the medical boards in
English; she would practise medicine into her eighties.) Wolf's father was
a well-respected lawyer. Wolf lived a happy-go-lucky life as a young child
in the care of the family governess, Maria, whom Wolf called Mia. It was
Mia who took him to school on his first day of school, not his mother,
and when Mia left service to get married, Wolf was distraught. One
day the well-to-do Edelsteins, who employed a full-time maid and cook,
accepted delivery of a newfangled refrigerator. 'When my mother showed
off our apartment to visitors, she'd show them the Frigidaire and make
excuses for having indulged in such a luxury – "it's to keep the children's
milk cold". The joke is that Gerd and I hated milk and never drank it.
In those days, milk was not pasteurized. It had to be boiled and then was

served warm with scum on top. Absolutely disgusting! I feel sick just thinking about it!'

Wolf started school at about the time racial laws were being enacted, in September 1934. One day a few older boys stopped him on the street to ask, 'Are you a Jew?' The scholarly Wolf said, 'No, the Jews lived 5,000 years ago', puzzled by such a silly question. A few days later, his teacher asked the children to bring in a family tree with religions next to the names. It was only then that he discovered that all his grandparents were Jewish. Upon the accession of Hitler, Wolf's father, in an act of defiance, joined an underground Christian church, the Confessional Church that had formed to protest the Nazi's conglomerate of 'official' Protestant churches. Wolf remembers enjoying Hitler's brass bands, the waving swastikas and extravagant displays of weaponry, but when he started school, he entered a period of bizarre and humiliating ordeals. The little boy was the only non-Aryan in his class. He was too intelligent to ignore some of the more blatant excesses of the school's propaganda machine. The Reich Minister of Science, Education and Popular Culture (onetime *Gauleiter* [provincial leader] of Hanover) and unemployed schoolmaster, having been dismissed in 1930 for 'certain manifestations of instability of mind', Dr Bernhard Rust perverted the entire German educational system from top to bottom, boasting that he succeeded in 'liquidating the school as an institution of intellectual acrobatics'. He forced teachers and professors to take an oath to be loyal to Adolf Hitler and he meddled with the curriculum, with catastrophic consequences for German education. Wolf endured the Nazi version of religion and paganist dogma the teachers slathered upon the children. 'The teachers opened each lesson with "*Heil Hitler*" as if voicing a religious incantation, and a new discipline appeared in the curriculum called *Rassenkunde* [racial studies]. In subjects such as German literature and history, Nazi doctrine prevailed.' Anti-Semitism was sanctioned by the teachers, and Wolf became 'the target of every bully', harassed and beaten. One day, a few boys pushed him down and urinated on him. 'I participated in interminable flag-honouring ceremonies (*Flaggenehre*), where teachers in SA uniforms with *Blut und Ehre* [Blood and Honour] daggers on their belts strutted about the school yard while we sang every verse of the "*Horst Wessel Lied*" and "*Deutschland Über Alles*".' Children picked on Wolf almost every day for one thing or another. One day, Wolf was given a moment's peace from his tormenters courtesy of an unlikely ally. A boy started to taunt him for having dark hair, but another boy rose to take Wolf's side. The defender was not just anybody but the son of the chief legal advisor to Hitler, Hans Frank. Little Norman Frank was indignant. '*Lass' ihn doch, mein Vater und der Führer haben auch schwarze Haare* [Leave him alone, my father and the Führer have dark hair, too].' Several years later, Wolf could not begin to describe the complex mix of nostalgia, revulsion and vindication that engulfed him when he learned from the safety of New York City that Norman's father was tried at Nuremberg and sentenced to hang for the crimes he committed as Governor General of occupied Poland.

Evenings over the dinner table, the Edelstein family talked about the sobering policies that were continually emanating from the Reich, such as the Nazi politicisation of organisations, a totalitarian philosophy termed *Gleichschaltung* [making things equal] that put every organisation (even the Protestant churches) under state control. The policy was so far-reaching that Wolf's father, a learned man with a wry sense of humour, joked that soon the name of the forest near their home would be dubbed the 'National Socialist Association of Trees'. Wolf noted, 'The Nazis never referred to themselves as Nazis but as National Socialists [*Nationalsozialisten*], NS for short. Motorists for example, were organised into the NSKK (*NS Kraftfahr Korps* – NS Power Vehicle Corps). Popularly, NSKK stood for '*Nur Säufer, Keine Kämpfer* [Only boozers, no fighters]'.

In August 1938, a couple of months after Wolf's tenth birthday, Hitler closed the public schools to the '*Nichtarier*' [non-Aryan] prompting Wolf's parents – at long last – to send him to a progressive school for non-Aryan children, the *Goldschmidtschule* in Berlin-Grunewald. During Wolf's short stay, the school operated out of its main building in Hohenzollendamm, formerly the mansion of the steel baron Hugo Stinnes, who had fallen foul of the *Führer*, and a subsidiary building nearby in the Kronberger-Strasse. Other houses were also acquired, one of which was later given to General Erwin Rommel, the Desert Fox. Today there is a memorial plaque on the wall of an upscale Greek restaurant that now occupies the site. It ends with the words '1939 *wurde die Schule durch die Nationalsozialisten geschlossen* [In 1939 the school was closed by the National Socialists].'[19] For the first time, Wolf found relief from his tormenters. He remembers being radiantly happy, if only for six months, until the Nazis closed the school and he was sent out of the country to England. Dr Leonore Goldschmidt (not to be confused with the great feminist Henriette Goldschmidt, 1825–1920) founded the Berlin school in 1934 for Jewish boys and girls in an apartment building. Like Stoatley Rough, this school forbade corporal punishment and did not tolerate abuse or fighting among the children. Male and female teachers conducted the co-ed classes in a relaxed environment, free of Nazi propaganda. Wolf studied English, natural science, history, music, handicraft and other conventional subjects that had been the fare of a pre-1933 German *Gymnasium* [secondary schools for boys]. Wolf learned for the first time about Judaism and sang Zionist songs.[20]

Wolf recalled that the Nazis classified one of the teachers at the Goldschmidt School as a *Mischling*, the Nazi term for the offspring of a mixed Jewish/Christian couple. 'Herr Lennert, my teacher [*Klassenlehrer*] at the *Goldschmidtschule* in Berlin was a *"Mischling"*. The Nazis decided he was too "Aryan" to teach in a Jewish school and too "non-Aryan" to teach in a public school. They solved his employment problem by drafting him into the Army. While he was fighting for the Führer, his fiancée, also a teacher at the *Goldschmidtschule*, was deported and murdered. He fought at Stalingrad and was never heard from again.'

On the night of 5 November, *Kristallnacht*, the sanctioned act of destruction and terror designed to intimidate the Jews of Germany, Wolf's grandmother's maid rushed to pound on the door of their apartment – the synagogue next to her house was burning to the ground. Wolf's father hastily packed and hid out with Aryan friends for a few days. It did not stop the Nazi thugs from repeatedly coming to their apartment and even striking his mother, once giving her a concussion. After *Kristallnacht*, the Edelsteins made plans to leave Germany. A distant cousin in England named Adolf Elston, (née Edelstein) agreed to pay for Wolf and Gerd's schooling and transport, and Dr Emmy Wolff arranged for them to enter Stoatley Rough. 'Adolf Elston's father was the brother of my great grandfather Gustav Edelstein, born in 1833, who moved to the north of England to start a wool business, and became a British subject. His story has an interesting twist. In World War I, Adolf joined the Royal Artillery, rose to the rank of major, and changed his last name to Elston. The name Edelstein was deemed too German for an officer on His Majesty's Service. That was the time when the royal house of Hannover-Sachsen-Coburg-Gotha became the House of Windsor and the Battenbergs became Mountbattens. I'm very grateful to Adolf Elston; I don't think Gerd, I or our parents would have survived if he and his mother had not paid our fees. I met him only once, shortly after arrival in England. I remember a portly gentleman in a double-breasted suit sitting in an alcove of the Sitting Room. He patted me on the head and told me to be a good boy.'[21]

It took Wolf's parents two years to make their way to America through unoccupied France, Spain and Portugal. 'To get out of Germany and to the United States, a person had to find someone who would guarantee the US Government by affidavit, $2,000 per person, equivalent today to about $40,000. The money had to be available, but was never, in fact, required. My parents got out via the wealthy financier member of the American Warburg family.[22] Acquiring a visa was a time-consuming, deliberately obscure process involving much paperwork and long lines. It was the official policy to impede and make it difficult for people to leave.' One official told Wolf's father that because Bettina Warburg had guaranteed so many visas already, his and his wife's could not be authentic. Wolf's father had the wit to appeal to the German's respect for the law, 'She signed a legal document, didn't she?' They got the visas. And then another German official did the family a great kindness. This time his father went to pick up a document stating they'd paid their taxes. The official slipped their paperwork to the bottom of the pile and issued a 'provisional' release which was enough for an exit permit. He said that he had orders to examine the file in detail and make as many difficulties as possible. He'd 'get to it in about a week' after Wolf's parents arrived in New York. After the war, the Edelsteins sent him Cooperative for American Remittances to Europe (CARE) packages.

Wolf arrived at Stoatley Rough late at night, 17 February 1939, and was put to bed in a room with several other little boys. In the morning, he woke to excited little voices. 'The first thing I heard when I awoke was the sound of boys yelling, "*Der Neue is da*!" [The new guy is here!] followed by a barrage of pillows. I returned fire, which made me part of the gang.' He had a great time with all the cheering, pillows flying, sheets tangling and blankets flung aside until a big girl rushed into the room and stopped the fun. Just days after such a spectacular welcome, Wolf was walking down Farnham Lane, happy to be heading into town to buy some penny candies. He passed Thursley Copse along the way, travelled about a mile, then turned left on the road that led past the railroad station and into the main street of town. The sun made the day unseasonably warm and as he marched along, looking forward to his candy, out of nowhere a sense of joy settled on his shoulders, enveloping him with warmth and hope. He was happy. He knew he was not going to be picked on again. He knew he should be homesick but he was not. He was exactly where he should be.

The swimming pool

Wolf and Martin and other boys in Wolf's dormitory soon became good friends. One mid-day they were having their main meal in the dining room when an exciting rumour circulated around the room. There was to be a swimming pool built on the property. A father of one of the few non-Jewish pupils at the school, a Mr Pniower, in England for the summer, knew how it could be done without spending large sums of money. (Mr Pniower would become Professor of Horticulture at the University of Berlin by 1948, in charge of restoring the *Berliner Tiergarten*.) All the bigger children would have to work hard to make the pool a reality. Wolf was thrilled. At last he could use his *Freischwimmen* [freestyle] certificate. Two summers earlier, he had practised endlessly in order to be allowed into the deep end of the local public pool near his home. He was crushed when they told him that being Jewish, not only could he not take the test, he was not going to be allowed into the pool any more. Luckily that summer his family went to a resort in the Italian Dolomites where Wolf had the chance to earn the certificate. He had carefully packed it in his suitcase on the chance he might need it in England, and here was the opportunity he had dreamt of. After he had finished eating, Wolf raced up to his room, dug the certificate out of his mess of books and papers, then ran around the house until he found Miss Astfalck, who looked at it, remarked what a nice certificate it was, and turned to another child clamouring for her attention.

Mr Pniower's plans placed the pool along the fresh water stream in the rear of the farm at the bottom of the property. The bigger boys and adults would dig out the large cavity and then line its walls with bundles of woven willow canes. It was an ancient technique (and one still used today to prevent erosion or to build temporary bridging by the military). It was backbreaking work. As the older ones toiled, the smaller children helped by hauling away the shovelfuls of the earth from the growing excavation or toted large bundles of rushes on their backs.

Dr Lion, accompanied by Dr Wolff, made the steep walk down the path to watch the progress of the construction. Her smile faded when she

discovered that the bigger boys were not working hard enough! Some
boys were talking off to one side, one even allowing a small boy to wield
his shovel. The two administrators were struck by what they perceived
as a very poor attitude toward the work. What business did those boys
have slinking away on long breaks while much younger children stayed at
the task? The two women made the steep climb back up to the main
house, feathers badly ruffled. Dr Lion was so disturbed that she wrote
about the problem in her *Rundbrief* [Round robin letter] of May in 1939,
stating that the older boys 'found it troublesome', to work, while the
younger ones, worked 'cheerfully'. She had a theory about these lazy
fellows, and she herself fell into the trap of eugenics at the time that
claimed in scientific terms that there were distinguishing characteristics
within each 'race' that could be classified, nailed down and documented.
Being Jews, Dr Lion decided, meant that these boys just had no flair for
manual labour (unaware that teenagers the world over will look to avoid
hard work whenever possible). She declared that their Jewishness
negatively influenced their work habits. 'As far as the non-Aryan boys are
concerned [she never used "Jewish" – it was always "non-Aryan"], going
back to the land ... presents a very difficult problem, because they have
*neither the right physiological nor right psychological attitude, nor
aptitude* [italics added] to enjoy the blessing of the earth.' She continued.
'Calculating and adding up is popular [with them].' She then said that
these boys avoided 'theoretical knowledge via books and other possible
opportunities ... [and they lacked] intellectual education and work
technique. Just these short-comings are also very obvious in school
children who today come from the German schools ... [there was an]
inability to do something for themselves with initiative and so to speak,
help themselves.' Strong words from the head of a school dedicated to
helping Jewish children to cope in a new country. It seems that in 1939,
Dr Lion was just fed up with a few of her teenaged boys, one of whom
perhaps had been rude to her. 'Very few boys get beyond their stamp
collection in their free time and few are impressed by the fairytale-like
gardens or the surrounding heath, impressions which could remain with
them all their lives.... The harmless enjoyment of discovering or inventing
something is often missing.' Dr Lion closed her diatribe by assuring her
readers that 'these defects were discussed at a Teachers Conference'.²³

Where did all this anger come from? In 1939, Dr Lion's school was
bulging at the seams. So many children were arriving. How would she
find the means to feed and house them? Perhaps her outburst had more

to do with stress than any deep-seated prejudices against Jewish teenaged boys. Wolf said in her defence that, 'There is evidence that Dr Lion mellowed after the war. A couple of my friends described her as motherly, which certainly was not the impression she gave in our day. In May 1939, Dr Lion was under great stress – besieged by desperate parents wanting to bring their children to safety. Perhaps the uncharacteristic rant at the time of the swimming pool dig shows that her nerves were giving way. I wouldn't blame her if they did.'24 Her *Rundbrief* written shortly after that incident was the only time Dr Lion expressed anything but comforting and encouraging words about her school.

When the pool was finished, Mr Pniower routed the little brook through it; it filled with clear cold water, and the children gleefully took to it like the proverbial ducks. The pool was such a success that Dr Lion decided to commemorate it, along with the school's summer holiday closing that year, with a gala Speech Day, just like the ones held in the best British private schools with their academic processions and awarding of prizes. Plans for a Speech Day at Stoatley Rough were drawn up, invitations were sent out, and the Household Girls (pupils on a special course) worked in the kitchen to prepare special treats. Someone with connections on the Board even arranged for a movie star to attend the ceremony, the blonde Elizabeth Bergner, lately of Berlin, who had been nominated for a Best Actress Oscar for her work in the British romantic drama *Escape Me Never* (1935). A Jewish refugee herself, the beautiful Miss Bergner went on to Hollywood, but never achieved the fame she had enjoyed in Germany and Great Britain.

A few days before the festival, a ten-year-old boy in the little German town of Bad Salzuflen, a mineral springs resort in northern Germany, was bidding farewell to his parents. Hans Obermeyer (nicknamed Obo by the boys and later, the Ginger Nipper by Mr Phillips) was an easygoing, red-headed boy with pale skin, a mouth always ready with a quip, a sturdy body and a level gaze. He loved a good joke and always had an arsenal of them at the ready. His father was the wealthy owner of a large hardware store that also sold milling machinery. Obo's house was the largest in the neighbourhood. When his mother packed his trunk, she filled it with more than enough clothing, books and toys for two boys, and even managed to ship his bike with him. Like many others who came to Stoatley Rough School, Obo was destined to travel by way of the *Kindertransport* [Children's Transport], a humanitarian programme that sent Jewish children to safety in England (a programme that would bring many of the Stoatley Rough population) that operated between December 1938 and September 1939. Among the nations of the world, Britain was the only one to agree to accept 10,000 children.[25]

Obo's family had lived in Bad Salzuflen for generations, as far back as the seventeenth century, and was highly respected in the community. 'The town was famous for its health spas and people would come from all over Germany to take the cure for digestive ailments and drink the nasty tasting and smelly waters which came from the salt wells in the ground. The town had a beautiful park with flowerbeds and trees and a lake with ducks, swans and rowboats', where Obo sailed his toy sailboat. Summers were pleasurable times, with candlelight festivals, concerts in the park with an orchestra or brass band that played every afternoon during the season. Obo had many friends in school, a few of whom were Jewish. Like other children in their first year of school, he had been proud to take the Horn of Plenty filled with candy for the others in his class. He attended the synagogue for religious instruction once a week. He received a beautiful bike for his eighth birthday in 1936, well into the era of Nazi consolidation of power, and then disaster struck. 'One day, a bunch of kids came running towards me shouting, "We hate you, you dirty Jew" pushing me to the ground, bending the wheels of my bike and making my knees and hands bloody. They then ran away laughing. I was crying and pushed my broken bike home and my mother comforted me as best as she could and called my father home. I asked them why this had happened and why they called me a dirty Jew? They explained to me that there were certain people in Germany who were suspicious of other people who were different from them because they believed in a different religion and that these "different" people were out to harm them and take away their possessions.'[26]

Obo's father was arrested during *Kristallnacht* and held in prison for several weeks. Obo was no longer allowed to attend his regular school, and his father had to sell his business at a loss. (Later, it was the Obermeyer home into which all the Jews in town were forced to move, crammed into every available room, closet and hallway, until they could be deported.) Up until 1938, Obo's parents had believed that the anger and persecution would pass. After *Kristallnacht*, they realised it was time to leave Germany.

Obo left for good on 4 July 1939, secure in his parents' promise to meet him in England as soon as they could leave Germany. His father took him to the train but his mother remained at home, unable to watch her boy actually board the train.

The school's secretary, Herta Lewent, met Obo at the Liverpool Street Station and took him straight to her parents' tiny flat in Hampstead. To make him feel welcome, she gave him Erich Kästner's *Emil und die Detektive*, a book which Obo probably knew well. Every German-speaking boy over eight, in 1939, knew this classic tale about a little boy who solved crimes, one of them even aboard a train.[27] The following Sunday, Herta gathered up Obo, his new book, his bike and his belongings, and together they boarded the train to Haslemere. It was the day of the Festival, Stoatley Rough's own Speech Day.

That morning, the children had been allowed to sleep until 8 a.m. Miss Graetz with the help of Putti Kassel and other pupils set up an exhibit of the children's art in the main house. At 3 p.m., the party began. First, the view of the exhibit was launched, followed by a performance of the children's choir, accompanied by Felix Schiller on the piano. The children then took up their various violins, recorders, flutes, triangles, kazoos, cuckoo clock and a bubbling water pipe (to represent the sound of a nightingale) and played their tongue-in-cheek performance of Haydn's *Toy Symphony*.[28] Accomplished musicians among the pupils carried the melody while other children chirped, burbled, pinged and rat-tat-tatted their parts. Wolf and a few of the boys lurked at the sidelines. Wolf did not think the performance was all that special, not the least because Dr Leven, who had arrived recently from Berlin to teach music, had kicked him out of the group just days earlier for being unable to keep to the rhythm. She had even asked him to stay away for this part of the festival. Miffed at the shabby treatment he felt Dr Leven had unjustly given him, Wolf stole upstairs to the second floor of the main house. He planned to deposit fake love notes under the pillows of some of the girls.

The party was in full swing. Three hundred distinguished guests, staff and children crowded the house, terrace and grounds. Obo must have been comforted to hear the familiar sound of German. Hardly anybody would have been speaking English except for the well-meaning British Committee members. When Elizabeth Bergner arrived to great fanfare, it was time for the academic awards. Elizabeth Bergner announced her gifts to the school: a pony and a ping-pong table, the latter, Dr Lion noted in one of her reports a few months later, 'used almost day and night'. Young Putti described Miss Bergner. 'She had blonde hair, a turquoise blue suit, a wine red blouse, gloves of leather and very nice shoes of the same colour as the gloves. Her fingers were of a different red. She enjoyed herself and acted naturally and sang all the German songs with us.'[29]

One of the Household Girls helped Obo take his suitcase and trunk up the stairs to Lookout, the dormitory/classroom (that later doubled as a dining room) on the third floor of the main building where Wolf and the other little boys slept. Obo recalls that it was the same spot 'where we later observed the dogfights between the Luftwaffe's Me 109 Messerschmitts and the RAF's Spitfires and Hurricanes as they were chasing each other through the valley below'. Freshened up, Obo walked downstairs and went out to the terrace. By then the whole assemblage was winding its way down the steep path to view the new swimming pool, resplendent in the waning sun, led by Susi Horn playing the accordion, followed by the children walking in twos, followed by the adults. At the pool, Miss Astfalck led some of the children in a folk dance.

At some point, either while the guests were still at the poolside, or after they had returned for refreshments – history is silent on this detail – Obo was still hanging around the main house trying to fit in, trying to find children his own age. He fatally struck up a conversation with the wrong girl. Ilse Bayer, unbeknownst to Obo, was two years older and a bully. She soon challenged Obo as to who was the stronger and they started to argue the point. Obo was determined to prove his manhood. Before he knew what was happening, he ended up in a struggle with Ilse on the terrace floor, thrashing about to get the upper hand in a fierce wrestling match. 'I think I was probably a little eager to establish myself as some macho kid which in retrospect I certainly wasn't then or now. She put some kind of headlock on me. I'm sure there were plenty of witnesses but I think Miss Astfalck broke it up pretty quickly.'[30]

Wolf saw the whole thing. 'Obo, your fight with Ilse Bayer did indeed have many witnesses; I watched from the second story window. As to what may have caused it: at one of the reunions, Ilse's older sister Ruth referred to Ilse as "a real tomboy in those days". I remember Ilse as having had a short fuse. About the time of your fight, when the girls were not in their dorm, a bunch of us boys snuck in and left fake anonymous love notes under their pillows.' As Miss Astfalck restored order on the terrace, Wolf finished his covert mission. 'Ilse correctly identified me as the author of her note and exploded in cold fury. She didn't hit me, though.'

And so it was, with much fanfare and possibly a bloody nose, ten-year-old Hans Obermeyer arrived at Stoatley Rough. Soon Obo, Wolf and Martin, along with other ten- and eleven-year-olds, were spending many hours every day that summer in the swimming pool, playing ping-pong or tramping around on the heath across the road. They knew that

war loomed ever closer on the horizon, just across the English Channel.
Yet they lived in a bubble of hope, protected by the kindness of their
caretakers and the innocence of their youth.

The calm before the storm

During the summer of 1939, the children at Stoatley Rough coped
with the discomforts of overcrowding, continually being forced to swap
rooms as others came and went. There was worrisome news on the
radio that told of the Rome–Berlin Axis (May), the German occupation
of Czechoslovakia (June) and Germany's move to close down all
Jewish businesses (July). The younger children like Martin, Wolf and
Obo swam, hiked, went scouting and visited the Haslemere Museum
to inspect its doll's house, the miniature furniture for sale, a 'poor moth-
eaten bear, the huge crab spider and of course, the mummy's exposed
toes'.[31] Martin's first encounter with the mummy had the unexpected
consequence of giving him nightmares. Visions of those desiccated, black
knobs haunted him for weeks.

Dr Lion not only educated her young charges, she also had to think
about preparing her older pupils for the day they would leave the school,
especially those who might not have parents to come to pick them up.
She had a long-standing policy of supplementing classroom studies
with guest lectures and many of them featured work available overseas.
In addition, there were plenty of evening activities for all but the smallest
of the children. Of particular interest were the nights when the school's
own Emmy Wolff read to the older pupils. Sometimes the children would
darn stockings or work on a sewing or knitting project as they sat around
the Music Room, a fire crackling in the fireplace, as she brought to life
various pieces of literature. Everyone listened aptly to her deep expressive
voice. During the winter of 1939, shortly after it was published, she read
Lotte in Weimer by Thomas Mann, a novelistic biography of Goethe
and the nature of genius, a subject dear to her heart. Dr Lion was present,
sitting and smiling as her friend's voice, filled with emotion, rendered
Mann's articulation of various political points of view through Charlotte,
the fictional lover of Goethe.

Dr Lion also tried to satisfy the practical needs of her older pupils.
She arranged for a 'Commissioner and Captain of Guides' to take a few
groups on weekly expeditions with the objective of developing their

powers of observation. 'This experiment is being made with the object of extending it to refugee children generally, as part of their training for life overseas.'[32] Indeed, in March 1939, seven of her pupils left the school to live in New Zealand, Australia, Brazil, Palestine and the United States. Other lectures at the school that year covered Syria, Iraq, South America, North America, India and Iran, along with such practical topics as kindergarten work, gardening, unemployment, Quakerism, country school homes and settlement work.

Dr Lion had hired a Mr S. Corfield as farm instructor who would oversee the ten or eleven boys who now lived in the new farmhouse that had been built with the assistance of a grant from the local Erla Balwin Fund. A poultry farm donated 100 fertile eggs. New students in 1939 boosted the residency level to '100 people, ninety of them pupils, farm students and domestic science students'.[33]

Dr Lion found it difficult to find sponsors for her children for the few weeks she needed to close the school that summer. It was too dangerous for children to return to Germany, and she wrote in one of her reports, that if they went to an English home, most 'came back too early'. Some parents came to collect their children for short vacations, but she worried about the 'fifty persons whose nearest relatives, father and mother are still in Germany'. There was a strange air of unreality, of blithe freedom for the children at Stoatley Rough that summer, while on the Continent, momentum toward war was accelerating.

Dr Lion rose to the occasion and defying any unwelcome thoughts of foreboding that might sneak into her school, took sixteen of the older children for an outing in London. Dr Wolff and two other adults also chaperoned. Their three-day excursion included the Science Museum (where the group was treated to a lecture on mineralogy, followed by a picnic), Victoria and Albert Museum, an open-air performance of *Twelfth Night* in Regent's Park, Westminster Abbey, the National Gallery, the Tower and St. Paul's Cathedral. Renate Dorpalen wrote, 'The last pre-war days at Stoatley Rough continued in their established rhythm of education, domestic life and recreational activities…. The magnificent weather of that summer was in perfect harmony with the bucolic, peaceful, life in Haslemere, though it was the calm before the storm. Those few months allowed me a glimpse of the school's rich, broad educational programme of didactic and applied teaching. The musical and theatrical performances, the visiting lecturers from all walks of life, the imaginatively planned festivals, and the visits to near and far places for cultural exchange were only some of the events to manifest the school's aims. Such excellence was never to be reached again.'[34]

There were no outings for young boys like Wolf, Martin and Obo. But as they whiled away the long summer hours, they invented a game that would absorb their attention for years. They called it 'The Lands'. Using plots 5 × 12 feet (1.52 × 3.66 metres) given to them next to the path that led down to the Farmhouse, each boy created his own imaginary country complete with castles, roads, armies, kings and subjects where they played for protracted sessions, manoeuvring toy soldiers, tanks and trucks, negotiating peace treaties, going to war and arranging for a real life 'protector' among the bigger boys. 'Boys would build roads, forts, castles and decorate with treelike plants. The whole project took on a somewhat military character. Boys would bring their toy cars, matches to act as men, small plants for camouflage. It was a matter of pride if the layout was particularly attractive or if a road had been built that could withstand someone's weight. Competition arose very early and with it, alliances. Pacts were drawn up, cooperative helping arrangements worked out and, as these progressed, the boys developed rules which governed the privacy of one's lands and it's defences. With all the play and the fun and the planning provided by these "lands", there was always a note of a war footing reflective of the atmosphere in which we were finding ourselves.... The owners gave themselves names of kings or emperors who, in turn, sought the advice of the next older group, which included me. We, the older boys, then became someone's prime minister, so you had the younger boys planning and plotting as well as the older ones. There were frequent conferences between these officials. These relationships, too, provided identity and for the younger boys, a big brother.'[35]

Obo called his Land Acropolis. 'We built buildings such as underground garages or defence buildings to house large armies of wooden soldiers which consisted of hundreds of used matchsticks painted with the national colours of each land. Most of us had some type of model cars, trucks or military vehicles which were mostly British made by Dinkey Toys or brought from Germany or Austria. Peter Rosenthal and Wolf Elston had a large assembly of German warship models and land vehicles. Needless to say they had to fight many wars to gain additional territory. Some made non-aggression pacts or alliances of two lands threatening to invade a third one. They printed their own money which allowed us to purchase things from each other. I remember spending many hours on my land during the darkest days of the war, probably in 1941, and I think we all acted out many fantasies as rulers of our lands.'[36]

Wolf said, 'In fact, we talked a lot and built very little, but that was not the point. Here we were no longer helpless refugees from terror: we were powerful rulers whose words were law in mighty states. Our fantasies allowed us to cope with grimmer realities.' A boy who joined the little gang of friends later in the year, Peter Gaupp, wrote in his diary, 'I think that my nicest thing here at Stoatley Rough is my Land. I have below the garden and, behind a fence, a piece of earth under a tree and there I build castles surrounded by towers (however, everything is made of sand, unfortunately!!)' Peter's older brother Dieter once found a dead bird which he buried on his plot, lined the grave with leaves, and called it 'Birdland'. Another boy, Hans Kornberg, wrote about his propaganda minister, W. F. Kerno, and his vice-emperor for *The Bridge*, a news-sheet the school published on two occasions during the war. (*The Bridge* was chock-full of stories of school life, short fictional pieces written by the children, staff and alumni, liberally illustrated with sketches.) In Hans's article, he not only abolished the League of Nations, but listed the imaginative names of the territories owned by himself, Martin and Wolf in the school magazine: '*Eratoquie*' [no translation], '*Rotgraben*' [Red Ditch] and '*Gelbbergen*' [Yellow Mountain].

Every summer since the school's founding it had held a German–English cultural exchange event. Although events on the Continent were heating up, the summer exchange of 1939 took place for the last time until the end of the war. Great Britain declared war on Germany on 3 September 1939, ending for good the halcyon days of Stoatley Rough. Mail services were disrupted, the Red Cross had not yet fully developed its messaging service and the children could only wonder what was happening to their parents. Now overcrowded and facing six years of rationing, the school would take an uncharted and sombre new direction.

Chapter 2

In the Beginning

Dr Lion slumped back in her chair. She sat at a small desk in her room
at the University Club. It was early 1934, and she had been in England
only a few weeks. She sighed. Building a school from scratch involved
so many things: facility, curriculum, supplies, pupils and staff. She sat
up straight. She had to prioritise. The first-order business was to acquire
staff. The Committee had agreed that German speakers would ease the
children's transition. She played with a strand of coarse grey hair that
had come loose from her bun. She knew she would need a curriculum but
that could come later. First, she needed a matron. Having little experience
with children, Dr Lion had no idea what they did for amusement or what
thoughts went through their little heads, but she knew a matron would
take charge of the children's health, listen to their problems and, of course,
keep them in line. She did not have to worry about this particular task,
because she knew just the person for the job, Eleonore Astfalck, a former
student at the *Jugendheim Charlottenburg* who had joined the teaching
staff after her graduation. Nore was a down-to-earth woman, a tireless
worker and someone who understood children. Nore was not Jewish, but
Dr Lion recalled that she had had some trouble with the Nazis recently –
she might be interested in getting out of Germany for a while. She wrote
to Nore outlining the job.

Dr Lion wished that the elegant Dr Emmy Wolff were at her side and
not in Berlin. After her few weeks in England, Dr Lion was profoundly
lonely, always feeling out of place at the fancy parties the wealthy benefactors kept throwing. She was homesick. And she missed Emmy. Emmy
was as neat and focused as (Hilde had to admit) she, herself, was
disorganised. She missed Emmy with her proud bearing and lovely
brown eyes that sometimes, when she was caught off guard, reflected
a private inner sorrow. Emmy knew what it was like to struggle in a
man's world when education and privilege were not enough. Dr Lion
missed their long talks about women's rights when they had lived
together. Dr Emmy Wolff might need to be rescued from the vile place
Berlin had become, where she was being forced to submit her articles for
Die Frau, a leading women's magazine, under her mother's maiden name,
Fleiss. How long would that last? The Nazis would discover her game

soon enough. Nothing escaped their attention. Dr Wolff would enjoy England, and from Dr Lion's point of view, she would be not only invaluable in planning the curriculum but would serve magnificently as a teacher of German and French literature and art appreciation. The Committee would love her. They had already approved bringing her over. Dr Lion pulled out another sheet of stationery and wrote to dear Emmy. When would she join her?

Dr Lion made herself a cup of tea on the small gas burner in her room, poured in a generous helping of sugar and milk, then settled down in the flat's threadbare armchair to read the brochure Miss Bracey and Miss Fearon had drafted. Her lips moved as she read the English words 'dedicated to helping German children to prepare for an English education; provide a sound education for children of all walks of life, denominations and nationalities; develop in its pupils' character … responsible and useful citizens wherever they may be, etc. etc.'. All well and good, but the real challenge was the English. The school needed a native English speaker. She would have to find someone not only academically proficient but also willing to live with the children after lights out and take on all sorts of extracurricular jobs. Since it was the Depression, she hoped there would be plenty of candidates.

Oh, look at the time! In an hour she was to meet Bertha Bracey for high tea. The Quaker activist had come up with one immediate solution to the crucial need for English language instruction: the well-off friends of the Committee and Council members who wanted to 'do something' would come to the school to conduct crash vocabulary training for the newcomers. Leave it to Miss Bracey to get things done. Dr Lion took a last sip of tea before depositing her cup in the small sink. She mused about the fact that there was no money for a cook or cleaning staff at the school. Thankfully, everyone had already agreed that the resident staff would share in the cooking and the children would help with the cleaning. She hoped the brochure would do its job in finding pupils. Even now, news of the school was circulating in Berlin and other large cities in Germany and Austria. She sighed again. If only Emmy would agree to come to England, she would have a friend at hand. Speaking English all the time was beginning to take its toll, even if she prided herself on her stamina. All those well-meaning women and men leaning in when she spoke, as if calling attention to her German accent, but too polite to ask her to repeat herself.

A week later, Nore's reply arrived. She would take the job but on one condition: the school must also hire her friend, Johanna Nacken. Dr Lion was not surprised. She was pleased in fact, that she was getting two hard-working, fair-minded women who would bring tremendous value to her staff. Hanna was an old friend of Dr Lion's, still working at the *Jugendheim* as a crafts teacher, and like Nore, she was a sister feminist. Dr Lion had even travelled with Emmy and Hanna to feminist rallies back when they were first at the Youth Home.

She put down Nore's letter and rubbed her eyes. She probably needed reading glasses. So much to do. She knew her instincts had been correct in selecting Nore for the critical post. Now, she had not only a new matron but, in the bargain, a new crafts and shop teacher. She yawned. Time to get ready for bed. Dr Lion moved to put her papers away in the desk. She may not have thought at the time of the importance of her decision to hire Nore. But if Dr Lion was to be the head of the school, Eleonore Astfalck would be its heart.

Everybody's substitute parent

The snow reflecting the alpine sun was blinding. Nore was about to hike up the mountain, skis on her shoulder, for the downhill race when Dr Lion's letter arrived, forwarded from Berlin. She put down her equipment and read Dr Lion's offer with interest. The job would mean a lot of work and virtually no pay. Dr Lion was careful to point out that Nore would only earn £2 per month under Britain's stringent conditions of immigration. Nore weighed her options. Since the Gestapo wanted to see her when she returned to Berlin, a move to England was a convenient way of staying out of sight until things cooled down. The Nazis would not be in power forever. She re-read the letter. She liked the idea of working with needy, homeless children.

One of the school's first professional English teachers on site, Margaret [Dove] Faulkner, described Nore as 'short, slender and dynamic ... everybody's substitute parent'. Eleonore Astfalck would become indispensable to Dr Lion in her ability to soothe, to make the children think that work was a game and to inspire them to set high standards for themselves. Nore was one of those rare people whose compassion was almost palpable. Growing up in Nuremberg with her two older brothers, Nore had been a busy little mother, so concerned for the welfare of others that she sometimes brought dirty, impoverished children up to her family's apartment for something to eat. When she was eight, she told her parents that she wanted to marry a criminal because 'when you love a person, then you love him even if he is a criminal'.[1] Classified as pure Aryans, Nore and Hanna should have had nothing to fear from the Nazi regime. But even the most casual association with the 'wrong' element of society in those days could have ruinous consequences. Nore's job in Berlin had involved running classes for out-of-work young men aged eighteen to twenty-five. She held afternoon and evening workshops teaching money-making skills useful in the Depression such as building a bird cage, crafting small pieces of furniture, putting together artificial flowers and learning the book-binding trade. Several of the men belonged to the Communist Party. One night, a Nazi thug shot at a couple of them working late through one of the windows of her *Jugendheim* social services centre, and shortly thereafter, someone broke into her office and stole her records. One book held incriminating details about the men, an association that made Nore look like a sympathiser. When she learned that the Nazis wanted to question her, Nore signed on to accompany the wealthy Strauss family to Switzerland.

Nore arrived in England first. (Hanna had to concoct an excuse to leave the *Jugendheim* before she could safely leave the country.) Hopping out of the car fresh from the train station, Nore tried out her halting English on the first person she met at Stoatley Rough, the Cockney gardener, Mr Phillips. Neither could understand the other. When Hanna arrived a few weeks later, she and Mr Phillips had no trouble launching into a lively exchange. Hanna had lived in Canada as an au pair and had the best English of the three German women at the school. The dour Mr Phillips later declared that Hanna Nacken was the only sensible person in the house and they became great friends. The Committee soon drafted Hanna into helping with the bookkeeping. It had not taken them long to realise Dr Lion was hopeless with money matters. She could be a bulldog collecting fees and tuitions or scrounging for a free medical examination for one of her children, but she was incapable of keeping proper records. Hanna agreed to take the job on a temporary basis until a permanent bookkeeper could be found. Six years later, she was still at it. One of the trustees wrote she needed to stay on, 'given Dr Lion's whimsical approach to fiscal management', and that Hanna was 'very sound on financial principles'. He kindly added (and one hopes she read his report) that she was 'entirely unselfish of herself'.[2]

Eleonore Astfalck's background in child development was impressive. She studied at the *Jugendheim* in Berlin in 1919, six years ahead of Hilde Lion, until she ran out of money. Nore returned to the institution in 1923 and, by 1929, had become one of its instructors. By then she had built an outstanding practical background in household management and child care, having participated in a work/student programme in Augsburg and, later, in a *Kinderheim* [children's home] for problem children in Rodaun, Austria, near Vienna. In a place where police sometimes brought in abused and neglected children, Nore managed the traumatised and unruly children without hurting them. 'It was then only natural that children were punished and even spanked quite hard. So in the beginning, to work in this house was very difficult, as the children would not believe that they could have a grown-up who would not spank them.'[3] The evidence of poverty moved her. 'We had children who were criminals and bed-wetters and children who had never met their parents, although they lived quite nearby.'[4] She never forgot the occasion when two gypsy children were deposited at the school, full of fleas. She said that the children were sewn into their clothes and that their parents never returned for them. There would be no corporal punishment anywhere the compassionate Nore worked.

Nore and Hanna began the task of converting the manor into a residential school. The house had been filled with knick-knacks from the Vernons's travels to India and China. Nore said that there were more than 120 precious objects that had to be packed up. Stoatley Rough was well suited to the needs of a boarding facility with its three storeys and large rooms. One entered the house from a small parking area off Farnham Lane. Leaded windows adorned a small vestibule. A few steps up and the visitor would be in the 212-square foot (20-square metre) 'Sitting Room', splendid with woodblock floors and a magnificent green-tiled William Morris fireplace. Just outside the large bay windows, the panoramic view of the verdant South Downs stunned every first visitor. A large flagstone terrace ran the length of the house, where children would gather in the years to come to sew, read, sort berries, talk or study and, on Saturday afternoons, consume hot cocoa. There were fireplaces in most rooms. Nore designated one of the larger rooms as a dorm for the anticipated small group of girls to arrive, smaller boys to go upstairs, while Nore and Hanna chose for themselves the room strategically located next to the main entrance to hear the comings and goings of little feet. At the other end of the ground storey towards the Phillips's 'Lodge' were the kitchen, the pantry, a sink and two toilets (one for teachers, located under the stairs, and one for boys, just off the kitchen). Staircases flanked each end of the house. A rear door off the kitchen led into an open courtyard, where young residents would soon be peeling the next day's lot of potatoes. A partial lower level carved into the hill at the front of the house held yet another large common room, boiler room, pantry and several stock rooms. This area eventually became an air-raid shelter.

The first storey had a large 'Music Room' with an even more magnificent view of the South Downs; several smaller rooms that were to become combination dormitories, classrooms and dining rooms; and a girl's bath, boy's bath, a boy's washroom and a girl's toilet. At the top, or the second storey, were four rooms with dormers, three overlooking the terrace and countryside and one containing a secret passage. Nore and Hanna found enough beds for the three residential adults and the few students who were expected in late spring, but they sent out word for donations of blankets, linens and other household items. Friends of the school duly delivered what was requested, and even more. Nore scrubbed the floors on her hands and knees and stocked the pantry, while Hanna brought out her carpentry tools and converted some old cupboards into wardrobes. (As the school grew, rollaway cots were purchased, which the pupils folded up and tucked behind curtains along the walls by day.) Dr Lion brought in carpenters to convert the stables at the far end of the gardener's house into a laundry room. Financial records of the spring of 1934 reveal expenses for 'sanitary closets' (either addition or repair), towels, blankets, mattresses, bedsteads, rabbits (!), an employment bureau fee for a cook, engine repairs, cutlery, cups, plates, pails, anthracite coal, a charwoman, 'medicaments', brooms, saucepans, gardener's wages, staff wages for Miss Ryecart (who would teach English) and Cook, stationery, postage, a year's worth of insurance (costing £1. 10s. for 'accident of the children') and food. The food was for five people: Dr Lion, Nore, Hanna and Mr and Mrs Phillips. In the next bill, the food item would cover thirteen.

The school opens its doors

Dr Lion moved from the University Women's Club in Chelsea into Stoatley Rough in the spring of 1934, after a brief recruiting trip to Germany.

Upon her return, she arranged for teachers of mathematics, rudimentary science and history to supplement the work of Miss Ryecart. Dr Lion also scheduled German-born Mrs List, a society lady who had given English lessons in Berlin to the brother of one of the future pupils and was now a member of the German–English circle in London. She would help teach English. The staff took turns in the kitchen, with Hanna Nacken designated to put the kettle on the stove in the morning. Mr Phillips was always up with the sun to keep her company. A local 'gardener's boy' kept the furnace stoked and the fireplaces replenished.

In April 1934, the school opened its doors. The founders had a sense of urgency; there were émigré children who needed lodging immediately. Committee member Miss Isabel Fry was elected to lead the school on a temporary basis. She was highly qualified owing to her prior experience as headmistress of two other experimental schools.[5] She wrote in her first report, 'The parents of some of these children have left Germany. One, a merchant, has gone to Africa with the rest of his family; another, who is a professor, has gone to India. One father, a younger man and a scholar, has lost all possibilities of earning anything at a university and does not know where to turn for employment of any kind. Some of the parents are still in Germany, but have to live under very changed standards of life.'[6] Seven German-speaking children comprised the first coterie of students: two small boys and five teenaged girls, recruited through the network of the Berlin Quakers and Dr Lion's former circle of friends and acquaintances at the Youth Home. The first girl, fifteen-year-old Gertrud Gans [Farnman], whose father, a dermatologist, had known Dr Lion in Berlin, arrived a month before the school opened and helped Nore and Hanna prepare the premises. Gertrud said later, the school was 'not what I thought it would be', perhaps expecting a traditional, English girl's boarding school. Yet she stayed for almost five years to become a much-loved mother figure to boys and girls. Gertrud briefly left the school in 1937, returned in mid-1938 and then left again to live in India with her new British officer husband and her parents, in 1939, just before the war broke out. (She and her husband later returned to England. In her nineties, she now lives in Limpstead, Sussex, not so very far from her first home in England.) The first boy to enter the school was Fritz Horkheimer [Fred Hawkes], who stayed exactly one year before emigrating to Kenya with his family. He later wrote to Dr Lion that at the ripe old age of nineteen, he had become an assistant manager of a coffee plantation, responsible for 1,500 workers and very happy with his lot.[7]

Other early pupils were Eva Feldmann, age unknown, who stayed until
1 November the following year. Ellen Isler, nineteen years old, arrived
in May and stayed for one year. Ayosdo and Alika Padolinsky, ages and
country of origin unknown (photographs show them to be around six
and seven), arrived on 10 May and stayed for one year and seven months.
Lotte Saul came in May, aged fourteen. It is not known when she left the
school. Lilian Chasanowich, whose age is unrecorded, only stayed for
three months, July through September, while Rosa Mazur [Hubner],
fifteen years old, arrived from Poland in August and stayed for two years.
Rounding out the enrolment up to December 1934, was Roswilla Looman,
who arrived in October 1934 and left in November 1935. (The pattern of
unpredictable, out-of-season arrivals and departures would characterise
the school through the war years, taxing the imagination and pluck of
its staff to maintain academic continuity.) News of the school spread
by word of mouth, through a modest lecture tour throughout Germany
by Dr Lion and through the work of the Quakers operating in Berlin.
By November of its first year, the number of residential pupils reached
eleven. At the end of the school year in the spring of 1935, Stoatley
Rough had an enrolment of thirty-six.

In the first two months of 1934, the pupils were given perfunctory
instruction, but most were there to learn English or to have a place to live
while their parents found a way out of their home countries. Volunteers
arrived from London and local environs to talk to the children. Dr Lion
decided to do some teaching of history and geography. She was more
comfortable with small children than with older ones but often talked
over the heads of the youngest. One little girl came away from a session,
believing that the Boer Wars involved Winston Churchill fighting wild
boars with a sword in the jungle. Everyone admired Dr Lion's intel-
lectualism, however, and enjoyed the company of the unpretentious
Headmistress.

Over the summer of 1934, almost everybody returned to the
Continent, giving the Committee the opportunity to focus on fund-
raising. The school needed to repay loans, however. The Committee
understood the problems in receiving full tuition from German families
since Nazi policies made it expensive to take money out of the country.
They decided to take advantage of the school's lovely locale. They would
turn the place into a vacation spot, a combination country inn and
cultural summer school with classes for children and adults. 'We are
expecting several holiday children and grown-ups to come from

Germany for a Summer School. They hope to meet English people here for a cordial exchange of views and for mutual practice in the two languages.'[8] The Committee used its connections to find scholars to lecture in both English and German. Eighteen German children came for the summer school in 1934, and forty-eight visitors attended for the entire six weeks. The Committee also implemented another money-making scheme in which they offered 'convalescence to specially chosen children from the East End of London. Pay by charity, ten shillings a week.'[9] The latter idea was short-lived. The (perhaps disingenuous) Committee's report of 10 November 1934, said, 'Re the future of the convalescent children – it is not too wise that too many East End children should be taken, as it is not fair for the German children to hear Cockney English.'[10] Meanwhile, the school also hosted 'a group of Germans living in London and one English guest'.[11] They came for 'the rest and the refreshment in the garden and the woods and especially … the fire-side talks in the evenings'.

The German–English cultural event raised local and London money by featuring music and literary readings from 28 July to 17 August. This cultural event became a tradition that would be repeated each summer until 1939, when it had to be suspended for the duration of the war. During the first summer exchange session, Dr Lion was introduced to Dr Luise Leven, holder of a doctorate in music, who had travelled from Berlin with an Aryan friend for the cultural exchange. Dr Lion was enchanted by this lively, dark-haired woman, so sure of herself, so full of confidence. The two women became friends. Dr Leven promised that she would return the following summer.

After one final event, recorded as a 'tea party' for a few dozen Haslemere residents, formal classes began in September. From the start, Stoatley Rough combined academics with healthy, outdoor extra-curricular activities, an approach rooted in the late-nineteenth-century progressive educational reform tradition of *Landerziehungsheime* [countryside educational homes]. Nore led the children every morning on a run down the path past the first tennis court to the second tennis court where she conducted calisthenics. Then it was back to breakfast and classes, with the main meal served at 1 p.m. Afternoons were for rest and homework but might include some sort of game or outing, music practise or crafts. Evening meals were informal and light.

Dr Lion's schedule was influenced by the work of the educationalists George Kerschensteiner (1854–1932) and Hermann Lietz (1868–1919), who introduced into Germany the idea of 'vocational' schools, an alternative to the traditional *Gymnasium* fare of classical languages, literature, mathematics and science, and the value of physical exercise and recreation, respectively. Indeed, these influences can be seen in the fact that all the children at Stoatley Rough were required to work at weekly chores such as dusting, setting the table, keeping the fireplaces filled with wood, doing laundry, and washing and drying dishes. They did gardening and later, when the school acquired livestock, cleaned the chicken coops and pigsty. On occasion, children helped to bring in crops. Far from being a formal school, Dr Lion's Stoatley Rough would offer a 'genial atmosphere of life in a happy, healthy environment'.

The school soon developed a pleasant, utopian quality. The Committee's first report, November 1934, waxed lyrical about children keeping Angora rabbits to use the wool for weaving and how each child spent a few hours at gardening, 'even the youngest ones had their own little plots'. It was cosy at Stoatley Rough, a family environment. The adults read aloud to the younger children after the evening meal as the older girls mended clothing or sewed. Literary fare included Sewells's *Black Beauty*, Kipling's *The Second Jungle Book* and Robert Louis Stevenson's *Travels with a Donkey*. The Committee was pleased with their 'community in which the children have their personal relationships so that no child feels itself [*sic*] a pupil only, but one of a community of real friends. Simple ethical reading before bedtime is meant to help these children to find their way and to clear their opinions about eternal truths.'[12]

Policies, symbols and a good first year

The formal school year began in September 1934, offering English language instruction, arithmetic, geography and nature studies. With so few children, Dr Lion had the time to plan for the larger enrolments that would materialise as the news of the school spread. What kind of a school would Stoatley Rough be? Was it to be a real school or just a safe haven? Unable to draw on tradition, history or established custom, Dr Lion and her Committee had to start from scratch, but they all shared certain firm ideals: communal work by staff and children, equality of the sexes, help for the smaller pupils by the larger ones and self-reliance. At a time when most private schools in England practised caning, perpetuated a rigid class system and tolerated anti-Semitic prejudices, the founders shared Dr Lion's belief in creating a school that would allow no corporal punishment whatsoever. It would be egalitarian. It would impart tolerance for difference. And it would be safe. Dr Lion may not have had experience with children, but she knew instinctively that they needed to feel safe. She wrote, memorably, that Stoatley Rough was a place 'where a child could grow up quietly'.

During their many planning sessions, the Committee and Dr Lion determined that Stoatley Rough would provide traditional education to children up to age sixteen, two years past the age required for government compulsory schools in England at the time. It was a logical decision since the school could not very well abandon otherwise homeless children younger than sixteen to fend for themselves. A thornier issue had to do with the higher level of academic preparation needed to enter a university. For such an objective, the pupil either had to do very well on the Cambridge School Certificate, a certificate of high-school completion, or had to take a stringent university entrance examination covering a wide range of subjects, informally known as the Matric (a 'matriculation examination'), which each university issued as its entrance examination. A Matric could be roughly compared with individualised scholastic aptitude tests (SATs) in the United States. Since funding was an issue, and the Committee sought accreditation and respectability, the Committee decided that advance preparation would be offered only to those 'deemed suitable'. The chance to sit for such an examination would be restricted to a few chosen ones. The Committee wrote that such a policy was good for everybody because it made sure that 'students [doing] intellectual work are not cut off from practical pursuits and the opposite is true for those engaged in practical or handicraft work'.[13]

Who was eligible for the Matric and who was not? The Committee did not know. They left that up to Dr Lion. She would judge a child's potential for higher learning. In hindsight, the Committee probably did not realise that it should have established criteria for eligibility for the Matric. They should not have left such a decision entirely up to Dr Lion's judgment. Dr Lion was a feminist social worker, not an educator of children. She had no background in elementary education or child development. With no criteria under which a child might understand his or her chances to prepare for the Matric, everything came down to Dr Lion's opinion, something she usually formed within minutes of a first meeting. She never changed her mind, either. (She even unconsciously rubbed salt into the wounds of those she judged unfit

43

for higher education by praising them with pronouncements, such as 'This is Inge, she's good with her hands.') Later, as the school filled with many impoverished but qualified children, those not chosen to be allowed to take the Matric took this judgment bitterly and felt discriminated against. Some could not help resenting Dr Lion's favourites, who were blessed with her clairvoyance as suitable candidates. They privately saw these children as teacher's pets. But in 1934, these problems were non-existent, undreamed of. The school had no candidates for the Matric then. It had five young ladies already finished with their education and two boys, nowhere near age sixteen. It all seemed workable.

During her first months on the job, Dr Lion set about establishing contacts with the Shottermill and Hindhead government schools and a few private schools (in Britain called 'public' schools) in the area and arranged to augment her meagre teaching staff with teaching volunteers and two paid instructors, the aforementioned Miss Reycart and Miss Postgate, who came several times a week to help the children learn English. Miss Hollick joined the teachers later in 1934. Part-time teachers Mr Owen and Col Hamilton were on the scene as instructors of mathematics and science. The latter, a retired officer and known as a kind gentleman, talked so loudly that when he gave lessons at one end of the school, people at the other end of the house could clearly follow his lecture through the open windows.

Dr Lion knew the importance of symbols. Someone – perhaps it was Dr Lion – designed an official emblem, a triangle enclosing three entwined circles representing Christianity, Judaism and Islam; the symbol said to derive from Gotthold Ehraim Lessing's play, *Nathan der Weise* [Nathan the Wise], one of the earliest pieces of literature to celebrate religious tolerance (1779). Lessing had expressed life as a pyramid (hence the triangle), the base of which represented the 'foundation broad and firm enough to let each person reach his or her fullest height, or potential'. Dr Lion, ever the intellectual, wrote in one of her many messages to the school's population about Goethe's subsequent use of the symbolic triangle when he wrote to the influential Swiss thinker, Lavater: '*Ich wünschte … Die Pyramide meines Daseins, deren Basis mir angegeben und gegründet ist, so hoch als möglich in die Luft zu spitzen*' [The pyramid of my existence, the basis of which is a given and well-grounded, I wished to point as high as possible into the air]. Dr Lion's allusion to Goethe reflects her passion for the power of ideas behind symbols. She knew the school needed its spiritual, non-religious base.

One day a package arrived by post, a 2-foot-tall (0.6-metre-tall), three-dimensional wooden signpost carved with the new emblem, showing in discs carved into the three-cornered piece bas-relief images of a girl reading, a girl at the kitchen range and a boy with a scythe. This hand-sculpted work of art had been created by the eminent German sculptor, Mr H. Nonnenmacher, who was living in exile with his Jewish wife in London. Mr Nonnenmacher was of such renown in Germany that the Nazis retaliated for his defection in 1934 by smashing his works from pedestals and branding his work 'degenerate'. The sculpted signpost was placed at the entrance of the school. Dr Lion later brought it inside to save it from the weather.

The Committee also endorsed a school uniform. Stoatley Rough could not begin to compete with well-endowed, established schools that housed upper-class English children such as the exclusive Royal School just down Farnham Lane. (Founded for daughters of naval officers in 1840 and still in operation today, it consistently rebuffed any formal contact whatsoever with Stoatley Rough.) But Stoatley Rough would have its own uniform. Dr Lion decided on simple navy skirt/trousers, white shirt and navy tie with silver stripes, to be worn on special occasions. 'These colours symbolise the dark skies of our time with – in spite of it all – the still existing silver lining on the horizon.' She knew uniforms would help to unify the student body in times when her ill-dressed assemblage came under public scrutiny. A uniform also served the significant goal of impressing the school's sponsors to whom she was ever attentive.

The school charter evolved. Various documents throughout the years show the school's changing identity. One letter to parents reflected the emphasis on the values of tolerance and strong character, e.g. 'The communal life of the boarding school will be shaped in such a way as to overcome the differences of creed, nationality and language. To achieve this aim, comradeship, initiative and self determined disciplined responsibility will be fostered.' One brochure stated the school's focus on English language and customs. Later the school was primarily a 'safe haven' from Nazi terror. After the war, the school was 'an international school'. Stoatley Rough existed for refugee children in a land dotted with wealthy, entrenched independent (public) schools. Dr Lion was always searching to maintain a balance between educational progressivism and proper curriculum. She made up the rules as she went along, redefining her pedagogical vision as economic challenges forced her to make constant adjustments, yet never failing her pupils in striving for quality.

Sometime in the 1930s, a school song came into being. Each of the
three verses ended with the refrain, 'God of the South, God of the North
| God of us all, we venture forth.'[14]

Stoatley Rough would always be a work in progress. In an anonymous,
undated sheaf of papers (probably written in 1937 since the writer puts
the school population at forty-two), the school is said to be 'an experimental school aiming at a thorough instruction in two languages, English
and German, combined with a methodical training in domestic science
and handicrafts'. It was also said of the school that it was a kind of
'educational hostel for German refugee teachers, students and
children'.[15]

Miss Isabel Fry turned over the reins of the school to Dr Lion
in December 1934. Some children were not sorry to see her go, having
little patience with her Quaker practise of holding a period of silence
every evening. Dr Lion was expansive in her praise of the experienced
pedagogue, 'for her willingness to come to our aid from the very first
and for staying with us for more than three months, organising and
teaching both staff and pupils. Living with us, she has been realising
an idea, and that meant more for us in this time and for the future than
we can say in this short report.'[16]

The school closed for two months over Christmas. The children who
could not afford to travel back to Germany or who had no family to go
home to were farmed out to English families. Two girls did housework
for their host families as part of a new programme Nore and Dr Lion
were launching at Stoatley Rough, the Domestic Sciences programme.
The school year started up again in January, and by the summer closing,
the pupil population was sixteen (ten girls and five boys with one English
day pupil). By December 1935, it was up to thirty-six. The numbers did
not reflect the same group of children but rather was merely a snapshot
of a rapidly moving current of children moving in and out. Pupils would
arrive and leave unpredictably, some staying for two months, others for
many years, and the original school functioned often as simply a way
station for many.[17]

During the summer of 1935, travel was neither restricted within
England nor prohibited abroad. Dr Lion went back to Germany again
on a recruiting tour, accompanying some children who would spend the
summer at home. The German–English school on the hill looked after
those who had nowhere to go, and the Committee continued to deal
with ongoing problems.

Around the time the school reopened in the fall of 1935, a crisis presented itself. Mrs Vernon had a potential buyer for the property. She wrote on 29 September 1935, 'I have had a rather urgent letter from the people who are finally going to succeed to the house and I have promised them an answer as soon as possible.'[18] Did the authorities still need the estate for their school? She might have been asking whether the sun rises from the east, since the answer was a foregone conclusion. Everyone was in love with Stoatley Rough. Dr Lion wrote a quick response with a perfunctory listing of the school's ongoing problems of space, the water supply and its 'antiquated sewage system', but it was clear that she did not want to leave. To her everlasting credit, Mrs Vernon did not evict the little band of refugees. Bertha Bracey articulated the case for staying at the property, reminding the reader that the school was a haven not only for the children, but for Dr Lion and her German cohorts. 'It is only right to consider what the beauty of the garden, and the situation with its beautiful views, has meant to just those people, older and younger, for whom the school was started. It has brought new hope and refreshment to many pupils, staff, casual visitors, and summer-school guests. From this angle the experience for so many is something for which we can be deeply grateful.'[19] In October, a new contract was drawn up for the lease of the property, 'for not less than five years with permission to sublet the house in case it was no longer wanted'. The terms of the lease recorded the fee of one shilling a year and reiterated the condition that Mr and Mrs Phillips would continue to live in the Lodge, employed for as long as they wished. The lease also stipulated that the internal and external repairs and maintenance would be the financial responsibility of the school. (In 1937, Articles of Association were drawn up and submitted to the Board of Trade with whom the school was registered. The school's Committee was incorporated into a Board of Governors.) To everyone's relief, Mrs Vernon's potential buyer was sent packing.

The Board Chair, Miss A.R. Fearon of Haslemere (no one seems to know what her initials stood for), was especially happy. This lady of means not only worked on strategic planning and fund raising, but enjoyed being around the children, often driving small groups of them to museums and zoos. Many remember one extraordinary act of kindness from Miss Fearon during the *Blitz*, the continuous attack on London by the German *Luftwaffe* that began in September 1940. As usual, the bell rang and the gong clanged over and over again, the signal to the children to walk quickly to the air-raid shelter at the lower end of the house. But that day the throngs were diverted from entering the rear door that led downstairs and were marched to the courtyard in the back where, after roll call, Mr Phillips appeared from around the corner, grinning broadly and pushing a wagon. Its cargo? An enormous pail of ice cream, courtesy of Miss Fearon. Everyone cheered.

The indomitable Miss Fearon chaired the Committee (later known as the Board of Governors), for the entire twenty-six years of the school's existence.

The household girls

When Gertrud Gans followed Nore around helping to set up the school in April 1934, the physician's daughter knew she was finished with formal education – there would be no *Lyceum* [finishing school] for her in England. She was stranded, penniless and struggling to learn the language of her new country. In their first report, the Committee conceded that 'the girls who come to us have all finished their school education, though some of them much too early'.[20] The five girls made the best of their situation. They understood that they were marking time until they could join their families or grow up enough to work and live on their own. As the fall classes began to take shape, the two new boys were kept busy with their studies, but the girls soon realised they had too much time on their hands. Gertrud and the others cornered Nore. Could they learn housekeeping from her? Could she train them to become real household managers? With certification, such a skill would land them good jobs – a fate preferable to ending up as an upstairs maid tucked away in some country estate evading the lecherous hands of the squire.

Why would teenaged girls from well-off families ask for such training? For one thing, it would keep them busy. For another, it might lead to a career. And finally, it had respectability. Far from being viewed as demeaning, expertise in housework had come to be perceived valuable and almost sacred, as if many 1930s-version Martha Stewarts had captured the hearts of that generation of women. A field of study sprang up influenced by science and technology that focused on women's work in the home. The movement was aimed at professionalising the status of housewife, applying scientific principles and discoveries to domestic labour. Achieving measurable standards in cooking, child care, sewing,

housecleaning, laundry, table setting, etc., national certification in the
Domestic Sciences offered the foundation of a career.

Dr Lion and Nore mulled over the idea. While the school had not been
designed as a trade school, perhaps such training could coexist with an
academic curriculum. Why not? Nore and Hanna, former instructors in
the field, certainly could provide the expertise required. The Committee
approved the idea. 'We have capable teachers who give those girls
instruction in everything that is necessary for the upkeep of our modern
English country house … an up-to-date kitchen, laundry, and garden.'[21]

As the population of the school grew, so did the need for girls who
would be called Household Girls or 'Big Girls'. The girls studied hard:
not only did they have English language and other academic subjects to
master, but also the specific classes in 'cleaning materials', 'stock foods'
and 'house furnishing'. Later, to qualify for Certification testing, a more
rigorous, detailed field of topics included the economy of heating fuel, the
importance of potatoes 'as an energy giving food', the economy in the use
of vegetable waters, the strengths of starches, soaking or boiling cottons,
rinsing woollens in lukewarm water, producing a good finish in ironing,
and so on.

Soon the girls wanted to learn child care; Nore and Dr Lion promptly
added kindergarten studies to the curriculum, the girls first practising
in neighbouring child centres. As more children arrived at the school,
they began to help the new younger children with their meals, grooming
and bedtimes. The girls were loving and, in turn, were loved by young
children lonely for their parents. The 'Big Girl' in charge of a young child
oversaw teeth brushing, bathing (once a week!), and tucking in. Martin
saw his 'Big Girl', Gertrud Gans, as a mother figure. Kate Lesser saw
hers, Lilli Wohlgemuth [Gluecksmann], as a source of security, having
left behind 'a Berlin of horror and darkness'. Kate wrote, 'It was to her
that I brought the Red Cross letter announcing the death of my
grandmother.'[22] Kate was only eight years old in 1939 when she was sent
off to England on the *Kindertransport*. Her arrival made her famous.
Sitting in Liverpool Station in London with the other children, Kate was
waiting for the next leg of her journey when she idly took out her violin.
A newspaper photographer for the *Evening Standard* had been covering
the arrival of a batch of children. 'I was asked whether I actually played
the violin, whereupon I played "God Save the King" to prove that
I did', to the delight and amazement of the photographer and crowd
of bystanders.[23] The *Standard* printed the picture of the unsmiling,

beautiful little refugee girl with her thick braids, legs akimbo beneath
a chequered smocked dress, violin in hand. Decades later, the enlarged
photograph of little Kate appeared as part of an exhibit at the National
Holocaust Museum in Washington, DC.

Household Girls helped children write to their families, an emotionally
charged, often difficult task. Nore recalled, 'There were many children for
years and years [who] never got mail. And some of them got regular letters
and then suddenly [they] stopped, which of course for those children was
more or less a terrible sign … we felt responsible. I remember we even
helped them a little because younger children always say, "Well, I don't
know what to write." I remember one day [telling them to] ask them this
or that. And then one of the young boys said, "Ask? But they are not
here." So I understood that for a child, this distance was something you
can't overcome.'[24] Martin never forgot the kindness of Gertrud Gans.
When she left to be married in India in 1939, he felt devastated. He
barely managed to adjust to his new surroundings, and the loss of her
left a lasting mark. 'I was heartbroken to lose my surrogate mother.'

It did not take long for the school to recognise the potential of
a Domestic Sciences programme to attract more students to the school.
The pool of pupils who could pay full fare was always limited, thanks to
the *Reichsfluchtsteuer*, the surcharge imposed by the Nazis, ten times any
amount the émigré wished to have transferred from German banks into
foreign countries. Only the very wealthy could fully fund their children
for the several years they would be in England. Bertha Bracey noted
in 1935, 'The transfer of money from Germany even for the education
of German children abroad is beset with difficulties and uncertainties.
These are beyond our control and the most persistent and patient efforts
to find a solution have only been very partially successful and in many
cases have failed altogether.'[25] Over time, a marriage of convenience
or a Faustian bargain (depending on one's point of view) was struck
at Stoatley Rough. The school needed labour to clean and keep the
house running, and Jewish girls from less than wealthy families needed
sanctuary. It was an opportunity made in heaven. Stoatley Rough School
began to offer free tuition, room and board in exchange for work.

Of the eight girls who had come to Stoatley Rough by December 1934
(known ages fifteen, nineteen, fourteen and fifteen in order of arrival and
all paying full tuition), at least four of them are known to have studied
Domestic Sciences. By the time Martin arrived in 1938, the school
counted twelve tuition-free Household Girls among its seventy-one

pupils. (The school also occasionally brought in English girls to help out, called 'Helpers', who played no part in the programme. There were five between 1934 and 1945; more Helpers were hired after the war.)

The school's brochure of 1938 described the fully developed programme:

The Domestic Science Course (Frauenschuljahr) (First year)

This training includes cooking, housework, laundry, handicrafts, needlework, arithmetic, book-keeping, and the care of young children. The aim is to give an all-round knowledge of work connected with house and nursery. English, written and oral, History, German Literature, Arts, Social Studies complete this year's general education.

Household Management Course (Second year)

Students continue their household work and specialise in management. This training provides the groundwork of experience in the organisation of hostels and homes.

Handwork Training

The course includes dressmaking, weaving, woodwork, cardboard-work, book-binding, pottery, basket-making, repairs and gardening.

The Care of Children

The pupils are systematically trained. They get some experience with our younger children and in a neighbouring Kindergarten Schools. Pupils who reach a satisfactory standard in private examination in theoretical and practical subjects are given a Certificate.

Girls in the Domestic Sciences programme received fifteen hours per week of literature appreciation, reading authors such as G.B. Shaw, Edith Sitwell, Robert Louis Stevenson, Joseph Conrad and D.H. Lawrence. They also wrote poetry and essays and studied shorthand, workshop, bookkeeping, music and 'games'. They learned scripture and child psychology. Thursday mornings were reserved for theory.

A report card from the time (kindly lent by the son of Ilse Kaiser [Neibert]) shows finely parsed categories of study:

English (Pronunciation, Use of language, Reading, Spelling, Composition and Literature)
European History
German
Shorthand
Arithmetic
Housework (Laundry, Ironing, Home Management, Odd jobbing)
Cookery & Scullery work (Applied Science, Hygiene)
Workshop (Needlework, Weaving; Woodwork and Bookbinding)
Gardening
Music
Gymnastics
Games
Condition of Health & Physical Culture (Carriage, Tidiness, Neatness, Punctuality, Attendance of lessons)
Willingness to Help
General Remarks, Hobbies and Special Courses

The Household Girls' curriculum for the winter of 1940 lists twelve Household Girls (Bauer, Bayer, Bing, Dorpalen, Kaufmann, Kaiser, Lilienthal, Klein, Neufeld L., Neufeld T., Steinberg and Koehler) and their curriculum: history, English, social geography and songs (English and American); their teachers were Miss Van Hollick, Miss Temple and Miss Humby. Miss Humby filed the following details:

A. Outline of American History and Civics
B. Dunkwalen's play *Abraham Lincoln* and Shakespeare's *Hamlet*
C. Practical descriptive and imaginative composition
D. Mathematics: frequent lists and accuracy
E. Some practical work in connection with housekeeping, e.g. cleaning materials, stock foods, house furnishing[26]

The girls did not study higher mathematics, sciences or French. When the girls turned sixteen, the lessons ceased while the work remained.[27]

Miss Astfalck's influence on the programme was enormous. Without her positive spirit and personal work ethic, it never would have flourished. She was popular and respected, and she got the best work from the Household Girls through her energy, praise and insistence on quality. Years later, Nore liked to say that Stoatley Rough was known as a 'clean house'. One girl recalled Miss Astfalck's admonishment: 'Whenever you have finished cleaning a room, before closing the door you must look around once more to see if the whole looks good.' Not only did Nore Astfalck set an example of diligence, cheer and fairness in her work, she assuaged the sense of social inferiority that inevitably was bound to surface. One girl said, 'I minded [being a Household Girl] at the time. We were all somewhat intellectually snobbish. But I did learn a lot from Miss Astfalck, especially organisational skills that I'm grateful for today.'[28] The girls took pride in their work. Ilse Kaiser [Neivert] recorded meticulous notes on the correct procedures for laundry and ironing. She used one whole page for her collection of tiny paper shirts, aprons, dishtowels and properly folded trousers pasted to the sheet. Each is a perfectly crafted tiny creation of origami.

National certification testers came to the school in 1941 to administer examinations; Nore's syllabus in hand stated that the 'Housecraft Certificate' training at Stoatley Rough took roughly a year, with eleven two/three-hour lessons per term, three mornings per week for lessons and one hour per week for theory. According to the National guidelines, each girl needed 200 hours of lessons. Nore explained to the examiners the uniqueness of the programme at Stoatley Rough: that her girls were more than just pupils. 'These girls run the house with the assistance on some days of the rest of the school. They do all the cooking, housework & laundrywork ... [and] work in groups, so that one group learns one thing one week & the other group the same thing the next. They gain a good grasp of the essential work – because the school must be run to plan ... theory is often taught whilst the cooking or laundry work is being done for the school.' The syllabus lists Miss Demuth, the school's cook, as resident 'Cookery Mistress' and Miss Astfalck as resident 'Laundrywork Mistress & Housewifery'.[29]

The national administrators were displeased with Nore's curriculum, pointing out that her 'Principles of Cookery, Cookery Methods and Kitchen Craft' were 'useless – the matter overlaps and is disjointed. For example, boiling, stewing, etc. cannot be separated from retention of juices, cuts of meat, meat cookery and stoves.'[30] They noted that in Laundrywork, processes should be taught in conjunction with the fabric 'being washed and studied. White cotton is never mentioned.'[31] Nevertheless, they decided to go ahead with the examination.

The Cookery examination was especially daunting. Liesel Neumann wrote, 'We did not know the recipes of all the popular English dishes by heart, and we were sure to get some of them in a test. The day before the exam one would see the Household Girls sighing over their recipe-books; but fortunately we only had to prepare some sponge and fruit pies, which are really quite simple. In spite of that the cookery was the worst part of the exam. We did not keep a careful enough eye on the pies, and the oven was not hot enough for the scones.'[32] There were also problems when the girls moved to Laundry and Housewifery. 'The tray cloth we had washed, starched and ironed, was not in perfect shape, and not shiny enough, [and] the metal polish was still seen in a corner of a candlestick.'[33] Afterwards, the examiners commented that 'some candidates were very extravagant with heating'. But it was not all bad. The examiner applauded the girls' knowledge of home-made cleaning solutions. Six girls passed. Before the examiners left, they noted that more 'practice in finishing finer articles and table linen would be helpful'.[34]

The Household Girls participated in the preparations for the traditional Christmas/Hanukkah celebrations the school held each holiday season. Miss Demuth hoarded sugar and butter (during the war years) to bake holiday cookies and cakes, and each spring Nore invited a few girls into her quarters to decorate Easter eggs. Inge Hamburger said, 'Each child would receive one egg, a treat, which some of us "secretly" decorated in Nore and Hanna's room. It was really enjoyable.'

Thus, the girls in the Domestic Sciences programme were able to adjust to their special status. In some ways, they were treated like adults and revelled in the extra attention and praise they received from Nore. In other ways, they were powerless servants with little choice but to do what they were told. And like the Farm Boys, another special category of pupil soon to arrive at the school, they were learning a trade while providing essential services to the school. Unlike most of their peers, they were not on the academic track – there would never be a Matric in their future. But like their peers, they were sheltered. Their goal was simply to grow up enough to get out on their own and then, if lucky, find work.

The farm programme

Although Dr Lion did not formally articulate a Farm programme
until 1938, she nurtured an idea for a training farm after well-meaning
benefactors donated a few cows and poultry to the fledgling school
in 1934. In some ways, the Farm programme mirrored the Domestic
Sciences course of work/study, yet it was much smaller and offered
fewer academic subjects. It was also less vital to the survival of the
school and more fluid in concept and implementation. Before the war,
having a farm allowed children to frolic with baby goats and puppies,
feed geese and chickens, and tend piglets. Once the war started, however,
practical considerations forced a new, focused activity, with serious crop
growing and a paring down to essential livestock that could help the
war effort. The farm provided milk, eggs, meat, vegetables and berries,
i.e. gooseberries, to the table.

The original farm course consisted of one and a half years of hands-
on training to prepare boys to work in 'a colonial settlement'. Dr Lion,
still reflecting her utopian vision, wrote in 1937, 'Our scheme of Small
Holding is to be started on the premises. We shall have an agricultural
teacher, as we wish to give the children growing up on such a beautiful
estate an idea what simple country life comprises. We should like to
make our boys and girls so independent that they will be encouraged
to leave the Old World.'[35] The 7 acres (2.8 hectares) of fields below the
manor house were dedicated to the farm. Boys received classes in English,
carpentry and something called 'sanitary instruction' and first aid.

A school brochure, c.1937, describes farm training as follows, listing
Mrs A.H. Railing as 'Chairman' of the department:

In its grounds of 24 acres the School has established a special course
for young people interested in agricultural and horticultural work.
The object is to give the pupils, who have for the most part been
educated in towns, preparatory instruction for life in an overseas
settlement. At the same time the aim is to teach them independence
and self-reliance and to make them familiar with the English
language and with British customs and outlook.

Gardening and Elementary Agriculture
Growing various crops, vegetables, flowers.
Keeping Livestock

Chicken-farming, pigs, goats, cows, calves, etc.
Carpentry, First-Aid, etc.

The school would not take anyone over age seventeen for the programme and assumed pupils would be 'physically and mentally fit'. Participants came in to the programme on a probationary status for the first three months. The school promised to utilise its connections with British overseas settlement organisations so as to facilitate the emigration of the pupils. By 1939, the Farm programme was fully functioning. Farm Boys did the heavier chores, while boys and girls living in the main house helped out with some routine chores and periodic harvestings of crops.

All the children at Stoatley Rough grew vegetables on individual parcels of land. Obo recalls, 'Our plots were given to us in the winter of 1939. At first we thought it was hopeless to cultivate pieces of land – it all was just one big piece of weeds, and high grass with a lot of frogs. Well, we started to trench (which means to dig the turf underneath, leaving the soil on top). It was really a nice job but tiring. The piece of land was divided into five plots, one being an experimental one.... We planted cabbages, kale, radishes, turnips, parsnips, mustard, cress, cauliflowers, Brussels-sprouts, beans and peas. But the cows broke through the fence and pinched many plants. We repaired the fence and the cows did not break through again. In autumn we lifted our potatoes which were of the "Red King" variety. It was a very good crop. Then we clamped them, which means that we put them on some straw on the ground and put straw all round them and then put earth on top. We left a chimney on the top to let the air out. All this was done to protect them from the frost.'[36]

The pre-war farm allowed the children access to pets such as dogs, cats and goats, all of whom were named. Dr Wolff recorded that Mindo had puppies (all the females were drowned) and that the 'happy' father was the 'ugly brown Bobby', Mr Phillips's dog.[37] By 1939, two breeding sows were in residence. Alexander Finkler enjoyed watching over the swine. 'It is eleven o'clock of a summer night. Inside the sty we find a happy mother surrounded by her numerous progeny; all struggling for milk. But there lurks in the background a policeman in the shape of a farm boy. One is reminded of a rush-hour in a big London store; the piglets are the pushing, excited queue of buyers, and the sow is the retailer, harassed by the unreasonable demands made upon the commodity she has to offer. Finally she rises, and kicks the impatient crowd away, and they are shepherded to safety by the watching farm boy. He must stay at his post until relieved at the second watch; then up the path he climbs with a great yawn. He drops into bed, and is soon asleep and dreaming of legions of suckling pigs.'[38]

Geese wandered freely. The unpredictable creatures had their favourites and also those they disliked among the pupils. One victim wrote, 'An aggressive goose, coming at you with neck extended and hissing, is a mean sight, resulting in bites to hands or legs if you were intimidated, but responding if one counterattacks.' One day, a goose turned up with a broken neck, and one older boy on the farm decided to try to cure her. He created a small splint, wound it around her neck and hand-fed her for a few days while she recovered. She returned to the farm as mean as ever, not favouring her saviour in the slightest. Wolff commented that, 'Elsewhere one might have turned such an accident into roast goose, but not here.'

Ilse Kaiser was sent to live on the farm upon turning sixteen. 'I did not know one end of the cow from the other, but ... I did fall in love with the two baby goats. I was put in charge of them and they started to follow me everywhere. Unfortunately Dr Lion did not appreciate it when they followed me to the house and ran back and forth on the terrace during dinner.' Miss Dove objected strenuously to the habit of Dr Lion taking the smaller children down to the farm to pet the baby animals since sometimes the animals appeared later as a main course. To make her point, and to Dr Lion's great disapproval, Miss Dove became a vegetarian.

In the 1930s and 1940s, farming was more a part of community life than now. Then the people lived close to the land and more people were being born on farms than in cities. The horse was still widely in use. When automobile plants in England were converted to provide *matériel* for the war effort in the late thirties, horses made a comeback, deemed essential in the drive for high levels of farm production. Even Stoatley Rough had its Black Beauty who was regularly hitched to a plough or wagon the kids called the Roman Chariot. Black Beauty hauled surplus kitchen refuse or made milk runs into town through back fields and gates. Obo recalled that the horse was temperamental, once giving him a swift kick. While the farm at Stoatley Rough was barely a real farm by most standards, it did train future farmers.[39]

Before farm managers arrived on the scene, the administrators were seriously invested in the farm, but they proved to be rank amateurs. In 1938, Dr Wolff wrote to her mother, 'We had some chicken experts here the other day; they were delighted with everything and explained, among other things, that the fencing chosen for the coming chickens was a paradise for – foxes!'[40] A year earlier, the farm's sole starter chicken met an untimely death, causing widespread consternation. Something got into the coop and ate, as Wolff put it, 'the entire stock of fowl'. The culprit was never identified; everybody except the administrators knew a fox had not breached the fence, but Mr Phillips's beloved Airedale mix, Bobby. Bobby went on to prey on a hapless moorhen who decided to nest next to the newly built swimming pool, giving rise to a wonderful irony. Wolf Edelstein [Elston] saw it this way. 'The Norwegian and Belgian campaigns ended in disaster, Dunkirk was evacuated, France fell, an invasion of England was expected at any moment, but the British authorities worried about protecting a moorhen. Later that summer the moorhen's gestation was terminated. It was blamed on a fox, but I suspect Bob, the fat mongrel. You may remember that the school farm was begun in 1938 with a single hen, carefully guarded by an enclosure guaranteed to protect against foxes. The moorhen was probably another victim of Bob, but no one ever knew for sure.'[41]

As she worked to establish the farm, Dr Lion consistently preached emigration. 'One boy works in the Haslemere Motor Works to get to know something about auto-engineering before he goes overseas.' She was creative in garnering resources to support her goals. 'Besides the English and other school lessons, a blind former County Council Agricultural Adviser comes up regularly to give farming lectures to the boys.'[42] She brought in experts to lecture on colonisation in Australia and India and made contacts with local area farms. 'In order to give our farm boys more experience, there were nearly only boys, they were sent for shorter or longer stays to farms in the neighbourhood and to Suffolk, where two of them had the great opportunity of being invited for ten weeks each and another one for three weeks. Besides the regular tuition, by an English farm teacher, we have enjoyed already for a month now the great help of an English builder who has been sent by Mrs Railing. He teaches the boy in erecting sheds, incubators, in altering the laundry with kind permission of Mrs Vernon. We have more livestock than before.'[43] She reported in 1938, 'We have nine little pigs from our old one; four of them have already been killed and provide the school with excellent meat.'[44]

When all was said and done, three boys emigrated to Australia, in 1938, to become farmers or farm managers, and in 1939, one boy went to New Zealand and one to East Africa. A few others (farm and non-farm children) went to Palestine. After 1939, the sea lanes were closed to passenger ships. After attending supplemental lectures at the Guildford Technical Institute, a few children passed examinations in poultry-keeping that were administered by the Board of Agriculture. Most in the Farm programme remained in England to work on farms until they could find other work.

Ordnung muss sein [Order must prevail]

In 1936, Dr Lion's friend, Emmy, arrived to teach and live at the school. She entered an entirely alien world and she had to struggle to adjust to a new, surprisingly unreasonable way of life. She did her best. After almost two decades in Haslemere, she left a legacy of respect for literature and art that lived long past her lifetime.

Stoatley Rough was on its way. In its second year (1935–1936), the school was a thriving little hideaway on the hill. The locals called it the German–English School. Enrolment grew steadily, reaching thirty-one pupils by December and forty by June. Payment for the services of two new women was recorded in the Board's report: Miss Billson, identified as a solicitor in the Board's report, and Miss Debenham, whose function is not specified but was probably an English teacher. The Board grew to fifteen members, and its new Articles of Association expressed the hope that 'one or two more Friends will consent to join the school'. In late winter of 1936, the school experienced its first infectious disease with seven cases of chickenpox, a calamity that spawned five weeks of quarantine until the Medical Office of Health pronounced that the 'sanitary arrangements of the house' were satisfactory. Someone gave the school a pottery wheel for art classes, but no one came to the rescue of the Science department. The Board claimed that it was unable to spare £15 for a piece of unspecified equipment. But Dr Lion was ever resourceful. With a captive group of pupils day and night, the school could offer a variety of informal learning opportunities within its flexible schedule: Dr Lion often held sessions in her room with a few small children, discussing subjects such as 'the Life and Work of Friedrich Liszt, or the German Customs Union and Development of Railways'; Nore Astfalck taught boys and girls to cook 'cocoa and an egg, cutlet and fried potatoes, soup for an invalid and chamomile tisane'. The curriculum now included Hebrew lessons, typing, shorthand, arts and crafts and natural sciences. Nature studies took the lower forms outdoors to collect specimens and make drawings of plants. A singing teacher stopped by with regularity, and the new second in command, Dr Wolff, was devoting four evenings a week to give readings in English and German literature as the older children darned. Eight visiting English speakers held regular hours of instruction several times a week, and books were donated to the new library, whose floor was now being polished with the new, albeit unwieldy floor polishers. Children sallied forth on educational excursions to a pottery factory, a laundry, a flower show, Arundel Castle, Windsor Castle, Eaton and Little Hampton. They also went to festivals, concerts and plays. In June, the school celebrated its year-end closing with a cultural weekend – a series of lectures followed by an evening concert of piano and violin and a children's choir – a performance held to the standards of excellence the school was becoming famous for attaining. The audience gathered on folding chairs outside on the terrace. Dr Wolff was moved to tears when the children sang '*Der Mond ist Aufgegangen*' [The Moon Has Risen] into the beautiful summer evening. The next day everyone enjoyed 'a genuine English tea – toast, sandwiches and masses of cakes', following a lecture on *Romeo and Juliet*. School was out for the summer.

Neither Dr Wolff, Dr Leven nor Dr Lion was temperamentally suited to the rough and tumble world of children. Dr Wolff, in particular, had to overcome her natural aloof and cool manner. Having left behind the quiet predictability of her literary work and intellectual circle of friends, she was overqualified to teach literature at Stoatley Rough. She was a real academic jewel but moving from a world of ideas and aesthetics to the literal-minded, unpolished world of children must have been shocking. She had grown up in wealth in Berlin and trained to handle a domestic staff she was expected to govern some day. She spent her days working on her needlework and practising the piano. Girls of her standing were not allowed to earn their living. 'This dictum caused me great suffering.'[45] After attending a *Lyceum*, she took an extra year to study more foreign languages, piano, needlepoint and literature. Then she made the courageous decision that put her (self) on the same path as Dr Lion. She defied her tyrannical father and left home to dive head first into social work and the women's movement. Like Dr Lion, she was determined never to marry. At the respectable age of twenty-five, she attended the *Hochschule für Frauen*, a school in Leipzig for women founded by the great feminist, Henriette Goldschmidt (1825–1920), and went on to undergraduate studies in Munich, where she came into contact with other influential feminists such as Gertrud Baumer (1873–1954). In 1922, she received her PhD from the University of Frankfurt/Main, where she and Hilde Lion became confidants and shared living quarters. Like Dr Lion, Emmy Wolff was passionate about women's political, social and economic equality; she wanted housework to be acknowledged for its value, 'even worshipped'. She chose prostitution as the subject of her dissertation ('A Girls' Hostel and the Origin of Its Members – A Contribution to the Problem of Female Dropouts'), in which she focused on a special hostel founded by feminist Bertha Pappenheim (1859–1939) to help girls from Eastern countries such as Russia, Romania and Poland who had ended up in bondage in Germany. As an assistant to Gertrud Baumer, Emmy Wolff held an important position in the feminist and literary world. She co-edited *Die Frau* and, for which, wrote dozens of articles and poems, and she lectured at educational institutions on youth literature and social work, including the *Deutsche Akademie für soziale und paedagogische Frauenarbeit* [German Academy of Women's Social and Pedagogical Work] then headed by Dr Lion. She wrote several books, including a collection of stories for children. Her formidable resume also listed the management of the Union of German Women's Associations (*Bund Deutscher Frauenvereine*), also known as BUND. After 1933 Dr Wolff was declared 'racially inferior', yet she continued to publish poems and essays in newspapers and journals under her mother's maiden name, Elisabeth Fleiss.

She always had a soft spot for children and enjoyed them, although she held a somewhat idealised view. She took children in small groups on outings and sometimes invited them in for cocoa and a feast of freshly picked mushrooms cooked in gobs of butter and onions. When she was assigned to drive a few children to Southampton for travel to Germany, she took a couple of their friends along. On the way back, they stopped to go rowing on the Wey, 'followed by cups of chocolate in an elegant tea room'.[46]

One of her hundreds of poems (undated, below, freely translated by the author) reflects a fairly sentimental Victorian worldview. The childless academic depicts her subject, a sleeping child, with exquisite imagery.

Das Kind
Niemals von der Mutter Mund
Fiel ein Lied in seinem Schlaf,

Sieben Engel Sangen
Selig ueber ihm.
Flaumiges Gefieder flog,
Rauschte weis und ahnungsvoll,
Sieben Donner brummten
Unter Blitz und Schwert.
Als am Regenbogenband
Sacht, so sacht die Wiege ging,
Legten sieben Leuchter
Lichtgold in sein Haar.

The Child
The mother
Never failed to sing a song as he slept,
Seven angels sang
Blissfully over him.
Downy plumage flew,
Rustling wisely and with prescience,
Seven thunders rumbled
Under lightning and sword.
As the cradle rocked gently, so gently
near the rainbow's ribbon,
Seven lanterns spread
Bright gold on his hair.

Dr Wolff had never held a mop in her hand before she got to Haslemere. She had never worked in a kitchen or spoken for any length of time to a small child. In her earliest letters home, Dr Wolff characterised Stoatley Rough as an exotic, daffy place, writing with detached amusement. 'For a little while now we have been enjoying the blessings of a potato peeling machine. The thing was expensive, but it is worth it. It washes and peels enough potatoes for about fifty people in about five-seven minutes. One boy turns the handle and then they plop into the bowl; one only has to take the eyes out.'[47] During the mid-1930s the school's population was so small that the staff, including Dr Wolff, was still taking turns preparing food for everybody. When it was Dr Wolff's turn to cook, she took the plunge with courage. Her job was to get the main meal on the table for around forty-five people by 1 p.m. As it was Monday, wash day, helping hands were absent that otherwise should have been available to assist her. Dr Wolff joked that her venture into the kitchen was the 'Great Cooking Day'. First she had the problem of not having anyone handy who knew 'beefsteak'; she had to fry 140 'minced corned beef patties' (we would call them hamburgers). She put her one experienced helper to work at the stove then turned to the great amounts of red cabbage 'straight from the garden' that she would have to cook with apples. Panic set in when about 220 pounds (100 kilograms) of potatoes failed to arrive early in the morning as scheduled until the delivery truck pulled up at 11 a.m., and she got the potatoes into the hot water she had started bubbling in large pots on the stove. She was in luck regarding the dessert. Yesterday's teacher on duty had prepared a fruit compote. As the potatoes boiled, Dr Wolff turned to the special requirements for the day. A certain amount of the cabbage and potatoes had to be made without salt for several 'diet eaters'; she also needed to cook tomatoes instead of cabbage for one of the adults on a gallstones diet. Dr Wolff then made a huge pot of tomato soup for the evening meal. Later she had milk brought up from the cellars for the early breakfast of the next morning that would be served to a select few: the girls doing the laundry, Mr Phillips, Bobby, several early-rising teachers and a couple of small children whose chore for that week was to spread butter on dozens of slices of bread. Since some children were allergic to milk, apples also had to be set out. Dr Wolff signed off with her letter to her mother with self-deprecation and a no small measure of pride at having conquered the stove. Grateful to Dr Lion and the Board for bringing her out of Germany, she was determined to fit in.

Dr Wolff enjoyed school life for the most part and entered into games and celebrations as happily as the children. She was playful and began to thrive in the environment of after-hours music and dance, encouraged to shed some of her natural reserve. One of her letters described several instances of dancing, including the time she led the children in a polonaise through the entire house to celebrate a fine job of cleaning. On another occasion the children danced in a conga line after refurbishing the Shed, an outbuilding down in the pasture area. The whole school attended that party with 'colourful snippets of tissue paper on string ... stretched across the room in all directions'. The children and teachers 'wound [their] way down ... in one long chain, singing away, the Shed "booming with folk dancing" '.[48] And then Dr Wolff described a curious ritual whose roots go back to medieval days. Beating the boundary occurred when peasants marked the limits of a particular piece of land, such as a farm, manor house or church, by pausing at certain trees, walls or hedges to exclaim, pray or 'beat' the marks with sticks of birch or willow. Dr Wolff vividly recorded that the Stoatley Rough children ran around the lower part of the Stoatley Rough grounds that night, beating the boundary and singing with a strumming guitar, *'und so zieht der Bauer durch den Matsch, Matsch, Matsch'* ['and so the peasant tramps through the sludge, sludge, sludge'].

From 1934 to 1938 the school functioned as a large family. Emmy Wolff recorded that there were Bible readings, work days ('our English historian was on her knees, scrubbing the dining room parquet flooring'), literary readings ('the children love anything like that and it does give them something to ... divert them a bit from their various manias'), a talk on the history of the Quakers, fire drills, impromptu plays (improvised Song of the Apple – an original composition), evenings of singing and playing, a bus excursion to hear a peace lecture, and so on. Dr Wolff wrote, 'The big ones entertained us with ... an original composition which they dreamed up yesterday over the potato peeling.... The little ones gave a gymnastic display, culminating in the presentation of all sorts of small gifts.'

As much as she worked at it, Dr Wolff's patience for children was not without limits. She once wrote home about the 'marvellous concert by the Busch Quarter here in the town – we were thrilled, about twenty of us went. German music only, Haydn, Beethoven and Schuman. We were in quite a different world and then we swept out into a beautiful evening, clouds scudding across the sky.' She concluded sombrely, 'Pity that up here so many different things happen to drive away the glorious impressions.'49

In another letter to her mother she wrote that Nore's birthday celebration was intimate and loving, a family experience. 'To mark Nore's birthday we have invited Ha No [Hanna Nacken and Nore Astfalck] for supper. (Does Dr Wolff mean a private supper with herself and Dr Lion and the two other women, or does it imply that Nore and Hanna did not always dine with the children?) Before that there is going to be a *"Ruepeltan"* [Dance of the Louts], which doesn't need much disguise, and a dramatised fairy tale – the Swineherd – to celebrate the occasion as a dramatic opera – and a marionette play – to be performed at the same time. Every now and again there just has to be something special. We packed Nore's presents into the huge porridge bowl from which she always serves in the mornings; when she dutifully marched to the serving table, instead of the customary porridge, her ladle found a cake and other goodies to the delight of the young ones.'[50]

Dr Wolff was happiest in the classroom. Angela Galligan, a post-war pupil, remembered her as someone who believed in order, who said '*Ordnung muss sein*'. 'It was her insistence in drilling us in French verbs that enabled me to master them and to make real progress in the subject; her enthusiasm for French poetry and literature inspired in me a similar response.'[51] Eveline Kanes concurred with the evaluation. 'I liked Dr Wolff the best; she helped me to re-learn German, and kindled my interest in German and French literature.'[52] Angela Galligan wrote of Dr Wolff's efforts to make the best of her new life. 'Emmy was once in the school kitchen, with a kerchief around her head, making Swiss *muesli*. On another occasion she invited students to her home in Hindhead where they were taking evening classes in typing and shorthand. She showed a photo of herself as a handsome young girl in leg o'mutton sleeves. She gave us a delicious home made bowl of potato soup.'[53] Angela Galligan also articulated the essence of the dignified expatriate who never relinquished her German citizenship, in the following tribute. She said that Emmy Wolff had 'all the Prussian virtues – honour, rigour, moral rectitude, orderliness and devotion to duty – without any of its vices'.[54]

The peaceable kingdom that was Stoatley Rough disappeared in the early months of 1939. Heartbreak, anger and recriminations were about to split apart the adult community just as the beleaguered women were trying to cope with increasingly limited resources. Children began to pour in from the Continent in droves, crowding the dining arrangements, overfilling classrooms and forcing a constant shuffling of sleeping arrangements. Against a backdrop of widespread fear with Europe on the brink of war, the arrival of a prickly new music teacher did little to quell the sea change about to happen at Stoatley Rough.

The interloper

The new music teacher ought to have fit right in with the other Germans on the campus; there were so many of them: Miss Demuth, Dr Bluhm, Therese [Thesi] von Gierke, Emmy Wolff, Nore Astfalck, Hanna Nacken. But it was not to be. Dr Leven made little effort to join the team and, in fact, managed to antagonise practically everybody almost at once. Yet she stayed at the school for twenty-one years and, along the way, bestowed a priceless gift on every child by raising music appreciation and performance quality to heights rarely found at any secondary school.

Dr Lion had been courting forty-year-old Dr Luise Leven for five years. Dr Leven recalled, 'In the spring of 1934, I chanced to read in Gertrud Baumer's *Die Frau* that a summer school for English and German grownups would be held in July, at the newly founded Stoatley Rough School in Haslemere, Surrey. I knew the name of the founder, Dr Hilde Lion, but I had never met her. My Aryan singer friend, Marta Zillesen, and I asked for admission. For a long time we did not receive a reply; her name and the fact that I was still teaching at the *Staatliche Musiklehrerseminar* [State Music Training School] roused suspicions. Only after a ... social worker supported the application were we allowed to come.'[55] Like all the others before her, Dr Leven fell in love with the scene. 'At our arrival, we were overwhelmed by the beauty of the place and the spirit of its inhabitants ... I repeated my visits ... each year – three times with my Aryan friend, until she was denounced in the *Stürmer*, the weekly anti-Semitic tabloid that published racist caricatures and obscene cartoons aimed to reinforce Nazi propaganda against Jews and other undesirables.'[56] Dr Leven concluded that Dr Lion continued to urge her to emigrate to England 'as soon as possible'.

Luise Leven was six years younger than Dr Lion and one year older than Nore Astfalck. She was 5 feet (1.5 metres) tall and, although originally slight, grew stout as she aged. She had an oval face of sharp features – sculpted lips, piercing eyes and short, dark, wavy hair streaked with grey. In contrast to the pudding-faced Hilde Lion, Luise Leven had been striking in her youth. A photograph taken in the 1920s shows a thin woman posing dramatically in black. Her bobbed hair is cut at sharp wedges and she stares coolly into the camera. To some, she looked mannish. Herta Lewent likened her to a bird of prey, 'perhaps a crow or raven'. Another pupil saw a Harpo Marx quality, 'he of the white hair and the zany look.... there was certainly a slightly zany gleam in the eye when she was conducting.'

She was born in 1899 in Krefeld, an ancient textile centre on the Rhine near the Netherlands. Luise Leven studied violin, piano and music theory. In 1919 she passed an examination at the 'A-level', higher than that achieved by either Dr Lion or Dr Wolff, a triumph that enabled her to enrol in the university in Frankfurt. Later she moved to Berlin to study science, the history of music and art and German literature. She received her doctorate in music in 1926, and after a brief stint in

Krefeld at the local conservatory, she relocated to Berlin to give lessons in piano and theory at the *Staedtliche Konservatorium* [State-supported Conservatory]. She was a leading singer, teacher and conductor of the women's choir, heading for a career as professor at the university. Then the Nazis came to power. Hypocritically, they excluded her as of 1 April 1933, from all official activities, yet, because she had been preparing music students for the Halle examination, the gold standard of exams for music teachers, the Aryan authorities asked her to stay on until her students could take the exam three years hence.[57] After that she returned home to become cantor in the Krefeld synagogue, but this occupation was closed to her in 1938. Five years after she had been booted out of her post in Berlin, Luise Leven ran out of choices.

The anguish she felt at separation from her home is apparent. 'I could not make up my mind to leave my parents in Germany – I was their only child.... However, after my father died in 1937 and my mother received a permit to emigrate to Holland into the neighbourhood of some of her Dutch cousins and, above all, after the events of Nov. 1938 [note: she refers to *Kristallnacht*] robbed all hope of a tolerable life in Germany, (and the Synagogue, the place was destroyed), I was grateful that Hilde Lion guaranteed my maintenance in England. In March, 1939, I entered Stoatley Rough for good.'[58]

Dr Lion's ability to offer sanctuary to Dr Leven demonstrates the wide latitude in decision-making she now had with her school board. That they allowed her to hire a full-time music teacher when the school was in need of a science laboratory also speaks to their commitment to music. In fact, music appreciation was a core value of the school. Familiarity with classical music was *de rigueur* for well-bred, upper-middle-class families in those times. By 1937, the school employed a teacher from the town to lead a school choir and teach piano, violin, records, guitar, a huge harmonica, mouth organ and recorders.

Dr Leven's arrival in 1939 coincided with dire events on the Continent. War was imminent. The spontaneous pleasures of singing and dancing ceased; music was now to be studied and mastered. The school had always had a high percentage of talented youngsters, many who arrived carrying their violins. Several were accomplished pianists, singers and artists. Children who expressed an interest in music (of course they had to pay fees) took music lessons from Dr Leven. Everybody practised seriously. People could use either of the two pianos in the house or, if they played recorder, flute or violin, various rooms and closets during afternoon free time. Once Dr Leven was in residence, music filled the house the year round. Hans [Goldy] Goldmeier, another boy who would join Martin's circle of friends in 1941, recalled, 'The large room was also used by our music students for practice sessions of violin or the piano. A grand piano graced the room near the large bay window. The students repeated over and over the difficult sections of Mozart or Beethoven sonatas, the music floating over the whole valley when the windows were open. I never resented the practicing. We always knew who was at the piano and who was playing the violin and the music students nearly always received the appropriate praise or teasing from the rest of us.'[59] The musicians sometimes had to fight for practise time in the finite spaces available to them, whether a bathing room, a room in the air-raid shelter, the elegant sitting room with its tuned piano or the school room with its dilapidated piano (destined to be dismantled in 1940 by a Shop crew) one floor below. An anonymous child wrote for *The Bridge*, 'Edith with her violin victoriously practices for one and a half hours from the green bathroom', and went on to describe the day a visitor toured the school. 'As we went along, the noise became worse, because we could hear the two pianos, quite distinctly. One person was playing Bach's "Italian Concerto" to the accompaniment of "The Village Green" on the other piano. A choir was rehearsing in one of the rooms, and then someone began scraping the C major scale on a violin.'[60]

Controversy surrounded the new music teacher. Eveline Landau [Kanes] wrote, 'Of the three, Dr Leven was the most difficult. She recognised I was musical but was impatient and dismissive with me when she tutored me in maths because of my inability to apply concepts to problems.... She embarrassed me greatly on one occasion when the orchestra performed in the sitting room, [calling out] "Miss Landau, your G-string is flat". At that moment I think I really hated her.'[61] One could never accuse Dr Leven of false praise. One day she was rehearsing the choir when Dr Lion walked in, beaming. She said 'Marvellous, marvellous', to which Dr Leven retorted, 'Terrible, terrible'. Some children were just plain frightened by Dr Leven. David Fielker, a post-war pupil, once played her a composition for piano he had written. Instead of praise came her response: 'Nobody writes like Mozart nowadays.' He later became a serious student of music with an encouraging mentor and wrote ' "After years of continual discouragement", I found someone who was "actually teaching me how to write music!" ', and he went on to write plainchant and organum, masses, fugues, impromptus and sonatas.[62] And then there was the time Dr Leven committed an appallingly selfish act. Wolff was the injured party. 'Here's my third reason for still being mad at Dr Leven: Once a year, surplus chickens from the farm were culled and we had a glorious chicken dinner with the pieces carefully counted. Chicken was a rare treat and I couldn't wait to eat. That day, Dr Leven was the disher-outer for one of the second-floor dining rooms and I was the server for her table. I noticed that she had set the biggest and juiciest piece aside. As the number of pieces on the serving plate diminished, I noticed with increasing anxiety that the count was short by one piece. At the end, only that big juicy piece was left but two people had not been served: Dr L and me. Without a word, she scarfed up that last piece for her own plate and handed me a plate of potatoes and veggies.'[63]

Dr Leven was not without her admirers. Lilly Henschel, who had left the school in 1944 to read medicine in Edinburgh, mentioned in a letter to Gerda Stein [Mayer] that Dr Leven had been kind to her, and that she felt one could rely on her as a friend. Wolff admits Dr Leven was 'a great teacher and I learned a lot from her, especially in those voluntary Friday night sessions on the history of art and music. I don't think she liked children, unless they had real musical talent. Then she went all out.'[64] Beate Frankfurter [Plonskoy] enjoyed her beginner's violin lessons with Dr Leven. 'Her teaching technique gave me a good foundation to build on and benefits me still; the choir singing, the recorder group and last but not least, playing the trumpet in a grand performance of Haydn's Toy Symphony.'[65]

Dr Leven babied her most talented youngsters. She would never have dreamt of stopping the car to pick up a child walking up the long steep hill to Stoatley Rough, but when her star performer needed a ride, it was different. Renate Herold [Richter] recalled, 'I was to sing a Mozart cantata, the *Freimaurer*, for a concert, a complicated piece that needed a lot of practice. A few days before the event I was called to London. [to bid farewell to her brother who was leaving for Normandy]. Several days before I was due back, Dr Leven telephoned me in a state of panic; I must go back immediately to prepare for my big solo performance. So back I went, to be met by the school car no less, an absolutely unprecedented honour, to be confronted by a near hysterical Dr Leven who proceeded to ply me with raw eggs which were supposed to be beneficial to the vocal chords.'[66]

Dr Leven took over art appreciation, formerly taught by Dr Wolff, sometimes catching a smart remark about this or that painting from a bored student. She offered a series of lectures on art history, held every Friday evening, and (brilliantly) made attendance by invitation only. Everyone wanted in. Wolff recalled, 'Art history is a subject unlikely to attract teenagers but Dr Leven used great psychology. There was no compulsion. On the contrary, attendance was by invitation, as a privilege one could earn after one's fifteenth birthday. Each illustrated lecture was a formal occasion, one of the few for which we had to wear school tie and blazer. I remember it so well, from Cimabue and Giotto to Gauguin and Van Gogh. Dr Leven opened up a new world to me and I pity any child raised in a school system that regards art and music as dispensable luxuries ... I really appreciated Dr Leven's lectures years later, in New York, when I took a required college course in art appreciation from a bored professor.'[67] Goldy Goldmeier concurred. 'I remember with special fondness the large drawing-room with the lead-framed windows looking out over the valley, used for special events, like "Friday Night", a two-hour period with our Music and Art teacher who, with her projector, showed us some of the great paintings from different periods going back to the Renaissance.... She also played classical music for us and explained it with the help of her wind-up phonograph.'[68]

The children sometimes had trouble following Dr Leven's rationale. She considered Uli Hubacher to be very gifted, yet he received no lessons; she gave Peter Gaupp violin lessons while excluding his brother, Dieter, who had years of piano lessons. The younger boys did not always revere good music. They found nothing more hilarious than to apply their words to classical tunes when Dr Leven was out of earshot. The adults still recall their version of 'The March of the Toreadors' with its perfect cadences: *Auf in den Kampf | Die Schwiegermutter kommt, Sieg – es – gewiss | Klappert ihr Gebiss* [On to the fight | The mother-in-law comes | Sure of victory | Her dentures clattering].[69]

When the Americans entered the war, they brought their jazz and swing to England. The boys listened avidly to Glenn Miller's US Army Air Corps Band, electrified by the exciting new beat. They also liked a British station, *Soldaten Sender Calais*, that pretended to be broadcast from France, actually beamed at German soldiers. It delivered the news of the war and also played the music of Benny Goodman, Arte Shaw and the rest. Dr Leven tried to stamp out this awful *Jazzgedudel* [pronounced Yuts-gu-doodle, meaning jazz tootling], but the kids were hooked and could be found running to the maps and geography books to find the exact locations of Chattanooga, Kalamazoo, Acheson, Topeka and Santa Fe.

Something magical sometimes took hold, thanks to Dr Leven. Peter Gaupp carries lasting and specific impressions. 'I have just tried to sing again "Lift Thine Eyes, Oh Lift Thine Eyes" from *Elijah*. The last time I sang this was with Goldy in about 1942–1943 when he recruited me to reluctantly sing in the Stoatley Rough choir because he felt alone. We were both sopranos. Soon after this he left the choir – asked to leave by Dr Leven because he was no longer a boy soprano – and that left me in the lurch. Needless to say I sounded a lot better in those days – but some of the music memory remains.'[70]

The end of the peaceable kingdom

Dr Lion met Dr Leven's train and drove her to the house next door to Stoatley Rough where she would live. She helped Dr Leven get settled and introduced her to the staff, and with some juggling of schedules, Dr Leven began to teach. The staff welcomed her into their small community, recognising Dr Lion's obvious fondness for the newcomer. And then came the all-school work day, the first Saturday of each month. Dr Leven was nowhere to be seen. Dr Wolff, Nore, Hanna and the other adults toiled alongside the Household Girls supervising the children's cleaning and polishing work. But where was Dr Leven? After dinner, Nore checked the roster, then quietly walked upstairs to Herta's room. Had Dr Leven's name inadvertently been left off the list? 'No', Herta replied, 'Dr Leven was not to be given household duties.' Nore made it a point to discuss the issue with Dr Leven. Did she understand that the morale of her Household Girls and the other children depended upon the perception that all the members of the community were pulling their own weight? Dr Leven was amused. What a ridiculous notion that she should have to do manual labour. She was the music teacher, not the cleaning lady. Besides, she did not even live in the main house. It was bad enough she had been asked to take on the art history. There was no way she would be involved in house cleaning. Nore returned to her room that night, shaken by the insouciance of the newcomer. Over Monday morning breakfast, Hanna lost no time discussing the issue – it was a question of school morale after all – with Mr Phillips and the Household Girls on laundry duty that day. Word went around.

Meanwhile, Dr Lion was letting her work slip. She began to disappear from the office for long stretches. One morning a call came in from one of the parents in Berlin. Herta left her office in the Bungalow after checking Dr Lion's bedroom. She ran over to the main building and checked the kitchen, library and dining/sitting rooms, then out to the terrace (but the Headmistress would not be outdoors in this weather) and then up and down all three floors of the main building. Next she marched across the lot, disturbing Mrs Phillips at her morning tea. Hating the thought of the steep climb back, she also loped down to the Farmhouse to see if, by any chance, Dr Lion had walked down to confer with the farm manager (a long shot, since Dr Lion avoided physical exertion whenever possible). There was only one other possibility. Herta walked over to Dr Leven's house, and sure enough, there was Dr Lion sitting close to Dr Leven on the couch, the heads of the two women bent together, as Liszt's *Piano Concerto No. 2* played on the phonograph. In the following weeks, Herta had never seen Dr Lion so happy. Come to think of it, she had started going around with an uncharacteristic grin on her face. The next time Herta had to get a signature from Dr Lion, she went straight to Dr Leven's residence.

In the weeks to come, things got worse. Dr Leven sat at Dr Lion's table every meal, while Dr Wolff ended up on the third floor supervising tables of eight-year-olds. Evenings after lights out in the main house were now lonely in the Bungalow. Earlier, Dr Lion had spent time each night talking with Emmy over a last cup of Ovaltine before bedtime. Now the Headmistress was almost never home, invariably over across the way with that woman, sometimes not even returning to the Bungalow until the wee hours. Dr Wolff became despondent, then angry, seeing her warm friendship with Dr Lion coming unravelled. Before long, matters grew worse, with an escalating war of arguments and hostilities that drew Nore into the fray. Nore was on Dr Wolff's side. One day, it was a Saturday, some older girls who happened to be working in the main house actually heard Nore and Dr Leven screaming at each other, going at it for all to hear. It was a shocking turn of events. Where was Dr Lion? How had things come to this? Herta recalled only 'being partly aware of the world of grown-ups – of small power struggles and big jealousies among the elders. I had some sympathy for Emmy Wolff when Louise Leven appeared on the scene – [when she] tried to and did in fact take over in many ways.'[71] The younger children, especially Martin, Wolf and the other boys who were only eleven at the time of Dr Leven's arrival, were less aware of the schism between the head and her second, but not entirely spared. Late one night, Wolf was rummaging around among the books in the library, downstairs when he should have been upstairs in bed. Unseen by the adults, he heard Dr Leven saying something, to which Dr Wolff replied in her deep voice. '*Sie haben mir die Hilde abtruennig gemacht!!*' ['You have alienated Hilde's affection']. There was a pause, a muffled response, and then, each word thick and ragged, Dr Wolff repeated, 'You ... have ... alienated ... her affection.' It was a shocking statement, notable that Dr Wolff uses the formal word for 'you'. Wolf sneaked back to bed, unable to get the hostile exchange out of his mind. For months an undercurrent of unease coursed through the school. The older pupils, especially the Household Girls, gave a wide berth to the adult German teachers.

Dr Wolff and Dr Leven were very different women. The aristocratic Dr Wolff with her warm brown eyes and aquiline nose was an impeccably groomed, elegant and intellectual woman. She always expressed herself calmly and was aware that she was a role model to the children. Not so with Luise Leven. She was impetuous and unfashionable and could be waspish and alternately irritated or exuberant. The character of each woman showed in her attitude towards the school. Dr Wolff had plunged into her new duties doing work she had never have touched in Germany. Dr Leven expressed little gratitude for her new life at Stoatley Rough and begrudged her extra duties. Her incomplete, unpublished, hand-written history of the school written in the 1950s often reveals a complaint just beneath the surface. 'I had to coach pupils in math and had to deal with the school's finances, which involved a great deal of work and responsibility.'[72]

Renate Dorpalen [Dorpalen-Brocksieper] wrote of the effect of Dr Leven's arrival at the school. 'The institution had been changed by cliques, rivalries and favouritism. Old friendships were challenged. A rift had opened up between Dr Lion and Dr Wolff because of the gradual but obvious intrusion into their friendship. Dr Lion began to isolate herself from the school's activities and withdrew into a life with Luise Leven off-campus. Dr Wolff was spending more time taking care of her ailing mother. Dr Leven, a talented musician but a rather self-centred, ungiving, antagonistic woman, had a condescending attitude toward anything non-academic. She showed little inclination to share in the daily activities of the school community, and lacked rapport with the students, except a few, whom she singled out for attention in most inappropriate ways.

She preferred to live outside the school complex, thus concretely separating herself from the school's life and emphasising a conduct foreign to the basic philosophy of the school. The adults and children began to suffer badly under these new developments. It was entirely due to Nore Astfalck and Hanna Nacken who were deeply affected by the tension, that difficulties were kept to a minimum and the school continued to function relatively well. For me, the shift in relationships meant new insecurities, and I experienced the total affair as another loss, as though I were the child of newly divorced parents. Once again, the world around me was collapsing. Aunt Emmy and Uncle Lutz were dead; except for a rare-outdated Red Cross message, I was totally cut off from my parents.'[73]

Dr Lion did not ask Dr Wolff to leave her quarters in the Bungalow, nor to abandon her post as second in command. Dr Wolff went on teaching and performing her normal administrative duties. But at the private level, the strife took its toll. The emotionally insecure Headmistress had a new confidante and companion. Dr Wolff had to soldier on alone. The rift between Dr Wolff and Dr Lion would not heal right away. A year later, a former employee and mother of two students at Stoatley Rough wrote to ask Dr Lion to accept her youngest, a five year old, as an evacuee from war-torn London. There ensued a flurry of correspondence among the three decision-makers: Dr Lion, the Refugee Committee representative and school Board member, Kathe Arndt. Who would pay for the girl? Kathe Arndt did some investigating behind the scenes, then wrote to the Refugee Committee (making sure to send a copy to Dr Lion) that 'a certain resident in one of the cottages on the school grounds might be willing to look after her'. It was a sly move. The 'certain resident' was Dr Wolff. The thought that Dr Wolff might sponsor the girl right under Dr Lion's nose galvanised Dr Lion into taking action. She quickly agreed to admit the girl on partial scholarship. Rather than giving Dr Wolff the satisfaction of being the problem solver, Dr Lion suddenly came up with the funding.

Dr Wolff had lost her only friend in England. It was a blow. Herta said, 'The relationship between Hilde Lion and Emmy Wolff deteriorated significantly when Luise Leven appeared on the scene. It was a hard time for Emmy Wolff, who was a slightly romantic person … she continued to live in the Bungalow in close quarters with Hilde. They each had their own room – but they often congregated in Hilde's room and I experienced them together there when they would give me dictation.'[74] Household

Girl Renate Dorpalen understood the tragic nature of the break in
friendship, now seeing Dr Wolff 'awkward and distant' in the presence
of children. The betrayal by Dr Lion crushed Emmy's spirit. Renate
'sensed quickly the misfortune of her [Emmy's] fate, which dislodged
her from former heights of professional standing.... I was often afraid
of her suppressed anger and moodiness.'

When Emmy retired in 1960, the acrimony had softened. It is especially
poignant to remember that all three women in this triangle were vulnerable
by virtue of their immigrant status. When things got bad, they had
nowhere else to go, no other job to apply for and no familial support
system from which to draw comfort. They were essentially alone, bereft
of their former careers, financial security and friends. Their plight
is something to be pitied on all sides.

Dr Leven's influence on Dr Lion is a matter for speculation. The
Headmistress encountered enormous stresses in the dark days of wartime
England and there is anecdotal evidence that she became less accessible,
perhaps more insensitive after Dr Leven arrived. Edith Hubacher
[Hubacher-Cristoffel] tells how Drs Lion and Leven took turns badgering
her for money. Her father worked in Thailand and was unable to send
her tuition until after the war. The harassment of the two women drove
Edith to leave the school at seventeen. Desperately lonely, Edith returned
to spend weekends with Nore and Hanna, sleeping on the floor in their
small quarters. It was preferable to being the constant target of the older
women.

By the end of the war, it was an accepted fact of life that there was
a rift between Drs Leven and Wolff among those students who were old
enough to notice. Gerda Haas raised the question of Dr Leven's negative
influence on Dr Lion in a piece written by Dr Lion she was translating
for the *Stoatley Rough Newsletter*, Issue 12, 1996. In her only comment
on the text, she pointed to Dr Lion's use of what appears a pejorative
term to describe the recently deceased Dr Wolff. Miss Haas wrote that
she found the term, 'firebrand' to be 'quite upsetting'. Miss Haas wrote,
'did Dr Leven help to word that article? A suspicion aggravating my
upset!'[75] The jury will forever be out on the question of Dr Leven's
influence on Dr Lion.

When the war ended and Nore and Hanna decided to return to
Germany, they were sent packing without a farewell party or public
words of gratitude from the Headmistress. The woman who had worked
tirelessly to manage the day-to-day functions of the school and whose

spirit had healed countless lost children for ten years had no bitterness. Nore wrote, 'We had told Dr Lion a long time ago that we were prepared to go back as soon as ever possible, to this bombed and destroyed and hungry country which was our country. But things turned out quite different. As you know, one of those other German schools closed down [she refers to Bunce Court] and there were a few people who were ready to come to Stoatley Rough. And so they gave us the "sack" without much ... talk about it. They said, "Well, there are some people who can take your place, so we think you should make arrangements to leave." '[76] Herta said, 'Hilde Lion treated Nore Astfalck and Hannah Nacken incredibly shabbily after the war.' One gets the sense that Nore was meant to feel like a traitor for wanting to return to Germany. It is hard to imagine how Hilde Lion could have countenanced such behaviour before the arrival of Luise Leven. Without Nore's tireless work and loving attention to detail and leadership, the school literally could never have functioned and Dr Lion knew this. Margaret Dove wrote about Nore and Hanna, 'the two of them really gave the school its unique quality and I cannot imagine what it was like without them when they returned to Germany after the war. I often wonder if Dr Lion realised how much she owed the two of them. She herself was not practical person and did not always understand the everyday problems that the rest of the German staff had to cope with.'

Dr Leven neglected to mention Nore and Hanna by name in her unpublished 'history' of Stoatley Rough, recounting the school's story as if the two women had never existed. Dr Leven wrote, 'A crisis developed immediately after the end of the war. The staff, especially the domestic one, who had been glad to live in a safe place during the bombing of the large [undecipherable] started to move. Some returned to Germany.'[77] Although some omissions in her history can be chalked up to a poor memory or lack of interest, Dr Leven must be called to task for failing to give Nore her due. The only reference Dr Leven made to the uproar that began with her arrival at the school in 1939 was a passing reference to the relationship between the Jews and the Christians. 'There was never the slightest friction ... though there were many frictions of a different kind especially among the grown-ups.'[78]

Dr Leven stayed on in her rental quarters until the deaths of Mr and Mrs Phillips and departure of Mr Phillips's successor, Miss Woolger. Then she took possession of the Lodge. Dr Wolff retired in 1956, ceding to Dr Leven at long last, the official mantle of 'second in command'.

What was it that had attracted Hilde Lion to the dynamic Dr Leven? Perhaps it was her self-confidence, coupled with a kind of glamour that the short, shy Headmistress was missing. Perhaps Dr Lion needed someone strong to help her make decisions. Four years into life at Stoatley Rough, bereft of family and friends, her school bursting at the seams, war about to break out, Dr Leven offered strength at just the time she needed it.

Dr Lion must not be judged by her personal relationships alone. Having absorbed a fair amount of educational theory in her professional life in Germany, Dr Lion built her school around the needs of the child, at the time a novel idea, and that ideal never faded. There is no doubt she liked children. She instituted communal work by staff and children, equality of the sexes and an ethic of self-reliance. That Dr Lion was impractical, unorthodox, quixotic and sometimes dictatorial was beside the point. Her secretary, Herta Lewent (Loeser), said that Dr Lion 'didn't even know if the children wore stockings or underpants'. Yet Dr Lion steered her school through twenty-six years of extraordinary political turmoil and social change.

Renate Dorpalen calls attention to the extraordinary contribution made by Drs Lion and Wolff, and to the same degree, Eleonore Astfalck and Johanna Nacken, hired with 'great wisdom and foresight', that their work is relevant to today's complex problems in the area of social services. 'This was the generation of the feminist and suffrage movements who worked for social reform and human rights.'[79] She points out that their philosophies were very much in line with those developed by the earlier feminists, Alice Salomon, founder and director of the first school for social work in Germany in 1908; Hildegard von Gierke, director of the *Jugendheim* that had been founded by Hedwig Heyl; all friends of Renate's mother. She points to the great tragedy of Dr Lion and the others who were dislodged suddenly from their prominent academic and writing careers, never to regain such status in their adopted occupations, in which they felt ill at ease for which they were poorly prepared. Yet they created in Stoatley Rough a living example of the great feminist principles forged a generation earlier by forever maintaining the founding principles, in spite of personal strife.

All three holders of PhDs – Lion, Wolff and Leven – brought high standards of literary and artistic excellence to the school. The two who supplied the emotional support to the children, Nore Astfalck and Hanna Nacken, gave the school its stability and sheltering atmosphere.

The distinguished British poet, Gerda Stein [Mayer], wrote a poem about the learned women (whom some, post-war, dubbed as the three 'Prussians'). The poem reveals as much about Gerda's happiness while she was at Stoatley Rough as about the personalities of Drs Lion, Wolff and Leven. Miss Mayer wrote the poem thirty years after she left the school.[80]

A Lion, a Wolf and a Fox
Stoatley Rough, Haslemere, 1942–1944

I went to school in a forest where I was taught
By a lion, a wolf and a fox.
How the lion shone! As he paced across the sky
We grew brown-limbed in his warmth and among the green leaves.
The fox was a musician. O cunning magician you lured
A small stream from its course with your *Forellenlied*,[81]
Teaching it Schubert; and made the children's voices
All sound like early morning and auguries for a fine day.
Now the wolf was a poet and somewhat grey and reserved,
Something of a lone wolf – thoughts were his pack;
There was a garden in that forest, walled with climbing roses,
Where we would sit or lie and hear the wolf recite.
And sometimes we would listen, and sometimes the voice
Would turn into sunlight on the wall or into a butterfly
Over the grass. It was the garden of poetry and so
Words would turn into flowers and trees into verse.
This morning I received the grey pelt of a wolf,
And the fox and the lion write they are growing old;
That forest lies many years back, but we were in luck
To pass for a spell through that sunny and musical land.

Chapter 3
The Child Workers

The girl with her slender body, piquant face and mounds of thick curly hair had something special about her, a directness that made one sit up and take notice. Facing her across the coffee table in the small hotel room in Berlin, Dr Wolff approved. This girl was not afraid of work, she was intellectually curious and obviously very smart.

'Herta, what are your favourite things to do when you aren't studying?'

Herta sat up straight. 'I used to play tennis, and only three years ago I was mad because they stopped letting us non-Aryans play sports. Before then I rowed and played *schlagball*.'

'Is that something you play with a ball and a bat?'

'Yes. Two teams of twelve players each compete. It's a little like soccer but one uses a bat. It's a lot of fun.'

Dr Wolff picked up a few documents, frowning as she read. It was the summer of 1936 – the Nazis in their third year in power – and already they had denied this girl sports programmes and had forced her out of the school system just for being Jewish. She flushed with sudden anger. These outrageous laws the National Socialist government kept passing. Would no one stop them? How could this country of Goethe and Schiller, of Beethoven and Haydn, sink to such madness? No one was safe any more. Dr Wolff reminded herself to step up her efforts to get her mother, staying with friends in Holland, into England as quickly as humanly possible. Dr Wolff looked up and spoke in English; her low, well-modulated voice was kind. 'I see that you have a fluency in English and also that you know English shorthand. Those are remarkable skills in one so young – you are only sixteen, is that right?'

'Yes ma'am, I like to keep busy, and when they kicked me out of school, I wanted to keep on learning. I also studied home economics, but I am more interested in secretarial work than household management. And I'd like to visit England. It would be fun.' Dr Wolff knew this was the girl she would hire – there was a sweetness and honesty that Dr Wolff knew Hilde would admire. Dr Wolff rose to her feet and switching back to German, asked Herta to bring her father into the room so that the three could discuss the conditions of the job.

Mr Lewent listened attentively. There would be no salary, of course –
British laws were strict about paying aliens. Dr Wolff hastened to add the
good news. Of course, Herta would receive free room and board for the
simple tasks of handling Dr Lion's correspondence, doing the filing and
answering the telephone. Mr Lewent sat back in his chair. He did not want
his little girl to be overworked. Dr Wolff assured him that Herta would get
time off and she should fit in nicely with the other children her age at
school. Mr Lewent, an engineer at Agfa, said that he and his wife,
an economist, were trying to relocate to England as well. Their son,
Helmut, planned to apply for Stoatley Rough's Farm programme. The two
adults and Herta concluded their meeting with handshakes all around.

Herta turned back when she reached the door, her curls incongruent
with the gravity on her face. 'Dr Wolff, please, I have one more question.'

'Of course, my dear.'

'May I bring my canary bird with me?'

The young secretary

Dr Wolff had been in Berlin the summer of 1936, just before Dr Lion was
to join her on the Continent for a six-week marathon of recruiting and
interviewing prospective pupils. She was greatly disturbed by the ugly
prejudice now openly expressed in Berlin, just one year later. In her talks
with the parents, she learned of the damage the Nuremberg Laws were
inflicting on the Jews in everyday ways – park benches restricted to
'Aryans', public places, such as swimming pools and theatres, closed
to Jews, Jews being depicted with leering, evil faces in the pornographic
and virulently anti-Semitic tabloid *Der Stuermer* [The Stormer], which
drew curious crowds along the urban streets. She was more than ready
to return to England.

Herta and her father arrived in Haslemere on 7 March 1937. They
took a cab up to the school on Farnham Lane, and after stopping in the
courtyard, Herta hopped out of the car and ran over to look at the view.
She saw there were two tennis courts just below the main house and
on the second court two people were engaged in a fast volley; she
couldn't tell for sure, but they seemed to be a teacher and a teenage
boy. 'A grass tennis court! I made a vow to myself that before the day
was over I didn't care what else I did, but I wanted to play tennis with
that boy.' And I did.' The boy was Hans Loeser, her future husband.

Herta, trusting and fearless, was prepared for her new life. Her association with Stoatley Rough would be unique not only because she was the first secretary of the school but also because her four years bridged both the pre-war period and the early wartime years. She arrived when the original child-centred concept of education was in full bloom, when the children had plenty of wholesome food and access to diversions across the English countryside, when Stoatley Rough was still a halcyon place. During her stay she would witness the hardships that going to war would bring to England, and she would help Stoatley Rough to cope. She was there when the children of Stoatley Rough, like millions of British citizens, faced physical deprivations and restrictions that changed the school into a less sanguine community than when it first opened.

Herta was born in 1921. She grew up with her parents and younger brother in an apartment in Berlin, happy to watch the streetcars and the occasional horse-drawn carriage from the balcony. Her assimilated, non-religious family attended services only on High Holidays, if at all. Herta had a pleasant childhood and was happy to spend summer vacations with her family in the mountains. Her father, an accomplished amateur photographer, would amble about taking pictures wearing his Loden coat, his baggy knickerbockers and special knee socks worn only on holiday. Her mother was more conventional in her dress, but Herta liked to wear her short socks called *Wadenstrumpfe*, which she had explained to Dr Wolff, were socks that 'just went up to your calf'.

Herta had been slated to enter the rough equivalent of eleventh grade in an American high school. The German educational system started children at six, offering four years of primary school. At ten, boys typically went on to the *Gymnasium*, while girls entered the *Lyceum*. Everybody went through *Sexta, Quinta, Quarta* [Sixth, Fifth and Fourth forms], then *Untertertia, Obertertia* and *Untersecunda* [Under-Third, Over-Third, Under-Second, Over-Second and so on, meaning first and second semesters of each year]. At sixteen, some children entered vocational training called *Berufsschule*. (Informally, the training was called the *Einjähriges* [One year], a military term.) Boys destined for a university education (and in rare cases, girls) took a stringent examination commonly called the *Abitur*.

Herta needed a trade. Her family sent her to learn home economics at a Jewish school (near the future site of the Sachsenhausen-Oranienburg concentration camp built in 1938, 35 kilometres from Berlin, whose commandant would be hanged for the shooting, hanging and marching to death of hundreds by war's end). Herta's father knew that she would need something practical and transferable if they needed to leave the country – there were few jobs in Depression-era Germany, regardless of an applicant's ethnicity. Herta studied English for six years at school, and while her aural comprehension was less than proficient, the plucky girl decided to take on English shorthand. She had no particular objective in mind. It was enough for Herta that it was challenging.

Herta moved into the room she would share with another girl her age, Barbara Gerstenberg [Prasse]. She unpacked her things and quickly made friends with her peers.

The boy on the tennis court was sixteen-year-old Hans Loeser, a tall, good-looking boy with a shock of thick dark hair and an unspoiled and generous personality. Although he knew why he had been required to leave Germany, he had cried the night before his departure, afraid he'd never be able to make the quips and jokes in English for which he was famous among his friends. He was afraid he'd lose his identity in the new country. His family owned a big department store in Kassel, a bustling city in the centre of Germany, once home to Jakob and Wilhelm Grimm. With a population of 180,000, Kassel had a thousand-year history. During the Second World War, the inner city of Kassel was reduced to rubble. Hans remembers that, standing in his bedroom's balcony, he could watch the ubiquitous streetcars clanging past the building with comfortable regularity, before 1933. With the election of the National Socialist party, however, the scene now included gangs of warring political parties engaging in hand-to-hand combat in the street, 'Nazis, Social Democrats, Communists, and right wing German nationalists led by Prussian Junker families and ex-officers.'[1] His parents did not keep a kosher kitchen and celebrated Easter and Christmas. His was a cultured family. His parents spoke French when they didn't want Hans and his big sister, Elisabeth [Fontana], to understand them. On the High Holidays, his father dipped his silk top hat as the family strolled to the temple to take their inherited seats. Herr Loeser played the violin and sang, a true son of the Gilded Age, and made sure Hans received violin lessons in spite of Hans' acknowledged lack of musical talent. It did not matter – children of his class played an instrument. Hans was thirteen in April 1933 when the storm troopers arrived at his father's department store and started telling the shoppers to leave, obscenely calling the Loeser family, *Scheissjude* [shit Jews] or *Stinkjude* [stinking Jews]. They used black, white and red paint to write *Jude* [Jew] on the plate glass.

One of the ironies of being a child in an oppressive state is the lure of the oppressor's culture. When his classmates became members of the youngest of the Hitler Youth groups, *Jungvolk* [Young People], Hans and other Jewish boys also wanted to join. The Hitler Youth wore black, very short corduroy shorts, and brown shirts with a black kerchief held in place by a Nazi swastika ring at the neck. The Jewish boys imitated the costume, wearing their own very short corduroy pants with knee socks. 'My military belt had a more neutral buckle than the *Jungvolk*'s swastika. But I have little doubt that, had we been allowed to join, we would have.'² Hans recalls that at first, the anti-Semitism at school was 'good-natured', but after 1933, when it became mandatory to greet teachers with a raised right arm and a '*Heil Hitler*', the six Jews in Hans' class of twenty-six children stood but were not allowed to salute. He recalled the small packs of Hitler Youth waiting to attack and beat up the unwary Jewish child riding a bicycle. His teachers became scornful and insulting. Birthday parties came to an end, and neighbours began to look away when they passed the Loesers on the street. At his violin lessons, his teacher greeted him with '*Heil Hitler*' to make him feel uncomfortable. After the collapse of his business, his father became depressed but soon rallied, as if exclusion from German activities heightened his sense of Jewish identity. The family began to observe the traditional Friday night ceremony of welcoming the Sabbath, lighting candles and saying *Kiddush* over bread and wine. They attended high-quality lectures for Jews sponsored by the newly formed civic organisation, the *JüdischerKulturbund*, because Jews were now barred from attending the opera and other cultural events. Some of Hans' uncles began to quietly transfer assets abroad and to nurture foreign business connections. In 1935, Hans' parents sent Elisabeth to boarding school in Northern Italy, and Hans followed, in 1936, to a fancy boarding school near Nyon on Lake Geneva. His father sold the business. Within days, the seventy-five-year-old business of Ferdinand Loeser and Company reopened under an Aryan name and customers flooded back. Five years later, the store was bombed to the ground.

Hans travelled by train, boat and again by train to London and somehow, with only two years of English (and utterly failing to understand any English that he heard in Paddington station), managed to find the train to Haslemere. He arrived at the school in April 1937. He took his violin in its shockproof case and his luggage to the school. 'Haslemere taxi drivers had learned by then that people with little or no English were to be taken to Stoatley Rough.'[3] Miss Astfalck and others received him warmly at the school. He recalled, 'God, what a relief it was to be back in a comfortable German atmosphere.'[4]

Herta and Hans made friends with other children their age, especially Klaus Zedner, a boy who had arrived in September 1935 and Barbara Gerstenberg [Prasse], who had arrived in August 1936. Room-mates Hans and Klaus slept in The Tin, a room at the end of a long corridor behind the kitchen, a relatively isolated den with its own entrance from the outside. 'One could slip in and out, day and night, unobserved and without having to account to anybody.'[5] The boys explored the house together, and then Hans noticed a most intriguing thing – a trap door in the ceiling of their room. They found a way to get up and through the trap door, landing in a hidden room under the eaves. The room, in turn, led to myriad crawl spaces connecting to other parts of the house. The excited boys soon pulled up mattresses, pillows and other items and proceeded to hold night parties in their ceiling lair they dubbed *Klingsburg* [*Burg* for castle, the meaning of *Klings* long forgotten] for selected friends, spending long hours discussing the mysteries of life. It did not take Miss Astfalck long to find out about the hideaway. 'She raised some hell over the unauthorized disappearance of useful things, but she also expressed admiration for our inventiveness and decorating skills. When we offered a deal, namely that she would be invited to our next party, she accepted – and did come. The extra pleasure of secrecy was now gone, but a new, conspiratorial bond had been established with Miss Astfalck which felt very good.'[6] Klaus and Hans must have discussed girls, although Hans claims that their talk was always respectful. But the fact was that Klaus Zedner and Barbara Gerstenberg became a couple. They took walks together, and when he gave her a wooden box he had made in shop class, she vowed to keep it forever. (She still keeps it in her dresser drawer, sixty-seven years later.) But their love was not to be. Before long, Barbara dropped Klaus for Hans. Their love was not to be either. In July 1938, Barbara left for the United States.[7] By now Herta had been at the school for over a year, rooming with Barbara until she left. Summer of 1937 arrived. There was a whole world to be explored. Hans and Herta were ready for adventure.

The two teenagers developed a special bonding with Nore Astfalck, who tolerated the penchant of some of the older residents for roaming the countryside far beyond the boundaries of Stoatley Rough. Miss Dove was a young English teacher who arrived in the fall of 1937. She wrote about the carefree times: 'The older pupils were given a great deal of freedom, or perhaps they just took it, I am not sure which.... On Sundays sometimes the older ones were given permission to go hiking all day since walking in the country had been very popular in Germany during the Weimar Republic. In actual fact, the pupils often hitchhiked all over the south of England, usually two by two, a boy and girl together – and no one came to any harm.'[8] Ilse Bauer (Feldstein) actually hitchhiked to Edinburgh with Katya Schaefer [Sheppard] to visit Lilly Henschel, a medical student there. The authorities allowed the older children to travel to London on their own. On 11 December 1936, a few Roughians, one wearing her Girl Guide uniform, stood most of the night outside Buckingham Palace to be in a good spot when the parade swept by bearing the Cinderella carriage of the new king, George VI, the father of Elizabeth II, who would be crowned on 11 May 1937.

Sometimes the children went on picnics to the nearby Waggoners Wells and Gibbet Hill. Laurie Halls described how the Roughian children tramped together over the heath, carrying their picnic baskets and singing '*Wir haben hunger, hunger / hunger haben wir*' [We are hungry, hungry / hungry are we] and other songs. (Eight-year-old Laurie, a poor English boy, was plucked from his home by one of the well-meaning board members to live with the pupils at Stoatley Rough to help them learn English; an arrangement Laurie found perfectly satisfactory during the two years he was there.) The Roughians were well ahead of their time in matters of environmental protection. They meticulously collected their trash after their picnics and carted it back home.

In the summers of 1937 and 1938, Herta and Hans hitchhiked around southern England, sometimes with others, sometimes just with each other. Nore felt that the experience was healthy. As a teenager, Nore had been part of an informal movement in Germany known as *Wandervogel* [Ramblers], groups of young people who went for walks in the woods equipped with rucksacks, guitars and cooking pots. In the days before the First World War, Nore's Sunday outings caused tongues to wag since there were usually more boys than girls, but Nore's mother was progressive and dismissed the gossip. Nore credited *Wandervogel* for giving her independence, self-confidence and enthusiasm for life. The experience was more than just walking around with other children carrying a guitar: 'We started … something quite new … it was not only an organisation for young people who wanted to be out of the towns and to live in the woods and meadows. It was much more than that.

It was a beginning; the aim was to start a new way of life in more freedom, not to follow the rules but to think of new rules, to create our own young life.'⁹ Herta and Hans benefited from Nore's liberal attitudes. They always reported their escapades afterwards, telling Miss Astfalck that they had gone 'beyond Liphook' (a village near Haslemere), code for going far afield. 'And [Nore] would know very well that we had been to the beach or some other fun place.' Herta loved Nore for her tolerance and trust in never knowing that the couple may have hitchhiked to Brighton Beach for a bracing swim in the ocean. As long as they were back in time for the evening meal, the outings were tolerated. Nobody even thought of the possibility of the danger of kidnappers lying in wait. It was the war, not fear of strangers, that would put an end to the fun. After September 1939, Roughians were not allowed to venture near the coastal regions newly designated as 'protected areas'. Such high-security places were forbidden to aliens.

Drs Lion and Wolff were still housed in the main building, as were Herta, Nore and her partner Hanna. But at the end of 1936, good news arrived for the two senior women on the staff. The board approved £550 to build a new building, to be called the Bungalow. It would have a bedroom each for Drs Lion and Wolff, a bathroom and a room for sick children. Almost as an afterthought, it would also have a tiny office for Herta with a window that looked out toward the main house and Farnham Lane. Herta would spend a great deal of time in that room, would see to the school's official business there and would witness the turbulent personal affairs that erupted when the new music teacher arrived in 1939, Dr Leven.

Halcyon days

School offices in 1936 were primitive compared to today's electronic operational centres. Herta had to type everything in duplicate using carbon paper, correcting her typos twice with a special eraser. Not even the machine that bridged the manual typewriter and the computer, IBM's Selectric, had been invented yet. Herta also sent out bills, sorted letters, filed correspondence and reports, answered the telephone and ran errands. She also typed official notices – the school did not get a duplicating machine until 1941. (People over sixty in the United States will remember seeing the boxy contraption in the school office, the teacher cranking away as the big drum churned out stencilled announcements for the children to carry home.) Herta called the school's duplicator a 'Gestetner multiplying monster' that got ink all over her hands. She itemised her duties in an article she wrote for the school newspaper, *The Bridge*, in 1941.[10]

'Passports and Registration Certificates need constant watching as they might want renewal. Lectures and Visits must be arranged and sometimes people who have left long ago want a testimonial.... The card index has to be kept up-to-date. Books are to be written for from various libraries and the days of return must not be forgotten. Timetables and lists of any kind are just another "source" for work. And in between the telephone rings.' Herta typed each pupil's report at the end of each term and issued circulars regarding holidays and travel. During the war, she cut out and organised food and clothing coupons from over 100 ration books; she saved stamps for the children's hospital and recycled paper for 'wrapping up parcels'.

Peak work periods, such as the end of a semester, kept Herta up all night with worry. 'This sounds rather a scrappy account, but that is just what a day in the office is like. There are so many little things to be thought of and so many people to be hunted after, because I must ask them one or the other question. But it can be very exciting too, if important messages and news have to be given out in time.' Looking back at all the work, it seems that Herta ran the place single-handedly.

While grateful to be safe in England, Herta felt thwarted and frustrated at not being able to further her education, especially since Hans, Barbara and Klaus were allowed to waltz off to class every day. She grew to resent Dr Lion's power over her future. 'Instead of taking the school certificate [Matric] which is what everybody took to enable you to go to the university, I had to take something that qualified you for English. I was really mad at them because I probably could have managed to attend school even if it had taken longer.... Dr Lion was narrow-minded in that she pigeonholed you. Once I went to take some sewing classes and she said "No, that is not for you." Sometimes I just went to classes and the telephone would ring.... And Dr Lion would have to go chasing after me and I'd have to drop what I was doing. "You can't take any classes. We've been looking all over for you." So I was exploited a lot. I had no money. They weren't really allowed to pay. All I got was a tiny, tiny pocket money.' The immigrant adults eventually received some form of salary. Herta never did.

Like the older Household Girls, Herta dwelled in an interim place
at the school between pupil and staff, preferring to socialise with girls
and boys her own age, yet technically a member of the staff. When she
entered the teacher's lounge for a morning break, only Nore and Miss
Dove welcomed her. 'We didn't have any money to pay so I couldn't
go to school. I was as mad as a hatter. I wasn't right away mad, I was
glad to be out, but I had to work for the headmistress.'

Herta had an especially tough challenge with one aspect of her work.
'I was told on the first day to keep all information confidential. And
I certainly kept to it. I had access to the confidential files on all the kids,
and I really wasn't any older than most of them. So that was a huge
burden, because whenever anybody asked me anything I always had
to say, "I don't know", so everybody had to think I was an idiot. But
it taught me a lot about confidentiality.' Her office was a small space
partitioned in the Bungalow. 'My office was cold, tiny and had a window
looking out on the path to the main building. I could see who arrived and
when, and who left. When it was cold I could use a little electric fire which
roasted me in the back and left my fingers frozen and full of chilblains.'[11]

Herta and Hans and others in their mid-teens especially enjoyed
wandering around at night after 'lights out', in what came to be known
as going on 'Night Walks'. Everybody sneaked out. They climbed out
of windows, tiptoed down hallways past snoring adults behind closed
doors and ran across Farnham Lane to the Heath. The key was not
to get caught. Children speaking German-accented English were not
favoured in an England mistrustful of anything German. The situation
worsened during curfew. Dr Lion was intensely opposed to night walking
not only because she feared unwanted pregnancies, but also because she
had to protect the reputation of her school with the locals. She feared
backlash, and rightly so, from any sign of disrespect for English law.
Only once did she deliver the ultimate punishment – expulsion – and
it was for someone who had been caught at a night walk. Her usual
reaction was to give the child or children a good talking to, and if the
truant was female, to assign her to sleeping quarters well guarded
against future escape.

Many Stoatley Roughians remember night walks. In 1941, Dieter
Gaupp went out walking with his friends to enjoy the fresh air on the
heath, look at the stars and watch the searchlights in the distance over
London drag their pale swaths of light across the black skies. A few of the
boys lit up forbidden cigarettes when on their return, they suddenly ran

into Dr Lion and another teacher. 'One of the guys jerked the cigarette from his mouth, sank it into his jacket pocket, and gave it a quick pat'. After a brief round of greetings, Dr Lion said, 'Carry on smoking.' Out came the cigarettes, passed all around and Dr Lion lit up the one offered to her by the boys. (Dr Lion, a notorious chain smoker, was known to shamelessly cadge a cigarette from anyone who offered her one, even taking a second one for later.) They all had a little chat as they smoked. Then everyone went off to bed.

Herta returned to her full-time duties when classes resumed in the fall of 1937 and Hans went back to his studies. Some of the older students left the school for weaving school, engineering school (evening classes) and apprenticeships in a carpenter's workshop. Two girls left for India and Palestine. Miss Margaret Dove settled in, and a Mr Basil Grimshaw and Miss Hetherington joined the teaching staff. There were many excellent teachers at Stoatley Rough throughout the years, but a few, such as Miss Dove, occupied a special place in the hearts of its pupils. Although her tenure lasted only two years at Stoatley Rough, Miss Dove, a tall slim lady 'of upright carriage', was always polite, spoke in a soft voice, doled out kindness to all and treated the children with sensitivity.

Herta passed her government English proficiency examination in 1938. By then Hans had finished school and passed his university qualifying examinations, the Matric. He went off to work at a department store in London, hitchhiking back and forth to the school on weekends. When London became unsafe during the Blitz, Dr Lion, who was fond of Hans, took him back and gave him a job as resident handyman. Herta likes to say that Hans worked for her as her office boy. 'We had a bell system that went from the main house to Dr Lion's bungalow. Hans had to fix the bell and I remember him, we had an attic above my little office, and he was sitting up there fixing the bell and taking an awful long time. He and I became very friendly in the course of his working for me, and he also became the school's driver, so that he was always allowed to take the car.'

To her credit, Herta made the most of life in the sunshine of her adolescence – she knew how to have fun and to take life head on. In 1937, she and Hans fell in love. She is frank about their relationship. 'I lived in a room called The Woods, above the kitchen. Just outside, it had a very nice lightning rod. Hans would come in through the window. The Headmistress had an absolute thing about boys and girls. In retrospect it is totally un-understandable to us why somebody didn't get pregnant. I mean, she had such a phobia about it all. Usually when you are so worried, it happens. She never quite knew what went on.'[12] Only one other couple married who met at the school: Lilly Wohlgemuth and Peter Gluecksmann. Like that of Hans and Herta, theirs was a lifelong union.

Herta and Hans understood that when a child was admitted to the school, he or she was escaping the Nazis. They did not know about death camps yet, but they knew, through Herta's access to Dr Lion's correspondence, that the situation on the Continent was deadly for Jews. Hans and Herta actively began to help children escape. Rescuing children was grown-up work, and they were aware that they were doing something important. 'By then it was becoming quite clear that things were getting worse and worse in Germany, and we took any kids that we could get into England and out of Germany and Austria. By that time there were some Committees in London that paid the school fees if the parents could not. We had very good connections to them, and the Headmistress, I told you, wasn't a very practical lady. So Hans and I figured out a way to get more children out. We were only seventeen and seventeen-and-a-half ourselves, but we made friends by mail with a British Consul in Berlin, and we worked out a system with him. If we could get any semblance of an affidavit from an English person who would say they would pay for a child … we would send the guarantee to this British consul, and he would immediately give the visa to get the child into England…. That way we must have gotten out something like twenty to thirty kids who wouldn't have gotten out otherwise. Our Headmistress was not very gifted for this kind of thing. We got it by writing. The Headmistress probably helped with that, and we had daily contact with the refugee Committees and got guarantees from them. But we were very imaginative about it all, and it was very exciting because we knew every time we got one of those letters off, we had another child out of danger.'[13] Herta approached this work with an adolescent's *joie de vivre*. 'There was a mailbox, halfway down Farnham Lane, and if we couldn't catch the mail going out that night then a whole day would be missed. So we got permission to use the school car so we could mail our letters at the post office in Haslemere. We almost always managed to miss the mail pickup on Farnham Lane, as you can imagine, and we had a very good time going down to the little town. It was very exhilarating…. This was the one time that Hans ever had an accident, not a very serious one, because he was driving with his arm around me.... We had to go home like two sheep and confess.'[14]

Hans and Herta sat down to the Christmas/Chanukah party in December 1939. It was a special breakfast with apples and lighted candles in front of every place setting, and each child feasted on hot chocolate and spice cake. In the middle of the table stood a pyramid of fretwork animals. It had become a tradition to have such a party and even in the worst days of the war, the school celebrated the two holidays jointly. Later that evening, Hans had news for Herta. He had learned that his visa had come through and that he would go to America with his family. In the two and a half years that they had been together at the school, Hans and Herta had developed a bond that became more than a passing infatuation. They were almost grown-up. Like millions of others at that point in history, they were captive to the larger events swirling around them. Like the lovers who would become famous in *Casablanca* a few years hence, personal plans were not 'worth a hill of beans' to these two Stoatley Rough teenagers. Neither questioned the fact that they would be separated, although they had told their respective parents that they wanted to get married (news which elicited the scoffing retort: it's just puppy love). Just before Hans was scheduled to sail, Herta landed in the hospital for a tonsillectomy. 'Hans came to visit me and I think he brought me a present. He was always a little embarrassed when he gave me a present, so he tossed me something, and it was a very nice fountain pen.' And then he left. Separated by a continent and a war, neither Hans nor Herta had any idea whether they would ever meet again.

Workers and scholars

One of Herta's best friends at school was Inge Hamburger [Pavlowsky], a talented artist who arrived as a Household Girl in February 1938, at age seventeen. Nore tried to fit the duties to each Household Girl's abilities and inclinations, and along with regular cleaning duties, she asked Inge to weave cloth and help Mr Obee, the school's handyman, with his repair jobs. Later, Nore promoted Inge to be Hanna's assistant in the shop, where she taught younger children crafts and woodworking on her own, working as a regular teacher. She found time to paint a decorative border around the shop ceiling. Like Herta, Inge and the other Household Girls had no real choices as to their duties, schedules or level of exertion required to perform their duties. No one escaped the hardest chores and some of the work was difficult, as Ilse Kaiser [Neivert] indicated, especially 'polishing floors with heavy polishing brushes, which one was pushing back and forth between stretched out legs'.

Once a month the Household Girls led the general clean-up morning. Children might help Mr Phillips in the gardens or work under the direction of Miss Astfalck in the main house. Dr Lion wrote, 'The whole school, including the teachers, have to do something practical; the little ones brush mats and clean the silver, the older ones look to the electric lamps.'[15] Standards were high. Maria Goldwater [Danziger] recalled that after leaving furniture polish on the wood around the door knocker she was cleaning one Saturday, Dr Lion chastised her. 'Na ja my dear, not even the poorest housemaid would do that!' Yet it was the Household Girls who did heavy cleaning every Saturday, rain or shine. Young Renate Dorpalen [Dorpalen-Brocksieper], described a typical Saturday morning.[16]

'Saturday morning! "Don't come through here! The other way round, please." Through the whole house you can hear this shouting of people who do not want to be disturbed while they clean the house.... One only can hear the running of water, the rushing through the house of household people, the rattling and clashing of pails. Beginning on the third floor and ending in the nursery they sweep and scrub, they dust and polish bathrooms, floors and lavatories. Nevertheless, you must sing and think of something nice – what it would be like to sit in the sun and to read a book. Don't dream too much, otherwise you may be blamed for forgetting something! Work begins. The first thing is to get enough pails [of water] to scrub with, otherwise you must start with a fight! Secondly if you need your neighbour's polishing brush, you go to her, ask for the brush, and say how nicely the floor is done, and that it looks awfully good and so on and then you have a chance of getting the brush. That is the way we fight over our work! In the cellars there are several larders, like dairy. There is one for food, of course, and one for soap and wax and Pulvo [a laundry power]. Nothing else is allowed in these cellars except one big trunk, which cannot go anywhere else. In this so-called soap-cellar, you can find everything you need and

on Saturdays it is a very useful place. Now the trouble is that you
cannot go into the house when they are cleaning and you are not
allowed even to walk through without a big struggle with the
household people. They clean the entrance, they close the door
and in the schoolroom there are lessons; sometimes you can rush
through the kitchen without further ado. At least at one o'clock
we have finished cleaning, the house looks tidy and nice for Sunday;
you can almost skate in the sitting room, the floor is so shiny.
Hardly anyone can believe that the cleaning is done only by the
Household Girls.'

Like Herta, the Household Girls were neither staff nor pupils. Their
average age was fifteen. While they all did cleaning chores, each had
additional special duties, such as caring for the youngest children
or taking over the kitchen every Tuesday, the cook's day off. One of the
more arduous tasks, reserved for older girls and performed rain or shine,
every week in the year, was laundry. They washed sheets and towels for
the entire Stoatley Rough population (which grew to over 100 in 1940).
Washing clothes could be considered primitive by present standards.
There were no synthetic, drip-dry, stretch or wrinkle-free fabrics. The
girls washed woollens, linens and silks in cold water, and they washed
cottons in boiling water laced with lye. There was no Woolite, fabric
softener or packaged stain remover to help the homemaker; there were
no colourfast dyes, pre-shrunk cottons or fleece. And, of course, Stoatley
Rough had no electric washing machines or dryers.

Their work seems like drudgery today, but the girls with laundry duty
enjoyed the camaraderie and the sense of accomplishment they achieved.
They felt privileged to share breakfast tea and bread with Mr Phillips,
Miss Nacken and other early risers; they were happy to sit in the cosy
kitchen with others who worked while the rest of the household slept.

The process was highly structured. The girls sorted and pre-soaked
sheets overnight in cold water and soda on Mondays. They washed the
laundry on Tuesdays, days when they rose early for their cosy breakfasts.
As the others lingered over a second cup of tea, one girl would leave the
group and let herself into the laundry room located next to the kitchen
door and off a small back terrace to start the fire going under the tubs,
a difficult task during the cold, dark winter months. When the others
arrived, they separated any overlooked woollens and silks from the
cottons and the large items from the small. Socks went into a special

lidded tub with four wooden blades rotated by a handle. After stirring the socks around for a while in the hot water, the girls fished them out, turned them inside out and then returned them to the soapy water for further agitation after which they transferred the socks to a clear-water tub to be rinsed. Sheets were wrung out between the rollers of the hand-cranked mangle and then put into water boiling in enormous tubs over a wood fire, then pulled out with wooden sticks and plunged into tubs filled with cold running water. Everything then went through the mangle. Selected cottons went into another tub of starch-infused water, and then everything was hung on clotheslines to dry (during winter, sometimes the laundry froze to the lines). Every other week the girls alternated between washing whites (mostly sheets and towels) and coloured items. Lacking rubber gloves, their hands would be red by the end of the washing cycle, and they would laugh and talk as they applied lotion in the evening. They managed what grew to be an enormous volume of bedding by an ingenious method: children transferred their top sheets to the bottom of their beds once a week and received a clean sheet for the top. (Fitted sheets had not been invented yet.)

It took almost a week to do a complete cycle of laundry. After the clothing and sheets were dry, everything had to be ironed. The girls placed heavy padding across a large table and worked with hot irons heated up on the coal-burning stove. They used sprinkling bottles of water to wet down the fabric. When her iron cooled, a girl would simply place it back on top of the stove and pick up another one, using a potholder since the handles were as hot as the irons themselves. When an inspector once asked why Stoatley Rough didn't use ironing boards (they did not have any) Edith Hubacher [Christoffel] piped up: 'It would be easier using ironing boards, but we don't have enough room.' Nore whispered, to her immense gratification, 'Good answer.' After ironing, the girls folded each piece to specification. Familiar with everyone's clothing, Nore would help the girls place items labelled with the students' names in the correct cubby holes located on the ground floor.

The programme that had begun as technical training, an experiment, inevitably led to a class system at the school. (The other large German-English school, Anna Essinger's Bunce Court in Kent, never asked its scholarship students to assume this type of essential work or tried to solve its domestic labour problem so creatively.) The Household Girls were not always invited to events open to other children, such as special outings or evening lectures, and along with the Farm Boys, were at the bottom of the implicit social hierarchy. Renate Dorpalen said, 'the designation carried a rather negative connotation among the student body and teachers, and it did little to strengthen my already fragile self-image.' Helmet Lewent (Herta's brother), a Farm Boy in 1938/1939, wrote (without rancour), 'There was always some rivalry between the farming department and the rest of the school. We farm lads were somewhat looked down upon, nevertheless we were still good enough to have English lessons by that indomitable Miss Dove and to enjoy Sunday breakfasts with real cornflakes and boiled eggs in the school dining room.' (Farm boys studied only one academic subject, English.) This sense of difference must have been particularly galling to the children, most of whom had come from upper-middle-class families. Renate Dorpalen wrote of class sensitivities in her own Jewish family, when she described playing a role in *Der Biberpelz* [The Beaver Fur Coat]. 'For once I had sanction to use Berlin slang, which fitted the character. In my family the use of slang had not been allowed, especially if it had any resemblance to Yiddish, which in the Berlin dialect was not uncommon.'

The Domestic Sciences programme begs the question as to how much work each day would have been fair. How hard were the girls working? Did they have choices as to what work they did? Did each work the same number of hours? Did older girls work more hours than younger ones? What were the labour laws of the time and who was monitoring the school? Over its ten years of operation, approximately forty European girls participated in the Domestic Sciences programme at Stoatley Rough, their ages ranging from thirteen to nineteen. To its credit, the school maintained a ratio of one Household Girl to every six students; as more students arrived, there were always proportionately more Household Girls. Yet who determined the fairness of that ratio in the first place? Who was looking out for the girls' interests? Child labour laws in England at the time (holdovers from the Industrial Revolution) dealt only with the knitting mills, where children were limited to twelve hours and to no night work but were silent otherwise as to children's rights.

The well-meaning committee always put a positive spin on the Domestic Sciences programme, reporting the work of the girls in terms of a learning experience rather than as a contribution to the school. Referring to the experiment (never repeated) of bringing convalescent children to the school from London in the summer of 1934, the Committee wrote that the incident provided 'excellent practical

experience in the care of the children for some of the older girls'.
When two girls were sent to do housework for English families one
Christmas holiday (receiving room and board and relieving the school
of its responsibility for their care), the Committee reported that the
girls 'were improving their English and [gaining] experience managing
an English household'.

Sometimes the Household Girls and Herta performed as real servants.
For example, the school's secretary who, like the Household Girls,
received no pay for five years of on-demand service had the duty
of awakening Dr Lion each morning by drawing the curtain in her
bedroom. Girls cleaned not only the rooms in the Headmistress'
Bungalow, but travelled to Hindhead to clean the house of Dr Wolf's
mother. The Household Girls were called upon to serve meals to
important visitors, at which times they wore the uniform of a servant,
a white apron. A little note was posted in the kitchen dated the spring
of 1940, admonishing, 'These aprons are only to be worn on special
occasions. They belong to the school and when you leave you are
requested to give them back.' Sometimes the girls were sent to work
for benefactors. Ruth Bayer [Tuckman] even became cook for a week.
'On my arrival at Miss Fearon's house, she told me that her maid and
gardener were also away on holiday and that a girl and boy from the local
Bernardo home (a mission house for homeless urchins) were taking their
places. She explained that as cook, I was in a status above the maid and
the gardener. I was to sit at the top of the table at meal times and socialise
with them as little as possible, an attitude that I not only found extremely
strange, but utterly alien to the way I had been brought up. Although
I obediently sat at the top of the table, I found both of them good
company.' She finishes her story with 'Most importantly, by the end of
the week I was paid ... and for now I could buy the soap and toothpaste
for my sister and me.... The less said about my cooking, the better.'[17]

It speaks of the leadership qualities of Nore Astfalck and Hanna
Nacken that any resentment that the girls might have felt was tempered
by a spirit of optimism and pride in their work. Former Household Girls
have claimed general satisfaction and immense gratitude for the
programme and, unlike Herta, have not written that they felt exploited,
probably because they were under Nore's tutelage (whereas Herta was
virtually on her own under the emotionally distant Dr Lion). There is no
question that the motives of the school's Committee and administration
were honourable, even heroic. They admitted Jewish girls who otherwise

may not have been able to leave the Continent. The programme saved lives. Yet the school benefited greatly by receiving inexpensive services that would have been otherwise done by salaried adults.

The school blurred the lines between expediency and socially acceptable pedagogy. We turn to the girls themselves for the last word on the programme. As adults, some former Household Girls recognised a modicum of unfairness in their fate, yet they recall having felt satisfaction and pride in their work. Writing for *The Bridge*, young Margot Silverbach [Kogut] expressed her joy at being given responsibility and receiving praise for a job well done, of belonging to a social structure in which their place was honoured. 'I must see that everything is OK. This includes such things as seeing where a table cover needs cleaning and replacing.'[18] Margot also saw herself as liberated. 'So I am now a real "housewife".' She was proud of learning handicraft 'so that I can do running repairs. I also enjoy the lessons in nutrition ... that have to do with chemistry and biology.' Referring to two new girls, she said, 'The expressions on their faces seem to say, "well, a modern girl has to know how to do this but later, in real life, it's going to be done by servants", but one has to be a modern educated girl, knowledgeable in household tasks.' Her words reveal the radiant influence of Nore. 'Yesterday I managed to do the whole house with only minimal help, in three hours. And so well that I got praised.'

Like the administrators themselves, the Household Girls had grown up with nannies and cooks and cleaning women, never having to do the duties they were now asked to perform. Yet they did not complain. Ilse Kaiser wrote with pride and humour about her work: 'I got to get up early on Tuesdays to help with the laundry. Mr Phillips' cups of early morning tea were wonderful. Someone always had to run down to the farm when the water tank ran over. I got my turn at cleaning Dr Lion's bungalow once a week. It was too bad that she did not appreciate my changing the position of her little wooden figure she used for sketching. In fact, I got into some sort of trouble with Dr Lion. I cut Lilly Wohlgemuth's long beautiful hair, much to Dr Lion's disapproval. Most of all, I did not manage to catch the mouse that had decided to run around the bungalow and the mouse turned up in her bed.'[19] Renate Dorpalen wrote to her mother cheerfully about 'dishes, knives, forks, spoons, pots and pans. I do the dishwashing and three or four other students do the drying. A person has to be quick and well organised to keep everyone busy and to get the job done as pleasantly and as fast as possible. Sometimes the work is accompanied by singing or good conversation.' Inge Hamburger [Pavlowsky] said, 'I came to Stoatley Rough as a Household Girl which in my mind is really a name of a low level, and in any case is much more interesting and valuable than it sounds.... What we learned was rather up to each person. But the possibility of feeling responsible for the work we did in order to make the school a new home for all the children – a place which was beautiful and agreeable, where the food was good, and where everybody had a task to play – was our mission.'[20] Miss Astfalck's spirit lives in Inge's words. Today, former Household Girls who have stayed in touch reflect with pride on their role, noting with satisfaction that the academic students also had to work. 'Peeling potatoes, doing the washing-up, sweeping the floor, laying the table, etc. was the work of all of us, students included, and [duties] changed once a week.... So it was not only the work of the Household Girls, as though they were the servants.'

Dr Lion made every effort to place the girls in good jobs after they left the school. She also maintained a warm correspondence with them. Although some girls found their way immediately into a university education after the war, almost none did so right away. First jobs for the Household Girls were more of the kindergarten teacher or 'lady cook' variety. One issue of *The Bridge* listed the occupations of former pupils under categories such as 'Farm Work' and 'Higher Education'. Dr Wolff, the editor, chose to fold 'Domestic Work' into the broader category titled 'Teaching – Social Work – Domestic Work', thereby granting the field a professional standing. Of eleven pre-war girls, four had nursing or teaching jobs; two were kindergarten teachers, one worked at the St. Bernardo Home for orphans, and one, in Buenos Aires, became a handicraft teacher (while finding time to be a 'champion javelin thrower'). One young woman administered a centre for mentally defective children, following directly in the footsteps of her mentor, Nore Astfalck. One conducted classes in sewing and clothing design. And the feisty Ursel Selo worked toward a certificate in Domestic Science, but they 'kicked her out for lack of room because of the war', and she only got a 'Housewife's Certificate' instead of the 'Housekeeper's'. During a class in shorthand, she wrote, 'Don't worry, I am not going into business as a typist or something equally horrid.' (The war effort apparently interfered with her plans; she signed up for Red Cross lectures in first aid and home nursing and was about to join a Voluntary Aid Detachment. She later became a nun and was known as Sister Mary Ester.)

Today the Domestic Sciences programme raises the question of fairness. Renate Dorpalen wrote that the programme 'was supposed to combine theory and practice and to include general academic subjects. In reality, the major responsibility of carrying out the household duties for the school rested on these young girls and adjunct staff. This programme offered little in the way of academic enrichment or systematic training. The workload was very heavy and the hours extraordinarily long, without remuneration except room and board.'[21]

The Household Girls played a crucial role in the history of a struggling school. Dr Lion's role in approving this work programme must be viewed in the larger context. She managed a school for over twenty-six years against a backdrop of constantly changing conditions and a never-ending quest for funds. It probably never occurred to her that the Domestic Sciences programme was exploitive. She saw it as a way to admit scores of refugee children, and her legacy, on the whole, burnished by the luminous leadership of the indefatigable Nore, is viewed favourably by the Household Girls. And Nore's role must be equally adjudged to be without blame. As the last to bed and the first to rise every day, she worked tirelessly and only asked the same of her Household Girls. In 2006 Renate Dorpalen said, 'I think without [the school] I would not have made it. The work and life was very hard and perhaps not always understood by me, who was too young to understand how the school served us all.' Even as a nineteen-year-old girl, Renate wrote, 'This community and its functions were created by great sorrow and misery.... Many children who had to leave their parents have found their new home here in the house I love.' She then refers to her role as a Household Girl. 'It is work which has the power of bestowing on the people in this house some kind of peace and which, in spite of the unquiet time, can give to all of us a certain inner content.'[22]

The Domestic Sciences programme at Stoatley Rough was discontinued towards the end of the war. No new Household Girls can be identified in the school's records after 1943. Letters from desperate parents had ceased to jam the mailbox; children had begun to leave. Post war, Dr Lion hired English girls for the larger cleaning jobs and instituted a benevolent prefect system that gave older children administrative tasks, such as managing the duty roster. Children may have continued to have weekly chores, but after the war, no child ever again had to do the school's laundry, help with the cooking, care for younger children or polish the floors.

Chapter 4
Their Finest Hour

Visiting day dawned grey and windy. Goldy's mother clutched her coat against her neck as she made her monthly trek the 2 miles (3.22 kilometres) up the hill from the train station to the school. Goldy waited for her in the Sitting Room already dressed in his blue wool jacket. Obo, as usual, had followed him up from the Hut, and he had his chequered green jacket with him. People said that the colour brought out the ginger in his hair, a fact that did not impress the unassuming, straightforward boy. Obo hung back as Goldy greeted his mother. He was not jealous. Some kids had parents in England, and Goldy was one of the lucky ones. Soon Mrs Goldmeier was urging Obo to come along with them – they were going to a restaurant in Hindhead for the midday meal. It happened every month. Obo never planned to spoil Goldy's time with his mother, yet he was unable to help himself. Thinking of his mother's cabbage specialty, *Sauerkraut mit Schupfnudeln*, he ordered a plate of bubble and squeak. But it wasn't the same.

On the muddy trek back across the Commons, Goldy and his mother took the lead, with Obo lagging behind, kicking at clods of earth along the way. Obo watched Goldy lean towards his mother and put his arm around her and a wave of yearning rose up and swept through him in a tsunami of loss and regret. His eyes watered and he saw for a moment the face of his own mother big as life and he smelled her scent of fresh cotton and lavender. His foot caught on a root in the path and he fell into the mud. By the time he caught up with the Goldmeiers, Obo had regained his composure; even his old sunny self-confidence. As the boys said goodbye to Mrs Goldmeier, Obo promised to follow her advice about treating his chilblains.

Goldy went straight back to the Hut, but Obo went into the main house. He would write his parents another letter. It had been a couple of weeks since their last postcard had arrived from Luxemburg. He hated the swastika covering the original stamp of the tiny country. He found a pencil. The faint odour of cooking onions drifted up from the kitchen downstairs and he heard a low murmur of voices, boys from the Farm arguing about who was going to have latrine duty the coming week. Someone was scraping away at a violin – probably Kate Lesser. Obo had learned to ignore extraneous noises. He fetched one of the squares of pastel papers they were supposed to write on, drew up a chair and tried to concentrate. He could use up to twenty-five words. It was funny. By the time he got through the Dear Mother and Father and the Love, Hans, there was not much room. He would not tell them about his near disaster last week with the crank handle: he had been revving up the ancient flywheel and almost had broken his arm when the engine backfired. Nor would he speak about the boil on his neck that would not heal or of his chilblains that turned one of his fingers greenish. Obo decided to report on the trip he had made to his distant relatives in Glasgow. While Dr Lion never let him ride out very far on his bike, for some reason she had let him take the train to Scotland all by himself.

Liebe Eltern, Danke für Nachricht. Besuchte Gumprich in Ferien. Sehr schön. Haben Kaninchen hier. Mir gehts gut…. Arbeite viel Farm. Lese viel. Küsse, Hans. [Dear Mom and Dad, Thanks for the news. I visited the Gumprichs on my holiday. Very nice. We have rabbits. I am well…. I work a lot on the Farm. I read a lot. Kisses, Hans.]

He would give Miss Astfalck the note, who would pass it to Herta to transcribe it into the official Red Cross form for posting. His parents should get it in a few weeks. He put down his pencil. The sun had almost set. A few wispy rays stole into the darkening room. Reaching out for a small patch of fireplace tile. Obo stared at the square of emerald brilliance, heedless of the squawking violin, the running feet on the terrace, the thudding of doors. Someone outside said, 'Has the gong gone yet?' He scraped back his chair, tucked the note in his pocket and walked outside. He needed to find someone to fool around with until it was time to eat.

The Calm before the Storm

A sense of unease hung in the air at Stoatley Rough throughout the summer of 1939. Wolf was especially unhappy, although it had nothing to do with the impending war. For no reason, Nore had made him move from the Hut back to the top floor of the main house into Lookout, the room for younger boys. Once again his routines would be supervised.

There was not much to do. Everybody knew the war was going to happen. They just did not know when. Wolf recalled those dog days: 'During the summer, a group of us used to meet in a clearing in *The Woods* and plot forbidden things. For example, we pooled our meagre cash and plotted to buy a can (oops, tin) of pineapple (about sixpence in those days). How we expected to do this is beyond me, as we eleven-year-olds were never allowed to go to Haslemere on our own. Nevertheless, the deed was somehow accomplished and defiance of Authority added sweetness to the pineapple. Another mystery: How did we open the tin?'

In August Dr Lion called the children back from their scouting trips and excursions. She fretted when two of her pupils, Beate Maier and Juergen Wolffson, left England for Holland and Germany. Obo's brother Arthur, who had been working in England, also left for Holland, planning to visit their parents. All were doomed. Renate Pniower also returned with her father, who was called back to Germany to enter the draft. She, her Aryan father and Jewish mother survived the war.

Juergen had been living in Lookout with Wolf. He had left behind his ticket and passport when he departed; it was discovered and someone from the school chased him after with the forgotten documents, enabling him to board. The loss of the twelve-year-old was especially hard on Dr Lion. Juergen Wolffson hailed from her own hometown, Hamburg, and she had known the distinguished family. Juergen was the grandson of one of the noted authors of the *Buergerliches Gesetzbuch* (BGB), the basic German legal code. Notwithstanding the predations of the Nazis on the German legal system, Wolf said, it had 'stood the test of time since its origin in the 1890s and even in New York, my father kept a copy of the BGB at his bedside and revered it the way Americans revere the Declaration and Constitution'. Yet Juergen Wolffson ran out of luck even before his final voyage home. He had somehow been sent to safety in England only to be placed in one of Dr Bernardo's homes, which according to Wolf was 'famous for the pedigree of their occupants: abandoned children whom the British in those days regarded as half-breeds, unwanted offspring of dark-skinned sailors from distant corners of the then British empire and English waterfront whores.' Nobody ever knew how this well-born German boy had managed to land in an English orphanage.

In 1937, a new building had been built on the campus next to Dr Lion and Dr Wolff's Bungalow. Called, simply, The Hut, it housed boys between twelve and fifteen years old. (Girls stayed tucked safely in the mansion on the upper floors.) Dr Wolff wrote to her mother about the new residence. 'Two nights ago the first two of the new rooms were inaugurated. After some real slog we improvised a moving-in celebration in the evening – ferns around the entrance, two girls welcoming the guests with Goethe verses. The company had progressed on its way, singing through the garden, and had danced German folk dances and the Hora under the big trees on the lawn. I read some pretty carpenter's verses by Uhland, somewhat reworked to fit the occasion. Then there was a feast of cakes and fruit juice, English and German songs.'[1]

The Hut was not luxurious. Dieter described it as 'a flimsy wood-and-corrugated iron barracks building left over from World War I, painted green with rooms for five and three boys'. The five-person room (Cornwall) had folding beds – like rollaway cots – which could be pushed under a shelf with a curtain and when unfolded allowed just enough space to get in and out of bed. The other room (Mark) had regular twin beds. Dr Lion named Cornwall after the location of the boy-scout camping trip that summer and Mark after the portrait of Frederick II (Frederick the Great) that someone had hung on its wall. 'Mark' was universally understood by Germans as the territory known as the March of Brandenburg. Wolf explained, 'The portrait of the great man was symbolic of the loyalty that still bound many Roughians to their German Fatherland in spite of persecution and exile. Some kid (I do not know who) carried the portrait into exile.' The Hut's quarters were cramped. According to Wolf, 'Between the two boys' rooms was a teacher's room so narrow that the adult could sit at a desk at night and pound on both walls without getting up.' The Hut's external walls were paper-thin. Wolf remembers hearing agonised cries of despair when Household Girls, who lived in an extension of the Hut (called the 'New Hut'), heard of the retreat of the Eighth Army after the surrender of Tobruk on their radio. There was a bathroom with the shower off the entry corridor and a furnace room in a small basement. A gong that could be heard all over the property summoned the boys to the morning run and meal.

Nore and Dr Lion were always shuffling the children around. (When they reached sixteen, Stoatley Rough pupils, boy and girl alike, were sent to the Farmhouse unless they were still taking classes and preparing for the Matric.) But for the younger boys of twelve like Martin, Wolf, Obo and Peter, to be promoted to the Hut was a rite of passage, a highly prized escape from the clutches of the Household Girls. Wolf said, 'A bathroom and a toilet all to ourselves were real luxuries, but they were our only luxuries. In the … rooms, the wind howled through the gaps between walls and ceiling. Winters were a perpetual battle between freezing cold and a temperamental coal-fired furnace. Each room was dimly lit with a naked 30-watt bulb. I loved it!' That summer Dr Lion had temporarily placed the eleven-year-old Wolf in the Hut to share quarters with thirteen- and fourteen-year-old boys, 'much older and more mature than I. They were in the throes of puberty, had heard of S.E.X. (which officially did not exist at Stoatley Rough) and had girlfriends (which was frowned upon).'

Within a year Wolf, Martin and all their friends were promoted to the Hut, and the few years they lived together in the badly constructed, primitive shelter were so intense an experience for them, that many years later they would always refer to themselves as the Hut Boys. Adolescent awakenings coupled with the excitement and fear of a war going on just overhead and across a few hills and dales in London were the fuel that forged the unbreakable attachments of virtual brotherhood for these boys. The Hut was the fertile grounds for young male bonding among pubescent boys with shared experiences as refugees living together with little supervision. There were, of course, the rare good-natured conflict. Austrians referred to the boys from Berlin as *Piefkes*, meaning a small boy who is quick with a fresh comeback, and the German boys retaliated by calling the Austrian snobs *Juenkes*, whose meaning is lost to history but was intended to be equally insulting. An occasional argument or wrestling match flared up over such weighty topics as failure to pick up one's clothes from the floor or who was the oldest member of the gang. When Martin and newcomer Peter Gaupp discovered that they had been born on the same day of the same year, each rushed to claim seniority by writing his mother requesting the exact hour of his birth. (Peter took in stride his harrowing introduction to school life when he was still in the Schoolroom, recording in his diary a 'Day of Great Disasters'. 'One of my roommates threw [*schmiss*] a pile of thirteen plates on the floor; and another one broke the wall in our bedroom. Not satisfied with this, he also broke my bed so that I had to sleep on the floor, but it was not cold since I got my mattress.'²) Obo once had a loud argument with Felix Schiller, a relative latecomer to the school, 'a gentle, polite, neat chap, a bit of a dreamer with a great sense of humour'. As their voices rose in angry dispute, the onlookers insisted that the boys settle it *mano a mano*. Obo recalled, 'It was a prospect neither one wanted but then it seemed unavoidable. So we talked about it and decided we would give them their fight. We rehearsed a staged showdown that would be the least painful, and then performed. I don't remember whether our room mates bought it.'

Informal social rules were used in The Hut. Dieter Gaupp wrote, 'Grouping by threes has never been a good idea and we found that frequently there were arguments or disputes pitting one against two. [But] overall the comradeship was close.... Each room had its own rules, arrived at by consensus.... For example, it [was] the norm to attack anyone's edible contributions received in the mail. Thus, a bar of chocolate was first tasted, courtesy of the recipient; followed by the rule that the "corners had to be cut," until there were no corners left, all despite the useless protestations of the owner.' The boys always shared packages of food from the United States – cocoa, canned fruit or candy. Wolf recalled receiving a can of Ovaltine: nobody had heard of it, but they knew it was edible. They produced spoons and ate it dry. Dieter continued

Once someone received a large tin of peaches. This was a novelty and it presented a serious practical problem. How do you open such a tin in your bedroom without a can opener? We finally managed to mutilate the tin enough so that it reluctantly yielded its contents.... Someone else once received a coconut, which was a complete mystery to all but one of us. The enlightened one (we think it was Felix) had heard that one needed to punch a hole in the nut, drink the milk and then break it up and eat the insides. Oh, how carefully we opened up that coconut and divided up the pieces. Someone saved the shell and tried to make something of it in the workshop. Another such rule concerned the neatness of the room. Everyone made his own bed and put up his clothes.... One of us had the weekly assignment of cleaning the room. It was never stated at what time the room had to be finished [yet] clothing not picked up on time was found hanging from the trees outside the window where they had been flung to clear the room, a sight greeting you as you ambled back from the main building. Retrieving those clothes and not tearing them (clothing was also rationed) was a chore. There was no recourse; it was one of those rules. Arguments and anger might result but the behaviour stuck.[3]

Mail was always welcomed. Sometimes what arrived was more than simply a letter. According to Wolf, his hutmate Hans Kornberg 'used to receive a newspaper from Berlin – the *Berliner Illustrirte* (spelled without the *e* before the *i*, the magazine's snobbish way of letting people know that it had existed before German spelling was standardised in the nineteenth century). Hans would take the paper in his cot and carefully unroll it. Pressed between the sheets of paper would be valuable stamps, an ingenious way to get money out of the country, which he would sell. Hans' parents, of course, took a terrible risk in smuggling those stamps out of Germany.'[4]

Most resident teachers had to take on a tour of duty in the Hut. Martin recalled that Miss Humby knew how to keep order, but Obo's favourite was Miss Eva Graetz, 'a gentle person, very sensitive, who tried to keep us under control but was overwhelmed'. (Miss Barnes, a Canadian woman who was not known for her physical beauty, took charge of the girls housed at the adjunct quarters called Rowallan for a time and was known to tell her fascinated female charges the details of her various dates with Canadian soldiers.) Mr Victor May also took a turn in the Hut until he was called up. A Mr Taylor was at the school for a very short time.

The teachers who lived in the Hut had their hands full. Miss Eva Graetz, according to Obo, 'although technically was supposed to be in charge of us, had to take a fair amount of abuse from us adolescents whose hormones were raging at that time.... I recall her wind-up portable phonograph and a wonderful collection of seventy-eight classical records. I well remember her evening concerts in Cornwall. What a treat they were! Tom asked for the *Fledermaus* "Overture" over and over again. Miss G was reluctant to comply, not wanting to wear out her record. Anyway, that's what she said. But Tom suspected that she didn't want Strauss' music to overly arouse his adolescent testosterone.' Peter said, 'She induced us to wash and go to bed in an orderly manner with the promise that if we did she would play a record for us. The one that stayed with me was the *Rosenkavalier*. I still think of her playing that for us with all of us sitting on our beds in pyjamas. Amazing how much of an impression something like that can have on a child.'

Miss Joan Humby was a thirty-something Oxford-educated woman who had spent a year in Germany on a farm programme, perhaps the only native English speaker on the staff who knew German. Wishing to learn German, in the 1930s, she had naively signed up for the *Reicharbeitsdienst*, the compulsory Nazi labour service, although she never converted to the cause. She took her Hut duty at Stoatley Rough seriously:

> One night I [Dieter] and another of my roommates had been visiting in the other room after 'lights out'. Miss H. asked for silence. We could have sneaked back to our quarters but the visit was too important, and we stayed and kept talking, in low tones. The wall was patted, then knocked, and finally Miss H. gave a last warning, followed by her coming from her room and telling us to stop forthwith. We hid under the beds, Miss H. returned to her room, and after a moment, we resumed our conversations; eight whispering boys just asking for it. Miss H. filled the doorframe once again and declared that she was going to stand there until it was completely quiet and we were all asleep. Sneakers did not amuse her and the room finally did become quiet: six plus two sets of lungs breathing as normally as possible. Those in their beds could even go to sleep; those of us under the bed couldn't. Miss H. stayed. We thought she would never leave. She never intimated if she knew we were there, [but] after that interminable night … we never did that again.[5]

Dieter Gaupp had recently arrived at Stoatley Rough, along with his brother, Peter, through Italy, having spent four years in the sun after moving from his birthplace, Berlin. Dieter was small-framed, wiry and tough, with sturdy shoulders and a long, mournful face that masked an understated, folksy sense of humour. He was independent, decisive and morally and physically courageous. Peter was a quiet and beautiful child with poster-boy Aryan looks – a shock of light brown hair, even features, wide, sensual mouth and big eyes that often reflected, in his early years at Stoatley Rough, great timidity, as if to ask what else was he going to have to face without his parents. The two boys spoke Italian together, Peter having almost completely forgotten his German. He was used to following Dieter's lead. The family was living in Florence when the boys learned that they would go to England. Dieter usually spoke German with his parents, but gradually became fluent in Italian, the language of his school, and he also knew passable French. Was there room in his head for one more language? Shortly after the decision to go to England, the family sat in the sunny kitchen of their villa. His mother opened a book. She was going to help Dieter get started with English. Now this word, she said, pointing to the numeral 'one' – is pronounced 'wun'. Dieter took one look at the book his mother held out to him and said, 'The heck it is', and slammed the book shut before making a fast exit from the room. Peter, hovering at his mother's elbow, was thrilled to learn a new language. Believing that 'eau de cologne' was an English word, he ran outside to ride around the neighbourhood on his bike, showing off his mastery of English. 'Eau de cologne', 'eau de cologne' he proclaimed to anybody he met.

The family had lived in a luxury apartment in Berlin in the wealthy borough of Steglitz. The boys' mother was a paediatrician, one of the first crop of female physicians in Germany. She was of Sephardic descent. Their father, not Jewish, was a senior editor at Ullstein, one of the largest publishing houses in Germany. His father had achieved modest fame for getting his company to publish Erich Maria Remarque's internationally acclaimed novel *All Quiet on the Western Front*. (Later banned by the Nazis, it was one of the books they publicly burned.) Soon after 1933 when nine-year-old Dieter showed eagerness to join the Hitler Youth, his parents shipped him off to friends in Italy to 'recover from appendicitis'. Left behind, five-year-old Peter was exposed to Nazi theatrics. 'In 1933 and 1934 I remember there being more and more loud parades along the *Mariendorfer Strasse* at the end of our block, with lots of loud band music and people in Nazi uniform.' The parents warned their sons. 'We had instructions to never open the door at night if we heard noises outside. We understood that if the Nazis were hauling away a neighbour and we saw them do it, we would also get hauled away.... We were told that someone might rush us or break in if we opened the door, and we should never repeat outside the house what our parents talked about – especially not at school.'

In school his parents registered Peter as non-religious, inadvertently causing the boy no end of discomfort. He stood outside his classroom once a week when religion class was taught. 'Very embarrassing!' Herr Gaupp's publisher did not support the Nazis in the elections, so his name ended up in the Nazi's 'little book', prompting the family to leave for a permanent vacation in Italy in October 1935. Thus, Herr Gaupp's initiatives to start a political opposition to the Nazis halted there. Peter remembered the interrogation his Jewish mother underwent at the police station when trying to get travel permits. 'Even at that age I knew that this was dangerous stuff.' He mourned having to give away his toys, 'for a seven-year-old that was more important than issues of political preference'.

The family moved into a villa in Chiavari on the Italian Riviera, where the boys spent the next four years in the sunshine, virtually unmolested in school. Every six months Herr Gaupp, who remained on the payroll at Ullstein and worked long distance, returned to Berlin to renew visas; on his return he sometimes brought an expensive camera to sell. 'These trips were obviously dangerous and Dieter and I were aware that my mother would be very worried when he made them, but our parents shielded us from much of this reality.'

The Fascist government of Mussolini (in power since 1922) did not intrude in the daily life of the Gaupp family. The only harassment the boys experienced was when they ran into some Italian toughs. 'I quickly learned not only formal Italian but also the street language and street gestures – of which there are many. Coming home from a good movie one day a bunch of boys threatened us and Dieter suggested that we quickly walk away from them. I was inspired and turned around and tried out a number of the most insulting gestures on those boys. Dieter was appalled! He yelled "Run for it!" and we did with those boys in hot pursuit.'

The family moved to Florence in 1938. One day Hitler made a state visit to Italy, starting with Florence. The authorities rounded up prominent Germans in the area as hostages to guarantee his safety. Herr Gaupp claimed that he 'met some of the nicest people in prison', one of whom offered him a teaching job in America. By 1939, the family were making plans to leave. The children would go first to England, to be joined by their parents, and then they would all sail to New York. But the war has a way of ruining even the best-laid plans. Just after the boys arrived, England closed its borders and the senior Gaupps managed to get the last train to Switzerland, where they waited out the war.

The Gaupps were well connected. A distant relative by marriage – Dr George Peabody Gooch (1873–1968), a distinguished British historian, political journalist and liberal member of parliament from 1906 to 1910 – sponsored the boys in England. During his brief political career Gooch criticised the policy that led to the South African War, ironically having been good friends while at Oxford with none other than Jan Smuts, who became the prime minister of South Africa in 1919.

Peter's trip to England was punctuated by one terrible scare, not from harassment by Nazis but because of Dieter's brazen stand against them. The boys' train had stopped at the Italian–French border. Peter recalled, 'Dieter announced with alarm that his bicycle was being taken off the train! He told me to stay put and ran off. My worst fears were coming true. Dieter, as always, was going to desert me.... There he was on the platform arguing with a bunch of train officials who would not let his bike through. I cared nothing about that bike. If only he would get back on the train. The French authorities evidently wanted to impose import duties on the bike, and since that was higher than the value of the bike, he objected. The Italian and French authorities argued with each other over the bike, and then the train started to move – just to the other side of the station, namely across the border.... and Dieter was not with me! It stopped again and after a while it started up again and we were off – without Dieter!!' The hair-raising finale to this drama (coming on the heels of his tearful separation from his parents) did little to put Peter at ease. As the train started to move, Peter sat frozen in his seat until Dieter opened the door to his compartment and came sauntering in. His bike was back on board, untaxed.

The boys spent the remainder of the summer at a boarding school in Watford, a town near London, before they would move to Stoatley Rough in the fall. It was then that they learned how it felt to be a German in England. They were in the headmaster's living room listening to the news of the German invasion of Poland on the radio (1 September 1939, two days before Great Britain declared war on Germany). The headmaster translated the words into French, which Dieter translated into Italian for Peter. The boys sat in shocked silence, stunned by the news they had dreaded. A shooting war was the least of it. Peter said, 'Suddenly the Germans were "they" and we did not have an identity.'

The boys fit right in at Stoatley Rough. Dieter went immediately into the Hut, and Peter to the top floor of the main house into Lookout with other boys his age, who would later give him a name they created – *Squink*, because 'Someone (not me) said we really ought to have nick names ... "cowboy" names, as they did in the movies, and this name seemed to have a real Western flair to it.'

War

Germany's invasion of Poland forced her treaty partners, Great Britain and France, to declare war on the aggressor on 3 September 1939. The news spread around the school in fits and starts. Herta was in her office when an 'icky little boy' came around. 'There was a little window that looked out on the path that led to the main building.... One day this horrible smirky little face appeared at my window and it said, "War's broken out" sort of triumphantly.... We had all been waiting for it, but it was such a yucky way of telling me; I mean, he almost sounded full of glee. He was an awful twerp.' Dr Lion turned on her radio in the Bungalow and as if they were gathering round to listen to fairy tales, children clustered under her window for hours. Wolf and his friends learned the news later that evening. 'It was school policy to give us as little news from the real world as possible. I don't know why. Nevertheless, we heard about Danzig and the Ribbentrop–Molotov pact and knew that war was very near. On Sunday, 3 September 1939, some of us boys (Peter Lassow, a non-Jewish boy from Munich, admitted for the summer programme, possibly Hans Kornberg, along with Obo, Martin, Francis LeMesurier and Peter Rosenthal) sat in a clearing in the woods above the farm and watched the RAF fly in the direction of France. We were too depressed to play. I had temporarily been transferred from The Hut back to Lookout to my unhappiness. That night Miss Astfalck came in, sat on a bed, and told us with a sad and tired voice that war had been declared. Her entire family was in Germany, as were my parents. Blackout curtains were hung on all windows. In the valley below, the lights of Haslemere disappeared and would not be seen again for five and a half years.'[6]

The day war was declared, a German U-30 submarine sank the British liner *Athenia* en route to America, killing 112 of her 1,400 passengers. Then the German navy sank the merchant ship *SS Rio Claro*. U-boats sank the aircraft carrier *Courageous* and, in October, the battleship *Royal Oak*, inside the main British naval base of Scapa Flow. After that, nothing much happened except for a few isolated incidents. So few skirmishes took place between the two countries in the next seven months that the newspapers began to say Britain was in a 'Phoney War' and commentators joked about the *Sitzkrieg*, and the 'Bore War'. As the nations went about building up their war machines, an unnatural calm settled in at Stoatley Rough. New rules were quietly implemented, such as restriction on travel from the school to within a 5-mile (8.05 kilometre) radius. The school's single car was not used for a few days. The constabulary confiscated the school's wireless sets and all the cameras only to return them within a few weeks. In October, twenty-seven Stoatley Rough students, all sixteen or older, joined the German staff and Dr Lion to go to the Guildford Aliens' Tribunal, where they were examined and then classified as category C Friendly Aliens. Thereafter, any pupil who turned sixteen was required to be evaluated for security trustworthiness. Renate Dorpalen recalled, 'I had to appear before such a tribunal in Guildford (in 1940) [but] Dr Lion's extensive connections to all levels of government, to refugee organisations, and to prominent, influential individuals, helped the school to remain intact. None of us was interned.' Christmas came and went, and there were sporadic skirmishes. When Germany invaded France and the low countries on 10 May 1940, the 'Phoney War' was over and the real one began in earnest.

Mr May joined up to become Lieutenant May, and Mr Taylor, a pacifist raised in China by missionary parents, arrived and was assigned to Hut duty. Wolf said, 'Mr Taylor went swimming in the dead of winter, insisted we keep all windows open on cold nights, tried to teach us Chinese, and was gone by the end of the year.' There were advantages to knowing two languages. The boys talked about Mr Taylor in his presence, confident that he knew no German; however, he finally noticed a certain word kept popping up in their conversation – *Schneider* [Tailor] – thinking that they perhaps were discussing the pre-war Schneider Trophy seaplane races. When he asked about the word, the boys had, according to Wolf, 'instant amnesia'. One more male teacher came to teach for a short while according to Wolf, a married man who tried to ogle the girls in their baths. Soon he 'was seen no more'. From that time on, all teachers were women, with the exception of Mr Hughes, the new Farm Manager. (Farm staff over the years included Mr Corfield, Mr Pniower (inventor, landscape architect and father of one of the pupils), Mrs Charlotte Weissrock (Farm Matron for a brief time), Mr Edward Hughes, a Mr Bibbe and, in 1944, the last manager, a former Farm Boy, Fritz [Fred] Dreschler.)

In London barrage balloons went up in parks (over 3,000 of them throughout the duration of the war), and anti-aircraft batteries appeared in Hyde Park, Windsor Great Park and Green Park. At Stoatley Rough, Herta and Nore passed out tan, square cardboard boxes with string handles containing gas masks, one for each child. The masks were a minor sensation, but within a few weeks, the children stopped carrying them around. (Wolf reported that at the end of the war, they were supposed to turn them in. He carried his now useless gas mask, rubber parts brittle and falling apart, to the ship in Scotland he would board for America. 'I left it with a pile of gas masks on the dock; nobody paid the slightest attention'.) Household Girls sewed blackout curtains

from old quilts and other bedding, and the chore of hanging them nightly
appeared on the duty roster. Inge Hamburger [Pavlowsky] helped
in designing a particularly decorative curtain with big appliquéd stars.
People learned to navigate through a black night, absolutely devoid
of light when the moon was new. One girl recalled how dark it was
to stumble over at night with no light to guide. She once bumped into
a 'soft thing', after which came a 'pardon me' and she went upon
her way.

The school maintained a steady-as-you-go course. As new clothing
and shoes became scarce, the school made every effort to become self-
sufficient. Self-sufficiency was dear to the hearts of Nore and Hanna,
who thrived on challenges as a matter of course. Even Dr Lion, who
frankly enjoyed the few luxuries afforded her (such as the occasional
special meal or the opportunity to arrange the flowers Mr Phillips
brought in season), embraced sacrifice. Uneasy with great wealth
and aware of the need for sacrifice, she once expressed her distaste
for living on 'millionaires' lane'. Reprising their *Jugendheim* days,
Nore and Hanna began to teach the children bookbinding and other
practical crafts. Children learned how to cut bowls and buttons from
coconut shells left over from care packages sent to some of the children
by American friends and relatives. The school would not neglect the arts,
not even for a war. Miss Sileezinski was brought in to teach painting
flowers and later a Miss Kaethe Wilcynski came in to teach oil painting,
the latter from Berlin who had come to England for an exhibition
of her work, having won the Rome Prize of the *Akademie fuer bildende
Kuenste* when Max Liebermann was its president. Later, she was known
as an illustrator of children's books. (Once again, the school benefited
from overqualified teachers!)

Appropriately, the administrators brought in a cobbler to teach shoe
repairing to the Household Girls. Ilse Kaiser wrote about the project for
The Bridge:

Eighty children! That means quite a lot of shoes to be repaired ...
our workshop was too small for us [and so] we moved to the so-
called nursery with our shelves and cupboards.... The children
themselves are very interested in the work and keep on asking:
'How do you do this?' and 'Why do you do that?' Even our little
Walter [at five, the youngest resident who lived at Stoatley Rough
for five years] is really anxious to know all we do. The boys know

all about the work 'of course' and should a girl dare to ask about
the soling of shoes, the boys are 'disgusted' and give a long lecture.
'Put a sheet of paper on the shoe and file round it, and you get the
exact shape you have to cut out of leather. Be very careful in cutting;
firstly it is War-time and we have to save every bit of leather.
Secondly the knives are quite sharp and our fingers do not like
to be cut. The pail with water is not there to splash other people,
but to soak your piece of leather. Later you stick and nail it on the
shoe after having taken off the old pieces. The very small pieces are
really given to us to play with, but generally our shoemaker thinks
it is worth keeping it. So we have to believe it. File the edges smooth
and lastly polish all round.' Then our little Walter is again given
the job of taking the shoes to their owner. Our boys really know
it perfectly, and if they go on like this in practice too, we will have
many good shoemakers in this school.[7]

There were formal personnel changes that autumn: a Mrs List started
giving English lessons once a week, and Martin's own Gertrud Gans left
the school to travel with her parents to India to marry a British officer
and wait out the war. (The former Household Girl later wrote to Dr Lion
about her difficulties in training her new all-Indian household staff.)
Miss Dove announced that she would leave to get married in December
in Dundee, Scotland.

That month, Stoatley Rough had its first air raid – a siren sounded
in the valley below in Haslemere that prompted a steady ringing of a bell
at the school. It happened early in the morning. Everyone filed down
into the lower basement of the large house into the large room called the
Schoolroom, in various states of dress – pyjamas, robes, hastily thrown
on clothes. Some tried on their gas masks. Marianne Gluecksmann
wrote, 'I felt for the first time the great responsibility which had fallen
on Dr Li and all the other teachers. In the first week we had every evening
some silent minutes in memory of all those people who must suffer
during the war.... We all felt a great unity. Correspondence with
Germany is becoming increasingly difficult. One loses touch with one's
relations. This makes for a growing community spirit. We have come
closer to each other. Thus we try to make our life a little easier in these
hard times. We don't forget the silver ray on the dark horizon.'

The experience was 'curious and sometimes even amusing', according
to one *blasé* seventeen-year-old identified as HP (probably Hans or

Heinrich Pachmeyr), who described for *The Bridge* how the Household
Girls lugged mattresses and cushions into the basement shelter:

> During the late summer the regular night raids on London began and
> we had an alarm almost every day between 8 and 9 o'clock in the
> evening, until 3 or 4 o'clock in the morning. People started early with
> getting ready for the night…. Everybody is provided with a book or
> some needlework. In the laundry cellar and in the box room the light
> is switched off at 9 o'clock and everybody is supposed to sleep. Many
> do, some don't. In the passage the light is kept on. A part of the staff
> and some of the older pupils are out here on chairs or improvised
> mattresses. They darn stockings, knit, read, or write letters on their
> knees. After two hours or so, Dr L. provides the awake people with
> a water biscuit. Then everybody tries to sleep a little until one
> of the guards in the stoke-room brings the news: ALL CLEAR!
> Rather drowsily you take your blanket and go to bed to sleep until
> 8 o'clock – Breakfast has been postponed after night alarms.[8]

During the Battle of Britain, August–September 1940, daylight raids
were common. Otherwise, alarms rarely set off during the day.
'If they did, lessons were continued in the basement. You could hear
mathematics from the box room, handicraft theory (as a substitute
for an underground workshop) from the laundry cellar, while
Shakespeare's plays were read in the passage.' The administrators
tried to keep the children from being frightened. HP continued

> For about a fortnight the siren was sounded almost daily at one
> of our mealtimes: Miss A. rings the bell and sounds the gong and,
> after having grumbled at the disturbance, we go down into the cellar,
> quickly swallowing another mouthful of bread and butter. In the
> cellar every available room is occupied. Some people even sit on the
> stairs. The box room has become an air-raid shelter for most of the
> smaller ones under the supervision of Dr W., and staying there
> became an envied thing for its German readings. In the same room
> Miss R., as long as she was here, used to play very exciting games
> with the children which were sometimes connected with so much
> noise that the roaring airplanes overhead were not to be heard.
> Outside the stoke room door two pails filled with water are put up
> with a stirrup pump next to them. Three or four people walk about

there enjoying the sunshine – they are supposed to watch but generally the planes are far enough away not to be dangerous.[9]

Wolf confirms that a certain jauntiness evolved at the school, a business-as-usual attitude towards the air raids. 'In the next nine months we had air-raid alerts almost every night and, at first, several times a day. I tried to count the number of alerts but they mounted into hundreds. We saw little of the fighting except for twisted contrails high in the sky. Sometimes, spent bullets and cartridges clattered on the corrugated iron roof of the Hut. We put pillows over our heads when we ran for our supposed shelter in the main building. After nights spent on mattresses jammed on cellar floors, we would march back to the Hut at dawn, singing, "Heigh-ho, heigh-ho, it's off to work we go" or "Good morning, good morning, we danced the whole night through" and other hits of the day.'[10]

The school rigorously followed wartime rules regarding rationing and extinguishing lights at night. HP wrote with great sincerity, 'We always look carefully to see that nothing is wasted in the house and that nobody is taking too much of the rationed food. All paper is put together and collected once a week.'[11]

That Christmas of 1939, the well-to-do Miss Fearon took it upon herself to invite some of the children to a special tea in her home. Dieter Gaupp, relatively new to the school, recalled the event for the utter generosity of the woman. 'She set beautiful tables in her large living room … with pretty napkins and glasses, a variety of cookies and cakes (again, remember this was a war time with rationing) and hot chocolate.'[12] She never mentioned the misunderstanding that must have been costly for her in what ensued during the meal. 'We admired the decorations on the table, small replicas of ancient galleons, carved in wood, handled them and played with them during tea. Somehow we gained the impression that these were for us to keep and many of us took them home…. Someone later pointed out that we were probably mistaken in our assumption; we felt bad but as far as I remember, we kept the ships.'[13]

Loveable misfit

In May 1940, Dr Lion's home of refuge was about to endure great strains as the war began in earnest. The event known as Dunkirk made British citizens realise that Germany was indeed dangerous. Furthermore, it opened up to the British the possibility that the enemy lived among them. British and French soldiers, The British Expeditionary Force (BEF), not only had been powerless to stop Germany's invasion of Norway, northern France, Belgium, Luxembourg and the Netherlands, but had been forced into a small pocket of land at the little French port town, Dunkerque, their backs to the sea. A massive naval response from the British merchant and private sector managed to evacuate over 335,000 troops, including 100,000 French. People saw for the first time the effect of fighting the invincible and cruel Germans: wounded young men, some of them disfigured, appeared in public covered in bandages and walking on crutches.

Rumours swept the nation. German paratroopers might be silently dropping into England by night to invade the towns and cities aided by unseen supporters – spies, secret agents – already lurking in Britain: a Fifth Column. Great Britain reacted swiftly and without hesitation to root out the evil in its midst. It suspended the practice of tribunals and locked up all aliens over the age of sixteen without the usual loyalty hearings. Six children – two Household Girls and four boys from Stoatley Rough, including Dieter – were swept up by this precautionary measure.

At about this time, Tom Wongtschowsky – a charming and intelligent boy, brought in by his overbearing and brilliant father – entered the school. Tom's mother had died earlier in Germany. Tom's neuroses were little understood by the adults. In today's world he may have been diagnosed and helped to live a satisfying life. While some children arrived at the school hurt by external events, others arrived just damaged, like Tom. Yet Tom was beloved by the other children, many of whom speak fondly of him to this day. The twelve-year-old arrived in May 1940, transferring in from another school in England, a dyed-in-the-wool Berliner who refused to speak English. From the day he showed up, Tom entertained the boys in the Hut with his thrilling disregard for authority. The other boys marvelled at what they perceived as courage but, in truth, were the actions of a deeply disturbed boy. The well-bred and polite boys who were raised in intact homes had no idea of the psychological basis of Tom's behaviour. They did not know what to make of someone who could get into trouble on a regular basis. Tom was never insolent or sullen. His anger was always directed towards himself. Dieter Gaupp said that he was 'very lonesome, unattached to any adult, basically hurt'.

Tom was fearless. When he read about the properties of conductivity in wood, water and metals, he decided to run his own experiment. One night he drew up a chair under one of the ceiling lights in the Hut, placed a rubber mat on it and set about to test the insulating properties of rubber. As others stood watching, he unscrewed the light bulb and put his finger in the socket. The current blew him across the room, leaving him with a burnt finger (but miraculously, alive). Another time Tom was talking fast to a friend. He absently put an open safety pin in his mouth and accidentally swallowed it. He landed in the Haslemere hospital, his bodily functions under intense scrutiny until the doctors were sure that he would not need surgical intervention. (For Christmas that year, the Hut Boys gave Tom a nicely wrapped box of rusty nails and pieces of metal with a little card offering him a hand-picked midnight snack.) It did not take Tom long to discover the space in the main house between the exterior and interior walls (the same gap discovered by Hans Loeser in 1937). Tom saw the possibilities at once, figuring that he could find his way to the ceiling above one of the girls' rooms. Great place for eavesdropping! Just before bedtime when the girls would be undressing, Tom wound his way to the room, inching across the fragile flooring. He made it halfway across when the supports gave way, chunks of plasterboard raining down. One of his legs suddenly broke through, Tom hanging on for dear life above, to the astonishment of the girls.

More than most, Tom suffered from chilblains during the cold, damp English winters. He once almost blew up the school to bring in more heat. Obo recalled, 'I was put in charge of supplying the "big boiler". It was located next to the "Schoolroom" a large room on the Lower Level. This work was under Mr Phillips' jurisdiction and as soon as I was strong enough to carry the heavy steel coal buckets from the coal cellar underneath the kitchen … to the boiler room, that job fell under my job description. Sometimes some of the other kids helped me "schlep" the buckets. He also showed me where all the main hot water valves and other devices were located and I guess I got what would today be considered a basic boiler operator's license at the advanced age of fifteen…. At any rate, one day Tom Wongtshowski wanted more heat and without permission, shovelled in more rationed coal than what was safe. He cranked up the lever in the main furnace room. The temperature got so high that it set off the safety valve and almost blew up the furnace. After that they installed an industrial grade padlock on the door.' (The boys used the boiler room as a refuge for the nefarious practice of smoking. Tom had introduced cigarettes to the boys – according to Goldy, Woodbines – 'the cheapest' and also the smelliest. Obo also blamed Tom for 'persuading us to "at least try it", getting us hooked very early'.)

Tom's bed was always unmade, his clothes were strewn about, and his things, like his life, were in disarray. Later on the Farm, some of the boys got so exasperated with him that they moved his bed into the feed room next to the pigsty. Tom's fear of water (Wolf called it *wasserscheu*) was legendary. While the other boys could not get in enough swimming time, Tom refused to go near the pool. One day Miss Astfalck had had enough. She insisted that he go swimming in the fresh water, probably thinking that a good dunking would do him good. Tom's flair for the dramatic surfaced. He went through the house collecting every hot water bottle he could find – four or five of them – and filled them with hot water. He then tied them to his body, venturing into the pool decked out like a Michelin tire man.

Tom was a fine musician and a connoisseur of classical music. Renate [Herold] Richter wrote, 'I remember Tom as an enthusiastic and gifted piano player, his favourite composer being Chopin. Once he drew up an alternative board game to "Monopoly", where the fields weren't street and road names, stations and hotels and houses, but names of *composers*.... The last, most precious field, instead of "Mayfair" ["Boardwalk" in the American version] was "Chopin"! What he used instead of houses and hotels and other value-increasing objects for his game, I just don't remember. But I learnt about a lot more composers playing the game than I had heard of before from Dr Leven; names like Glinka, Mossorrgsky, Borodin, Mascagni, Donizetti, Leoncavallo, Respighi, and of the "lighter" muses like Adam, Franz v. Suppé, Lortzing, Offenbach, Auber, Reznicek. These were Tom's Boardwalk properties.'

Tom's father was often invited to give violin concerts at the school, but Tom never performed with him, complaining that his thick short fingers held him back. He played the piano to entertain himself and sometimes accompanied Renate Herold when she sang.

Tom liked girls and girls liked Tom. Obo remembered, 'One girl, Ruth Deutsch, a Viennese girl with long pigtails, became the object of his affection. [She is the girl in the photo selected for the cover.] Tom told us he was able to kiss her after presenting her with a bar of Cadbury chocolate, a rationed treat that we all treasured dearly. It was just one more act that we would have liked to carry out ourselves but didn't have the guts to do.' Renate claimed that she loved Tom madly until she caught his attention and then she moved on to another conquest. Gerda Stein [Mayer] was a steadfast friend of Tom's, remaining in contact with him for many years. The distinguished poet was surely thinking of Tom when she wrote the following:

Chopin's Minute Waltz[14]
First love
who played it
with learner fingers
> slow ten
> > der notes drif
> > > ting in
to the garden...

Wolf recalls that Tom talked incessantly at night. 'Tom had the most complex love life, with not one but two girlfriends. He'd keep Obo and me awake at night, talking about it. One of the two actually kissed him (or he, her).' Tom always spoke in German and could be crude. He had a particular proclivity to talk on and on until nobody answered, on the verge of sleep. Tom would pause in his monologue for a moment, and then say, '*Arschloch*?' [Asshole?] as if addressing one of the drowsy room-mates. Whoever answered, of course, would pay the price. Wolf says that Obo was the one who always answered, '*Wer*?' [Who?], to which Tom would retort in triumph, '*Du*!' [You!] Wolf claims, 'Obo fell for it several times until he caught on.' Obo disputes the story.

Tom's humour was almost always self-deprecating. Long after he had left Stoatley Rough, he wrote from London to Wolf, by then living in Albuquerque, New Mexico, about a female pen pal who lived in West Africa whom he had acquired. Her letters to Tom had begun with formal pleasantries, but as the months went on, she became more and more friendly, going from 'Dear Mr Warner' to 'Dear Thomas', then 'Tom', 'Tommy', 'Dearest Tommy', 'Tommy, Darling', and so on. One day she announced that she was coming to England to meet him. The fateful day arrived and they met at a restaurant. Tom concluded his letter with the outcome: 'She took one look at me and disappeared.'

It was not unusual for Stoatley Rough pupils to be related to each other. Several in the Stoatley Rough community were connected. Wolf was related, through his maternal grandmother, to Dr Wolff's father. A true nephew of Dr Wolff, Gerhard Wolff, who ended up living in Israel, also attended Stoatley Rough. (One of Wolf's aunts, Tante Erna, was a well-off lady who dismissed her maid in Berlin, escaped to England and entered Mrs Marjorie Vernon's household as a maid herself. After the war she emigrated to America and lived to be a hundred.) Renate Dorpalen's father, a physician, had delivered Gina Schaefer's little brother. There were siblings, cousins and, in Tom's case, second cousins at Stoatley Rough.

Tom's genealogy carries special pathos. The grandfather of one of the Household Girls, Ilse Kaiser, had married a sister of Tom's grandfather Dr Adolf Wongtschowski. In 1955, one Charlotte von Mahlsdorf, a German transvestite who had survived the Nazis and the post-war East German Secret Police, the Stasi, published *I Am My Own Woman*.[15] The man, born Lothar Berfelde, had grown up in Berlin. He became estranged from his abusive father in the early 1940s, just as the Nazis were rounding up Jews in earnest. Lothar left home and began dressing as a woman, calling herself Charlotte. She lived hand to mouth in the streets in war-racked Berlin. (She confessed in her memoir, perhaps spuriously, that she killed her father and hid his body, never to be brought to trial for the crime.) At the height of the deportations, the young vagrant was hired by the Nazis to enter and report the contents of the empty houses of the deported Jews. (Later, this slight unassuming man, who always wore plain housedresses, built a collection of furniture and decorative objects from the *Grunderzeit* period (1850–1914), which, after the war, she made into a museum in Denmark, where she lived out her days.) In her book she describes her grisly work for the Nazis. One day she entered the Adolf Wongtschowski apartment in Berlin and found evidence of a swift departure. On the floor were two items: an autograph book and a First World War medallion, lying there as if their owners had considered taking them and then abandoned them at the last minute. The book's handwritten contents identified the owner of the house as one Dr Adolf Wongtschowski.

Ilse Kaiser's son, Peter Neivert in America, whose mother had been Tom's cousin at Stoatley Rough, read Charlotte's book in 2004. Astonished to see the name of his mother's great-uncle mentioned in the book, Peter corresponded with Charlotte in Denmark, identifying himself as Adolf Wongtschowski's sister's great-grandson. He learned that Charlotte had also corresponded with Tom Wongtschowski's father, Karl, in England when the dentist was in his seventies. 'Charlotte wrote in one of her letters to me that she sent the diary and medallion to Karl, Adolf's son, and Tom's father, in London. It was not really a diary, but a "Poesie Album" in which family members or friends would write short poems and then sign them. It's really more of a signature booklet.' In her book Charlotte recorded her emotions upon reading the name of this particular victim, noting, 'Over and over you heard the harmless phrase, "called for". The words sprang readily to the mouths of neighbours, as if the Wongtschowskis had been called for and taken to a little party by dear friends. Only this time, they had been "called for" to be murdered.' Adolf Wongtschowski and his wife, Blanca Pniower Wongtschowski, died in Theresienstadt in 1943. Charlotte von Mahlsdorf died in Denmark in 2000.[16]

Tom's stay at Stoatley Rough ended sadly. In 1945 Dr Lion expelled him. He had gone on a prohibited night walk with Eddie Behrendt, one of the younger Hut Boys, and one of the girls. Eddie Behrendt said, 'We got picked up in the middle of the night in Hindhead by one of the local watchmen. He thought he had caught a bunch of "German spies" from "that foreign school" and treated us accordingly.' The arresting officer 'made a big fuss and thought of himself as a real hero. He called Dr Lion from the phone box and woke her in the middle of the night. We were carted back to school and met by Dr Lion who was furious. Furious because we were outside, furious because she had been routed out of bed in the middle of the night, and above all, furious because she said we were ruining the STR reputation with the locals. It was right there and then when she told us about having to expel Tom to make an example.' (Dr Leven expressed regret for the decision many years later.)

Only sixteen, Tom was sent packing. Refusing financial help from his wealthy father, he worked at odd jobs until he landed the job of zipper salesman. In 1988, forty-four years after he had left the school, Gerda Stein Mayer, who had been at the school at the same time as he and the Hut Boys, invited him to a dinner party at her home because Wolf and his wife, Lorraine, were in town from America. Tom brought to the party his partner, a blowsy woman eighteen years his senior. He also brought a book to return to Wolf, *Immensee*, that he had borrowed from Wolf in 1943. It had been a gift to Wolf for his fifteenth birthday from Dr Emmy Wolff, and Wolf had never had a chance to read it. It turned out to be a frustrating if happy reunion for all. A few months after the dinner party, Tom suffered a fatal stroke. The sad thing is that his elegant companion not only failed to notify Gerda Stein Mayer of his death until after the funeral had taken place, but was purported to have missed a chance to save his life in her delayed call for help. All who had known Tom mourned. Tom's estranged father's grief was so profound that the writer of his obituary, upon the old man's death a few years later, recorded in the paper that Dr Wongtschowsky had never recovered from his son's untimely passing. Gerda Stein Meyer wrote an unpublished poem about her maverick friend shortly after his death.

School Casanova
The school – Casanova.
All the little girls who loved you
grew up
long before you did.
At twenty already
too adolescent:
(I say! – he's the same
old Tom.)
Then plain girls and
the plainly awful;
girls with problems
alighted, departed.
Wifeless, childless,
jobless, penurious
you died
a juvenile sixty.
Old flame,
dear chump, my
almost-brother,
I cry …
How handsome your
teenage photographs;
how silly your
teenage letters;
How suddenly recent
youth.

Interned on the Isle of Man

In the spring of 1940, several children turned sixteen, an event that normally involved a routine trip to the Haslemere police station for a perfunctory Tribunal. Eleven days after Dieter's sixteenth birthday, Dr Lion summoned him and three other boys who turned sixteen to her office. They were to be interned and they needed to pack. This time there would be no Tribunal. Every German alien (who had not already been cleared in a Tribunal) was classified as 'Category C' or 'enemy alien' and was to be locked up. The boys left her office, and next she called in two more sixteen-year-olds, Household Girls, Ilse Kaiser and Liesel Neufeld. Inexplicably, she failed to tell them to pack and merely directed them to report to the Haslemere police station. This act, whether because of absentmindedness or miscommunication, turned out to be a spectacular gaffe. The girls walked into the town in their summer dresses and were immediately carted away. It was a dark day for the school when people learned of the forced internments, according to Margaret Dove, it was 'the saddest time when the staff had to help some of the pupils through the double trauma of being persecuted as Jews in Germany and as Germans in Britain, while gradually many of them came to realise that they might never see their parents again'.[17]

The boys were taken to nearby Guildford, issued blankets and placed in a school under guard by British soldiers. Over a hundred other men and boys were milling about. Dieter and the other three boys did not know what to make of their predicament. 'I encountered for the first time in my life Orthodox Jews who practiced their rituals at appointed times daily [and] men obviously fearful and nervous, others who considered the whole experience a joke. Some ... wanted to be helpful with us boys; others wanted to impress us.... No one could know whether there was any stopping the enemy and to some, the thought of a German invasion of England produced talk of suicide. On the other hand, it never occurred [to me] that England could lose the war and [even though] we were non-British subjects, we hung on every word spoken by Winston Churchill.'[18] A week later, the internees were transferred during a rainstorm to Huyton, a suburb of Liverpool, where the boys shared a tent for two more weeks. 'Everyone was interrogated with the result that some were taken away including the colourful Captain von Rintelen, a German agent of World War I vintage, whose nefarious work resulted in many Allied merchant ships being burned in mid-ocean.'[19] Then they were shipped to the Isle of Man, a crown dependency of 221 square miles (572.39 square kilometres) in the Irish Sea, and assigned rooms in hotels encircled by barbed wire in Douglas, the main city.

Meanwhile, the two Household Girls were driven to a boxing ring in Reading and, after spending the night on the floor with a few hundred women and crying children, were immediately ferried out to the Isle of Man. The girls threw their identity cards into a large wicker basket and were assigned a room in a hotel, each with a double bed and washstand.

Boredom was the biggest problem, for the girls were used to heavy work schedules. Ilse wrote to Dr Lion, 'Two weeks ago we have left. You really can't imagine what it means for me to be unable to do anything. We just sit around and have no possibility of work ... could you please send something to work.... some recipes and how to scrub [sic] the floor for instance. I'm afraid I will forget otherwise.... Our washstand was our salvation. We washed our clothes in the evening and hoped they would dry by morning. When our clothes were still wet we could not go to the dining room for breakfast. Sometimes we had enough dry things for one of us to go, so that one would try sneaking some food to the room for the other.'[20] Three weeks later clothing arrived. 'Dear Dr Lion. Thanks very much for the suitcase, unfortunately s6.4d had to be paid, so we borrowed the money. We'll have to give it back as soon as possible. So if you would kindly send it on quickly, and you might even be so kind as to send us a little more, as we have no money at all (for stamps, shoesoles, etc.). May I ask you for something else? Poor Ilse [she coyly refers to herself] didn't get any underwear nor socks or *bathingkostuem* [her German-English word for bathing suit] and dresses. Would you please send this and more dresses and shorts for both of us, in a parcel (cost 6d or 1s.) We are very well but wish we were back in school.'[21]

Dieter's quarters were on the opposite end of the island from the women's barracks. The men and boys were shown how to make their bed and fold blankets and towels according to army regulations. Each house appointed a leader and chief cook and in this one detail, Dieter was lucky – his cook had once been a chef of the Ritz Hotel in Paris. Among his housing cohorts were a former German chess champion 'who played with us frequently' and an elderly man who taught the boys Ju Jitsu. 'This made us physically very fit.... We worked to build up our abdominal muscles and learn the art of falling on ... [the] mattresses on the floor.... Our instructor demonstrated his firmness by letting us punch him as hard as we could into his stomach, which resounded like a hollow drum.... To practice with knives or guns we used sticks or rubber knives, learning to parry, unbalance and throw our opponents, pin them to the ground, disarm them, render them harmless, and so on.... We learned to dive, tumble and somersault on piles of mattresses, on our own.'[22] After a few weeks, Dieter sank into depression. He wrote to Dr Gooch, his patron. He wanted to join up. At least fighting Germans would get him off the island. 'I was hoping I might be able to train as a fighter pilot and shoot some of those Germans down'. But the only avenue open to aliens was the Pioneer Corp, an option Dieter rejected because British nationality was not given to its volunteers and 'moreover, the uniforms were baggy'. The Corp engaged mainly in road building and other manual tasks, were not issued arms and were under the direction of officers unwanted in the regular army.[23]

Tensions were high. Men talked about their wives interned on the island and discussed endlessly what would happen to them if the Germans invaded England. One man had been in a concentration camp. 'He had his face slashed from one eye to his mouth, with his face muscles pulled to one side and a resulting speech impediment. He also walked with a limp. He spoke forcefully, saying he would rather take his life than wait for the Germans, and several agreed with him. To him, the invasion was imminent and once the Germans were on English soil their advance would not be stopped. It was a sobering assessment though most of us never believed for a moment that England would fall or that we would lose the war. Was it faith, deep conviction, or were we avoiding reality?'[24]

Among those interned on Man was the German sculptor Hermann Nonnenmacher, who had carved the beautiful wooden sign donated to Stoatley Rough in its early days.[25] The best part of the day for Dieter was after dinner when a couple of the prisoners gave impromptu concerts with accordion or violin accompaniment. 'The tenor's voice was, indeed, wonderful. His favourite song was Romberg's "Be My Love …". We all cheered and asked for more. What was most memorable was the fact that on the other side of the fence stood the British in a large group, taking it all in, joining us in the applause. Sometimes the British were already waiting when the musicians arrived. It was an odd feeling that we should all be on the same side … but here we were separated by tall fences of barbed wire.'[26]

One day a large white ship showed up in the harbour. The authorities told Dieter and the other Stoatley Rough boys to get on board. They were going to Canada. As they were unpacking in their cabin, there was an announcement that only one thousand passengers would fit on the ship; two hundred would have to stay behind. The passengers would choose. Two boys chose almost immediately to go on, afraid of the upcoming invasion of England. Perhaps in Canada they could enrol in the service. (Klaus Zedner, out of school and interned at the same time, chose to go to Canada. He later returned to England to work on a farm.) 'Eddie [Eduard Roussel], the third guy, and I were ambivalent. The discussion went back and forth. I had Peter in England, my parents were in Switzerland and the prospect of additional separation did not sound good. There was also the possible danger from U-boats on the high seas.... Ironic enough, the decision was made for us since Eddie and I had combined our packing into one duffel bag, and we had to stay together, or so we thought. So we stayed.'[27] The next morning the white ship carried away two of the boys from Stoatley Rough, while Dieter and Eddie returned to a joyous welcome from their former housemates. A week later Dieter received his identity papers, a train ticket and some cash and was shipped back to the mainland. From London, Dieter boarded the train to Guildford, where he planned to catch the Haslemere train. Halfway en route, he stayed in the wrong car when an engine was added and cars were switched. By nightfall, the exhausted teenager was stranded at the end of the line in Aldershott, the site of England's largest military training establishment. It was a Saturday night. Dieter was in a real pickle. An alien with a German accent surrounded by drunken and boisterous military men should not be in Aldershott. He crept along the streets looking for a room. Eventually a policeman rescued him and gave him one of the high-security cells for the night. After breakfast, Dieter boarded the right train to Haslemere and walked the 2 miles (3.22 kilometres) back to the school.

Ilse and Liesel were released after two months of internment, receiving their identity papers and fare to London. Ilse used her lucky shilling to get to the school. 'My friend told me: "Put it in your shoe and it will bring you luck." My friend had joined the British forces and was killed. His shilling, however, was enough to get me back to Haslemere.'[28]

The internment of the six pupils received scant notice in the October minutes of the board meeting; it neither named those interned nor offered an explanation. 'Then came the first internments, but thanks to the great effort of some of you here, we have now got all our pupils back except for two, who have been shipped off to Canada before news of their release could reach them.'[29] The two boys who opted to go to Canada were interned once again. One disappeared into the Canadian wilderness, and the other committed suicide after the war upon learning that his mother had died in a concentration camp.

Wolf offers his thoughts. 'At age fourteen we were issued Alien Registration Cards which identified us as "enemy aliens". They were an ironic counterpart to our German passports, which had been stamped with a big scarlet letter J. Regardless of our official classification, the people of Britain and of Haslemere in particular continued to treat us with remarkable understanding and consideration throughout the war. I learned to admire their innate sense of decency and fair play.' During the war, about 8,000 people were interned in Britain, many on the Isle of Man.

Why were the Stoatley Rough children allowed to be scooped up by the authorities? The Tribunals were orderly hearings, for which Dr Lion always supplied documentation attesting to the children's security fitness; she always had time to prepare adequate documentation. According to Herta, Dr Lion was afraid of authority, 'a very Germanic thing'. She believes that Dr Lion's fear rendered her unable to push the right buttons to protect her children from the 'C' classification of 'unfriendly alien'. Renate Dorpalen also wonders, 'Why did not Dr Lion intervene, or the governing body of the school? I cannot imagine they did not care, but perhaps they did not care enough. The school was not without connections to prominent, influential figures.'[30] In her defence, Dr Lion had plenty on her plate in the spring of 1940. As long as the war lasted, she would have been highly protective of public opinion towards her Germanic 'family'. It may have been that she simply did not understand what would happen to the children or that she did not have the resources to get the paperwork together on time. Wolf remarked that after the fall of France, Churchill was so busy that when asked what to do about the refugees, he merely said, 'Round 'em all up'. The matter was raised in the House of Lords, but eventually the refugees were released. Wolf points out that even in America, he had to get permission from the District Attorney's office to travel more than 50 miles (80.47 kilometres) and that the Canadians were even more paranoid – upon landing in Halifax in April 1945, 'we were put on a train and guarded by soldiers with fixed bayonets.'

The children who returned to Stoatley Rough tried to pick up their lives where they left off. All three, Dieter and the two Household Girls, Ilse and Liesel, were sent to live on the Farm. Worse, they learned that they would not be allowed to continue taking classes. Dr Lion would not allow Dieter to prepare for the Matric. By her decision – one that would not change in spite of the intercession of Dieter's sponsor, a member of her own board, the esteemed Dr Gooch – Dieter was deemed unsuitable for a university education. 'This was the only time ... that I remember being truly angry but discussions with Dr Lion, Dr Wolff and others made no difference. I was stunned.'[31]

The consequences of the board's decision to give Dr Lion unilateral sway over the fate of her children were felt by many others besides Dieter over the years. A child could never recover from or move up in her estimation. Hans Loeser recalled, 'I liked her. It also didn't take long for me to find out that I was one of the favoured ones. She was a strong, commanding woman, with powerful ability and desire to do good. That quality was dominant, but she was also able to make life hard for those whom she didn't like for some reason or – more often – those whom she had wrongly pigeonholed as, say, potential farmers, or not suited – or only suited – for academic work, etc. Once one became classified in her mind, it was hard to break out even though the classification didn't fit.' Inge Hamburger once wrote about dining table assignments, always posted for the children to read, and never to be altered. 'Some children often sat with Dr Lion, but others were never given the privilege, and what made it worse is that I felt I deserved to be disliked.'[32]

Dieter, devastated, moved his belongings from the Hut into the Farmhouse. Was it his fate to become a farm labourer?

Banished to the farm

There were two jobs Dieter hated more than anything – hosing the manure from the cowshed and slopping the portable toilets. 'While the floors were concrete and we had big rubber boots on our feet, the hosed manure had to be swept towards a tank in the ground which was teeming with worms. It turned my stomach.'[33] On the first morning of his stay on the Farm, he saw that he had been assigned toilet-bucket duty. He and his teammate, one of the Farm boys, decided to get it over with first thing. The Farm boy handed him the two poles that would be used to carry the waste containers. The two boys had to slip the poles through the handles of the buckets the size of a small oil drum, then move them one at a time to the manure pile. One of the boys would climb the manure pile and then, both the boys striving to keep the bucket from sliding down towards the one on the lower plane, together they would overturn the contents. The trick was to get the bucket to the manure heap without letting it slide. The climate was warm when Dieter first time had this job, but in winter he knew that there was the risk of slipping on the ice. The manure heap was several feet high, a stinking hill laced with straw mucked from the cowshed. 'It was teamwork, and the close calls were many.' (During the war, the system changed and human waste was dumped into a large hole on the premises.) Dieter had one good thing to say about the general plumbing setup on the Farm. 'The toilets were certainly of a higher standard than many rural outhouses.' But, he continued, using the toilets at night without any light was iffy. Sometimes the boys just 'opened the window in the hall'. Wolf recalled that the girls also had to carry their buckets. 'One of them tripped one night outside the open window of the boys' room, and the bucket spilled. Phew-eee!'

Sixteen-year-old pupils not preparing for the Matric were sent to live in the farm house. With the school's population at its all time high, there was no room in the main manse. There were now one hundred people living and working at Stoatley Rough: 'sixty-one school children including two non-resident [day] pupils; nine Household Girls, seven helpers (girls paid to come in and work during the day); ten farm pupils, two evacuees and eleven teachers'.[34] Within a few months in 1940 the school took an additional seventeen children from the New Herrlingen School at Bunce Court; they had been evacuated from their Kent home owing to its proximity to London. No one could see the farm house from the main house, but since everyone got together for the main meal of the day, Farm boys had to make the arduous ascent once a day. Going back to the farm, according to Dieter, was a breeze. 'We negotiated the shortcut at a good speed, knowing when to brake or skirt a tree without losing the rhythm of the run, somewhat like a skier on a slalom run. The walk up took several minutes, the run down took less than one. Once, I was galloping down the trail while enemy planes overhead were being pursued by fighters. Suddenly one dived out of the sky towards the farm.... I was distracted just as I was about to make a tight turn around a tree. I crashed but wasn't hurt. Another time I almost reached the bottom when I caught my foot on a rock and went sailing through the air [doing] a complete flip, landing on my feet below the steps.'[35]

Dieter described his new home. 'It was probably a converted army hut, which included a kitchen, a living room, a bathroom and two toilets.

Central heating of steam heat, generated by electricity ... [kept] the outer parts of the room much warmer than the central areas ... a good [arrangement], since our beds were against the walls.... The toilets were primitive seats on portable drums which had to be cleaned daily. The walls were made of some kind of particle board which in damp weather assumed the consistency of cardboard; in both damp and freezing [weather] it could also become brittle, causing cracks, bulges and breaks.'[36] There were several feed and animal sheds nearby and near the end of the path, an old fashioned generator, a primitive one-cylinder diesel engine, dating from 1896, with an enormous flywheel that provided water to the main house.

In the summer of 1940, the Household Girls did their daily work, but most children had little to do. Foot travel across the heath was constrained because of the radar towers that would provide decisive defence against air strikes by the German Luftwaffe in the coming months. Dr Lion continued to bring in guest speakers for Friday evening lectures: 'Weather in the Making' was met with great success, and a Mr Kewley (whose wife would help prepare the Household Girls for the King's College Housecraft exam in 1941) came in to give travel talks. Some of the Farm and Household workers passed the national poultry certificate examination that summer after attending poultry lectures at Surrey County Council at Guilford Technical Institute. Among them was one girl who had only taken the training to improve her English. The school sold sixteen pigs to the government.

In the fall, classes started again and Nore moved the children in the big house from the upper floors into lower rooms, where windows were taped to prevent flying glass. Residents of the Farmhouse apparently never used the air-raid shelter they had worked hard to dig into the side of the hill early in the war. In October, the school was recognised as 'efficient' by the Board of Education, a rating most welcomed by Dr Lion and her board. The school was now accredited.

Dieter and three of the full-paying academic boys lived in the Farmhouse, alongside six boys, most of them tuition free, who were training to be farmers. Caring for livestock and tilling and harvesting of fields gave everybody plenty to do. Now the school kept livestock only if it was practical – for example, a flock of ducks that refused to lay went under the knife. The pet goats and their kids (with one exception) disappeared. The Shetland pony was also sold. Animals remaining on the farm were 'Black Beauty', or, according to some, 'Betty', the horse that hauled a cart into town on a regular basis to fetch pig food or to take away trash; two milk cows named 'Suzi' and 'Hannah'; two heifers and a calf; a pony; a goat; four sows with 'innumerable piglets'; fifty Rhode Island Red and Light Sussex Breeder chickens; and a pair of geese. There were also puppies from Fred Dreschler's long-haired mutt, Betty, sired by Hanna Nacken's Welsh terrier, Keedah, who dug under the chicken wire to get at her when she came into heat. Miss Nacken tried to deny that her dog would do such a thing, but one of the litter, a little thing who was the spitting image of Keedah, became Keedah's best friend in the ensuing months.

Sometimes someone would refuse to do a chore. After a series of farm managers, young Mr Edward Hughes from Wales was in charge by 1940; he was a man who did not countenance rebellion. He tried to head off resistance with a 'Don't argue with me', but usually both parties stormed up the hill to Dr Lion's office for resolution. Mr Hughes spoke with a broad accent and possessed, to Dieter, 'a strong physique and stubborn mentality',[37] and he provided a vital masculine role model. Dieter wrote, 'Sometimes the farm boys played soccer with Mr Hughes on an uneven pasture staked out with improvised goals and sidelines. Competition was fierce. There were no set teams, but whoever played against Mr Hughes relished the chance to beat him or outfox him. They took the risk of fierce physical contact and many a time Mr Hughes and one of the big boys would find themselves in a shoving match that, in turn, sometimes degenerated into animosity. Such an instance would be cause for intense discussion later among the boys. Lacking fathers, they found in Mr Hughes the much-needed strength against which to test themselves. Good sportsmanship was the rule, and the games provided a necessary outlet.'[38]

Mr Hughes had a sense of humour, luckily for Wolf. One summer day Wolf had the audacity to push Mr Hughes into the swimming pool. Mr Hughes, who had been wearing his swimming trunks, nevertheless emerged unsmiling from the water and grabbed Wolf by the scruff of his neck, marched him to the changing booth. Wolf reports that Mr Hughes 'stood by me with his hand raised in a threatening manner while I changed back into my swim trunks, marched me back to the pool and chucked me in' to the delight of the onlookers. There was never rancour between them over the incident, and Wolf admired the man. Like others, Wolf could produce an excellent imitation of Mr Hughes' heavy Welsh accent. Rolling his *r*'s and broadening his *a*'s, Wolf went around chanting, 'the r-r-rahbbits, the r-r-rahts, and cahterpillars have bahdly dahmaged the cahbbages'.

The boys on the farm were known to have daily rounds of amiable fighting with each other. Alexander Finkler made light of the almost daily combat in his ironical commentary on school life pegged to the alphabet. '*A* – America seems to be a glorious country and it is so exciting to have a visa to the United States.... *E* – Education. The manners of the farm boys are said to be atrocious. Efforts have been made to improve them. Now everybody has to feed the pigs in evening dress.... *I* – Imagination. Our milkman dreams that he is the dairy owner.' When he gets to *U*, he targets the roughhousing on the Farm. '*U* – Unity under the farm boys is excellent. Every day is a fight and some people feel that the walls will soon look like Swiss cheese.'[39]

In 1940, the school acquired a tractor from a wealthy gentleman who had an 'iron horse' to spare. An unidentified farm boy wrote about the gift in *The Bridge*. 'Imagine, a tractor as a present! It was brought over in a butcher's van. I do not know whether you can call it amusement or disappointment which the boys felt.... The tractor had firstly only two wheels, secondly [could get] only eight h.p., and third, it [was so small that it] could enter the horse-stable and still leave room for the horse! The engine was probably the greatest attraction and [at the same time a] bother. It was pretty strong and difficult to handle once it worked. I say "once it worked" because it was often a long time before it worked.'[40] In 1941 another tractor arrived. Dr Lion said, 'The greatest surprise for everybody was the present of a real tractor worth a hundred pounds or more. It was given to us by a personally unknown friend of our cause, after we have been struggling for some time.' Wolf remembered that he earned three pence per hour for weighting down the bouncing mowing machine that Mr Hughes pulled with the tractor over a hummocky pasture, giving him a sore bottom. Dr Lion also wrote, 'the first real Land Army girl, [Miss Woolgar] a girl who really wants to do farming and is going to take it up as her career, has arrived recently and does her pioneer work quite bravely'.[41]

Mr Hughes maintained a farm diary, filling it with rich details about the farm which by then had become though small, a productive entity with a serious purpose. Pages from his farm diary show that he collected wild bees with 'a smoker', a skep [wicker beehive], a white sheet and a short knife; he took a crossbred (Guernsey-Shorthorn) bull calf and a sow and five pigs to market; he was pleased that the ordinary and 'not a pedigree' Red Poll cow, 'frequently milked by different milkers often inexperienced', was yielding three to four gallons daily. 'In the spring he noted that carrots, swedes (rutabagas), peas, onions, leeks, sugarbeet, beans and potatoes [were] all in the ground. He also noted in midsummer that the workers were gathering hay into stacks'.[42]

Birgitte Heinsheimer, the girl who took poultry classes to improve her English pronunciation, was an enthusiastic worker. 'We have an incubator where, I hope, we shall very soon rear some more chickens. All our birds are kept out-of-doors and the ducks enjoy a nice pond next to the swimming pool which was made by the boys last year. Now for the cheese, I do not know, how many sorts of cheese there are, and from white cheese to gorgonzola every country has her own secret way of production. The white cheese [cottage cheese] is the simplest to make; it is the sort which we had last summer and which we saw on the tables in the evening. How we did like it! It tasted so good and is so easy to make; pour the sour milk into a thin cloth, hang it up and let the milk water drain away, and mix what remains with salt, with cream, if you have it, and with caraway seeds.'[43]

Farm work was strenuous. Weekly duties consisted of preparing breakfast, cleaning the building and emptying the toilet tanks; children had to bring in the cows in the morning, milk them, feed them and clean the sheds, sties and chicken coops. Dieter liked caring for the hogs, although the less-experienced children had to be careful not to get caught between a hog and the wall of the pen. One night Dieter stayed up with another boy to tend to a sow who was about to have a litter. She gave birth to one pig after another, frequently standing up to count them and then dropping back on her belly to continue the process. The boys had to rescue the piglets that might otherwise have been squashed by her ponderous body. The boys made their own swill in a large iron kettle over an open fire fed with wood that they had chopped earlier. 'We used all leftovers and trimmings of vegetables from the kitchen, vegetables that were not fit for the kitchen, and special potatoes purchased for hog consumption only. The odour from the cooking was as from the best of stews.'[44]

The worst job was harvesting cabbages in the winter that were destined to be cowfeed. 'The cabbage heads were frozen and wet and we had to cut them from the stem with the cold seeping through my gloves.'[45] Dieter also hated cleaning out the chicken coop, the odour clinging to his body and clothes, which he imagined was not always cleansed away with a shower. Another unpopular job was exterminating mice and rats who invaded the feed shed, rodents entirely at ease with two cats who spent their time dozing in languorous comfort inside the farm house. It became an ongoing sport. The boys tried inserting an air rifle into one of the holes then shooting, but they never hit anything. They could not use poison because it might affect the feed, so they began to set traps. Freeing and re-setting the traps became one of those rotating assignments that nobody wanted.

Farm people ate breakfast and supper on the Farm. 'Breakfast duty had its hazards. First of all, farm schedules are strict: cows need to be milked at the same time daily, without exceptions. School begins for certain people at a given time … and food had to be on the table and ready on time…. There was [always] the risk that the porridge might not be ready because the fire would not burn or it became burned on the bottom of the big iron pot, giving rise to grumbles and complaints. We laid the fire for the next day's breakfast the evening before. The wood had to be chopped, the paper and matches available, the pots and pans ready…. It was strictly wood burning fire and one always hoped that the wood was dry enough to burn, hard enough to last, and of sufficient quantity…. The tables had to be set, the milk had to be filtered by those taking care of the cows … Once the porridge was on the fire it needed frequent stirring. We were about fifteen to twenty persons at the table, all hungry and hard working, all critical if not satisfied…. I always felt the horde's restlessness close behind.'[46]

Taking advantage of their access to the farm kitchen, Dieter and his friends developed what they called Our Weekly Meal plan, OWM for short, for their weekly special meal when they would cook up something the rest of the school's population did not have in the main house. One summer day they made an egg custard by using eggs and milk from the farm, unrationed custard powder and blueberries from the surrounding woods. They put the blueberries into the hot yellow custard and let it stand overnight in the cold pantry. In the morning they eagerly fetched their treat and discovered the gelatinous treat had turned 'richly green'.[47]

Everything was recycled. Manure and chicken droppings became fertiliser; Mr Hughes, the only one strong enough to work behind the horse pulling a heavy, one-bladed plough, churned crop remains back into the ground. Weeding, cultivating and digging out produce were done by hand, a challenge in the thin soil strewn with rocks. Dieter said, 'We'd set aside the rocks we had dug up, the following season there were just as many as before.'

Later in the war years, Dr Lion suggested that Mr Hughes grow sugar beets. It sounded like a great idea. By producing their own sugar, the school could supplement their rationed allotment and satisfy the children's constant craving for sweets. In the spring Mr Hughes duly put in a crop of beet plants. They grew to maturity and then were harvested (with great difficulty, since they grow with multiple roots and cannot be pulled up like carrots) and mashed. The farm boys set up a large cauldron to boil down the pulp. Upon tasting the outcome, there was disappointment. Unfortunately, they ended up making an 'inedible concoction with a bitter aftertaste'. Determined not to waste food, the authorities instructed Miss Demuth to serve some of the mash to the children. Nobody touched it. Undeterred, the cook then stored the bitter syrup derived from the mash in a large barrel in the kitchen, ostensibly for cooking. Nobody recalls that it was ever used.

Mr Hughes left Stoatley Rough in 1941 to continue his training at Culham Training College in Arlingdon, Berkshire. He was replaced by a Mr Bibbe. Mr Hughes wrote to Dr Lion on 18 September 1941 that he was 'learning, even though it is the toughest clay I have ever met with', and he included a recommendation that Dr Lion not sell the old sow. She seemed, in his opinion, 'fit for another season'. He concluded with words of gratitude. 'I often think of you all and shall never forget how much you did to make a very lonely man very comfortable. I only hope that, when I have completed my training here, I shall secure a good appointment with as happy a home as I found at Stoatley Rough.'

The droning of bombers

The spring of 1940 was brightened with the arrival of the duplicating, aka mimeograph machine that Herta dubbed the 'Gestetner multiplying monster'. Dr Wolff set about reprising her former job as magazine editor by producing a cheerful newsletter called *The Bridge*, which she called a 'magazine'. With the exception of Mr Obee and Mr Phillips, almost everyone connected to the school contributed. In her article, 'A Glimpse in the Office', Herta explained that the school had time to publish a magazine since mail deliveries were down to one delivery per day. And besides she said, 'Something good must come out of the war,' unconsciously channelling the words of her adult bosses. Herta typed the nearly forty single-spaced pages of the first volume, and Dr Wolff put the pages together with the artwork that some of the talented youngsters at the school such as Inge Hamburger [Pavlowsky] and Lili [Putti] Kassel [Wronker] produced. Charming drawings of ducks, shoes being repaired and children diving into the pool, dancing, waiting for a haircut or studying – all grist for the mill. Dr Wolff fed the masters into the big drum, Herta turned the handle, and out came the freshly inked copies. Sadly, only two editions of *The Bridge* saw the light of day, Volume I, issued on 14–15 May 1940 and Volume II, numbers 1 and 2, issued in August/September 1941, but they offer a window into school life in their German or English articles, almost each page bearing some kind of illustration.

In the first issue, Dr Lion, now in her seventh year in England and forty-seven years old, addressed the war with eloquence and passion. She recalled having been a teenager during the First World War and offered the benefit of her experience. 'We knew our own lives were unimportant at a time when masses were suffering. But we were quite confident, because we felt that we had run into the path of a new wind, which – although it sometimes blew against us – would in the long run, help us on our way.' She then referred to a picture, famous in its day, that she had placed in the school library. It was Max Liebermann's (1847–1935) '*Netzflickerinnen*' [The Net Menders], a scene of white-capped peasant women handling huge piles of brown fishing nets under a cloudy blue sky. 'It expresses what I want to say. "Wonder is the beginning of worship." And Stoatley Rough was a wonder for all of us, coming after the darkest days of our lives. It has kept its overwhelming beauty, not only on this exceptional spring Sunday on which I write, but on every day in the year.… We have not lost a single of our old friends since war broke out and of that we are glad because we have had to fight still harder for our existence and for the welfare of our younger children. Many of them are entirely separated from their relatives and it is still more important for us to provide the "home" where they can be quietly growing up.'

On other pages, children wrote about trips to the museum, working in the garden, baking cookies. One poignant section was devoted entirely to essays about homes left behind. And, of course, they wrote about the war.

Children expressed their feelings in their English composition classes. The following piece by Inge Schleimer [Wurm], fourteen, appeared in *The Bridge*. She began by invoking the newly fallen Christmas snow that covered 'not only the houses, mountains and all the other concrete things, but also the evil of all living creatures. I sat at the window and looked at the white town thinking of that which belonged to the past and to that which was to follow. My thoughts presented themselves to me as a great question-mark. There was a sound like soft music as if chimes rang. Without noticing it I closed my eyes, and then everything became light and I saw one image after the other passing by. There was the ship which was to carry us to America, and when at last we stood on American ground, our father met us. Naturally we had much to tell each other after such a long separation ... and we went by car to our simple but pretty little house.... Then I passed over many years and saw myself going for a walk with my children followed by a small puppy. I saw how I kept the house, cooked for my family and prepared surprises on Christmas Eve, lit the candles and ... everything vanished. Through thinking of Christmas I was brought back into the tangible present.'[48]

Hitler had decided to invade Great Britain through the English Channel in 'Operation Sea Lion', first by launching a massive effort to cripple the Royal Air Force. While the German air force bombed British air fields, factories and cities in what was known as The Battle of Britain, it began to concentrate on London in what would be called 'The Blitz' [Lightening (strike)], a sustained campaign of night-time bombing that lasted from late summer of 1940 until May 1941. Luftwaffe Chief of Air Staff, Hans Jeschonnek, rashly predicted that the invasion of Britain would take about six or seven weeks, but Commander of the Luftwaffe, Hermann Goering, knew better. 'An Englishman is like a wounded bull, he is most dangerous when he is injured.'[49]

What relative peace the pupils may have enjoyed in the summer of 1940 was over. Only 40 miles (64.37 kilometres) from London and located along a major flight path, the school provided a front-row seat to the action. Renate Dorpalen recalled, 'We heard a buzzing as if from innumerable bees in the sky above. It was the sound of squadron after squadron of Spitfires and Hurricanes taking to the air and flying towards the English Channel. Searchlights probed the sky for Nazi bombers droning overhead until, finally, an All Clear was sounded and we emerged from the cellars.... The German bombers came seldom in bad weather but were certain to show up in full moonlight. Standing on the heath near the school we could see the stars and watch the searchlights crisscrossing the sky in a frantic hunt for bombers. We could hear the approaching roar of enemy planes and then see their flares. First would come the lead plane, which set flares at four points to mark the target zone, followed by the squadrons. Their incendiary bombs lit up the area in the distance. We could watch the bombs falling and, moments later, hear the faint sound as they hit. Occasionally there would be aerial dogfights. Each time a German plane was shot down cheered and mourned the loss of an RAF plane.'[50]

Children at Stoatley Rough saw flames in the horizon by night as whole neighbourhoods in London lit up from direct hits by incendiary bombs. The bombardment lasted over fifty-seven straight nights. Articles written for *The Bridge* during this time show that the response to the drama the children were witnessing was varied, ranging from indifference to amusement to fear. Creature comforts came to an end as a steady flow of refugee children came and left; children constantly moving into the shelter each night to sleep in a mad game of musical beds, alerted by the school's air-raid signal, a sustained bong-bong of the gong and ding-ding-ding of the bell. Wolf wrote, 'Before the war, girls slept in rooms on the second floor (c.1938) and boys on the third, but when the war came it was deemed safer to move girls to the ground floor and boys to the basement next to the "Schoolroom".'[51] Children slept on mattresses on the floor packed in like sardines and also on the shelves normally used for sorted laundry. Renate Dorpalen recalls that she moved nine times during her six-year stay at Stoatley Rough. Air raids became routine.

Martin and the other Hut boys at twelve, found the Blitz exciting, especially the dogfights. After the sound of planes faded into the distance, they would run outside to pick up spent cartridges, which they traded with each other. A trip to London yielded other treasures: pieces of molten land mines, shrapnel from bomb casings and shreds of silk parachutes. Obo said, 'We used to look for and PICK UP exploded smoke bombs and what might have been anti-personnel bombs that had been dropped on the Heath, not realising what mortal danger we put ourselves in. When I think about this now I can only say that someone was looking out for us.'

With the exception of the gentle Peter Gaupp who lacked interest in fast-moving machines as a matter of principle, the boys became intensely involved with airplanes. They educated themselves with official pictures and small metal-cast models of airplanes and warships. Dieter wrote, 'The plane models, made by Dinky-Toy, were very good scale models and augmented our avid interest in plane identification. Some models were harder to obtain than others. Sometimes we would project the images of these planes on a wall in a dark room with a flashlight and have the other person guess what we were showing. The models of warships came from boys who had brought them from Germany. While we had no occasion to see warships, we could talk authoritatively about them when they were reported on the evening news or in the newspapers.'[52]

It is hard to imagine the intensity of the attack as experienced by witnesses on the ground. The Germans committed 625 bombers and 648 fighters to The Blitz, sending them across the Channel two hundred and three hundred at a time. The boys had plenty of chances to identify the planes. Over the five years of war, the boys learned to recognise each type and version of British, German and, later, American aircraft in the sky. Sometimes their experience with the planes and their pilots was weirdly intimate. Goldy recalled, 'The view into the valley (from the manor house) was beautiful and our strategic position high up above the valley enabled us to look down into the cockpits of passing fighter planes when they flew low. None could go faster than about 400 miles per hour. When the pilots were taking a training flight through the valley we could usually wave to them and they would sometimes wave back.'[53] The German air force was divided into *Gruppen* [groups] much like the RAF with its Fighter, Bomber, Coastal, and Training Squadrons, Groups and Commands.[54] The boys could distinguish one from another. Today they easily detect errors in the old Second World War movies where directors have substituted aerial footage. Wolf avers, 'I'm appalled by the sloppy way *The History Channel* makes up collages of alleged events in the air war in WWII and to my surprise, P-51's suddenly morph into Spitfires, B-24's into Lancasters, etc.'

The boys saw so many airplanes because not only was Haslemere situated between Portsmouth and London, it was also close to the two largest air force bases in England – Biggin Hill and Croyden. The first, the 'aerodrome' Biggin Hill, in northern Kent, 20 miles (32.19 kilometres) southeast of Central London, was supposed to protect London. Its hangers, workshops, mess halls, shelters and married quarters were made ready by 1938. Biggin Hill was to be one of the most important bases during the Battle of Britain.[55] Croydon was 15 miles (24.14 kilometres) south of London. Imperial Airways was founded at Croydon in 1924, and many aviators started or completed flights there, including Charles Lindbergh, who landed the Spirit of St Louis at Croydon amidst a crowd of 100,000 excited spectators May 1927.

The Hut boys lost their soccer, kick-the-can and hiking grounds (parts of Hindhead Common and Gibbet Hill) when the RAF cordoned the areas off with barbed wire to become lookout stations. Radar, a potentially powerful technology, was a potential target of the German air force. It more than proved its worth during the Blitz in its ability to warn of incoming planes, allowing the RAF to be ready when the German planes appeared on the horizon.[56] Even closer was the RAF Experimental Station at Farnborough, enclosed by a thick hedge to protect top-secret designs from prying eyes. Wolf recalls that there were gaps in the hedge, and the boys would slow down their bikes, hoping to get a glimpse.

As the Hut boys grew older, the school expected them to honour the custom of helping the younger children, a duty that sometimes involved the simple act of giving comfort. One day, Nore asked Goldy to leave the Hut on a temporary basis to sleep with a roomful of small boys in the manor house. Goldy recalled, 'The German planes [sometimes] came closer to Haslemere than usual and there was some anti-aircraft fire and concussions from bombs which made the birds chirp even at night. (Bombs can sound just like thunder, especially when far away, but apparently there are differences in the atmospheric pressure that make birds chirp when there are bombs but not when there is thunder.) One night the bombs seemed louder than usual, and one of the boys came into my little room as if to ask me to stop it all. He was afraid too and asked to stay.... I remember getting his mattress and putting it on the floor next to me, holding his hand from my bed until he fell asleep.'[57] The boys also remember some close calls. Dieter was lying in bed on the Farm one summer night when an air raid sounded. As usual, the Farm kids had not bothered to put up the blackout curtains and the windows were open. Dieter was lying in the dark watching the searchlights of London sweep the sky. Then came the sound of an airplane. A single bomber was approaching Haslemere. Dieter saw a big flash of light over the sleeping town followed by the burst of a bomb. The flimsy farm building shook and his bed shook. Then there was an awful quiet. The next day, he learned that a German bomber under pursuit had jettisoned its bomb while trying to hit the railway yards. Instead, he had scored a near miss on the little Haslemere museum. There were no casualties. Another time, a bomb fell into the courtyard of the Haslemere Hospital and did not explode. It became exhibit number one in a subsequent war bond drive.

The maintenance man and general factotum Mr Obee was an official airplane spotter. He came to the school a few times each week to do the odd job and was much admired by Dr Lion for scrounging parts to keep things running. The boys admired him because he belonged to the Royal Observer Corps – that is, he was a spotter for enemy aircraft. Wolf recalled, 'We all read his copies of the *Aeroplane Spotter* avidly and all of us became expert spotters.' Obo said, 'when Mr Obee brought us our copy of the weekly *Aeroplane Spotter* tabloid, we would first turn to the quiz on the back page to see who first could identify the Friend or Foe partial plane views'. Renate Dorpalen described the little handyman with fine detail. He was 'a friendly talkative handyman with ill-fitting dentures and a Cockney accent who lived in a nearby town. [He] consumed quantities of tea before contemplating [any] task as did his ever-present dog who was provided with a special saucer near his master. The genius of this man lay in his ability to make any repairs presently, which usually meant some time, often never. He seemed to be as puzzled about us as we were about him. Later, however, he proved to be a vital resource when things got scarce during the war, for he always had a friend who just happened to have what some of us needed.'[58] He was famously known for the following line regarding his dentures: 'Somebody asked me if they were my own teeth. I told 'em: "they jolly well ought to be, I paid fifteen quid for 'em!"'

In his youth Mr Obee had travelled the world as a soldier and as an evangelical missionary, but what the boys liked about him was his ancient Vauxhall, a rattletrap that somehow he had been allowed to keep. (It was rare to have a car since gas was rationed.) Dieter marvelled, 'the fact that it functioned at all often seemed like a miracle to us, though we knew nothing about cars. First of all, it looked old, of a bygone vintage. Secondly, it sounded old. It put-putted. At times it roared. It had squeaks. Most remarkable was its ignition system. I am not sure if I have the sequence correct, but it seems that to start the car (if it did not turn over the first time), the hood had to be raised, the radio turned on, the windshield wipers activated, followed by a lunge to a location under the hood (bonnet) to catch the spark which would start the engine. Given that Mr Obee usually wore a jacket, the added sight of coat tails flying made the performance all the more fascinating.'[59]

13 August 1940 was a day Wolf would never forget, since it was not only his twelfth birthday but also 'Adlertag' [Eagle Day], the official opening of the Battle of Britain and the prelude to invasion.

[We were] awakened about 6:00 a.m. by the throbbing of many aircraft engines. It was some time before we spotted dozens of silvery dots, high in the sky and in neat geometrical formations. A few moments later, a pair of Hurricanes swooped over our heads and climbed out of sight. We heard distant machine-gun fire and thuds. Only then did the sirens of Haslemere sound the alert, followed by the school alarm signal, the alternate sounding of a gong and ringing of a bell. We dashed over to the main building and were told to take shelter in the coal cellar, probably the most unsafe place around. Someone remembered that it was my birthday and everybody sang 'Happy Birthday to You' and 'Hoch Soll Ehr Leben' [High Should He Live, the German equivalent of 'For He's a Jolly Good Fellow']. I thanked Hermann Goering for providing fireworks for my birthday party. Later … Miss Evans took us to Frensham Pond which was being drained because it was a landmark for German bombers. We splashed and crawled through the mud of the remaining puddles, collecting fresh-water mussels and minnows. Mr Obee had agreed to pick us up in his ancient car. Instead, he took one look and said, 'Oh no! Not in my car you, don't!' After we had scraped off most of the mud, he allowed us to stand on the running boards all the way back to school.⁶⁰

Mr Obee will be remembered most for having once faced down the British army. Dieter tells the story:

Mr Obee had to go to Hindhead from time to time which entailed crossing the dirt road across the 'heath'. The actual distance was probably no more than five miles, but the trip was slow. Frequently the road sank between two banks to a point where it could not be seen. On one side of the road was the expanse of heath, on the other, a rolling slope. Tanks for practice runs and manoeuvres frequently used the site. On this particular day, Mr Obee was returning from Hindhead and had reached the sunken part of the road when, up ahead, a column of tanks was advancing in the opposite direction. For each this was a one way road. Mr Obee had been in World War I – he had fought in Gallipoli among other places (where he said he spent much of his time on his stomach overlooking the harbour, according to Wolf) – and perhaps because of this experience, he was not impressed. I believe that a certain British pride may have motivated him. He continued on his appointed route. He could have done little else, other than retreat until there was sufficient space to leave the road, but he didn't. The car was rocking along, slowly, hitting boulders and rocks as it went, emitting its usual range of sounds. The tank leader soon realised that there was no solution available, other than to reverse. Thus the entire tank column, some six or more vehicles, put their caterpillar tracks in reverse and retreated in the face of Mr Obee's relentless progress! Whether greetings were exchanged, I don't know; Mr Obee never stopped.[61]

From 24 August to 6 September the Germans sent over an average of a thousand planes a day. On 15 September 1940 the British RAF intercepted, diverted or shot down seventy-six bombers, escorted by three times as many fighters and routed a second wave of two hundred more. Historians write that Goering's bombing of London extended the time for Britain to manufacture armaments and planes for future warfare on the Continent. But the attack exacted an immense toll. Intense bombing lasted until May 1941, leaving 375,000 Londoners homeless. Hitler's bomber losses over England had been so severe that the *Luftwaffe* never fully recovered from the blow it received in the skies over Britain that late summer and fall. The Battle of Britain was effectively over (although the Blitz continued). Damage had been inflicted on Buckingham Palace, Westminster Abbey and the Chamber of the House of Commons. After June 1941, air raids became sporadic as the *Luftwaffe* turned its attention to the Soviet Union and the Mediterranean. The schoolchildren at Stoatley Rough were left to deal with the psychological consequences of the German's attacks. For the rest of their lives, they would not forget that they had witnessed Britain's 'finest hour'.

Coping with fear

While plane spotting may have been exciting, fear lurked beneath the surface of daily life at Stoatley Rough School.[62] Dorit Bader Whiteman

famously noted that survival from the Holocaust did not mean that
'nothing happened' to the Jewish refugee children.[63] Not only were the
children at Stoatley Rough uncertain whether their parents were alive,
they also thought they might be attacked: a German plane might drop
a bomb or paratroopers might land on the heath bordering the school.
And then there was the insurmountable problem of nationality: they
were, after all, Germans and Austrians, the enemy. Finally, when the first
serious bombing began, the school was still on holiday and quite a few
children had gone to London and Dr Lion called them back. Wolf recalls
that it was 'too late for some of the younger ones – they would have
screaming nightmares for a long time'. Fear might have destroyed
the slender thread of courage that sustained the children but for the
discipline of hard work and shared responsibilities that Nore and the
others imposed on the children each day. Hope kept everyone going,
regardless of realities. Typical was Ernst Wohlgemuth, a young boy from
Germany, who said many years later that he 'wrote to his mother every
day since he first came to Stoatley Rough and never saw her again.'[64]

Renate Dorpalen, at seventeen, arrived from Berlin in May 1939,
typifying many Roughians as a child of privilege who suffered
a wrenching loss of family and moving on to a new life, alone even
at Stoatley Rough but for a few close friends. Renate's wealthy family
had lived in the Charlottenburg district of Berlin, the same area where
Dr Lion and her German staff had lived and taught. Her father was
a gynaecologist; her mother sat on several charitable boards of directors,
including one of the three Pestalozzi-Froebel Houses in Berlin through
which she came to know Dr Lion, who had spent time there as a teacher.
In her capacity, Renate's mother introduced young Renate to several
leading feminists of the time: Dr Lion (who had been in her home), Alice
Salomon and, in particular, Hildegard von Gierke, the great educator
and a close friend of Renate's mother. The family was assimilated and
staunchly patriotic, with banking money on Renate's mother's side, law
and commerce on her father's. Another key member of this close-knit
family was the housekeeper, Martha Grams, whom they called 'Mürt',
who also lived in the spacious apartment with the family and a few
domestic staff. Mürt was a fair-haired woman with greyish eyes and
a long braid, a poster-woman for the healthy Germanic Aryan.

Everybody in Renate's family played an instrument and spoke fluent
French. Unlike many Jewish children who were schooled in the public
system, Renate did not experience harassment at her post-primary

school, a Huguenot school, the *Hohenzollern Oberlyceum* in Berlin-Weilmersdorf, where everybody spoke French. During *Kristallnacht* her father fled to the country home of an Aryan patient. During that long night young Renate watched Mürt politely admit the Nazi police into the house several times to allow them to search the premises. (Owing to Mürt's age at the time, fifty-seven, the Aryan servant had been allowed to remain in service to the Jewish Dorpalens.) After *Kristallnacht* the family broke up. One brother was sent to the United States to live with an uncle; another to England into British military service; the third ended up starting a business in South America. Renate would go to Stoatley Rough, and her parents would stay in Berlin to wait for visas to the United States. On 28 May 1939 Renate's father accompanied her to Hamburg, where she would set off to England. They stayed in the best hotel in town. She was surprised to see him wearing his Iron Cross pin in his lapel in an effort to ward off suspicions. By then, Nazi bullies were openly arresting Jews right off the street, night and day. Renate's trepidation about the impending voyage took away her appetite, and she found it difficult to converse with her father that night. When they said goodbye the next morning, her father told her she was loved no matter if they ever saw each other again, and when her bus pulled away, he waved his handkerchief at her according to the custom of the day. She arrived in Haslemere the next day. Dr Lion received her warmly. At first she went to work typing for Dr Wolff, but Renate soon tired of the isolation of the job and became a Household Girl, welcoming the long hours of hard work. From then on she kept to herself, plunging into work and studies without forming attachments, finding solace in the many letters from home and her brothers who were now scattered in various parts of the world.

Like Renate, the children at Stoatley Rough seldom talked about their fears with the brisk and sensible adults, who marched them through their daily routine. Goldy wrote, 'Denial was the main psychological mechanism used by the children. Some had not heard from their parents for months, even years; others received a card through the Red Cross from parents pretending that all was well. It was already known that the Germans were killing people but the children whose parents were in danger seemed to totally ignore this. As for how all this applied to me, I still find it hard to understand how I could watch in the distance the red clouds over London, the result of flames from the air raids, without it occurring to me that Mother or Ralph would be in the thick of this. I was too occupied watching as the searchlights tried to pick out the

German airplanes and wondering how many would be shot down.'[65] Wolf
remembered that the school's response was something between 'Prussian
discipline and the British stiff upper lip'. Boys had been taught to keep
their emotions to themselves. Any show of emotion was met with '*Stell'*
dich nicht so an!' [Don't make a fuss!]. He concludes, 'when I reached age
sixty, I decided I'd earned the right to make a fuss (or to "*stell' mich an*")'.

Sometime in the spring of 1942, the messages from Renate's
mother stopped coming. Her parents had been deported to
Theresienstadt, a concentration camp designed to house privileged
Jews from Czechoslovakia, Austria and Germany. A year later,
in August 1943, Mürt, who had remained in Berlin, wrote: 'My beloved
child, news from Alice [Renate's mother]. Deeply saddened: Georg
[Renate's father] died on December 13. God be with her and us.'[66]
After the war, Renate held in her hand the postcard her mother had
sent to Mürt from Theresienstadt about her husband's death. She noted,
'A reply to the card could be sent only via the *Reichsvereinigung der*
Juden [State Association of Jews] in Germany, Berlin-Charlottenburg
two, Kantstrasse 158 – not very far from where we used to live. My
mother's message was written in pencil, almost illegible and with spelling
errors.' Her mother had addressed Mürt with the familiar 'du', which
profoundly upset Renate, remembering the strict relationship once
maintained between the mistress of the house and her servant.

Renate reflected on the situation:

> It was truly symbolic of Nazi aims and left me in a quandary
> about my mother's feelings, almost more so than about any other
> deprivation or degradation she had suffered. I grieved for the
> woman she no longer was…. Mail had [been] a tangible sign
> of their presence in our separation. Separation allowed for hope,
> my struggle between hope and despair was present at all times.
> And now my father had been dead for almost a year when I thought
> him alive. How does one mourn such a loss, hidden beneath the
> fragile hope of a reunion? What had happened to him? And what
> about my mother? To picture her apart from my father was
> inconceivable. I did not want to think what life was to be without
> my parents. In reality I had been alone for more than four years.

Renate soldiered on with her household chores and her studies, refusing
to give in to despair. She articulates her uncertainty, dread and lack

of control over events at the time: 'But the tears did not come and life at Stoatley Rough continued in its daily rhythm of hard work and the caring for others. By year's end a clamouring for change grew slowly in my mind but uncertainty about my mother held me in check. As long as she knew where I was, I thought we had a chance to be reunited.... Was this uncertainty a disguised fear of the unknown and had I become totally dependent on Stoatley Rough? More likely mental depression was the ultimate cause.'[67]

Renate began to hoard her weekly ration of one small Cadbury chocolate bar and her clothing coupons. She was saving them to give to her mother.

The authorities at the school ignored or suppressed self-pity and despair, wisely. They, themselves, had much to grieve for. After an initial attempt to suppress news of the war, they allowed the children access to world news. Before each dinner hour, radio broadcasts from the BBC informed the assembled children and teachers about 'the numbers of dead and injured soldiers and civilians ... the military advances and losses, the sunken ships and the never-ending reports of how many tons of bombs were dropped on our cities and elsewhere' (and, of course, the bracing rhetoric from the great Winston Churchill).[68]

During the Blitz, the Household Girls noted an increase in laundry chores, the result of bedwetting by transient children recently evacuated from London. Hard work helped, but depression was contagious. Renate recalled, 'Most of the children experienced separation with intense longing and sadness. Often they did not understand the reason for the break-up of their families. I remember a young couple whose small children [at Stoatley Rough] ... were soon informed of their mother's death. Such devastating news affected all of us.'[69] Some children found resiliency, their spirits braced by the no-nonsense leadership of Nore Astfalck, who whisked away doubt and worry. Martin recalled, 'The Matron and Headmistress never pitied or comforted the children. We all dealt with our loneliness alone, although the Household Girls in charge of the younger ones provided selective comfort. I think that they felt that if they had shown any sympathy, the children would never have been able to endure the separation from their parents.'[70]

Renate confirms Nore's healing influence. 'Routinely we spent our nights in the cellars, where the small children were bedded down in safe corners. Thanks to Nore Astfalck's extraordinary organisational skills and reassuring manner, there was never panic or overt anxiety about the real danger of a direct hit by bombs on the school. Somehow that likelihood was blocked out of our minds in spite of the daily reports about disastrous bombing effects all around us. Perhaps the fact that the older pupils were responsible for the younger ones strengthened our ability to master our own worries and thus extend comfort to our charges.'

The older the child, the greater the fear. Seventeen-year-old Inge Rothschild and her friend Edith Hubacher (still friends, sixty-eight years later) were on the heath 'ablaze with purple fragrant heather, our favourite place for walking'. Inge was worried. She had not received any mail from her mother for two weeks. She recalled Edith's breaking-off the conversation at the point, asking, 'What are you afraid of?' Her response was one of silence. Unable to articulate her fear, Inge recalled, 'I couldn't go on.'

While the chances that a German paratrooper would land anywhere near Haslemere were slim, the possibility existed. In 1943 with Martin and Goldy now fifteen and old enough to be appointed Air Raid Messengers, they never knew who might be hiding in the dark blackout of night. Martin recalled, 'We took turns usually at night, getting up when the air raid siren announced the beginning of a raid. We wheeled our bikes through the dark gardens to a neighbour's house while the searchlights probed the sky and sometimes, anti-aircraft guns boomed. Our job was to run messages down Farnham Lane on our bikes in case the Germans knocked out communications. The neighbour was the Air Raid Warden, and we remained at his house until the "All Clear" sounded. It was scary. The thought of an enemy soldier lurking behind the bushes was never far from our minds. Thank goodness I never had to run a message down the lane.'[71] One time Goldy was taking a bath when 'there was a terrific explosion.... I crouched almost below the water level ... [then] after awhile I put on my clothes and with soapy hair, put on my steel helmet to report to my civil defence station. I was a fire-bomb messenger and had to be ready to get on my bicycle to call the fire engines if telephone connections were cut. We later learned that a German plane with a full bombload had crashed into Hindhead across the heath.'[72]

Children feared not only the parachutist lurking just beyond the hedges, but injury from an exploding bomb. When Goldy was put in charge of the blackout curtains for the large dormitory in the main building, 'that meant that I had to climb on the window sills of the long bay windows to fasten the curtains which were always open to allow for fresh air. If a bomb would have dropped at the moment I was standing there so exposed, it could have been serious because of flying glass. I was afraid to do this chore but gathered up my courage when I had to do it.'[73]

There were times of intense excitement at Stoatley Rough, times when spectacular events captured everyone's attention. Haslemere lay along the flight path between London and the naval base in Portsmouth. An American bomber, a B-24, had crashed in the streets of Haslemere, one of its engines ploughing through the roof of the Rex Cinema during a matinee show, setting fire to the theatre. Large parts of the engine burned outside on the street. Two groups came to the rescue: Canadian soldiers from their barracks in Hindhead, 3 miles (4.83 kilometres) from Haslemere, and the Haslemere fire brigade. The Canadians rushed to unleash carbon tetrachloride on the smouldering debris from their side, while the Brits feverishly ran out their hoses. It was not long before the Canadians mistakenly gassed some of the English firefighters in the process. There were no casualties reported.

British children were taught to put out fires with buckets and stirrup pumps, owing to the German habit of dropping incendiary bombs as beacons for navigation. When the school's notorious pump house with its nineteenth-century flywheel caught fire in 1945, the drill turned out to be of real use. The children knew exactly what to do, their efforts to be especially vital since the site was almost impossible for the Haslemere Fire Department to reach. Hanno Pilatz said, 'As regards the fire we did completely extinguish it before the fire brigade could get there, and what a fire it was. At the end Dr Lion had got more or less the whole school to the blaze and organised a chain of buckets to supply us with water from the swimming pool. Of course as a result of that fire all the main fuses for the farm including our Black Hut [an outbuilding near the farm house that became a dwelling for some of the pupils towards the end of the war] were destroyed and it took a few months for the current to be restored.'[74] Uli Hubacher added, 'We successfully fought the fire in the pump house on the farm, and practically extinguished the actual fire before the (poor) fire brigade, with no proper access road in the farm valley, reached the site.'[75] The fire chief later praised the children in the local newspaper. Earlier the children had fought a large brush fire on Hindhead Commons just outside the school's gates. They fought with 'buckets, brooms, anything handy' according to Wolf, who said, 'we speculated that it could have been set by German bombers – to light a beacon or destroy the Gibbet Hill radar station'.

There were times of genuine panic. One day a six-year-old walked into the dining room carrying an unexploded 20-millimetre shell exclaiming, 'Look what I found.' With such events, it is hard to imagine the steadiness these conditions demanded of the adults. Common sense usually prevailed. One girl remembered watching a dogfight overhead. 'We watched the first dogfight between a German plane and a Spitfire in bright daylight, until somebody rushed us inside.'[76] Each of the Hut Boys remembered watching various air battles between planes until being hustled into the house, sometimes cheering as a German plane went down in flames. On one such occasion – a night-time occurrence – one of the adults gently admonished Wolf with the sobering thought that 'the pilot might very well have been a former neighbour of yours'. Wolf later wrote, referring to the puzzling complexities of their situation, 'we weren't pampered or spoiled or spared much. Not at all.'

In spite of all the chaos, the Hut Boys grabbed at every opportunity to have fun. Wolf recalled one prank. 'We found an empty smoke bomb on Hindhead Common, probably left behind from a Canadian Army exercise. We got some black paint (where?) and wrote on it something like *Achtung! Nicht Anfassen!* [Attention! Don't touch!] Then we planted it – I can't remember whether it was on the path outside The Hut or The Bungalow. At any rate, our teachers were not amused.'

One day the dinner time was interrupted by a particularly horrific event. The mealtime had started out perfectly well, with everybody enjoying at least two items that were standard fare during wartime – potatoes, always part of the main course, and sometimes stewed prunes for dessert, considered a treat. (Canned prunes in syrup would have been a luxury.) Wolf was at Dr Lion's table, and he recalls, 'Dr Lion had the habit of looking around to see what the rest of us were eating and, if she liked it, would consume a generous portion on top of her diet ("I'll try just a little bit").' On that day Dr Lion contemplated the prune pits in her bowl for a moment, then turned to Wolf. 'Hmm, *Kinder*, I have an idea. I want you to collect all prune pits today and from now on, and use them for paving the muddy path that leads to the Bungalow and beyond, to the Hut.' Wolf stopped eating, mid-bite. 'My immediate reaction was a vision of a forest of plum trees sprouting out of the path. I did some quick mental order-of-magnitude arithmetic: Assuming that 100 people consume five prunes each fifty times a year and that each prune pit occupied one square centimetre. Of a path fifty meters long and one meter wide, how long would it take to collect the required pits? The answer: twenty years (check it out).' Wolf did not collect any pits that day and went about his business. A few days passed, then Dr Lion mentioned the project to Wolf once more. He mumbled some response, intending to stall as long as possible. And eventually either Dr Lion came to her senses or she forgot all about it. At any rate, the prune project died.

That day at dinner something else happened – the war paid them a direct visit. While some ate in the Sitting Room or smaller adjutant rooms, Dr Lion and Wolf were seated in Lookout that day, the big dormitory on the second floor where the little boys were placed when they first arrived at Stoatley Rough. Lookout had an enormous picture window that gave a panoramic view of the South Downs, a dazzling vista of forests and hilly lands stretching before the eye at great distances. As everyone was finishing dessert, a noise from outside penetrated the quiet hubbub of conversation. Diners turned towards the window to see what was happening. Barrelling straight at them was an American bomber, a B-25, with propellers churning on its distinctive gull wings. The bomber was travelling at about 300 miles (482.80 kilometres) per hour, having failed to lift up to avoid the promontory upon which Stoatley Rough perched. Everyone stopped talking. At the last minute, the plane veered up and flew over the house in a tremendous roar of its engines, pulling out just in time. Nobody could finish their prunes that day.

Nore Astfalck could not ever completely assuage all the children's fears, nor could anyone change the fact that they were Germans in an England at war with their motherland. In 1941, as if the reality suddenly scared the authorities, the school adopted the questionable policy that the pupils should shed all vestiges of their Germanic heritage. No longer would the school overtly cherish its Germanic roots. Children were instructed to throw away all their letters from home and, thenceforth, to speak only English. (Many defied this directive and kept their letters.) At last they were supposed to become English. The German teachers started exhorting the children more forcefully to '*Sprecht Englisch!*' Subdued, the children took care not to speak loudly or often when they ventured into town, fearful that their accents would give them away as aliens, but among themselves they still spoke German until 1942 or so. But those children old enough to understand the implications of both a possible invasion and hostility from the town folk were now confused.

Renate recalled the situation: 'The school told us to destroy all letters and items linking us with our German past.... I was puzzled to know how our pronounced accents could be hidden. And accents we all had, some of which were acquired from the extraordinary pronunciations of the German staff. The atmosphere in the school remained predominantly German, with German customs and traditions, and with the German language as the chief mode of communication, particularly among the German educators. This was, in some small way, comforting in my transitional phase. But acclimatisation was far more difficult.'[77] Renate tried to become English overnight. 'I frantically learned to knit and eat "the English way", and very conscientiously counted in English.... Each night I repacked a small suitcase in preparation for sudden flight to whereabouts unknown. But my decision about what was most important to me – and it changed every day – led eventually to the awareness that nothing really mattered. Finally, I did not pack at all.'[78]

Digging in – The hardships of 1941

Almost two years into the war, the material deprivations, the overcrowding and the constant fear of attack settled around Stoatley Rough like a thick London fog. Miserable conditions permeated every activity, threatening to blot out expectations for the future. Early on, Germany had blockaded shipping lanes with their U-boats, making it difficult for England to import, among other goods, food, wool, cotton and oil. (By cutting off Atlantic travel, Germany could not only prevent America from entering the war but force Britain towards surrender.) In January 1940, Britain began to ration basic foodstuffs (meat, eggs, butter, sugar, tea, milk, cheese, jam). In 1941, clothes were rationed. In 1942, sweets and chocolate, along with petrol joined the list. In a letter to her mother, Renate Dorpalen described how rationing worked at Stoatley Rough. Each pupil received 'eight ounces of sugar, four of butter, four of tea, two of bacon and one shilling and ten pence worth of meat per person per week.'[79] Later, the meat ration was cut to two pence worth of Argentine corned beef. Imported fruits became a thing of the past. Eggs, according to the boys, rationed as 'one egg per person per week perhaps' were preserved in water glass (sodium silicate) brine for the winter months. Even hot water became scarce. The bathtub was to contain no more than five inches of 'tepid' water. The pre-war

porridge (in German, according to Wolf, known as the off-putting
Haferschleimgruetze) [gruel groats][80] seemed a veritable luxury now that
it was no longer available. Now the children were eating 'boiled oats
intended for animal feed' for breakfast. On Sundays the former treat
of corn flakes was replaced with puffed barley, a food so strange to the
boys that they called it *Ammeisen* [ants] since the grains were oblong in
shape. Gone was the newfangled delicacy of corn flakes, once described
to parents as *gequetschter und gebackener Mais* [squashed and baked
corn], unknown on the Continent. Yet all was not lost. Under the new
rationing, Miss Demuth kept finding creative ways to please the children,
her 'yeast balls' a perennial favourite. Wolf recalled

> The remarkable thing: rationing was never unpopular during the
> war (that changed when it continued for years after the war.)
> Lord Woolton, Minister of Food, was very popular. Much of this
> probably had to do with the pre-war class system. The upper
> classes were, by European standards, grossly overfed, drawing food
> from all over the empire and the world. The working class had
> a notoriously poor diet – chips with everything, no fruits, veggies,
> an aversion to things green. The German name for rickets (Vitamin
> D deficiency) is *Englische Krankheit* – English disease. The war
> brought on a social revolution – a great levelling experience. His
> Lordship got the same rations as his scullery maid. With lots
> of government propaganda, working class diet improved. Full
> employment helped. Of course, the rich still ate better, especially
> if they had access to Scottish salmon streams, etc., or could afford
> to pay £7 6d ($1.50) for *one* hothouse peach, pre-inflation, about
> $15.00 today. In addition to fixed rations, there was a points
> scheme (a much more generous version existed in America): thirty-
> two points per person per month. A pound of beans might be two
> points, a can of salmon or peaches in heavy syrup sixteen points
> (that's why we never got canned fruit). I remember seeing a big sign
> in a department store in late 1944: New-Americans love it! Peanut
> butter, only six points for eight ounces! Try it!

Along with the bombing, the air raids, the blackout curtains and animal
feed for breakfast, the students endured poorly heated rooms and illness.
Peter Gaupp recorded in his diary at the time that he was 'forever being
dragged out by Miss Humby to go on walks when I wanted to be inside

where it was warm'. He also noted that the school was quarantined around 20 January and that the 'cold water pipes froze and some big boys came and thawed them out'.[81]

The older girls noticed that some children received more attention than others, that the sense of fairness and equality formerly paramount at the school was diminished. Renate Dorpalen wrote, 'Many of the children were highly gifted and came from educated professional families. Those of lesser endowment, or lack of competencies, or coming from more modest family backgrounds adapted less successfully to the new environment. Though the children were tolerated, they were rarely rewarded with deep human relationships or recognition. They suffered silently and their symptomatic behaviour often worsened their vulnerable position. Perhaps there was a certain harshness towards psychological difficulties on behalf of the school. Could it be that no-one was able to face and deal with the enormous emotional reactions produced by the reasons for the school's existence? Expectations were for excellence, acceleration and proficiency at all cost. The adults, as substitutes for the lost parental figures, were hard pressed to meet all the children's needs in addition to coping with their own problems.'[82]

The school carried on. In the annual report of February 1941, the school's population was listed as holding 'fairly even' with eighty-seven permanent residents, two day pupils, two visiting teachers. Of the seventy-four pupils, including the Domestic Science group and a few helpers, there were six farm pupils and two London evacuees. Six of the children were attending elementary schools in Haslemere.[83] In September the school relinquished its lease on Thursley Copse and the Austrians moved back into the main house. Martin was glad to be able to live with his friends in the Hut. Some of the older girls moved into a few rooms at another nearby house, Rowallen. A new German teacher arrived in 1941, a PhD in Mathematics, former *Direktorin* [principal] of a large, girls' secondary school or Lyceum, *Oberstudienrätin* Bluhm, who became the mathematics and science mistress. Dieter recalls, 'Dr Bluhm had been a professor of some sort in Germany. I would guess she was in her late forties–early fifties when she came. She did speak English quite well, with less of an accent than some of the other leaders. She made the subject interesting and challenging, making you think and being supportive rather than intimidating.' Science was problematic for the school, since it required expensive facilities. Dr Lion notes, 'The need of a small laboratory is felt ever more, and we are trying to collect some funds for it.'[84] Dr Bluhm converted Dieter's fear of all things mathematical to 'fascination'. That year Dr Lion also engaged a retired professor in Haslemere to give a few weeks of practical instruction in chemistry and physics. A small group of older boys, including Dieter and the Pachmayr twins, walked into town a couple of times a week to experiment with litmus paper. They mixed chemicals to produce intense heat and performed other wonderful experiments. When Dieter went on to college in the United States, he found that his academic preparation at Stoatley Rough had been more than adequate with just one exception: true biology.

General Rommel began to consolidate his *Afrika Korps*, while back in Haslemere, the children continued to track the war on the map. There was always anxiety. Wolf Edelstein worried about his parents. 'The *Luftwaffe* robbed us of sleep during that winter of 1940–1941, the RAF was keeping my parents awake in Berlin. Like so many at Stoatley Rough, I watched daily for the little red Royal Mail van with the G VI R cipher.'[85] Early in the war, a few letters originating in Germany or Austria penetrated censorship, those forwarded by friends in Sweden and Holland. After Norway and Holland fell, children (rarely) received the twenty-five-word Red Cross messages from their parents, many coming in weeks old. Months of silence was the norm. One day in March 1941, a telegram from Spain arrived unexpectedly for Wolf. Miraculously, his parents were on their way to America through occupied France, unoccupied Spain and Portugal. Wolf knew that he was among the lucky ones. Worse news awaited some of the children. According to Nore Astfalck, 'there was one famous saying in these Red Cross letters, "*Morgen muessen wir verreisen*" [Tomorrow we have to take a trip] … and everybody knew what it meant'.[86]

Because of the volume and frequency of correspondence to and from Stoatley Rough, the school became a 'Bureau' of the Red Cross Message Scheme in February 1941.[87] Messages went from the school to Red Cross headquarters in Geneva for distribution. Dr Lion's responsibilities now included passing along Red Cross updates to letter writers in the community at large, the steady stream of official notices that were continuously citing new rules as the war raged through Europe and elsewhere. One early Red Cross dispatch forbade anyone to write information about a member of the armed services, for example, rank, number, address and regiment. Another came along to amend the preceding rule: 'Senders of messages may state the *county* in which they

or any friend or relative are living but not special part of the county
(e.g., North or South).' Lists of allowed languages were distributed and
updated. As of October the Red Cross started to accept letters written
in Finnish.

To conserve paper, the pupils wrote on scraps of very thin paper, some
coloured pale blue or yellow. Even Dr Lion used thirds or half pieces of
paper, neatly trimmed, for her correspondence. The children's messages
were copied onto the official forms and sent through a clearinghouse
to be reviewed by the British censors before being sent across the Channel
for delivery. The Red Cross asked for brevity on 30 July 1941. 'You may
write up to twenty-five words on purely personal and family matters
on the back of the enclosed Red Cross message form.' The school kept
a file of a subgroup of missives entitled 'ENQUIRY FOR MISSING
RELATIVES', something probably unofficial, for Dr Lion's eyes only.

The tone of the Red Cross notices was businesslike, disconcertingly
neutral. One dated 19 November 1942 (after the Allied landings in
French North Africa and when the Germans occupied all of France that
had previously been unoccupied), stated: 'all postal communications
with Vichy France have now ceased, and we can therefore extend the
Red Cross Message Scheme to what was "Unoccupied France". You
can now dispatch messages to the whole of France, including Corsica
and Monaco.' Another, dated 24 April 1945, said, 'In view of persistent
rumours that the internees have been moved elsewhere and of the
uncertainty of communication, we very much regret that we consider
it is now useless to accept any further messages for the Theresienstadt
camp. Moreover, we are unable at the present time to institute enquiries
for persons known or believed to be in Theresienstadt.'[88]

The school collected small sums of money to help the war effort,
including the Red Cross Penny-a-Week Fund, to which it sent in January
1942 £19.0s 31/2d. Later that year the school sent roughly £3 to the
Red Cross and St. John Fund, for which it received this response:
'On behalf of the Duke of Gloucester, I acknowledge with grateful
thanks your contribution to the above fund.'[89] Once, the school
received a gracious letter from HRM the Queen.

Dr Lion asked the Red Cross if the children might fill out the forms
in their own handwriting. She knew what it would mean to the parents
and family. The request was denied. Dr Lion saved these small scraps
of paper, dozens of bits of yellow, white and pale blue paper covered
in a scrawling child's script, most in German. Sometimes the address

is longer than the message itself. Some messages reflect yearning or fear, but most are childlike, simple, blithe recitations of activities, a poignant display of innocence.

> *Liebe Muttile, Brief erhalten. Nett beschenkt würden. Alle gesund.*
> *Roma grüsst. Wohne nähe ihr. Geburtstagsglückwunsche. Grüsst*
> *alle, Küsse. Hannele.* [Dear Mommy, Letter received. Everybody's
> fine. Roma sends greetings. I live near her. Happy birthday.
> Greetings to all, kisses, little Hanna.]

> *Lange nichts gehört. Hoffe alle gesund. Ruth macht Examen fur*
> *Krankenschwester im Mai. Schreibt bald. Küsse.* [Long time that
> I haven't heard from you. I hope everyone is well. Ruth will take
> the exam for nursing in May. Write soon. Kisses.]

> *Liebe Eltern, Ich gehe Anfang Sept. auf eine Fröbeltagung, habe 14*
> *Tage Ferien hoffe Korri Lisa zu sehen. Heute freier Sontag, darum*
> *besonders herzlichen grüss.* [Dear Parents, I am going away for
> a Froebel Conference at the beginning of September. I have fourteen
> free days I hope to see Korri Lisa. Today is a free Sunday, with
> especially warm regards.]

The last of these messages is from one of the Household Girls, who would learn about the deaths of her parents from a couple of strangers. After being imprisoned in Theresienstadt, a severely malnourished man and his wife had managed to get to England through Switzerland after the war. They travelled by train to Haslemere to tell the girl about their friendship with her parents and the circumstances of their deaths. As free Europe slowly shut down, the news worsened. One day the Red Cross wrote: 'We have decided that the time has now come to stop Red Cross messages to those parts of enemy and enemy-occupied Europe that still remain under German control. This is in view of the rapidly changing war situation and the extreme difficulty of the I.R.C.C. at Geneva maintaining communication with these territories.'[90]

The sporadic nature of communications was unsettling for the children whose parents were still on the Continent. Inge Hershkowitz, whose father had been forced to continue to manage his factory in Germany for the war effort, recalled, 'for two weeks I had not heard from home. My mother always wrote twice or three times a week. Not to have a letter made me feel out of touch with my family. I was very upset. When another week went by without a word from home I became frantic. What could have happened? … For no one to get in touch with me must mean something happened to all three of them. I feared the worst.' She comforted herself by imagining walking through the rooms of her former home in Cologne. 'In the music room I touched our Bechstein piano. I looked out of the bay windows at the tree-lined street below … in the living room I lingered over our mahogany book cases, opened one of the glass doors and soothed myself by reciting Goethe's poem: *Dem Schnee, Dem Regen, / Dem Wind entgegen* [The snow, the rain / Against the wind].'[91]

The bombing of London continued through May 1941 at which time Germany abruptly turned its attention to the East, to the Soviet Union. While the intense attacks on London ceased, the war was by no means over. Occasional night raids, little Blitzes, were to continue through 1944. The fear of an internal Fifth Column among the British citizens caused no end to Dr Lion's worry that her little German-speaking community could stoke the embers of anti-German sentiment that understandably smouldered in Haslemere. This concern grew as the war dragged on. As early as 1936 nightwalks had been forbidden for the children, and not just for their safety or out of fears of sexual activity. Dr Lion was trying to protect her community. One day someone finally came under suspicion of the Haslemere constabulary. It was not a pupil, but the second in command herself. Wolf recalls, 'Emmy Wolff (who, you remember, had a deep voice and a heavy German accent) went to visit her mother in Hindhead, bundled up against the cold in a heavy coat, hat and muffler. At a bus stop apparently she spoke to someone and immediately was suspected of being an infiltrator. She was surrounded by a muttering crowd when the policeman came by to tell the crowd, "It's OK, they've caught him." A German bomber had been shot down the previous night, the crew had bailed out and one of them had not yet been accounted for.' On another occasion, again it was a staff member who was caught outdoors at night. Joan Humby was questioned after being discovered wandering around Hindhead Common clad in her black velvet dressing gown.

Summer arrived easing some of the hardships. (The alumni of the school refuse to admit they suffered, determined to draw a distinction between their plight and that of concentration camp victims.) The pupils exhibited their home-made arts and crafts in a nice show – cotton shirts, picture frames, table mats – a myriad of useful things, all made by the pupils. Ilse Kaiser, something of a beauty and the object of several boys' fantasies, presented a shirt to Dieter Gaupp, who, a couple of years earlier, had struggled to close the top button on a shirt that he had received from America. Younger than Ilse by two years, Dieter was stunned by the unexpected gift.

Since no one could emigrate from England to join his or her family on another continent or go home to German-dominated Europe, Stoatley Rough became everyone's year-round home in the summer of 1941. Dr Lion realised that she could no longer farm out an entire school full of children. A new challenge arose. How were the children to spend their summer days? Not wanting to leave the children idle, Dr Lion came up with an idea (short-lived). The children would take up hobbies. Gina Schaefer [MacKenzie], in *The Bridge*, wrote, 'Miss Astfalck passed around a big sheet of paper which went around each classroom and everyone put down a choice of hobby, be it pottery, kitchen, farming or weaving.' The thirteen-year-old girl then added wistfully, 'I think it is a pity swimming is not a hobby, but perhaps it is a good thing, or our swimming-pool would be overcrowded.'[92] Another (unidentified) child wrote that 'bookbinding is also a nice hobby and there is about half of our library to be repaired.' The scheme died out pretty quickly – perhaps none of the adults had the interest or energy to keep it going – but some children took up pottery and worked in the shop over the summer. Good news sometimes arrived from abroad: the Free French and British took Syria on 14 July. But the evil of Hitler's regime was in its fullest bloom: as the children in Haslemere laboured over their woodworking and sewing projects, Hermann Goering was instructing Reinhard Heydrich to prepare for the Final Solution (31 July). On 1 September, the Nazis ordered Jews to wear yellow stars on all outer clothing.

Dr Lion sought to raise flagging spirits during the dark days of 1941, quick to report on the successes of her pupils, to praise those who received school certificates or who passed the Board of Agriculture's poultry-keeping examination. She reported the news that 'best of all, one farm-pupil has passed the Royal Horticultural Society's Examination as the seventh out of 130 candidates.'[93] She maintained cheer and praise for her community. In her *Rundbrief* [Letter for general distribution] of late 1941 she expressed her gratitude for 'the life we are allowed to live here ... for the vegetable garden and farm, the use of the piano (fought over for practicing time) and the handwork departments which are continuing to supply us with furniture either new or repaired'. She ends on an upbeat note. 'A home-made armchair with weaving out of old stockings has been given me at Christmas, though I am afraid it has disappeared now since some farm-boys sat on the arms instead of in the chair!'

Thus was life at its lowest point at Stoatley Rough during the war years. While children dealt with their fears of attack from invaders from Germany as best as they could, interestingly for some there was no fear at all. The fear of attack in Britain paled in comparison to what they had experienced while in Germany at the hands of their hate-filled schoolmates and teachers. Wolf remembered, 'I was never in fear of attack. None of this compared with what we had experienced in Germany.' He concludes, revealing the true extent of the children's ordeal at the hands of their countrymen, saying, 'In Britain, we were in the same boat as everybody else.'

Hard landings

Not every child came directly to Stoatley Rough from the Continent. Some first bounced around between sponsoring families, government institutions and other schools. Gerda Stein [Meyer], for example, was eleven when she left her family in Czechoslovakia. For five years she lived in an English preparatory school, then a Council school, then a traditional English boarding school. Gerda was one of the 669 Czech children saved by Nicholas Winton, the young stockbroker who had been summoned to Prague by his friend Martin Blake ('don't bother bringing your skis') to help save Czech Jewish children not eligible for *Kindertransport*. Other children of Stoatley Rough known to have been saved by Winton were Laura Selo, born in Berlin, but living in 1939 in Prague, and Rosemary Gumpel.[94]

Ten-year-old Hans [Goldy] Goldmeier was not a Winton child, yet he, too, came to Stoatley Rough via a circuitous route, faring badly during his first months in England. His story provides a window into the trauma experienced by many refugee children who were denied safe landings, whose residence with English families was marked by disappointment, exploitation and sometimes abuse. (Even children at Stoatley Rough were not entirely safe from exploitation in homes opened to them for holiday breaks. Barbara Gerstenberg [Prasse] was farmed out to a British family for Christmas 1936, into a family that made her work for her keep. 'It was not a happy experience.... I had to get up early, start the fires in the kitchen and living room, start the breakfast and was kept busy working most of the time. My bedroom was cold, and I got a terrible cough.' Hans Loeser came to her rescue after an impromptu visit. He located an elderly couple on the southern coast of England who would take her. Barbara lived with them in a residential hotel for the duration of the holiday.)

Goldy was the last of the Hut Boys to arrive at the school. His story was one of trauma followed by rescue followed by trauma followed by sanctuary. Goldy, a tall boy with a slender build, prominent nose, soft brown eyes and thick wavy hair, was considered cautious, studious and passive. He was also kind to the bone, a gifted raconteur and enormously popular for his clever, understated wit, and ability to deliver a funny story. He was the one who paid for the *Sunday Express* on the boys' weekly forays to the Hindhead Corner shop. Goldy might have been a comedian with his witty views and killer delivery had he not been raised so strictly, to mind his manners, to behave, to avoid risk. His mother admonished him that 'Please', 'Thank you' and 'Excuse me' were the most important English phrases he needed to survive in England. He and his older brother, Ralph, arrived, extraordinarily, by airplane from the Frankfurt airport late in 1938. Upon learning how difficult it was to book passage by sea, his grandmother sensibly bought two tickets on fledgling Sabena Belgian airlines for her two grandsons. Off they went, flying low in the two-prop plane, 'making the countryside and ships in the channel visible like a toyland'.[95] Goldy recalled the cunning with which his mother prepared for his trip. 'Jews were forbidden to take more than the equivalent of about $5.00 out of the country and that was all the money in our pockets when we left. However, the Germans probably overlooked that one could ... take a bicycle and an unlimited supply of clothing as long as it was not "new". Because we all realised that buying clothes in England as we grew out of what we had would not be possible, mother took us on shopping sprees for every item of clothing imaginable. Both Ralph and I had two sizes in our luggage, and the clothing was carefully marked with labels that said HG1 and HG2 for Hans, and RG1 and RG2 for Ralph.... Mother planned this so carefully that I needed no new clothing the whole six years in England. To hide the fact that we did buy new clothes, tags were taken off, creases made, and my job was to rub dirt from the garden on the shoes.'[96] (The senior Goldmeiers also emigrated to England. Goldy's mother joined the ranks of those immigrants who, having dismissed their own maids, became maids in England. Goldy's father failed miserably at his own job as valet and died from a heart broken before the war ended, a heart attack brought on by the stress in which he lived.)

The boys landed at the Croydon airport, London's major civilian airport, took the train into London, then changed trains for the small town of Sunderland in County Durham. Friends of their cousin had guaranteed their visas. The new hosts were Rosie Wolfson, a Jewish schoolteacher and her husband George. Goldy had been stimulated by the flight and train ride, but when he arrived at the Wolfson's, the 'full impact of our separation from our parents and the uncertainty of what was to happen next … hit me like a proverbial ton of bricks'.[97] The row house was filled with many relatives. 'Not long after we took our coats off and were introduced, Ralph and I were told that we would be separated, that I would be staying with George's parents, the older Wolfsons.' Goldy continues: 'I felt a sense of betrayal. We had been told in Germany … that we would stay together. However, remembering Mother's admonitions that I should always be appreciative for what people were doing for me, I said nothing. Still, I could not stop the tears that started coming down and so as not to embarrass myself I excused myself to go to the bathroom. There I really burst out crying. After a while people knocked on the door and asked what was the matter. I was quiet, hoping my tears would just dry. They did not, and when I emerged, I think I did admit that I was unhappy about the unexpected separation from Ralph…. After a few minutes of conversation – it seemed the whole idea must have been concocted on the spur of the moment – the subject of our going to different homes was dropped and my sadness lifted.'[98] After five months, the Wolfson family was notified by the British government that they would need to evacuate the 'danger area'. They had falsified their address by making it seem that they were inside one of the targeted areas unsafe for children, seizing the opportunity to get rid of Goldy and Ralph. 'We obviously were not part of their evacuation plans. That said, I must hasten to add that the Wolfsons did not desert us and, in fact, kept in touch with us. I also cannot blame them for perhaps being intimidated by the likelihood that, what at first may have looked like a temporary stay while we were waiting to go to America, could turn into something much longer.'[99]

Refugee officers placed the Goldmeier brothers on a farm in Bellerby near Leyborn, in North Yorkshire with a kind family named Scott, where they would remain for the next two years. Goldy and Ralph attended the government school and participated in healthy, summer farm work. They would always be grateful to the Scotts, and they did not forget the Wolfsons. 'When we were evacuated to Yorkshire, they [the Wolfsons] regularly sent us pocket-money, enough to go to a movie now and then and buy our two ounces of candy rations allotted to each child every week.'[100] That the Wolfsons belatedly realised that they were not equipped to keep two German boys is instructive. Well-intentioned English families did not always know what they were getting into when they offered to take refugee children. There were plenty of stories of a darker nature during these times of escape 'into the arms of strangers', of people who used refugee children as unpaid labour and worse. The Wolfsons illustrate that the families who took in children did make a tremendous sacrifice of time and money that could last for years.

Goldy had started school, the *Farntrappschule*, in Frankfurt the city in which he lived until he was ten. 'I remember arriving at the school on my first day with a "*Zuckertuete*" as was the custom, a paper bag of elliptical shape which was filled with candy that we all shared. I was about five years old at the time, but I was immediately aware of changes, such as being required to remove the old red-white-and-black flag of the old Germany which had decorated our balcony on national holidays. Our parents were not about to display a flag with the swastika that everyone else, except the Jews, began to hang out. One day a Jewish boy told me that Jews were no longer German citizens. I asked him what that meant, but he couldn't tell me.'[101] (Regarding the flag of the old Weimar Republic, it was symbolic of the loyalty to that period. Wolf himself never saw the official flag as well. His family, too, preferred to display only the one of the empire.)

For Goldy, travel to school became dangerous. 'There might be an innocent question by some Nazi who would stop us, like did we get enough to eat. If you did not answer this question correctly ... someone [might come] to the house to arrest a parent for black marketing or other trumped-up charges. We were taught what to say: never volunteer anything and always be non-committal. Bands of Hitler Youth boys could also beat one up if provoked or for no reason at all. There was no winning these fights because if one defended oneself, the boy could complain to his father who might make things disagreeable.'[102] Goldy became wily, spotting the hooligans before they spotted him and ignoring their shouts of abuse. 'Our parents said name calling didn't really hurt us, and they felt they could nullify ignorant or abusive statements, but irrevocable injuries were hard to reverse. They always said it was the mean boys who had the problem, not us.'[103]

Goldy was happy to sing '*Deutschland über Alles*' in the mornings at school. In 1935 the official Nazi Horst Wessel song was added, and as in Wolf's school, the children had to hold up their arms in the Nazi salute, 'not easy when one is only seven. When I finished first grade, my grades were nearly all "C's." I received "B's" for religious studies which were offered during regular class hours by Jewish religious teachers who already taught us Hebrew at that early age. Christian children received Christian instruction as there was no separation of church and state. All Jewish children received "C's" because the teachers were ordered to give "C's" in reading, writing and arithmetic.'[104] Goldy's parents raised no objections as long as their children were learning.

Then the teachers decided to segregate the Jewish children, prompting Goldy's parents to send him to a new Jews-only school, the *Philantropin*, located on the other side of town. During his last year, when he was nine, a group of boys ambushed him while he was riding his grand *Adler* [Eagle] bike home from school, a normal ride of thirty-five minutes. 'I had no escape route, I was stopped and my bicycle was vandalised. The boys threw the valves of the tires into the bushes and they wanted me to go find them. I knew instinctively that it would be asking for trouble if I did this as I could be more easily attacked there. The boys, however, had so much fun doing it that they let me go, throwing curses at me and then stones.... I wheeled my bicycle away as fast as I could. The principle of "Don't provoke" had worked again. I found my Uncle Jakob's house where I was soothed and collected by my mother.'[105] Arbitrary indignities abounded. Goldy recalled seeing a crowd gathered in the *Opernplatz*, the central square of Frankfurt. 'Always curious, I investigated and found ordinary people laughing hilariously. Then I heard abusive names hurled at a number of Jewish men who must have been stopped on the street a little earlier and then given toothbrushes with which to clean the sidewalk. When I saw what was happening, I crept away as unobtrusively as possible lest someone would pick on me.'[106] The hardships of 1941 did not curtail the opportunity for religious instruction for children at Stoatley Rough. Christian children were allowed to attend services in Haslemere and to prepare for confirmation, and even some of those with no religious background received instruction. Peter Gaupp relates that in 1940, his parents wrote from Switzerland via Portugal to their guardian, George Gooch, that it was time for the boys to join some sort of church. Since Mrs Gooch was a strong German Lutheran by background, Dr Lion chose the Haslemere Congregational church for them. The boys 'had to attend private tutoring classes with the very nice scholarly Reverend Isitt, a displaced New Zealander'. Wolf recalled Pastor Isitt as a man with a sense of humour and a 'true Non-Conformist, in the tradition of the Pilgrims who crossed the ocean rather than submit to a state-sponsored church ... I was impressed by his attitude toward the war: A great evil to prevent even greater evils, but an evil nonetheless. When the Church of England asked people to pray for victory, he suggested that people should instead pray for God's forgiveness, for allowing such terrible evils to exist. Those weren't the exact words of his sermon, but it was the point he was trying to make.'

Although the school was formally secular, Dr Lion never abandoned her Jewish roots nor did she ignore those of her pupils. Periodically she arranged for each crop of boys to be prepared for *bar mitzvah*. When Martin, Goldy and Obo turned thirteen in 1941, they were scheduled for lessons with Dr Stein, who came twice a month by train from Oxford to teach the basic ritual prayers a year prior to the actual event. Dr Stein was a German Jewish refugee who earned a PhD from University College, London, in 1963. Besides preparing boys for their *bar mitzvahs*, the rabbi taught religion to fifth formers. Gerda Meyer [Stein] – no relation to the rabbi – remembered him for teaching 'at a far higher standard than required by the modest demands of the School Certificate'.[107] Dr Stein only ate Kosher meals, requiring Wolf or another to fetch eggs from the farm. Goldy, the future rabbi, received special, more arduous private lessons.

It was perhaps logical for Dr Lion to point Goldy to the rabbinate, but not entirely justified. Goldy had come from a traditional and religious family, and he tried to follow the rules. After the death of his father in England, Goldy believed that he should join a group of ten men and say *Kaddish* every day for eleven months, although it is not clear whether his mother instructed him to do so or Goldy was trying to follow the Hebraic laws on his own. Saying *Kaddish* every day for eleven months was impossible. 'For a while that was OK, but then, in the normal course of "grief work" I forgot more and more often. This started me thinking about ritual and what else there was to religion.'[108] Goldy made sacrifices for his beliefs, on one occasion refusing the rare opportunity to attend a show at the Rex Theatre of recently released *Pygmalion*, starring Leslie Howard and Wendy Hiller. Such entertainment was not allowed in the year of mourning. Goldy became proficient in Hebrew. One day Dr Leven handed him a transliterated Hebrew text to sing for a recital for which the chorus was practicing. He handed it back to her, to her great surprise, saying that he could pronounce the Hebrew text without props.

Goldy mused on his Jewish identity many years later. 'When I went out with a non-Jewish girl [after the war in New York] she was generally ready to convert to Judaism even though I was not necessarily close to proposing marriage. However, it must have been clear that I was giving out signals that religion was important to me even though I was not a very observant Jew. At the point where the girl was willing to convert I would often flee.' He entered psychoanalysis, searching for reasons for why he was not finding a suitable mate. He wrote, although 'it might have seemed logical that my experiences as a child, growing up in Germany and England at a difficult time, would leave some effect on my sense of identity as a Jew', they never did. 'I was more interested in the present.'[109]

Nineteen forty-one came to a close, bringing the moment of Martin's and Obo's *bar mitzvah*. Goldy had his own *bar mitzvah* at another time and place, with his mother and his older brother in attendance. For Martin and Obo, there would be no family. The date was set for Saturday morning 13 December 1941 at St John's Wood Synagogue on Abbey Road in Hampstead in north-western London. Although the boys recognised the solemnity of the occasion, Obo reminds us they were also, first and foremost, males in their adolescent years. 'After the ceremony Dr Lion, who accompanied us by train to London, took us to a beautiful private home of a Jewish family I think nearby, where we had a luncheon with some St. R. people and others and I especially remember Marianne Glücksman [a Household Girl] whom I especially asked to be there, because she always took very good care of me at school and, besides, I had a mad crush on her.'[110]

When they were sick

When he arrived at the school, Goldy was immediately accepted by Wolf, Martin, Obo and Peter, along with other boys. He quickly became one of the gang. But conditions at the school were deteriorating in the winter of 1941. A rash of infectious diseases tore through Stoatley Rough. The school existed in a kind of frozen cocoon, remote from daily English life, and even the milder weather below. Snow and ice might blanket the grounds at Stoatley Rough, while below in Haslemere, it had turned to slush.

The United States declared war on Germany on 11 December, news that the school received with joy. Yet fever, coughing and vomiting reduced the joy. The crowding, cold and wartime diet were taking their toll. One girl inexplicably put herself on a strict vegetable diet and became so weakened that she had to be institutionalised. The children did not have the luxury of galoshes or boots and after a walk outside in the snow or rain, their shoes became soaked. Even socks failed to dry overnight in the chilly dormitories. The furnace often went on strike in the Hut, and heating in the main house was so minimal that many children began to suffer the ugly purple and green sores of chilblains, ulcerations of the fingers and toes that produced painful itching. (It was not the only time the children were cold. The winter of 1939 had been the coldest in Europe in forty-six years, freezing the water pipes.) Children coped as best as they could. Renate Dorpalen sometimes wrote her letters to her family huddling under a pile of blankets. One night, the water in her rubber water bottle turned to ice overnight. Renate's father forwarded to her brothers a dire account of a day in the life of a Household Girl based on Renate's news from Haslemere. 'Her day from early morning until nightfall is filled with work. Then back … to her unheated little room, half the size of Martha's [their housekeeper]. The kerosene stove, adored by Renate and her roommate, is used to heat water for the hot-water bottles. Attired in thick pyjamas, a bed jacket, a bathrobe, stockings and gloves, she sits in bed to maintain her correspondence.'[111] In 1941, at least two-thirds of the pupils and several teachers contracted a nasty intestinal flu. Wolf Edelstein [Elston] recalled, 'To this day I don't know which was worse: being sick or working as a member of the mop-and-bucket brigade. The epidemic soon passed. The relentless *Wehrmacht* [German Army] finally ground to a halt in Russian snow and African sand. Better yet, America entered the war. Our health improved as the sun returned and as rare lend–lease delicacies like Spam occasionally appeared on the menu.'

Wolf described the school's nostrums. 'The stock preventative against all ills was a daily dose of cod liver oil in malt (Ugh!!) and the stock remedy for feeling unwell was to put us to bed for twenty-four hours, with only dry toast and chamomile tea at mealtimes. Very effective for curing tummy-aches, diarrhoea or straightforward malingering. (To this day, Martin will not go within sniffing distance of chamomile tea.) The children suffered from boils as well. Wolf had some on the back of his neck, Martin also had one on his arm 'which one of the matrons squeezed, popping the pus sky high.'[112]

The children received regular dental care at Stoatley Rough from a visiting dentist. Martin said, 'The dentist was always pulling my teeth. I have my wisdom teeth but a couple of molars are gone. He used laughing gas. One time I woke up and I was crying.' The drill was something short of a medieval torture instrument. 'This was in the days before sophisticated electric equipment and unfortunately I had one or two cavities at the time. A treadle drove the drill. As [the dentist] stepped on the pedal and activated the belt which drove the drill, he also had to bend over me and apply the drill where needed.... The speed of the drill surged and waned with each stroke of the pedal, as did the accompanying hum of the drill which at times became quite hot, and then got ... cooling from a squirt of water.'[113] Household Girl Ilse Kaiser wrote for *The Bridge* her experiences with corralling the children for the dentist's visits. Note her barely concealed *Schadenfreude*:

It is sad to look at the children's faces when the drilling machine has to be fetched across! Now all is ready and we are only waiting for the dentist to arrive. We hear the noise of his car. He is here! With all his drills and tools he goes over and now he can start. The worst part is the waiting outside and hearing the groans from within. Poor dentist! We aren't easy patients. Glad, because a small boy's tooth has been pulled out without any tears, he throws it into the pail. But now the boy starts to cry terribly. The dentist looks at him in surprise. 'What is the matter? It can't hurt now'. 'No', says the little boy, 'It doesn't hurt, but my mother wants to keep my tooth and you threw it away.' So our dentist has to recover the tooth and with contented smile the boy puts it into his pocket and goes off. 'Next one, please!' This patient sits down and looks only at the drilling machine. There is still the hope that nothing need be done. But alas! He has a big hole. Then: 'Can't you fill the hole without any drilling?' Poor dentist. But the next one is a little girl. He looks at her mouth. He thinks, he will be very kind to her and tells her that nothing need be done. But that is the wrong thing too. The drill machine is just the thing she likes. Poor, poor dentist. He will never get it right. And this is what always happens when the dentist comes.[114]

The administrators minimised pain and distress as much as they could, but their limited funds made them err on the conservative side when it came to actually taking a child to the doctor. Gut-wrenching stories of suffering are all the more poignant in the light of the child's forgiving nature. 'Once I had a terrible toothache and even a fever. So Dr Lion and Dr Leven plus the matron at that time were worried. They took me for a walk on the Hindhead Common hoping to alleviate the awful pain. I was also given aspirins.... And so we walked up and down 'til finally the pain got better. The next day I was sent to an ear, nose and throat specialist and it transpired that I had an abscess on the eyetooth and my eustacean tubes were closed. The treatment I got was most unpleasant. I fainted in the doctor's office but he also cleared my sinuses and voilà, I was better.' She adds with perhaps intended irony, 'Both Leven and Lion were delighted and said the walk helped and cured me!'[115] At least one pupil is not so forgiving of the school's leaders. Post-war pupil Jan Schneider wrote that the 'doctor-ladies' [referring to Drs Lion and Leven] raced past in their car the time he was walking his sick sister up Farnham Lane on a return trip from the doctor's office in Haslemere, at least a 2-mile (3.22 kilometre) walk. 'The Austin climbed the hill, drew alongside, and passed us without a glance from the doctors. Clearly there was no room in the car for a small sick child.'[116] He reports not without irony that later that season he had been walking along the same road, this time hand in hand with a blonde pig-tailed girl from his class. Again Dr Lion happened by in the Austin. This time she stopped the car and rescued the girl, insisting on driving the maiden back to the school without further discussion.

While the years brought chicken pox, impetigo and the need for delousing at regular intervals, Eddie Behrendt recalled that certain diseases landed children into quarantine. 'As for the mumps, it was the usual story of multi cases of an illness where kids gather closely together. There were one or two new cases almost daily. Those with mumps were isolated from anyone else. We didn't have much supervision, so that could have been fun. However they put real greasy stuff on your neck which stunk and felt awful and then covered that with a couple of layers of woollen scarves or similar materials. Ugh! No one was anxious to "pretend" to have the mumps.'[117] Susi Weissrock was only five years old when she joined the ranks of the ill and recalled wearing a wool scarf that held a hot poultrice and tied on top of her head, making her look like a 'comic book character'. She also discovered that 'blue paint was nice and sweet' and ate her way through a whole paintbox.[118]

In mid-July 1941, there was an outbreak of whooping cough. This time the children were put into a section of the ground floor of the manse. Liselotte Kauffman wrote, 'We live in a sort of protected area. That means a place where there is one string behind which we stand, and then there comes another string, where all the others stand. In the middle of these two strings, there is nothing. Our life is not so bad, first of all, we have a very nice room which is called the "Tin". It is very airy. Of course we have no proper drawers, so all our things have to be put where there is enough room, the books on any chest-of-drawers, our dishes on the window, covered with a clean dish-cloth, our bathing-tub behind the bed, also covered. We have everything we want, even too much. We have four injections, one every second day, and we hope that it helps a lot.'[119] During the darkest days of the war, many children were discovered to have head lice. Eddie Behrendt wrote, 'As for the lice, well, that affected only the girls. The longer the hair, the more lice. All the hair on a girl's head would be cut short and greasy stuff was put all over her head. The difference was that with mumps we were more or less together and yet isolated. With the lice, once the hair was cut short and greased, the girls had to run all over school that way and continue to try to live more or less normal lives.'[120]

Even when the children were healthy, clashes occurred within the boarding environment, where living in close quarters sometimes provoked quarrelling. There were differences of opinion among the staff too, petty grievances about privilege and belonging. And as we have seen, sometimes the boys on the farm had fist fights. Miss Dove, who left in 1939, reported on 'many weaknesses at Stoatley Rough'. Although she praised the school as a safe place and admired 'a belief in the importance of art, of thorough scholarship and solid hard work', she was critical of the 'lack of balance' at the school, referring to the children from London's East End, who found temporary refuge at the school, whereby the school mixed 'highly-intelligent German-Jewish children with a handful of British ones of a completely different level'. She discerned 'a certain hardness towards emotional and psychological difficulties', on the part of Dr Lion and criticised the policy of selective opportunities to take the Matric, 'the unnecessary pride which allowed no one to sit an external examination without a ninety-nine percent chance of passing'. Also she noted the physical hardship in having 'growing teenagers trying to study late at night without so much as a warm drink to help them along'.[121]

Christmas of 1941 inspired the children to patriotic acts. Dr Lion recorded that, instead of making presents for each other, 'the children and grown-ups prepared parcels with garments (sewn and knitted) and toys (for the larger part home-made) for bombed-out people and evacuees'. Dr Lion then told a story of sweet unselfishness. 'The nicest gift came together with the following letter. 'Dear Dr Lion, Here is a contribution of 3s6d for the Red X Fund. It has been collected from members of an organisation called the "Secret Help." This particular organisation was founded in order to aid people who are in need of help. We kindly request you not to investigate or try not to find out who we are, because we want to keep matters secret. Yours faithfully, "Secret Help".'[122]

Remainders pie

Preparing appetising meals at Stoatley Rough was a challenge for Miss Demuth, but to her credit, the Hut Boys claim that they never went hungry. She received help from some of the older girls, who, either indulging a nurturing instinct or simply watching their weight, often scraped their shares onto the boys' plates. After dinner, leftovers never went to waste. During the earlier years, the Household Girls used to hand out 'bread and dripping' after meals to their friends, who, in turn, fed scraps to small children waiting just outside the kitchen door. Sometimes the whole school population went on excursions to pick wild blueberries, blackberries or other wild fruit, the bounty of which would become the object of steamy canning sessions for the Household Girls. Sometimes the children ate what they found outdoors. Susi Weissrock [Rice] reported eating 'sour yellow blossoms and sweet red berries of forbidden yew trees; bilberries, black berries, beechnuts and sour clay [*sic*] meaning *Sauer Klee*, an edible wild plant that looks like clover – every walk was primarily a search for edible experiences.'

While the farm supplied milk, eggs and some meat and poultry, most of the food consumed at Stoatley Rough was delivered to the kitchen

by truck (lorry). One day Inge Hamburger [Pavlowsky] overheard
Miss Demuth ordering in her accented English 'tepid water', which the
person on the other end of the line kept asking her to repeat. 'God knows
what she did mean, but at least it's an indication that food was ordered
by phone.' Some foods became so scarce to become treasured, horded,
relished. Rarely a treat might arrive from relatives in the United States.
The treats took months to cross the ocean and there would never be
fresh fruit, but this fact did not stop children from dreaming. Once
Wolf overheard Dr Bluhm conversing loudly at a nearby table about
pineapple, in German, and stating with authority that one 'must peel
the tough skin'. Since any pineapple served at Stoatley Rough came
from a can, the image of a fresh pineapple was one of overwhelming
richness to the growing boy. Wolf recalled, 'the chances of encountering
a pineapple in wartime Britain were about as likely as meeting
a visitation of angels.'

Eggs were doled out at one egg once or twice a year per child during
the war. Months after the war ended, Wolf, now living in America, had
not yet become accustomed to the bounty of his new country, post-war.
One day some friends took him and his brother Gerd on a picnic by the
banks of the Hudson River. When they unpacked the food, one of the
hard-boiled eggs in the basket was discovered to have a crack in it. Their
friend held the egg for a moment, frowned, then hurled the offending egg
into the river. Speak of culture shock! Wolf and Gerd stared at each other,
speechless. 'If the man had flung a diamond ring into the river, we
wouldn't have been more surprised.'

Eggs were served at the annual Easter breakfast. Although there was
no acknowledgement of Easter's link to Christianity, the staff made
a great effort to make a special Easter breakfast every year, reading the
Oster Spaziergang [Easter Walk] from Goethe's *Faust* that celebrated the
resurrection of the Lord, a truly ecumenical gesture as well as a reminder
of the richness of the German culture. Goldy recalled, 'There had to be
one continuous table and we were all to sit at it. I am sure that the littlest
ones did not participate at this time but otherwise all of us were there.
It was incredible how crowded we sat together, our elbows in our laps
and our hands barely able to reach our plates. Why this practice I don't
know.'[123] The tables were always cheerfully decorated with 'egg trees'
(sets of parallel/horizontal rods on a pedestal) from which were hanging
hand-painted Easter eggs, usually empty shells blown out by the kitchen
helpers and painted by hand by various artists. In addition to the

hard-boiled egg, each child received toast and jam and perhaps a slice
of coffee cake. When he was eleven, Peter Gaupp recorded that the
Easter breakfast also included a piece of Matzo. The best part for
him was the session of games held after the feast.

> The whole school met at the tennis court. Miss Astfalck explained
> that everyone must participate in running an obstacle course.
> Everyone who won got a prize [in 1939 it was Cadbury's crème-filled
> chocolate eggs] as well as those who did not win. It was very
> exciting. One had to summersault. Then one had to crawl under
> a board, then one had to jump over a rope. Then one had to bind
> a shawl around someone else. Then one had to run through a
> swinging rope and jump on a table. On this table was a ladder
> on which one had to climb and jump down into a sand pit. Then one
> had to run between sticks with a bucket full of water. Then one had
> to sit down at a table and write out on a piece of paper one's name
> and address. After that, one had to creep under a structure, step into
> a sack and hop. Then one had to try and throw a soccer ball into a
> net. Then, as quickly as possible, one had to run around a special
> place and jump over a bench. Then came the winning post. I was
> once first, once third. After that there were egg races. I was fourth.[124]

Standard meals at Stoatley Rough were neither sumptuous nor elegant
but always filling. Porridge evoked strong feelings. Some, like Wolf,
found the smell sickening. Others, like Edith Hubacher [Christoffel]
loved porridge:

> I loved its rich oaty taste and smell. That is, I loved it when it
> happened to have turned out well; as it was, there were innumerable
> contingencies that had to be thought of by the distressed porridge
> cook, there were innumerable hazards that could lead to failure,
> there were multiple variations of making that nutritious dish
> unpalatable. And so our morning porridge was, more often than
> not, either too thick or too thin, there was either too much salt
> in it or none at all, it was either raw or – and that was always
> a negative climax – the taste and smell of the burnt crust at the
> bottom of the cooking pot pervaded the whole lot and forty or
> eighty pupils and teachers had to eat it willy-nilly. Just think how
> difficult it was for the house girl on breakfast duty to prepare the

enormous quantity of porridge needed every day. The pot required
was huge and, filled to the brim, was really too heavy to lift for
the slighter editions of seventeen-year olds. When the mixture
of rolled oats, water and salt reached a certain temperature, it had
to be stirred continuously to prevent burning; that was heavy work.
At the same time the coal fire under the pot had to be kept up, and
all the other preparations for breakfast had to be tended to. And
so of course it was a rare stroke of luck if the result of all these
exertions was neither too thin nor too thick, neither too salty nor ...

Others disliked the porridge. Herta said, 'I know that at my first
breakfast I nearly fainted because we all got porridge, slimy, wet porridge
with brown sugar. And I hated every spoonful of it.' Martin liked its taste
well enough but was unable to eat it if it was lumpy, in fact, claiming
that the lumps made him gag. During the war years, the Hut Boys started
saying, 'Porridge really isn't as bad as it tastes.' (Another comment
made the rounds at the same time: 'Hindemith's music isn't as bad
as it sounds.') The brown-sugar topping was, of course, never refused
and was never enough for Peter. He recalled that when Wolf had the
job of ladling it out, passing it around in an aluminium bowl under the
teacher's watchful eye – one heaping teaspoon per person – he was sure
he would get more. 'I thought oh good, I know this guy is going to treat
me well.' It did not happen.

All the cooking for the main meal was done on the huge coal-filled
range and an electric range in the kitchen. Edith recalled, 'Mr Phillips,
our wonderful gardener, came early every morning to get a fire going,
and I will never forget how once he swore at "that bloomin' teaspoon"
of a coal shovel which was really much too small for a decent portion
of anthracite lumps.' She also remembered that Mr Phillips' dog Bobby
sometimes got into the groceries. Wolf corroborates, 'On at least two
occasions, our rations were shortened by Mr Phillips' dog Bobby, who
discovered that food deliveries were sometimes left outside the back
door of the kitchen. One time, he made off with a beef roast intended
for Christmas dinner. On another occasion, a large fish mysteriously
disappeared until I found its chewed-up remains in the bushes.'

Drs Leven and Lion ate a somewhat different menu than that of the
children. The blackboard in the kitchen always listed the day's menu,
and at the bottom, the notation for the two women's food was always
marked with 'Dr L^2'. Peter was once sitting next to Dr Leven, who was

eating toast spread with marmite, a dark-brown spread made from yeast, something akin to peanut butter.[125] He recalls he was always hungry for more bread but was put off by the looks and smell of the spread. 'I never could make up my mind whether to be envious or disgusted at what she was served.'

Wolf took spectacular risks with his pranks, even risking Dr Lion's displeasure in dining. 'One day I found a stone in the garden that looked remarkably like a small steak. By current wisdom, it was probably a piece of calcite (white, like fat) with reddish-brown stains (hermatite, lean meat). When it was my turn to serve, I carefully put it on a plate and added potatoes and veggies. Dr Lion's countenance lit up; "Ah, steak!" (a rare delicacy, even for the privileged). It turned to dismay when she tried to cut it. Luckily for me, she joined in the gales of laughter at her table. It was my first successful geologic experiment.' She was quite tolerant. On one occasion, one boy decided to improve upon the table service by installing a small electric train on tracks that ran around the table. They used the device to send the condiments on a little car that sped around on its tracks for a few days until everybody was tired of the novelty.

Once the authorities went too far in their belt-tightening. Wolf recalled, 'There was no refrigeration and in summer our carefully hoarded butter ration was rancid by the end of the week. One hot summer day, a pig from the farm was slaughtered and some of the meat spoiled. It was served anyway; its offensive smell sickened even those of us who had not been raised in kosher homes. Complaints were met with reminders about the starving children of China. We laughed about that (how could our eating of stinking meat help the children of China?) but in our hearts we knew we really were privileged.' Goldy balked. Raised in a kosher household, he proclaimed that he could not eat any of the pork, rancid or not. One of the teachers insisted that he take a bite. He resisted, was pressured and gave in. No sooner had he swallowed than he immediately vomited. Nobody ever tried again to make him eat anything he did not want to eat.

The children especially disliked the infamous 'remainders pie' (in America it would be 'leftover pie'). Such a dish had been a staple of the Stoatley Rough kitchen since earliest days and before the war was a tasty treat. In 1938 Emmy Wolff wrote

Unser Betrieb ist trotz Erschwerungen recht gut belaufen. Jeder strengt sich eben ganz vergnueglich an. Diesen Dienstag habe ich

*zum Abendessen von uebriggebliebenen Kartoffeln, die ich
stampfte, three Riesenbadewannen Kartoffelauflauf gebacken –
mit Milch, Eiern, geriebenem Kaese und etwas kartoffelmehl, dazu
Tomatensosse. Alle nahmen 2mal davon.* [Our establishment in
spite of aggravations is running along smoothly. Everyone is trying
hard. On Tuesday I baked supper from leftover potatoes which
I mashed and filled three giant washtubs – with milk, eggs, grated
cheese and a bit of potato flour and tomato sauce. Everybody had
two helpings.][126]

But during wartime, remainders pie (missing the eggs and cheese) was
less palatable. The boys called such a dish (which apparently could
contain any item served the prior week) *gedraengte Wochenuebersicht*
[condensed review of the week]. They sometimes also pronounced it
'Remainder Spei' [*spei* – spit; *spien* – to spit out, vomit]. Wolf described
one such offering. 'It had an appetising crust, which turned out to
be mashed potatoes browned in the oven. Underneath was a gloppy
mixture of porridge or worse, boiled barley, mixed with spinach.
The entire mess was called "remainders pie". The poor children
of wherever would probably upchuck at the sight of it.'
  Lest we feel too sorry for the children of Stoatley Rough, one
of them who spent time at a boarding school in Ware before arriving
in Haslemere, claims the food was pretty good by comparison. Andreas
Pilartz (known as 'Hanno' to the boys) remarked upon one difference
between Stoatley Rough and the boarding schools he had experienced.
'One of the most incredible differences for me was the food. In
St. E[dmund's] the cooking was very English and did not agree with
me at all. Every term I spent at least ten days in the infirmary and
that meant ten missed classes. In Stoatley Rough I had no trouble.
The cooking was continental and really excellent.'

Chapter 5
We'll Meet Again

Martin was set to sail. Alternating currents of foreboding and pleasure coursed through his mind, exhausting him. First he'd feel disappointed at not being able to take the Cambridge Matric, then he'd feel relieved – no more studying. He looked forward to seeing his family in New York but was afraid of losing his independence. He suddenly realised he fiercely loved England and that Americans spoke atrocious English. On the other hand, Americans had lots of fresh fruit, eggs and meat. They had big cars and movies and Benny Goodman. *Begin the Beguine!*

He was supposed to go on a night walk with Odette one last time. It was all so hopeless. He felt dizzy as he left the breakfast table, his porridge untouched. He pawed through his clothes wondering if he could fit them all into his steamer trunk and then went uphill again to spend a few hours in the shop. He skipped the main meal, took a nap back in the Farmhouse and, still with no appetite, also skipped evening tea. When he caught up with Odette that night, the itching on his chest was starting to drive him mad and he had a sore throat. Damn, he couldn't even touch her, let alone kiss her goodbye. Her parting words were 'Go see Miss Astfalck'. He traipsed back up to Miss Astfalck's room. She knew at once what was wrong. Several of the third formers were down, too. Martin had chicken pox. He was not going anywhere – not to the dining table where he might contaminate others and not on a night walk with Odette. And certainly not to America.

* * *

Wolf peeked in on Martin the day before their ship was to sail – Wolf had been booked for the same passage. Martin roused himself to promise to meet as soon as he made it to New York. After Wolf left, a stillness settled over the Farmhouse, the kind of quiet that a windless, bright warm spring day brings when the world is waking from hibernation. Martin lay back in his bed and watched the ray of sunshine on his blanket, trying not to scratch at his scabby sores. He was oblivious to the cackle of a hen pecking around outside. He'd long gotten used to farm sounds (and to its ripe odours of dung and feed). Martin fingered the frayed edges of his blanket sending the faint scent of mothballs up his nostrils. The grey fibres of the blanket were thick and hoary in the sun, silvery bristles, even pretty. He struggled not to scratch at his chest. Miss Astfalck had told him to apply cool wet compresses every few hours but it wasn't working. He hurt. He hoped she would come down again to the Farmhouse with some Calamine lotion.

Martin sighed, raised an arm to make sure his glasses were still tucked behind his pillow, and pondered his future in New York. Lisa would be eleven now. Martin would have to change his name to Martin Field-Owens. What would that feel like? What would it be like to see his mother again? He dreaded her tears. He fought against feeling sorry for himself, all alone in the empty dormitory. When they first put him in quarantine, he'd felt like a prisoner. But he was getting better – a stirring of something deep inside began to radiate little tics of strength outwards to his limbs, and lying there in the sunlight, new possibilities streamed into his consciousness, sparking dreams of a new adventure.

He exhaled loudly and picked up his airplane magazine. At least he wouldn't have to muck the pig sty while he was sick.

Kinder, sprecht Englisch! [Children, speak English!]

Ich bin in den 'Mud' gefallen! ('mud' in German is *Schlamm*). This mixture of German and English was likely to reverberate around the school well into 1941 until, with anti-German sentiment in England threatening the very existence of the school, Dr Lion had, at last, put her foot down. From now on children were to speak only English. Although English had always been the top priority ('Our most important task is to teach our German children good English …')[1] for much of the school's existence, German had echoed through the house night and day, with the German adults the worst offenders, speaking German most of the time together, often shutting out the English teachers. Their English was heavily accented and poorly enunciated. One day, a Miss Krohn (a refugee temporarily housed at the school) was struggling with some containers in the kitchen and she shockingly asked Wolf to 'help me empty my bowls', pronouncing the last word to rhyme with 'owls'. It amused the Hut Boys to hear their betters constantly hectoring them to '*Sprecht Englisch!*'

A key strength of Stoatley Rough had always been its Germanic linguistic and cultural environment, offering a great measure of security for the children who had lost everything else. As Dr Lion wrote for a lecture dated 24 November 1937, 'We consider it our foremost duty towards these children to cherish and preserve all the good and great essentials of the German culture whilst teaching them to recognize, appreciate and accept those of their foster country.'[2] The children read great German classics in Dr Wolff's class and had to recite from memory passages of classic German poetry, even the English pupils (who had no idea what they were saying). The multicultural experience was reinforced through the efforts of the English teachers, who taught the boys not to click their heels when being introduced and the girls to desist from curtsying. The children learned to eat with the fork held upside down, never to say 'bloody', and so on.

Those few who found the school too Germanic, fled. Hans Kornberg left at age eleven after only a year. 'Even if one does not want to forget one's German origins, one does not want always to be reminded of them – and the still-German atmosphere, with German customs and German language as the common modicum of communication – became burdensome to me.'[3] Renate Solmitz [Frankenstein] also stayed for only one year because she 'had some feeling I ought to really become part of the English culture, language, etc. At Stoatley Rough everyone did talk with an accent (and I still do!).'[4] While Edith Hubacher [Christoffel] also recognised the liability of speaking accented English, she was financially unable to move to another school. So she did the second-best thing. She befriended a refugee who had spent a year at a traditional English girls' boarding school, newcomer Katya Schaefer. Hearing Katya's beautiful English made her aware of her own strong accent. It was not long before Katya was giving weekly lessons in correct pronunciation to the grateful Edith. After a few years working in England, Edith returned to her native city, Zurich, where she lives today and more than fifty-five years later, Edith speaks the beautiful English of the educated classes. Hans Loeser doesn't regret his accent. 'Nothing would have made me give up voluntarily the warmth, the feeling of comfort and home that Stoatley Rough meant to me. As it turned out, I traded a lifelong accent in speaking English for a home at a crucial time in my development. I think I got the better end of the bargain.'[5] Herta Lewent [Loeser] concurs, 'One reason ... we have our accents (I, even more than Hans, because later he lost some of his in the army) [is that] most of the people in the school with very few exceptions were refugees themselves.... Since we were in that school way up on the top of the hill, we really did not get to meet many native people from Haslemere.... We would go into the village, but basically we were exposed to bad English spoken by people who spoke it only a little bit. That's really the reason why we never lost our accents.'[6]

Martin and any who entered the Haslemere school system such as the Shottermill School also escaped the burden of a lifelong German accent. The occasional Britishism, however, still escapes his lips. He might say 'learnt' instead of 'learned' or call his wife 'Love' instead of the more common (American) term of endearment, 'Dear'. But he can pronounce a word containing the deadly 'th' with the best of them. Not so with his friends. Peter Gaupp, highly educated, refined and intelligent, speaks a delightful Texan English overlaid with a German accent. Or is it a German-accented English spoken with a drawl?

How did the children manage the shift to English? They arrived speaking German and they left the school speaking correct, if accented, English. The school provided not only English literature and grammar, it also had a vigorous writing programme rooted in the ability to form a précis of any paragraph. The new arrivals at Stoatley Rough first gained listening comprehension, the easiest of the four general categories of mastering a new language: listening comprehension, reading comprehension, writing and finally speaking, in that order. Miss Fearon bragged in her first term report on the school in 1934 that 'after a bare three months for most, and less for some, all the children understand any English conversation, even those who did not know a single word when they came'.[7] The more-active speaking and writing skills would have taken longer to acquire, somewhat complicated by the fact that they had learned to write using a German script called 'Sutterlin', a script based on a centuries-old 'Fraktur' or broken script, so-called for its ornamental serifs, that was taught in German and Austrian schools (Polish, Czech schools too where German was spoken) during their era (although some had started to learn Roman script in their English classes). This meant that the children had first to learn to reproduce the slightly different Roman alphabet, both as print and cursive. In September of 1938, one of the part-time English teachers noted in her monthly report, 'The handwriting of the children is a mixture of script and flowing hand. Much practice is needed.'

Wolf Elston muses on the subject of speaking English. 'It must have been about 1941–1942 that English became our language of choice [but] in 1939, German was commonly used in the Hut. Mr May, who [having joined up and] had been assigned to a West African unit, wrote back to Stoatley Rough that his new charges in the army were much like his old at Stoatley Rough; he had to admonish them to speak English.'

In the 1930s and 1940s, language training largely depended on dictionary-aided translation and rote memorisation. At Stoatley Rough, children were simply thrown into English: they were assigned to read age-appropriate literature, put through vocabulary drills, given papers to write and encouraged to perform in numerous plays and skits. Dr Lion's approach was progressive in a way. She wrote (unconsciously assigning 'child' the genderless 'it' as it is in German, '*das Kind*'), 'we do not believe in teaching language chiefly through … grammar, but … through doing a thing, as they pick up colloquial English more quickly in that manner…. It is a very delicate job to teach a child a foreign language when it has lost its home, so as not to also give it the impression of being deprived of the possibilities of expressing itself in its own mother-tongue.'[8] Dr Lion explained how English was taught at the school. 'The children began by using English at the table, at washing and dressing, and … at games…. Of course slang expressions are most captivating and it is a real fascination for them to repeat ("You lazybones!").' She also mentions that some of her pupils had received in other schools the French 'Globule' (or cobweb) method, and the use of Beacon readers. Some children arrived learning phonetic reading and insisted on knowing the sound of each letter. 'Jessie, eight, distinguishes the eight different types of the German alphabet and the English one with its different pronunciation, as well as reading and writing in both languages. Those children who had already mastered the rudiments of reading in Germany are capable of reading and writing English nicely after some months.'

In the early days of the school, thoughtful British volunteers, while untrained in pedagogy, did their best. Cesia Szajnzicht [Rothbart] recalled a Miss Pelmare who would walk around the grounds pointing to things, naming them and having her repeat the words. Miss Pelmare 'never scolded for mispronunciation and always encouraged us for words remembered. Crumbs of kindness very much appreciated.'[9] Dr Lion was not to know that not every effort was successful. Beate Frankfurter [Planskoy] recalled a Miss Bewley, 'a thin elderly woman, with brown eyes, a deeply lined, brown face, greying brown hair [who,] dressed in brown tweeds and sensible shoes, took us for nature walks in the countryside. She had a mousy looking lady assistant whose name I can't recall. The pair were not on the staff of the school but, I think may have had some connection with the Quakers and in teaching us were doing their bit for refugee children. I remember that Dr Lion enjoined us to be especially well behaved and polite on these walks, implying that these two ladies were doing us a favour. In any event, they appeared to be very knowledgeable about the area and about plants and animals and took a great deal of trouble to teach us, but as I knew no English most of what they said passed me by. In order to hide this fact and not cause offence by looking bored, I learned to keep a fixed, polite smile on my face, an expression that came in useful on many other similar occasions in the classroom during the next few months where I was equally at sea.'[10]

Curriculum notes from 1940 refer to a teaching manual that recommends various exercises such as pointing to items and asking the students to name them, but there is no evidence of any formal speech/language methodologies at play. In fact, the teachers like Miss Dove had arrived at the school ready to teach literature, not language, and they were forced to devise their own methods to teach children at the start of a semester who had no English at all. It was a process that depended on a child's innate ability to learn quickly, a cumulative process that might allow Miss Dove within a few weeks to ask the children to describe a circular staircase without using their hands. Alternately, the pupil would just listen in class until he or she could pick up a few words. Ruth Bayer [Tuckman] wrote in 1990 to her former English teacher, Miss Dove, mentioning not only her lack of English but also a political scare the new teacher had unwittingly caused. She said, 'You may not recall a slight, thirteen-year-old with black hair and very dark eyes whose knowledge of English was non-existent. I never uttered a word in your lesson and was incapable of writing an essay. But indelibly imprinted in my memory is one of my early History lessons in which you spoke most disparagingly, to the point of derision, about the Hanoverian kings. Having just come from an educational system that had nothing but praise for the rulers of Prussia in general and for Fredrich the Great in particular, I feared for your safety; You cannot imagine my relief when you, kind and cheerful Miss Dove, appeared unscathed at supper time.'[11] (Later the school created ever-shifting English classes to conform to the language ability of its newer pupils. An eleven-year-old newcomer like Peter Gaupp could end up in a class with six- and eight-year-olds until his grasp of English had sufficiently matured.) The Hut Boys joked about the funny new words they were learning. Goldy came up with a few definitions: 'Icicle' is a bicycle with one wheel. A 'public conveyance' was a toilet. The older students helped the newcomers, even in language learning. Ilse Bauer [Feldstein] remembered when Hans Loeser spent time at Thursley Copse to teach English. 'I have never forgotten your vivid explanation of English plurals: tooth-teeth, goose-geese, you said exasperatedly, "but look, it is just like in German – *der Fuss, die Fiess*." '[12] [The joke is that the plural of the German word for 'foot' is *Füsse*, while *Fiess* is a common dialect.]

While the children were reading Goldsmith's *She Stoops to Conquer* or, for the younger ones, Kipling for homework, they preferred German books in their free time. Many girls devoured the popular *Nesthakchen* book series. The *Nesthakchen* or 'baby of the family or pet' was a slim, golden-haired girl named Annemarie Braun who, over the course of several books, grew up and took a job while not forfeiting marriage and children. She was a breathtakingly modern role model and the books are still read today. The series was written by a young aristocrat, Else Ury (1877–1943), who would die in Auschwitz.[13]

The boys read books by Karl May, a German author (1842–1912) whose stories were (and still are) wildly popular in all of Europe.[14] Based on *The Last of the Mohicans*, James Fennimore Cooper's masterpiece (known to the Hut Boys as *Der Letze Mohikaner*), May's hero was a German do-gooder named Old Shatterhand who had a sidekick, an Indian named Winnetau. Old Shatterhand was so called because he 'knocked out a bruiser with one blow.' Although May had never been to America, his books perpetuated a mystique of the old west that had fascinated Europeans since Cooper introduced Hawk-eye and his cohorts to the world in 1862.[15]

As the Stoatley Rough boys grew older, they were happy to switch to reading in English primarily because they discovered penny dreadfuls. Wolf tells us that, 'By the summer of 1940, monthly magazines for boys, like *Adventure* and *Hotspur*, began to displace Karl May.' These cheap publications provided serialised escapist stories of superheroes, the more fantastic the better. George Orwell explained in an essay of 1940 that 'boys at certain ages find it necessary to read about Martians, death-rays, grizzly bears and gangsters.'[16]

The magazines gave the boys inspiration, escape from uncertainty and loss, and feelings of helplessness. Again, Orwell captures the lure of the cover illustrations: 'On one a cowboy is clinging by his toes to the wing of an aeroplane in mid-air and shooting down another aeroplane with his revolver. On another a Chinese is swimming for his life down a sewer with a swarm of ravenous-looking rats swimming after him. On another an engineer is lighting a stick of dynamite while a steel robot feels for him with its claws. On yet another a man in airman's costume is fighting barehanded against a rat somewhat larger than a donkey! This character is intended as a superman, whose usual method of solving any problem is a sock on the jaw.' Orwell nails the salutary effect of these stories for the boys in the following conclusion: 'At the same time the scenes of violence in nearly all these stories are remarkably harmless and unconvincing.'[17]

By 1942, the preferred reading of the Hut Boys was in English. Wolf said that 'only a die-hard Berliner like Tom Wongtschowski would insist on speaking German.' Of course the school authorities frowned on the penny dreadfuls and assigned only approved age-appropriate classics of English and German literature. Wolf recalls that 'Our teachers regarded penny dreadfuls as trashy literature which, of course, made them all the more attractive.'

At any rate, roughly two years into the war, the children at Stoatley Rough began to speak English with regularity. Wolf said, 'It is … difficult to remember when my private thoughts and dreams switched from German to English; most probably it happened about age fourteen (1942).' Wolf had had to work hard at his English. 'To overcome my heavy German accent, I was put in special speech class taught by a prim English lady whose name I have forgotten (Miss West?) but to whom I am very grateful. She made us repeat words like "hyacinths" and "chrysanthemums" endlessly, saying, "You'll pronounce it correctly, or you shan't have any tea". In England, tea is not just a beverage but the principal meal of the day, which made this a very serious threat to a growing boy. Without her perseverance, I would today probably sound like Henry Kissinger.'[18] But Wolf's real trial in his acquired language was yet to be faced when he began life in New York. 'I had arrived at Stoatley Rough as a German in language and thought. On leaving, I was not exactly an Englishman but had acquired fluency in the English language and a lasting understanding of British ways. Americanisation followed gradually. Upon enrolling at the City College of New York in 1945, I was required to read aloud from *The New York Times* to demonstrate proficiency in English. My pronunciation of "aircrahft were sheduled to fly to Schenectahdy" landed me in Remedial English, along with natives of Brooklyn and the Bronx. This came as a shock, as I had regarded myself as the only one in the place who actually spoke English!'[19]

Newcomers sometimes got into trouble not knowing English. Ilse Steinberg [Braude] took newcomer Wolf into town to get a haircut after he had just arrived. While walking across Hindhead Common, Ilse entertained him, in German of course, with a blow-by-blow account of an exciting book she was reading for English class, *Tom Sawyer*. They arrived at the barbershop and Wolf was seated in the chair. The barber started in with pleasant small talk, asking Wolf questions as he trimmed this side and that, turning him in the chair, snipping away. Wolf tried to be pleasant by answering 'Yes' each time the barber paused.

The barber said, 'Did you bring your comb?'

Wolf answered, 'Yes.'

'Well, where is it?'

'Yes.'

'I said, where's your comb?'

'Yes.'

'Are you trying to be a smart aleck with me?'

'Yes.'

At that point, Ilse woke up, put down her book and broke into the exchange to explain to the barber Wolf hadn't the slightest idea what he was saying. The barber finished the haircut in silence.

Household Girls were sometimes assigned special work on the Farm, such as helping to paint a room or bring in a harvest. Birgitte Heinsheimer [Pring-Mills] had just arrived from Germany. 'I was sent to work on the farm (perhaps because I had grown up in the country?) to help with the building of a stable. The instructor had a most beautiful singing voice. [She refers to Mr Hughes, the Welsh Farm Manager, who succeeded Mr Corfield. He spoke no German.] And the picture I remember is of both of us hammering laths onto the roof, and my asking whether he would teach me that song. He did. I thought it was beautiful, and fifty years on I still think so. I learnt it, and next day, on kitchen duty with Lizzi Loebl, I tried it out on her and asked what my pronunciation of English was like. "Can't tell", was the sobering answer, "You are singing it in Welsh." I have now forgotten the Welsh text, but the song was "All Through the Night".'[20]

Goldy, who was ever alert to propriety, said about learning English, 'There was teasing at times when we mispronounced certain words, but people really tried to help us master the language, especially the "r" and the "the" sounds. One tricky aspect of learning a new language, mainly from other twelve-year-old boys, was to discriminate acceptable from unacceptable words, like swear words, which should not be repeated at home.'[21]

The children performed often in plays. The alumni cite many instances in which they successfully played roles, perhaps showing the importance to them at the time of their small moment in the sun. Dieter said, 'On one occasion I was cast in the part of the Miser (L'Avare) in the play of the same name by Moliere. This was in the original French. I don't know how many people who watched it understood us but I imagine most people had been briefed beforehand and we all enjoyed it.'[22] He liked the period piece in which he played a German lord. 'I had only a few lines ... I was drunk most of the time and what I had to say came out accordingly. It brought a lot of laughter.... When I left the school Dr Lion gave me a letter of recommendation in which she mentioned my stage activity, saying she thought I was quite gifted. I don't know what a prospective employer was to do with that.'[23] He once had the occasion in which familiarity with Shakespeare provided an amusing moment in class. English teacher Mr Taylor had arrived late to class that day, so late that the children were out of their seats, running around and talking loudly, doing what children do when the teacher's absence provides a mandate for cavorting. Mr Taylor soon restored order but one child remained behind a curtain in the room, creating great suspense. 'We wondered how things would develop. Mr Taylor, generally ... a friendly but also controlling schoolmaster, made some comments which led him to talk about *Hamlet*, the play in which there was a scene where Polonius, hidden behind a curtain, was stabbed while trying to hide.... The missing student emerged, much to everyone's amusement.'[24]

There is at least one instance when it is clear how difficult the nuances of spoken English must have been for the German children. Wolf was only eleven or twelve and had walked down to the Farm to watch the older Farm boys dig out the side of the hill to make an air-raid shelter (which apparently was never used). The boys were hard at work on it, hacking at the earth with various tools. 'Someone called to the digging crew: "Have you got any pigs here on the farm?" The answer by one of the Farm boys: "Ve haff two big sows and a dozen little picks."'

Confessions of an army cadet

In September 1942, Dieter left the school. He had turned eighteen in May and it was time for him to find work. Gerd Edelstein [Elston] knew of an opening in the optical factory where he was working, in Offenham in Worcestershire, about a hundred miles north-west of London. Soon Dieter was making spectacle frames from plastic. His building was used for Home Guard practice raids and he recalls times when he would look up from his workbench to see troops slinking along the wall outside. He often joined his friend Gerd to go to concerts while there. In 1944, Dieter joined the Home Guard himself, 'feeling we needed to do something tangible for the war effort ... we were issued real rifles, though I don't know if they had firing pins in them.... Our rifles were made for giants, were longer and heavier than regular rifles – I can't imagine what their initial purpose had been. They were obviously not wanted by the regular army. We drilled with them, specially marching and cleaning. That's as far as it went as we ordered uniforms which never came because in a week or two after that the Home Guard was disbanded.' While he was at the factory, Dieter received a scholarship to a Youth Leadership course in 1946 at the University of Bristol for running (with the help of Gerd and Miss Jenks, a local schoolteacher) a youth club.

Dieter's departure gave Peter, still at Stoatley Rough, pause to consider his own status. When his friend, Michael Strauss, proposed they transfer to a 'real' English school, Peter agreed. With Dieter gone, he had nothing to lose. The two fourteen-year-olds enrolled in Shoreham Grammar School, an independent school in Shoreham-by-Sea, on the south coast.[25] Peter left Haslemere thinking he would become more self-sufficient away from the warm nest of Stoatley Rough and in a very real sense, he got his way.

For the first time in his life, Peter experienced the cruelty that boarding children are capable of inflicting on outsiders. Peter was German – that was bad enough. Worse, Peter was also a Jew but not really, because worst of all, he wasn't even a real Jew but a *Mischling*, the product of a marriage between a Jew and a Gentile.[26] Peter found himself thrown into an elegant purgatory, mired in the finely tuned nastiness of prejudice that was prevalent in many public schools then. His situation was exacerbated by the existence of what was known as the prefect system. Supposed to build character, the prefect system conferred privileges and responsibilities on upperclassmen and heaped punishment and humiliation on the younger set. The prefect, a privileged senior boy, was allowed to wear clothing that would distinguish him from the rest of the boys and had the power to bully lowerclassmen (sometimes called 'fags') and even to consign them to canings administered by teachers.[27] 'I was harassed badly by the other kids as a "Nazi", and since I was such a shy character, did nothing about it.'

Shoreham's system of rewards and punishments brings into sharp focus the benevolent atmosphere that Peter had abandoned. Stoatley Rough fostered, if nothing else, a relaxed environment of non-competitive, positive encouragement. Discipline at Stoatley Rough consisted of sending children to bed early or remanding them to Dr Lion for a stern talking to. Roughian children certainly were capable of mischief; they could be rude to their teachers; they were known to steal food, fight with each other and break rules such as taking a night walk. But as long as Miss Astfalck reigned, physical punishment was unimaginable.

Peter himself became a prefect in his last year at the school but there seems to be an element of sadomasochism in the attitude taken by his elders. 'Caning was a part of the school principal's options. It did not happen very often, but I was caned the evening of the day I was made a prefect. The boys in my dorm room decided to have a pillow fight at night, in which I was really not interested, when Mr Bruder opened the door just as I finally sailed a pillow in his direction. I know he thought it was funny in a way, but invited me to his study for a caning anyway. After all, I was supposed to set an example … or something like that.' Peter continues with more graphic examples. 'There were always rumours that he "chalked" his cane, even though that was never proved. Chalking the cane was a barbaric system which assured that one hit the identical spot over and over again, inflicting maximum punishment. It was a widely held belief in British schools that principals did this. I was never certain whether mine did or did not. I suspect that since he was basically a rather decent fellow, that he did not – but the myth prevailed. The trouble is that while one is bending over, it is hard to look behind to make sure! And afterwards most kids don't really want their peers to examine the injured article.'

The educational systems in the United States sanctioned corporal punishment in the 1930s and 1940s, but 'caning' (as opposed to spanking with a hand or ruler) conveys an approach to punishment that employs humiliation and fear. Peter recalled that he was frightened by the mere presence of a cane at his elementary school in Germany. 'The male teacher always walked around with a cane under his arm, a clear suggestion that he would use it if we misbehaved. I never saw him use it and my parents said that he was actually a very nice man – but

I was awed!' Wolf's teacher also used a cane but Goldy, Obo and Martin have no memory of caning punishments on the Continent.

Andreás [Hanno] Pilartz's first school was St. Edmund's College, Old Hall, in Ware, the oldest Catholic boarding school in England. 'We played cricket and rugby, had boxing, and luckily I was very good at that, which allowed me not to be pestered by the others. There were prefects (upperclassmen) who could punish you by giving you lines to write say forty or eighty times, "I must not do this or that, etc.," they could also send you up, which meant that you had to report to your House Master after supper. So after supper you went up to your House Master's rooms, there were usually three or four others waiting and that, in a way, was the worst moment – the actual waiting and maybe hearing somebody else being caned. Eventually it was your turn to go so either you were told off or you got it. There was a big armchair and you had to put your knees on one arm and bend over to put your hands on the other arm. There were different thickness of canes, normally there were three strokes but sometimes there were six. You could have it with your trousers down or up. Six is the maximum I ever had, but apparently in the not so distant past, twelve strokes and even in one case there had been twenty-four strokes, and that in public. Of course when you came out of the room one had to have a smile on one's face.' Hanno concludes, 'They told my mother that they thought it might be better for me to change schools.... Of course my first impression was what a curious place, no discipline; no real punishment. I soon got used to it, and in the end I got so much more out of Stoatley Rough than I would have done in St. Edmund's.' David King, a post-war pupil, testified to the existence of sadistic behaviour in his English school before he arrived at Stoatley Rough. His poem, 'Six Whacks with an Old Gymshoe', described a teacher who inflicted pain 'like six lightening sparks' on children's behinds. The teacher 'always had the same ones up to beat/He made them think it was a special treat'.[28]

Another post-war Stoatley Rough pupil, Franceska Amerikaner [Rapkin], started out her British education at the exclusive Polam Hall School (Darlington, Durham), a place distinguished by the fact that the fathers of most of the girls were still in the armed services. She learned early that she was 'the enemy, if not because I was German, then because I was Jewish and the Jews had killed Christ, hadn't they?' She was 'taunted and tugged, pulled and shouted at'. This refugee child suffered for two years, coming home to her mother, 'dirty and dishevelled, with

so many detentions and bad reports', and 'never invited to parties'.
She was asked to leave after she had inexplicably stolen a hockey
stick from one of the other girls. She reports about the goodness of
Stoatley Rough, 'The school may not have been known for its academic
achievements, but my goodness, it prepared us for life and taught
us decency and I will be ever grateful for the opportunity that I was
given … to leave my traumas behind me and to develop my potential
as a human being.'[29]

Peter persevered. He would see the last three years of Second World War
at Shoreham. He joined the school's branch of what was called the Army
Cadets, a programme roughly comparable to the U.S. Army's Junior
Reserve Officers Training Corps (ROTC). No mere play-act, Army
Cadets were expected to be a rear-guard deterrent to a real enemy should
it appear on English soil. Michael Strauss, who seems to have led Peter
off the straight and narrow path again and again, had volunteered for
the Cadet programme and become a Quartermaster with the rank of
Sergeant. He arranged for Peter to become his assistant. 'I was promoted
to the rank of Company Quartermaster Corporal – a rank which actually
did not exist. I was told that it was especially created for me. Then
I found out that there *was* one other person with such rank: he was
in charge of the queen's horses at Buckingham Palace!' The following
is a verbatim account of Peter Gaupp's adventures as a Cadet.

My British Army career in the Cadets during World War II was
a little like being around the Keystone Cops. To all intents and
purposes we were the Home Guard for the area while living at the
Shoreham Grammar School. One day the great General in Charge
of the Southern Command (i.e. all of Southern England) came by
to inspect our company. There was a formal inspection in which
we looked all polished up and stood forever in the broiling sun
for the great man to come. I was the company 'spotter' which
means I was the one in a position around which the rest of them
organized the straight ranks, etc. It was hot! With my friend the
Quartermaster I had scavenged beautiful Canadian uniforms for
us which were designed for arctic conditions. Great in the winter,
but in the summer … After standing at attention for what seemed
like hours waiting for the great man, he finally turned up and
started walking along the ranks until he came close to me when
I fainted in front of him. Some impression!

Illustrations

1. Stoatley Rough School, *c.* 1935.

2. Dr Hilde Lion, post-war.   3. Eleonore Astfalck, pre-war.

4. Dr Emmy Wolff, undated.

5. Dr Luise Leven, undated.

6. Johanna Nacken, pre-war.

7. Sitting Room with Morris Fireplace, Peter Strauss on chair, *c.* 1939.

8. Inge Hamburger [Pavlowsky] with unidentified child, *c.* 1938.

9. Renate Dorpalen [Dorpalen-Brocksieper]
age 19, 1939.

10. Ten-year-olds on the heath, 1938.

11. Luggage of new arrivals, undated.

12. School sign sculpted by Hermann Nonnenmacher,
c. 1938.

13. Hans Obermeyer with his horn of plenty on his first day of school, Bad Salzuflen, Germany, 1934.

14. Kate Lesser in Liverpool Street Station, August 1939, upon arriving with 150 other children from Berlin.

15. Lisel Loeser and Wolf Edelstein [Elston] building the swimming pool, 1938.

16. Cadets Peter Gaupp (left) and Bruce Main, Shoreham, 1944.

17. Dieter Gaupp, age 15, 1939.

18. All-school Easter game, undated.

19. Boy studying, undated.

20. Haymaking on the farm, pre-war.

21. Hans Loeser and Herta Lewent on their wedding day, 11 December 1944.

22. *Left to right*: Peter Gaupp, John Obermeyer, John Goldmeier,
Martin Friedenfeld [Owens], Wolf Edelstein [Elston] celebrating their
50th birthday in Columbia, Maryland, 1978.

We were told that the German invasion seemed to be imminent.
Then the General stood on top of a high cliff in the Liphook area
and pointed towards the broad valley below it and said something
to the effect that if the Germans came through there we were
in charge of seeing that they were stopped. One has to remember
that we were a bunch of teenagers with long Enfield rifles from the
Boer War, with no rifling left and no firing pins. During the deadly
silence which followed he added that our principal role would
be to be artillery spotters in that event. Otherwise we would be
in charge of field communications. Perhaps that was because we
could do semaphore? We had antiquated battery operated field
telephones from WWI which required wires to be laid out in order
to connect them. I suspect that had we ever been required to do this,
we would have had a high casualty rate just from the accidents
we used to have laying that wire!

Every now and then we went on manoeuvres preparing ourselves
for the great invasion. One time I found myself sitting in a small
forest at night in charge of a platoon. Word came that German
parachutists with evil intent were thought to have dropped in the
area. One of my 'men' came to me and whispered that there were
people moving around on the other side of the broad meadow.
So, what does one do? One captures the parachutists … with Long
Lee Enfield rifles! Talk about terror. I ordered my men to sneak
carefully towards that area and then I shouted 'charge!' What we
found as we broke into the clearing was a herd of cows, placidly
moving through the field. We won the battle of the cow. But, I think
some of us died on the way there. I don't remember reporting this
story to my commander.

One day, in the middle of classes, the principal, who was also
our Company commander, told us to quit school and get into our
uniforms and be ready to board lorries in thirty minutes. Now, there
is excitement. We boarded and rolled out in what seemed like
an endless, very bumpy trip towards Western England. At night
we drove into a large British Army camp while the Army rolled
out in a long row of trucks and tanks. We were told that we were
in charge of the camp. Every morning the Germans were said
to send over a small spotter plane to take pictures and it was our

job to make it look like we were the busy army still occupying the camp. Most of my time that night was spent peeling an endless supply of potatoes while my friends stood guard around the camp. When I was really sleepy, I was told to take my turn as a sentry and once again we were told that there were rumours of German parachutists in the area and to keep a sharp look out. I don't remember the details but still have a vivid memory of being told that those parachutists could be real mean and slit your throat without your knowing it had happened. Next morning we were all over the camp looking 'busy' while the army rolled towards the coast and 'D Day' was on. Next day we marched around and I remember going past a farmer's field with lots of tanks and airplanes on it. We looked at them up close. They were made of plywood and painted very realistically. Again, the object was to deceive that spotter plane. (This was one of many fields, also described in Ken Follett's book *The Eye of the Needle*.) We really did not know why we were asked to do this strange and demanding thing until quite some time later.

Our Company took its obligation to stop the [German] invasion very seriously, except that we really had nothing much to fight with. Our original uniforms were Boer War uniforms with puttees to wrap around the legs and other strange things which were totally obsolete. My genius friend, the Quartermaster, concluded that it was up to us to outfit the company since nobody else would do it. He dreamed up the idea of visiting the various army camps which surrounded us, an English one, a Canadian one, and an American one. He would secure beer and we would carry it to the Quartermasters in those camps who, to my amazement, would tell us to take whatever we wanted! That's how we got those uniforms. Then we started collecting weapons and ammunition and grenades of all kinds. It was amazing how easy it was. Then we had everyone train with these wonderful modern things and, like teenagers, we did very silly and dangerous things with the explosives. One day we decided to carry out a beautiful, large Bren Gun [a light machine gun] plus wonderful heavy Canadian Ross rifles. The MPs stopped us. The next thing I knew that our principal had been called and we returned very sheepishly. He had accepted all we brought home in the past, including a gorgeous Canadian uniform for him and had never questioned it! Now we were in really hot water with him. But, as I remember it, all the stuff we had scrounged in the past we kept throughout the war and were possibly the best equipped Home Guard unit in the region. Certainly, the inspecting General was impressed but evidently did not ask how we got all that stuff. In the midst of war there is always some idiocy.[30]

The birds and the bees

In the halcyon days of the school when there were far fewer pupils than during the war, Herta said that policies regarding sexual contact were 'relaxed to non-existent'. According to Hans, 'Dr Lion … had fears, and we sensed them and even respected them (largely by way of caution), but at least at our time there were dances in the School Room attended by Astfalck and many co-ed parties which were well known to Astfalck. Dr Lion's stricter code emerged only when the student population swelled and she no longer had the close contact with each student she had formerly enjoyed.' Since there is no record of any unwanted pregnancies (with the exception of a rumour that one precocious upper-level pupil had a liaison with a soldier during the war and had to be sent away, which Wolf debunks as having been started by a notorious liar), Dr Lion had success with her approach.

After 1939, the prospect of large numbers of adolescents of both sexes growing up together in her school caused Dr Lion no end of anxiety. She was determined nobody would get pregnant on her watch. In part because the 1940s fostered a general atmosphere of naiveté and censorship (everyone knew that sexual activity could lead to pregnancy and ruined reputations), but more because she herself did not have any experience with adolescents, she sensibly created an environment least conducive to romance. She would not countenance public displays of affection, prohibited dancing (except for conga-line or folk dancing) and maintained constant vigilance. She was known to save more than one girl from a fate worse than death. Driving along Farnham Lane, if she spotted a boy and girl from her school walking along holding hands, she would screech to a halt, order the girl into the car and whisk her back to safety.

But children are curious and will learn about sex by hook or by crook. Tom Wongtschowski, although no more curious than the rest of the Hut

Boys, was certainly the boldest. Even as a little boy in the Schoolroom in the manse (a large room holding rows of beds for the boys), he was not above peeping. There was one screened-off corner of the room where the Household Girl in charge had to sleep and keep her clothes and belongings. Wolf said, 'The screen had more or less conspicuous holes, and the curtains on the doorway tended to leave a small gap when closed, which gave little boys an opportunity to ogle big girls undressing. One night Tom Wongtschowski hit the jackpot by getting a good glimpse of one of the older girl's pubic hair.'

Renate Dorpalen [Dorpalen-Brocksieper] reported that when she stumbled upon a source of forbidden knowledge, Dr Lion nipped it in the bud. She loved cleaning Dr Lion's bungalow because 'she allowed me access to her extensive library. I could read to my heart's contentment late at night, much of the time by flashlight.... One day I selected Ina Seidel's *Das Wunschkind*, the story of a love-child born out of wedlock.' Dr Lion confiscated it. 'I was surprised at her restriction, the first I had ever experienced in my life. It was years later when I was in graduate school that the book fell into my hands and I became aware of the reason for her prohibition and of the suppression of sexuality in the school.'[31] Wolf recalled, 'by the time I reached the farm, at age fourteen, I'd picked up all sorts of sex information from raising rabbits, observing farm animals and by learning from other boys. The Cockney Boy Scouts from the East End of London, with whom we camped, were a great source of information. In many ways they were our opposites: Heroes of the Blitz, but scared to death of spiders; ignorant in all that Stoatley Rough taught, but sophisticated in the ways of sex. Eventually someone on the farm acquired a Ministry of Information brochure on Sex Education. The Ministry did a good job. Anyway, we boys and girls knew about sex but stressful situations at the school were rare.'

Scandal was partly avoided owing to the phenomenon that makes pals and buddies out of people who live closely together, for example co-ed college dorms. The student body at Stoatley Rough was family to each other, and it was only a newly arrived girl or boy who attracted attention. In his teens, Martin had one girlfriend after another, most of whom were recent arrivals. Goldy wrote, 'Sex seemed to be totally ignored as well, at least for us boys. The girls and boys in the school were often more like brothers and sisters to each other, even though teenage romances blossomed here and there. For us boys it was sometimes difficult to ignore our sexual urges when the developing girls were wearing sweaters which they had long outgrown but could not replace because clothing was rationed.… We often had crushes for the same girl, but that did not seem to matter because such things had to be kept very secret. The response to these awakening sexual feelings was to basically ignore them and to discourage situations where a boy and girl would be left alone too often and for too long. We did receive dance lessons by one enterprising teacher but the preferred dance was mostly the waltz because the centrifugal force of spinning a girl around almost eliminated body contact. Certainly the tango would have been frowned on.'[32] Peter adds, 'In a setting where boy-girl relationships were not encouraged nor special opportunities for such provided, the pool was one of the few places where the teenager could daydream.' Wolf believed that 'the sexual restraints which seem odd in retrospect were as much caused by inexperience, lack of information, the students' acute sense of insecurity as to their future and intuitive understanding that making commitments was too risky, as by School-imposed restrictions'.

Night walks gave children freedom to explore relationships. Although Dr Lion prohibited them, Nore, the enforcer, turned a blind eye. Many Roughians have written of those hours on the heath under the stars. Edith Hubacher [Christoffel] recalled having to be awakened to go on the night walks because she was always falling asleep before the appointed hour. She tied a string to her big toe and hung it out of her window. When her friends tugged on the string, she woke up and joined them. Barbara Gerstenberg [Prasse] wrote, 'It is hard to describe our friendship given the ethos of today's teenagers. It was caring, loving, tender and very romantic. Surprisingly enough, we were so young that we never went beyond a chaste kiss or an embrace.… We set an alarm and snuck out a kitchen window and then walked in the surrounding commons open fields and sat on a bench in the moonlight. When Ed and I went to Haslemere in 1972, I found the bench still there.'[33] As noted earlier, at least two liaisons led to marriage: Herta Lewent and Hans Loeser, and Lilly Wohlgemuth and Peter Gluecksmann (both lifelong unions).

With no access to mass media (except the BBC radio) to enlighten youngsters about adult sexuality, childhood was extended compared to that of children in today's world. Physical and emotional maturity occurred much later in the 1940s, than today where many children (some blame it on the steroids in processed meats) reach pubescence at ages nine or ten. The authorities also shifted children around, policies that discouraged intimacy, even in same-gender friendships. Barbara Gerstenberg [Prasse] wrote, 'I did not make any close girl friends at school, in fact, I believe we were not encouraged to do so. We were moved around, so that we always had different roommates and never became too close to any one.'³⁴

Teachers handled questions in class about sexual matters with more evasion, conflation and denial than are wielded by today's most skilful politician. Wolf was once sitting in class when the following dialogue took place. Our teachers were not particularly informative about matters of sex. In English literature one day, we were discussing Pope's 'Rape of the Lock'.

Girl Pupil: 'What does "rape" mean?'

Teacher: 'Rape is, you know, it's just one of those words that want to make you squirm!'

On another occasion, the word 'virgin' had come up:

Girl Pupil: 'What's a virgin?'

Teacher: 'A virgin is a young girl who hasn't, you know, who doesn't – well, you're a virgin and Elsie (not her real name) here, she is a virgin.'

Elsie: (waking up from a daydream, emphatically): 'I am *not*!'

And then there was the discussion during one of Dr Lion's occasional classroom appearances, about the great German philosopher, Emmanuel Kant. Wolf recalls, 'I don't mean to imply that the girls were more naïve than the boys. One of the more sophisticated girls broke into uncontrollable giggles in class when Dr Lion told us about a man who had devoted his life to studying Kant. She was speaking English but pronounced the philosopher's name correctly, in the German manner.'

The authorities were determined to keep the facts of life away from the younger students yet toward the end of the war, they allowed unsupervised teenagers of both sexes to live in the Farmhouse. Wolf reminds that 'any reader who expects lurid confessions will be disappointed. The atmosphere of Stoatley Rough simply did not lend itself to improprieties. How, then, did we handle our growing sexual awareness? Simply getting information was a hit-or-miss affair. In a school run entirely by single women, we could sense stresses and strains among the staff. Sex was so delicate a topic that it was best avoided.' At least once, Stoatley Rough offered a version of sex education that may have raised more questions than it answered, in Wolf's opinion. 'Shortly after my arrival at age ten, the boys of my class were one day separated from the girls and confronted by a formidable

German-speaking lady who announced that she would enlighten us
("*aufklären*" [clear up] was the word.) She solemnly produced a large
German book with pictures of human foetuses in the womb, in various
stages of development. How they got there, she did not say. She left us
with the admonition not to play with ourselves ("*Also, hört zu! Vor
Allem: Spielt nicht!*") [So Listen up, all of you! No playing!]. A few years
later, the girls were taken aside by the Haslemere District Nurse. Wolf
reported, "I don't know what she told them, but for a couple of weeks
the girls gave us boys a wide berth and strange looks."'

To the boys, anything with the slightest connection to sex was
infinitely fascinating. In the summer of 1944, Martin got a part-time
gardening job at a place in Haslemere known euphemistically as a 'home
for wayward girls', where unmarried young women stayed for the
duration of their pregnancy. Every day he would return from work
to his friends, who always asked the same question: what did you see?
Every day came the same answer: nothing. It didn't matter. The subject
was so full of potential that the boys speculated endlessly during the
three months Martin's rather dull job lasted.

Wolf was once subjected to an agonising experience that only a young
man in the throes of adolescence could appreciate. Dr Lion had made
an arrangement with a private girls' school nearby that started having
groups of girls walk over to swim in the pool once a week. A new boy
had joined the Hut, Herbert Zwergfeld [Fielding] whom, having arrived
with a mop of long hair, the boys instantly dubbed 'Beethoven'. Wolf
moved to live on the Farm along with Beethoven early in 1943. 'When
Beethoven and I were on the Farm, we noticed that, on a certain
afternoon of the week, our swimming pool would be visited by girls
from Inval St. Hillary, a girl's school so strict that no contact with males
was allowed. (My brother, Gerd, took his School Cert. exams there,
in segregated conditions and under guard.) Under those circumstances,
there was no need for the girls to have bathing suits. And they didn't.
Beethoven managed to borrow a pair of high-powered binoculars from
Mr Obee, issued to him by the ROC [Royal Observer Corps]. Then
he spent the afternoon by a window of the farmhouse, ogling the girls
cavorting at the pool. BUT THE STINKER WOULD NOT SHARE THE
BINOCULARS WITH ME! (He claimed that Mr Obee had made him
promise not to let them out of his hands!)'

There were the occasional accidents, when boys and girls were
rewarded a brief glimpse of each other in the nude. Peter Gaupp

remembered, 'For some reason the boys and girls had to switch baths for a time, and the boys got to use the larger one.... There was great excitement among the boys when they learned that out of habit, one of the younger boys had barged into the Girls' bathroom. He was said to have seen a number of naked girls. The girls were reported to have been outraged that he just stood at the open door with his mouth open while they screamed for him to get out. The older boys declared the incident was "wasted on him". Once a girl barged in on Peter himself when he was sitting in the tub – fortunately with his back to her.'[35] Another time Wolf burst into the Girls' bathroom expecting to see the barber. He was stunned to see a naked girl 'facing me, standing up. I couldn't recall a thing. She later confessed to having blushed "all over".' The younger boys played a game with the girls called 'ball-over-the-string'. They were awed when the girls provocatively caught the ball against their chests. And then there was the time that Peter had to endure the same face-off with the same tomboy who had wrestled Obo to the ground two years earlier. It seems the girl liked to pick on the newcomers. Peter was standing near a group of thirteen-year-old girls on the terrace, waiting for dinner. The tomboy called him over. At eleven, Peter was shy and unsure of how to act, but dutiful and curious, he approached. The girl told him she was sure she could wrestle him to the ground. Peter prided himself on his wrestling skills, but this was an outrageous idea. He had been brought up with the idea that one did not ever touch girls. He tried to find excuses but they shamed him into accepting the challenge. So, he asked himself, how to wrestle a girl without touching her? Several children watched from the terrace as he and the girl squared off on the lawn. She had her arms about him and he flailed, trying not to put his hands on her. As he put it, 'It was a terrible way to wrestle' and she had him down in no time. She even sat on him. Peter concludes, 'No greater shame has a boy endured than that.'

Sometimes someone fell in love, sometimes fatally. Wolf reports. 'One of my classmates was smitten by a somewhat older girl [Ilse Kaiser] who kept her distance. He literally pined away in the classic manner, becoming pale, thin and distracted. This was serious because he was due to take the school-leaving exam, the School Certificate. It was a matter of great pride to Dr Lion that no Roughian had ever failed the School Cert. The boy's love eventually literally rendered him "pale and lifeless", a true Byronic lover suffering from unrequited love. I worried that he'd become a ghost of his former self, and it got so bad that Dr Lion gave me five shillings ($1.00) to take him to the movies in an effort to shake him out of his depression. The film version of "Pygmalion" was showing in Guildford, so we cycled there, saw a matinee and dined off fish and chips served in folded newspapers. My companion passed the School Cert and I returned about a pence in change to Dr Lion.'

The wartime environment did not favour innocuous pranks by randy teenagers. The military base of Canadian soldiers in the small town of Hindhead, a few miles from Haslemere, was a particular source of concern to mothers and of course, to Dr Lion who warned her girls to avoid any contact with the soldiers. Wolf describes an innocent prank that backfired when carried out in the generalised atmosphere of fear that prevailed at the time.

It was 1944. I was living on The Farm, where Fred Drechsler was supposed to be in charge. He was the last Farm Boy, about nineteen. The ambush was his idea. To house an overflow, the school had rented a house on Farnham Lane, 'Rowallan', for some of the older girls (about my age, fourteen to sixteen). Miss Barnes was in charge. She had been raised in Canada and knew how to handle Canadians and would regale wide-eyed girls with her adventures on dates with Canadian soldiers. I'm sure Dr Lion never heard these stories. Also those Canadians must have been pretty desperate for female companionship – Miss Barnes was a large lady with a moustache. Anyway, the girls became apprehensive about their nightly trek to Rowallan in the blackout, about a half mile or more. Fred D. rounded up Beethoven and me (possibly someone else) to hide in the bushes and waylay the girls. When a group approached, he said, 'Hello, Sweetie' in his best North American, probably picked up in movies. The result was explosively dramatic. The girls turned on their heels and ran back to school, screaming at the top of their lungs. We ran after them to shut them up. The girls never looked back to see who was pursuing them, just ran faster and screamed louder. By the time we caught up with them, neighbours had called the police. Fred had made himself scarce (we didn't squeal) leaving Beethoven and me alone to face the music. We weren't punished but Dr L's wrath was unmistakable. One of the girls was Gerda Stein [Meyer]; I don't remember the other victims.

Of such importance were girls to the boys (and vice versa) that one day, the Hut Boys decided to deal once and for all with the mysterious creatures at their school. Peter recalled,

> One day five of the Hut Boys were lounging, staring out of the hut window towards the front entry of the school, when someone announced that they had heard or read that we were of the age when one is supposed to have a girlfriend. A novel idea which had not crossed our minds before. There was some disorganised ruminating as we tried to digest this. We did not question it; rather, it was startling news. So what do you do with this? It was actually a rather frightening proposal. Girls were confusing. It was all right to share classes, work, and even games with them, but nothing too close. In retrospect, I have the feeling that none of us were too enthusiastic about the business. (Note: By the age of thirteen, quiet Martin, along with Tom the Boldest, already had girlfriends and were the envy of the others.) Someone came up with a brilliant idea. Why not pick one girl, who could then be everyone's girlfriend? Sounded good and nominations were in order. Someone suggested Gina Schaefer. At first that had unanimous support. She was cute, our age, and friendly. But then a challenge came up. 'We can't do this because she is Felix's girlfriend.' No question about it. We knew he had expressed some interest in her and we had all witnessed him talking to her, in public, in the driveway by the front door. That clearly meant he had first claim and no gentleman interfered with that. As we pondered again, we looked across at Dr Lion's bungalow. That was the answer! Mischi had recently been moved into the classroom which was at one end of the Bungalow 'because she was growing up'. We weren't quite clear about all of that but knew enough not to bother Mischi. In other words, her bedroom was directly in front of our window! She was nominated and, in a rush, approved as the group girlfriend. Next came the pledge to never tell her or anyone else. In a way this was a great relief. We had done our duty and as far as I can remember, the subject never came up again. If there were fantasies which followed this, they were personal and nobody's business. I don't remember if we ever told the other Hut Boys that they now had a girlfriend. They probably never knew that we had taken care of this for them.[36]

Felix and Obo were attracted to the same girl at the same time but the coincidence was scarcely a problem and in fact, it probably bonded the boys more closely together. Obo recalls, 'We became aware of girls like Rosemary Ward, a very pretty English girl, whose reason for being at Stoatley Rough I never knew, and we would find excuses to follow her when she went riding and discovered that she looked very sexy in her riding outfit. Then our interest of the opposite sex took a quantum leap to a very attractive young blonde English teacher named Miss Bailey (not Miss Bates). I don't know what she taught but she came to Stoatley Rough probably in late 1944 and had among other things, a great sense of humour and for some reason liked us. I remember that she must have been in the women's branch of the RAF because we thought she looked "smashing" in her uniform. Felix and I would frequently cross the Heath to the Corner Shop in Hindhead where we bought our cigarettes (where did we get the money?) and thought we were really going to score big points when we attempted to present Miss B with a five-pack of smokes which of course she promptly refused to accept.'

While the Hut Boys pondered the mysteries of adulthood, the war ground on. In January 1942, the first American forces arrived in Great Britain, bringing a whole new array of airplanes to be identified. Rommel began offensives and counter-offensives against a sequence of British generals in North Africa. In one of the countless shameful public acts of the Third Reich, SS Leader Heydrich held the Wannsee Conference, just miles from Wolf's former home, to coordinate 'The Final Solution of the Jewish Question'. Meanwhile the school carried on, continuing to cope with its high turnover of students. The boys in the Hut acquired a new supervisor, Miss Graetz (later would come Mrs Herman). Wolf recalled, 'She was in her early twenties; the Hut Boys were advancing through puberty and beginning to value privacy. Only her sense of humour saved her and us from embarrassments.' The boys had begun to care about their personal appearance, and Goldy's hairnet became an object of particular interest, something he wore at night to tamp down his especially bushy mane. 'We remember that Goldy wore a hairnet to bed to keep his hair neat. Such garb was a novelty to the rest of us. As long as the girls did not see us wearing the hairnet, some of us occasionally borrowed the net after washing our hair.'[37]

The boys followed the field action on maps. German troops overran Odessa and reached Sevastopol in the Soviet Union in July 1942, while the Americans began to conduct sporadic air attacks on German-held cities in Europe in August.[38] The decisive months were October with Montgomery's victory over Rommel at El Alamein and early November with Eisenhower's landing in then-French North Africa. By the end of the year, the Russians had surrounded the German Sixth Army at Stalingrad. Goldy recalled, 'We had maps with little flags where we followed the Russian, North-African and European theatres of operation as the front-line see-sawed back and forth. We learned the names of towns and cities where there was fighting, many that no one can recall any more. The big armies we followed were like the sports teams that we follow today.'[39]

Every fourth Sunday was visiting day. Goldy's mother (who had found work as a day domestic servant nearby) would visit Goldy and notice Obo hanging around. In fact, she and Goldy might start to take a walk in the grounds, and there would be Obo, following them like a duckling follows its mother. The kindly woman began to include Obo in the little trips she made with Goldy outside the school. She knew that while letters kept arriving for Martin, Wolf and the Gaupps, there were none for Obo. No one ever spoke to him about this worrisome fact. There was always hope. He knew his parents had by now joined his brother Arthur in Holland and presumably were safe. They just didn't have time to write. Obo continued to write letters to his parents and Arthur through the Red Cross.

In June 1942, six months after Pearl Harbor, Herta received the news from Hans that he had enlisted in the US Army, a patriotic act that made him a citizen of the United States. In September 1941, Herta had left the school and was living with her parents while doing secretarial work in London. Hans wrote about his new experience with the military, that he felt he was 'an odd bird' with his German accent, but noting that the men seldom made fun of him. (He told Herta later that after basic training, he was assigned to the military police and spent several months escorting ranking officers around town or riding shotgun on one of the trains that carried boisterous troops between southern training posts and New York.) It was wonderful to hear from Hans. Herta would never forget him, but now she had moved on and had begun to date young men she was meeting through friends in London. The pair had not pledged fidelity to each other when they had parted in late 1939, neither knowing if they would ever meet again. Herta wrote back to Hans about her job and of her life in the big city and about their mutual acquaintances. Neither dared to make long-term plans. Their relationship remained suspended in the vacuum created by the intrusive, overshadowing, ever present war. All they could do was let their lives unfurl. And wait.

Big jobs

In 1943, sixteen new students entered Stoatley Rough, and some of them were British. For the first time, children from the school's host country comprised a quarter of the total incoming group. The next year six, or about a third of the nineteen new students, were English. In 1945, of twenty-six newcomers, nine were English and by the end of the decade, England would be the predominant country of origin of the incoming pupils. Each year after 1943 the school's overall population declined, starting with the drop in 1944 from sixty-five to fifty-two pupils.

In 1943, the Hut Boys were fifteen, speaking with newly deepened voices and requiring longer sleeves and pant-lengths. Supplementing their weekly chores came new responsibilities and new privileges. Wolf said, they now 'could walk to town by ourselves or ride our bikes. A group of Hut Boys would walk to the Hindhead Corner Shop (now gone) on Sundays, to buy the *Sunday Express*. Goldy paid for it. I remember reading the exciting news of the victory of El Alamein and the Allied landings in North Africa. By 1943 I would regularly cycle to Haslemere at least once a week to run errands and replenish supplies for The Shop, run by Gina Schaefer [Mackenzie] and me.'

The war was far from over. Early in 1943 United States and Commonwealth troops were heading for Sicily, still to fight many bloody battles. Wolf reminds us that 'The U.S. Army under Patton and the Commonwealth Eighth Army under his arch-rival, Montgomery raced to Palmero, with Patton winning by a couple of hours. In the meantime, the Germans escaped by sea in their version of Dunkirk.' At this time came the news Wolf had been waiting for with a mixture of elation and dread. He would leave the school. With his parents safely in the United States, they had been able to get visas for the whole family to join them (although travel by sea was still prohibited as it was highly dangerous). Dr Lion promoted Wolf to a higher Group level in order to help him get ready to take the school certificate examinations. 'I was deemed to have outgrown the Hut and was transferred to the Farm. The Hut Boy gang broke up, as *Squink* (Peter Gaupp) left Stoatley Rough [for Shoreham] and Obo and Tom joined me on the farm.' Long-haired Beethoven, after living on the Farm for two years, would leave within a few months. Wolf learned the pleasures of listening to the radio (for there was very little other entertainment for the children aside from the occasional excursion

to the Rex Cinema). 'The radio gave electric shocks to anyone trying
to tune it, but it allowed us to keep up with the BBC news, listen to ITMA
("It's That Man Again", the Tommy Handley Show), enjoy the latest hits
played by Geraldo and his Band and the voice of Vera Lynn ("The Forces'
Sweetheart") and wait for Vic Oliver's inevitable father-in-law joke. Vic
Oliver was the stage name of a fellow-refugee from Vienna who had done
very well for himself. Everyone knew that his father-in-law was Winston
Churchill. After the invasion of Normandy, we could listen to Captain
Glenn Miller and his Band on the Allied Expeditionary Forces Program
of the BBC until the sad day when Captain Miller was reported missing,
presumed dead.' The boys loved swing music. Wolf continued, 'Another
favourite radio station was *Soldatensender* Calais, a BBC station
masquerading as a German station for the *Wehrmacht*. Its barracks-
room German made a nice contrast to genteel BBC English.'[40] Martin
said, 'The program was broadcast widely on the Continent, intended
to discourage German soldiers by giving real news about German defeats
and Allied victories, all interspersed with skits, jokes and music.'

Martin remained in the Hut with Felix, Goldy, and Francis Le
Messurier, but older girls and other friends were also sent to live on the
Farm, such as Ruth Ultman [Lichtenstein] and Ilse Meyer [Morgenstern].
Mr Hughes, the sturdy Welshman, had left by then to further his farm
training. That left eighteen-year-old Fritz Drechsler [Fred Drexler] in
charge, the last of the original 'Farm Boys', who still ran what was left of
the farm. With wonderful common sense logic (after all, the kids had
now been living years without parental supervision), the new 'man' in
charge made no attempt to enforce the rules that still reigned up at the
main house. Wolf said, 'Fred lived in a small room off the common room
and had no objections to anything we did, as long as he was invited.'
Wolf also informs us that by then, 'the Farmhouse also housed Benjy the
Cat, and Fred's nervous dog, Betty, and her two pups, Winston and
Franklin. I now had what I valued most: freedom from supervision.' Such
freedom once led to a mistake in judgment. Wolf and Beethoven decided
they needed to do something about the cold. Beethoven went to the pump
house to scrounge some diesel fuel. Mistakenly, he took petrol intended
for the tractor. He 'chucked it onto the wood stove and whoosh, the
flames roared up to the ceiling'. Some of the fuel spilled onto the floor
and the wooden planks began to burn. The boys worked feverishly
to extinguish the fire. Wolf grabbed a coat belonging to one of the Farm
boys that hung on a hook near the door and began beating the flames.

After a few minutes, the boys managed to put out the flames, burning their fingers in the process. They looked around at the damage, acutely aware that not only had they almost burned down the building, but that they had done so with rationed fuel, a serious matter. They set to work. First they scrubbed the floor clean of any charred remains and then checked the coat. Remarkably, it was not ruined. They managed to remove most of the gasoline smell from it with soap and water, and when the hapless owner came back, they concocted a story delivered so well that the boy believed them. They were able to expunge the gasoline smell in the room by putting wet leaves on the fire, leaving the top off the stove and filling the room with smoke. Disaster had been averted, and no one in authority ever knew of the incident. Wolf remarked with no facetiousness, 'With Fred Drechsler in charge, nobody was in charge.' The general lack of supervision of the Farmhouse children presaged an atmosphere of freedom that would characterise the school after the war.

The Hut boys took on new and larger responsibilities. Obo, in particular, was given more duties than seem reasonable today. In one of Dr Lion's intuitive (often mistaken) and irrevocable decisions about a child's future potential, she assigned Obo to be an apprentice to Mr Phillips. Obo not only was destined to help with the gardening in the summer but had to feed the coal furnaces in the winter. The 'Ginger Nipper' so fondly named by the old man graduated, at fifteen, to a more dangerous responsibility – the operation and maintenance of the ancient kerosene-powered engine located just off the path to the Farm. This engine drove a deep-well water pump that served the main house. It had an enormous flywheel, a heavy wheel that spun and moved a belt that energized a pump that pumped water to the main building. 'I don't know how I qualified for these pyrotechnic activities but I did learn something without ever becoming a fireman or arsonist.'[41] This contraption was anything but safe.

At the bottom of the steep path just above the farm house was an old corrugated steel shed which housed a large horizontal single cylinder, kerosene fired engine with two 6 or 7 feet (1.8 to 2.1 metres) in diameter flywheels c.1895. In order to start this engine, a small chamber on the opposite end from the flywheels had to be preheated in order to compress the gasses derived from the kerosene. Once the kerosene was hot enough to give off the desired compressed gas mixture, Mr Philips used a removable handle which

he attached to the end of the fly wheel drive shaft and slowly started
to turn it until the pressure of the compressed gas took over and
the engine gained momentum, removing the handle as it came
up to speed. He later showed me how to do this whole process and
when the engine backfired, which it did quite frequently, it scared
the hell out of the young Ginger Nipper and I ran for the door more
than once. Talk about OSHA, I think they would have put a large
padlock on the door. One of the flywheels drove a flat leather belt
which in turn drove a pulley shaft, which in turn drove another
shaft and pulley. That arrangement drove the water pump which
supplied a good part of the water to the large tank on the top floor
of the main building several times a week as well as a small tank
located just outside the shed from which we got the farm house
water supply. There were also the remains of a pedestal which
at one time had a dynamo/electric generator mounted on it which
presumably provided electricity to a large storage battery in the
main house but this had not been there for many years.... This
pump, so necessary to the operational life of Stoatley Rough,
was one of the things that I remember vividly and really got
me interested in all things mechanical in later life.[42]

The Hut Boys had been Boy Scouts since late 1942, garnering merit badges.
Martin recalls, 'The Haslemere Fire Brigade trained us to fight fires. One
Saturday we learned how to hook up a hose, jump from a tower into
a round canvas held taut by waiting men below and to carry each other
up and down ladders.' Martin was teased because during the instructions
on handling the hoses, he called out, 'Water on!' while pointing the nozzle
straight at his face. 'If they'd turned the water on at that moment, it would
have knocked me clean into next week.' Scouting was not just a casual
dalliance. The school must have recognised that scouting gave the boys
male role models but also a way to earn recognition.

After one summer at a Zionist camp Martin became fanatical about
the Zionist movement. He wrote, 'During this time, I became a boy
scout, patrol leader and then troop leader. My patrol was the Stork
Patrol whose colours were blue and white, the colours of Israel.' He
thrived in scouts. 'Our scoutmaster was a gem from Haslemere where
he worked in a plumbing supply house. I remember he once took me for
a ride in a truck and the gas tank was right under my seat. The gasoline
leaked as I sat there, and my bottom was sore for days. We were an active

troop, taking a lot of merit badges. We took the fireman's merit badge and also the handyman's badge. We learnt to tie knots behind our backs and we drilled, marching some intricate formations, which we exhibited, in town. I thoroughly enjoyed scouting and the drilling.' Martin became a King's Scout, the equivalent of an Eagle Scout in America, an achievement of which he is still proud. Some time after Wolf had left the school in 1944, the Hut boys/boy scouts were granted permission to ride their bikes into London and back, a trip of 40 miles (64.37 kilometres) one way. (Earlier attempts to get Dr Lion's permission had been unsuccessful.) The merry pack set off with the promise to return in time for evening tea. They rode as far as Hyde Park in downtown London and stopped en route to look at the King's Beasts at Hampton Court Palace. The trip was arduous, legs pumping, sweating bodies, up and down over many hills along the way. On the return home, Tom Wongtschowski ran out of steam and fell behind. He dismounted, defeated, as the others circled around, egging him on. It was the good-hearted Goldy who chose to stay with Tom, coaxing him along, while the others heartlessly forged on towards home.

Martin and Goldy, at fifteen, became air-raid messengers, a job that forced them to confront their fear. Air raids now occurred on an average of once every two weeks (although from August 1940 to May 1941, there were hundreds). After the Battle of Britain the air raids became sporadic, they happened at night, and children only heard the airplane motors as search lights swept across the sky. The job of the air-raid messenger was to show up at the closest neighbour's, the Air Raid Warden, just beyond the Farnham Lane estates, during each raid and carry messages by bike in case the telephone lines went down. The boys took turns getting out of bed and walking their bikes through the dark, blacked out landscape. The Air Raid Warden's wife always gave them a cup of hot tea and cake before they returned home, but neither enjoyed the trip, going or returning – after all, a German parachutist might lie in wait just beyond the next hedge.

Wolf described the experience of the war in early 1944. 'London had formidable defences and the northern horizon (towards London from the school) would be red with flashes, probably from rocket and AA batteries (mostly in parks – all that hardware had to come down). There would also be flares, probably from German planes trying to locate landmarks. The morning after, we'd pick up strips of aluminium foil with paper backing (as in candy wrappers, but long and narrow) dropped by bombers to confuse radar. In 1943 while in bed on the Farm, I watched a German Dornier bomber (we learned its identity later) crash in flames. In 1944 we cycled to the Beacon Hill Golf Course, near Hindhead, to look at a crashed Heinkel 177, one of the few German four-engined heavy bombers. Dr Lion heard about it and was not pleased.'

Wolf began studying for his Matric, and Dr Lion asked him and Gina Schaefer [Mackenzie] to co-manage the Shop. The Shop was an essential institution at the school, operational almost from its inception. Wolf recounts the details of his responsibilities:

> My period on the farm was one of maturing in matters other than sex. Although my National Geographic card file showed little progress [Dr Lion had asked Wolf to catalogue the contents of a huge pile of the old magazines], Dr Lion promoted me to a position of real responsibility. Gina Schaefer (Mackenzie) and I were put in charge of the Shop, a weekly Wednesday evening affair, where pupils and staff could buy necessities like pencils, toothbrushes, and the like. Most important of all, I was put in charge of the sweets (candy) ration of three ounces per person per week. One ounce was dished out free of charge for dessert, the other two were sold in the Shop. I was entrusted with the sweets-rations coupons for the entire school. The exercise of this new responsibility required much diplomacy. Gina and I operated under supervision of Miss Nacken, who believed in high thinking and plain living. Her idea of sweets was something nutritious, like plain dark chocolate. The kids much preferred something gooey, like Mars bars, even though they were said to cause pimples and rotten teeth. With Solomonic wisdom, I tried to get one-third of the ration in plain chocolate, to be handed out free of charge as dessert, and the rest as candy bars, which had to be bought with our meagre pocket money, half-a-crown per month (fifty cents at the then prevailing rate of exchange). The soap ration was another point at issue. The plain soap that was issued free of charge was sufficient for us boys, but the girls had reached an age at which they demanded some choice. Miss Nacken approved, provided the alternative was a strong disinfectant soap. That was not what the girls had in mind. To please everybody, we carried two kinds of soap: a daintily perfumed variety, which sold briskly, and a smelly carbolic soap for Miss Nacken's eyes and nose. Nobody ever bought a piece, not even Miss Nacken.[43]

Wolf and Gina employed creative (but scrupulously honest) bookkeeping. 'Miss Nacken taught Gina and me a simple kind of double-entry bookkeeping and inspected the books at the end of every month. Our total capitalisation was exactly £11. 1s. 6d. (about $45, pre-inflation) and on inspection day the value of our stock of merchandise plus cash in hand had to total that magic number. After much sweating, Gina and I always managed to balance the books, at which point I had a great urge to kiss Gina. I was much too shy and never did. Gina, what would you have done if I had?' (Fifty years later, Gina met Wolf at a reunion and responded, 'I would have been honoured.' Wolf's own response: 'Life's saddest words … Checkhov wrote plays about situations like this.')

I will now reveal another secret for the first time: our books never balanced precisely; we were always a few pence over or under £11 1s. 6d. Unknown to Miss Nacken, Gina and I had an old cigar box, into which we deposited the surplus of good months and from which we made up deficits. Fortunately, the box never ran out of change. It's too bad that the US Treasury can't operate on the same principle. The shop gave me a great opportunity to get away from school and supervision. On Thursday afternoons, I regularly cycled down Farnham Lane to Haslemere, to replenish our inventory. Word soon got around and I was handed many other errands … shoes to be repaired, stamps to be bought, prescriptions from Boots the Chemist, groceries for the kitchen, etc. I got to know and respect many of the local tradesmen, like Boots' the chemist, which moved to the opposite side of High Street as of 2004; Nobs the Stationers, still in business as of 2004; and Metcalf and Yates, the butchers (their former shop is now an expensive Italian restaurant). The carrier on the back of my bike was always loaded. Once, my cargo included a sick little girl to take to the doctor. She was obviously frightened to death but never let out a peep, even when the bike blew a tire. Another time, Miss Demuth asked me to pick up an order at the butcher's. It turned out to be about thirty pounds of bloody lengths [of oxtail] very difficult to balance on the back of a bike. They fell off a few times but made good soup anyway.

Sometimes the administrators asked the boys to pick up cigarettes for them. Obo recalled, 'I think Dr Lion smoked DuMaurier Ovals which came in a square box and the smaller quantities came in a cardboard box.

I do remember going to the sweet shop next to the Haslemere railway station to purchase smokes for her. I don't know why the man, then already elderly, somehow didn't ask me how old I was. If I had discovered wine and beer I wonder what would have happened if I'd tried to buy some from him.' Wolf remembered Dr Lion making a little joke while buying candy in town. 'Even before they were rationed, the limited supply was restricted to people with children.' Not aware of the restriction, she tried to buy some and was asked, 'How many children do you have, madam?' Her answer was, 'Oh, about one hundred.'

Wolf reminds us that the children always walked or rode bikes; the single car at the school was the exclusive provenance of the adults. 'The trip home was always the hardest since it was uphill all the way. Occasionally Dr Leven would zoom by in the school car (grey Austin 8 convertible, license plate HPL 715 – another piece of remembered trivia). She never stopped and never offered to carry my load, let alone the bike and me.' In our era, where most parents have become obsessed with children's safety, it's hard to imagine the risks the staff allowed the children to take. Cycling into town with its numerous traffic junctions and roundabouts was potentially dangerous, yet according to Wolf it was not dangerous at all, just 'little Haslemere with little civilian traffic'. He was nevertheless not immune to the dangers of being hit by a vehicle. One day he was riding on what was called the High Pavement. 'The narrow roadway was (and still is) flanked by a brick embankment more than 6 feet high. Unexpectedly encountering an outsize tank while riding a bike, a split-second choice had to be made: Get squashed or bail out and hit the bricks. I made the right choice but required stitches on my forehead. If you look carefully, you can still see a faint scar. The tank was unhurt.' Wolf's comment about the incident: 'I didn't feel that I almost got killed, just that I had made an obvious choice. In view of all the risks of the times – Nazis, bombs, etc. – the ordinary risks of daily lives seemed so trivial that we gave them little or no thought.'

The Hut Boys recognised the historical significance of the war and the impact upon their lives. Wolf said, 'In the midst of a pervasive war, we did not look on ourselves as sheltered. Planes, most of them friendly, were always within earshot as were training exercises of the Second Canadian Armoured Brigade. One beautiful summer day, somebody remarked that "if it weren't for the gunfire, you wouldn't know there's a war on". No irony was intended. The Springs of 1943 and 1944 brought "little *Blitzes*", when the night sky was lit by flares and tracers and glowed red in the direction of London. One night, a flaming German bomber spiralled to earth. In excitement and immaturity, I cheered. The next day, one of the grown-ups sharply reminded me that men had died in that plane, men who might once have been neighbours. The incident brought home to me the dilemma of our times; our former neighbours served a cause dedicated to our extermination; the men who risked their lives to save ours might look on us as enemy aliens. We did not lead sheltered lives.'[44]

Wolf began to think like an adult. 'After our fifteenth birthdays, we became fire guards and stayed up all night once a month in an air raid; we were supposed to get on the roof of the main building and watch for incendiary bombs. Fortunately, there were no air raids when I was on duty, and I could use the long nights to satisfy my thirst for modern history in the school library.... I tried, and am still trying, to discover the reasons behind the events that had placed us where we were. Nothing I read, then and since, has come close to conveying the feelings of what we saw and lived every day.' Obo expressed similar thoughts. 'I often think, what did we really know and understand and relate to with regard to these horrific events during our stay at Stoatley Rough? For that matter, what did the staff know and what should they have told us and if so, were we ready to understand and relate to it?'

In 1943, the Hut Boys were still speaking too much German with each other. Dr Lion made them an offer. If they spoke only English for six weeks, she would reward them with cash. The boys decided to take up the challenge (in spite of the fact that Tom Wongtschowski might be a holdout). For those six weeks they had no trouble keeping their pledge during daylight hours, but at night with the lights out, Tom was always lapsing. By and large they managed to convert him and they were rewarded with a modest sum. They held a caucus to determine what to do with their winnings. After much deliberation, they decided to become entrepreneurs. They would raise rabbits. They bought two females. Someone found a pamphlet on raising rabbits (probably a free pamphlet issued by the Ministry of Food) and the boys learned how to determine the gender of a rabbit through all that black and white fur. The boys built a hutch in front of the Hut and took turns rising at the crack of dawn to search for dandelion leaves or to beg vegetable scraps from the kitchen. When the does were old enough, they took them to a Shottermill school friend who owned a buck. 'It was slam, bam, thank you ma'am, very educational.' The stud fee was one of the litter.

One day, Peter saw a young one fighting with one of the does. 'We tried separating them but it did not work. And then, a few weeks later, one of them started getting fat – it was pregnant. It turned out to be female and the fighting wasn't fighting at all.' One of the male offspring had impregnated one of the does (one hopes not its own mother).

Over time, the boys grew tired of raising rabbits but for awhile, there was a time of real, if paltry, money-making. The first time they decided to sell a rabbit to the butcher in town, Wolf was chosen to take it in. He borrowed a bike, popped the rabbit in a burlap-covered box and cycled into Haslemere to the butcher shop. He carried in his bundle and handed it over, expecting to be paid and to get out the door. It was not to be. 'The butcher dispatched it with a quick chop before my eyes, as soon as I handed it to him.' Wolf was still in shock when the butcher handed over the money. 'He paid us five shillings, equivalent to two months' pocket money.' The rabbit family multiplied and Wolf got used to delivering the rabbits to town. One day he carried two rabbits in the burlap box. Riding down Farnham Lane, he met two strangers who stopped him for directions. He got off his bike and put the box on the ground. As he stood chatting, the box started jumping up and down 'to the astonishment of the onlookers' until Wolf explained its contents. Even on their last journey, the doomed rabbits had found love.

The enterprise lasted through the next year, Obo and Wolf taking the rabbits with them to the Farm. When Wolf left the school in the Fall of 1944, Obo became the sole proprietor of the remaining stock. It's not clear how many generations of rabbits the Hut Boys raised, or how successful an enterprise it was. We know that at least one time a rabbit ended up on the boys' dinner table.

Obo picks up the story. 'The party was on the night of 5–6 June 1944, for my (June 2) and Martin's (June 16) birthdays. Afterwards, boys and girls went for a moonlight walk, interrupted by low-flying (under German radar) RAF heavy bombers, heading for Normandy. After awhile, we heard rumbles of distant explosions. As a joke, somebody said, "it must be the Invasion". (We had waited for years and wondered if it would ever come.) The next day the sky was full of American and British planes, their wings painted overnight with black and white recognition stripes. The first news of the Invasion came from the German radio, but gave the wrong location, a successful Allied feint.' Life was about to take a new turn for the denizens of Stoatley Rough.

But on the night before the invasion, the teenagers had their party. One of the Farm boys butchered one of their rabbits for them while a few girls 'liberated' some shortening and sugar from the kitchen. Still others stole apples for the feast they planned. The boys fried the pieces in stolen margarine. They all sat down at the table. Martin, unaware of the project, arrived from the Hut and sat down at the table, commenting on the delicious aroma of the 'chicken'. 'When they told me what the main dish was, I was appalled. How could they have been so heartless? I jumped up and left the table, refusing to eat the vile thing, raising hoots and jeers from the others.'

D-Day

Nineteen forty-four saw German losses (Italy had suffered defeat in 1943 and was out of the fight). Wolf recalled that some Italian POWs worked on nearby farms), with Soviet troops advancing into Poland and Italy becoming the new major battleground. The British prepared to drop 3,000 tons of bombs on Hamburg as the Allies entered Rome. The sixth of June 1944 was momentous. It signalled the invasion of the Continent by way of Normandy – the push to Paris.[45] D-Day (not 'debarkation' day but merely a military shorthand to name events before an event such as D-3, D-2) was not only a thrilling turning point but also a time of reflection for the children at Stoatley Rough. It marked the beginning of the end of their lives under the sheltering wing of their school and home. With the end of the war they would have to leave Stoatley Rough with its routines, familiar surroundings, friends and reliable and kindly adults. A reunion with family was a prospect loaded with uncertainty. Few wished to leave the security, the predictability and the familiar. Each child experienced this knowledge in his or her unique way.

The pupils knew for well over a year that the Allied attack was imminent. The build-up was all around them. For weeks the Allies had been steadily bombing the coastal areas of France, only 75 miles (120.7 kilometres) away from Stoatley Rough (35 miles [56.32 kilometres] to Portsmouth, 40 miles [64.37 kilometres] across the channel). Goldy wrote, 'We had been used to the constant sound of Allied planes which often had their rendezvous above us before they set out to bomb Germany as we guessed where they were going. Around D-day it was a little different, however. For one thing, the activity was so frequent that most of us had to sleep through it if we were to have any rest at all. It continued daily and by night for perhaps four weeks. Only on D-day was everyone up to watch a sky constantly full of planes, the DC-3's [C-47's] pulling gliders so low that the trees bent in their wake.' The children saw massive ground mobilization as well. 'D-day, and the days before and later were exciting ones for us. Tanks, trucks and masses of troops, mostly British, Canadians, and Americans, were noisily making their way down the crowded Portsmouth Road to the coast and this traffic went on forever.'[46]

On the day before D-Day, the pupils and teachers listened to the radio as usual in the large Sitting Room, grouped in front of the large bay windows or by the fireplace; they stood or sat tucked in various places in the next room; some were on the terrace. Quotations were recited for the amusement and enlightenment of the pupils and of those who lived and worked on the Farm as well as of the teachers and staff standing in attendance. Then Dr Lion turned on the radio, the moment all had awaited. Would today be the day? The broadcast began with the usual anthems of the nations comprising the Allies. It was a game among the children to be the first to match the country to the anthem. Then came national and international events. (People living on the Farm were accustomed to listening to a second helping of news every night on the radio and, old enough to understand the larger dimensions of the war, they hung on every word, interjected their reactions, and held long discussions in the evenings when the news was over. They also greatly enjoyed the German propaganda broadcasts and scoffed loudly at their former countrymen.) But on that day, there was no news of invasion and everyone filed up the stairs to their designated tables. Dinner was served. The day ended and everyone went to bed wondering if the next day would be the day they had been waiting for. The next day around mid-morning, the children learned that the invasion had indeed begun. And during the mid-day news of 6 June, the Supreme Commander of the Allied Forces, General Dwight D. Eisenhower, came on the radio to announce the great offensive. When he finished talking, Beethoven's Fifth Symphony flowed majestically through the airwaves.

That night, some of the boys went to the Cooney's house on the edge of the Farm to listen to their radio. Once again Eisenhower's high-pitched, constricted voice filled the room, and someone said, 'He sounds just like Donald Duck', and someone else said, 'Yeah, well he's American, isn't he?'[47] Donald Duck, Mickey Mouse and the rest of the Disney gang were world-famous in the 1930s, so famous that the youngest child could recognise the voice of the frustrated duck. (On the same token, Laurel and Hardy were also loved, even by the Germans who called them *Dick und Doof* [Fat and Silly]. But the voice of Donald Duck was the most imitated and many children tried to produce the sound. Before the war, the very young Peter Gaupp – he must have been six or seven – had gone to see a movie with his mother. The newsreel featured Joseph Goebbles, Hitler's powerful minister of Nazi propaganda, who also had a high voice. 'I asked in an apparently loud voice if that was Donald Duck. We left very quickly.') The comments made that evening in the Cooney's kitchen about Eisenhower's voice intended no disrespect, although Wolf points out that the Cooneys weren't only making fun of Americans and their accents. King George VI came in for his share of unwished-for attention. The warmly regarded king had struggled all his life against stuttering and any public appearance must have been an agony for him. On that evening broadcast, the king momentarily had to pause in the middle of his address. One of the Cooneys remarked, 'Shouldn't we now be singing *God Save the King*?'

Obo heard the aircraft that morning and had run outdoors. 'On the morning of 6 June 1944, we saw thousands of Allied planes with black and white stripes painted on the underside of their wings, headed for the south coast of England. We knew then that D-Day had come and the Allies had landed on the coast of Normandy in France. Although the war was far from over, we could feel for the first time in five years that it was coming to an end.' The planes carried tons of bombs intended for Normandy beaches, the largest of which could carry around 8 tons. Painted stripes on the planes were intended to prevent them from being shot down by Allied guns. Martin, standing a little apart from the others, gazed up in wonder. His focus was on the hundreds of gliders being towed by the DC-3s that he knew transported men. There were thousands of missions flown on D-Day by US and British planes, mostly fighters, with light and medium bombers and transports. The boys and girls saw it all.

D-Day brought private sorrow for more than a few. Fifteen-year-old Ruth Ultman [Muessig] had lost her mother several years before she came to Stoatley Rough, but her father and young brother had made it to England. Her father planned to take the family to America where they would 'have a future'. She resisted the idea, but he was adamant – he would go and she would have to decide whether to join him. She had no intention of going to America, a country she knew nothing about. All she wanted to do was to live at Stoatley Rough until she could find work in England. D-Day destroyed her security. She recalled, 'We were waiting for the news to begin and the usual voice came on: "This is the BBC Home and Forces programme. Here is the news and this is Robert Robinson reading it. Allied forces have landed on the beaches at Normandy and are making their way to the capital, etc. etc." He spoke about soldiers being greeted by children strewing flowers on them and women throwing kisses as they marched towards Paris. There was a hush in the room and the next thing we heard was *The Marseillaise*. I for one silently burst into tears. I realised instantly it was the beginning of the end, and I was torn because I knew that it also meant I would have to leave the family who had taken me in as one of their own, Stoatley Rough, my "other home" and England which I loved so dearly. To this day I cannot hear the French National Anthem without thinking of that day. I know exactly where I was standing (in front of a bookcase next to the curtain that divided the Zoo from the Bower [girls' sleeping quarters in the manse] and I was not paying attention as usual, daydreaming, not even facing the way I was supposed to be until I heard those fateful first words. I remember later that day running out into the garden to be alone and going to the bench under the wall facing the Downs. I looked hard at them, because I wanted to remember them forever and I told myself that was what I was doing, memorizing that one peak on the right-hand side and the built-up part in the middle with the depression on the far left.'[48] Stoatley Rough remained with Ruth long after she left the school. 'One reason my little house here in Connecticut attracted me right away was that it faces a mountain, the Sleeping Giant, and it looks remarkably like the Surrey Downs. When my Public Radio station plays Beethoven's Fifth Symphony and I look out of the window, I am back in the Music Room at Stoatley Rough.' (Ruth crossed the Atlantic on the Cunard liner, *Aquitania*, that had been converted into a troopship, in April, 1945.) Later, Wolf, by then also in New York, occasionally ran into Ruth at the Times Square subway station. 'She'd be heading downtown to work and I'd head uptown to City College.... I too was homesick for England in my first months in America.... The smug attitudes of Americans toward the war – distant from the action, safe, well fed, obviously prosperous – came as a shock after the sacrifices and privations of shabby, rationed, blackout and bombed Britain.' Wolf adds with uncharacteristic bitterness, 'I was *never* homesick for Germany.'

Wolf expressed his feelings about American attitudes towards the world wars. 'The differences in experiences between Europe and America lie at the root of current attitudes and conflicts. Two world wars, with millions of dead on both sides, have devastated and traumatized Europe. On the plus side, the Europeans will not fight each other in a major war for the first time since the collapse of the Roman Empire.... By comparison, America got off lightly in two world wars and mostly remembers the Greatest Generation, John Wayne and inevitable victory. For experiences comparable to the European, one has to go to the South after the Civil War. When I was in the Army, stationed in Virginia 1952–1955, the time of *Brown v. Board of Education*, we were treated as the Yankee Army of Occupation.'

After the invasion started, life changed for Stoatley Rough, although the children would have plenty of time to adjust. The war still had to play out to its bloody (albeit inevitable) conclusion for almost another year, with squadrons of airplanes still blanketing the sky and convoys of war vehicles constantly moving through Haslemere. Goldy recalled, 'I was at the Haslemere train station a few days after D-Day and saw long lines of ambulances, most of them American, waiting to pick up the wounded who were expected by train from Portsmouth.'[49] Although it may have seemed that the end was in sight, there was much more blood to be shed, many more buildings to be destroyed. Wolf wrote, 'For nearly two months, the German lines in Normandy held and the battle was in balance. Many more battles were to follow, e.g., the Battle of the Bulge. For America, especially, the climax came after D-Day. Until that time, British and Commonwealth troops had outnumbered Americans in North Africa and Europe. From the build-up after D-Day, Americans became dominant in numbers and in casualties.' The war wasn't over and the children came to fear one last act of evil from the hands of Hitler via his new bomb, the V-1 rocket, or 'doodlebug'.

During the summer of 1944, the same summer the Nazis liquidated the town of Oradour-sur-Glane in France in retaliation for the murders of SS officers by guerrilla resistance fighters, they also unleashed their first doodlebug on Britain, also called buzz bomb by American reporters. The bombs came flying towards London from various sites held by the Germans in Belgium and France in the form of small unmanned jet planes (the V-2 was a rocket), kept level by simple gyrocompasses. The bombs made an odd putt-putt sound before their motors stopped, ominous because one could hear it coming, then its motors conked out just

before it hit, and one never knew exactly where it would explode.⁵⁰
The children of Stoatley Rough experienced sufficient near-misses
to have good cause to be afraid. David King, who as a seven year old,
was living in London at the time, was home alone when his house caved
in around him. Instructed always to go under the big oak table if there
wasn't enough time to get to a shelter, he dutifully had crawled under the
oilcloth tablecloth taking with him his toy soldier, his little lead spitfire
airplane, one blade of the propeller missing, and his 'special torch which
had a shaded light beam and a kind of brown paper over the glass'. Ten
hours later, he was rescued, unhurt, covered in plaster and dust, saved
by the table that had withstood the blast that took down the rest of his
house. He recalled the sound of the V-1 with clarity. 'It starts to splutter
when the propellant runs out. Then there is a terrifying silence; it lasts
forever, or so it seems. This is followed by a screaming dive as the flying
bomb heads for its target. If you hear the next thing then you live; it's a
deafening explosion.'⁵¹ Obo remembered, 'We could hear these pilotless
bombs passing overhead and when their engines stopped we would hold
our breath and hope they would glide far enough away so that when they
hit the ground and exploded, we would have been able to take shelter.'
Martin happened to be standing in for an ailing teacher with a class
of young children when the distinct sound of a doodlebug filled the
school. At sixteen, Martin not only held the honour of being head
of student council but also had earned the rank of Boy Scout Senior
Patrol Leader, both achievements of which made him feel 'very
important'. Things were well underway in the classroom when the
buzzing started then stopped. All eyes looked toward the window.
Martin yelled, 'Dive!' Everyone disappeared under the table, waiting
for the explosion. They waited and waited, and nothing happened.
'Eventually I crept out from under my desk, the rest resumed their
seats, and I finished the class. Afterwards I learnt to my embarrassment
that it hadn't been a doodlebug at all, but rather a B-17 that had lost
a propeller as it flew by.'⁵² At the same time, Wolf had been in Dr Wolff's
French class. She was so absorbed in the literature that she failed to note
at first that the students had all scuttled under the table. 'When the noise
stopped, we all dived for cover. Dr Wolff, who was hard of hearing
but refused to admit it, hadn't heard a thing. She got excited and angry.
She thought we were playing a trick.'

The summer months proved to be a time of contemplation and anxiety
for those who knew they would leave. Wolf wrote, 'What I had heard

about American high schools was not reassuring and I was determined to finish my secondary schooling in Britain. My goal was to take the School Certificate Examination in June 1944, two months short of my sixteenth birthday. The School Certificate, I should explain, was then the standard school-leaving examination throughout the British Empire. It was set by the universities (Cambridge, in my case) and, if passed at a high standard, entitled one to matriculate at a university. In order to prepare, my period of contemplation came to an abrupt end in late 1943. For many months, I studied hard far into the night. The time of the exam coincided with the weeks immediately after D-Day and the beginning of the V-1 flying bomb ("doodlebug") bombardment. A V-1 exploded during one of the tests; it raised adrenalin levels and cleared the brain. I passed with flying colours.'

In the over twelve months prior to the exam, Wolf spent his afternoons at the Farm purportedly to study. 'The greatest contribution to my maturing was the isolation of life on the Farm. On most days I went there after lunch ostensibly for prep. Actually I did very little work. Sometimes I read a non-required book; I remember pondering *The Bridge of San Luis Rey*. More often, I just wandered off. By the stream that fed the swimming pool, I watched frogs mate, tadpoles hatch, and newts and salamanders crawl. Mostly, I just walked and thought about whatever was important to me at the time. The thoughts allowed me to come to grips with who I was and how to cope with cruel and unusual times. My schoolwork suffered. Today, I would probably be classified as a withdrawn underachiever and potential candidate for the teenage ward of a psychiatric clinic. At Stoatley Rough I enjoyed a rare opportunity to mature at my own pace.'[53]

A few months before his exam, Wolf began to study very hard. He passed the Matric and realised he was ready to leave Stoatley Rough. He was no longer a student there, and although Dr Lion offered to let him stay to attend Godalming High School to study while working part-time on the Farm, he felt it was time to leave. 'The expected journey to America did not materialise because wartime conditions prohibited civilian travel. After much soul searching, I decided to leave Stoatley Rough, accept an invitation from relatives to live in Surbiton (a suburb of London) and attend Kingston-upon-Thames Technical College to make up deficiencies in physics and chemistry.' Wolf left the school 8 October 1944. The next Hut Boy to leave the security of Stoatley Rough would be Goldy. Meanwhile, Hans Loeser was on his way from the United States back to Germany seven years after he had left. He was now a member of the Allied army that was on its way to crush the army of his former countrymen.

A roughian returns as a yank

One of the more dramatic moments in the history of Stoatley Rough was the day Hans returned to the school in the uniform of an American Army officer. Not only would he go on to take part in the Battle of the Bulge but the former Roughian was on a personal mission. He was to meet Herta Lewent in London.

Three years earlier, on 3 September 1941, Herta had given her notice after four years of service to Dr Lion. (Katya Schaefer took her place.) At twenty-one, Herta had been more than ready to move out into the world. She took a secretarial job in London but continued to maintain contact with her friends, who included Nore Astfalck and Hanna Nacken, and she often returned to the school on weekends to sleep on the floor of their small room in the manse. Herta also did 'war work' in Dundee, Scotland, for a stint, living with Margaret Dove [Faulkner] and her husband.

There are boundless stories of quiet sacrifice in wartime, and in 1939, Hans' family had benefited from one unsung hero, a lowly waiter, who lived in Philadelphia. 'My parents found a black sheep cousin in America, a banquet waiter in Philadelphia, who gave an affidavit of support for the entire family. It was a generous and unselfish act by a virtual stranger. Supplemented by money from Walter Curchard, a second cousin, it did the trick.'[54] The parents, who had emigrated to Tel Aviv, Palestine, while they awaited visas to America, sold the Biedermeier furniture they had managed to save from their home in Kassel and booked passage on the Dutch liner *Staatendam* bound for New York for themselves and their two children, Hans and his sister Lisel who had been working in England while Hans finished his studies at Stoatley Rough. They all docked in New York in December 1939 to start afresh in America.

As the first bombs of the Battle of Britain dropped on to London and Stoatley Rough prepared its air-raid shelter, the Loeser family were settling into an austere apartment in Long Island City, New York. Hans and Lisel [Elizabeth Fontana], who also had attended Stoatley Rough for a brief time, took low-paying jobs while their father became a door-to-door Fuller-Brush salesman, enduring a humiliating and exhausting role that slowly killed the soul of the former owner and manager of his important department store in Kassel. This educated, elegant man, fluent in French, barely spoke the language of his new country. He later upgraded to another sales job, but like many refugee parents of Stoatley Roughians, he never adjusted to his reduced circumstances. 'Though my father was saved from extinction in a place such as Auschwitz, he was clearly a victim of the Nazis. His six weeks in Dachau did impair his health, robbed him of energy and resilience, and speeded up the loss of self-confidence and belief in the future which had begun with the sale of his business.'[55]

In the Fall of 1940, Hans enrolled in the City College of New York night school and Lisel learned she had received a full scholarship to Smith College. It had been arranged for her through a friend of Hanna Nacken who happened to be the president of the college. It's noteworthy that Lisel's academic preparation at Stoatley Rough was so good that she entered college as a junior. Hans worked by day restocking wallets and key cases in the luggage department of Gimbels' Department Store on thirty-fourth street, next to Macy's on Herald Square. He attended school at night. He learned a new skill: how to interact with Americans by 'kidding around'. He saw in this 'important facet of American life the necessity for surface friendliness with everybody.'[56] The family moved to Jackson Heights, made friends and assimilated, shedding their German clothes which represented the formality of the life they had left behind. (We are reminded of Wolf's father's displeasure when Wolf started wearing polo shirts and khakis to college classes. The old gentleman had the impression that Wolf had lowered himself by dressing like a 'member of the proletariat'.) Hans was promoted to assistant buyer at Gimbels (gone since 1986). All the while, he and Herta maintained their correspondence.

Five years and over 400 letters later, Herta knew Hans was coming to England. She must have wondered about his fate as she watched the planes fly overhead on D-Day (just a few weeks before Hans was to arrive). Hans was now a part of military intelligence. It had taken the army a few years to appreciate what they had in him: After basic training, the army assigned him to the military police; then they sent him to language school to learn Moroccan Arabic to prepare for the North Africa invasion (which happened before he graduated, in November, 1942). At last they placed him where he should have been all along, in Camp Ritchie, the military intelligence training camp in the Blue Ridge Mountains near Washington, D.C., a unit unique for its high number of future academics who 'attained fame in the 1950s and 1960s'.[57] Camp Ritchie was filled with other immigrants from Europe, like Hans, who would be used in the interrogation of captured Germans. A movie was made about these refugees who returned to Germany as US soldiers, called, appropriately, *The Ritchie Boys*.[58]

Hans' orders were to report to a private house in the small town of Broadway in the Cotswolds. Once he unpacked, the next action of the new Second Lieutenant was to secure a jeep, drive to a nearby town to find a telephone, and arrange to meet with Herta in London. Uncertain with each other at first, they soon discovered that five years of separation had not diminished their love. They knew that 'their lives belonged together'. Under military rules, they had to wait ninety days before they could marry. So Herta went back to work while Hans joined the Eighty-Second Airborne Division of seasoned veterans who had spearheaded the Normandy landings the night before D-Day. Accompanying them on their push through the Netherlands, Hans would interrogate prisoners of war with regard to the positions of their units and other such details, reading and analysing written material that had been seized by the advancing American armies. Hans spent time translating captured German documents, and practiced riding in gliders that carried a squad of twelve men plus a pilot and co-pilot. While the uninitiated might think of a glider ride as a quiet, meditative experience, Hans reports that the ride was anything but silent or gentle, with the prop wash of the tow plane making any loose canvas slap against the steel frame, whipping the gliders up and down and sideways with sickening consequences to the passengers.

On 16 September 1944, his division joined the 101st Airborne's assault to retake Holland in what would be known as Operation Market-Garden, portrayed in the Cornelius Ryan book of 1977, and later in the film *A Bridge Too Far*.[59] His glider unit joined hundreds of planes and gliders in an enormous formation, his plane arriving in the second wave (which Herta and most residents of south England surely watched), a horde of planes with parachutists and planes towing gliders as far as the eye could see. Hans wrote, 'As we headed towards the Continent hundreds of fighter planes came from all over England to fly cover above us and our fighter bombers paved the way below us. It was an unbelievably spectacular event. I know that many people in England who saw it from the ground will never forget the sight.'[60] He described the flak around the plane once his glider plane passed the coast.

One didn't hear them and seldom saw the flash of the gun muzzles. What we did see was the puffs of smoke in the air where the shells exploded. Occasionally, we saw a plane or a glider get hit and go down, but mostly the formation held.... Very shortly before we got to our drop zone, my tow plane's right wing was cut off by what looked like machine gun fire from the ground. There were certainly no German fighters in sight. We saw it happen and our pilot cut us loose, putting us in a steep dive down while the formation went on very briefly and then cut loose its gliders and dropped its paratroopers. We could see this in the distance as our glider lost altitude.... A slow landing glider is a sitting target. Our pilot headed for what seemed like a lonely farmhouse, tried to land in its garden, but would have hit the house if, in the last minute, he hadn't been able to lift the plane just over the roof of the house with its last bit of lift and then plunked it down in front of the house.... The farmer and his wife were flabbergasted to see us there but once they collected their wits were enormously helpful.... We managed to tow the glider, the canvas of which was in shreds, into a barn tail first, with the wings sticking out. We packed down a lot of bushes and trees to cover the wings ... so that they would not be easily discerned from the air.[61]

Hans and his comrades soon caught up with his division, and then he settled in a Dutch house at Nymegen for work as an interrogator of German prisoners for the next two months. Later he relocated to Reims, France. 'Life was easy, the champagne flowed freely. Officers were given a free ration of two bottles of liquor of their choice per month and could buy more at the PX or from the French people. The great champagne cellars of Reims had been raided by the first troops.... You waded in champagne. The soldiers had often broken the necks off bottles, drunk a little and tossed them away. Much went on that, in retrospect, one couldn't be particularly proud of. French girls were hungry and lonely and Americans were big and well fed and had food and nylons to give away. The synergies were clear.'[62]

In December 1944, the ninety-days waiting period was up. The Chief of Staff of his Division summoned Hans to his office. 'Lieutenant, do you still want to get married?' 'Yes sir.' 'All right. There is a troop carrier command pilot who also wants to get married.... I will issue orders for both of you to proceed to England on temporary duty.... Your duty will be to get married as promptly as possible, have a few days with your bride and then get your asses and the airplane back here to us. Take off!'

Hans could not return to England without paying a visit to Stoatley Rough. He drove up and we can only imagine the excitement in the school, the younger boys crowding around the grown man who had once been a Hut Boy like them, one of their own returning as an officer in the US army. Wolf recalled, 'I remember his visit. I was greatly impressed by his reappearance in the glamorous uniform of an American officer, made familiar by Hollywood. I suspect we all were. Here's a fantasy I cherished every time I pumped up Farnham Lane on the heavily laden one-speed bike borrowed from Felix (a green Hercules), after my weekly quest to replenish The Shop: One day I'd return, rich and famous, in a plush car. I wonder if Hans felt a sense of fulfilled fantasy.'[63]

After a civil wedding on 11 December 1944, and a brief honeymoon in Torquay on the south coast of England, 'the warmest place we could think of in England in December', Hans and Herta finalised their vows in a Jewish ceremony in London performed on 14 December by a Catholic US Army chaplain. Hans returned to take part in the Battle of the Bulge (Battle of Ardennes), in a region covering parts of northern France, Belgium and Luxembourg. Hans was based just behind the lines.

> There was deep snow on the ground and we had to sleep in foxholes in the snow and mud. It was cold and miserable.... We were under almost constant artillery fire. Day in and day out and throughout the night shells landed haphazardly among us, causing serious casualties even at Regimental Headquarters level. The combination of being cold and wet and being shot at is not a good one. The nights in particular were miserable and scary.... Yet once again I must emphasise that what I suffered was nothing compared to the front line troops who lived in equally miserable or worse foxholes but were, in addition to artillery fire, exposed to machine gun and small arms fire, had to go on nightly patrols to feel out where the enemy was, and were constantly subject to being attacked, overrun and killed by the still advancing Germans.... One night we ran into and captured alive the German Adjutant of a regiment of the 2nd S.S. Panzer Division. He was riding in a motorcycle side car. He had

on him … detailed plans … their routes to Liege and on towards
Antwerp. My men and I were the first to understand the significance
of that capture. It proved of great help to our superiors. All our
training and experience paid off generously that day. We were
delighted and were commended, though the real commendation
and medals went, as they should have, to the patrol that captured
that officer and his driver alive. [64]

A new kind of danger took centre stage. Hans spoke English with
a German accent. It was a chilling fact that Germans deployed men
in American uniforms who spoke perfect English. Hans once ran into
a group of such men with their throats cut, killed by US paratroopers.
(A similar murder of Germans masquerading as GIs is depicted in
Episode Three of 'Band of Brothers', the eleven-episode series produced
by HBO in 2001.) Richie Boys such as Hans were instructed never to
stray from the base, nor to walk alone. On New Year's Day, 1945, the
Battle of the Bulge was over. There were 80,000 American casualties,
of whom 16,000 had been killed.

For the victorious troops, life became easy (in stark contrast to the
fate of the vanquished German citizenry). Hans had a treat when he was
in Reims. Ingrid Bergman staged a special performance for the troops.
It gives you an idea of the confidence of this man when he relates that
he asked her to dance at the party afterwards, and she accepted. Later
he was sent to Cologne where he learned FDR had died. By then, the war
for him was 'almost fun'. There was little resistance as the Allies moved
towards Berlin, and much of the German army consisted of 'pitifully
young and old men, the old ones looking to surrender, while the sixteen-
and seventeen-year-olds were still fanatically loyal to the Reich'.[65]

Hans, however, was not allowed to escape one horrifying reality of the
war. On 2 May 1945, the US Eighty-Second Airborne Division liberated
3,500 survivors of the Wöbbelin concentration camp, a satellite of the
Neuengamme extermination camp near Ludwigslust in western Germany
near Hamburg. 'The stench alone was so strong that the protestations
of the Ludwigslust inhabitants that they knew nothing of what went
on were laughable. There were hundreds of dead bodies in the striped
concentration camp uniforms stacked up several meters high and deep.
There were also hundreds of almost starved to death people within
the camp. It cured our GIs at least for some time from having any
relationship with the Germans. We brought out the entire population

of the town at gunpoint, paraded them past the bodies, facilities and survivors, then had them dig graves in the most beautiful place we could find, the estate of the Duke of Mecklenburg. Many threw up as they were forced to bury the bodies, at the butt of the rifle. Every last person of the town was forced to attend the funeral.' Hans' division was selected to guard the American sector of Berlin, an honour, and when Hans arrived, he found the city 'one huge pile of rubble, nothing standing in the centre of town'.

Herta asked Hans to find Nore Astfalck's brother and his wife and to deliver food packages to them. German civilians were starving. He did so, and he also located an old school friend of Herta's, Gabi Landsberg, in a miserable basement room. She was half Jewish but had survived. The Germans in Berlin were in rags, starving gaunt shadows of people, pushing carts of pitiful belongings. Russian soldiers were everywhere, and everybody dealt with the black market, trading watches, army issue underwear, and other scarce items. Hans found himself translating for Russians (those who knew German) as well as for Americans, but one incident soured him. An American soldier had complained that a Russian MP had forced him to hand over his watch at gunpoint. A Cossack Brigadier took the GI and Hans to find the man and there he was, still directing traffic where he had taken the watch. 'The General got out of his Jeep, walked up to the MP and spoke to him in Russian. Then we saw him pull out his revolver and shoot the man dead at point blank range. Then he came back grinning and said, "That's what we do with thieves in our army". Undoubtedly, he wanted to impress us. We were shocked to the core but there was nothing we could do. All this for a lousy GI watch.'[66]

The Wannsee Yacht Club, where the Wannsee Conference of 20 January 1942 settled on the logistics of carrying out the Final Solution (the various family men representing the railroads, post office and telephone communications, etc. referring to their victims as *Stuecke*, i.e. pieces), now became an officer's club for the Allied Forces. Formerly owned by a wealthy Jewish family, the mansion had been turned into an R and R resort for SS officers. It is now a museum that Wolf visited in 2002 as a guest of the city of Berlin. Hans took out a sailboat many lazy afternoons while posted there. He worked in prisoner interrogations and became disgusted with those who said they didn't know or hadn't wanted to know what had happened to the Jews. 'It was obvious that thousands of people were involved in loading and driving and scheduling

the trains that ran endlessly to the extermination camps, others were
involved in the arrests and in providing guards and the meticulous
planning that went into the construction and erection of the camps and
ovens. These people knew; they were not just SS members. They were
civil servants and employees of companies and government agencies who
did the dirty work.'[67] Hans also took time to revisit his old hometown
of Kassel. In a tragic twist of fate (and not uncommon), he located an old
friend and was able to rejoice with him for having survived Auschwitz.
The tragedy was that the friend's son, who had escaped to the United
States before the war, had joined the army and returned to fight
in Holland, and died in battle. Thus it was that Hans, as authentic
an American soldier as one could be, had a front-row seat in the
liberating of Europe from Hitler.

In order to live with her new husband, Herta joined the US army
in the fall of 1944 as a mail censor, went to Paris, and managed to get
assigned to Munich. Hans had himself transferred out of the Eighty-
Second and moved to Munich as well ('only a little sorry that he had
to leave the Eighty-Second since it had been selected to lead the great
VE victory parade planned for New York'). The couple worked side
by side, she as a censor, he as a de-Nazification officer, and they 'had
a wonderful time'. In 1945, they sailed to Boston and Hans prepared
to enter Harvard Law School, their first child on the way.

Leaving Stoatley Rough

In December of 1944, as Hans left Herta to join the Eighty-Second
Airborne Division in the Battle of the Bulge, sixteen-year-old Goldy
was at last ready for his Cambridge University Matriculation. 'This
exam included Math (Arithmetic, Algebra and Geometry), English
(writing, grammar and comprehension), English literature including
thorough knowledge of two plays by Shakespeare (*Hamlet* and *Richard
II*, that year) British and European History from 1689 to 1914, and
German as a foreign language.' Goldy was also tested on his electives,
French and Scripture. He had prepared himself during a winter
of deepest deprivations at the school. Renate Dorpalen [Dorpalen-
Brocksieper] wrote, 'Christmas was very cold and the most miserable
one of the war. Five years of marginal diet, bombing and humiliation
made everyone feel that his strength was sapped. There was only one

wish – for the war to be over.'[68] After his exams, Goldy celebrated with
his teachers at Stoatley Rough over tea and 'biscuits' (cookies) in the
school library. It was a bittersweet time for the boys because now Goldy
was soon to leave. After him, only Obo and Martin would be left at the
school from their gang of Hut Boys.

U-boats menaced the Atlantic to a lesser degree than in 1944, and
consequently, visas to the United States came through for Goldy's mother,
Goldy and his brother Ralph. (In fact, however, commercial ships were
not safe on the water. Wolf's ship – in April 1945 – the *Aquitania*, was
chased by U-boats, only to be rescued by the arrival of ships of the Royal
Canadian Navy from Halifax, Nova Scotia.) Travel was contingent upon
the availability of berths on the liners that had begun to cross the Atlantic
again. Britain meted out arrangements for passage. People were not told
ahead of time the name of their ship or the port of departure for security
reasons. Although the war was winding down in the European theatre,
a certain number of German U-Boats still prowled the Atlantic, mostly
still out there trying to avoid prosecution. Granting of visas was not
a predictable or timely process and people had no choice as to the carrier
they were assigned to. Instead of waiting at the school, like Wolf before
him, Goldy felt it was time to leave Stoatley Rough, allowing himself
a short period of respite between the rigour of his final studies and the
voyage that would begin his new life in America. He made his farewells
and boarded a series of trains toward Yorkshire. His former hosts met
him at the station and kept him well-fed on their farm for a few months.

On 2 February 1945, Goldy, his mother and Ralph reported to
Paddington Station to learn the point of departure of the ship assigned
them. Their ship was in Wales, a 12,000 ton Cunard merchant ship that
once had carried bananas from Jamaica. It now carried coal. There was
room for only 150 passengers. The little family made the trek to their
port in Wales and watched, for seven days, as coal poured into the hold
from freight cars making a 'deafening noise'. Goldy picks up the story.
'We moved out into the Atlantic Ocean where we circled until we were
about sixty ships, mostly going to the United States in convoy.' The ship
cruised by the Azores where they picked up air cover and then went
to Bermuda for more air cover. En route, an enormous storm overtook
the voyagers. 'It tossed the ship like a cork, plates crashing, and waves
so high that they reached above the bridge. A day or two later we were
almost alone in the ocean. The convoy had dispersed to avoid collisions
and every ship was on its own. We zigzagged north along the American

coastline, and while aboard, I tasted Coke for the first time and ate a banana, something I hadn't had for six years. The captain piped music and news from local stations through our public address system.' After twenty-five days at sea the ship docked in Halifax. The family still had to catch a train to Montreal, from which they went to enter the United States through St. Albans, Vermont. It was decidedly unglamorous to arrive in the United States in the middle of the night, with no vision of the Statue of Liberty to cheer them on. But the unsentimental Goldy and his family pushed on. With little fanfare he wrote, 'Finally, we were in America. We arrived about 8 a.m. at Pennsylvania Station in New York City and were met by Uncle Carl and his wife Alma. So here we were.'[69]

With victory in Europe a certainty, many other residents of Stoatley Rough were making plans to leave. Since the prior September, the blackout in Great Britain had been officially relaxed to dim-out, with some street lighting allowed. The English began to feel fairly sure that enemy planes would no longer approach their country.

The Board of Governors of the school took up an important topic at their spring meeting. Should the school continue or was its work done? When the war ended on the European front, the other large German-English school, Bunce Court, was quickly disbanded and its leader, Anna Essinger, was more than happy to retire and return to Germany. She had helped over 800 Jewish children who otherwise might have perished. Her work was done. But Dr Lion was younger than Miss Essinger and was not ready to retire. She saw her work unfinished. The indefatigable Miss Bracey sided with her. 'Did we wish to carry on with our experiment as it is now or should we wish to include it into a larger Scheme? The future need would be very great in the matter of the care of children from the Occupied Countries, International Centres of Education for Children and Adults and the vast problem of the Orphans in Europe.'[70] The Board decided that the school would forge ahead, offering a new kind of refuge while at the same time, assuring Drs Lion and Leven and others of continued employment.

Meanwhile, the war raged on. In the first months of 1945, the Allies successfully rolled back the Germans. The Russians advanced from the east, and the British and United States closed in on Berlin from the south and west. This was good news. There was also bad news, as word began to trickle in about the death of parents of Roughian children. It was to be a terrible time at the school for many. It was a spring day that

Renate Dorpalen had been dreading. 'I remember the day I received the letters as vividly as few others. It was one of those sparkling spring days that only England can offer, with the warm air permeated by the scent of blossoming bushes. The meadows were covered with bluebells, cowslips and primroses and the greening trees were full of chirping birds. In this incredibly peaceful atmosphere, in a quiet corner of the garden, I read and reread the shattering news of my parents' death in a grim, hostile environment.' What is particularly poignant is the fact that Renate's mother had been dead for almost two years.

Renate also received lengthy accounts from friends of her parents who had survived Theresienstadt (her mother died a year and a half after her father). These pages only reached Renate on 27 April 1945. She wrote later that when the films came out about the German concentration camps, 'the picture of what my parents' last months of life might have been like was to become my recurring nightmare for years. Often in my dreams I was with them in the camp.'[71] On 7 May, Germany surrendered unconditionally to the Allies, the same day Theresienstadt was liberated by the Soviet army, 'where of more than 140,000 deportees to the model ghetto, 33,529 had died of overcrowding, disease and starvation and another 88,000 had been sent to the gas chambers in Poland'.[72] Renate was able to share her grief with one of her brothers who had fought with Patton in the American army and by then was stationed in England. The Western world was celebrating what everyone called V-E Day (Victory in Europe). Three months later on 6 August, the United States dropped the A-Bomb, 'Little Boy', onto Hiroshima, killing 70,000 people, followed by 'Fat Boy' on 9 August, which devastated Nagasaki. Japan surrendered on 15 August.

Stoatley Rough was not to be left out of the victory party. Renate recalled wild celebration all over England on V-E Day. Stoatley Rough threw a festive picnic, 'dipping deep into our food ration reserves'. Some of the younger boys were emboldened to scale the steep roof of the mansion to hoist the Union Jack and a Scout flag. Hanno explains their adventure. 'We (Andreas [Hanno] Pilartz, Uli Hubacher and Eddie Behrendt) climbed out of the "Lookout" window to hoist the only two flags we could get hold of (a Union Jack and a Scout flag) onto the pinnacle of the building. We floodlit the flags by converting a number of pineapple tins into spotlights, providing enough light to make the flags visible from downtown Haslemere.'[73] When she learned of such foolishness, Dr Lion gave them a dressing down about climbing on the roof. Yet she was pleased. The stunt 'even received a favourable mention in the *Haslemere Herald* the following day'. Eddie said, 'The [flags] were put up, along with the lights, to celebrate the end of the war and the end to blackouts. I seem to remember the lights as more important then the flags. I am not sure, but I don't think that I was all that patriotic. It was a big and very exciting lark for me. To this day I remember being somewhat scared climbing along the roof. It was of course a very crazy thing to do, but I had done it a couple of times before successfully, so that I didn't have to think about it too long. This time though I seem to remember it was dusk whereas the other times it was on a weekend during daylight. One could only get on the roof through the "Lookout" Window which was rather small and I believe had a couple of bars across it which we had to wiggle through. It was a typical thing for me to do since I was considered more of a mischief maker than someone worthy of education at the time. I was nearly always in trouble.'[74] The same troublemaker loved to tell people the last thing Dr Lion said to him before he left the school: 'Eddy, you will make a fine practical worker.' Eddie went to America and received a master's degree in social work, Dr Lion's own field. The 'practical worker' went on to build a distinguished professional career and became the well-known founder of the American Kindertransport Association, established in 1989.[75]

After war's end, Hanno and Uli were granted the privilege of living in an outbuilding of the farm called The Black Hut, a shed in which one kept hay for the horse and the cow. Part of the shed had been fixed up as a hideaway for Nore and Hanna in happier days. 'It was a sort of Paradise for us – we even installed a cooker.'[76] One day a few months after the war had ended, the boys encountered a serious brushfire on the lower property. 'Dr Lion got more or less the whole school to the blaze and organised a chain of buckets to supply us with water from the swimming pool.... All the main fuses for the farm including our Black Hut were destroyed and it took a few months for the current to be restored.' Uli wrote, 'We ... practically extinguished it before the fire brigade, with no proper access road in the farm valley, reached the site.' Wolf, who by then had left the school, explains, 'It would indeed have been a difficult place to reach by fire truck – up Bunch Lane and then muddy farm paths, through several gates.'

With the war over and the oceans once again reasonably safe, the mass exodus began. Those who were too young to live on their own and whose parents had not survived stayed on at the school, and some children left to live with relatives who found their way to England or sent for them. For any student who had matriculated, there was no delaying. It was time for the Hut Boys, the Household Girls and all the others to leave. 'We'll Meet Again' was played over and over on the radio (sung by Vera Lynn, the 'Forces' Sweetheart') as if to chronicle the inevitable end of an era and the parting of fast friends.[77]

We'll meet again/Don't know where/Don't know when.
But we know/We'll meet again/Some sunny day.

The young people at the school had a sense of foreboding about the future. Peter Gaupp recalled, 'None of us had any idea of what was going to happen to us after we finished school. I had a very quiet terror about the uncertain future. Who would tell me where I should go, how I would earn a living, how I could survive without adults telling me what to do? I certainly had no idea of going on to higher education since I was very doubtful that I would pass the School Certificate Exam. Who would find me a job and a place to stay? After all, I had been a shy, retiring child and teenager and totally relied on adults for every decision up to now.'

Nore Astfalck and Hanna Nacken prepared to return to Germany. They both had parents and brothers still in Germany and they were eager to help their former countrymen. Immediately after the war, expatriates were not allowed back into the country right away and the women had to wait for the bureaucracy to give permission. Under mysterious circumstances, they left Haslemere for London under a cloud as the bureaucracy processed their applications to return. There was no going away party for either woman. Nore spoke frankly of leaving the school without ceremony, without formal acknowledgement and gratitude and without even sufficient time to pack. In fact, once they had made their intentions to return to Germany clear, she and Hanna were asked to leave before they were ready to do so. Dr Lion failed, in the end, to acknowledge the invaluable contribution Nore had made to the school (see 'The Interloper'). She and Hanna left the premises quietly in the summer of 1945 and took lodgings in London. Quakers in London asked 'whether we were willing to help them in training German people who wanted to go to do the most urgent things in the way of social work. We agreed, and we also found a very good opportunity to work as helpers in the wartime kindergarten of Anna Freud. Then we moved to rooms in the settlement in Hoxton, the working class district of London.'[78] They had to wait for more than six months. With the help of Hans Loeser, who by then, as an officer of the occupation army in Bavaria knew how to pull strings, they were finally given the go-ahead. 'Miss Nacken and I and two other people were the very first permitted to go back to Germany to stay there.' They left, as she quaintly phrased the date, 'on Whitsuntide, in [19]46'.[79]

It was not unusual for children who had found sanctuary at Stoatley Rough to regret having to leave. Barbara Gerstenberg [Prasse] (who, like Hans and many others, left for America before the war began) wrote about the pain of leaving, of real trauma.

I did not want to leave Stoatley Rough. It was home! I had had to learn to live without my parents and was apprehensive about moving back into their lives. I did not want to go to America. It seemed so far from not only England, but from Europe. But, of course, I could not stay and so in August of [19]38, I had to say 'goodbye'. I have come to the conclusion that I have had too many goodbyes in my life, too many times of putting down roots and having to tear them up again. It hurts to do that. Stoatley Rough had been home and I had to leave it … I do not recall that anyone at the school, i.e. any one of the adults helped me or others to understand or to deal with our feelings. It was not only the British 'stiff upper lip' but in retrospect there must have been other reasons. Perhaps it would have been too overwhelming to take the cork out of the bottle of all those pent-up feelings of displaced, confused and often, I am sure, homesick children. There were no support groups, no therapy sessions, no reflections on what was happening to all of us. We simply went on with our lives as best as we could and maybe that was the only way to cope. In any case, I could not really voice my conflicting feelings about leaving Stoatley Rough and I do remember crying into my pillow the last night there, trying not to wake Herta, who was my roommate. I have no recollection where I sailed from or how I got there. My memory stops with that last night at the place that had been my home for two years and starts again with the next chapter in my life, i.e. America.[80]

It was Obo's turn to leave. 'Since any funds that were deposited for me for tuition and board at Stoatley Rough were gone, Dr Lion said rightfully that it was high time for me to earn a living. So in April 1945 I was sent to a youth hostel where a counsellor found an apprentice job for me at the British Small Arms (BSA) factory (a former bicycle factory) that made mechanical and hydraulic components for military equipment. I started out by sweeping the shop floor, grateful to have been given a chance to make a new life for myself. I knew that this was the first step to a profession. Pretty soon I graduated to operating some of the precision metalworking machinery and apparently I was pretty good at it so that they enrolled me in their apprentice program and sent me to night school, the British Central Technical College.' Obo wrote to Dr Lion at the time, complaining, sounding a bit snobbish, about the types of people he had to work with. 'I do not like the people because they are honestly very uneducated, especially the girls. In other words a bit common I suppose. [They like] dancing, pictures, Jazz, etc. That's all for them.'[81]

Three weeks after Obo left the school the International Red Cross confirmed that his parents and brother Arthur had died in a concentration camp. He was an orphan and most of his friends had already gone to America. Obo was invited to move to the United States.

> Meanwhile my father's brother, who had escaped from Generalissimo Franco's Spain to New York, asked me whether I was interested in coming to the US. In December of 1946 I received my immigration documents and $10 'travelling money'. I boarded a US Liberty ship which was returning GIs home from World War II. The eight-day voyage was, for the most part, uneventful and not particularly luxurious. One of the things I was unable to understand was the segregation of the 'coloured' soldiers from the white, especially those 'coloureds' who were returning home with their British and other European war brides.... I arrived in the early morning hours of 29 January 1947 and after the excitement of seeing the Statue of Liberty and the lower Manhattan skyline, had the feeling that I was going to like my new home in a new world full of excitement and opportunities.... It was not easy to bridge the age gap between an eighteen-year-old boy whose hormones were racing and was eager to start a new chapter, and an old world seventy-year-old intellectual gentleman [and newly discovered uncle] who was now deprived of all the comforts and culture to which he had been accustomed for much of his life in Europe. But we worked it out.[82]

Wolf and Goldy (and later Martin) re-established contact with Obo in New York, and others came to frequent reunions: Susanne Horn [Schapiro], Ruth Lichtenstein [Ultman], Evi Cassel and Putti Cassel [Wronker], Hanna Untermeier and Hanna Katz. The boys' families treated Obo as one of their own. A photo dated just after Obo arrived in the United States shows a group of young people – the girls inordinately pretty, the boys smiling and handsome – looking sleek, affluent and confident in their futures.

It is well-established that many displaced children of the Holocaust and their parents who reunited years later suffered a special kind of hell, arising from the inability on both sides to bridge over the estrangement that had occurred during their period of separation. Diane Samuels' play, *Kindertransport*, explores this theme. It depicts a grown survivor who, as a girl, had been sent out of Germany to live with an English family. Now a middle-aged matron, she has blocked out her entire German past until her daughter finds a box of letters that reveal the fact that her mother is not the person she believed her to be, but a child of the Holocaust. Flashbacks in the play depict the naturalised English woman as a teenager rejecting her birth mother who has returned from a concentration camp to claim her. The girl finds her birth mother a stranger and wishes only to continue in her present life. She even tells her birth mother that she already has a mother, her English foster mother. The pain experienced by both of the mothers and the refugee daughter is wrenching to witness.[83]

There was at least one such case at Stoatley Rough, documented in the archives and probably dozens of others left unrecorded. In September 1945, a certain young woman's mother wrote from Hamburg asking Dr Lion to intercede for her: her daughter (whom we shall call Lisel Goldschmidt) did not want to see her. The mother wrote to the child's sponsors who suggested that she reassure Lisel that there was no question of her returning to live in Germany. The mother wrote, 'It is very hard to understand from a mother's point of view whose child is her own flesh and blood.... I think I will find a way to approach Lisel and ... will come to England when travelling possibilities will be available again.... It is not my intention to take the child back to Germany or to interrupt Lisel in her education ... for which I have to be extremely grateful to you for ever.' The mother then asks Lisel's sponsors to discuss the matter with distant relatives as intermediaries. The sponsor then became angry and wrote to Dr Lion: 'Lisel is not going to be tricked or exploited by anyone, myself included. LISEL WILL DO AS SHE WISHES WHEN THE TIME COMES. If Lisel of her own free will elects to keep in touch with her mother I have no objection but I do object to intimidation or any interference. Do you think you could write to her mother pointing out the legal position, and ask her to stop meddling!' The sponsor's wife adds her own hand-written thoughts, 'After being with us for six years, as you can imagine, she has completely forgotten her mother, and showed not the slightest interest when we told her that her mother was alive and well. Her only reaction was that she did not want to go back. Her father died in 1942.' Dr Lion wrote the sponsors that she understood 'a mother's longing for her child after all these years', and that she also understood the sponsors' 'being anxious not to let the child get back to Germany in the near future'. She referred them to a woman of the Refugee Children's Movement, Bloomsbury, House 'who will probably have a number of similar cases'.[84]

Wolf was worried. 'One cause for emotional turmoil was the realisation that I would soon be reunited with my parents in America. How could I relate to them? Our experiences of the intervening years had been so different. Would they still look on me as the ten-year-old they had last seen in 1939? ... I had mixed feelings about emigrating to America. How could I adjust to yet another country?' It turned out that Wolf's reunion was fine. 'It went smoother than expected even though there were rough spots. I had adopted English (and later, American) ways of thinking and behaving. My parents were forty-six years old when they came to America and set in their German ways. (Even today, when I visit Europe, I feel at ease in England and like a foreigner in Germany, even though linguistically I could more easily pass there as a native. In England, my acquired American accent would give me away as a foreigner.) The actual meeting with our parents in Penn Station was easier than [expected].... We recognised them right away (they had sent us pictures from America). Mainly I remember strange sounds coming from my father – a mixture of laughing and sobbing. The taxi ride to our new home was terrifying, all that NYC traffic on the wrong side of the street. Mainly I remember being dirty and dead tired after three nearly sleepless nights. During our last night at sea, we had to sleep in our clothes with life preservers at hand. That was followed by two nights of sitting in a train [entering the US from Montreal, by the back door, at St. Albans, Vermont], and there was no chance for shaving (by that time I needed to do that) or shower.'

Dieter and Peter Gaupp would also go to America, but having left Stoatley Rough earlier, did not express anxiety or sorrow, but rather eagerness to see their parents again who had waited out the war in Switzerland. While working his day job at the optical company in Bristol, Dieter took correspondence courses and passed the Matric. Peter also passed the Matric and stayed on at Shoreham for one more semester. He floundered, unable to attend Cambridge or Oxford, the colleges for which he had qualified, because of the planned trip to America. 'They did not know what to do with me. I waited to be told. I was called into Mr Bruder's office (Headmaster) who asked me what I wanted to do with my life.... In desperation I said I wanted to be an engineer and build bridges. So they kept me on for that extra summer, the only student at an empty school, while Mr Bruder gave me science tutorials in the laboratory. I walked his Corgi [and] helped him clean his fish tank.... Eventually he told me he had enrolled me in the Joseph Lucas Trade School in Birmingham (England) where I could learn to be a toolmaker [while I took] engineering courses at night.... In some ways it was almost an Oliver Twist experience. Sometimes I would miss some meals to save enough money to go to a concert with Obo and Dieter. (Obo was working at the local BSA factory.)' Peter concludes this phase of his life with characteristic wit. 'The J. Lucas administration was impressed with my IQ testing and proposed to train me to become their director of research to help them move into the jet propulsion field. I was terrified.'[85]

Since the elder Gaupps would leave for America before the boys' visas were available, the family arranged to meet first in Switzerland, the first time they would be reunited after six years of separation. The brothers took a train to Zurich and when they arrived they began searching for their parents in the crowded station. They were looking for the tall, robust people they had last seen so many years earlier. Their parents were looking for their two little boys. When they all finally found each other, Peter was shocked to discover 'two people who looked not as I remembered them at all but two aged, small people'. The senior Gaupps, in turn, said they were amazed to see not little boys at all, but nearly grown men.

Visas arrived in September 1947. Dieter and Peter set sail on a freighter headed for Georgetown, Texas, home to Southwestern University. Herr Doktor Gaupp was already there with his wife, ready to start his position to teach German (and Italian Renaissance history,

if the college required it). It was when Herr Gaupp had been incarcerated
in Italy upon the occasion of Hitler's state visit that he befriended the
people who arranged for his teaching post in America. Knowing little
English, he tried to learn the new language en route on his ship to
America using a child's US history book. He facetiously quipped
about the United States, 'I did not know they *had* any history.'

The Gaupp brothers were unfortunate to have been assigned to
an empty freighter returning from Holland after having hauled carbon
black from the Gulf coast. Peter recalled, 'The crew kept busy trying
to clean up the carbon and Dieter and I started looking like coal haulers.
Everything one touched turned black. There were about eight of us living
in the officers' quarters. After we passed the half way mark, things
changed amazingly. The crew started playing children's games (dominos)
and the Captain's Table served curried rice for breakfast EACH
DAY. (I still shy away from curry.) Then we started to run away from
a hurricane and headed towards Galveston. That poor old ship had
been through rough wear and it shook noisily as it tried to get up speed.
The vibration and noise were scary – I kept wondering if things were
going to fall apart. It did not help that one of the sailors, who I had
befriended because he said he was a Boy Scout Ranger, told me that
things were not holding up too well in the engine room. There was
a period when the waters got rough and we were told to keep in our
bunks … hard on the stomach! Well, the ship did hold together and
we eventually enjoyed watching the dolphins escorting us into the
Gulf of Mexico. Seeing the lights of Galveston from the distance was
emotional. We parked a long way away from the coast and next morning
we were told to appear in the Captain's cabin to meet with American
Officials. SCARY! I don't know about Dieter, but I saw visions of being
turned away. They were public health officials who checked out if we had
the uglies … and passed us! Eventually we got to a cargo dock and exited
on wooden planks.' Peter adds to the story that when their parents met
the boys, they hardly recognised them for the black grease on their faces
that had not come off with soap and water. It took days to get the carbon
black off from their skin and hair.[86]

Martin's departure was without incident. His crossing, in fact, was a
sublimely happy one. 'I planned to take my matriculation for Cambridge
University in June 1945. In March of that year, however, I received notice
that I would leave for the United States to join my family in April. It was
a big adjustment for me to give up my Cambridge plans, on the one hand,

while contemplating leaving England [along with] all my friends. Perhaps it was that conflict that gave me the chicken pox, causing me to miss the boat I'd been booked for (the *Aquitania*). I did, however, catch the next one in May, the month the war ended in Europe, and I left on a troop ship that carried happy members of the US Army Air Corps. They were forever arguing about the merits of the airplanes that they had flown, notably the B-17 and the B-24. They were a very funny bunch and I literally laughed my way across the Atlantic. They also taught me to love Peppermint Patties. We were in one of the last convoys because there were still U-boats out there and we were the slowest ship in the convoy. It took us eleven days to cross from Liverpool to Brooklyn where we landed at the Army Base. Also on the ship was Susi Horn from Stoatley Rough. She was older than I, and she fell in love with one of the airmen who promptly jilted her the moment the ship docked.'[87]
When Martin's ship landed in Brooklyn, he disembarked and stood amidst the swarming crowds on the pier with his luggage, searching for a familiar face. There was no sign of his mother or sister or his mother's new husband, Henry Owens (née Oppenheimer). Most of the crowd disappeared. Still no family. Then he heard a cry. It was his sister who had spotted him. 'A budding twelve-year-old, wide-eyed and adoring. Apparently, they had almost given up finding me among the throngs.' There was discomfort in the reunion. Like the character in '*Kindertransport*', Martin felt estranged. 'My mother seemed capable of picking up where we had left off seven years earlier when I was ten, and tried to baby me. To me, she was almost a stranger.'

(Martin and his parents never discussed how they came to their decision to send him away. He does not know who in fact sponsored him, whether it was a family friend or one of the relief agencies. The family never talked about their uprooting; Martin says he does not recall his mother ever asking him about his seven years in England, leaving him with a measure of disappointment and a sense of something left unfinished with her. Understanding that she herself faced tremendous hardship after losing her privileged status in Vienna, he says she acted as if the hiatus in their lives had not happened at all, tucked under the rug and forgotten. For the rest of her life, his mother tried to baby him although to Martin, she was never again the beloved *Mutti* he had left behind in the *Bahnhof*.)

Wolf's tale of leave-taking of a month earlier had the greatest poignancy. He had enrolled at Kingston-upon-Thames Technical College, and while he was living with his relatives, a doodlebug hit his home. 'After much floundering', he moved to a boarding house in Guildford, near Haslemere, 'for 30 shillings a week (meals included)' and started taking classes at Guildford Tech. In late March 1945, his visa cleared and he was assigned to his ship. He had to say goodbye to the boys and to the teachers, to Dr Wolff and especially Dr Lion, who had been so tolerant and indulgent of him as he grew into manhood. 'I received word to report forthwith for travel to America. One last time I cycled 12 miles to Stoatley Rough to say goodbye to friends and teachers. The last one was Dr Lion. She met me at the door of her Bungalow and, as always on emotional occasions, spoke in Hamburg German. "*Na, Junge, mm, mm, mach's gut, halt' die Ohren steif und nimm dich vor den Weibern in acht!*" (Difficult to translate; approximate meaning: "Now, boy, good luck, don't let anyone get you down, and be on your guard when it comes to females!") With that advice, she sent me out to face the world.'[88]

Epilogue

Stoatley Rough School 1945–1960

The end of the war began the last of three phases in the life of Stoatley Rough School. Phase 1 was a harmonious, utopian experiment that unfolded from 1934 to 1938. Phase 2 began after the historic events of the *Anschluss* and *Kristallnacht*, when the small Camelot was replaced by an overfilled institution struggling to make ends meet. With several houses full of children, the school's leaders gravitated to the expedient and the practical, having to balance strict child-centricity against dwindling funding and provisioning. The shift between Phases 1 and 2 that happened when war broke out was noticeable. Those who had been at the school in the early days had to realign their priorities and to expand their circle of care and responsibility. Renate Dorpalen [Dorpalen-Brocksieper] arrived in 1939, on the cusp of the change. 'I felt like an outsider and intruder…. With wartime, there were no more festivals and summer holidays. The new order of business at the school was to make do, to scrimp, sacrifice and to perform that wonderfully British activity of carrying on…. After 1939 the school adapted to a very different mission … [of] providing a safe haven for children who had often suffered severe emotional trauma.'

Phase 3, which spanned 1945–1960, saw a virtually new school. In 1945, Dr Lion was fifty-one. She never considered returning to Germany, although she was too young (and lacked the means anyway) to retire. She faced substantial challenges in both staffing and recruiting for her school now that sanctuary was no longer the first priority of potential pupils. Through word of mouth, modest brochures and British relief agencies for displaced people, she kept the doors open by admitting significant numbers of day students. Annual enrolments between 1945 and 1960 averaged around seventy pupils, with a ratio of boarding to day pupils around four to one.[1] When the school closed in 1960, there were only thirty-six boarders (one as young as five) and about the same number of day students. It was tough sledding. Dr Lion wrote in 1952 that she would take children 'with nervous conditions' but not ones with serious mental illness. There is no evidence she brought in specially trained staff to deal with children who might have had emotional problems.

The post-war population was a diverse group. At first comprised of foreign students, refugees, children of refugees and the deserving English poor, it evolved to encompass day pupils from nearby towns who either took cabs, carpooled or walked up Farnham Lane from the bus stop each day.[2] Dr Leven wrote that the post-war students 'came from a lesser educated background than the refugee children, [which] made teaching, organising, the relationships between pupils and grown-ups often more difficult'. The graduates of the post-war era have written that they felt they had 'a certain inferior status' to those who had come before them, deferring in newsletters to war-time pupils whom they perceived to have suffered more. Some felt that their experiences were 'trivial' in comparison to those of earlier pupils.

The post-war school's identity was no longer based on shared suffering and displacement. In fact, by the early 1950s, the historic roots of the school seem to have been (consciously or inadvertently) suppressed. Surprisingly, some post-war pupils never knew why the school had been founded and had no idea of its links to the Third Reich. Dr Lion spoke accented English, wrote herself notes in a mixture of German and English and usually spoke German to German-speaking refugees and Dr Leven. Yet, the entire *raison d'être* for the school and its tumultuous history were ignored, forgotten or simply considered inconsequential. Richard Greenwell, who attended Stoatley Rough between 1954 and 1958, mused, 'I don't recall hearing anything at all about the Holocaust while at Stoatley Rough, directly or indirectly. The Holocaust (actually this specific term wasn't yet being used at that time) was never discussed in any class that I had, and no teacher or fellow student ever mentioned it.... To me, Stoatley Rough was simply another (my third) boarding school that I had lived in since I was about six years old – although I was much happier there than at the others – and I had no knowledge ... that its creation had anything at all to do with Nazi Germany.' He then explains that he 'must have led a very sheltered life at Stoatley Rough. In fact, I sometimes wonder if, by the mid-1950s, that's what Dr Lion may have wanted, in order to protect us a little from even the knowledge of such evil.' This gentleman studied twentieth-century German history to compensate for all that 'youthful ignorance' and, as an amateur historian, he reported, 'the World War II section of my personal library contains about seven hundred and fifty volumes (including on the war's causes and aftermath), about eighty volumes of which deal specifically with the Holocaust'.[3] The school never lost its association with the wider world. Brochures in the late 1940s and 1950s claimed that Stoatley Rough would 'provide a sound education and training for children of both sexes and more especially … for the children of parents who are or at any time were refugees in England.' According to the school's alumni historian Michael Johnson, by 1959 the school had become 'an international school following a grammar school curriculum with special stress on languages and music'.

The post-war school suffered from the absence of Nore Astfalck's powerful and positive presence. A social chasm grew between the boarding and the day pupils. Michael wrote that it took courage for a day pupil to ask the residents for the location of the day boarders' loo. Along with the loss of the Farm programme and morning run, perhaps most significant, the school lost its sense of community. Now boarders and day pupils formed their own groups. An older boy supposed to be Michael's big brother told him on his first day that children were locked into the Schoolroom as punishment – ' "been there myself several days", he said cheerfully' – leaving Michael with a slight fear of incarceration throughout his years at the school. The ethic of looking out for the smaller, younger ones had vanished, at least in this case.

One thing did not change: music. Dr Leven's influence spread wide and deep, perhaps the single most conspicuous characteristic of the school's lasting legacy. The custom of quotations also survived. The school inched towards incorporating the character of traditional English boarding schools. It started a prefect system whereby older children performed administrative duties. Dr Lion was no longer as strong a presence in the day-to-day affairs of the school, and without Nore's omniscient presence, the train now headed down the tracks almost on its own momentum. No longer did the adrenalin born of survival and idealism fuel the decisions of the aging headmistress – she delegated many of her responsibilities. An open, casual, almost unstructured atmosphere took shape with diminished supervision of the children, a situation that most children loved yet one that allowed corporal punishment to creep in. At least once, a sadistic teacher administered a brutal beating to a boy who had thrown spit balls at a girl during church services, as others, waiting their turn just outside the closed door, bolted in fear upon hearing the dreadful cries of the victim. It is doubtful that Dr Lion

was ever made aware of the incident. Academic standards slipped.
In 1950, a letter to Dr Lion from parents reported bullying at the school.
Dr Lion wrote at least one letter to a former student forbidding him from
bringing his friend to the grounds again for some unnamed but serious
prior misdemeanour.

That the school's academic and general environment had deteriorated
from its pre-war standard is evident in the alumni evaluations of the
school reported in the newsletters. Yet, there was something special
about the school that transcended the usual features by which
a school is judged. The fact is, post-war pupils simply loved Stoatley
Rough. Stefan Lacey recalled, 'an indifferent education, awful living
conditions and an administration which almost fifty years later I still
consider a disgrace.... I always had the idea that the school was way out
of their control.' Yet the same boy went on to say, 'I feel honoured and
lucky to have spent my youth there; without doubt, it was one of my
father's best decisions to send me there.... It taught us self-reliance, to
deal with the knocks of life without fluster, to try, try and try again till
we succeed – to view a task or problem in different lights and angles,
to perceive a solution where few others could.' In fact, the majority
of post-war pupils fiercely defend their years in Haslemere as happy
and worthwhile, as if original values of self-esteem and independence
had seeped into the walls of the structure itself and had gone on to
nourish its post-war children. David Kirby-Burt called Stoatley Rough
'a shambolically happy place', and many others exulted in the open
environment. Ruth Morgan [Roberts], a day student, wrote, 'I actually
loved the school so much I begged to board and came up voluntarily
on Saturdays and stayed as late as possible after school.'

Early in the spring of 1960, Dr Lion, now sixty-seven years old
(Dr Leven was sixty-one), circulated a letter declaring her retirement and
the closing of the school.[4] She asked that there be no special celebrations.
She helped pupils to find other placements, and the school closed for
good that summer.

As a headmistress, Dr Lion was flawed – insecure in her personal
relationships, capable of taking vengeance. She was judgemental and
often wrong in evaluating a child's potential. She showed unhealthy
favouritism towards some pupils, and she may have pushed the law
to the limit in her use of Household Girls. Yet, she also did the best she
could with a fate she had hardly imagined for herself, let alone had been
prepared for when as a young intellectual, she first launched her career

in welfare and women's issues in Germany. This shy, physically
unimpressive woman was supposed to live out her days writing and
managing teachers like herself, dedicating her life to women's issues.
Instead, she ended up in the midst of displaced children with needs that
only her school could uniquely meet. At forty, she built a school from
scratch in a new country. She kept her board happy, acquired and
monitored an ever-changing stream of dedicated and often superb
teaching staff, and showed a willingness to improvise to achieve her
goals. No mere ideologue, she was also practical in her own way, yielding
to the forces of history that could have swamped the school at any point.
She had to badger, bully and scrounge, but she kept her school running
for twenty-six years and she did so with honour. She saved many lives,
helped hundreds to find jobs and loved her large brood even more after
they had left her protection. Most who passed through her tutelage
express undying appreciation for her efforts. She never lost her love
of growing things and always appreciated the humorous and the ironic.
She wrote a letter to Peter Strauss in 1948: 'The garden has improved
since last year, especially our vegetable garden now under the care
of a former MP, who puts his potatoes in such order, just as if they
had to go on parade with the parsnips and the radishes! At the moment
we are over-run with lettuces but luckily some raspberries picked from
the garden break the monotony in the diet of spaghetti and tomato juice
and a rather dry second course.'[5]

It is much to the credit of Dr Hilde Lion that the pupils loved the school.
Former Roughian Edith Hubacher [Christoffel] made up a word to express
her feelings about Stoatley Rough School: *Zusammengehörigkeitsgefühl*.
The word comprised of three German words: *Zusammen* [together],
Gehörigkeit [sense of belonging together] and *Gefühl* [feeling, emotion].[6]

The buildings

In March 1945, Mrs Vernon transferred the use of her property
'by deed poll' to the religious order of St Mary's Convent in Wantage,
Oxfordshire. This Anglican community nurtured overseas communities
in India, Madagascar and South Africa. A Mr Jeffries, whose notes
on an earlier history of Stoatley Rough are filed with the school's
archived materials in the London School of Economics, wrote that
the transaction was complicated, the legal status of the house 'being

almost "entrusted" to the new owners' who allowed the school to remain without incident. In 1963, after the closing of Stoatley Rough School (Mrs Vernon died exactly one year after Stoatley Rough closed, in June 1961), a new school moved in. It was part of the Ockenden Venture, a charitable organisation formed in 1951 to care for Latvian and Polish girls from displaced persons camps. The mansion became known as 'Quartermaine House.' The Venture eventually took in other children under the War Charities Act of 1940, turning Stoatley Rough into a 'reception centre', for Vietnamese 'boat people' between 1979 and 1988. When the Ockenden organisation moved its operations overseas, the buildings in Haslemere lay empty and in disrepair for almost a decade. Various businesses examined the site, but because of a dispute with the National Trust about the access rights over common land, many 'baulked at the asking price of £530,000'.7 In early 2001, a development corporation bought the land and buildings and converted the original building into three luxury condominiums. The new owners tore down the Bungalow, Hut, Farmhouse, pump house and other out buildings and converted Mr Phillips's cottage, the Lodge, into a fourth luxury condominium. They restored the landscape. Thanks to the efforts of Chris Townson and other trustees, the new owners agreed to install a plaque at the entrance stating that the site was once Stoatley Rough School.

Today, the estate is as grand as ever. The façade of the building is impressive, the view over the Downs still takes one's breath away and the small brook still runs at the base of the property. A quiet reflecting pool sits where once children cavorted in the home-made, sometimes slimy swimming pool. Today, its tranquil waters are guarded by a pair of long-legged brass herons. The fields are wild.

In 2004 the Stoatley Rough School Trustees organised a reunion in Haslemere. (The first of several reunions was held in November 1990, in Guildford, Surrey.) The condominium owners were kind enough to open their homes to the crowds of aging alumni and their partners for an afternoon of reminiscing. In attendance were people in their seventies and eighties who had been at the school in the 1930s as well as the younger post-war Roughians. John and Lyn Orrick, owners of the largest condominium, gathered the large group in the sitting room and fed them refreshments. Everyone then watched a video of a black-and-white film made in 1937. With the still lovely tiles of the William Morris fireplace a shining backdrop, Roughians chortled and exclaimed,

laughed and clapped as a sprightly thirty-something Nore Astfalck
led the morning run and a beaming Dr Lion read to children sitting
cross-legged by the Polynesian shack. On seeing the film,
Mr Orrick declared on the spot that he would restore the gazebo,
thatched roof and all.

The view from the mossy-walled terrace (now carved into three
terraces partitioned by brick walls) still commands attention, although
some alumni reported that the general tree line looks higher now from
the third floor than it had sixty years earlier. The main building remains
magnificent – quietly imposing, elegant, restful and ageless – rising
high above the cobbled pavement that leads in from Farnham Lane.
It is comforting to be there. One feels as if the house itself is comfortable
in its own remarkable history and will be forever infused with a special
peace.

Dr Lion and Dr Leven

Upon retirement Drs Lion and Leven became naturalised citizens of
Great Britain, a decision that allowed them to travel to Italy in 1948 and,
later, to Switzerland, the United States (twice) and Canada. The couple
also spent time each winter in Las Palmas (Gran Canaria) visiting Hilde
Lion's half-brother. She had written about her half-brother's son in May
1941, in one of her *Rundbriefs*, 'My nephew came in full uniform
to see us and to let us share a little in his military life.'

One occasion reconnected Dr Lion and Dr Leven with their past.
They returned to Krefeld, Dr Leven's hometown, in September 1951,
to celebrate the seventieth birthday of a close friend who had asked
Dr Leven, who was fifty-two at the time, to conduct a Women's Choir
for an audience of over four hundred. She was to lead the singers
in a composition she had conducted in that town in 1931. Dr Lion, fifty-
eight, who travelled with Dr Leven for the performance, was profoundly
moved by the experience. Unprepared for the flood of memories, she
found forgiveness in the experience. There is wistfulness in her report,
a passion in her words that shine a light on the emotional cost of her
exile. 'A thunderous, nearly tumultuous applause spontaneously
broke loose.... Tears came to my eyes.... The hall was filled with
an atmosphere of veneration. The last remnants of suspicions, distrust,
petty excuses were blown away, we were no longer accusers or accused

by human beings before a new beginning. On this summer night one had the feeling of suddenly being young again as in the spring of one's life.'[8]

In 1960 the women used their reparation monies and pensions ('shockingly small' according to Dr Leven) to build a house with two self-contained apartments at a 'beautiful and secluded' site in Hindhead. They received many former pupils (some of whom had financed one of their trips to the United States). Dr Lion died at the age of seventy-six, on 8 April 1970. Dr Leven wrote to Martin explaining why she had been unable to visit with him when they were in Boston and enclosed a clipping from the local newspaper about Dr Lion's death. True to form, she complained that the reportage had been inadequate. She concluded, 'Life is hard for me now. We built a beautiful house in Hindhead in 1960 and enjoyed it and the garden for nine years. Now I am alone and must let the furnished top-flat which, fortunately, has its own kitchen and bathroom, before the winter.'

Dr Emmy Wolff

Dr Wolff never took British citizenship. She clung, to the end, to her idealised vision of a Germany resplendent in literature and culture, willing the beauty of art to transcend the ugliness of history. She managed to bring her mother to England during the war and would never return to Germany. After serving for twenty-two years at the school, she retired in 1956 and continued to write poetry. She died on 9 September 1969 in Haslemere, leaving more than four hundred poems, translations and articles. In a letter to a mutual friend, Dr Lion wrote that Emmy was 'a fire-brand, often torn to and fro between the loyalty to the country she had to leave, the land of German Humanism, and England, the land of tolerance and freedom.... Several times a week Emmy visited her mother, usually on her own, without a hat in all weathers. On her way she recited poems from Goethe to Ricarda Huch and on to Rilke, poems of early French to Verlaine, from Shelley to Auden. She has been an excellent translator, and some of her translations have been published in England and Germany.... The inner richness helped her to accept her gradually increasing deafness and loneliness. She never talked about it. She was [un]compromising – at times stubborn, she was fond of her friends and she loved her family, keeping in close touch through unusual vividly descriptive and deeply moving letters. She was a fearless woman who slept alone in her house with windows wide open throughout the night.'[9]

Eleonore Astfalck and Johanna Nacken

Nore and Hanna were among the first expatriates to re-enter Germany after the war, bypassing the red tape for most returnees with the help of First Lieutenant Hans Loeser. After they visited Hanna's parents in Wurtemburg and Nore's brother in Berlin, the two women set about helping where they could do the most good. The educator Minna Specht, also having returned to Germany from exile, asked them to help her reclaim the *Odenwald Schule* near Heidelberg, a facility that had become a Nazi boarding school and, later, a hospital.[10] (While Nore does not specifically address her relationship with Minna Specht while in England, she implies in her oral history that there was communication among the various German refugee educators. Dr Lion was a firm friend of Bunce Court's Anna Essinger and probably corresponded with Minna Specht as well.)

Nore wrote about the deprivations of war-ravaged Germany. 'Everybody got one potato and some boiled turnips for lunch and we had to scavenge the nearby woods for fuel but it was stripped clean.'[11] She recalled that there were only enough boots or shoes for half the school, and so they made the children share, some going around unshod while the others went on an excursion wearing the shoes. Even one of the male teachers could not go to a conference because, he said, 'I have no shoes.' She wrote of the importance of CARE packages from America that brought honey, corn flakes and dried milk.

In 1950, Nore was asked to direct the rebuilding of *Immenhof*, part of a larger worker's welfare organisation, the *Arbeiterwohlfahrt*, a self-help organisation like the Red Cross. The *Immenhof* offered Kindergarten, speech therapy and even a walking school for people injured during the war. It also brought in troubled girls formerly living in foster homes, aiming to educate them without locked doors and windows. Later the *Immenhof* offered domestic science training and provided a home for poor mothers to have a holiday, *Muttergenesungswerk* [Mother's Recuperation], a brainchild of Nore's. Over the years, the indefatigable Nore instituted other programmes: training for mothers of handicapped children, a recreation programme for blind mothers and experimental programmes dedicated to giving very poor people a holiday.

Hanna died in April 1963, in her sixty-seventh year. Drs Lion and Wolff had known Hanna as a feminist activist in Berlin. The two collaborated on a tribute, harkening back to their own salad days. The following was translated by Martin [Friedenfeld] Owens: 'We knew Hanna in the days of the youth movement when she was still wearing wooden beads in her hair. She had the simplicity and love of nature of a *Wanderfogel*. She associated with the social youth organisations ... expressing a new generation. We worked then at practical tasks and also tried to solve philosophical issues ... Hanna, the daughter of a pastor, was opposed to strict and narrow religious dogmas. Inner truthfulness ... was something she did not question.' In their final lines of tribute, Drs Lion and Wolf paid respect to Nore as well: 'Hanna had no visible ambition. She was more capable than her modesty allowed, she was clever, musical and had good taste. With her Rhenish humour and sharp wit she laughed difficulties away. For those she loved, her financial largess knew no bounds. She and Nore helped so many not just with advice but also with action.'

Nore was now alone. She stayed on at *Immenhof* for seven more years. In 1970, at seventy, she planned to retire and join her brother and his wife in Berlin. But she had more to give. She took a job at a *Schule fuer Frauenberufe* [School for Women's Professions] that provided training for social workers and household workers and offered cooking and sewing lessons. She worked full time for another seven years. Still healthy, she started a children's club for Turkish and German children. According to her, what was most valuable about her work was reaching out to the parents of the children. In her eighties, she met a convict (she was doing volunteer work at a prison) who needed someone to accompany him when he travelled under his parole rules. They became friends. She enjoyed travelling with him for several years. She often said that there was no such thing as old age. When she mused about the role ordinary Germans played in the war and the Holocaust, she refused to heap blame on her countrymen. She said, 'You can't pass on what really happened, because if you are honest with yourself, you have to say you cannot understand it. It's not possible to understand what human beings have done to other human beings even when they were not forced to do it.'[12]

Eleonore Astfalck, a most loving woman, died in her sleep during her ninetieth year of life. Months before, she had been fêted at a reunion of Stoatley Roughians in Guilford.

The Roughians

Students who passed through the hallways and dormitories of Stoatley Rough dispersed widely across the five continents. Many acquired new surnames and new identities. Some totally disassociated themselves from Stoatley Rough. Many, of course, have died since 1960, including at least four who are known to have committed suicide. Nevertheless, a core group of Roughians still retains an active connection with the school through the newsletters and occasional reunions. A steering committee (Board of Trustees) still meets regularly to preserve the legacy of Stoatley Rough School. While Dr Lion's file-keeping was anything but meticulous, she knew that her school records had historic value. Upon retirement, she placed the school's files and letters in the archival department of the London School of Economics and Politics, in London. The Trustees of Stoatley Rough raised sufficient money from the alumni to catalogue this large body of materials; today all but the personal files of individual pupils are open to researchers.

Certain general statements can be made about the alumni of Stoatley Rough based on their writings, documents in the archives and aural reminiscences. For one thing, the majority loves the school; they uniformly express gratitude to the people of Great Britain for taking them into their country. They have a lifelong appreciation for classical music and art; they revere neatness, thrift and recycling. Many share a philanthropic, politically liberal attitude towards the less fortunate. Many have maintained their ability to speak and read German, many have shared their histories with high-school students, and many have returned at least once to inspect their former homes, each in his or her own way attempting to come to terms with what happened.

Many went on to higher education, some receiving PhDs. Taken as a whole, a high percentage of Roughians rose to some level of prominence in education, literature and science, and many have entered the healing arts as physicians, psychoanalysts and social workers. A smaller percentage became lawyers, university professors, high-tech workers, business managers and bankers. Women who followed their hearts into marriage and homemaking uniformly seem to have given considerable service to charitable causes.

What follows is a detailed look at the lives of a few who have voluntarily shared their stories for this book; many of them offer a final word about the impact of Stoatley Rough on their lives. The profiles appear in the order in which the survivors arrived at Stoatley Rough School.

Hans Loeser (Arrived, April 1937; left, June 1939)

Hans graduated from Harvard Law School in 1948 with honours, having been given the prestigious invitation to edit the *Harvard Law Review*. Although offered a position with a prominent firm in New York City, Hans chose to join Foley, Hoag and Eliot in Boston, which he helped build into one of Boston's major firms. (He commented that in the early years, some large firms 'wouldn't look at Jews'.) He became partner in five years and went on to serve as managing partner for many years. Hans presided over the Cambridge Civic Association and the Arts and Crafts Council. He opposed the Vietnam War in the 1970s by helping to put a referendum on the ballot asking for the end of the war. While privately accepting many pro bono cases along the way, he was proud to have managed to get himself onto Nixon's enemies list after forming the group, Lawyers against the War in Vietnam. Hans felt that the 'establishment was not being heard enough' and became instrumental in the publication of full-page advertisements in the *New York Times* and *Los Angeles Times*, in which recognised people protested the Vietnam War.

Hans co-founded Lawyers Alliance for Nuclear Arms Control. He was Special Assistant to the Dean of Harvard Law School for long-range planning and was appointed honorary consul for the Republic of Senegal. One of his most gratifying moments came the day his client walked into the room where three Securities and Exchange Commission (SEC) lawyers waited, prepared to do battle. Hans' reputation for fairness and intelligence was such that upon seeing him, the lawyers clapped their hands in appreciation. 'At that point, my client relaxed.' In 2007, at eighty-six, this robust gentleman finally gave up his yearly ski trips to Europe. For many seasons he and Herta met Inge Pavlowsky [Hamburger] (now living in France) and the twins, medical doctors Henry [Heinrich] and Hans Pachmayr still in England, to ski together. Hans drives to his law office in downtown Boston every day except Wednesdays and continues to provide guidance and consultations to his younger colleagues.[13] Hans recently published his memoirs focusing on his life before he arrived in the United States, *Hans's Story*, iUniverse, 2007.

Herta Lewent [Loeser] (July 1937–September 1941)

Herta worked as a civilian in US uniform from 1944 to 1946 in Munich after she married Hans, 'helping tend to the needs of the hordes of refugees then flooding Bavaria'. She was official translator/censor of German mail in the US army, Civilian Censorship Division, and she helped survivors search for relatives. In 1946, she left her parents and brother, Helmut, in England and moved with Hans to Cambridge, Massachusetts, where their first child, Helen, was born. Harris and Thomas followed. Today, the couple have eight grandchildren, all of whom enjoy visiting them in their Cambridge home or at their retreat on Martha's Vineyard.

Profoundly affected by the Women's Liberation Movement in the late 1960s, Herta came home one night and said to Hans, 'there's a revolution going on'. She became involved in helping women find meaningful work, either for pay or through volunteerism, echoing Hilde Lion's own activities at the same age. Herta has always felt grieved by her fate not to have been afforded a university education, yet she more than made up for any lack of paper credentials by taking leadership in a variety of volunteer positions. She put the Society of Arts and Crafts on the map in Boston. It is difficult to overstate this woman's strength of character and leadership skills.

After spending a few years in part-time work with an antiques dealer, Herta was asked to co-chair Boston's Civic Center and Clearing House, an organisation that placed volunteers into the hundreds of charitable opportunities available in greater Boston. She received the prestigious honour of admission to the Radcliffe Institute for a year during which time she wrote *Women Work and Volunteering* (Boston: Beacon Press, 1974), illustrated by her friend Inge Pavlowsky [Hamburger], who had settled with her husband, Maurice, in France. The book sold over 4,000 copies before going into paperback. Herta developed an internship project for seniors in high school until she was offered funding to start Project Re-Entry for women to get back into the workplace. She became the president and director of the Society of Arts and Crafts, America's oldest non-profit crafts organisation in Boston, 'happy that I knew very little about running

a craft gallery'. This gallery, a women's guild of artists, was located
in a lovely old building on Newbury Street, a trendy section of Boston,
offering food, clothing and artefacts for sale long before 'wearable art'
was fashionable. Herta rescued the fine institution from going under by
raising its standards, and for over ten years she steered it comfortably in
the black. Herta spoke about the difficulties she faced. 'Everything we did
had to be fought for and it was never, as I said, credentialed; it was always,
in my case at least, hit or miss and unconventional.'[14]

On her growing-up in Germany, Herta commented that 'In many ways
I didn't really know my father very well because I left when I was sixteen.
In Germany you didn't mingle the way we mingled with our children.
The grown-ups were much more separate. And the children were
tolerated but they were perfectly nicely told to stay out of the way,
to do their own thing, to come in when asked, to speak when asked, to
talk when asked and not to take over. I don't think we ever had the kind
of conversations with my parents that we have had with [our] children.
In Germany we were too young and the situation was too lopsided.'
Profoundly affected by her experience of being wrenched away from
home so early, she noted that travelling later in life was not easy. Her
memories of taking leave from Germany and her family are still residual
and overwhelming, decades after the events. 'Even now when we go off
to Greece and everybody says how wonderful … it's always difficult for
me…. I think that it has to do with having to go on a big trip and never
being able to go back.'[15]

Martin Ludwig Friedenfeld [Owens] (September 1938–May 1945)

Martin headed for New York to live with his mother, new stepfather,
Henry [Oppenheimer] Owens and sister, Lisa, in the Jackson Heights
section of Queens. (His father, John Field, also remarried and lived in
New Jersey.) Before entering college, Martin attended summer school
to study American History, a course he needed for graduation. After
a semester at Elmhurst High School he passed the Regents Examinations,
gaining admission to Queens College from which he graduated in 1951
with a degree in Psychology. Martin would always be grateful for his
stepfather's commitment to Martin's continuing education, since it was
not easy for any penniless newcomer to get through those years. Martin
worked as a shipping clerk in his stepbrother's ballpoint-pen factory, but

his favourite job was as a searcher at the New York Public Library. He served on a committee that persuaded Boris Karloff to attend a gala staff party, and he found Frankenstein's monster the kindest, most courtly of gentlemen. Martin spent other summers working, along with Obo and Wolf, as a busboy at the Breezy Hill Resort in the Catskills, a resort populated by German–Jewish immigrants, where German was the preferred language. Martin says that it only slightly resembled the resort made famous in the movie *Dirty Dancing*.

The Korean War heated up and the draft loomed. After a one-year deferral to attend graduate school at Western Reserve University in Cleveland, Martin volunteered for the Air Force and received one-year training as Electronics Countermeasures Officer. He flew as a first lieutenant out of Puerto Rico for two years on very large airplanes, RB 36's, spending thirty-six-hour stretches flying up and down the east coast of the United States locating and analysing radar signals. He married Jane Passant of Connecticut, and the first of his five children, Joan, was born on the island. After a transfer to Topeka, Kansas, where his son Peter was born, he left the Air Force in 1956 and joined the System Development Division of the Rand Corp as a programmer trainee for the SAGE system, the first automated air-defence system. Martin worked in military systems development for the next thirty-seven years, serving the last twenty-seven with the MITRE Corporation in Bedford Massachusetts, during which time three other children, Suzi, Ethan and Emily, were born. He has thirteen grandchildren.

A mark of the influence of Stoatley Rough on Martin is not only his neatness, drive for punctuality and preparedness (he packs for travel several days before the event) but also his love of classical music. He became president of Adventures in Music, a volunteer group that organised symphony orchestra concerts for middle-school children of Boston's western suburbs while he lived in Lexington. Today he lives in Acton, Massachusetts, with his current wife, Barbara Kirk Wolfenden. He said, 'Stoatley Rough made me a responsible person. People were counting on me doing my part, and I couldn't let them down. I could count on others to do theirs. In my adult life I brought my children up to be responsible. Stoatley Rough, not to mention the country of Great Britain, provided a means for my parents to rescue me from the Holocaust and get a reasonable education. I am grateful to Stoatley Rough for the appreciation of art, literature and music I received, and most of all, for the friendships with the Hut Boys.'

After retiring Martin began to devote more time to his two passions, sailing and skiing. A self-described 'aging jock', Martin, at seventy-nine, teaches skiing at the Nashoba Ski Area in Westford, Massachusetts. He skis annually in Europe, partaking of the Continental cuisine with special gusto, but has only returned twice to Vienna. Although his favourite musical is *Sound of Music*, he has no wish ever to see his homeland again. 'That duplicity of the Austrians made a profound impression on me, and I never wanted to return to Vienna to those two-faced people. It took me fifty years to muster the courage to return. I have been to Vienna twice since, and I still do not like the people. I admire the buildings and historic palaces, and the coffee houses and the food, but I can't ever forgive the Viennese for giving up their country to Germany so easily.'

More than the other Hut Boys, Martin has chosen to leave behind his past. He has never tried to keep up his German (although he speaks it well enough to get around on the Swiss ski slopes). With his anglicised name and the lack of accent, Martin is always taken as American born and reveals his past only to friends. He has never taken part in Jewish religious or cultural events, and his children were raised as Christians. Yet if you ask him for his primary identity – Austrian, British, American – he answers he is a Jew. He has a formal manner and bearing and an uncommonly quiet, non-threatening nature. A new friend of his once remarked that Martin had the exquisite manners of an Austrian and the formality of an Englishman. Martin recognises that he is a private man. Having lost so much so early in life, he says that today his greatest fear is of losing people who are dear to him.

Martin is a national officer in the United States Power Squadrons, a volunteer organisation that teaches boating safety. His wife, the author, to whom he has been married for thirteen years, sails with him on their 32-foot Erickson sloop, *Pamina*. He commented for this profile that she [the author assumes he means her] 'gives me much joy'.

Wolfgang Edelstein [Elston] (February 1939–October 1944)

Wolf graduated *cum laude* from City College with Honours in Geology in 1949, earning the Ward Medal. At first he worked summers as a busboy in the Catskills, then as a shipping clerk in Martin's stepbrother's ballpoint-pen factory. He later taught evenings at City College of New York (CCNY). He did projects for the mining industry to pursue graduate studies at Columbia. 'Warm bodies were desperately needed in front of classrooms jammed with returned GIs.' A Fellowship from the State Bureau of Mines took him to New Mexico for the 1950–1952 field seasons, for which he received $1 per month. After earning his PhD in July 1953, he was drafted into the US Army the day after commencement to become a 'highly educated dishwasher, potato peeler and cleaner of grease traps in the mess hall of Camp Crowder, Missouri.... I went in as a private, came out as a private two years later because I was classified SPP [Scientific and Professional Personnel], which kept me from getting a permanent assignment until two weeks before discharge. No assignment, no promotion. I was, however, eligible for a Low IQ Discharge because I hadn't made PFC in eighteen months. (I was tempted to apply).' Meanwhile Wolf married Lorraine Hind, a journalism student from Columbia, and followed his 'inglorious military career as a tester of nylon socks and petroleum products'. Always one to spot the absurd, Wolf tells of the day a general came to inspect the military sock test site. The great man appeared in the door, looked around and barked, 'Are these socks mercerised?' Wolf snapped to attention. 'Yessir!'

Wolf began work as assistant professor at Texas Tech in Lubbock, Texas, and in 1957 he accepted a position at the University of New Mexico, where the couple raised their two sons, Richard and Stephen, and where Wolf still resides.

He holds numerous academic honours: Founder and Coordinator, University of New Mexico–Los Alamos National Laboratory Volcanology Program, 1990–1999; fellowships from the Geological Society of America, Society of Economic Geologists, American Association for the Advancement of Science and the Meteoritical Society; the New Mexico Museum of Natural History dedicating a symposium to him in 2001; received a tribute at the annual meeting of the Geological Society of America in Denver in 1999, the same organisation that had dedicated a guidebook to him a decade earlier, also granting him honorary life membership.

The boy who once slipped a rock onto Dr Lion's dinner plate has now numerous publications and consultancies and currently works on a project in the Bushveld in South Africa, thinly slicing rocks for scrutiny by electronic microscope. 'I have found evidence that an asteroid or comet disintegrated before hitting Earth two billion years ago, made holes over an area bigger than New England and melted the Earth's crust.' He says, 'I'm one of the lucky people whose vocation is also their avocation.' He suffered the dual losses of his wife of over forty years, Lorraine, in 2000, and his second son, Richard, 'a brilliant astronomer', in 2004, but wrote, 'Family, caring friends (notably the Hut Boys and their wives) and active professional life have helped me to cope'. He said, 'An academic career has given me the freedom to pursue interests in volcanology on this and other planets, at home and in Hawaii, Australia, New Zealand and South Africa. Having arrived in Britain as a stateless child refugee in 1939, it was a thrill to return in 1986 with a Research Fellowship from the Royal Society.'

Wolf speaks fluent German and has a prodigious memory. 'The five and a half formative years at Stoatley Rough have remained a powerful influence on my life. Without knowing it, we Hut Boys were a support group without equal; it's no wonder we have remained friends for life. The strong women who ran Stoatley Rough had their quirks, but where would we have been without them? They not only gave us a safe home, they put us on paths to productive lives. Concerns for others that was instilled by community life at Stoatley Rough have prompted modest efforts in furthering minority students and in speaking to school children about a childhood in Nazi Germany. I still maintain the appreciation for German language and art instilled by those old rivals, Emmy Wolff and Luise Leven. Bilingual readings in modern history are unfolding the tragedy that once sank the gifted "*Land der Dichter und Denker*" [Land of Poets and Thinkers] into savagery and have awakened me to responsibilities as a witness. My public presentations end with a troubling question: How would I have acted if fate had given me ancestors considered "Aryan" by Hitler's perverse definition?' Wolf continues with an expression of gratitude. 'I'm deeply grateful to the people of Britain, who accepted us "enemy aliens" at a time when their own national survival was at risk. America has become my country; it has given me home, family, citizenship, social acceptance and incredible educational and professional opportunities. As a child it was described to me as "*das Land der unbeschränkten Möglichkeiten*" [the land of unlimited possibilities], and so it has turned out to be.'

Hans Max [John] Obermeyer (July 1939–April 1945)

Obo arrived in the United States in January 1947, to live with his elderly uncle, after the war, his only living relative, a man who had escaped while

travel was still possible. Obo worked at various jobs in New York City
while attending a vocational trade school taking machine shop and
related courses. In October 1950 Obo was drafted into the US Army and
was sent to Germany for two years, still awaiting citizenship. Laws after
the war dictated a five-year wait. When he learned that he would be sent
to Germany, he wrote, 'My feelings were of course very confused. On the
one hand the nightmare of having had to leave my parents some eleven
years earlier and having learned of the horrors of the Holocaust and the
death of my family at the hands of the people to whose country I was
about to be sent still plagued me. On the other, I had escaped … and
I was grateful for having been given a second chance at life in my newly
adopted country.'

His return to Germany was difficult. 'After a military parade down
lower Broadway from New York City Hall to the battery, we … crossed
the Atlantic and landed in Bremerhaven and then went by train to a tent
city in Mannheim where I had my first contact with Germans. I heard
an all too familiar language and all that conjured up in an instance.
Most of my fellow infantrymen knew that I understood the language and
I had to interpret for them, especially when the NCOs and the officers
wanted to know where the nearest pubs were located.… I overheard the
Germans on public transportation as we were passing through the still
partly destroyed neighbourhoods, talking about how tough they had had
it during the war and what the Allies and especially the Amies (GIs) had
done to their beautiful cities and how stupid those soldiers were. I stared
them in their faces and left no doubt that I understood what they were
saying. I think one time I spoke up and said how unfortunate it was that
the Russians didn't advance far enough to the west. More than once
I was asked to accompany the military police, when they were called
out to defuse a fight between the GIs and the local police at pubs and
elsewhere.' Obo revisited Bad Salzuflen. 'Note I am avoiding the word
"Hometown".… Basically very little had changed except that my parent's
nice stucco house was now a private hotel presumably still owned by the
Nazi hotel family to which my father had to sell it in 1937.… Everything
looked grey and depressing and badly in need of a coat of paint. We drove
to my father's former place of business, a hardware and housewares store
which he was forced to sell at a ridiculous price. After wrestling with my
thoughts I went inside and immediately recognised a number of former
employees who, presumably because I was in GI uniform and all grown
up, at first did not know who I was. When I identified myself they seemed

genuinely happy to see me and were glad that I had survived the war. They then wanted to tell me about their experiences under the Nazis and who of the former staff was killed on the Russian front. By then I was more than ready to leave town.… It was not until 1977 that I paid the town another visit, then with Joan and I had matured and had a different slant on life.'

Obo spent time casting about for the right job, at one point travelling to Holland to learn the rawhide trade. In 1956 he married and had two children, Peter and Vickie. He ended up working for the DoAll company, a distributor of machine tools, living in various parts of the country, selling industrial metal-cutting machinery, such as metal-cutting band saws, lathes and drilling and grinding machines. When he accepted a management position in Baltimore, he moved to Columbia, Maryland, just a few blocks away from where Goldy had settled a few years earlier. Obo still lives in Columbia with his current wife, the former Joan Berger, having retired after thirty-one years with DoAll. He enjoys spending time with his grandchildren, one of whom is only two years old and, with red hair, the spitting image of Obo. Having become a grandfather for the first time when he was seventy-seven, Obo dotes on the new little 'Ginger Nipper'. Obo serves on the board of his condominium association and attends concerts and theatre in Washington, DC and Baltimore. 'Thanks in part to Dr Leven at Stoatley Rough much of my daily life includes listening to good classical music. I exercise regularly, enjoy retirement and keep busy everyday.' He remarks on his past life. 'Through the "miracle" of the computer I keep in touch with several of the Hut Boys who have remained my best and lifelong friends. I have attended some of the reunions and have told my story to various groups of school children and adults as part of the *Kindertransport* experience. Stoatley Rough School was a positive and vital part of my early life and I hope to continue to keep it alive for the students as long as I can. Life has been good to me after an uncertain and perilous start both in England and [in] the US. I am thankful to Great Britain for saving my life and the US for having given me the opportunity to build a career and the security everyone can achieve in this country if one is willing to work for it.'

Dieter Einhart Gaupp (September 1939–May 1942)

Dieter enrolled at Southwestern University in 1947 and received his undergraduate and masters degree in social work. He became a social worker in the Dallas area. One summer three co-workers invited him to join them in a cross-country trip to California. On the way home, he fell in love with one of the travellers, Fannie Belle Peak, a native of Texas; they have been married for over forty-six years. They had a child, Bill, and bought a small farm along the way. Dieter's career was launched firmly in the public-service camp: he ran children's agencies, worked at a medical school in Dallas evaluating children and became coordinator for clinics for the state. He never forgot his Stoatley Rough introduction to carpentry. He has enjoyed wood-making projects throughout his adult life, forever indebted to his earliest mentor, Hanna Nacken, for showing him the intrinsic beauty of wood.

Dieter had an opportunity to heal old wounds within the Gaupp family that had been inflicted over Nazi membership. While his mother had been born Jewish, his father's people were Aryan, and certain broken allegiances through the years remained unhealed when the war ended. Dieter had never returned to Germany. In 1970, he took his family to Europe to travel around Luxembourg, Liechtenstein, Switzerland, Italy and England, but he avoided Germany. Then in 1979, he and Fannie Belle travelled to India to meet an elderly aunt, a deaconess of one of the Christian Protestant denominations in that country. She encouraged him to re-establish contact with an estranged cousin whose father had been a member of the Nazi special security force, SS. On their return Dieter and Fanny Belle stopped over in Berlin. 'There we met my cousin, embraced and have been very close ever since…. When he came to the States he asked if he could meet my mother. She welcomed him into her home, whereupon he burst into tears.'

Dieter lives with Fanny Belle in the Dallas area, and visits their son, Bill, as often as possible. He currently edits and produces the *Stoatley Rough Newsletters*. He wrote, 'While I was at STRS [Stoatley Rough School] less than three years, my experiences there have lasted me a lifetime. I have valued what I learned, both formally and informally, and the relationships established, some of which are still ongoing. Having come to the school some five years after leaving Germany, it took me some time to integrate back into a German culture and I did not embrace it readily. I also felt at times that the adults in charge did not really understand me as a teenager, so that the close bonds I formed with friends offered me the security I needed and a way to express myself. Looking back, it seems that I was asked to conform and to be dependent when I still had a close relationship with my own family. I am not complaining about this; I know the staff did their best and meant well and cared about me; they just didn't quite know what to do with me. Thus, when I was ready to take the Matric exam, they did appreciate that I could do so with success but instead, denied me the opportunity. Stoatley Rough was for me a very special place and a very special part of my life.'

Peter Georg Gaupp (September 1939–December 1942)

Peter enrolled in Southwestern University almost immediately after arriving from England and studied physics, mathematics and, later, sociology and psychology. 'The Dean's secretary was a stunning redhead and a music education major and I married her.' With his bride in tow, the former Jo-Lou Meitzen, Peter went to work as recreation worker at a large children's institution. He later moved to Austin, Texas, where he earned a master's degree in social work after having held various jobs as a Boy Scout camp programme director, liquor and shoe salesman and recreation therapist with adolescents who were emotionally disturbed. After a stint as a child-welfare worker in East Texas, he became a psychiatric social worker in a Federal research psychiatric prison hospital for narcotics addicts. The couple by then had two children, daughter Robin and son Andrew. In 1964, Peter entered the University of Pittsburgh and earned a PhD in community planning, research and public health. He returned to Dallas to direct a psychiatric research foundation and later worked as a community health planner, 'developing innovative public services such as the first family court services in this region'. He is most proud of his efforts to develop *avant-garde* public services, such as the first regional mental health and mental retardation centre system and a network of community health centres for the poor. 'These efforts were controversial and political pressure forced my job to be cancelled.' He joined the faculty of the nearby State Graduate School of Social Work, where he taught postgraduate and doctoral students, did research and organised a state-wide planning and development agency within the university. He established services in public health, preschool education, housing for the poor, delinquency prevention and banking for the poor. He received a commendation medal from the US Surgeon General and retired as a Professor Emeritus in December 1993. He and Jo-Lou live in Arlington, Texas. 'It's interesting and gratifying how several of my programs, so controversial when I first developed them, are now well-accepted mainstays of the community and doing a great job. The primary health care clinics I developed, for instance, significantly brought down the infant mortality rates, which is wonderful. As I had hoped, they also have done such a good job among the poor that now the middle class wants them and industry is incorporating them into their own operations. And … my principal opponents claim that they did it all.'

Peter is an active member of the church he joined while in England, the Congregational Church, which, he reports, 'is considered one of the most liberal Protestant denominations with a long history of fighting against slavery, homophobia, etc.'. He never lacks the time to visit and support his three grandchildren and to spend time with his close-knit immediate family.

Renate Dorpalen [Dorpalen–Brocksieper] (April 1939–September 1945)

With one brother in the United States, another in Buenos Aires, Argentina, and a third in the American military (who served under General Patton, at one point writing her from 'somewhere in the Ardennes Forest'), Renate was alone after the war. She went through her daily chores at Stoatley Rough on autopilot with no plans, no sense of what she should do with her life. Mürt, her beloved housekeeper, was still in Berlin. Inspired by the biography *Eglantyne Jebb* that Dr Lion gave her (the remarkable Ms Jebb had founded the Save the Children Fund in 1919), Renate applied for a job with one of their Relief Missions on the Continent. She was rejected because she was 'stateless'. Determined to get back to Germany, she became a postal examiner, part of a group of civilian personnel attached to the US Army's Operation Civil Censorship Division. They assigned her to a suburb of Munich. When she notified Dr Lion of her plan to leave the school, Dr Lion objected and tried to convince her to remain, unwilling to lose her best worker. 'Dr Lion did not approve of my plans, but she did not suggest any alternative and we parted, regrettably, in disagreement…. I walked down Farnham Lane to the railroad station for the last time. I felt a sense both of relief and [of] sadness. It was one of those moments in which I sensed the magnitude of being alive and well, and all because above

LITTLE HOLOCAUST SURVIVORS

all nations there is humanity.' Through her brother in the military, she set about to find Mürt. She was not prepared for the wasteland that Berlin had become, her former home now a part of the rubble.

> I had returned after seven years that seemed an eternity. How often had I pictured in my mind this return, never with the reality that was to confront me. In my dreams time had stood still.... The bombed-out cities of England, the ruin and rubble of Munich, had not prepared me for the destruction of Berlin. The formerly vibrant city was barely surviving. Once-crowded streets were empty, filled with silence, the avenues, robbed of their majestic trees, were overgrown with weeds; the parks had turned into wasteland.... The few passers-by hurried along with downcast looks as if they dreaded to leave the safety of their shelters.... children were rummaging for food everywhere, or begged for cigarettes, which had become legal tender on the black market.... The silhouette of the mighty tower of the Kaiser Wilhelm Memorial Church stood ghostlike above the ruins of its sanctuary, looking down the *Kurfürstendam* that had also lost its soul. The jagged tower had become a memorial to the drama performed by fearless, unshaken ministers of the confessional church and other righteous Christians.[16]

Renate struggled to articulate her feelings during the long hours she stayed with Mürt. She recalled sitting outdoors on a curb with the aging housekeeper who had received and relayed messages to various parts of the dispersed family and who had notified the surviving children of their parents' deaths in Theresienstadt. The old woman was dressed in proper black with a white-lace collar, her cane and pocket book beside her, while Renate, young and fresh in her American military uniform, sat by her side. Able at last to unburden her heart, Renate reminisced about the life she had left behind. 'My dominant feeling on encountering German men and women was one of distrust, as I could not help but wonder what part they had played in the sadistic drama. What I felt most, however, was an immense sadness.'

Renate wrote of meeting the 'wrecked members of the master race.... I felt no pleasure in watching the misery of the masses, who had once shouted "*Sieg Heil, Jude Verrecke*" [Hail Victory, Jew die]. They were not reduced to suffering the fate of the haunted, the displaced, the homeless. Here were people who had willingly followed their Fuehrer to conquer the world; these people who years before treated me as an outcast were now ingratiating themselves to me. It was such a strange situation that I could hardly interpret my own feelings. I was supposed to hate them with all my strength. But I could not hate, or was it in the face of such suffering hatred was silent? I would neither sit in judgment nor would it be in my power to forgive and forget.'[17]

Renate moved to New York City in 1947, and worked as a governess during her first summer. She too had to pass the American History course to gain admission to college. She worked in New York City's Settlement House by day (one of several centres established to help recent immigrants to acclimate) and attended Hunter College by night. She graduated with a BA in sociology and history in 1950. She went on to Western Reserve in Cleveland, Ohio, on a full two-year scholarship, where she earned an MA in social work. She moved on to postgraduate work at the University of Michigan, where she met her husband who was completing his PhD. When he moved to Yale University, Renate accepted a position as a social worker in the department of psychiatry. The couple had one son, George, who now works in Branford, Connecticut, near Renate's home in New Haven, Connecticut, where she still lives. She frequently 'babysits' her teenaged grandchildren.

Renate has always been a volunteer. She served on one of the planning committees for the Special Olympics World Games in New Haven in July 1995 and was a delegation host for the German team for that event. She learnt valuable lessons. 'Meeting, mingling and mixing with people from 140 countries and our own fifty states not only highlighted that people from diversified cultures and ethnic backgrounds can get along … but that people with developmental disabilities can become valued citizens.' She recalled having witnessed the 1936 Olympic Games in Berlin as a child. 'All signs of Jewish persecution disappeared temporarily. From the balcony of friends on the *Kaiserdamm* I saw the marathon runner carrying the torch to the stadium…. Jesse Owens, a Negro on the United States team, won four gold medals, astounded the world and upset Hitler's Aryan theories of superiority. While practically living with the German team for ten days on the Yale University campus, I surprised myself once again with thoughts of wondering what part the grandparents, maybe great-grandparents of the athletes, their coaches and the German officials had played in the sadistic drama of Hitler's "Thousand Year Reich". Reconciliation with our past is an intellectual accommodation but will never let us forget the emotional experiences.'[18]

She was a working mother and volunteer for much of her adult life. Widowed many years ago, she wrote, 'for many of us who have pursued professional careers as well as volunteered to fight injustices or to improve the lives of people in need … it was a constant juggling act. Many times I took myself on guilt trips feeling I was short-changing one or the other. I have never forgotten the many people who had helped and supported me … often at risk to themselves. They too were fighting for causes and their belief in righteousness and the goodness of man saved many lives. In their memory I have tried to return to society what had been given to me so generously.'

Hans Ludwig [John Goldy] Goldmeier
(September 1941–December 1944)

Goldy emigrated with his mother and brother to New York. Ralph, his brother, was inducted almost immediately into the Army, and his mother found work as a secretary and nurse. His family had expected to claim a cache of $200 his father had entrusted to the brother of a friend in England, now living in New York. When the man denied receiving the money, the Goldmeier family resorted to the ancient custom of Beth Hadin, a Jewish system of justice in which three rabbis decide disputes. 'This system still existed in New York and had been a way Jews solved legal problems in Russia and other countries where they wanted to remain inconspicuous or thought they could not obtain justice from biased judges in the regular courts.' The Goldmeiers won.

The diligent Goldy embarked on a rich succession of part-time jobs, from apprentice diamond cutter to fur-coat salesman. In that capacity, he caught a glimpse from his showroom of Frank Sinatra being mobbed by screaming girls. 'It made me think that American girls had lost their sense. I did not realise yet that in life there have to be distractions and sometimes it is fine to indulge them, provided they are not harmful. For me, life had always been serious.'[19] Goldy attended evening classes at City College in New York City over the next several years, all the time working a dizzying string of occupations: retail-clothing clerk, door-to-door magazine salesman (he never sold one subscription), pots-and-pans salesman, peep-hole salesman ('a product I really believed in and I felt that the security it afforded would be helpful to the customer. And one could be honest and sincere when selling'). He became a waiter.

'My biggest problem on this job was … other waiters taking away
my orders if I wasn't watching. It was New York all over – dog eats dog.
Also they offered too many pies that I did not know, like lemon, apple,
cherry, lemon meringue and so on. When I could not recognise one, I just
said we had run out, an evasion that worked until a customer noticed his
pie being delivered to another table. So this job ended.' As process server
(he once served a summons to the Broadway theatre owner, Mr Shubert),
he was paid to shout 'present' when the case was called, after which
he called the lawyer on the pay phone to come to court. He worked
summers in the Catskills with Martin and Obo at Breezy Hill Hotel
and with Wolf one summer at the Majestic Hotel. 'We all had to speak
German so that the guests could feel free to speak German … they had
definite habits, from the food they ate to what time they would get up
in the morning.… If someone wanted fish or something not fried, that
could be arranged and people had their bottle of wine at the table just
like in the old country. These hotels were thriving enterprises until
people started to vacation again in Europe and gradually were ready
to see more of the United States rather than huddle with each other.
As for our working conditions, we cheerfully lied to the Department of
Labour inspectors that we had a day off when we never did and that our
accommodations were fine when we were really crammed like sardines
into hot lofts.'

Goldy entered Tulane's graduate programme in social work to defer
his draft for a semester. He received his master's degree in social work
in 1952, returned to New York City and entered military service as
a heavy weapons infantryman. He qualified as an interpreter in French
and German and was sent back to Germany, to Bremerhaven. 'It had only
been fourteen years since I had left as a child and I was ambivalent.' He
decided not to remain in Germany, so he got himself transferred to La
Rochelle, a French port, receiving his commission as a second lieutenant
in 1953. He transferred to La Chapelle St Mesmim, where he was put to
work in the neuropsychiatry department, troubleshooting mental-health
problems. His one 'MASH' incident came about the night a big-shot
general called to demand a veterinarian. The general's dog had swallowed a chicken bone. Goldy and his buddies searched all the bars in
the area with no luck. 'We all made a strategic decision to let the dog run
around a bit longer, coughing away. The story ended happily; the dog got
rid of the bone and the General went away pleased.' In 1955, Goldy left
the Army and returned to New York City to work in the school system

with multi-problem families. He spent 1961 at Columbia University, and in December 1961 married Dotty Fried whose parents had been born in Breslau and Kaiserslautern. The couple had three children: Barry, Karen and Susan.

Goldy earned a PhD from the University of Chicago, School of Social Work, in 1963. He moved to Columbia, Maryland, to take a position as associate professor in the School of Social Work at the University of Maryland and later became full professor, publishing many articles in journals and books and teaching for thirty years. Dottie recalled, 'John was proud that his writing of a grant for a halfway house for mentally ill offenders became a successful halfway house that continued for over thirty years. He was very involved with the running of this facility and worked closely with the Clifton T. Perkins Hospital, a Maryland state hospital for mentally ill offenders. He had intended to continue to be of service to the community, after retiring from the University.' Goldy wrote in the *Newsletter* that although he never became a rabbi, he was grateful for the ideas that Dr Lion 'seemed to espouse and try to promote in others. I mean the idea of open inquiry, respect for others and seeing the dignity of people in a world where this was all but forgotten at the time. I am grateful for that.'[20]

In 2001 Goldy died before he could pursue this final dream of wanting to 'pay back' for the many opportunities that he was granted to advance himself in his life.

Timeline

This story ties into the segments of the twentieth century known as the Holocaust and the Second World War. Salient events of each appear below to help the reader position the narrative of Stoatley Rough School's history within the context of its larger framework.

28 June 1919	Treaty of Versailles ends the First World War
29 October 1929	Stock market on Wall Street crashes; world wide depression
14 September 1930	Nazis become the second largest political party in Germany
30 January 1933	Adolph Hitler becomes Chancellor of Germany; politicisation of all governmental agencies; Dachau concentration camp opened
March 1933	Enabling Act makes Hitler dictator
April 1934	Stoatley Rough opens doors to its first pupils
25 July 1934	Nazis murder Austrian Chancellor Dolfuss
15 September 1935	Nuremberg Race Laws are enacted by the German Parliament
1936	Germany occupies the Rhineland; Mussolini takes Ethiopia; Civil War erupts in Spain; Olympic Games are held in Berlin; first of several 'reconnections' of territories holding significant German-speaking populations
12/13 March 1938	Bloodless takeover or *Anschluss* [Union] with Austria
9/10 November 1938	*Kristallnacht* [Night of the Broken Glass]
December 1938– September 1939	*Kindertransport* – over 10,000 refugees children taken in by Great Britain via special sealed trains
15/16 March 1939	Nazis take Czechoslovakia, close borders
1939	Spanish Civil War ends; Nazis sign pacts with Italy and Soviet Union, invade Poland; British fleet mobilises

1939–1940	Stoatley Rough reaches peak enrolment of over 100 children
3 September 1939	Britain, France, Australia and New Zealand declare war on Germany
8 January 1940	Rationing begins in Britain
10 May 1940	Winston Churchill becomes British Prime Minister
1940	Nazis invade Denmark, Norway, France, Belgium, Luxembourg, Netherlands
Late May to early June 1940	Dunkirk Evacuation of British Expeditionary Forces
10 July 1940	Battle of Britain begins
7 September to 30 December 1940	Blitz
1941	Battles take place in North Africa, Greece, Yugoslavia; Stoatley Rough School becomes Red Cross Message Centre; Roosevelt and Churchill announce the Atlantic Charter; fighting begins in Soviet Union
June/July 1941	SS begin mass murders; Göring instructs Heydrich to prepare for the Final Solution
1 September 1941	Jews ordered to wear yellow stars
1941	Roosevelt and Churchill announce the Atlantic Charter
7/8 December 1941	Pearl Harbor is bombed; the United States declares war on Japan
11 December 1941	United States declares war on Germany
1941	First all-American attack in Europe; Rommel driven back by Montgomery in North Africa; Fermi sets up atomic reactor in Chicago
21 January 1942	Wannsee Conference coordinates logistics of 'Final solution to the Jewish Question'
June 1942	Mass murder of Jews by gassing begins at Auschwitz

1943	Germans surrender at Stalingrad; Montgomery takes Tripoli; Jews rise up in Warsaw Ghetto; Allies land in Sicily
1944	Allies land in Anzio near Rome; Hamburg bombed with three thousand tons; Germans surrender in the Crimea; Nazis liquidate Polish concentration camps; Americans recapture France; Soviet pushes from the East
6 June 1944	D-Day landings
13 June 1944	First V-1 (Doodlebug) rocket attack on Britain
17 September 1944	Allied Airborne (eighty-second) assault begins on Holland
16–27 December 1944	Battle of the Bulge in the Ardennes; Concentration camp victims force-marched away from the camps
11–15 April 1945	Allies liberate Buchenwald and Bergen Belson concentration camps
28 and 30 April 1945	Mussolini captured and hanged; Hitler commits suicide
8 May 1945	V-E (Victory in Europe) Day
9 August 1945	Second atomic bomb dropped on Nagasaki, Japan
2 September 1945	V-J (Victory over Japan) Day
20 November 1945	Nuremberg war crimes trials begin

Background and Sources

Is one death less significant than, perhaps, 2,000? And is the life of one murdered victim more significant than the life of someone who survived the same persecution? As noted earlier, in *The Uprooted: A Hitler Legacy*, Dorit Bader Whiteman refutes the idea that Holocaust survivors who never spent time in a concentration camp didn't really suffer – that 'nothing happened' to them. She claims that everyone whose life was scarred, interrupted or otherwise injured by the evil perpetrated in the name of Aryan supremacy suffered in one way or another. Survivors come in many stripes. The survivors depicted in this book are small in number and most were young when they attended Stoatley Rough School. Some saw their parents again; none endured unspeakable physical cruelties. Nevertheless they suffered. While the book tends to reflect happier memories, the facts are that the children at Stoatley Rough endured great hardship: homesickness, cold, poor sanitation, substandard nutrition and grinding fear. They lost more than can be assessed, accounted for, tallied or compensated for. These children lost their childhood. Yet those who have written and spoken of their days in England retain many positive memories. In the face of their suffering, the fact that they can smile is owed to a small school on a Surrey hillside where, decades ago they spent their few years in refuge growing up. The Headmistress, the Matron, the faculty and, in no small measure, the architecture and gardens of the site itself – all helped to make their survival not only tolerable but a healing experience.

I am grateful to have had the privilege of knowing some of those survivors, of having had access to the stories of others, and for the support and encouragement of yet others who helped me write this book.

Sources

The material in the book comes from the spoken and written words of the alumni and staff. The most voluminous supply has been the Stoatley Rough Newsletters, collections of reminiscences, archived materials and news published by alumni for alumni. This material is the stuff of memory and time. It took the Roughians many years before they could settle their new lives to the point where it was safe to turn around and look back. Barbara Gerstenberg [Prasse] wrote, 'For so many years I repressed most of my life prior to coming to America and focused on being a good middle western wife and mother.'[1] Once those people began to write, however, they poured out great quantities of rich stories, too many to capture in one book.

I had access to the Stoatley Rough School correspondence, records and reports housed in the London School of Economics, which yielded information about the board of trustees during the critical start-up years, as well as other important clues to the school's inner workings. Another valuable resource was Katharine Whitaker and Michael Johnson's excellent short history, *Stoatley Rough School 1934–1960*, illustrated by Chris Townson, written for the Sixtieth Anniversary Reunion of May 1994. Many alumni granted me interviews in the United States, England and Switzerland. Autobiographies, memoirs and oral histories have also provided crucial details that bring the stories to life. On the occasion of the first 'official' reunion, Hans Loeser and Herta Lewent Loeser had the foresight to record and distribute such documents as *Oral History of Eleanore Astfalck* and *Since Then* (a collection of stories by alumni about their lives after leaving Stoatley Rough).

The views in the book are not the whole story. Countless former students remain unrepresented, some of who may disagree with my interpretation of the school. The views reflect the thoughts of those who survived to write, of those who chose to write and as I interpreted them. I tried to stay as close to the facts as possible and apologise if there are omissions, half-truths or just plain untruths in this accounting.

Refugee Schools in Great Britain Contemporaneous to Stoatley Rough

A few other schools for child refugees were established in Great Britain, most smaller than Stoatley Rough School.[2] In response to Nazi policies, more than twenty schools were founded worldwide, largely boarding schools oriented towards the German progressive educational reform tradition of *Landerziehungsheime* (countryside educational homes). They all had one common task: 'to support the uprooted and confused refugee children as they developed a new and complex identity, and as they came to terms with an alien environment'.[3]

Anna Essinger's Bunce Court in Kent, England, was the largest school with roughly 900 students over nine years. (Next came Stoatley Rough, with a cumulative student count of around 800 over its twenty-six years.) Bunce Court began life in Germany and was transplanted to England.

Miss Essinger, with the help of two sisters and her physician brother-in-law, started the school in Ulm, Germany, in 1929 as an alternative to traditional German pedagogy. Like Hilde Lion, she was a progressive educator who believed in child centred, non-punishing methods of teaching, and she combined vocational training such as carpentry, sewing and cooking, with academics. In 1933, Miss Essinger moved Bunce Court with the heroic help of the Quakers and wealthy Jewish benefactors from Germany to England, just one step ahead of Nazi defilement. (Tamar Duke-Cohan wrote in her unpublished document, *Our Family, Part I: The genealogy and history of the Essinger, Levistein, Oppenheimer, Gottheiner, Seeligsohn and Ostberg families*, that one of the school's buildings was later given to General Erwin Rommel, the Desert Fox, who in 1944, while recovering from war wounds, was taken from that house and forced to commit suicide in the local hospital.)

Bunce Court settled in England on property that dates from the time of Henry VIII. The school resembled Stoatley Rough in many ways: it used play performance to teach English; it held non-denominational, cultural celebrations; it depended on benefactors to house children during holidays; it struggled with getting the children to speak English, to name a few similarities. In June 1940, the British army requisitioned the Bunce Court estate, forcing most of the school to move to Trench Hall in Shropshire. Stoatley Rough even housed a contingent of Bunce children on a temporary basis at that time. The school continued to operate until June 1946, accepting prisoners from Nazi concentration camps. By 1948, Anna Essinger, almost seventy, closed its doors. Her students remembered with gratitude the kindly Anna Essinger without whose efforts they would have perished.[4]

Other exile schools in England included the Beltane School, moved by its founders Ernst and Ilse Bulowa from Berlin to Wimbledon where it housed thirty children. It closed in 1941. Another famous exile school was Gordonstoun, near Abderdeen, Scotland, still very much in existence. Known for its famous pupil, Prince Charles, and for having educated other members of the British royal family as well, Gordonstoun was founded by Dr Kurt Hahn, an exiled German Jew, in 1934. Modelled on the first school established by Hahn, Schule Schloss Salem, Gordonstoun preached self-realisation through community service and a spartan lifestyle. The school moved to Wales during the war and has evolved to become an important independent educational institution today.[5] Another school, smaller, was Camp Hill House, founded by

Karl König, who moved fifteen of his colleagues to Aberdeen to form an educational workshop for handicapped and non-handicapped children;[6] Minna Specht's *Landerziehungsheim* (countryside educational home) school named Walkemühle, was founded in Denmark, then moved to Wales, and finally occupied a country house near Bristol called Butcombe Court in 1938. It closed in 1940, although Minna Specht herself continued to educate children in a camp school on the Isle of Man. (Ms Specht's school building on Man was later used by Quakers to care for half-Jewish survivors of Theresienstadt.) Towards the end of the war, a group called the Free German Cultural Alliance created the Theydon Bois School near London under the directorship of Hans Schellenberger. Its purpose was to prepare young German and Austrian refugees for their return home.

Specialised Diction

Nazi

Hitler's political party was the *Nazionalsozialistische Deutsche Arbeiterparteir*. People called them Nazis for short, much as Socialists (*Sozialistische Partei*) were called Sozis. The Nazis called themselves NSDAP and used the prefix NS for organisations, for example, *NS Frauenschaft*, the Women's Organisation.

Headmistress versus Head of school

In the 1930s, the female head of any independent school was known by the gender-specific title, headmistress, a term shunned usually today in favour of the more neutral term, head or head of school.

Matron

We think of a matron in connection with prisons; yet the term is still used outside the United States quite normally to describe a job at an independent boarding school. A matron today is expected to love children and be able to listen to them, represent to them an authority figure, have responsibility for their day-to-day needs and their physical welfare and possibly to know first aid and have the ability to plan menus of nutritious meals. The matron at Stoatley Rough covered most of that ground (except for the meal planning) and in addition, taught classes and managed a unique housekeeping training program.

Pupil versus Student

In the 1930s student was a word reserved for those studying at a university. Pupil is used to describe children at Stoatley Rough.

Manse, big house, main house or country house versus mansion

The students never thought of Stoatley Rough's main dwelling as a mansion. A mansion carried the connotation of something much grander, a building or complex of buildings more on the scale of a residence owned by someone extremely wealthy or titled. The Vernons were very wealthy but unpretentious. Stoatley Rough was their country house.

Aryan and non-Aryan versus Jew and Christian

The National Socialists cared greatly about genealogical lineage and came up with 'Aryan' (a Sanskrit word meaning noble, used to describe the ancient inhabitants of northern Europe), to distinguish true Germanic blood from Jews. The headmistress and her cohorts always used the terms 'Aryan and non-Aryan', never 'Jewish' or 'Christian' to describe themselves and their young charges.

Birth names, married names and new names after immigration

Many students anglicised or changed their names after leaving Stoatley Rough School. I have retained the original German name in referring to them, and included, at first mention only, their (new) anglicised name in brackets. This holds for married women as well – the use of their original maiden name, followed by their married names in brackets, e.g. Renate Dorpalen [Dorpalen-Brocksieper] or Herta Lewent [Loeser] and Martin Friedenfeld [Owens].

List of Illustrations

1. Stoatley Rough School, c.1935. Hanna Nacken, SRS Archives, London School of Economics (LSE)

2. Dr Hilde Lion, post-war. Photographer unknown, SRS Archives, LSE

3. Eleonore Astfalck, pre-war. Photographer unknown, SRS Archives, LSE

4. Dr Emmy Wolff, undated. Photographer unknown, SRS Archives, LSE

5. Dr Luise Leven, undated. Photographer unknown, SRS Archives, LSE

6. Johanna Nacken, pre-war. Photographer unknown, SRS Archives, LSE

7. Sitting Room with Morris Fireplace, Peter Strauss on chair c.1939. Johanna Nacken, SRS Archives, LSE

8. Inge Hamburger [Pavlowsky] with unidentified child, c.1938. Johanna Nacken, SRS Archives, LSE

9. Renate Dorpalen [Dorpalen-Brocksieper] age nineteen, 1939. Johanna Nacken, SRS Archives, LSE

10. Ten-year-olds on the heath, 1938. Johanna Nacken, SRS Archives, LSE

11. Luggage of new arrivals, undated. Photographer unknown, SRS archives, LSE

12. School sign sculpted by Hermann Nonnenmacher, c.1938. Photographer unknown, SRS Archives, LSE

13. Hans Obermeyer with his horn of plenty on his first day of school, Bad Salzuflen, Germany, 1934. Collection of John Obermeyer

14. Kate Lesser in Liverpool Street Station, August 1939, upon arriving with 150 other children from Berlin. Appeared in the London Evening Standard, collection of Kate Lesser

15. Lisel Loeser and Wolf Edelstein [Elston] building the swimming pool, 1938. Photographer unknown, SRS Archives, LSE

16. Cadets Peter Gaupp (left) and Bruce Main, Shoreham, 1944. Collection of Peter Gaupp

17. Dieter Gaupp, age fifteen, 1939. Johanna Nacken, SRS Archives, LSE

18. All-school Easter game, undated. Johanna Nacken, SRS Archives, LSE

19. Boy studying, undated. Johanna Nacken, SRS Archives, LSE

20. Haymaking on the farm, pre-war. Johanna Nacken, SRS Archives, LSE

21. Hans Loeser and Herta Lewent on their wedding day, 11 December 1944. Collection of Hans and Herta Loeser

22. *Left to right:* Peter Gaupp, John Obermeyer, John Goldmeier, Martin Friedenfeld [Owens], Wolf Edelstein [Elston] celebrating their 50th birthday in Columbia, Maryland, 1978. Collection of John Obermeyer

Bibliography

Baer, Elizabeth R., and Goldenberg Myrna, eds. 2003. *Experience and Expression: Women, the Nazis and the Holocaust*. Detroit, MI: Wayne State University Press.

Bielenberg, Christabel. 1970. *The Past Is Myself*. Oxford: Clio Press.

Clare, George. 1983. *Last Waltz in Vienna*. New York: Avon Books.

Elston, Wolfgang E. 1987. 'Goldschmidtschule, Berlin-Grunewald, 1938–39'. In *Passages from Berlin*. Edited by Steve J. Heims. South Berwick, Maine: Atlantic Printing.

Epstein, Helen. 1979. *Children of the Holocaust*. New York: Penguin Books.

Epstein, Helen. 1998. *Where She Came From: A Daughter's Search for Her Mother's History*. A Plume Book. New York: Penguin Books.

Feidel-Mertz, Hildegard. 2004. 'Integration and Formation of Identity: Exile Schools in Great Britain'. *Shofar* 23/1: 71–84.

Fox, Anne L. 1996. *My Heart in a Suitcase*. London: Vallentine Mitchell.

Goldhagen, Daniel Jonah. 1997. *Hitler's Willing Executioners: Ordinary Germans and the Holocaust*. New York: Vintage Books.

Goldmeier, John. 2000. 'Memoirs', Part 1. Columbia, MD [unpublished].

Gorell, Lord. *A Great Adventure: The Story of the Refugee Children's Movement*. London: Bloomsbury House.

Holton, Gerald, and Gerhard Sonnert. 2003. 'What Happened to the Austrian Refugee Children in America?' A report from research project 'Second Wave', June, Department of Physics, Harvard University, Cambridge, MA.

Jeffreys, D. 1965. 'Some Earlier History of Stoatley Rough'. *Stoatley Rough School Archives*, File 11/12, London School of Economics.

Kubicek, Peter. 2002. *1000: 1 Odds: Memoir of a World War II Childhood*. New Canaan, CT: Information Economics Press.

Laqueur, Walter. 2001. *Generation Exodus*. Tauber Institute for the Study of European Jewry Series. Hanover, NH: Brandeis University Press.

Leverton, Bertha, and Shmuel Lowensohn, eds. 1990. *I Came Alone: The Stories of the Kindertransports*. London: Book Guild, Ltd.

Loeser, Hans F. 2001. 'Legal Oral History Project'. Interview dated March 2. The University of Pennsylvania Law School [unpublished].

Loeser, Hans F. 2007. *Hans's Story*. Lincoln, NE: iUniverse.

Loeser, Hans F., and Herta Loeser, eds. 1971. *Since Then … Letters from Former Stoatley Roughians*. Boston, MA [unpublished].

Loeser, Hans F., and Herta Lewent Loeser, eds. 1991. *Reminiscences*. Boston, MA [unpublished].

Loeser, Hans F., Herta Loeser, and Eleonore Astfalck. 1990. *Oral History of Eleanore Astfalck, 1900–Recorded July 1985*. Cambridge, MA [unpublished].

Loeser, Herta, and Tom Loeser. 1988. *Oral History Recorded during the Winter of 1988 between Herta and Tom Loeser*. Cambridge, MA [unpublished].

Megged, Aharon. 2002. *The Story of the Selvino Children: Journey to the Promised Land*. Translated from Hebrew by Vivian Eden. London: Vallentine Mitchell.

Meyer, Gerda. 2005. *Prague Winter*. London: Hearing Eye.

Milton, Edith. 1993. *The Tiger in the Attic: Memories of the Kindertransport and Growing Up English*. Chicago: University of Chicago Press.

Samuels, Diane. 2000. *Kindertransport*. London: Nick Hern Books.

Segal, Lore. 2004. *Other People's Houses*. New York: New Press.

Seligmann, Matthew, John Davison, and John McDonald. 2003. *Daily Life in Hitler's Germany*. New York: Thomas Dunne Books, St. Martin's Press.

Shirer, William L. 1960. *The Rise and Fall of the Third Reich*. New York: Simon & Schuster.

Simmel-Joachim, Monika. 1993. 'Background of the Five Principal Refugee Teachers of Stoatley Rough School from Nazi Germany'. *Ariadne* 23, 23 May.
Speer, Albert. 1970. *Inside the Third Reich*. New York: The Macmillan Company.
Whiteman, Dorit Bader. 1993. *The Uprooted: A Hitler Legacy: Voices of Those Who Escaped before the 'Final Solution'*. New York: Insight Books, Plenum Press.

Newsletters from Stoatley Rough School 1934–1960

Vols 1–23, December 1992–September 2004.

Web References

On Other Schools

Duke-Cohan, Tamar. 'The Essingers', Part 3. Boston, MA.
http://www.egu.schule.ulm.de/wsignals/wsignals9/aessi04.htm (cited November 2004).
Jüdische Privatschule von Dr Leonore Goldschmidt. Luisenstadt edition, 1998–2003.
http://www.berlin-geschichte.de (cited 10 November 2007), http://www.luise-berlin.de/
Gedenktafeln/cha/j/juedische_privatschule_von_dr.htm cited (cited 28 October 2005).

On the Battle of Britain

Battle of Britain Historical Society, Education and Research for Students. 'The Battle of Britain: 1940'. http://www.battleofbritain.net/0020.html (cited 11 April 2005).

On the Quakers

Traces: We Bring History to Life. 'Quaker Refugee Projects'.
http://www.traces.org/quakerrefugeeprojects.html (cited November 2004).

On the Blitz

EyeWitness to History. 2001. 'The London Blitz, 1940'.
http://www.eyewitnesstohistory.com/blitz.htm (cited October 2004).
The Wiener Library, Institute of Contemporary History. www.wienerlibrary.co.uk (cited 13 June 2008).

Other Books Consulted

Bikales, Gerda. 2004. *Through the Valley of the Shadow of Death*. Lincoln, NE: iUniverse.
Glassner, Martin Ira, and Robert Krell, eds. 2006. *And Life Is Changed Forever: Holocaust Childhoods Remembered*. Detroit, MI: Wayne State University Press.
Nicholas, Lynn H. 2006. *Cruel World: The Children of Europe in the Nazi Web*. New York: Random House.
Silten, R. Gabriele S. 2004. *Is the War Over? Postwar Years of a Child Survivor of the Holocaust*. McKinleyville, CA: Fithian Press.
Tayar, Enzo. 2004. *Days of Rain*. New York and Jerusalem: Yad Vashem.
Winter, Miriam. 1997. *Trains: A Memoir of a Hidden Childhood during and after World War II*. Jackson, MI: Kelton Press.

Notes

Chapter 1: Sanctuary

1. Hilde Lion, quoted by Monika Simmel Joaquin in her paper delivered at the Seventieth Anniversary Reunion 22–25 October 2004, Haslemere, Surrey, entitled 'Background of the Five Principal Refugee Teachers of Stoatley Rough School from Nazi – Germany: Dr Hilde Lion, Dr Emmy Wolff, Eleonore Astfalck, Hanna Nacken and Dr Luise Leven'. The quotation, translated by Dr Simmel-Joaquin, appeared in Manfred Berger's work, *Hilde Lion, in Christ und Welt* 5/1995, p.167. 'M. Berger holds several papers of many women in the history of welfare in his private "Ida Seele Institute."

2. The *Jugendheim* was founded in 1898 by Anna von Giercke (1874–1943) who became Hilde's mentor and friend, who ran it largely by and for women. It offered training to the general population in nutrition, counselling, day care and job skills and functioned primarily as a teacher training institution for careers for women in social work, kindergarten and child care.

3. Susi Weissrock [Rice], 'The Story of Gabi, Susi and our Mother', *Stoatley Rough Newsletter*, Issue 4, February 1994, p.10.

4. Miss Bracey found Dr Hilde Lion through her Quaker colleagues, Corder and Gwen Catchpool, in Berlin. Not many people knew that a Berlin International Centre was established after the First World War to promote reconciliation between England and Germany. Bertha Bracey would be awarded the Order of the British Empire (OBE) in 1942 for her humanitarian work during the Second World War. Another key founder of Stoatley Rough was Mrs Anna Schwab of the Jewish Women's Committee and Chair of the Hospitality Committee of the Refugee Committee. A native of Frankfurt am Main, she had not only worked with German refugees in England during the First World War but was instrumental in converting the B'nai B'rith rooms in a building called Woburn House in London into a refugee organisation that would assist the entry into England of many Stoatley Rough children during the Second World War.

5. Eleonore Astfalck, *Oral History (1990)* [unpublished].

6. Council members/benefactors included Miss Bertha Bracey, Miss E. Day, Sir Wyndham Deeds, Professor G. P. Gooch, Leonard Monfiore, Sir Walter Nicholson, Lady Parmoor, Lady Pentland, famous for her work with Lord Pentland in raising money for a hospital ship for the people of Madras, and Lady Sprigge who, with her husband, Sir Squire Sprigge, worked to discredit the false science of eugenics, or race-classification.

7. Original Committee members included Miss Bertha Bracey, Miss B. Alexander, Miss Isabel Fry, Dr Mary E. Gilbert, Miss Mary Hayward, Ms Omerod and Mrs Marjorie Vernon.

8. Mr Vernon spent a few years after the First World War as financial advisor to the government of Iraq. Then, after a lifetime of service, he was paralysed from the waist down after a plane crash in Palestine. He died in 1942, predeceasing Mrs Vernon by almost twenty years. The couple had one adopted daughter, Sally. Mrs Vernon, who, upon her death in June 1961, was colourfully characterised in the local newspaper as 'a bit of an autocrat and contradictory', to which, as if to mitigate his dubious description, the writer hastens to add, '[but] generous'. Apparently she was not an infinite source of funds for the school, however. In a letter to Dr Lion dated 16 February 1935, she writes with great cordiality, 'Dear Dr Lion. Thank you for your letter. I'm afraid the income tax is yours! Also you will have to pay the tax for the two gardeners – I return the form, also the telephone receipt.'

9. Obo wrote that Mr Phillips was succeeded by a 'Miss Woolger who lived in his nice cottage with her big Irish Terrier dog. She was a very nice lady, always wore riding boots, and was a good horticulturist.'

10. Mr Arthur Leon moved his family from Russell Square, London, to the Haslemere house in 1889. His parcel of land on the farthest end of shady Farnham Lane was one of the prettiest sites in the county, formerly owned by a Quaker surgeon, Jonathan Hutchinson.

11. Rapturous descriptions such as that of Beate Frankfurter [Planskoy] describe 'high-growing bracken and yellow flowering gorse, bilberry and blackberry plants.... I shall also never forget the beautiful terraced gardens with the tall mature trees, the flowering rhododendron and wisteria, and the many secret places where one could hide when in need of solitude. In the winter the branches of the trees were heavy with snow and the landscape took on the magical appearance of a Hans Anderson fairytale.' The house offered a spectacular view of many of miles of verdant countryside. The poet and Roughian Gerda Meyer [Stein] recalled, 'It may need saying, for the sake of the younger reader, that the world – visually and aurally at least – was an altogether prettier and quieter place than now. But even by the standards of those days, Stoatley Rough must be reckoned to have been uniquely beautiful.'

12. In a letter to her mother dated 20 November 1936, Dr Emmy Wolff wrote that Phillips had won ten prizes in Haslemere's vegetable and flower show that year: 'two firsts, four seconds and four thirds for the lovely vegetables (especially the English celery), pears and a rare form of chrysanthemum which he cultivates'. 'We Lived at Stoatley Rough', translated by Katya Schaefer [Sheppard], *Stoatley Rough Newsletter*, Issue 8, June 1995, p.16.

13. Gerhard [Gad] Wolff, 'A Traveller's Tale', *Stoatley Rough Newsletter*, Issue 19, August 1999, p.49.

14. Martin Friedenfeld [Owens], unpublished memoir, *The Journey*, 1988.

15. Hilde Lion, 'Letter to Principal of Shottermill School', *Stoatley Rough School Archives*, Box 1/1 (ii), London School of Economics.

16. Ibid.

17. Martin's *Kleine Omi* and *Opi* also escaped, but his *Grosse Omi*, the maker of *apfelstrudel* [apple strudel], chose to stay behind. She died in Theresienstadt. Over the course of the war, 65,500 Austrian Jews were deported and perished as victims of the National Socialists.

18. The researchers studied the effects of the social, psychological and economic effects of the Holocaust on Austrian–Jewish children in America. They found resiliency and other abiding values, yet there were scars. 'They, their families and many of their friends were suddenly considered outlaws, thrown into dreadful turmoil by the persecution, assaults, expulsion from their schools – while their parents, with some most honourable exceptions, were made to experience much worse.... The National Socialist regime and a hostile population in Austria learned in days what had taken years in Germany.' The authors list possible traumas: firing of teachers; prohibition from using theatres, playgrounds, parks; exposure to assault by mobs and uniformed men; takeovers of apartments, offices, shops and other property. On 26 April 1938, the vicious newspaper, *Volkischer Beobachter*, widely read in Austria as well as Germany, even ran an article, 'How Can We Get Rid of the Jews?' While the study found that Austrian refugees did relatively well economically and led productive lives (and described positive effects of their early experience on their attitude, stating that 'success was the best revenge'), others were demoralised by Nazism, became depressed in the new world and, over the years, have suffered in later life anxiety, panic attacks, fear of abandonment and suspicion of all authority.

19. Wolf Elston, in an email to the author.

20. Coincidentally, two other people at Stoatley Rough shared a common history with the Goldschmidt School. Eva Graetz was only nineteen when she was hired to teach at the Goldschmidt School, requiring Dr Goldschmidt to give her lessons in teaching techniques. The assistant principal of the Goldschmidt School was Herta Lewent's uncle. Dr Kurt Lewent, a noted scholar of medieval Provençal literature, was known to children

like Wolf as *Kinderschreck* [Frightener of Children]. Wolf said, 'He went around with a pained look on his face and attitude of stern discipline.... He was in fact, in constant pain, the result of wounds from his services as an officer in WWI, fighting for his *Kaiser und Vaterland*. Eva Graetz was so young that one day Dr Lewent encountered the young teacher in a school hallway during classes and bawled her out (*Er hat Sie angeschnauzt*, as only a German teacher can do), mistaking her for a wayward pupil.' A small group of Hitler Youth tried to attack the school on 11 November 1938 just after the *Kristallnacht* siege when one half of the male teachers were arrested. Miss Graetz wrote 'Dr Goldschmidt called up all the women teachers begging them to come and ... let the show go on. Many of the [children's] fathers had been arrested. Everybody tried to prepare for emigration. The present and future of these children spelled danger and insecurity, but if they came to school, one part of their life would continue, business as usual. Needless to say we, the women teachers, were all glad to come. [It was characteristic of Dr Lewent that he] insisted on completing his French class while a mob was threatening to burn down the school. Only after the closing bell did he finally lead the quaking kids to safety out of the back door, and go into hiding himself.... Dr Leonore Goldschmidt saved the school by selling it for 10 Reichsmark to Mr Whooley, one of the British teachers [who had been hired to prepare] us for our future in an English-speaking country. That placed the school under the protection of His Britannic Majesty and the Nazis did not dare to provoke an international incident.' In 1939, the SS occupied the site of the school and the students moved to Kronberger Road. Leonore Goldschmidt was unsuccessful in moving the school abroad. She escaped as Dr Lewent stayed on to oversee the school's closing on 30 November 1939. Dr Lewent eventually escaped the country and resumed teaching Provençal literature at the New School in New York.

21. Wolf Edelstein [Elston], in a note to the author.

22. Bettina Warburg's father Paul had helped to set up the Federal Reserve for Woodrow Wilson. She and her husband Kubie co-chaired the American Psychoanalytic Association's Emergency Committee on Immigration that helped people in the medical profession leave Germany.

23. Hilde Lion, 'Round Robin Letter', *Stoatley Rough School Archives*, Box 1/1 (i), London School of Economics.

24. Elston, in an email to the author.

25. The idea for of a train to remove children from harm's way originated with the British Committee for the Jews of Germany and became known worldwide as the *Kindertransport*. Jews, Quakers and Christians of many denominations helped in the courageous and heroic work, especially the Berlin Quakers, a hardy but tiny band of friends that actually increased in numbers during the Nazi years who challenged officials time and again to right the wrongs they saw, sometimes losing their lives in their efforts to speak truth to power. England, alone among the countries of the world, agreed to accept 10,000 children. Private citizens or organisations had to guarantee to pay for each child's care, education and eventual emigration from Britain. In return for this guarantee, the British government agreed to permit unaccompanied refugee children to enter the country on simple travel visas. The nine-month rescue operation brought between 9,000 and 10,000 children into the country, some 7,500 of them Jewish, from Germany, Austria, Czechoslovakia and Poland. The last transport from Germany left in September 1939, just before the Second World War began, and only a few months before Obo boarded his train. The last transport from the Netherlands left on 14 May 1940, the day that country it surrendered to Germany. Eighty percent of the *Kindertransport* children never saw their parents again. About half of the children (some older ones carried refugee infants placed aboard the trains by parents) ended up in the homes of foster families, some of whom immediately put the children into service as farm workers or domestics. Others treated the children as their own. Some *Kindertransport* children stayed clustered in communal hostels

and on farms throughout Britain. And some came to Stoatley Rough. (Obo was on one of the special railway wagons which took the children via Bergen, Hanover, to Hoek van Holland or Flushing and on to Harwich in England.) A committee then distributed the children at Liverpool Street Station in London. The *Kindertransport* Association (KTA) website, http://www.kindertransport.org/history.html (accessed November 2007).

26. Hans [John] Obermeyer, From notes of talks about his life before the Holocaust delivered over the years to schools in the Baltimore area.

27. Erich Kästner's classic tale of a boy who falls asleep on a train and awakens to find his money gone. The boy enlists a gang of Berliner children to track down the thief. Written in 1929, this story is seen to attack Hitler's totalitarian regime with humour and pacifist ideals. The author also wrote *Baron Munschhausen* and several other popular tales. 'Books and Writers', http://www.kirjasto.sci.fi/kastner.htm (accessed June 2003).

28. Haydn's *Toy Symphony* was a mainstay of Stoatley Rough's musical repertoire, first performed in 1937 for Dr Lion's birthday, when Nore Astfalck joined the performers by clicking keys on her typewriter. Peter Gaupp recalled the school performed it the following year, when Dr Leven allowed Wolf to participate. 'Wolf played the nightingale using a type of water pipe with water spewing all over the place. "I think I had the tambourine at one time and then was demoted to the triangle when I could not get my act together."' The *Toy Symphony* was performed many times at the school, always tongue-in-cheek. Once it was performed as a surprise wake-up for Nore Astfalck's thirty-seventh birthday. The performances took place with one or two actual musicians playing the melody, while many other children played the kazoo, triangle, toy trumpet, drums and a bubbling waterpipe that was supposed to suggest a nightingale's song. Wolf remembered that the school did one more concert in Haslemere during the war. 'Dr Leven had kicked me out the choir, without warning or explanation (as usual). I had thought my singing was just great and I'm still mad.'

29. Lily (Putti) Cassel [Wronker], 'Life at Stoatley Rough', *Stoatley Rough Newsletter*, Issue 26, November 2007, p.13. Taken from a letter in German written home, translated for this book by Martin Owens: '*Sie hatte blonde Haare, einte tuerquise blaues costume, eine weinrote Bluse, Handschuhe aus Wildleder und sehr huebsche Schuhe aus der selben Farbe, die Fingernaegel aber in einem anderen Rot. Sie unterhielt sich sehr nett und natuerlich und sang alle Deutschen Lieder mit.*'

30. Hans [John] Obermeyer, in an email to the author, October 2005.

31. Ruth Morgan [Roberts], 'Letter to the Editor', *Stoatley Rough Newsletter*, Issue 9, October 1995, p.13.

32. 'Committee Notes', January meeting, *Stoatley Rough School Archives*, File 1/1 (i), London School of Economics.

33. Ibid.

34. Renate Dorpalen [Dorpalen-Brocksieper], 'Stoatley Rough Remembered', *Stoatley Rough Newsletter*, Issue 6, October 1994.

35. Dieter Gaupp, 'Reminiscences', *Stoatley Rough Newsletter*, Issue 12, October 1996, p.34.

36. Hans [John] Obermeyer, 'I Remember', *Stoatley Rough Newsletter*, Issue 17, June 1998, p.10.

Chapter 2: In the Beginning

1. Eleonore Astfalck, *Oral History (1990)* [unpublished], pp.1–16.

2. 'First Committee Report', *Stoatley Rough School Archives*, File 1/1 (i), London School of Economics, 10 November 1934.

3. Astfalck, *Oral History*, pp.2–9.

4. Ibid.

5. Isabel Fry (1869–1958) was an educationist and social activist. She founded, and was headmistress of, The Farmhouse School, Mayortorne Manor, Wendover and, later, Church

Farm, Buckland, Aylesbury, Buckinghamshire. She came from a famous reforming Quaker background and was the daughter of Sir Edward Fry (1827–1918), jurist, and sister of (Sara) Margery Fry (1874–1958), penal reformer, and Roger Eliot Fry (1866–1934), artist and critic. http://www.ioe.ac.uk/library/archives/fy.html (accessed 24 September 2007).

6. 'First Committee Report', *Stoatley Rough School Archives*, File 1/1 (i), London School of Economics, 10 November 1934.

7. Fred wrote he was well paid; had his *shamba* [land], where he grew spinach, lettuce, asparagus and cabbage; and had six chickens for breeding. He walked to work 3 miles (4.8 kilometres) away where he did office work and where he 'engaged' or 'sacked' the labourers and listened to their troubles. 'I have no paper, no wireless, and am free from political worries', *The Bridge*, vol.2, August–September 1941, pp.66–67. (Other early agricultural students were Ernst Wilzek, who emigrated to New Zealand and became a land surveyor in 1939 before the war. Klaus Zedner was interned and sent to Canada and later returned to England to work on a farm before the school lost track of him.)

8. 'First Term Report of German–English School', *Stoatley Rough School Archives*, File 1/1 (i), London School of Economics, 10 November 1934.

9. Ibid.

10. Ibid.

11. Ibid.

12. Ibid.

13. 'Committee Meeting Notes', *Stoatley Rough School Archives*, File 1/1 (i), London School of Economics, 7 October 1935.

14. Stoatley Rough School Song:
    Gladly we join to sing our song
    We who to Stoatley Rough belong
    Proud, we display our circles three
    Bound by a chain which makes us free.
    God of the South, God of the North,
    God of us all, we venture forth.
    Many the kinds of work we do
    Kitchen and farm, and classrooms too
    All to the common good shall give
    Learning together how to live.
    God of the South, God of the North,
    God of us all, we venture forth.
    Silver and blue our colours are
    This is the news they spread afar
    Dark through the clouds of pain and fear
    Silver, the ray of hope shines clear.
    God of the South, God of the North,
    God of us all, we venture forth.

15. *Stoatley Rough School Archives*, File 1/1 (i), London School of Economics.

16. Katharine [Meyer] Whittaker and Michael Johnson, illustrated by Chris Townson, 'Stoatley Rough School 1934–1960: A Short History', *Stoatley Rough School Archives*, London School of Economics, 1994.

17. The enrolment numbers cited in this book are approximate, gleaned from a list of students put together from the confidential files now in the London School of Economics archives. The list was created by Katharine Whitaker and Michael Johnson as a compendium to their short history, which they distributed in May 1994, for the sixtieth Anniversary Reunion in England. I extrapolated milestone enrolment numbers from the ages, dates of arrival and dates of departure noted on the Whitaker/Johnson list for each student who attended the school up to 1945. Some pupils' names are missing since some

records are missing. The school lacked permanent lists and records, perhaps owing to the fluid nature of the arrival and departure of the pupils.

18. Whittaker and Johnson, 'Stoatley Rough School 1934–1960', p.11.

19. Bertha Bracey, 'Letter to the Committee', *Stoatley Rough School Archives*, File 1/1 (i), London School of Economics, 7 October 1935.

20. 'First Term Report of German–English School', *Stoatley Rough School Archives*.

21. Ibid.

22. Ibid.

23. Kate Lesser, in an email to the author.

24. Ibid.

25. Astfalck, *Oral History*, pp.6–8.

26. *Stoatley Rough School Archives*, File 4/13, London School of Economics.

27. Yet another lesson plan of 1940 lists the German literature that Dr Wolff would teach. Summer Term: Thomas Mann, *Unordnung und fruehes Leid; Schiller, Don Carlos* [Disorder and Early Sorrow (fiction); Schiller, Don Carlos]. Winter Term: *Der Biberpelz; Gelesen und Aufgefuehrt; Bahnwaerter Thiel; Naturalismus und Realismus* [The Beaver Coat (play); Read and Performed; Signalman Thiel; Naturalism and Realism].

28. Inge Rothschild [Hershkowitz], from a letter to the author dated December 2004.

29. *Stoatley Rough School Archives*, File 1/1 (i), London School of Economics.

30. Ibid.

31. Ibid.

32. Liesel Neumann, 'Domestic Science', *The Bridge*, vol.2, August–September 1941, p.16.

33. Ibid.

34. *Stoatley Rough School Archives*, File 1/1 (i), London School of Economics.

35. Hilde Lion, 'Dr Lion's Lecture, Notes of a Lecture Given by Hilde Lion on November 24, 1937', *Stoatley Rough Newsletter*, Issue 3, October 1993, p.7.

36. Hans [Obo, Ginger Nipper John] Obermeyer, 'Our Plots', *The Bridge*, August–September 1941.

37. Emmy Wolff, 'Extracts from Letters from Emmy Wolff to Her Family, August 1934–February 1939', translated by Katya Shepard [Schaefer], *Stoatley Rough Newsletter*, Issue 1, December 1992, p.8.

38. Alexander Finkler, 'Drama on the Farm', *The Bridge*, vol.2, August–September 1941.

39. An early participant in the Farm programme, Klaus Zedner, is a case in point. He left the school at seventeen in 1938 with an uncertain future. He joined a government programme designed to train refugees to become farmers or farm managers in Australia. They were supposed to work on a real farm with eighteen other boys from Austria and Germany. They would have been sent to Australia if the war had not interrupted the scheme. The programme attracted the attention of the press. He later wrote to Dr Lion. 'After some time our training farm became well-known, so much that for a fortnight or more we spent most of our time giving interviews to reporters, posing for press-photographers and answering all sorts of questions. Two sound films were made of us. Later we went to a cinema to see and hear ourselves as stars on the screen!' 'Farmwork in England', *The Bridge*, vol.1, May 1940, p.35.

40. Wolff, 'Extracts from Letters from Emmy Wolff to her Family'.

41. Wolf [Elston] Edelstein, in an email to the author.

42. 'Dr. Lion's Semi-Annual Report', *Stoatley Rough School Archives*, File 1/1 (i), London School of Economics, 1938.

43. Ibid.

44. Ibid.

45. Manfred Berger, 'Emmy Wolff, Her Life and Her Achivements', article reprinted in *Stoatley Rough Newsletter*, Issue 13, February 1997, p.13, and Issue 14, May 1997, p.28,

translated by Gerda Haas. Manfred Berger, distinguished scholar and founder of the Ida Seele archive dedicated to the history of the kindergarten in Dillingen, Germany, wrote about many pioneering feminists of the Weimar era, including Johanna Goldschmidt, Alice Salomon, Luise Froeberl, Anna Warburg, Gertrud Pappenheim, Maria Montessori and Hildegard von Gierke.

46. Gerhard [Gad] Wolff, 'A Traveller's Tale', *Stoatley Rough Newsletter*, Issue 19, August 1999, p.49.

47. Emmy Wolff, translated by Katya [Schaefer] Sheppard, 'We Lived at Stoatley Rough', *Stoatley Rough Newsletter*, Issue 1, December 1992, p.8.

48. Ibid. p.10.

49. Emmy Wolff, translated by Gerda Haas, 'We Lived at Stoatley Rough', *Stoatley Rough Newsletter*, Issue 8, June 1995, p.16.

50. Ibid. p.18.

51. Angela Galligan [Roberts], 'Not So Prussian As All That!', *Stoatley Rough Newsletter*, Issue 12, October 1996, p.9.

52. Eveline Kanes, 'Remembering Stoatley', *Stoatley Rough Newsletter*, Issue 18, September 1998, p.49.

53. Ibid.

54. Galligan, 'Not So Prussian As All That!'

55. Dr Luise Leven's unpublished notes on the history of Stoatley Rough School, Stoatley Rough School Archives, Box M3253, London School of Economics.

56. Wolf Edelstein [Elston] talks about the tabloid mentioned by Dr Leven. '*Der Stuermer* was a viciously anti-Semitic paper published by Julius Streicher, the corrupt and sadistic *Gauleiter* (Nazi Party Governor) of Nuremberg. He was so notorious that even a lot of Nazis were disgusted by him but he retained Hitler's confidence in return for total loyalty. He had been at Hitler's side during the failed 1923 uprising in Munich. Streicher was one of the defendants at the original 1946 Nuremberg Trial, convicted and hanged. *Der Stuermer* was displayed all over Berlin (and other towns, I imagine) in framed public bulletin boards called *Stuermerkasten* [*Kasten*=box] (not many solid citizens would have wanted to be seen buying a copy at a news stand). As it combined anti-Semitism with pornography, it was very popular with *Gymnasium* [secondary schools for boys] students; the kind who waylaid me on my way home from the *Goldschmidt-Schule*. For this reason, I had to avoid one corner of a city square, the Elsterplatz. The *Stuermerkasten* at that corner faced a Jewish *Altersheim* [Home for the Aged]. Today the building has a plaque in memory of its staff and residents, who were deported and murdered in 1942.'

57. The ancient city of Halle, near Leipzig, is the home of the distinguished Protestant College for Church Music, still a respected institution.

58. Leven's unpublished notes on the history of Stoatley Rough School.

59. John [Goldy] Goldmeier, *Memoirs*, Part 1 [unpublished], p.51.

60. Pupil identified as S. L., 'Sounds, Sights, and Smells at Stoatley Rough', *The Bridge*, vol.2, August–September 1941, p.9.

61. Kanes, 'Remembering Stoatley', p.51.

62. David Fielker, 'What Did I Want to Do When I Grew Up?' *Stoatley Rough Newsletter*, Issue 10, February 1996, p.34.

63. Elston, in an email to the author.

64. Ibid.

65. Beate Frankfurter [Plonskoy], 'A Few Memories and Bits and Pieces', *Stoatley Rough Newsletter*, Issue 23, September 2004, p.5.

66. Renate Herold [Richter], in an email to the author.

67. Elston, in an email to the author.

68. Goldmeier, *Memoirs*.

69. The boys took great delight in putting words to classical music. Other entertaining versions included the following:

From the seduction aria from *Don Giovanni* [Mozart]
Gieb mir die Hand, mein Leben,
Komm auf mein Schloss mit mir.
Ich will dir Bratwurst geben
Und auch ei-ein Glaessche-en Bier
Give me your hand, my Dearest
Come to my castle with me.
I want to give you bratwurst
and a glass of beer.
From Schubert's 'Unfinished Symphony'
Frieda, wo gehst Du hin,
Wo kommst du her,
Wann kehrst Du wieder
Frieda, where are you going?
Where do you come from
When are you coming again?
From Handel's 'Daughter of Zion Rejoice' (from *Elijah*)
Tochter Zion, Freue Dich,
Doktor Lion, Freue Dich
Daughter of Zion Rejoice
Dr Lion, Rejoice

70. Peter Gaupp, in an email to the author.

71. Herta Lewent [Loeser], Oral History Recorded during the Winter of 1988 between Herta and Tom Loeser [unpublished], Cambridge, MA, 1988.

72. Leven's unpublished notes on the history of Stoatley Rough School.

73. Renate Dorpalen [Dorpalen-Brocksieper], 'Stoatley Rough Remembered' (continued from Issue 7), *Stoatley Rough Newsletter*, Issue 8, June 1995, p.25.

74. Lewent, Oral History Recorded during the Winter of 1988.

75. Gerda Haas, note to the reader regarding her translation of Monika Simmel-Joachim's article, 'Hilde Lion – For the Centenary of Her Birth', *Stoatley Rough Newsletter*, Issue 12, October 1996, p.27.

76. Astfalck, *Oral History*, pp.1–16.

77. Leven's unpublished notes on the history of Stoatley Rough School.

78. Ibid.

79. Renate Dorpalen [Dorpalen-Brocksieper], 'Letter to the Editor', *Stoatley Rough Newsletter*, Issue 8, June 1995, p.6.

80. 'A Lion, a Wolf and a Fox' was first published in *Meridian* magazine, 1974.

81. German for 'Trout song', a reference to Schubert's famous quintet.

Chapter 3: The Child Workers
1. Hans Loeser, *Hans's Story* (Lincoln, NE: iUniverse, 2007), p.50.
2. Ibid. p.53.
3. Ibid. p.72.
4. Ibid.
5. Ibid. p.74.
6. Ibid. p.77.
7. Stoatley Rough was a powerful influence in her life, as it was for so many of its pupils. Not only did Barbara save the little wooden box, but she carried the imprint of William Blake's majestic old standard, *Jerusalem*, she had learned while at Stoatley Rough. 'There was a big event to which patrons and supporters of the school came and we had all learned to sing

it. Several years ago, the movie *Chariots of Fire* used it in its closing scenes, with the school-boys amassed in the chapel and the organ booming. It stirred some very deep memories as I viewed it in the theater. I could still remember all the words to it.' Living in Connecticut, she remains friends with Hans and Herta in Cambridge, Massachusetts.

8. Margaret Dove Faulkner, 'Refugees Meet Again After Fifty Years', in *Reminiscences* (collection) written in connection with a School Reunion held in Guildford, Surrey, 9–11 November 1990 [unpublished], Boston, MA.

9. Eleonore Astfalck, *Oral History (1990)* [unpublished], pp.5–14.

10. All quotations in this section appeared as part of Herta's article, 'A Glimpse in the Office', *The Bridge*, vol.1, 14–15 May 1940, p.10.

11. Chilblains is a condition that causes hands and feet to swell painfully, itch and produce purple or green sores, sometimes treated with applications of iodine.

12. Herta Lewent [Loeser], Oral History Recorded during the Winter of 1988 between Herta and Tom Loeser [unpublished], Cambridge, MA, 1988, pp.2–10.

13. Ibid.

14. Ibid.

15. Hilde Lion, 'Dr. Lion's Lecture', *Stoatley Rough Newsletter*, Issue 3, October 1993, p.7.

16. Renate Dorpalen [Dorpalen-Brocksieper], 'Work of the Domestic Science Group', *The Bridge*, vol.1, May 1940, p.12. Renate omits the fact that once a month general cleaning was undertaken by the whole school.

17. Ruth Bayer [Tuckman], 'Memories', *Stoatley Rough Newsletter*, Issue 7, February 1995, p.12.

18. Margot Kogut, 'Letters Home' (from a letter she wrote home on 1 April 1935), *Stoatley Rough Newsletter*, Issue 3, October 1993, p.29.

19. Ilse Kaiser [Neivert], 'Reminiscences of Stoatley Rough', *Stoatley Rough Newsletter*, Issue 21, October 2002, p.43.

20. Inge Hamburger [Pavlowsky] from a letter to the author dated November 2004.

21. Renate Dorpalen [Dorpalen-Brocksieper], 'Stoatley Rough Remembered', *Stoatley Rough Newsletter*, Issue 7, February 1995, p.15.

22. Renate Dorpalen [Dorpalen-Brocksieper], 'The House I Love', *The Bridge*, vol.2, August–September 1941, p.53.

Chapter 4: Their Finest Hour

1. Katya Sheppard [Schaefer], tr., 'We Lived at Stoatley Rough', letters from Emmy Wolff to her family, 10 July 1937.

2. Peter Gaupp, *Stoatley Rough Newsletter*, Issue 22, December 2003, from his diary an entry dated 9 January 1941.

3. Dieter Gaupp, "Excerpts from Autobiography", *Reminiscences*, 1991.

4. Hans [John] Obermeyer, in an email to the author.

5. Gaupp, "Excerpts from Autobiography", *Reminiscences*, 1991.

6. Wolf Edelstein [Elston], 'Memories of Stoatley Rough School', in *Reminiscences* (collection) written in connection with a school reunion held in Guildford, Surrey, 9–11 November 1990 [unpublished], Boston, MA.

7. Ilse Kaiser, 'Shoe Repairing', *The Bridge*, vol.1, no.2, August–September 1941, p.18.

8. H. P. (Hans or Heinrich Pachmayr), 'Shelterlife in Stoatley Rough', *The Bridge*, vol.2, August–September 1941, pp.5, 6.

9. Ibid.

10. The two American songs were featured in movies, the first from *Snow White and the Seven Dwarfs* released in 1937. Modern audiences associate the other song with the 1952 movie *Singin' in the Rain*, yet it was first sung by Judy Garland (her co-star was Mickey Rooney), in the movie *Babes in Arms* in 1939. 'Heigh-ho' was composed by Frank

Churchill with lyrics by Larry Morey. 'Singing in the Rain' was written by Nacio Herb Brown, lyrics by Arthur Freed.

11. H. P., 'Shelterlife in Stoatley Rough'.

12. Dieter Gaupp, 'Reminiscences', *Stoatley Rough Newsletter*, Issue 10, February 1996, p.12.

13. Ibid.

14. From *Time Watching* (London: Hearing Eye, 1995). First published in *Dancing the Tightrope* (London: The Women's Press, 1987).

15. The book was later made famous with the Pulitzer Prize-winning play in 2004, *I Am My Own Wife,* by Doug Wright (Faber and Faber, New York).

16. This anecdote was related to the author by Peter Neivert, Ilse Kaiser's son, who contacted Charlotte after reading her biography.

17. Margaret Dove Faulkner, 'Where School Was Home', *AJR Journal* (1990) [issue unknown].

18. Dieter Gaupp, *Stoatley Rough Newsletter*, Issue 15, October 1997.

19. This former officer of the Imperial German Navy had developed a small cigar-shaped incendiary, composed of two chemicals that when fused, provided an intense fire, which could easily be smuggled among the cargo being loaded in the United States. He wrote a book about his espionage, *Dark Invader,* which Germany refused to publish or sanction. He turned against his former country, went to live in England, befriended one 'Blinker' Hall, his former captor, and asked if he could don a British uniform and join the fight against Germany in the Second World War. He was widely respected by the British. Editorial review of *The Dark Invader*, http://www.amazon.ca/exec/obidos/ASIN/0714647926/702-3183931-0806431 (accessed 18 June 2006).

20. Ilse Kaiser's letters, collection belonging to her son, Peter Nievert, Providence, RI.

21. Ibid.

22. Dieter Gaupp, 'Reminiscences', *Stoatley Rough Newsletter*, Issue 15, October 1997.

23. Originally formed in 1917, this group performed jobs such as engineering, road clearing and other manual tasks for the British military. They were later known as the Royal Pioneer Corps. 'Some six "alien" pioneer companies were set up in the 1939/1940; they were not issued arms but expected to engage in road construction work, setting up Nissen huts and other such works … The officers appointed … were those unwanted in other parts of the army. Their camps were miserable…. They were not given British nationality upon enlisting, which meant that they would have no protection if they were taken prisoners of war.' Walter Laqueuer, *Generation Exodus* (London: I. B. Taurus, 2004), p.74.

24. Dieter Gaupp, 'Reminiscences', *Stoatley Rough Newsletter*, Issue 14, May 1997.

25. In her on-line memoirs, Sheila Lahr relates that her father was a friend of Nonnenmacher and was also interned. There were many artists on Mann who found themselves bereft of tools and art supplies. Miss Lahr tells the story of how the many interned artists improvised their art supplies. They used 'oil paint made from crushed minerals, dyes abstracted from food rations mixed with oil from sardine tins, paint brushes from Samson Schames' strong and wiry beard'. She names various artists and their scrounging activities: 'While artists Dachinger and Nessler collected gelatine from boiled-out bones and mixed it with flour and leaves to size newspapers, and so made paper on which to draw with burnt twigs for charcoal. The artists of Onchan used also the reverse side of wallpaper, and having stripped one room completely, formed a human chain along the walls with each artist drawing a portrait of his neighbour on the bare wall, to form a continuous frieze. Lino from corridors and kitchens was used for linocuts. And Weissenborn manufactured an enduring printing ink by mixing crushed graphite from lead pencils with margarine. Kurt Schwitters made use of ceiling squares of a composite material to paint portraits and landscapes.' http://www.militantesthetix.co.uk/yealm/CONTENTS.htm

26. Gaupp, Stoatley Rough Newsletter, Issue 14.

27. Ibid.

28. Ilse Kaiser, conversation with Iam Holmby, author.

29. 'Board Meeting', *Stoatley Rough School Archives*, File 1/1 (i), London School of Economics, 6 October 1940.

30. Renate Dorpalen [Dorpalen-Brocksieper], 'Letter to the Editor', *Stoatley Rough Newsletter*, Issue 14, May 1997, p.8.

31. Dieter Gaupp, 'Reminiscences', *Stoatley Rough Newsletter*, Issue 16, February 1998, p.20.

32. Inge Hamburger [Pavlowsky], *Reminiscences* (collection) written in connection with a School Reunion held in Guildford, Surrey, 9–11 November 1990 [unpublished], Boston, MA. At the Stoatley Rough reunion in England in 1990, Inge learned that her tablemate at one of the meals felt she had suffered a similar fate from Dr Lion. Inge said with a smile, 'So it was not me, after all.'

33. Gaupp, *Stoatley Rough Newsletter*, Issue 16, p.22.

34. 'Board of Governors Meeting', *Stoatley Rough School Archives*, File 1/1 (i), London School of Economics, 6 October 1940. That year a list was kept of the Farm Boys: Heinz Pachmyr, Fritz Drechsler, Franz Otto Ernst, Heinz Guggenheim, Goetz Houser, Hans Heinz, Helmut Lewent (Herta's brother), Peter Rosenfeld and Ernst Roussal.

35. Gaupp, *Stoatley Rough Newsletter*, Issue 16, p.20.

36. Ibid.

37. Ibid.

38. Ibid.

39. Alexander Finkler, 'Stoatley Rough Farm Alphabet', *The Bridge*, vol.1, 14–15 May 1940, p.14.

40. Author unknown, from *The Bridge*, vol.2, August–September 1941, p.19, 20.

41. Dr Lion, 'Rundbrief', *Stoatley Rough School Archives*, File 1/1 (i), London School of Economics, 20 May 1941. Women who took over men's jobs on farms during the war were part of the Women's Land Army (WLA) and widely known as 'Land Girls'.

42. Edward Hughes, portions of his farm diary reproduced in *The Bridge*, vol.2, August–September 1941, pp.17–19.

43. Bridgitte Heinsheimer [Pring-Mill], *The Bridge*, vol.1, 14–15, May 1940, p.14.

44. Gaupp, *Stoatley Rough Newsletter*, Issue 16, p.23.

45. Ibid.

46. Ibid. p.24.

47. Ibid.

48. Inge Schleimer, 'The Past – Music', *The Bridge*, vol.2, August–September 1941, p.54.

49. Battle of Britain Historical Society, 'The Chronology', p.23, http/www.battleofbritain.net/0023.html (accessed 19 May 2008).

50. Renate Dorpalen [Dorpalen-Brocksieper], 'Stoatley Rough Remembered', *Stoatley Rough Newsletter*, Issue 7, February 1995, p.22.

51. Wolf Elston, on the occasion of Nore Astfalck's 90th birthday.

52. Dieter Gaupp, 'Reminiscences', *Stoatley Rough Newsletter*, Issue 12, October 1996, p.35.

53. Hans [John Goldy] Goldmeier, *Memoirs*, Part 1 [unpublished], January 2000, p.49.

54. At first, the British planes were no match for the Messerschmitt Bf 109 and 110 fighters, and later the Focke-Wulfs. British aircraft developed during the 1930s such as the Bristol Bulldog, the Hawker series and the Gloster Gladiator (including some old biplanes), initially slow and cumbersome, were soon upgraded. Airplanes began to roll off the assembly lines: The Boulton-Paul 'Defiant' (1936), the Bristol Blenheim (1938), the Hawker Hurricane (1936), the Supermarine Spitfire (1938), the Bristol Beaufighter (1939) and the DeHavilland Mosquito (1942) along with constant upgrades of the others. After 1941, the Americans filled the skies with Corsair, Tomahawk and Mustang airplanes.

55. After the war, Biggin Hill became an RAF hiring centre and, until the late 1970s, the site of an annual air show on Battle of Britain Day, 15 September. The RAF left Biggin Hill in 1992, leaving behind St George's Royal Air Force Chapel of Remembrance to honour those who died defending Britain from the airfield, http://www.bigginhill.co.uk/ (accessed June 2008).

56. While British radar technology was superb, the country recognised early on that its supply source was inadequate. In 1940 the British made an informal arrangement with top US military and industrial leaders to share their technology for mass production processes supplied by the Americans. The agreement saved the day.

57. Goldmeier, *Memoirs*. Wolf later wrote that the noise came mostly from the British defensive planes. 'After the 1940–41 Blitz, there were "little Blitzes" in the springs of 1943 and 1944. By that time, British defenses were formidable. That's where most of the noise came from. Then, in 1944, shortly after D-Day, came the V-1s and (later) V-2s.'

58. Renate Dorpalen [Dorpalen-Brocksieper], 'Stoatley Rough Remembered', *Stoatley Rough Newsletter*, Issue 5, June 1994, p.41.

59. Dieter Gaupp, 'Reminiscences', *Stoatley Rough Newsletter*, Issue 10, February 1996, p.10.

60. Wolf Edelstein [Elston], 'Memories of Stoatley Rough School, Haslemere, Surrey, England 1939–1945', in *Reminiscences* (collection) written in connection with a school reunion held in Guildford, Surrey, 9–11 November 1990 [unpublished], Boston, MA, p.8.

61. Ibid. Wolf Edelstein [Elston] adds that the army was probably the Canadian army; the second Canadian Armoured Brigade had its headquarters in Hindhead and would become famous after the Normandy D-Day.

62. Wolf believes that although the children were frightened on a regular basis, they were not 'continually on the edge of our seats, worrying about bombs, safety, being taken for spies, etc.' He wrote, 'The wonder is how normal our lives were in the midst of horror. That was the school's principal achievement.'

63. Dorit Baden Whiteman, *The Uprooted: A Hitler Legacy* (New York: Insight Books, Plenum Press, 1993).

64. Margaret Dove [Faulkner], in a letter to Herta Lewent [Loeser], 31 March 1990.

65. Goldmeier, *Memoirs*, p.55.

66. Renate Dorpalen [Dorpalen-Brocksieper], 'Stoatley Rough Remembered', *Stoatley Rough Newsletter*, Issue 9, October 1995, p.30.

67. Ibid. p.32.

68. Renate Dorpalen [Dorpalen-Brocksieper], 'Stoatley Rough Remembered', *Stoatley Rough Newsletter*, Issue 6, October 1994, p.35.

69. Ibid.

70. Martin Owens, unpublished memoirs.

71. Ibid.

72. Goldmeier, *Memoirs*, p.59.

73. Ibid.

74. Hanno Pilartz, in an email to the author. The Black Hut was one of the sheds on the farm. Hanno and Uli were allowed to live in this shed after the war and, apparently, it had also been commandeered as a getaway for some of the teachers at the school.

75. Uli recalled that Dr Lion was pleased that the local newspaper reported the quick action of the boys. The Haslemere Fire Department later gave formal commendation to Dr Lion.

76. Inge Wurm [Sloan-Schleimer], 'Stoatley Rough Remembered', in *Reminiscences* (collection) written in connection with a School Reunion held in Guildford, Surrey, 9–11 November 1990 [unpublished], Boston, MA.

77. Dorpalen, 'Stoatley Rough Remembered', *Stoatley Rough Newsletter*, Issue 7, p.18.

78. Ibid. Wolf Edelstein [Elston] has no memory of being told to destroy letters.

79. Dorpalen, 'Stoatley Rough Remembered', *Stoatley Rough Newsletter*, Issue 7.

80. Components of this word mean roughly grain, soft mass and cereal.

81. Peter Gaupp, 'Notes from a Diary, 1941–1942', *Stoatley Rough Newsletter*, Issue 22, December 2003, p.37.

82. Renate Dorpalen [Dorpalen-Brocksieper], 'Stoatley Rough Remembered', *Stoatley Rough Newsletter*, Issue 5, June 1994, p.38.

83. 'Annual Meeting of School Board', *Stoatley Rough School Archives*, File 1/1 (ii), London School of Economics, 26 February 1941.

84. Ibid.

85. The embossment G IV R stood for George IV Rex. It could also be found on other governmental property such as mail boxes.

86. Eleonore Astfalck, *Oral History (1990)* [unpublished].

87. The material that follows was found in *Stoatley Rough School Archives*, M3207 Box 2, London School of Economics & Politics.

88. Ibid.

89. Ibid.

90. Ibid.

91. Inge Hershkowitz, 'Shattered', *Stoatley Rough Newsletter*, Issue 22, December 2003, p.11. Her parents survived the Nazis because her father was made to continue manufacturing a compound he had devised that was equal to crude rubber, of vital importance in the war to the Nazis. The poem she quotes is from 'Restless Love' by Johann Wolfgang von Goethe (1749–1832).

92. Gina Schaefer [MacKenzie], *The Bridge*, vol.2, August–September 1941, p.14.

93. Dr Lion, in an article written about the school's status in *The Bridge*, vol.2, August–September 1941, p.3.

94. Along with private school instructor, Trevor Chadwick, the three well-heeled men set up a rescue organisation for the thousands of Czech children they had discovered not eligible for *Kindertransport*, working night and day to save them. Great Britain would only admit children for whom homes were found and guarantees deposited – £50 for each child – an enormous sum. Raising money, cutting through the red tape, even forging Home Office entry permits, Winton and his helpers succeeded in getting the first transport by airplane out of Prague in March 1939 with several trainloads in the works. The effort was short-lived. The last trainload of children left on 2 August 1939, while one month later, a large transport of children was shut down when Hitler invaded Poland and closed the borders. Winton returned to England, married and carried on, never mentioning this part of his life, even to his wife. In 1988, almost 50 years after the fact, she came across a scrapbook dated 1939 in their attic, with the Jewish children's photographs and names. He was to be honoured by the world. Honours included those from Yad Vashem (Holocaust Martyrs' and Heroes' Remembrance Authority, located in Israel) who named him a Righteous Citizen of the World; he was made an Honorary Citizen of Prague; received the MBE (Member of the British Empire); was awarded the Order of T. G. Masaryk by the Czech Republic. In 2002, he was knighted by Queen Elizabeth II. Winton's story is the subject of two films by Czech filmmaker Matej Mináč: *All My Loved Ones* and the award-winning *Nicholas Winton: The Power of Good*. Today, Sir Nicholas Winton, age 97, lives at his home in Maidenhead, Great Britain. A ring given him by some children he saved is inscribed with a line from the Talmud, the book of Jewish law: 'Save one life, save the world'. Nicholas Winton, 'The Story', The Power of Good website, http://www.powerofgood.net/story.php (accessed 10 November 2006). Roughian Laura Selo attended Sir Nicholas's 95th birthday party hosted by the Czech Embassy. BBC History, 'WW2 People's War: Three Lives in Transit', www.bbc.co.uk/ww2peopleswar/stories/82/a6988882.shtml (accessed 24 October 2007).

95. Goldmeier, *Memoirs*, p.25.

96. Ibid. p.26.

97. Ibid.

98. Ibid.
99. Ibid.
100. Ibid. p.35.
101. Ibid.
102. Ibid.
103. Ibid.
104. Ibid.
105. Ibid. p.21.
106. Ibid.
107. Gerda Meyer [Stein], 'Professor Siegfried Stein', *Stoatley Rough Newsletter*, Issue 9, October 1995, p.20.
108. Hans Goldmeier, 'Religion at Stoatley Rough', *Stoatley Rough Newsletter*, Issue 18, September 1998, p.31.
109. Goldmeier, *Memoirs*, p.101.
110. Hans [Obo, Ginger Nipper, John] Obermeyer, in an email to the author.
111. Dorpalen, 'Stoatley Rough Remembered', *Stoatley Rough Newsletter*, Issue 6, from a letter written on 24 November 1939, by her father to her brother.
112. Stoatley Rough children fared better than their counterparts in Bunce Court, Kent, at least in its early years. In 1933 the school's first year in England, the crowded living conditions at Bunce Court gave rise to a few cases of diphtheria and scarlet fever. That terrible year, one boy even died from polio, placing the entire school into isolation for weeks, forcing tradespeople to leave provisions at the gates and restricting short meetings with parents or relatives to the open November air. 'Quaker Refugee Projects', We Bring History to Life, http://www.traces.org/quakerrefugeeprojects.html (accessed 19 May 2008).
113. Gaupp, *Stoatley Rough Newsletter*, Issue 12, p.31.
114. Ilse Kaiser [Neivert], 'The Dentist Is Coming', *The Bridge*, vol.1, 14–15 May 1940, p.20.
115. Rosemarie Gumpel, 'Letter', *Stoatley Rough Newsletter*, Issue 21, October 2002, p.21.
116. Jan Schneider, 'Letter, 1945–1947', *Stoatley Rough Newsletter*, Issue 5, June 1994.
117. Eddie Behrendt, in an email to the author, 13 May 2005.
118. Susi Weissrock [Rice], 'Reminiscences of a Roughian', in *Reminiscences* (collection) written in connection with a school reunion held in Guildford, Surrey, 9–11 November 1990 [unpublished], Boston, MA.
119. H. W. and B. L., 12 and 13 years old, 'Our Whooping-Cough Isolation', *The Bridge*, vol.2, August–September 1941, p.13.
120. Email from Eddie to the author.
121. Margaret Dove [Faulkner], *Since Then … Letters from Former Stoatley Roughians*, edited by Hans Loeser and Herta Loeser [unpublished], 1971, p.16.
122. Dr Lion, 'Old Roughians', *The Bridge*, vol.2, August–September 1941, p.2.
123. Goldmeier, *Memoirs*.
124. Peter Gaupp, 'Notes from a Diary, Jan. 1941–Jan. 1942', *Stoatley Rough Newsletter*, Issue 22, December 2003, p.39.
125. Marmite has a strong, slightly salty flavour and is loaded with vitamins B2, folic acid and B12. A love-it-or-hate-it type of food, it has an addictive quality. Children in Britain are fed it from the time they are weaned.
126. Emmy Wolff, *Wir Lebten in Stoatley Rough*, letter dated 25 March 1938, p.12 (translation by the author).

Chapter 5: We'll Meet Again

1. Taken from an early brochure, cited by Katherine Whitaker, *History of Stoatley Rough*, p.24 from her research; Adenda, *Stoatley Rough School Archives*, File 6/117,

London School of Economics & Political Science.

2. Dr Lion, 'Dr. Lion's Lecture', Notes of a lecture given by Hilde Lion on 24 November 1937, *Stoatley Rough Newsletter,* Issue 3, October 1993, p.8.

3. Sir Hans Kornberg, *Since Then … Letters from Former Stoatley Roughians*, edited by Hans Loeser and Herta Loeser [unpublished], 1971, p.49. His English schooling served him well. After working for one year in the biochemistry laboratory of Sir Hans Krebs (1945–1946), Hans graduated from the University of Sheffield (UK), received his PhD and conducted research at, among other institutions, Yale in the United States and the University of Oxford. He headed up the Biochemistry department at the University of Cambridge, became Master of Christ's College at Cambridge and was knighted by Queen Elizabeth II, in 1978, 'for services to Science'.

4. Renate Solmitz [Frankenstein], *Since Then … Letters from Former Stoatley Roughians*, edited by Hans Loeser and Herta Loeser [unpublished], 1971, p.87.

5. Hans Loeser, *Hans's Story* (Lincoln, NE: iUniverse, 2007).

6. Herta Lewent [Loeser], Oral History Recorded during the Winter of 1988 between Herta and Tom Loeser [unpublished], Cambridge, MA, 1988.

7. Miss Fearon, Archive STR 1/1 (i), London School of Economics & Politics.

8. Dr Hilde Lion, 'Dr. Lion's Lecture', *Stoatley Rough Newsletter*, Issue 3, October 1993, pp.9–11. The quotations in the remainder of this section come from this paper.

9. Cesia Rothbart [Szajnzicht], 'I Remember', *Stoatley Rough Newsletter*, Issue 17, June 1998, p.12.

10. Beate Frankfurter [Planskoy], 'A Few Memories and Bits and Pieces Related to My Time at Stoatley Rough School (1939–1944)', *Stoatley Rough Newsletter*, Issue 23, September 2004, p.6.

11. Ruth Bayer [Tuckman], letter to Margaret Dove Faulkner, dated 26 March 1990, from her home in Israel.

12. Ilse Bauer [Feldstein], *Since Then … Letters from Former Stoatley Roughians*, edited by Hans Loeser and Herta Loeser [unpublished], 1971, p.5.

13. The Ury series is still popular in Germany. Else Ury's *Nesthäkchen* is a Berlin doctor's daughter, Annemarie Braun, a slim, golden blond, quintessential German girl. The ten-book series follows Annemarie from infancy (*Nesthäkchen and Her Dolls*) to old age and grandchildren (*Nesthäkchen with White Hair*). The first was published in 1906. *Nesthäkchen and the World War*, the fourth volume in the series, is the tale of a pre-adolescent girl growing up in Berlin at the outbreak of the First World War. A recent survey of German women revealed that 55 percent had read Else Ury's *Nesthäkchen* books. Even more had heard them read over the radio or had seen the television serialisation, and feminists at the beginning of the twentieth century had even read them, finding inspiration in the bold idea that Annemarie could have it all, meaning get both a degree and a husband, http://stevenlehrer.com/nesthaekchen.htm (accessed 4 January 2007).

14. The works of Karl May (1842–1912) have thus far sold over 100 million copies across the globe, his sixty novels having been translated into over thirty languages, including a recent series in Chinese. Born into a poor family in Hohenstein-Ernstthal, while imprisoned for petty theft, May began to write his books most likely inspired by *The Last of the Mohicans*. Danica Tutush, *The Strange Life and Legacy of Karl May*, http://www.cowboysindians.com/articles/archives/0999/karl_may.html (accessed May 2005).

15. Wolf Elston, a resident of Albuquerque, New Mexico, for most of his life in America, sets us straight about Old Shatterhand. 'Karl May didn't get all his American geography and ethnology right. Winnetou's home was supposed to be a pueblo on the Pecos, near the present Roswell (famous crash site of space aliens). There were no pueblos on the Pecos and, anyway, the Apaches were nomads who didn't live in pueblos. However, an Apache band, the Mescaleros, live in the vicinity to this day. They own much of the resort area in the mountains around Ruidoso, NM. This is where Texans come in droves to do all the

things that at home are either impossible (like skiing on 12,000-ft Sierra Blanca) or illegal, like playing the horses at Ruidoso Downs or gambling and boozing at the Inn of the Mountain Gods, the fanciest (and most expensive) resort in New Mexico. Recently the Apaches voted to offer their reservation as a site for a nuclear waste dump. What would Old Shatterhand say to that?'

16. From George Orwell, 'Boys' Weeklies', *Horizon*, March 1940; *Essays and Journalism*, http://www.netcharles.com/orwell/essays/boysweeklies2.htm (accessed February 2005).

17. Ibid.

18. Wolf Elston, upon the occasion of Nore Astfalck's ninetieth birthday.

19. Ibid.

20. Birgitte Pring-Mills née Heinsheimer [in 1990 *Reminiscences*]. 'All Through the Night' is an ancient Welsh song, 'Ar Hyd Y Nos', the most popular version in English by Harold Boulton that begins with, 'Sleep my love, and peace attend thee / All through the night'. Folk Songs of England, Ireland, Scotland and Wales, http://www.contemplator.com/wales/allnight2.html (accessed October 2006).

21. John Goldmeier, *Memoirs*, Part 1 [unpublished], Columbia, MD, January 2000.

22. Dieter Gaupp, 'Reminiscences', *Stoatley Rough Newsletter*, Issue 12, October 1996, p.36.

23. Ibid.

24. Dieter Gaupp, 'Excerpts from Autobiography of Dieter Gaupp', in *Reminiscences* (collection) written in connection with a School Reunion held in Guildford, Surrey, 9–11 November 1990 [unpublished], Boston, MA. The following plays have been mentioned by various students as having been performed over the years at Stoatley Rough. This information appeared in newsletter accounts, interviews and articles in *The Bridge*. *Julius Ceasar* (excerpt) was apparently performed in parody. An unidentified child wrote 'Since I have been in Stoatley Rough, I have seen in the summer of 1940, two plays on the same day. It was on Dr. Li's birthday. One of them a gay, bright play of a stolen princess, was acted by Group V on the second tennis-court with Miss Evans as producer. The other was a somewhat odd parody of *Julius Caesar* performed by older boys and girls. Other Shakespearean efforts included scenes from *Hamlet*, (excerpt) and *Henry VIII*, both performed by the farm boys and directed by Miss Humby.' When the farm boys played a scene from *Richard II*, it was reported in *The Bridge*, unkindly, that 'they had trouble pronouncing their W's, K's, O's and R's'. For the production of *Midsummer Night's Dream*, Peter Gaupp played Oberon, Uli Hubacher was in charge of props and Wolf Elston was Bottom, who wore the ass head. Wolf says the kids commented that he didn't need a fake head to play the part. Wolf also appeared in *Richard II*, and Martin Friedenfeld [Owens] was Sir Tobey Belch while Felix Schiller played Sir Andrew Aguecheek in *King Henry IV, Part 1* (subplot). The children also performed scenes from Dickens' *Nicholas Nickelby* and *Captain Scuttleboom's Treasure*, the later only interesting in that its playwright, Ronald Gow (1897–1993), was married for fifty-six years to Wendy Hiller, the star of the original *Pygmalion* film. The children performed *Turandot* for which, as reported in *The Bridge*, 'wings were painted and many a young man's head popped up on the wall. The performance would have been excellent except for the laughs certain actors had to give at their own dramatic speech'. Students performed the comedy *Tovarich* in English. Yet another play is mentioned by Barbara Gerstenberg [Prasse], *Victoria Regina,* in which she played the queen in a role that made Helen Hayes famous. The children also performed two other plays that we know of: *Le Voyage de Monsieur Perrichon*; performed in French, to which apparently the students initially objected, putting up a 'strong and vigorous protest'. Miss Humby, producer, director-stage-manager-dress-maker-arranger persuaded them to tackle it, which the reporter claims was great fun to rehearse, and a play entitled *Der Biberpelz* [The Beaver Coat], a comedy performed in German.

25. The school was relocated to Liphook, Hampshire, close to Haslemere, during the war. Afterwards, the school became Shoreham College, relocated in Shoreham-by-Sea, a small coastal community near Brighton, West Sussex.

26. Peter found a book that describes *Mischlings* that also contained information about his family name. 'This morning I had a surprise phone call from Ralph Gomar (formerly Goldmeier), Goldy's older brother. Sounded just like Goldy to me! He had read a book (Bryan Mark Rigg, *Hitler's Jewish Soldiers*, University Press of Kansas) which describes the treatment of "*Mischlinge*" (i.e. part Jewish) who were in the German army during WWII. Somewhere in there is a photo of one Peter Gaupp, "*Soldat*", and I gather there are several other mentions of this person who was interviewed. He must have been about ten years older than I was. He wanted to make sure it was not me (and remembered that he had met me at Stoatley Rough when he visited with his mother) and to see if I knew anything about him. So far I have found references to twenty Peter Gaupp's in my family tree collection, the earliest going back to the 1500's. So, it was a fairly well used name. There are also references to intermarriages with Jewish spouses. My father used to say that probably all "Gaupp's" are interrelated somehow, and I am inclined to agree. Of course the relationship could go back a few hundred years!', in an email to the author, June 2005.

27. In many British public schools, prefects, usually sixth formers, have considerable power. They effectively run the school outside the classroom. Corporal punishment administered by a prefect is now abolished in the United Kingdom. There may be a senior prefect known as the *Head of School* (colloquially, *Head Boy* or *Head Girl*) who carries some responsibilities, but gone is the ability to inflict bodily punishment on younger classmates.

28. David King, 'Six Whacks with an Old Gymshoe', *Stoatley Rough Newsletter*, Issue 9, October 1995, p.27.

29. Franceska Rapkin [Amerikaner], 'How I Came to Stoatley Rough', *Stoatley Rough Newsletter*, Issue 7, February 1995, p.26.

30. The entire story 'Confessions of an Army Cadet' appeared in the *Stoatley Rough Newsletter*, Issue 23, September 2004.

31. Renate Dorpalen [Dorpalen-Brocksieper], 'Stoatley Rough Remembered', *Stoatley Rough Newsletter*, Issue 7, February 1995, p.15.

32. Goldmeier, *Memoirs*, p.55.

33. Barbara Gerstenberg [Prasse], 'Dear Stoatley Roughians', in *Reminiscences* (collection) written in connection with a School Reunion held in Guildford, Surrey, 9–11 November 1990 [unpublished], Boston, MA.

34. Ibid.

35. Peter Gaupp, 'Adolescent Awakening', *Stoatley Rough Newsletter*, Issue 17, June 1998, p.29.

36. Ibid. p.30.

37. Wolf Edelstein [Elston], Martin Friedenfeld [Owens], Hans [John Obo] Obermeyer and Hans [John Goldy] Obemeier, 'Lifelong Friends', *Stoatley Rough Newsletter*, Issue 19, August 1999, p.56.

38. Wolf adds details of early American efforts in the war, hoping to counter one-sided perceptions borne in the movies. 'The American raids of 1942 were feeble, ineffective, and costly, mainly for propaganda purposes. One exception: the disastrous raid on the Roumanian Ploesti oil fields, from North Africa. The US Eighth Air Force didn't become effective until 1943. That's when we saw lots of B-17's.'

In 1942 the RAF began major night raids (1000 scraped-together planes hit Cologne), with heavy losses. The RAF night raids didn't become effective until 1943 (air-to-ground radar, tin foil counter-measures); to this day there is controversy whether the enormous diversion of Britain's limited industrial resources harmed the Allies more than it hurt the Axis (Singapore lost in 1942 with 80,000 men for want of a few fighter squadrons while 1,000 bombers failed to cut Germany industrial production in Cologne). Beginning in 1943, the U.S. daylight offensive, like the British night offensive, was enormously costly. Churchill estimates both Allies between them lost 160,000 men (against fewer than 5,000 Germans in the Battle of Britain); about 600,000 German civilians were killed. The U.S. daylight raids became effective in 1944 after the Packard Motor Company in Detroit manufactured Rolls Royce Merlin engines under license. P-51's with Merlins and fibre-glass disposable extra gas tanks (build by British manufacturers of small boats, on the spot) were able to escort B-17's all the way to Berlin and back. At that point, Hermann Goering ... conceded that the war was lost but kept that piece of news to himself. In 1944–1945, American daylight raids finally picked a truly decisive target, the German synthetic oil plants. Eventually, the German military literally ran out of gas.

Wolf adds the following to make his point. 'I saw the first few American planes – P-47 Thunderbolt fighters – on 15 August 1942, the day of the disastrous Dieppe raid – thousands of Canadians lost in their first European engagements. I mention these details to straighten out the current American impression of World War II: Things went badly until John Wayne and Steve Spielberg led the Greatest Generation to victory. The reality: along bitter and bloody struggle, with many blunders.'

39. Goldmeier, *Memoirs*.

40. Wolf Edelstein [Elston], 'Memories of Stoatley Rough', in *Reminiscences* (collection) written in connection with a School Reunion held in Guildford, Surrey, 9–11 November 1990 [unpublished], Boston, MA, p.17.

41. Hans [Obo, John] Obermeyer, *Stoatley Rough Newsletter*, Issue 19, August 1999. Wolf noted in an email to the author that the diesel engine was a true museum piece. 'Unfortunately it was junked after the war. Its date, 1896, from memory, showed it was one of the first diesel engines made in Britain. Rudolf Diesel took out his original German patent in 1892.'

42. Hans [John Obo] Obermeyer, in an email to the author.

43. Edelstein, 'Memories of Stoatley Rough'.

44. Wolf Edelstein [Elston], 'Memories of Stoatley Rough School, Haslemere, Surrey, England, 1939–1945', written in honour of Nore Astfalck's ninetieth birthday and dedicated to the entire staff of Stoatley Rough, Albuquerque, New Mexico, December 1990.

45. Hans Loeser points out that D-Day does not mean 'Debarkation Day' but rather simply 'day'. It is merely the military's way of marking a planned event, to lock in a date without disclosing it, hence three days before the event is called D-3, then the next day is D-2, and so on.

46. Goldmeier, *Memoirs*, p.59.

47. Wolf makes it clear that there was no disrespect meant towards Eisenhower on D-Day. 'People joked about speeches by big shots. That included King George VI, who manfully tried to control his stutter. When he momentarily had to pause, one of his loyal subject said: "Shouldn't we be singing God Save the King?".' The point is that there was no universal reverence or unalloyed admiration for the Americans in the war.

48. Ruth Ultman [Muessig] never fully accepted having to leave England in 1945. She reported from her home in Connecticut that after her husband had died, after her children had grown and after she had become a grandmother, that she had never felt at home in America, that her heart remained in England and that leaving had been a lifelong regret. Ruth Ultman [Muessig], letter to Martin Owens, dated 17 October 2001.

49. Goldmeier, *Memoirs*, p.59.

50. 'The V-1 was an unmanned, unguided, flying bomb. Although primitive by today's standards, it was the first of what we now call a "cruise missile." The Germans called it *Vergeltungswaffe* or "retaliation weapon," designated V-01 because it was the first of its

kind. The V-1 was a liquid fuelled, pulse-jet drone aircraft that could carry a 2,000 lb warhead. There was no navigation system, so it was simply pointed in the direction of its target. Simple gyrocompasses kept it level and range was controlled by the fuel supply. Its typical target was a city in southern England.' http://www.aviation-central.com/space/usm10.htm (accessed 27 May 2005).

51. David King, 'Buried Alive for Ten Hours', *Stoatley Rough Newsletter*, Issue 18, September 1998, p.22.

52. Martin Friedenfeld [Owens], *Stoatley Rough Newsletter*, Issue 10, February 1996, p.14.

53. Elston, 'Memories of Stoatley Rough School, Haslemere, Surrey, England, 1939–1945'.

54. Loeser, *Hans's Story*.

55. Hans' mother was responsible for getting her husband out of concentration camp. She approached the official with documents giving permission to emigrate to Palestine. By merest coincidence, years earlier the Loesers had donated money to plant a grove of trees in Palestine. This act made them eligible as landowners to enter Palestine. In New York, Hans' father suffered from depression. He died of a heart attack at fifty-six, in 1943, never to know of the victory of the Allies over Hitler.

56. Ibid.

57. Walter Laqueuer, *Generation Exodus* (London: I. B. Taurus, 2004), p.83.

58. This film by Christian Bauer is the 'untold story of a group of young men who fled Nazi Germany and returned to Europe as soldiers in US uniforms. They knew the psychology and the language of the enemy better than anybody else. In Camp Ritchie, Maryland, they were trained in intelligence and psychological warfare. Not always courageous, but determined, bright, and inventive they fought their own kind of war. They saved lives. They were victors, not victims.' http://www.ritchieboys.com/index.html (accessed 19 April 2006).

59. The 1977 film directed by Richard Attenborough. Its stellar cast, including Michael Caine, Sean Connery, James Caan, Dirk Bogarde, Anthony Hopkins, Liv Ullman and Gene Hackman, portrayed the failed attempt to capture several German bridges. The Internet Movie Database (IMDb), http://us.imdb.com/title/tt0075784/ (accessed 10 January 2007).

60. Loeser, *Hans's Story*, p.119.

61. Ibid.

62. Ibid. p.108.

63. Wolf Edelstein [Elston], in an email to the author, 21 April 2006.

64. Hans Loeser, *Hans Story*. The entire account of Hans' experience with the Battle of the Bulge is taken from his memoir.

65. Ibid.

66. Ibid. p.118.

67. Ibid. Hans' experience confirms Goldhagen's thesis in *Hitler's Willing Executioners*.

68. Renate Dorpalen [Dorpalen-Brocksieper], 'Stoatley Rough Remembered', *Stoatley Rough Newsletter*, Issue 9, October 1995, p.35.

69. Goldmeier, *Memoirs*, p.63.

70. *Stoatley Rough School Archives*, File 8/2, London School of Economics.

71. Dorpalen, 'Stoatley Rough Remembered', *Stoatley Rough Newsletter*, Issue 9, p.40.

72. Ibid. p.43.

73. Andreas Pilartz, in an email to the author.

74. Eddie Behrendt, in an email to the author, 13 May 2005.

75. With help from the Simon Wiesenthal Center, Eddie set up the organisation to search for Kindertransport children living in America. The mission was to provide a venue for reunions, to educate and inform the next generation about the Kindertransport and Holocaust, and to provide funds for needy children regardless of race, creed or country of national origin. After four years in the United States Army, he served as Director

of Personnel for the American Home Products (Wyeth) Corporation in New York for many years, but it was his role as teacher of the truths about the Holocaust that led him to travel the country to speak to high-school students for several years as part of a programme he founded from Eugene, Oregon, known as 'Reach and Teach'. He died in November 2006. 'His fervor for the world to know and accept responsibility for the mass annihilation of a people was overwhelming.' The Kindertransport Association website, http://www.kindertransport.org/eddy_behrendt.html (accessed 2 August 2007).

76. Uli Hubacher, in an email to the author, 12 May 2005.

77. Written in 1939, the music was written by Ross Parker and words by Hughie Charles. A movie of the same name came out in 1942, starring Miss Lynn.

78. Eleonore Astfalck, *Oral History (1990)* [unpublished].

79. Whitsunday is the seventh Sunday after Easter; 'White Sunday' commemorates the emanation of the Holy Spirit to the apostles in the Christian doctrine. Whitsuntide would be the week in which this celebration takes place. Wolf adds, 'Whitsunday (*Pfingsten* in German) was (and probably still is) a popular holiday in Germany. Easter often is too cold for outings that are traditional at *Pfingsten*.'

80. Barbara Gerstenberg [Prasse], 'Reminiscences on the Occasion of the School's 1990 Reunion'.

81. Hans [John Obo] Obermeyer, 'Letter to Dr. Lion', *Stoatley Rough School Archives*, File 3/28, London School of Economics.

82. Hans [John Obo] Obermeyer, in an email to the author, 21 April 2006.

83. The play, *Kindertransport*, deals with the theme of separation and reuniting of children and parents after the Holocaust. 'Ratcatcher' is a man who steals children and whose role is based on the Pied Piper myth. Miss Samuels dedicated her play to the 'Jewish Kinder Who Caught the Trains in 1938–39', http://www.carpentersquare.com/shows/show_kindertransport.htm (accessed 29 May 2005).

84. 'Letter in Dr. Lion's File', *Stoatley Rough School Archives*, File 3/4 (ii), London School of Economics.

85. Peter Gaupp, in an email to the author, 21 April 2006.

86. Peter Gaupp, in an email to the author, 18 January 2007.

87. Martin Friedenfeld [Owens], *Recollections* [unpublished memoir], 3 July 2004.

88. Elston, 'Memories of Stoatley Rough School, Haslemere, Surrey, England, 1939–1945'.

Epilogue

1. In 1949, there were seventy-three pupils (sixty-two boarders, eleven day). By 1954, the numbers dropped to sixty-five pupils (fifty boarders, fifteen day).

2. In 1951, Dr Lion wrote, with a touch of cynicism, that her pupils were 'partly those of refugee parents and partly those who are sent by Authorities in the new boarding out scheme – children deprived of home life who are supposed to be worthy of grammar school education'.

3. Ignorance can never be overestimated. This Roughian had the good fortune to be seated next to Elie Weisel, Nobel Prize winner and professor of Humanities at Boston University, on an airplane. He mentioned to the flight attendant that there was a celebrity on board, but when he mentioned the name, she said, 'Oh, is he a rock star?' He relayed this fact to Dr Weisel, who commented, 'I suppose I missed my calling.' Mr Greenwell would always be grateful that he had had the opportunity to tell the story to the 'distinguished humanist'. (From *Stoatley Rough Newsletter*, Issue 7, February 1995, pp.10–11.)

4. A draft of Dr Lion's announcement read, 'Dear Parents and Friends, It is with great regret that we announce that Dr L. Leven and I want to retire at the end of the summer 1960. The School will cease to exist. This decision has been taken after careful consideration with our Chairman and the other members of the Bd. of Governors....

We were glad, Dr. Wolff included who had to retire earlier – that we could help in a small way, children and this country. Difficulties for the working of an independent school are mounting and we are not as young as 25 years ago – May we thank our most helpful board, esp. Miss Fearon, for their continued assistance. Stoatley Rough has been our life, now we want to have an active retirement. Please, remain our friends!' *Stoatley Rough School Archives*, Box 1/1 (ii), London School of Economics.

5. Hilde Lion, 'Letter to Peter Strauss', *Stoatley Rough School Archives*, Box 3/45 (iii), London School of Economics, 15 July 1948.

6. 'I just made up a word that expresses the way Roughians feel about each other', Edith Hubacher-Christoffel quoted by Wolf Elston in *Reminiscences*, 1992.

7. Chris Townson, 'The Sale of Quartermaine', *Stoatley Rough Newsletter*, Issue 8, June 1995, p.12.

8. Dr Lion, 'Luise Leven's Story', *Stoatley Rough Newsletter*, Issue 18, December 1998, p.17.

9. Dr Lion's letter was reported by Manfred Berger, whose original document appeared in the Ida Seele Archive for the Research of the History of the Kindergarten in Dillingen, Germany. It was translated by Gerda Mayer and reprinted for the *Stoatley Rough Newsletter*, Issue 14, October 1997.

10. With the rise of the Nazis in the 1930s, Minna Specht moved her *Landerziehungsheim* school from Germany to Denmark and then to Butcombe Court in Bristol. She married an English headmaster while waiting out the war in England, returned to Germany and became a member of UNESCO's committee on Education.

11. Eleonore Astfalck, *Oral History (1990)* [unpublished].

12. Ibid.

13. Hans Loeser. Some of the information has come from his book, *Hans Story*, and some from a recorded interview taken 2 March 2001, 'Legal Oral History Project', Pennsylvania Law School.

14. Herta Lewent [Loeser], Oral History Recorded during the Winter of 1988 between Herta and Tom Loeser [unpublished], Cambridge, MA, 1988, p.8.14.

15. Ibid. p.6.13.

16. Renate Dorpalen [Dorpalen-Brocksieper], 'Stoatley Rough Remembered', *Stoatley Rough Newsletter*, Issue 9, October 1995, p.45.

17. Ibid. p.15.

18. Ibid. p.18.

19. John [Hans Goldy] Goldmeier, *Memoirs*, Part 1 [unpublished], Columbia, MD, January 2000, p.67.

20. John [Hans Goldy] Goldmeier, 'Religion at Stoatley Rough', *Stoatley Rough Newsletter*, Issue 18, September 1998, p.34.

Sources and Acknowledgements

1. Barbara Gerstenberg [Prasse], *Reminiscences*, p.3.

2. Hildegard Feidel-Mertz, 'Integration and Formation of Identity: Exile Schools in Great Britain', *Shofar*, 23/1 (2004): 71–84.

3. Ibid.

4. Anna was a friend of Dr. Lion's. They corresponded during the war years and she was a founding Trustee of Stoatley Rough School. Alan Major, 'Bunce Court & Anna Essinger', *Stoatley Rough Newsletter*, Issue 14, May 1997. The article first appeared in *Bygone Kent*, a monthly journal of all aspects of local history, volume 1, number 8, August 1989.

5. Dr Hahn is credited for having founded Outward Bound, originally created in 1941 for British soldiers facing battle.

6. A first cousin of one of the students at Stoatley Rough (Renate Dorpalen [Dorpalen-Brocksieper]) was sent to the Camp Hill School and remained there until she died.

Index